Labor Under Fire

TIMOTHY J. MINCHIN

Labor Under Fire
A History of the AFL-CIO since 1979

The University of North Carolina Press *Chapel Hill*

Set in Arno Pro by Westchester Publishing Services
Manufactured in the United States of America

The University of North Carolina Press has been a member of the
Green Press Initiative since 2003.

Library of Congress Cataloging-in-Publication Data
Names: Minchin, Timothy J., author.
Title: Labor under fire : a history of the AFL-CIO since 1979 /
    Timothy J. Minchin.
Description: Chapel Hill : University of North Carolina Press, [2017] |
    Includes bibliographical references and index.
Identifiers: LCCN 2016042815 | ISBN 9781469632988 (cloth : alk. paper) |
    ISBN 9781469632995 (ebook)
Subjects: LCSH: AFL-CIO—History—20th century. | AFL-CIO—History—
    21st century. | Labor unions—United States—History—20th century. |
    Labor unions—United States—History—21st century.
Classification: LCC HD8055.A5 M56 2017 | DDC 331.880973—dc23
    LC record available at https://lccn.loc.gov/2016042815

Jacket illustration: Solidarity Day—lead group. Courtesy of Special Collections,
    University of Maryland Libraries.

Chapter 3 was previously published in a different form as "Together We
Shall Be Heard: Exploring the 1981 'Solidarity Day' Mass March," *Labor:
Studies in Working-Class History of the Americas* 12, no. 3 (September 2015): 75–96.
Portions of chapters 9 and 10 were published in " 'Labor is Back?': The AFL-CIO
during the Presidency of John J. Sweeney, 1995–2009," *Labor History* 54, no. 4
(October 2013): 393–420, and "A Pivotal Role? The AFL-CIO and the 2008
Presidential Election," *Labor History* 57, no. 3 (July 2016): 299–322. All material
used here with permission.

To Anthony John Minchin

Contents

Illustrations

Acknowledgments

This book would not have been possible without the help of friends, colleagues, and institutions in the United States, UK, and Australia. While it is impossible to acknowledge all those who have assisted me, I would especially like to thank the Australian Research Council (ARC), as *Labor Under Fire* is the main outcome of a three-year discovery grant that the Council awarded me for this project. This book could not have been contemplated—let alone completed—without the ARC's generous support. Prior to this, I was assisted by a grant from the U.S. Studies Centre at the University of Sydney, where I was a "researcher in residence" in July 2012. During this fellowship, I formulated the ideas behind the book and conducted early research. I am especially grateful to Brendon O'Connor and Shane White, Sydney-based scholars who encouraged me to pursue the project. I would also like to thank La Trobe University for its consistent support, especially in awarding me a period of research leave during the writing process.

The research for the book was underpinned by a series of lengthy research trips to the United States, particularly Washington, DC. On my travels, a number of former AFL-CIO leaders and staff were enormously helpful. Tom Donahue—who served as AFL-CIO secretary-treasurer and president—put me in touch with many retirees and was extremely generous with his time. He also shared his personal papers, including original material on the 1995 leadership contest. Special mention should also go to Lane Windham and Joe Uehlein, who helped arrange a number of interviews, especially with staff from the John Sweeney era. In addition, I should thank Mark Anderson and Steve Rosenthal, valuable interviewees who also gave me access to personal written material.

At the AFL-CIO headquarters, Pat Lleras and Angie Forsythe gave me a place to work and helped with interviews, while Arlene Holt Baker, Liz Shuler, John Sweeney, and Richard Trumka were especially generous with their time. Several former leaders of Change to Win, particularly Anna Burger and Andy Stern, also agreed to be interviewed and were very helpful. All of these people—and many more—helped make my trips to Washington, DC, productive and enjoyable. They ensured that I came away with more interviews than I had anticipated, providing a rich resource that complemented the detailed archival records.

Throughout this project, many librarians and archivists were also very helpful. In particular, I would like to thank Jen Eidson and Lauren Brown from the Hornbake Library at the University of Maryland. Jen and Lauren provided speedy access to the AFL-CIO Papers when they were moved from the George Meany Memorial Archives in 2013. With their assistance, this relocation was not as disruptive as I had feared. Jen also helped me to navigate the post-1979 part of the collection, a vast resource that the AFL-CIO kindly gave me permission to use. In addition, I would like to thank Sheryl Vogt and Jill Severn from the Richard B. Russell Library for Political Research and Studies at the University of Georgia, and the staff at the Ronald Reagan Presidential Library in Simi Valley, California, for all of their help.

At the University of North Carolina Press, Brandon Proia was very encouraging and saw the manuscript through to publication with admirable efficiency. Several other Press staff—especially Jessica Newman—guided me through the publication and permissions process. My Australian-based research assistant, Bronwyn Hislop, worked with me throughout the project and did a great job of organizing a vast amount of material. Early on, Jeremy Bigwood, Patrick Funiciello, and Jon Keljik collected material from the AFL-CIO Papers, helping to get the project off the ground. One of my graduate students, Holly Wilson, took time out from her own research at the Dwight D. Eisenhower Presidential Library in Abilene, Kansas, to copy material for me. Throughout the project, Mandy Rooke tackled the transcribing of interviews with skill and dedication. I am grateful to them all.

Conversations with colleagues were also formative. On a visit to Melbourne, David Garrow unexpectedly put me in touch with Tom Donahue, a crucial early breakthrough. In Washington, DC, I had a number of enriching conversations with Joe McCartin from Georgetown University. Several other colleagues, including Tony Badger, Roland Burke, Clare Corbould, and John David Smith, guided and supported me. I also benefited from fruitful discussions at the conferences of the Australian and New Zealand American Studies Association, allowing me to test and improve my ideas.

As ever, close friends and family were also vital. Penny and Chris Harvey provided me with a home away from home in Sydney. Chris VerPlanck and Abby Bridge did the same in San Francisco. When I was devising the project, John Salmond—who sadly passed away before its publication—provided valued friendship and wise guidance. My wife, Olga, has been enormously supportive throughout, while our three children—Alexander, Natasha, and

Anton—have been very tolerant of their father's idiosyncrasies. I would also like to thank my parents, Tony and Christine Minchin. I would like to dedicate the book to my father. Throughout his long life, he has taught me a great deal about labor history and social justice, and I am very grateful.

October 2016
Melbourne, Australia

Labor Under Fire

Introduction

On July 1, 2008, Richard Trumka gave a remarkable speech to the United Steelworkers convention in Las Vegas. Speaking to a packed auditorium composed largely of white men, the secretary-treasurer of the American Federation of Labor-Congress of Industrial Organizations (AFL-CIO) made an impassioned appeal. A few weeks earlier, Barack Obama had won the Democratic nomination for president, yet he was struggling to win support from working-class white voters, especially men. Some commentators feared that Obama would lose if this did not change.[1] A burly former coal miner, Trumka tackled the issue head on. "There is not a single good reason for any worker, especially a union member, to vote against Barack Obama," he asserted, wagging his finger and mopping sweat from his brow. "There's only one really bad reason to vote against Barack Obama. And that's because he's not white." To illustrate the issue, Trumka related an encounter he had with a woman he had "known for years" in his hometown of Nemacolin, Pennsylvania, a lady who had been "active in Democratic politics when I was still in grade school." Speaking during the crucial Pennsylvania primary—which Obama had lost— the woman admitted that there was "no way that I'd ever vote for Obama." Trumka asked why. The woman initially alleged that Obama was a Muslim and that he was not patriotic, charges that Trumka refuted. Dropping her voice, she then admitted that she did not trust Obama "because he's black." Pointing out that Nemacolin was a post-industrial "dying town," Trumka rebuked the woman for refusing to support Obama, a politician who was "going to fight for us," simply because of his race. "You won't vote for him because of the color of his skin," he replied. "Are you out of your ever-loving mind, lady?" The woman, he concluded, was typical of how many white voters felt, and the labor movement could not "tap dance" around the fact.[2]

Trumka's speech had a significant impact, especially when it was uploaded online. "By summer's end, the speech had gone viral," summarized the *Washington Post*. "And by election day, the worries about how Obama would fare with working-class whites had been largely laid to rest, thanks in part to his strong showing among union families."[3] Trumka's impassioned address galvanized the AFL-CIO's election campaign, highlighting to many white members the importance of backing Obama. Running the biggest election campaign in its history, the AFL-CIO played an important role in mobilizing white voters behind Obama, and the results were impressive. Exit poll data gathered by Peter D. Hart Associates—a leading survey research firm—found that Obama won among white men who were union members by 18 points, yet he lost that same group in the broader population by 16 points. Obama also won among union members who were white weekly churchgoers, veterans, and gun owners, and among whites who had not graduated from college, yet he lost each of these groups in the general population. The AFL-CIO's targeted campaigning—and its 250,000 volunteers—had also helped Obama to win the swing states of Florida, Michigan, North Carolina, Ohio, and Pennsylvania. In Pennsylvania itself, organized labor's efforts over the last two months ensured that support for Obama among union members rose 16 percent, for a 68 percent to 24 percent advantage. Over the country as a whole, union members and their families comprised about 21 percent of voters, and a striking 69 percent of them backed Barack Obama. Union members, thought the *Post*'s Michael A. Fletcher, had played a "pivotal role" in Obama's victory.[4]

Citing similar data, Trumka—who became AFL-CIO president in 2009—agreed. "He (Obama) doesn't win without the Labor Movement," he asserted later. "He loses that election, the first time around, without the American labor movement." Even labor's opponents gave it considerable credit. In the *Washington Times*, conservative editorialist Gary Andres wrote soon after the election: "No special interest group deserves more credit for electing and expanding a Democratic majority in Congress than organized labor. Unions infused Democrats with money, manpower and message support across America. Their resources are both concentrated and large, and they continue to provide electoral and legislative lifeblood."[5]

The role that the AFL-CIO played in the 2008 election highlights the continuing impact that labor has on U.S. political history. As the story of the election shows, unions remain a vital political force in twenty-first-century America, and this is especially true of the AFL-CIO, the largest labor federation in the country. In many standard accounts of the 2008 election, however, the AFL-CIO is only mentioned in August 2007, when it sponsored a debate among the leading contenders for the Democratic nomination.[6] In a broader sense, much remains to be learned about the history of the AFL-CIO, particularly in the difficult decades prior to the 2008 vote. Most writing has focused on the AFL-CIO under George Meany, a well-known figure who served as president from 1955 to 1979. Overall, scholarship on the AFL-CIO illustrates historian David M. Kennedy's observation that "the history we know least well is the history of our time."[7]

Labor Under Fire aims to correct this imbalance. It provides the first general history of the AFL-CIO in the turbulent era after Meany's retirement, a time when the Federation operated in a hostile political and economic climate. By providing the first history of a major American organization in this period, this book contributes to an emerging body of scholarship on U.S. history since the 1970s. In important works, a range of historians—including William Chafe, James T. Patterson, Daniel Rogers, and Sean Wilentz—have begun the periodization of the history of this era. For progressive groups such as the AFL-CIO, what Wilentz has called "The Age of Reagan" was a difficult era, yet throughout it the AFL-CIO fought hard against the many challenges that it faced, and the period contains a lot of rich—and little-known—history.[8] In September 1981, for example, the AFL-CIO organized Solidarity Day, a mass protest in Washington, DC, that was the largest labor march in U.S. history—some 400,000 people took part. It was also perhaps the largest single protest gathering ever in Washington. In 1982, 1983, 1984, and 1991, the AFL-CIO also organized sizeable follow-up marches—the 1991 rally alone had 250,000 participants—yet none of these protests have received scholarly attention. In national elections, the AFL-CIO also remained a significant force; as well as helping elect the first African-American president in 2008, for example, the Federation also played an important role in the Democratic sweep of the House and Senate two years earlier.[9]

Of course, these are recent events, and it is understandable that they have yet to receive extensive scholarly analysis. The task for any historian writing about such a big and decentralized organization as the AFL-CIO is also daunting. This account, however, is based on detailed research into the AFL-CIO's papers, particularly a large body of underutilized—and unprocessed—material on the post-1979 era. While the Federation's papers prior to 1979 have been used quite extensively, the more recent, restricted material has been overlooked.[10]

In addition, *Labor Under Fire* draws on other archival collections, particularly the records of several presidential libraries, including those of Ronald Reagan and George H. W. Bush, key Republicans who had a strained relationship with the AFL-CIO. It also utilizes other political collections and the personal papers of Federation leaders, including Thomas R. Donahue and Mark Anderson.[11] I use these documents to examine the record of Meany's immediate successors, Lane Kirkland (1979–95), Donahue (1995), and John

J. Sweeney (1995–2009). These leaders, however, cannot be assessed without some understanding of the earlier period, especially as both Kirkland and Donahue had worked for Meany. As a result, the AFL-CIO's history between 1955 and 1979 is summarized in a detailed opening chapter that concentrates on Meany's legacies. The main body of the book concludes with Sweeney's retirement in 2009, the last date that archival records were available. Although it is an evolving story, the post-Sweeney period—or the Trumka years—is surveyed in an epilogue.[12]

Throughout this work, I have also drawn on my own oral histories, including interviews with the current AFL-CIO president, the two surviving former presidents, and a wide range of retired staffers and union leaders. Overall, I conducted sixty interviews, and they shed light on the Federation's history in new ways, enriching the written record and bringing through the human agency of key players. Through interviewing, I was also able to include the voice of more women activists, and to give closer detail to the Federation's efforts to diversify its leadership, particularly at the Executive Council level. These initiatives began tentatively under Kirkland but gathered pace significantly during the Sweeney presidency. Newspapers, including the conservative and business press, are also mined extensively throughout.[13]

Drawing on these records, *Labor Under Fire* presents a fresh interpretation of the AFL-CIO's history. To date, most writing about the AFL-CIO has been highly critical, if not hostile. While general studies have been rare, particular aspects of the AFL-CIO's history have been closely scrutinized. The Federation's civil rights record, for example, has often been lambasted—with some justification. In 1961 NAACP labor secretary Herbert Hill charged that the AFL-CIO had "failed to eliminate the broad pattern of racial discrimination and segregation in many important affiliated unions." Until his death in 2005, Hill—first as an NAACP official and later as an academic and commentator—repeatedly highlighted the gap between the AFL-CIO's egalitarian policies and its actual practices.[14] While more favorably inclined toward the labor movement, other scholars, particularly David Roediger, Michael Goldfield, Bruce Nelson, and William Gould, have emphasized the racism and hypocrisy that existed in the House of Labor, and in the white working class generally. In the Kirkland-Sweeney era, the AFL-CIO battled with this history of discrimination, and was slow to address it. While early efforts were halting, over this period the Federation made substantial progress in diversifying its leadership, especially during the Sweeney era. By 2013, the AFL-CIO was still led by a white man, but its two other top officers were Elizabeth Shuler, a white woman, and Tefere Gebre, an Ethiopian-American man. Both Shuler and Gebre were also in their forties, much younger than the Federation's leaders had been in the past.[15]

A second group of scholars have explored how the AFL-CIO supported U.S. foreign policy throughout the Cold War, implicating itself in the overthrow of several democratically elected governments in the process. A lot of this work has also been highly critical of the Federation. In his seminal *American Labor and United States Foreign Policy* (1969), written at the height of New Left revisionism, Ronald Radosh asserted, "From World War I to the present era of the Cold War, the leaders of organized labor have willingly offered their support to incumbent administrations." For Radosh, the AFL-CIO represented "corporate unionism" and failed to present a "Socialist alternative to American workers." More recently, the Federation's foreign policies have come under fresh attack. Under Meany and Kirkland, asserts sociologist and labor activist Kim Scipes, the AFL-CIO pursued a "reactionary" foreign policy that saw it support the overthrow of several democratically elected governments, particularly in Brazil in 1964 and Chile in 1973. "AFL-CIO foreign policy leaders," charges Scipes, "support and have worked to extend the U.S. Empire."[16] Other work has shown how the AFL-CIO slavishly adopted the prevalent anticommunist ideology of the Cold War era, often putting it ahead of solidarity with workers in developing countries. Labor historians have also criticized the Federation for its "hawkish" stance throughout the Vietnam War, showing how staffers even orchestrated "hard hat" rallies in New York City in 1970 in order to shore up support for the war.[17] While some of the more recent scholarship—such as work by Geert Van Goethem, Yevette Richards, Quenby Hughes, and others—has been more nuanced and sophisticated, the focus on the AFL-CIO's support for U.S. foreign policy during the Cold War has remained. The Federation's domestic history, especially its legislative and lobbying work, has been comparatively neglected.[18]

A third group of scholars have explored the decline of the labor movement. This literature has not focused exclusively on the AFL-CIO, and does not explore its experience directly, as *Labor Under Fire* does. Rather, activist-oriented scholars have generally concentrated on exploring possible solutions to labor's predicament, arguing that the labor movement needed to be more radical in order to reverse the fall in union density—the proportion of the workforce that was unionized. According to this analysis, the AFL-CIO is primarily to blame for its own problems.[19] In *Taking Care of Business* (1999), for example, socialist writer Paul Buhle offers a blistering critique of the AFL-CIO and its most prominent leaders. He dismisses George Meany as "a

sputtering, foul-mouthed conservative," and a "badly-aging, ill-spirited chief."
Lane Kirkland fares little better, blasted as a dull champion of "inside-the-
Beltway policy maneuvers," a remote bureaucrat with "no actual, personal
history of unionism." Overall, the AFL-CIO represented "business unionism,"
a conservative philosophy inherited from AFL founder Samuel Gompers
that led to its decline. In a series of books and articles, labor journalist Kim
Moody has repeated similar charges. For Moody, the AFL-CIO also represented "business unionism," a stale and conservative philosophy that cut its
leaders off from their members, ensuring that the movement gradually ossified and declined.[20]

All of these criticisms have a lot of validity, and this scholarship has helped
to enrich the field. Overall, however, I argue that the AFL-CIO deserves to
receive a more balanced treatment than it has so far, one that recognizes its
achievements *and* its limitations. In the detailed treatment of Kirkland's
presidency provided here—the first to draw extensively on archival sources—
the former Merchant Marine officer from South Carolina emerges as a more
complex and talented figure than his critics allow. While he was reserved,
Kirkland was also intelligent, committed, and capable of innovation. As
Solidarity Day highlighted, the AFL-CIO under Kirkland was not just a bureaucratic organization that was far removed from those it represented; it
could also mobilize its members. Kirkland was also successful in holding the
Federation together at a hostile time, securing the re-affiliation of several
unions—most notably the Autoworkers and Teamsters—that had been outside the fold. Under his leadership, the AFL-CIO achieved an unprecedented
degree of unity.[21]

Existing scholarship has also only covered small parts of the AFL-CIO's
history. More work is needed, especially given the prominent role that the
AFL-CIO played in national life. In many other Western countries, national
union federations have been written about in some detail, their histories covered closely.[22] The size of the AFL-CIO ensures that it deserves more historical attention. In 1955 Meany claimed that the AFL-CIO's 15 million
members made it "the largest trade union center in the free world." Closer
examination reveals that this was no idle boast. In December 1955 the *New
York Times* found that the AFL-CIO was the "largest national workers group
in the free world," noting that its membership easily exceeded that of the British Trades Union Congress (8 million members), as well as trade union federations in West Germany (6 million members), Brazil (1.6 million), and
Japan (1.85 million). While much of the AFL-CIO's dominance derived from
a larger population—and Great Britain had higher union density—its power

was undeniable. The Chinese communist workers' federation, with 12.45 million members, was a rival, but this organization—like its counterpart in the USSR—was government-controlled, ensuring that the AFL-CIO was the biggest labor federation in the non-Communist world.[23]

Despite falling union density, the AFL-CIO's absolute membership held steady. In 1982 the Federation still had around 15 million members, and it represented "virtually all" of America's labor unions. In 1989, following a decade that saw unions come under attack from both employers and the White House, the AFL-CIO had a per capita membership of 14.15 million, partly because several re-affiliations had compensated for the loss of members.[24] Even after the end of the Cold War, when the pace of globalization accelerated, the AFL-CIO remained the largest labor federation in the Western world. In 1995 membership stood at 13 million, while in 2011 it was 12.2 million.[25]

Throughout its history, the AFL-CIO concentrated heavily on legislative work. Because affiliates had a considerable amount of autonomy, especially when it came to organizing and collective bargaining, the AFL-CIO was primarily a Washington-based organization that focused on providing a legislative voice for its members. As staffer Craig Becker put it, the AFL-CIO had "limited authority" over affiliates, with politics being the main area "where the value is added by a federation." In 1955 the merger of the AFL and CIO was partly designed to increase labor's political power, and Meany promised a heavy emphasis on political mobilization from the beginning. "The scene of battle is no longer the company plant or the picket line," he explained. "It has moved into the legislative halls of Congress and the state legislatures." Meany's successors shared this mantra.[26] As a result, this book focuses heavily on how the AFL-CIO at the national level, and particularly its leaders, interacted with various presidential administrations and with Congress. In order to maintain this focus, and to keep this account relatively concise, the AFL-CIO's history outside the United States—a huge topic in its own right—is only summarized briefly, chiefly when it impinges upon domestic events. These international efforts have also been scrutinized well by others.[27]

At the same time, this work tries to move beyond Washington, to convey how the American workplace changed over time and how workers on the ground experienced these shifts. The history of the AFL-CIO indeed provides an excellent lens through which to view many important economic and social changes of the postwar period, including the entry of women and racial minorities into the workforce, and the growth of the service and retail sectors. These developments had a profound impact on the Federation, particularly after 1979, when major shifts in the economy—especially deindustrialization and globalization—forced the AFL-CIO to reach out beyond its manufacturing base. By 1995, when Sweeney became president, the biggest affiliates were government and service sector unions, and they proved crucial to his ability to wrestle the presidency from the Kirkland-Donahue team.[28]

In seeking to provide a more balanced view of the AFL-CIO, *Labor Under Fire* argues that the Federation was an important institution because it did not just speak for its members but sought to represent *all* American workers. When it was founded in 1955, the AFL-CIO called itself "an expression of the hopes and aspirations of the working people of America." The new organization was committed to serving "the interests of all the American people," not just at the collective bargaining table but also in the community.[29] Its long-standing goal, as Kirkland reiterated in 1993, was to be "the genuine voice of working American men and women." Located on Sixteenth Street, the AFL-CIO's headquarters were in the heart of Washington, DC. One side of the building—occupied largely by the president's offices and associated meeting rooms—looked directly over the White House, a proximity that graphically illustrated the Federation's mission. In a political system increasingly dominated by corporate lobby groups, the AFL-CIO was important. As prominent journalist John Judis summarized in 2005, "Since its founding in 1955, the AFL-CIO has provided the largest counterweight to business interests, both in the workplace and in Washington." Despite business opposition, for example, the Federation consistently fought for health care reform, and it played an important role in the eventual passage of the Affordable Care Act in 2010.[30]

In many other areas, the Federation has been a major force in national life, influencing legislation that helped all working Americans, particularly during the presidencies of John F. Kennedy and Lyndon B. Johnson. Recognizing the Federation's importance, former president John F. Kennedy termed the AFL-CIO "the people's lobby," a mantra that it embraced.[31] The Federation pushed for most of the important social legislation of the 1960s, including the Elementary and Secondary Education Act, the Voting Rights Act, and the Social Security Amendments of 1965. When he left office in January 1969, President Johnson presented the AFL-CIO with 100 signed pens that symbolized the group's "contribution to legislation beneficial to all Americans." Each pen carried the name of a piece of legislation passed during Johnson's presidency. In the 1970s, the AFL-CIO wielded a considerable amount of power, particularly within the Democratic Party. As President Jimmy Carter wrote Meany in September 1978, the AFL-CIO had provided "a voice for millions of workers who might otherwise not be heard," helping to "uplift the standards of living and of work safety for America's workers." According to Carter, "most of the major social advances of the last fifty years," particularly in areas such as civil rights, welfare, health, and education, "would have been impossible without the able assistance of the organized labor movement."[32]

Even in the more challenging climate that it confronted after 1980, when changes in the workforce and an increasingly conservative political climate led to steady falls in union density, the AFL-CIO remained a powerful force in American life. Solidarity Day highlighted the Federation's ability to mobilize its members, causing real concern at the Reagan White House. There were also successes abroad; it was the AFL-CIO that was one of the main allies of the Solidarity Movement in Poland. Even when it proved unable to pass domestic legislation, the Federation had a lot of defensive power, and it repeatedly resisted attacks on vital social programs, particularly Social Security. It also consistently fought—with some success—to raise the federal minimum wage, an effort that helped millions of low-paid workers.[33]

Conservative and business groups certainly recognized the AFL-CIO's importance. In December 1997, for example, *Fortune* magazine ranked the AFL-CIO as the third most influential lobby group in the country. Based on extensive research among elected representatives, their congressional offices, and White House staff, the survey gave the AFL-CIO a high ranking largely because it could mobilize grassroots Americans. In 1993 this capacity was evident when the Federation launched a high-profile national campaign against passage of the North American Free Trade Agreement (NAFTA). It was also apparent during the presidencies of George W. Bush and Barack Obama, when a massive campaign for labor law reform fell agonizingly short. Under John Sweeney, the AFL-CIO also built a sophisticated and effective political program that helped the Democrats to regain control of the House in 2006 and the presidency two years later. Clearly, the AFL-CIO still had clout.[34]

The failure of the labor law reform campaign, however, highlighted how the AFL-CIO's power had been undermined by the steady decline in union density. While the AFL-CIO's membership held relatively steady throughout its history, its influence waned as a new, non-union workforce grew around it. Statistics reveal that although decline framed the entire history of the AFL-CIO, it became a real problem after 1979—highlighting the importance of understanding this crucial era. In 1955, when the AFL-CIO was founded, union density stood at 32 percent. Falling slowly, it stood at 24 percent in 1980.[35] By 1989, just 16.8 percent of American workers held union cards; in less than a decade, union density had fallen by almost as many percentage points as in the entire first twenty-five years of the AFL-CIO's history.[36]

These conclusions engage with important scholarship about the roots—and the course—of labor's decline. In influential works, Judith Stein and Jefferson Cowie have both argued that the 1970s represented a critical turning point in the history of labor. According to Cowie, the "hope and possibility" of the early part of the decade gave way to "despair" in the second half. Both see the decade as one in which labor was broken, or what Stein has termed a "pivotal decade." In contrast, Nelson Lichtenstein has argued that the changes in the 1970s reflected broader political and economic developments. In addition to these labor-focused works, other historians have devoted increasing attention to the 1970s, insisting that it was more than a weak relation to the more glamorous 1960s, and was a decade that witnessed both important social and racial protests and the rise of conservatism. With so much attention focusing on the "hot" 1970s, however, subsequent decades have been comparatively overlooked, especially by labor scholars. While some of the roots of the AFL-CIO's problems in the Kirkland-Sweeney era did lie in the 1970s, *Labor Under Fire* asserts that the climate really changed after 1980, when Ronald Reagan was elected president. After 1980, labor's decline accelerated rapidly. While this shift had important precursors, the AFL-CIO went into the 1980s with considerable strength, with a new leader and a favorable administration in Washington. By the end of the decade, however, organized labor had been greatly weakened, as the density figures document.[37]

Density continued to decrease in the 1990s and early 2000s, dropping from 14.5 percent in 1995 to 12 percent in 2009. After 1995, the pace of decline slowed partly because of the efforts of John Sweeney, who poured resources into organizing and encouraged affiliates to discuss—and address—decline. Even Sweeney, however, could not grow the labor movement and turn around the AFL-CIO's fortunes.[38] This outcome is not surprising, as the decline in union density was an international phenomenon that was linked to broad forces, particularly the changing attitudes of management to work organization, rising government opposition, and the decline of heavily unionized manufacturing industries. "Trade unions in Britain and the West are continuing to decline considerably in membership," summarized the London *Times* in 1985, "but show no signs of withering away." Between 1979 and 1983, union density in the UK fell from 54.3 to 49 percent, while in Italy it dropped from 43.8 to 40 percent. In most Western countries, decline accelerated in the 1990s, placing the AFL-CIO's experience in an international context. In the overseas media, stories about unions' "membership crisis" were also widespread.

The pace of decline was especially marked in the United States, however, where the labor movement enjoyed less regulatory protection compared to other developed nations. Employer opposition to unions was also greater. Particularly exposed to the key causes of decline, the AFL-CIO provides an important case study.[39]

In the story of the AFL-CIO's decline—a theme that runs through this work—I argue that there were a number of turning points that together illustrate the need to explore the decisive period after 1979. The 1980 presidential election, which was closely followed by President Reagan's dismissal of over 11,000 striking members of the Professional Air Traffic Controllers Organization in 1981, was especially important. These events were responsible for greatly accelerating the AFL-CIO's decline, establishing the 1980s as a critical decade in the Federation's history. In the early 1990s, following a partial recovery from its darkest moments, the passage of NAFTA was another big blow.[40] NAFTA accelerated the demise of core manufacturing industries that were heavily unionized. After some promising changes in the early years of the Sweeney presidency, the contested presidential election of 2000 and the terrorist attacks of 9/11 again turned the domestic political climate, and the Federation found itself under renewed fire. After 2005, Sweeney's reforms were further undermined when several large affiliates, including his own Service Employees International Union, left the AFL-CIO and formed Change to Win, a rival federation. Many Federation staffers felt that Sweeney's leadership would not have been challenged if Al Gore had won the 2000 election.[41]

As he sought to reform the AFL-CIO, Sweeney was also hurt by the legacy of the past, and it is clear that the Federation must bear some responsibility for its problems. Prior to Sweeney's presidency, labor leaders were slow to recognize the gravity of the situation, or to recommend solutions. Under George Meany, there was little discussion of decline or how to reverse it. The Executive Council, the Federation's key decision-making body, remained all-male throughout the Meany years. While recognized as important, organizing was largely left to the affiliates, a policy that reflected the AFL-CIO's decentralized character. When Meany stood down in November 1979, he predicted in his final speech that the AFL-CIO would grow in the years ahead. Public sector and service workers were joining unions in record numbers, he explained, and the Federation was strong and united. "I am confident that the labor movement is about to embark on another period of significant growth and expansion," he declared.[42]

In retrospect, Meany's speech appears ironic. Rather than an era of expansion, the 1980s proved to be an incredibly harsh time for the AFL-CIO, which came under fire from both the Reagan administration and private employers. As union density dropped at an unprecedented pace, Kirkland was pushed to initiate some reforms—including setting up a committee that studied the decline issue for the first time. He also placed the first woman on the Executive Council, a limited breakthrough, and increased the emphasis on organizing, especially after the formation of the AFL-CIO's Organizing Institute in 1989. Kirkland primarily responded to the harsh climate, however, by calling for unity, and the theme of solidarity defined his presidency.[43]

Many international union presidents felt that these reforms did not go far enough, and in 1995 they backed reformer John Sweeney. Sweeney prevailed over Tom Donahue in the first contested election in the AFL-CIO's history. Drawing on new archival sources and interviews with the main participants, this bitter and important contest is explored in detail here. Under Sweeney, an increased emphasis was put on organizing and political mobilization. For the first time, decline was also discussed in explicit and candid terms. In 2001, when Sweeney addressed the Federation's biennial convention, he sounded a very different tone than Meany or Kirkland. "We have declined in union density from representing one worker in three to now representing only one worker in eight," he acknowledged. "That single fact is the harshest judgment history can make on our collective leadership of the labor movement." The American union movement had stood still, Sweeney noted, representing roughly the same number of members while the economy created millions of new jobs, most of them non-union. The AFL-CIO had not organized the new service and white-collar workers in the way that Meany had predicted.[44]

All through this period, however, the AFL-CIO also carried out a lot of positive work, particularly in the legislative sphere. For most of its history, the Federation has been on the defensive, but in the process it has helped to ensure that crucial laws—including the Occupational Safety and Health Act and the federal minimum wage—have remained on the books. By focusing largely on the Federation's flaws, it is easy to overlook this. "The AFL-CIO has always had to fight," recalled retired staffer Susan Dunlop. "We've *always* had to defend. With health and safety, or minimum wage, or hours, or whatever it is, and it's still going on. So at least there's somebody here that's doing it." Ultimately, the Federation provided an important voice for working people at the national level. As former staffer Barbara Shailor put it, the Federation was "a progressive organization on many issues . . . minimum wage, health care, issues that were well beyond just the desires of its own members. So I think it's the major progressive force in American politics."[45]

On some occasions the AFL-CIO was also much more than a national lobby group—it was truly capable of mobilizing working Americans and their community allies on the national stage, and exerting real political power in the process. Key events—especially Solidarity Day and the 2008 election campaign—illustrated this well. When the AFL-CIO was founded in December 1955, moreover, it was a major institution in American life, a strong, new force that was determined to press—and not just defend—a progressive agenda. If we are to understand the Federation's more recent history, this formative period is the place to start.[46]

CHAPTER ONE

The Roots of Decline

The AFL-CIO in the Meany Years

At 9.30 A.M. on December 5, 1955, the AFL-CIO was born when AFL president George Meany and CIO leader Walter Reuther brought down a single gavel at the Seventy-First Regiment Armory in New York City.[1] With this simple act, a former plumber from the Bronx and a one-time auto worker from Detroit created the largest trade union federation in the Western world, one made up of 141 affiliates from craft and industrial unions. Both men recognized the significance of the moment. The formation of the AFL-CIO, thought Reuther, represented "a great, new beginning," while for Meany this was "the most important trade union development of our time." At 2.30 P.M., President Eisenhower saluted the new organization in a telephone call from his headquarters in Gettysburg, Pennsylvania, where he was recuperating from a heart attack. In a warm congratulatory message, Eisenhower claimed that the labor movement had made a "unique contribution to the general welfare of the Republic." Messages of congratulations were delivered by several other prominent figures, including NAACP special counsel Thurgood Marshall, U.S. presidential candidate Adlai Stevenson, and former First Lady Eleanor Roosevelt. "I am very happy to be here at this historic meeting when the two great labor groups in this country are coming together to join their forces," commented Mrs. Roosevelt. "The growing strength of labor," she added, had "given us strength as a nation."[2] A few months later, a healthy Eisenhower attended the dedication of the Federation's headquarters in Washington, DC. Because the impressive eight-story building was located at the foot of Sixteenth Street, straight across Lafayette Square from the White House, Eisenhower walked to the ceremony.[3]

Eisenhower's actions illustrated how the AFL-CIO occupied a place at the very heart of American life. As Pulitzer Prize–winning reporter C. P. Trussell noted in the *New York Times*, the new federation represented "perhaps the greatest union force in United States history." At the time, the creation of a 15 million-member labor body caused some concern. Reporters asked Eisenhower whether the new organization was too powerful, yet the president insisted that the American people were too "independent" to be bossed around. Even the liberal press discussed the dangers of a "labor monopoly," yet Meany was having none of it. "How can there be too much power if the power is for good and is used only for good?" he replied.[4] A few years later, the blunt leader dismissed renewed claims that the AFL-CIO was too influential as "a lot of bunk." There was, however, no doubt that the Federation began life as a political force to be reckoned with. According to respected labor writer A. H. Raskin, the AFL-CIO was "the new colossus of American labor."[5] As President Eisenhower told the Federation's founding convention, "Never before have so many people banded together in a single organization to promote their mutual welfare." Eisenhower urged the AFL-CIO to use its power wisely, and expressed his hope that it would grow.[6]

On the surface, the next twenty-four years—the Meany years—were the AFL-CIO's heyday. Throughout this period, the Federation remained a major force in American life, an influential lobby group that helped to pass a lot of progressive legislation, especially during the Kennedy and Johnson administrations. Even in the 1970s, as the economy weakened and Meany became increasingly frail, the Federation retained a lot of power, especially within the Democratic Party. On the eve of the 1976 presidential election, Jimmy Carter addressed the General Board, deferentially telling its members that they were "always in the forefront in battles for minimum wage, health care, social security, public education, fairer tax laws, strong national defense, job opportunities, housing and the quiet dignity of free human beings." Throughout the Meany years, presidents, cabinet officials, and White House aides all courted the Federation. Former AFL-CIO staff also remembered the influence that they had over Congress, where the Democrats controlled both houses from 1954 to 1980. According to retired lobbyist Jim Kennedy, the AFL-CIO really functioned as a "People's Lobby" during these years. "We were powerful," he recalled. "It's hard to consider today's circumstances, and remember that in 1965 and for many years thereafter we were the people's lobby. I mean we used it as a term, but we actually functioned that way." A lobbyist in the legislative department in the 1960s, Ray Denison added that the Federation worked closely with House Democrats to push—and often pass—important legislation. "There were victories and defeats, and thousands of hours of painful, ever-so-slow stitching together, like needlepoint, the fine points in bill after bill," he recalled. Sitting in an office overlooking the White House, Denison felt that he was at "the center of power in Washington." As another former staffer summarized, the AFL-CIO in these years had "tremendous power."[7]

Beneath the surface, however, all was not well. For some critics, the Federation's closeness to the White House was problematic, symbolizing the way that its leaders acted more like lawmakers and lobbyists—with whom they

spent most of their time—than the workers they represented. More importantly, the Federation failed to keep up with the growth of the economy,
which created millions of jobs in the white-collar and service sectors. Union
membership was concentrated in manufacturing, yet in the three decades
after World War II blue-collar jobs expanded by just 19 percent, much less
than the 32 percent average for all jobs, and four times less than the growth
rate in clerical posts. Between 1958 and 1978, the Federation's membership
increased only slightly, from 13.8 million to 15.5 million, largely because of the
growth in the economy.[8] The changing nature of the American workforce
meant that union density—the key indicator of union influence—declined
from 32 percent in 1955 to 24 percent in 1979. The AFL-CIO had become
trapped, its membership concentrated in a dwindling sector.[9]

While the drop in union density was not as rapid as it became, corporate
opposition to organized labor was increasing. Between 1955 and 1980, the
Federation reported that National Labor Relations Board (NLRB) complaints against employers for illegal dismissals during organizing campaigns
rose by 600 percent. The percentage of representation elections won by
unions fell steadily over this period, from around three-quarters to little more
than half.[10] The Federation's figures also showed that a number of affiliates,
especially in manufacturing, lost members under Meany, chiefly because of
rising import competition and automation. Between 1955 and 1975, membership in the Textile Workers Union fell from 203,000 to 105,000, while the
Garment Workers lost one third of its membership, or about 150,000 workers,
between the late 1960s and the early 1980s. Imports also hurt affiliates in the
electrical and furniture industries, while declining passenger numbers led to
membership falls for the railroad unions.[11]

Throughout this era, however, Meany refused to be concerned about decline, insisting that the Federation was strong and healthy. To be sure, much
of it was, at least on the surface. While significant decline was concentrated in
industries that were particularly sensitive to imports, membership in other
large industrial affiliates held steady. Between 1955 and 1977, the membership
of the United Steelworkers dropped only slightly, from 980,000 to 954,000,
while the comparable figures for the Machinists were 627,000 and 653,000.[12]
Most affiliates concentrated on servicing their members rather than recruiting,
a pattern that Meany did not challenge. "Why should we worry about organizing groups of people who do not appear to want to be organized?" Meany
told a reporter in 1972. A skilled political operator, Meany concentrated on
wielding power in Washington. While the AFL-CIO president bequeathed
Lane Kirkland a federation that still had considerable power, it was ill-

equipped for the more hostile political and economic climate that it would soon face. Meany also left other legacies, including a deeply anticommunist foreign policy—which Kirkland embraced—and a fractured organization that had expelled some major affiliates, something that he was determined to fix. Finally, Kirkland inherited an organization that had been slow to reach out to women and non-white workers. While he moved to address this, his efforts were not as rapid as many would have liked. Kirkland's presidency was thus shaped by the troubled legacy he inherited from Meany.[13]

At the time of the AFL-CIO's foundation, however, the mood was upbeat. On June 4, 1956, when the eight-story headquarters was formally dedicated, it was a proud moment for Meany. The new building, he noted, would be the place where the labor movement would secure "even greater advances by American wage earners in the years to come." To mark the occasion, Meany secured a permit to close off an entire block of Sixteenth Street for two hours during the dedication ceremony. The building's centerpiece was "Labor is Life," a huge mosaic mural that greeted visitors as they arrived. Seventeen feet high and fifty-one feet wide, the marble and gold masterpiece was one of the largest single panels of its type. Created by artist Lumen Winter, it celebrated the diversity of workers' jobs and the way that unions had helped many different groups.[14] In August 1957 the Executive Council also approved the purchase of the large adjoining property, increasing the Federation's street presence and expanding its operations.[15]

The dedication of the building was the culmination of a merger process that had taken several years. In 1935 dissident industrial union leaders had broken away from the timid, craft-dominated AFL because of its reluctance to organize mass production workers. In the years that followed, significant differences between the two groups remained, especially when the CIO undertook mass organizing drives in the late 1930s and early 1940s.[16] After World War II, however, with the main parts of the industrial economy solidly organized, this militancy dissipated. By the early 1950s, both the AFL and CIO had new leaders—George Meany replaced William Green, and Walter Reuther succeeded Philip Murray—and this allowed for some of the divisions of the past to be set aside. With the CIO well established, most of its unions concentrated on serving their large memberships. "The organizing fervor that marked the early days of the CIO died out during the war," thought labor writer A. H. Raskin. In addition, both Meany and Reuther wanted an increased emphasis on political action, sharing a desire to tackle a rising tide of conservatism that had seen Congress enact the Taft-Hartley Act of 1947, which significantly pared back the freedoms given to workers under the landmark National Labor Relations Act (NLRA) of 1935. During what he later described as "many months of tedious, patient conference negotiations," Meany also stressed the necessity of ending twenty years of division in the labor movement. To meet the challenges of the postwar era, it was vital to create a powerful and united "trade union center."[17]

During the winter of 1954–55, the agreement to bring the AFL and CIO together was drafted. On February 9, 1955, it was approved by the Joint Unity Committee and signed by Meany and Reuther. Under the agreement, the "integrity" of affiliates was closely protected, a core provision. Furthermore, this was a voluntary federation; affiliates could leave at any time without penalty, and most jealously guarded their autonomy. As former staffer Gerry Shea explained, "The AFL-CIO is a federation of independent national unions, who prize their independence . . . in many cases more than solidarity." While the merger agreement declared that affiliates should not conduct raiding against each other, there was no enforcement mechanism or mention of penalties for those who did. Interunion rivalry would be a constant problem under Meany.[18]

Several other parts of the merger document were particularly significant. In a landmark clause, the agreement recognized the right of all workers, "without regard to race, creed, color, or national origin" to share in the "full benefits" of membership in the new organization. Despite this breakthrough, an enforcement mechanism was again lacking, and the remaining AFL affiliates that continued to bar or segregate blacks were not compelled to end these practices. In contrast, both the merger document and the Federation's constitution contained clear procedures—and penalties—for dealing with affiliates that were tainted by corruption or Communist influence, two areas that Meany was particularly interested in.[19]

Despite affiliates' autonomy, the running of the AFL-CIO was highly centralized. The new organization had two executive officers, a president and a secretary-treasurer, who were elected at the biennial conventions. The president had considerable power, including the "conclusive" authority to interpret the constitution between meetings of the Executive Council. The president played the decisive role in setting policy, although the independence of affiliates often constrained his ability to implement it.[20] In addition to twenty-seven vice presidents, the executive officers made up the Council, the body that ran the AFL-CIO between its conventions. In establishing the Council, which met at least three times a year, the merger document guaranteed the dominance of the numerically larger AFL, decreeing that its unions would contribute seventeen vice presidents and CIO unions just ten. The constitution also established a General Board, which was composed of Executive Council members plus one representative (usually the president) from each of the affiliates. The Board met at least once a year to decide "all policy questions referred to it by the executive officers, and the Executive Council."[21] Funding for the new Federation was provided by the assets of the AFL and CIO, as well as by a per capita tax payable by national and international unions—and organizing committees—of four cents per member per month. In its first full financial report, submitted in August 1956, Secretary-Treasurer William Schnitzler—the burly former leader of the AFL Baker's Union who Meany had picked as his deputy—reported that the AFL-CIO had total assets of $8.33 million, an increase of $1.39 million since merger. After liabilities were accounted for, the Federation had a net worth of $4.73 million.[22]

Cementing the authority of the AFL-CIO president, Meany ran the Executive Council with an iron fist. Although he was not young—he was sixty-one in 1955—much of Meany's authority derived from his physical presence. "In appearance he is a cross between bull and bulldog," wrote A. H. Raskin, "with resolute head set on short, massive neck, powerful hands and a bulk that bespeaks solidity rather than flabbiness." Meany was "two hundred and fifty pounds of Bronx granite," and his strong leadership was central to the AFL-CIO's ability to become a respected force in American life. As *New York Times* reporter Kenneth Noble observed, Meany became known for "his bulldog scowl, omnipresent cigar and irascible temperament."[23] An unmistakable figure, he shaped those around him, inspiring loyalty and affection. He had a particularly decisive influence on Lane Kirkland and Tom Donahue, who both worked as his executive assistant (though not concurrently). Meany, thought Donahue, was as "tough as nails," especially when sparring with reporters and congressional committees. Widely respected by the press, Meany had a prominent media profile.[24]

Meany also had lesser-known qualities. Staffers remembered his intelligence and activism, attributes that outside observers often missed. Aide Susan Dunlop cited Meany's backing of a long organizing campaign among migrant farm workers, a campaign that pitted impoverished Latino grapepickers against powerful agribusinesses. Meany was "one of the strongest supporters of the Farm Workers Union," she recalled. In February 1959 the AFL-CIO pledged to mobilize its "full resources" behind a campaign to organize hired farm workers in the fields and packing sheds. Facing determined resistance from growers, the Federation backed the campaign into the 1970s, spending over $1.4 million in the process. Overseen by the charismatic Cesar Chavez, the campaign culminated in a mass boycott of table grapes that

George Meany. Courtesy of Special Collections, University of Maryland Libraries.

aroused considerable sympathy for the labor movement. As a result, by 1970 the AFL-CIO's youngest union had signed more than 300 contracts, covering over 30,000 members.[25] In a broader sense, staffers insisted that Meany was not remote from the rank and file, and never forgot his roots. "Somebody made the mistake one time of calling him a Brooklyn plumber," related staffer Jim Kennedy, "and he got furious—not with the 'cigar-chewing,' and 'a plumber,' and 'a meat-head,' and all that, but that they had the temerity to say he was from Brooklyn. He said: 'God damn it, I'm from the Bronx!'"[26]

Above all, however, Meany was known for his forthright leadership of the labor movement. Less than two years after the founding convention, for example, Meany expelled the large International Brotherhood of Teamsters (IBT), as well as several small affiliates, due to evidence of corruption in their ranks. As labor historian Robert H. Zieger has observed, Meany's ejection of the Teamsters was an "unprecedented exercise in central authority." It also meant that Meany bequeathed Kirkland a divided labor movement.[27]

From the beginning, the AFL-CIO took a strong position against corruption. In January 1957 it adopted a strict—and ominous sounding—"Code of Ethical Practices With Respect to Racketeers, Crooks, Communists and Fascists." Clearly, none of these groups was welcome in the new Federation.[28] The spotlight quickly fell on the IBT, which was the subject of a Senate investigation at the time. Chaired by Arkansas Democrat John McClellan, the Senate Committee on Improper Activities in Labor and Management exposed some vivid and damaging details about the IBT's leaders. In particular, President Dave Beck and Vice President Jimmy Hoffa had both used union funds for their own purposes, with Beck later agreeing to repay $370,000 to the union. Vice President Frank Brewster, meanwhile, admitted to the Senate Committee that he had used union funds for a variety of personal purposes, including making a down payment on a home and paying travel expenses and hotel bills for his race horse trainer and other associates. Conducting its own investigation, the AFL-CIO's Ethical Practices Committee also found that Hoffa had "associated with, sponsored, and promoted the interests of notorious labor racketeers."[29] In its files, the Executive Council listed a range of items that had been purchased with Teamster funds. Totaling more than $85,000, they included sizeable consumer goods such as a washing machine and vacuum cleaner, as well as more bizarre entries such as twelve pairs of binoculars, a bulk order of diapers, and $54 worth of golf balls.[30]

Meany was not afraid of making tough decisions. At the second convention in December 1957, the Executive Committee, citing the Teamsters' refusal to address the charges against it, recommended the union's expulsion. According to the Committee, the IBT's leaders had "blackened" the name of their union and the AFL-CIO had to act to protect the labor movement's credibility.[31] Around the same time, several small affiliates were also investigated on ethical grounds. While a few were placed under trusteeship, others—including the Bakery and Confectionery Workers and the Laundry and Dry Cleaning International Union—were expelled. The debarred unions represented over 1.436 million workers, reducing the Federation's membership to a lower level than it had been at the time of the merger.[32] The loss of the Teamsters, probably the strongest union in America, was particularly damaging in this regard. In 1959, the Federation admitted privately that the exclusions for unethical behavior had resulted in significant "membership loss."[33]

The Teamster case also attracted a lot of negative publicity. Many Americans came to associate organized labor with corruption, undermining the AFL-CIO's reputation—despite its swift response. The press reported the Teamsters' excesses in lurid detail, explaining how union funds had been used to build a $5 million marble-and-glass headquarters that incorporated such luxuries as a 472-seat auditorium with twenty-three-carat gold leaf walls, as well as a penthouse lounge and roof garden. A range of popular books on the Teamster case soon followed.[34] Out in the field, the impact was clear. In

December 1957 a convention discussion about organizing noted that the McClellan Committee investigation had been "used with telling effect against union campaigns in recent months." In 1960 Meany told the Executive Council that the corruption stories had hurt the AFL-CIO as it tried to sign up new members. For "three years," he noted, "the Labor Movement has been subjected to unfavorable publicity because of the exposures of corruption and wrong-doing."[35]

In the organizing field, labor had many other problems. From the beginning, the AFL-CIO struggled to connect with the fastest-growing sections of the labor force. When it was established, the Federation had 15 million members, out of a total workforce of 64 million. The six largest affiliates all came from the industrial or manufacturing sector. The biggest, with 1,239,000 members, was the Autoworkers, followed by the Teamsters (1,231,000) and the Steelworkers (1,194,000). The Machinists, the Carpenters, and the Electrical Workers completed the group. These six unions accounted for almost 40 percent of the Federation's total membership.[36] The biggest affiliates came out of industries dominated by white men, shaping the labor center's identity. As the founding convention documented, women constituted one-third of the labor force, with most of them concentrated in nonunion industries, especially in the service sector. When it was founded, the AFL-CIO only had a small number of members in areas where women were concentrated. In May 1957, Carl J. Megel, the president of the American Federation of Teachers, told the Council that there were 1.25 million teachers in the United States, but 96 percent of them were unorganized. The Federation also had limited representation among government employees, while the Building Service Employees International Union—a forerunner of the Service Employees International Union (SEIU)—had just 205,000 members. The United Food and Commercial Workers International Union, another mainstay of the later years, did not even exist at this time.[37]

Meany recognized the need to organize more, at least verbally. At the time of the merger, he proclaimed that he wanted to double the Federation's membership within ten or fifteen years, an aim that Reuther strongly supported. For Reuther, the creation of the AFL-CIO provided "an unparalleled opportunity" to organize "millions of unorganized workers." It was clear that realizing these goals would be very difficult. Few gains could be expected in the industrial sector; of 13.4 million factory workers, nearly three-quarters of them already belonged to unions. Expansion into the fast-growing South and West, where unions were less common, would also be hard. Eighteen states already had "right-to-work" laws on the books, and most were in the

South. Although labor was expected to increase its efforts in the region, many employers—both in the South and elsewhere—were adept at avoiding unionization by using both carrot and stick tactics. Better prospects for growth existed among the 5.75 million workers in service industries and the 7 million government workers, yet unions in these sectors were small and lacked the resources to launch massive organizing drives.[38]

Unions with a strong organizing record were also outnumbered in the new Federation. The AFL—which was generally more conservative—was the dominant partner in the new structure. The older Federation went into the merger with about twice as many members as the CIO, allowing its leaders to secure the top two positions. The AFL also supplied 109 of the new organization's 141 affiliates, including four of the six largest affiliates.[39] At the time of the merger, CIO unions pledged $4,000,000 to a special organizing fund, but AFL unions were reluctant to match it. The organizing skills of the AFL unions, thought A. H. Raskin, were "atrophied," partly because most had been established decades earlier. Since affiliates were autonomous, all that the AFL-CIO could do was call upon them to contribute to a new Organizing Fund Raising Committee—it could not compel. As part of the merger, the CIO established an Industrial Union Department that was only open to industrial unions. While the IUD forcefully promoted organizing, it faced an uphill battle, especially as the AFL affiliates were beyond its reach.[40]

Despite the official rhetoric about the importance of organizing, actions behind the scenes told a different story. In 1955 the AFL-CIO started life with 335 organizers on staff, but the AFL's dominance soon asserted itself. By August 1956, fifty-six of these staff members had been retrenched. "The Department is working on a program of assisting international unions in their campaigns rather than originating and conducting campaigns itself," reported Director of Organization John W. Livingston to the Executive Council.[41] In February 1959 Livingston related that there were 157 men on the organizing staff, a further significant cut. The drop in staff numbers—and the apparent absence of any female organizers—did not evoke concern or discussion. Livingston added, moreover, that 50 percent of staff time was spent on service work with affiliates rather than actual organizing. Even when this was not the case, Federation staff generally assisted organizers of affiliated unions rather than undertaking "direct organizing work."[42]

Meany was crucial in setting the tone. "It was always the policy of the Federation that the main responsibility for organizational work rested with the affiliated organizations," he told the Executive Council in May 1960. "While the national center had an organizing staff, its function was to give

assistance to the affiliated organizations, and not to carry the full organizational responsibilities of the Trade Union Movement."[43] When organizing
was carried out, progress was not dramatic. Between 1956 and 1959 members
of the Field Staff helped affiliates contest 16,662 NLRB elections, with labor
winning 9,656 of them (58 percent). The winning percentage increased
slightly over this period, something that Livingston termed "the most favorable aspect of organizational activities." About 800,000 new workers were
brought into the AFL-CIO, and Meany claimed that "substantial progress"
was being made. Still, the economy was creating jobs at a much faster rate
than the Federation was able—or willing—to organize.[44]

The organizing cuts also reflected the priority that was given to political
action, and in this area the AFL-CIO was more successful. In its political work,
the Federation strove to speak for all workers, not just its members. Highlighting this, in early 1956 it established a number of committees geared to key
legislative goals, including a Social Security Committee to defend the vital
program and an Economic Policy Committee that advanced the Federation's
positions in favor of job creation and worker protection. In addition, a Fair
Labor Standards Committee pushed for increases in the minimum wage.[45]

The Fair Labor Standards Committee illustrated the Federation's "People's
Lobby" mission well. Although very few union members worked in minimum
wage jobs, this was still a high priority area. In March 1956, following extensive lobbying, the AFL-CIO welcomed an increase in the minimum wage
from 75 cents to $1, a move that helped some two million workers. At the
same time, it pressed for a substantial broadening of the law's coverage, as
millions of workers, especially in agriculture, were still excluded from its provisions. "Extension of minimum wage coverage should be an item of top-
most priority for the present session of Congress," declared an Executive
Council statement in May 1956.[46] A year later, the Federation reiterated these
calls. While the Eisenhower administration proposed some improvements in
the law's coverage, its recommendations—which failed to set a maximum
hours limit—were "grossly inadequate."[47]

Undeterred, the Federation pressed on. In February 1959 the Council
urged Congress to correct "glaring deficiencies" in the Fair Labor Standards
Act. The minimum wage should be raised to at least $1.25 an hour, and cover-
age should be extended to many of the twenty million workers—including
employees in retail stores, laundries, large farms, and canneries—not covered
by the law. Most of these workers, the Council pointed out, were unorganized, so there was no one else to speak for them. Despite these pleas,
Congress—responding to business arguments that a higher minimum wage

would raise inflation and jeopardize economic growth—took no further action in the Eisenhower years.[48]

Workplace safety was another key issue. From the outset, the Committee on Safety and Occupational Health called for much stronger federal action in this area. In particular, the limited Occupational Health Program in the U.S. Public Health Service needed to be expanded significantly. The Federation's work in this area was very important, as the United States continued to lag behind other Western countries in its record of workplace safety. This was graphically highlighted in January 1957, when nine female apparel workers were killed in a factory fire in New Haven, Connecticut. A subsequent investigation revealed that fire escapes at the factory were "far below standard," and some fire exits—as had been the case in the chilling Triangle Shirtwaist Company fire in New York City in 1911—were locked. Following the New Haven fire, the AFL-CIO called for "concerted action" to strengthen public inspection laws. All American workers, it insisted, deserved a safe workplace.[49]

In these years, the AFL-CIO established its interest in a vast number of topics, including many that were far removed from workplace concerns. As the Executive Council summarized in September 1959, the Federation had "broad social objectives" that included "housing, social security, education, civil rights, and mutual security." The AFL-CIO fought consistently—and successfully—to defend the Social Security system, arguing that maintenance of the program was in the public interest.[50] At the same time, the Federation also carried out a lot of close-grained work on behalf of workers. Despite some resistance in Congress, where southern Democrats often sided with Republicans over labor issues, there were important "occasional victories." During the Eighty-Fifth Congress, the Federation helped to pass twelve bills that assisted government workers. In one example, the Federation played a crucial role in securing a pay increase for postal workers.[51] There were also gains at the state level. Between December 1957 and June 1959, pressure from the AFL-CIO ensured that six states acted on minimum wage legislation. In particular, North Carolina became the first southern state to pass a minimum wage law, setting a 75-cent minimum that went into effect on July 1, 1960.[52]

While relations with Eisenhower were always cordial—the president accepted the AFL-CIO's place in national life and spoke of the "essential teamwork between management and organized labor in American industry"— following John F. Kennedy's narrow victory in 1960, the Federation's legislative work received a boost. In 1964, moreover, Lyndon Johnson's landslide victory transformed the political climate in labor's favor. During the Kennedy-Johnson era, the Federation was able to shape an unprecedented amount of legislation. Staffers recalled the era fondly, eulogizing it as a time when, in the words of Gerry Shea, the White House "checked with the AFL-CIO before they did much of anything."[53]

During the Kennedy administration staffers worked closely with the White House, drafting and passing several pieces of legislation. Particularly important were improvements to the minimum wage in 1961 and passage of the Equal Pay Act of 1963, which barred the widespread practice of paying women less than men for equal work. The 1961 minimum wage amendments extended coverage to large retail and service enterprises, as well as those employed in local transit, the construction industry, and gasoline service stations. In all, around one million new workers received the minimum wage of $1.15 an hour, and they also saw their work week cut to forty-two hours. As President Johnson noted in a subsequent letter to Meany, these improvements reflected the "aggressive role played by the AFL-CIO" in pushing for change.[54]

A consummate politician who had served as Senate Majority Leader and Majority Whip, President Johnson passed a wave of progressive legislation that pleased the AFL-CIO, with whom he had a very close relationship. One apt example was the 1966 amendments to the minimum wage, which extended coverage to many state and federal government employees. As a result, some eight million new employees were brought under the law's protection. In 1966 the minimum wage was also raised to $1.60 an hour, a substantial boost. "Congress recognized that an increase in wages for millions of Americans, working at substandard wage levels, was one immediate and effective way to help reduce poverty," declared an ebullient Executive Council. "We in the AFL-CIO are proud to have helped millions of Americans move a step or two above the poverty level."[55]

Meany took a close interest in legislative work. He had regular meetings with key powerbrokers, both at the White House and in Congress. Much of his political work was also carried out on the phone, the prevailing medium of the day, and President Johnson operated in the same way. As Federation economist Rudy Oswald recalled, Johnson and Meany "spoke frequently."[56] Recognizing his importance, Johnson invited Meany to attend the signing of many of the major bills passed during his administration, including the Voting Rights Act, the Housing and Urban Development Act, and various anti-poverty measures.[57] Meany's invitation to the signing of the 1965 Elementary and Secondary Education Act, for example, proclaimed that the AFL-CIO had played an important role in passing the law. The "labor-endorsed" bill

Lane Kirkland with President Lyndon Johnson, who worked closely with the AFL-CIO. Courtesy of Special Collections, University of Maryland Libraries. Copyright 2017 University of Maryland.

was very significant, as it was the biggest aid to education legislation ever to be considered by Congress. In its first year alone, the Act provided more than $1.3 billion to try and overcome the educational disadvantages of children from urban and rural slums.[58]

Other legislative breakthroughs were more labor-focused. The AFL-CIO was the driving force behind the Service Contracts Act of 1965, which required that employers who provided service or maintenance work on federal contracts that were worth $2,500 or more must pay their blue-collar workers wages and fringe benefits that were at least equal to those given to other workers doing similar work in the locality. The law also stipulated that all federal service contract workers must be paid at least the minimum wage, extending minimum wage coverage to contracts of less than $2,500. The Act was a significant step forward. Prior to its passage, federal service contractors had often secured work by cutting employees' wages and benefits. Large numbers of workers on government-contracted jobs, including janitors, food service workers, and maids, had struggled by on low wages and did not receive any benefits. "I was very happy with the passage of the Service Contracts Act," recalled Rudy Oswald, who saw it as one of the main achievements of his long career at the Federation.[59]

While the Federation took its "People's Lobby" mission seriously, some legislative work was designed to improve the organizing climate, paving the way for the Federation's growth. Even in the mid-1960s, however, the limitations of the AFL-CIO's political power were obvious, especially in the key area of labor law reform. Here, employers mobilized to keep organized labor confined to its traditional strongholds. In 1965 a variety of business groups fought the Federation's efforts to repeal section 14(b) of the Taft-Hartley Act, which allowed states to outlaw the union shop.[60] For business groups, the AFL-CIO was a grubby "monopoly" with excessive influence, a group that—in the words of the Committee for Constitutional Government—had "the greatest concentration of political and economic power in the United States of America."[61] Particularly important was the Citizens Committee to Preserve Taft-Hartley, an umbrella group that included a number of prominent corporate leaders, including Winn-Dixie president A. D. Davis, R. J. Reynolds Tobacco Company president A. H. Galloway, and Montgomery Ward chairman John A. Barr. The group's honorary leader was Fred A. Hartley, the conservative former congressman from New Jersey who had co-authored the Act. Influenced by these groups, Senate Minority Leader Everett M. Dirksen led a filibuster that blocked labor's efforts to repeal 14(b). Organized labor had also agreed to President Johnson's request for a delay on 14(b) until after he had pushed through his Great Society program, increasing the likelihood of a filibuster. It acceded to Johnson's request partly because it prioritized the broader progressive agenda over its own interests. After three unsuccessful attempts to end the filibuster, the AFL-CIO had to accept defeat, and it would never again come close to repealing 14(b). In October 1965, a livid Meany blasted the outcome as "a travesty upon the legislative process," but there was little that he could do about it.[62]

This failure was important. By 1965, nineteen states had used 14(b) to ban the union shop, and virtually all of them were in the South. The clause made it hard to organize or build strong unions in the region.[63] As a result, an increasing number of companies moved their factories to Dixie, undermining the AFL-CIO's base. In 1965 one Federation study focused on firms that had moved from Pennsylvania to "right-to-work" states, highlighting the problem. It found that, in 1964, wages for production workers in nine southern "right-to-work" states were $1.93 an hour, whereas in Pennsylvania the average was $2.55 an hour. While the list of companies included in the study represented "merely a small sample" of those that had fled the Keystone State, it still ran to seven pages and counted forty-four firms. "Low wages are not the only attraction," concluded the study. "The anti-union atmosphere that 'right-to-work' laws engender and perpetuate help produce lower fringe benefits and substandard state social welfare legislation as well. These all serve as a lure to plant runaways." The flight of jobs from unionized areas was already a concern, causing "personal tragedies" that the Federation linked directly to the existence of 14(b). The outcome graphically highlighted the need to organize the South.[64]

Section 14(b) proved to be a thorn in the Federation's side. The provision undermined its efforts to build a base in the South, and forced it to fight expensive defensive battles in states that tried to pass new right-to-work laws. In November 1964 Meany candidly told the Executive Council that the Federation's inability to repeal 14(b) had really hurt, especially as labor had spent "millions of dollars [and] limitless time ... fighting against Right-to-Work laws in various states." In Oklahoma alone, the AFL-CIO expended at least $550,000 to thwart a proposed right-to-work law. More companies continued to move their factories to the South, accelerating union decline in the Northeast and Midwest. Throughout the Meany years, the South's economy grew about 30 percent faster than the national average, and the region also had the lowest rates of unionization in the country. This was a grave problem that Meany's successors would have to tackle.[65]

Capital flight was also becoming a broader problem. In the 1960s, the Federation raised concerns about the flight of jobs to Mexico, especially as a border industrialization program was already offering tax and tariff concessions to American firms. In 1963 Item 807 of the U.S. Tariff Schedule gave incentives to U.S. companies who wanted to move manufacturing abroad, especially in the apparel industry. Under Item 807, American apparel makers would cut the cloth needed for garments in the United States and then export it to an overseas factory where the clothing was assembled. Finally, the U.S. apparel company would import the finished garment, paying tariffs only on the value added, or the cost of the labor required, to assemble the garment. Companies in a range of industries—but especially apparel and electronics assembly— were attracted by the much lower wages in Mexico. What the *American Federationist* called "low-wage lures South of the Border" were already a concern, another warning sign.[66]

Despite the AFL-CIO's agreement with Kennedy and Johnson over most domestic issues, they disagreed over trade policies, establishing important themes for the future. Principally concerned with international affairs—and with building a strong economy that would prevail in the Cold War— President Kennedy promised to open up foreign markets. These policies were continued by his successors, including Richard Nixon, Gerald Ford, and

Jimmy Carter. In the early 1970s, as historian Judith Stein has shown, the AFL-CIO helped to write the Foreign Trade and Investment Act—the Burke-Hartke law—which would have ended the tax advantages enjoyed by multinational corporations and given the federal government extensive powers to regulate imports. With the Democratic Party divided over Vietnam and Watergate, however, Nixon repulsed this challenge, and the subsequent Trade Act of 1974 reaffirmed presidential authority to reduce trade barriers, this time with "fast-track" procedures. While many unions did not yet appreciate the dangers posed by foreign competition—the free-spirited UAW opposed Burke-Hartke partly because auto jobs were not yet threatened—the dissonance between labor and the White House over trade was already clear. In the Kirkland-Sweeney era, it would have damaging consequences for the Federation.[67]

Even in the 1960s, some AFL-CIO leaders recognized that more needed to be done to avert decline. From his base as president of the UAW, Reuther led a sizeable dissident faction that wanted to give more emphasis to organizing. At the 1967 AFL-CIO convention, the UAW submitted a resolution that claimed that the Federation lacked the "social vision" and "crusading spirit" that it needed to meet the challenges ahead. Rather, Meany was an autocratic leader who was too closely associated with the Johnson administration. The UAW called for a quarter of the Federation's income to be spent on a "massive organizing crusade," and pressed for stronger links with community groups.[68] Using the convention as his springboard, Reuther repeated many of these allegations two years later.[69] In response, Meany stressed the autonomy of affiliates, arguing that they did not want a heavier emphasis on organizing. He bluntly rejected charges that his leadership was undemocratic, arguing that the younger Reuther just wanted his job. "I think he is interested only in being head of an organization," he asserted.[70]

While there were clear policy differences, the split between Meany and Reuther also reflected personal rivalry. Indeed, the 1967 resolution was preceded by a history of jealousy and conflict that dated back to the AFL-CIO's foundation. According to Joseph Goulden, Meany's biographer, the two men shared a "mutual distrust" that had "weakened the AFL-CIO from the very first days of its existence."[71] In the mid-1960s relations between Reuther and Meany worsened considerably. In November 1966 Secretary of Labor W. Willard Wirtz reported to President Johnson, "The split between George and Walter is real, and probably permanent." The two men had disagreements over international issues, with Reuther disliking Meany's avid support of U.S. foreign policy. By June 1967, personal relations between Meany and Reuther were so poor that Meany refused to serve on any committee that contained Reuther.[72]

Once again, Meany acted decisively when challenged; in July 1968 he summarily suspended the UAW from the Federation, prompting the UAW to disaffiliate from the AFL-CIO. The move led to a bitter exchange of letters between the two leaders. Calling the action "regrettable," Reuther argued that the Executive Council should have called a special convention to discuss the UAW's reform proposals. Meany, however, was clearly angry with Reuther, slamming the "UAW's record of denouncing the AFL-CIO," and its willingness to advertise its "so-called 'proposals for reform and revitalization'" in the press. Although his letter was signed "fraternally," it ended with the pointed assertion that the UAW had been suspended because of Reuther's "apparent unwillingness" to listen to the views of other union leaders.[73]

Meany was unable to put the split behind him. In September 1968 he supported the UAW's ejection from the International Confederation of Free Trade Unions (ICFTU), a large grouping of non-communist national union federations. Upholding the ICFTU's decision, Meany cited the "continuing efforts of the UAW to split the American trade union movement."[74] Even when Reuther was killed in a plane crash in May 1970, Meany reacted cautiously. In a concise Council resolution, Reuther was called a "leader of unique capability," but no mention was made of his role in the foundation of the AFL-CIO. Overall, the Meany-Reuther split was a significant distraction, consuming much of the Federation's energy at a time when it needed to be tackling the roots of decline. Observing these events, Lane Kirkland learned the importance of unity.[75]

Meany and Reuther also differed in their reaction to the civil rights movement. Although the AFL-CIO's early years coincided with an upsurge in civil rights protest—the Federation was born just four days after Rosa Parks' dramatic arrest in Montgomery, Alabama—Meany was wary of direct action protests. Internal records illustrate that the Federation was especially divided in its response to the landmark March on Washington in 1963. The march was strongly endorsed by Reuther and Brotherhood of Sleeping Car Porters' (BSCP) president A. Philip Randolph. Randolph was an experienced and talented black activist; in 1941, for example, he had announced plans to bring 100,000 marchers to the nation's capital to protest against the discrimination faced by black workers in defense industries, especially in hiring. In order to head off the protest, President Franklin Roosevelt issued an executive order that created the Fair Employment Practices Committee (FEPC), an important body that—while its powers were limited—showed that the federal government was aligning itself with the aspirations of black workers. A significant precedent for the equal employment provisions of the Civil Rights Act, the FEPC also encouraged the March on Washington.[76]

Although the march occurred in the summer of 1963—a time when civil rights protests were gripping the country—Meany's cautious stance won the day. Meeting on August 12, the Executive Council discussed the upcoming rally. Seizing the initiative, Reuther and Randolph spoke first. "The AFL-CIO," thought Reuther, "must identify itself with this demonstration." Meany was clearly reluctant, and once he spoke discussion revolved around, as the minutes put it, "whether we want to be identified with a public demonstration initiated by others and over which the AFL-CIO has no control." Fearing violence, the Council—which was dominated by elderly men—refused to endorse the march, although affiliates were free to participate. This position disappointed the progressive wing of the Federation. National Maritime Union president Joseph Curran, a dogged activist with a CIO background, was particularly outspoken. "It seems to me," he charged, "that by this failure, the Labor Movement forfeits the position of leadership which it has always held in the struggle for human rights and social justice." When the march took place on August 28, Meany refused to join Reuther and Randolph in the front ranks. Former staffers also recalled—with some embarrassment—that the AFL-CIO building was locked during the protest. These actions showed the limitations of the AFL-CIO's support for civil rights, especially when it came to direct action protest.[77]

In the legislative arena—where Meany and his staff were in their element—the AFL-CIO's support for civil rights was more effective. The March on Washington had been designed to mobilize support for President Kennedy's civil rights bill, a comprehensive measure that finally took decisive federal action against de jure segregation in the South. Although President Johnson used the mood of mourning after Kennedy's assassination to mobilize support for the bill, its fate still hung in the balance, especially as southern Democrats retained a lot of power. In early 1964, as the bill was debated in Congress, the Federation's legislative director, Andrew Biemiller, seized the initiative. Working behind the scenes, Biemiller wrote hundreds of letters to Representatives and urged their support. According to Biemiller, the bill, which the AFL-CIO was supporting without amendments, was "the most important moral issue on which members of the House will vote this year." Biemiller described the equal employment opportunity provisions—which were included in the final bill—as "especially meritous." The proposed ban on discrimination in public accommodations, he argued, would mean little if blacks did not earn enough to use public facilities widely.[78] The ILGWU's legislative representative, Evelyn Dubrow, also dispatched scores of letters. Both staffers educated union members about the Federation's position and tried to neutralize opposition, especially in the South. "Please inform your members that the AFL-CIO wholeheartedly endorses the civil rights bill," wrote Biemiller to all officers of state and local central bodies, "and urge them to communicate their support of the bill to their United States Representatives and Senators."[79]

While the Federation had long tolerated racial discrimination in its ranks, it played an important role in passing the Civil Rights Act of 1964, which had to overcome a long Senate filibuster led by southern Democrats.[80] On July 2, 1964, President Johnson finally signed the measure into law. For AFL-CIO staffers, it was a proud moment. "We were there," summarized Jim Kennedy. Once the law was passed, Meany quickly convened a national conference of affiliated unions and state central bodies, which was designed to establish a program of compliance. In a tacit acknowledgment of ongoing discrimination within the ranks, Meany admitted that the law was a "challenge" to the labor movement, and he called on affiliates to increase their efforts to destroy racial barriers "at every level." There was, however, no mention of penalties for those that refused to comply.[81]

Although they welcomed the AFL-CIO's support for this legislation, critics argued that the Federation should have done more to tackle discrimination in its ranks. By the early 1960s, they stressed, African-Americans made up at least a quarter of the AFL-CIO's membership, yet few blacks were represented at the top, even within former CIO affiliates. In 1960 black activists set up the Negro American Labor Council (NALC), with Randolph serving as the first chair. The role allowed the eloquent orator to expose the flaws in the Federation's civil rights policies. At the 1961 convention, Randolph declared that the status of nonwhite workers in the labor movement was one of "second class citizenship." Insisting that the basic problem was "race bias," Randolph called for the Federation to adopt much more forceful civil rights policies, including the abolition of all segregated local unions. The Federation resisted most of Randolph's specific demands, however, including his call for the expulsion of unions that practiced discrimination. In 1961 Randolph was also censured by the Executive Council for publicly criticizing the Federation's civil rights record. Again, Meany reacted forcefully to a perceived challenge to his authority.[82]

Despite the Federation's support of civil rights legislation, concrete action to address discrimination in the ranks was limited. At the 1961 convention, one composite resolution—reflecting pressure from Randolph and BSCP colleague Milton P. Webster—recognized that labor's civil rights record contained "serious shortcomings and deficiencies." It also called for continued vigilance to eliminate discrimination. Nevertheless, the resolution repeated Meany's assertion that the AFL-CIO was "in the forefront of the civil rights revolution in our land."[83] Meany remained happier supporting national civil rights legislation rather than discussing the Federation's own racial record. At the 1963 convention, held at the end of a year that had witnessed extensive civil rights demonstrations, Randolph tried to put Meany on the spot. "The labor movement is now called upon to take a stand on the civil rights revolution that has gathered pace during the past year," he declared. In response, an irritable Meany defended the Federation's record, insisting that it had made substantial progress on the race issue. "I refuse to accept the idea that the American trade union movement should be scolded and berated because it is not doing enough," he retorted.[84]

There were good reasons why Meany preferred to keep discussion focused on external civil rights developments. By his own admission, in 1963 nineteen international unions—including the paper workers, tobacco workers, and various railroad crafts—still had segregated local unions. There were at least 172 segregated local unions still in existence, yet Meany stressed that there had once been many more.[85] In other parts of the labor movement, the problem for African-Americans was not segregation but gaining admission. Powerful constituencies within the Federation, the craft and construction unions remained virtually all-white enclaves even as the AFL-CIO supported national civil rights legislation. In many of the building trades, labor apprenticeship programs helped to freeze out blacks. One 1967 survey showed that, despite years of pressure, blacks made up only 1.6 percent of the membership of the Electrical Workers, 1.7 percent of Ironworkers, 0.2 percent of Plumbers (Meany's own union), and 0.2 percent of Sheetmetal Workers. Even in the UAW, where Reuther endorsed many of Randolph's demands, institutional barriers kept most African-Americans out of leadership positions. In 1968 one UAW survey found that although blacks comprised one-third of the union's membership, they held just 75 of 1,000 union staff positions. Some of the problems dated back to the expulsion of the Communist-oriented unions, as the Communist Party had been a strong rhetorical supporter of racial equality, and the pro-Soviet unions had been generally more willing to recruit blacks.[86]

Although the Civil Rights Act prohibited discrimination on the grounds of gender as well as race, the early AFL-CIO also struggled to connect with women workers. At its founding convention, the Federation opposed the

Equal Rights Amendment—which sought to guarantee formal equality for women—arguing that it would jeopardize labor-endorsed laws that protected women against "substandard" wages and working conditions. This position reiterated the AFL's policy. In December 1956 the AFL-CIO issued its first policy statement on women workers, endorsing the need for federal legislation to provide equal pay for comparable work.[87] Meany, however, apparently resisted calls by civil rights director Boris Shiskin to develop programs aimed at eliminating the discrimination faced by women workers. He also knocked back suggestions to appoint a "qualified woman trade-unionist" as a presidential assistant for women's affairs. Only much later would the AFL-CIO's civil rights programs be expanded to cover women, even though Shiskin noted that many affiliates wanted stronger action.[88]

Meany's AFL-CIO failed to keep up with the increasing feminization of the workforce, bequeathing a troubled legacy to Kirkland. In 1920 women had comprised just 20 percent of the workforce, but by 1976 this figure had increased to 41 percent. Organized labor, and especially the AFL-CIO, was clearly not doing enough to mobilize this vast group. In 1970, of the approximately 34 million women in the labor force, just 4.3 million belonged to unions, out of a total membership of 19.4 million.[89] Following the emergence of the modern women's movement in the 1960s, demands for change began to affect the labor movement. On March 23 and 24, 1974, 3,200 trade union women met in Chicago and formed the Coalition of Labor Union Women (CLUW). According to its founding statement, CLUW's "primary purpose" was to "unify all union women in a viable organization" that could determine their common needs and "develop action programs within the framework of our unions." The group was specifically designed to change the labor movement from within.[90]

The CLUW expressed the dissatisfaction felt by many women workers—the fact that although they were getting more jobs, they still earned significantly less than men.[91] It also criticized the underrepresentation of women in the labor movement. In September 1974, for example, a CLUW resolution declared that although women had surged into the workforce, "not all unions" had actively recruited or trained women for leadership positions. As a result, participation by women within the labor movement's bureaucracy was "inadequate." In the Meany era, appointing women to union leadership positions was "just something that wasn't done," recalled Barbara Easterling, who had to wait until 1992—when she was close to sixty—before she became the first female secretary-treasurer of the Communication Workers of America.[92]

Although CLUW sought to transform the labor movement from within, it had its work cut out. Even when Meany left office in 1979, the Executive Council was all-male, largely because the president endorsed the tradition that no union could have more than one representative on the Council. Another custom decreed that this representative had to be a union president, positions that were monopolized by men. Women who held elected offices—but who were not union presidents—were unable to get on the prestigious body. Some union leaders also stayed on the Council after they had retired, and Meany refused to move them on—even if they were octogenarians. "There's nobody going to be asked to leave the council," he explained.[93] Many women shared the frustration of Donna Mobley, a CLUW member in New York who wrote at one chapter meeting in 1977, "When is CLUW going to get a woman on the AFL-CIO Exec. Bd.?" Despite these appeals, many unions, particularly in the powerful building trades, continued to resist. Even affiliates with many female members, recalled Lenore Miller from the Retail, Wholesale, and Department Store union, "had an awful lot of male leadership." Miller, who later became the first female union president to serve on the Council, recalled that it "took a very long time" to bring change to this area.[94]

Another legacy that Meany bequeathed to Kirkland was a fiercely anticommunist foreign policy. Coming out of a conservative craft union, Meany was a committed anticommunist, and in the early Cold War era the AFL enthusiastically embraced the U.S. government's containment policy. In 1949–50, however, the CIO had also expelled eleven unions with the most pro-Soviet records, a move that reflected the increasingly anticommunist emphasis of U.S. foreign policy, as well as bitterness from the 1948 election, when the pro-Soviet faction in the CIO had broken with the Democratic Party and endorsed third-party candidate Henry A. Wallace. "The anticommunism was just as strong, I believe, in the CIO as it was in the AF of L," thought Tom Donahue. Inheriting anticommunism from both of its predecessors, the AFL-CIO quickly laid down its opposition to "free labor" having any contact with official workers' organizations in Eastern bloc countries because these unions were government-controlled. Kirkland subsequently upheld this hard line. At the 1957 convention, Meany detailed the need to combat the spread of Communism. Speaking just a few weeks after the Soviet launch of Sputnik, the first artificial earth satellite, Meany warned, "This is no phantom danger . . . we face the advocates of world communism dominated by Moscow. . . . We face a militant ideology geared to war, continuous war with any and all means, against the free democratic way of life." The AFL-CIO had a duty to resist.[95]

Under Meany, every foreign policy issue was viewed through an anticommunist lens. Communism, Meany declared in 1955, was the "totalitarian threat of our day." Believing that the Communists—short of war—could only seize control of a country by subverting its mass labor organizations, Meany insisted that the AFL-CIO had a special duty in this area, and his strident beliefs consistently drove Federation policy. In 1958, for example, the Council argued that the "racist" policies of the South African government, including denying recognition to African labor unions and preventing them from striking, were "playing into the hands of Communists."[96] In the late 1950s and early 1960s, as demands for national independence swept across Africa, the AFL-CIO was on guard. "The political awakening of Africa," it noted, should be encouraged so that these new nations could quickly develop "viable democratic institutions." Otherwise, the Soviets would step in. "Only free trade unions," it declared, could "prevent the growth of totalitarianism in Africa." The Federation took a similar line in Asia and Latin America.[97]

In July 1962 the AFL-CIO set up the American Institute for Free Labor Development (AIFLD), a Cold War body that aimed to further what Lyndon Johnson would later term "the development of free and democratic trade unionism" in the American "Hemisphere." The AIFLD was established as part of the Kennedy administration's Alliance for Progress, which tried to build democratic institutions in Latin America in the wake of the Cuban Revolution.[98] Between 1964 and 1968 alone, Meany's Executive Council gave $300,000 to AIFLD "impact projects," which were designed to provide immediate aid to non-communist unions across Latin America. In all, the Council approved 159 projects in nineteen different countries. For critics on the Left, the AIFLD was controversial, especially as its board included executives from U.S. companies that fought unions. Furthermore, most of the AIFLD's budget derived from federal funds, especially the U.S. Agency for International Development. While much of the AIFLD's work focused on education, there was some validity to critics' charge that the Institute went much further, especially in supporting anticommunist dictatorships. For Meany, however, these important programs achieved valuable results, especially as they fended off Soviet-style unionism. "We have helped workers in the newly emerging countries," he asserted, "we have made a great contribution in Latin America, Africa and Asia. . . . More and more, the unions are beginning to look a little bit like our unions."[99]

Under Meany, the AFL-CIO was also an enthusiastic supporter of U.S. intervention in Vietnam. In December 1965 a key convention resolution pledged "unstinting support" for all measures that the Johnson administration might find necessary to halt the spread of Communism in Vietnam. The Federation shared the common view that America had to take a stand in South-East Asia. "In Viet Nam," declared the Executive Council in 1966, "our country is fighting for the entire free world." Meany recognized that the costly war had a "heavy bearing" on the AFL-CIO's domestic program, which called for more spending on job creation and antipoverty programs, yet he opposed efforts to end the war. Even when the antiwar movement grew, Meany stuck by LBJ. "There are those who insist the war must be stopped, on any terms, so that domestic progress can continue," he wrote Johnson in December 1967. "They claim to be the voice of liberalism, yet they are blind to the first essential without which liberalism cannot exist—human freedom."[100]

Voices of dissent—especially those of UAW secretary-treasurer Emil Mazey and American Federation of State, County and Municipal Employees (AFSCME) president Jerry Wurf—were again sidelined. Although there was a significant and growing antiwar faction in the labor movement, the former AFL unions supported Meany, and there was little change in the Federation's policy right through to the end of the war. Even in February 1973, when the war came to an unsatisfactory end through the Paris Peace Accords—which failed to effectively guarantee the future of the Republic of Vietnam—the Executive Council claimed that the United States had emerged from the messy conflict with "unimpaired credibility" and had preserved the "sovereignty and independence" of South Vietnam. "In this light," proclaimed the Council, "the AFL-CIO has correctly and steadfastly supported the basic Vietnam policy of three Administrations." Meany's Vietnam policy severed ties with the Left, tainting the AFL-CIO's reputation for decades. "To a generation of progressive-minded unionists and intellectuals," observed historian Edmund F. Wehrle in 2005, "the federation's hawkish stance on Vietnam seemed an unforgivable error, the product of a mindless anticommunism that poisoned dreams of an activist labor movement working in coalition with a revitalized Left."[101]

Meany also ensured that the early AFL-CIO placed a heavy emphasis on servicing members. Coming out of the conservative plumbers union, Meany had spent almost his entire career in the labor bureaucracy, and he was proud of it. Shortly after the creation of the AFL-CIO, Meany told a meeting of the National Association of Manufacturers (NAM) that he "had never been involved in a strike and had never belonged to a union that had called one." For many observers, the remarks illustrated that Meany—rather than proselytizing—wanted to work with management and secure gains through collective bargaining.[102] In this area, the AFL-CIO was very successful, especially during the 1950s and 1960s, when the economy grew. As a result, Meany was able to emphasize positive news and strengthen his position with many affiliates. In December 1965 a confident Meany declared that, after its first decade, the AFL-CIO was "stronger and healthier than at any time in the history of the American labor movement." Gains were particularly strong in the collective bargaining area, where Meany claimed that the Federation had raised workers' real wages by 19 to 30 percent. Clear improvements had also been made in pension benefits, health and welfare plans, job security provisions, and supplemental unemployment benefits. Furthermore, the Federation had reached a "new peak" in membership, with most affiliates having gained members. This was, however, partly a product of the economic conditions.[103]

While some of the Federation's claims—particularly in regard to membership—may have been overstated, there was no doubt that the AFL-CIO was able to deliver unprecedented economic benefits to its members. Throughout the 1950s and 1960s, the strength of the economy helped large affiliates to make major gains at the bargaining table. Between 1961 and 1965, the weekly pay of steelworkers increased by over $20, and fringe benefits also jumped sharply. In June 1965 the average hourly wage in the steel industry was $4.43, close to the peak in U.S. industry. Unemployment in the major steel centers of Gary, Indiana, and Youngstown, Ohio—communities that would later become symbols of economic devastation and deindustrialization—stood at just 3.2 percent and 3.8 percent, respectively. As a Johnson administration memo in June 1965 summarized, "Steelworkers have scored great gains in the present record expansion."[104] The steelworkers' experience was not unusual. In the 1960s basic wage rates for production workers, which were negotiated between major employers and the industrial unions, rose 44 percent. Even allowing for inflation, workers made strong gains, and the AFL-CIO ended the decade on an upbeat note. By October 1969, when the eighth constitutional convention met in Atlantic City, it noted that while income inequality was a problem, American workers were enjoying "the highest standard of living ever known by mankind."[105]

In the major manufacturing industries, national bargaining increased labor's leverage and helped it to secure substantial gains for all workers, whether they were union members or not. In the spring of 1965, for example, the United Rubber Workers' union reached an agreement with the major rubber firms, securing a twenty-eight-cents-an-hour package of wage and welfare improvements for 52,000 workers. The deal—as was commonly the case—was reached a few hours before a strike deadline. Such gains pleased

Meany, who viewed the delivery of economic benefits as the AFL-CIO's prime purpose. In an April 1971 address to members, he summarized this philosophy: "Our business is jobs and decent working conditions on the job and an adequate income as our share of the wealth that the economy produces. This has always been our business. And everything we do—organizationally, legislatively, politically—is directed toward this basic simple idea—decent jobs at decent pay and a fair share for the worker in the economy."[106]

In the 1970s, however, the economy weakened, partly because of the costs of the Vietnam War. As inflation and unemployment rose, workers suffered. Continuing to seek improved pay and benefits, the AFL-CIO clashed with the Nixon and Ford administrations. The Federation was fundamentally opposed to the "Nixon game plan," which tried to revive the economy by freezing wages and restricting prices. The Federation also claimed that employers were using Nixon's economic controls to attack unions. In the early 1970s the weak economy, combined with a long period of Republican dominance of the presidency, hurt the AFL-CIO. "The policies of the Nixon-Ford Administration," summarized Meany in 1975, "have plunged America into the worst economic crisis since the 1930s."[107]

The 1970s still produced victories for the AFL-CIO, reinforcing Meany's sense that all was fundamentally well. Even during the Nixon and Ford presidencies, a Democratic Congress secured the passage of important progressive legislation. In 1970 and 1971 the AFL-CIO helped to secure the passage of the landmark Occupational Safety and Health Act, as well as a five-year extension of the Voting Rights Act. It also advocated for a public service employment bill, which Nixon reluctantly signed at a time of high unemployment.[108] Both Nixon and Ford also took the AFL-CIO seriously. Meany went to the Nixon White House regularly, and even played golf with the president. Nixon later wrote that, while his relationship with Meany was "tempestuous," he respected the "tough, smart, and combative" labor leader. Despite policy differences, Meany had a constructive dialogue with the Nixon and Ford White Houses, who saw the AFL-CIO as a constituency that could not be ignored. The two groups also shared common ground in foreign policy. "We want to keep open and friendly communications [with the AFL-CIO]," summarized Nixon's Special Counsel, Charles Colson, "notwithstanding any political differences."[109]

Under Nixon and Ford, the Federation carried out its "People's Lobby" role effectively. In 1972 the federal minimum wage stood at $1.60 an hour, and it covered some 45 million workers. The Federation pushed for coverage to be extended, and for a $2.20 minimum wage to be adopted by 1974.[110]

In that year, Congress—following lobbying from the AFL-CIO's legislative department—raised the minimum wage to $2.00 an hour, with a further increase to $2.30 scheduled within two years. In addition, the law was amended to cover federal, state, and local government employees, as well as domestic workers. The improvements in coverage represented a major breakthrough, and were secured despite objections from the Nixon White House. At the state level, collective bargaining laws for public workers continued to spread, often because of pressure from state labor federations. In 1978, following a campaign by government unions, the Federation also secured collective bargaining rights for federal workers in the Panama Canal Zone.[111]

Helped by the new laws, government workers flocked to unions. Between 1964 and 1981, the American Federation of State, County and Municipal Employees grew from 240,000 members to almost 1 million. Throughout the 1970s, the union was picking up 1,000 new members every week. The affiliate's growth was also linked to the dynamic leadership of its president Jerry Wurf, an outspoken Jewish American from Brooklyn. Unlike private companies, government agencies did not usually oppose unions, while the influx of union-minded African-Americans into government and service sector jobs further boosted organizing. In this era, notable gains were made among African-American hospital workers, many of whom had been politicized by the civil rights movement. "The lowest paid hospital workers, all over the country ... were African-American workers, and so it [organizing] was sort of on the heels, it was seen as part of the civil rights movement," recalled Karen Ackerman, who organized hospital workers on the East Coast at this time.[112]

Other affiliates also benefited from these changes. Between 1969 and 1977, membership in the SEIU jumped from 352,000 to 505,000. The union quickly became a major force in the Federation, admired for its ability to innovate and grow. It was a heady time, recalled former staffer Bob Welsh, as the union benefited from highly favorable conditions: "Our problem always was we had too many opportunities to choose from, and actually having enough resources to ... take advantage of any one opportunity, was a major problem for us. ... The public sector, where state collective bargaining laws were being put in place, we would go in as a sort of second union, behind AFSCME in many places, and be part of organizing in those states, and in some states we would dominate." In June 1979, moreover, the merger of the Retail Clerks and the Meat Cutters helped to create the United Food and Commercial Workers International Union (UFCW). With 1.3 million members, the UFCW was the AFL-CIO's newest and largest affiliate. Like the SEIU and AFSCME, the

UFCW was committed to organizing, and its membership included large numbers of women and racial minorities. A different kind of AFL-CIO was taking shape.[113]

Despite the growth of particular affiliates, on the whole organizing was getting harder, especially in the private sector. Between 1969 and 1979, the AFL-CIO claimed that NLRB unfair labor practice complaints against employers jumped by 250 percent. One prime example was J. P. Stevens, a notorious textile firm that violated the NLRA on fifteen different occasions between 1965 and 1976, paying out over $1.3 million in back pay as a result. For the AFL-CIO, Stevens was "the Nation's No.1 labor law violator," and its example was influential, especially in the South. Openly flouting the law, companies like Stevens were able to kill organizing drives, a trend that worried Federation leaders. "Union-busting is a growth industry in America today," asserted the Executive Council in February 1979. Another disturbing development was the growth of consultants who advised firms on how to avoid unionization, usually by skillfully blending reprisals and inducements. "Worker protections geared to the conditions of the 1930s are inadequate in the face of employer tactics of the 1970s," noted the Executive Council in 1977. "Gone are the employer's goon squads and the billy clubs; today's union-busters wear business suits and carry attaché cases."[114]

In an effort to tackle these problems, in the spring of 1977 Meany initiated a major fight for labor law reform. Calling the NLRA "a hollow shell of its 1935 promise," Meany's reform bill mandated quick elections and allowed the labor board to issue "self-enforcing orders" in unfair labor practice cases, ensuring that workers fired for union activity would be quickly reinstated. Penalties for violating the law were also increased. Privately, Meany admitted that the bill's provisions were "ambitious," but he hoped that the AFL-CIO's "many friends in Congress" would carry the day.[115] Even Meany knew that he could not just rely on high-level lobbying. In an unusual move for the era, every AFL-CIO member was written to and urged to support the campaign. "America's workers have a tremendous stake in this campaign," explained Meany. The Federation also prepared a detailed Speakers' Handbook and other educational materials for use by interested activists. Despite these efforts, contacts between Federation staff and grassroots members were limited. For many members in established unions, moreover, organizing was not a top priority.[116]

Labor's opponents were also well organized and powerful. Increasingly unified, groups such as the Business Roundtable, the National Association of Manufacturers, and the U.S. Chamber of Commerce lobbied intensively against the AFL-CIO's proposals. The legislation, they charged, was designed to "enhance the power of labor unions," especially as it also included provisions that allowed unions to be recognized on the basis of signed authorization cards. Rather than making such controversial changes, employers argued, it was better to maintain the status quo, which was proven to protect "employee rights." In this way, business groups cleverly separated unions from "employees," portraying the former as a special interest only concerned with amassing power. It was a strategy that would be used frequently—and successfully—in the years to come.[117]

On the surface, the Carter administration supported the labor reform effort. The president even urged the AFL-CIO to keep up the fight. "We who are working for Labor Law Reform," Carter wrote Meany in June 1978, "must counter the emotionalism and misinformation of the opposition with straight, honest talk about the real need for reform and the real effect on American businesses of this modest reform legislation." At the same time, the mobilization of the business community, including small businesses, concerned the administration. In June 1978, 5,000 small business owners marched on the U.S. Capitol to protest against the proposals. Seeking to respond, several of Carter's aides, including Secretary of Labor F. Ray Marshall, met with march leaders and promised that they were "flexible as to several 'small business amendments.'" Responding to business concerns, congressional supporters also agreed to several modifications to try and ensure that the legislation passed.[118]

Led by the increasingly influential National Association of Manufacturers, the corporate campaign carried the day. By 1977, the NAM represented more than 13,000 companies and 15 million workers, making it a formidable opponent. Charging that the bill benefited unions rather than workers, the NAM fought the AFL-CIO in every available forum, including the media and Congress. Even Meany admitted that the intensity of these efforts caught him off guard. "What I did not expect and what I find unexplainable," he commented at a White House breakfast in May 1978, "is the campaign of opposition from the blue chip corporations of America—the campaign financed by the most 'responsible' corporate leaders in this country."[119] Eventually, this opposition persuaded the AFL-CIO to admit defeat, bringing its two-year fight for labor law reform to an end. In June 1978, after six failed efforts to break a Senate filibuster, the *New York Times* pronounced the "death of labor law reform."[120]

While the labor law campaign was unsuccessful—and the AFL-CIO was also disappointed that its full employment legislation was watered down significantly—the Federation still ended the Meany era with a lot of power, and in an upbeat mood. Few staffers anticipated how hard things were to become in the 1980s, and there were no specific reforms to address declining union density, which was not seen as a major problem. "In the sixties and the seventies," recalled Gerry Shea, the AFL-CIO remained "really strong." Despite their awareness of negative trends, leaders rarely discussed the decline issue. In February 1972 one reporter asked Meany why the labor movement was not growing as fast as the country's workforce. "I don't know. I don't care," he snapped. Even as ominous trends accelerated in the 1970s, Meany did not seem concerned. "Frankly, I used to worry about the membership, about the size of the membership," he added. "But quite a few years ago I just stopped worrying about it, because to me it doesn't make any difference." As evidence mounted that employers were becoming increasingly sophisticated and united as they fought unions, Meany continued to insist that organizing should be left to affiliates. What was needed, summarized the Executive Council in 1973, was "more participation by the unions and expansion of organizing efforts."[121]

In Meany's later years, the emphasis on publicizing good news increased. In 1975, as the Federation reached its twentieth anniversary, the president insisted that the overall trend was positive. "During that period," he proclaimed as he reviewed the years since the merger, "we have seen significant progress toward a better life for all Americans. Despite setbacks and reverses, from time to time, the overall movement has been forward."[122] Even in the late 1970s, with union density clearly in decline, Meany and his staff asserted that all was well. In February 1979 organizing director Alan Kistler reassured the Executive Council that it was important not to "write the labor movement off as far as growth is concerned." Although density had dropped, unions were maintaining membership. Meany again dismissed reports of decline, pointing instead to positive developments such as the growth of service sector and government unions. In 1979, as Meany's health failed and he prepared to step down, the mood at the Federation was generally optimistic. The octogenarian leader submitted his final convention report "with confidence in the future of the labor movement." The years since the merger, he reasserted, had been "productive ones for the American labor movement."[123]

Even in the private world of the Executive Council there was almost no discussion of decline, with Meany insisting that fundamental changes were not necessary. By the late 1970s, moreover, organizing was rarely mentioned.[124] On the ground, there was some dissatisfaction. At the 1979 convention, Harry Van Arsdale, Jr., the leader of the powerful New York City Central Labor Council, called for the AFL-CIO to give more support to affiliates that wanted to organize. According to Van Arsdale, major recruiting campaigns "should not be taken for granted as the sole concern of the individual unions," and needed more AFL-CIO involvement. Despite these recommendations, the Federation failed to change long-standing organizing policies.[125] Union leaders in the fast-growing service and government sectors grew especially frustrated. "We realize, and I think everybody in this room should realize, we have forgot how to organize," SEIU president George Hardy told the twelfth constitutional convention in 1977. Within the labor movement, the dominant feeling was that "now is not the time to organize." In reality, claimed Hardy, "any time is the time to organize."[126]

Meany did not share this sense of urgency. Rather than organizing, he remained focused on political and legislative work, an area that bore more fruit. Through the 1970s, Meany took pride in the way that the AFL-CIO was able to fend off efforts by the National Right to Work Committee to pass new "right-to-work" laws. In the mid-1970s the National Committee tried hard to push through restrictive laws in Idaho and New Mexico. Placing full-page advertisements in national newspapers, the Committee was confident of victory, but a determined counterattack by the AFL-CIO ensured that both bills were defeated. Following Jimmy Carter's victory in the 1976 presidential election, moreover, Meany enjoyed another close relationship with a Democratic White House. After eight years of Republican administrations, this change meant a lot to him.[127]

Like their Democratic predecessors, Carter's aides took the AFL-CIO seriously. Although there were tensions over the president's incomes policy—which targeted the industrial sector in an effort to control inflation—his papers reveal that the administration forged a closer relationship with labor than many outsiders realized. In September 1977 Carter's chief domestic policy adviser, Stu Eizenstat, wrote a colleague that the administration had a "very positive working relationship" with the AFL-CIO. Throughout his presidency, Carter addressed Executive Council and General Board meetings. "I have gotten to know many of you personally," he told the General Board in September 1980, "and I have benefited from your advice."[128] This relationship was not just symbolic. During the Carter years, the AFL-CIO was the driving force behind a series of increases in the minimum wage. In early 1977, as the administration devised its minimum wage policy, Secretary of Labor Ray Marshall held extensive discussions with the AFL-CIO, particularly Kirkland and Donahue. This dialogue helped the Carter administration to agree to a minimum wage hike that it termed "the largest single increase in history." Between January 1977 and January 1981, the minimum wage jumped from $2.20

Lane Kirkland with President Jimmy Carter. Courtesy of Special Collections, University of Maryland Libraries.

to $3.35 an hour, with Carter terming this a "dramatic breakthrough." The administration and labor also worked to defeat efforts by congressional Republicans to exempt young workers by paying them a lower wage. Clearly, the Federation remained an effective "People's Lobby."[129]

Much of the AFL-CIO's power, however, was linked to Meany. As two of Carter's domestic advisers wrote in 1978, Meany was "an extremely respected member of the political community," a veteran powerbroker who could "influence the political climate with an off-the-record remark." Aides prepared detailed memos for Carter to illustrate all he was doing for organized labor, and they recommended that he stay in regular social contact with Meany. For many Americans, the twelve-term Meany—an unmistakable figure—*was* the AFL-CIO.[130] In contrast, Secretary-Treasurer Lane Kirkland was an anonymous man, a behind-the-scenes operator with little public profile. He was, summarized the *New York Times*, a "mini Meany." Meany finally stepped down in November 1979; he was greatly affected by the death of his wife, Gina, in March, and his health declined sharply after this. When Meany stepped aside, all the focus was on the retiring leader, his long record of achievement. For the understated Kirkland, stamping his authority on the AFL-CIO presidency would be an uphill battle. While the Federation retained considerable power, particularly in the legislative sphere, Kirkland also inherited an organization that had not tackled decline, had not reached out to its members, and had failed to diversify at the top. It was riddled with internal divisions, especially as two of the largest founding affiliates were no longer members. Many challenges lay ahead. The Federation was also about to come under fire in new—and unexpected—ways.[131]

CHAPTER TWO

A New President and a New Decade

In November 1979, when Lane Kirkland became president, the mood at the AFL-CIO was upbeat. Kirkland began his presidency during the closing days of the Carter administration, enjoying a brief, deceptive honeymoon. Despite differences over industrial and incomes policies, the Federation's leaders enjoyed a constructive working relationship with the Carter administration, and Kirkland was a friend of the first family. Federation officials praised many presidential appointments, calling NLRB General Counsel Bill Lubbers "outstanding" and Ray Marshall "the best Secretary of Labor in the history of our government."[1] In the fall of 1979, Carter accepted the invitation to address the AFL-CIO's thirteenth constitutional convention, declaring that he was "honored" to be invited. In his speech, Carter praised Meany and Kirkland as "old friends," adding that his administration had a "solid working relationship" with the AFL-CIO. The president also reiterated his determination to pass "strong labor law reform."[2]

Once Kirkland was in office, the situation changed quickly. Two events—the 1980 election and the 1981 PATCO strike—transformed the political climate, placing the AFL-CIO on the defensive. Kirkland's presidency was thrown into crisis, his leadership questioned. It was the start of a new era, one in which the AFL-CIO operated in a hostile economic and political climate. For Kirkland, the turnaround was a shock, and he struggled—at least initially—to respond.[3]

In many ways, Kirkland's background had not prepared him for the adversity that would characterize his presidency. Reflecting his internal connections, Kirkland's ascendancy to the top job occurred quietly, largely behind closed doors. "George Meany sort of tapped him (Kirkland) to be president," recalled Markley Roberts, a former staffer in the Public Policy Department. After Meany took the microphone at the 1979 convention and nominated Kirkland as his successor, the handover was a formality. Meany was aware that it was not customary for the chairman to make nominations, yet he noted—with customary assertiveness—that there was "nothing" in the AFL-CIO Constitution that prevented him from doing so. Meany gave a glowing endorsement of Kirkland, praising his early work as a researcher and speechwriter for the Federation. He also extolled Kirkland's success in establishing a close working relationship with the Carter administration. "Lane," he declared, "has finally got across to the White House that they can have American labor as a partner . . . not a junior partner, but a real partner who has something to contribute." Meany clearly wanted an inside successor, one who could carry on the political work in Washington that he valued so highly. After Meany praised Kirkland's "great integrity," as well as his dedication, experience, and knowledge, he was elected unopposed. Officials from Kirkland's own union, the International Organization of Masters, Mates and Pilots, seconded his nomination. Kirkland's running mate, Tom Donahue, was another insider. Meany's executive assistant, Donahue was more outgoing and charismatic than Kirkland, and had a clearer speaking style. "Lane made a very, very good decision in getting Tom Donahue as his secretary-treasurer," related Roberts, "because . . . Tom Donahue has that Irish capacity to identify, shake hands."[4]

For three decades, Meany had trained Kirkland, and it was difficult to imagine anybody better placed to protect his legacy. As Meany's assistant and later as secretary-treasurer of the Federation, Kirkland had forged close relationships with key power brokers in Washington. Kirkland dealt frequently with White House aides, and he also gained regular access to presidents, especially Democratic ones. One example was his relationship with Democratic Party powerhouse Lyndon Johnson. In one typical exchange in the wake of the 1960 presidential election, the vice president-elect thanked "Lane" for his "most helpful" work during the campaign. "I know you share with me the deep satisfaction of seeing our efforts crowned with success," he added. When LBJ became president, Kirkland arranged regular meetings between the Executive Council and the White House, helping him to forge his reputation in Washington.[5] Meany worked regular office hours and prized his evening privacy, whereas Kirkland started and finished later. As a result, it was Kirkland who often took Johnson's restless late-night phone calls, rather than Meany. After Johnson left office, Kirkland continued to field evening calls from the White House.[6]

Long before he became president, key outsiders had predicted Kirkland's ascendancy. In 1970 Charles Colson, a top aide to President Nixon, described Kirkland as "Meany's heir apparent." To well-placed observers, Kirkland's rise up the AFL-CIO bureaucracy was seamless. In 1960, while still in his thirties, Kirkland became Meany's chief assistant, while nine years later he was appointed secretary-treasurer by "unanimous action," Meany having put his name forward. There was no discussion of Kirkland's merits, and no alternative candidates.[7] Meany valued Kirkland's political skills, as well as his fierce

Secretary-treasurer Kirkland meeting with President Richard Nixon. Courtesy of Special Collections, University of Maryland Libraries. Copyright 2017 University of Maryland.

anticommunism. To Meany, Kirkland was "a strong and vigilant defender of liberty, at home and abroad." He was also a faithful deputy. Even in the late 1970s, as Meany's health began to fail, the secretary-treasurer quietly bided his time. In 1977, when another AFL-CIO convention passed with Meany still in charge, Kirkland joked that he was "the world's longest permanent heir-apparent."[8]

Filling Meany's shoes was a tough assignment. Describing the Federation's top decision-making body, Charles Colson observed, "Meany still runs a one-man show and fully controls the Council." It was fitting that even when Meany stood down as a frail eighty-five-year-old, during his last official act as president the wooden block on which the gavel rested fell and broke in half.[9] Meany, summarized staffer Susan Dunlop, was a "labor icon." At the start, Kirkland deferred to his predecessor, and seemed reluctant to step out of his shadow. "I cannot promise to match, or even approximate, the record of George Meany," he noted meekly.[10] Some commentators questioned Kirkland's autonomy, dismissing him as "a carbon copy" of his former boss and a "mini Meany."[11]

In the early days of the Kirkland presidency, Meany was also a visible presence, and his shadow often seemed to engulf his successor. Meany was made President Emeritus and continued to receive a remuneration package that was equivalent to "the highest salary paid to the president of the

AFL-CIO." Even when Kirkland chaired Executive Council meetings, he sat under a woodcarving—in profile—of his rumbustious predecessor.[12] Two months into the Kirkland presidency, Meany died from cardiac arrest. Meany's passing, while paving the way for Kirkland to assert himself, also robbed him of attention. Tributes poured in for Meany, whose body lay in state at the AFL-CIO headquarters. As President Carter commented, Meany had been an "American institution," a man who had changed the country through "the force of his character and the integrity of his beliefs." Upon Meany's death, Carter decreed that flags on all federal buildings should fly at half-mast, an honor also given to Meany by his home state of New York.[13]

Kirkland, however, had some clear differences from Meany, traits that were often missed by outside observers. In particular, a softer—and more collaborative—leadership style reflected a very different background. A native of South Carolina, Joseph Lane Kirkland was born in the small town of Camden on March 12, 1922. Like Meany, whose Christian name was William, Kirkland was always known by his middle name. The similarities, however, ended there. While Meany had been a Bronx plumber, Kirkland was descended from southern aristocracy, a highly unusual background for a labor leader. South Carolina was also one of the least unionized states in the country. Kirkland's great-great-grandfather, Thomas Jefferson Withers, signed the Declaration of Secession that took South Carolina out of the Union, and he subsequently served in the Confederate Senate. Kirkland grew up in the mill town of Newberry, South Carolina, an experience that provoked his interest in workers' struggles. His father, Randolph Withers Kirkland, was a cotton buyer, and Kirkland remembered going to the public schools with students who worked in the mills at night. In the process, he heard how unorganized workers could be fired at the company's whim, losing everything—including their company-owned house—in the process. "There's no better way to get an education in becoming a liberal than to be exposed to those sorts of things," he reflected later.[14] Still, Kirkland had much better opportunities than most of his classmates. Drawing on his grandfather's large library, the youngster read widely, providing an escape from the poverty around him. "Scientific, historical, the classics. I went through all of those," he recalled later. After high school, Kirkland found that a year at the local college "wasn't very fulfilling." He added, "If you live in a little town and you don't want to work in the mill, you spend a lot of your teen years figuring how to get out of town and what to do with your life. I wanted to be a ship's captain."[15]

Benefiting from a New Deal program that provided special training for merchant ship officers, Kirkland joined the Masters, Mates and Pilots union as an 18-year-old Merchant Marine Academy cadet. His naval papers described him as 5 feet 8 inches tall, with auburn hair and a "ruddy" complexion. According to Tom Donahue, Kirkland's years in the marine union gave him solid "trade union experience" that outsiders often missed, and were highly formative.[16] Graduating in 1942 under an accelerated wartime curriculum, Kirkland served as a deck officer throughout World War II. His first service was aboard the SS *Liberator*, which docked at Baltimore, Houston, and New Orleans. As a cadet, Kirkland recalled that he came "within an inch" of joining the Communist Party, which had an active cell on his ship, but the Party's volte-face—which he saw as unprincipled—after the Nazi invasion of the Soviet Union dissuaded him, helping to breed a fervent anticommunism. After leaving the *Liberator*, Kirkland served in every major theater of the war, and his ship frequently came under heavy fire. In January 1944, for example, Kirkland took part in the Allied beach landing at Anzio, Italy, where German precision bombers effectively targeted American ships.[17] In 1946 Kirkland came ashore, attending Georgetown University's School of Foreign Service at night and working for the Navy's Hydrographic Office during the day. A man of considerable intelligence, he did well at Georgetown, securing high marks in political science courses, as well as an impressive 94 percent for Economic History. Based on his strong academic record, Kirkland received an offer to join Pi Gamma Mu, the National Honor Society in the Social Sciences.[18] He graduated from Georgetown in 1948, the same year that AFL president William Green spoke on campus. It was a key incident in the young man's life. "Bill Green came one night to speak to a class that I was a member of at Georgetown," Kirkland recalled in 1996, "and I told him that I was the only union member that he would find there. He told me to come by and see him after I graduated, and I did, and he offered me a job on the staff, and I thought I would try it for a little while, and I have been there ever since. I found a home."[19]

Throughout his union career, Kirkland referred to his experience in the merchant marine. While generally not prone to self-reflection, he once described himself as a "maritime buff."[20] As former staffer Ray Denison recalled, a Greek fisherman's hat was Kirkland's favorite headgear, and he was fond of a sculpture that depicted the AFL-CIO as a ship being ably guided by Captain Kirkland's "firm grip." From the start, Kirkland also used nautical images and metaphors to describe his leadership.[21] His wartime experiences were especially formative. As a deck officer, he recalled, he spent time in the North Atlantic on convoy runs. He took part in the Arctic convoys that supplied the Soviet city of Murmansk, runs that were particularly dangerous, and shuttled ammunition between North Africa and Italy, an important part of the Mediterranean campaign. These experiences of danger shaped Kirkland, equipping him with a hardness that was easy to miss, as well as a balanced perspective and an appreciation of the importance of sticking together. Throughout his life, Kirkland was proud of his wartime service; in 1992, for example, he ordered a series of medals from the Office of Maritime Labor and Training that highlighted his decorated military record. They included the Atlantic War Zone Medal, the Merchant Marine Defense Medal, and the Pacific War Zone Medal.[22]

Shaped by his southern upbringing, Kirkland always had sympathy for the underdog. Despite their lineage, Kirkland's family were not wealthy, and his formative years in Newberry had exposed him to the poverty of the town's mill operatives, who were some of the lowest paid industrial workers in the country. Across the South powerful mill owners bitterly—and successfully—opposed workers' efforts to unionize, leading to frequent and violent labor conflicts. Explaining what motivated him to work in the labor movement, even when it was under fire in the 1980s, Kirkland was fond of quoting Meany's mantra that "the key role of the trade union was to see that the big guys didn't kick the little guys around."[23] There was, he noted in 1990, "an absence of a strong, declared political force in the United States that is clearly on the side of working people," and for this reason the AFL-CIO was vital, especially during harsh times. Kirkland's understanding of adversity—both in his upbringing and in his military experiences—shaped his emphasis on unity. "Solidarity," he declared, "is the essence of our strength." Kirkland's politics, however, eluded easy categorization. As Tom Donahue recalled, Kirkland was never connected with a political tendency but he was a "staunch Democrat" who had been greatly influenced by President Franklin Roosevelt's New Deal. Through the A. Philip Randolph Institute, Kirkland also became good friends with Bayard Rustin, yet he avoided formal affiliation with Rustin's Social Democrats, a successor to the Socialist Party. Kirkland, remembered Susan Dunlop, often talked with her about his youth in South Carolina, and how New Deal programs, particularly its electrification efforts, had improved the lives of the citizenry. While Dunlop emphasized Kirkland's complexity and independence, she noted that he was proud to call himself an "unreconstructed New Dealer."[24]

When he was elected, Kirkland immediately appealed for reunification. It was the theme that would define his presidency, from his success in bringing numerous unions back into the fold, to his calls for solidarity in the face of Republican attacks, through to his work in support of Solidarnosc in Poland. "All sinners belong in the church," he explained in a key early speech, "all citizens owe fealty to their country, all workers belong in the union of their craft or industry, and all real unions belong in the AFL-CIO. . . . Neither pride nor pelf should keep them away."[25] For Kirkland, internal unity was the best way of protecting the labor movement from outside attacks. Rather than organizing, the labor movement should stand together against the storm. In retrospect, several of Kirkland's staffers argued that he had successfully carried out this vision, especially as he secured the re-affiliation of the UAW and Teamsters. As former executive assistant Jim Baker put it, Kirkland was able to "protect" the union movement during the Reagan-Bush era, the "years of devastation" as the *AFL-CIO News* put it.[26] "There'd been a number of defections," recalled aide David St. John, and reunifying the AFL-CIO was consequently "important." Even those who were not big supporters of Kirkland, such as Joe Uehlein of the Industrial Union Department—which called for more organizing in these years—gave him credit in this area. "He did reunite the House of Labor," admitted Uehlein, "and that was a great thing."[27]

While Kirkland had a less forceful personality than Meany, he relied on a strong intellect and well-crafted speeches and memorandums, most of which he wrote himself. "He is a completely different personality than George Meany," commented one Federation official. "With George you have the feeling that he was in absolute control. Lane picks up support for his positions by the extent of his knowledge and the force of his presentation."[28] Kirkland, wrote Philip Shabecoff in the *New York Times*, was "slow-spoken and quiet-voiced," relying more on "sardonic wit rather than flamboyant oratory." Staff who had worked for both men remembered their very different personalities. "George Meany was a larger-than-life figure," summarized Susan Dunlop, "and Lane wasn't that kind of person. But he was tough, and . . . in his own way he was a fighter." Kirkland, who was fond of Meany's dictum that "labor never quits," was more resilient than he appeared.[29]

With the election of fresh leadership and the start of a new decade, there was considerable optimism at the Federation. As the new decade began, the *AFL-CIO News* was much more positive than it would be later. "The AFL-CIO moves into the 1980s with new leadership, strengthened resources and a renewed determination to deal effectively with the challenges of the decade," noted Saul Miller in a key article. As the gavel was passed to Kirkland, the new president was also upbeat. Drawing on his nautical background, Kirkland confidently set the course for the Federation as "full ahead, steady as she goes."[30]

In the early months of his presidency, Kirkland enjoyed a honeymoon, and there was little sense of the crisis that lay ahead. He basked in the congratulations that he received from around the world, keeping many of these letters carefully in his files. Reaction to Kirkland's election highlighted his links with diplomats, corporate chiefs, and international political leaders, as well as his labor friendships. Among those who congratulated him were the American ambassador in Moscow, Thomas J. Watson Jr., Israeli Prime Minister Menachem Begin, General Motors Chairman Tom Murphy, and Forbes CEO Malcolm S. Forbes Jr. "I hope kind words from this quarter won't damage your standing among your colleagues!" Forbes told Kirkland. "They couldn't have a finer person," wrote Ambassador Watson, adding that he knew that Kirkland's "deep interest in international affairs" would continue.[31] Kirkland also received congratulations from Bob Hawke, the president of the Australian Council of Trade Unions and a subsequent prime minister of Australia. He had met the gregarious Hawke on several occasions and the two had got along well. Noting that he was about to become active in politics, Hawke hoped that his "close personal relationship" with Kirkland could continue. Warm greetings also came from President Carter, who called the AFL-CIO presidency "one of the rarest honors in the world." Carter hoped to continue the "strong partnership" he had forged with Meany.[32]

As Carter's entreaty indicated, Kirkland took over an organization that still had considerable power, both at home and abroad. Stockholm's *Dagens Nyheter* even described Kirkland as "the world's most powerful trade union leader."[33] At his first full Executive Council in February 1980, Kirkland reported that the AFL-CIO had 13.7 million members and a net financial worth of over $21.4 million. Absolute membership had held steady since the foundation in 1955, when there were 13.5 million members.[34] In many ways, the Federation was in robust shape, something that Kirkland and Donahue—a former SEIU leader from New York City who worked as Meany's executive assistant in the 1970s—emphasized. While it would later struggle to support one publication, for example, at this time the AFL-CIO published both the *American Federationist*, a high-quality monthly with detailed articles on economic and labor trends, and the newspaper-style *AFL-CIO News*, which came out weekly.[35] Despite the decentralized nature of the AFL-CIO, the president also retained real power, especially in running the Executive Council. As former staffer Denise Mitchell recalled, in the Council meeting room the president's seat was elevated, a clear visual cue: "All the chairs were the same height, except one; Kirkland's chair was a little taller than all the rest, which he probably inherited from Meany, but you did not disagree with him. And so I sat in that room, around the margins of staff sometimes, and was just amazed, having heard people disagree before they went in the room, and then they went into the room, and they would go around the table, and nobody disagreed!" Kirkland also routinely called Council members prior to meetings and secured commitments about how they would vote, ensuring that opposition was minimized.[36]

When he took over Council meetings, Kirkland took immediate steps to introduce more diversity. For more than two decades, Meany had presided over a thirty-five-member Executive Council that was entirely composed of men, steadfastly resisting any change. Although A. Philip Randolph was on the Council from the beginning, he was surrounded by a large phalanx of suited white men. "The Executive Council was always a club of white males," admitted Donahue. "I mean that, because those were the presidents of unions. . . . When Kirkland became president, in '79, he said: 'We've got to do something about this, we have to bring diversity to the council.'"[37] At his first Council meeting, the new president signaled the need for reform, telling the group that it should explore how the contribution of women and minorities could be "better reflected" on the body. After an extended discussion, Kirkland received the authority to appoint a special committee to oversee the change. Made up of fifteen vice presidents, the committee included strong representation from the service and retail unions, large affiliates with many female members.[38] In February 1980 the committee reported to the Council, recommending that two positions on the body should be exempt from the "general precedent" that candidates needed to be the president of their union. This exemption should stay in place until "adequate representation" of women and minorities had been achieved.[39]

Despite resistance from conservative affiliates, particularly in the building trades, Kirkland and Donahue were determined to diversify the Council. In August 1980 Joyce Miller, a fifty-two-year-old vice president of the Amalgamated Clothing and Textile Workers Union (ACTWU), made history when she became the first woman to serve on the Council. Kirkland and Donahue hoped that the change would help them to recruit more members, especially as Miller—who had been president of CLUW since 1977—was a forceful promoter of efforts to unionize women. In December 1979 Miller wrote in the *American Federationist* that more than 50 percent of American women held paid jobs. They comprised 40 million workers, yet less than 20 percent of these women belonged to unions or associations. "Although there has been an improvement in the status of women in the labor movement," she wrote, "it is not yet good enough. There is an absence of women at the top level of the labor movement."[40] By breaking Meany's tradition of only electing one representative from each union—ACTWU president Murray Finley was already on the Council—Kirkland had stepped out of his mentor's shadow. Miller would serve on the Council until 1993, when—appropriately enough— she became director of the Glass Ceiling Commission in the Department of Labor, an initiative that sought to increase the number of women and minorities in management positions.[41]

Throughout his first year in office, Kirkland enjoyed other challenges that came his way. Foreign policy developments played to his strengths. Over the winter of 1979–80, the Soviet invasion of Afghanistan increased Cold War hawkishness in the United States, and Kirkland was well placed to speak out. In February 1980 the Executive Council called the invasion "the greatest threat to the free world since the end of World War II." It subsequently gave strong support to President Carter's call to boycott the Moscow Olympics in protest, solidifying the relationship between the AFL-CIO and the White House.[42] Domestically, there were some important positive developments. As late as October 1980, the labor movement received a major boost when textile firm J. P. Stevens agreed to settle its long-running dispute with ACTWU. The historic settlement, under which the company finally agreed to a contract at the sites where the union had won bargaining rights, brought to an end a dispute that dated back almost two decades. Since 1963, Stevens had committed widespread violations of labor laws in order to thwart a major organizing drive launched by the Textile Workers' Union of America, ACTWU's predecessor. The settlement was partly due to a labor boycott of Stevens' products, a key component of an innovative corporate campaign that was endorsed by the AFL-CIO. In addition, the retirement of CEO James D. Finley, who had taken a hard line against the union for more than a decade, paved the way for an agreement. Kirkland was delighted, calling the outcome "a major victory for all of the working people of America." In a speech to ACTWU's convention, he used the settlement to predict improved times for American labor. "I firmly believe," he declared, "that because the union members at Stevens would not quit, and because their fellow workers and trade unionists would not abandon them, that better days are ahead throughout the American textile industry and throughout all other industries."[43]

The climate, however, would be transformed by the results of the 1980 presidential election. Going into the election, the two candidates stood poles apart on labor issues, presenting what the Federation termed a "stark" contrast. As governor of California, Republican candidate Ronald Reagan had amassed a poor record on labor issues, and he now supported right-to-work laws and opposed labor law reform. His platform, thought the AFL-CIO, was "anti-worker, anti-union, anti-government, and anti-poor." In contrast, President

Carter supported both labor law reform and programs to help the disadvantaged. Just prior to the election, he had also issued an Executive Order that applied OSHA safety and health standards to federal work sites. In their discussions, AFL-CIO leaders recognized that much was at stake in the election. At the General Board meeting in September 1980, for example, members warned that a Reagan victory would signal a disastrous turning point. "The 1980 election is the most important for workers and their families in many years," it declared.[44] Kirkland also knew that his leadership was now about to face the sternest possible test. The forthcoming election, he warned, would determine "the course of the nation for the next four years and, possibly, for the next generation." Under Carter, the AFL-CIO's voice had been heard at the "highest levels" of government. This would not be repeated if the GOP won. "Who will be listening if Ronald Reagan wins the White House?" he asked. "Within his Administration, we can expect no opportunity to be heard, no role in shaping the 1980s." It was a prescient warning.[45]

The election results were a disaster for the AFL-CIO. As the historian William Chafe has noted, in the presidential campaign Reagan skillfully offered "a message of revival" to a country experiencing an economic recession and foreign policy reverses. The charismatic Republican challenger won forty-four of the fifty states, and the GOP also picked up twelve seats in the Senate and thirty-three in the House. In the election Reagan was also backed—at least tacitly—by a number of major unions, including the Teamsters, the International Longshoremen's Association, and the National Maritime Union. Several of the unions that endorsed Reagan were not affiliated with the AFL-CIO, highlighting the need to unify the Federation.[46]

It was the backing that Reagan received from union voters that was the most damaging aspect of the result, especially as it meant that the Republican felt that he had been given a mandate to speak for workers. In the election, noted the *New York Times*, "millions of union members ignored their leaders' advice and voted for Ronald Reagan and other Republicans." According to a poll carried out by the *Times* and *CBS News*, some 42 percent of voters in union households had backed Reagan, compared to 49 percent for Carter. A further 7 percent voted for Republican congressman John B. Anderson, who ran as an independent. Even liberal observers found it hard to sugarcoat the outcome. As the *Times* acknowledged, much of labor's political power had been "sapped" by "the widening gulf between the top union officials and their members." The AFL-CIO, concluded respected *Times* reporter Philip Shabecoff, had suffered a "disastrous defeat."[47]

It was hard to find any positives. Reagan won 489 presidential electoral votes, giving him a large victory margin, and the Republicans also secured control of the Senate. With a 53–47 majority, the Republicans controlled the Senate for the first time since 1952. In seven Senate races that were decided by two percent of the vote or less, Republicans had even won with the help of union votes. Although the Democrats retained control of the House and had more success in state races, the Federation knew that it faced a hostile political climate. In the House, the Democrats lost 33 seats, leaving them with a fragile majority of 243 to 192, especially as a rump of conservative Democrats were lukewarm—at best—to organized labor. As even the *American Federationist* acknowledged, Reagan had achieved a "sweeping victory" in a "pivotal" election.[48]

Reflecting on the election, Kirkland acknowledged that the Republicans had been effective in recruiting union members. Helped by a candidate who was a talented communicator, they had been successful at "broadening their base." The union movement had also made mistakes. Kirkland felt that the AFL-CIO's policy of staying neutral during the primaries should be reviewed, and that the Federation needed to exercise a "more forceful leadership role" in its approach to the presidential candidates. He promised wholesale changes in the Federation's approach to the nomination process.[49] Overall, the period straight after the election was a dark time for the new AFL-CIO president and his staff. "This was the best effort we ever fielded and to lose so badly is hard to take," admitted a candid Alexander Barkan, the director of the Federation's Committee on Political Education (COPE).[50]

The outcome reflected not just Reagan's popularity, but also the ambivalence that many union activists felt towards Jimmy Carter. Despite a constructive working relationship, especially at the national level, there was little personal warmth between Carter and most labor leaders. Kirkland, a southerner, got on quite well with the former peanut farmer from Georgia, but relations between the president and the rest of the AFL-CIO leadership were cool. The problem was partly Carter's reserved character. Unlike Lyndon Johnson, another southerner, Carter was inexperienced in Washington, DC, and he was unable to bond with key Democratic power groups, especially in Congress. Many in the Federation struggled to relate to Carter. Like so many of the AFL-CIO hierarchy, former staffer Jim Kennedy was a plainspoken Irish-American from New York City. "Carter," he summarized, "was not one of us."[51]

There were also clear policy differences. The failure of labor law reform strained the relationship between the AFL-CIO and the Carter administration.

In August 1978 Meany commented that the demise of the labor law bill could be attributed to the administration, claims that annoyed even Secretary of Labor F. Ray Marshall. "This is just not true," replied Marshall. "I devoted my full energies to trying to pass this bill." Marshall blamed "difficult times" in Congress for the legislation's failure, and suggested that the AFL-CIO should have been more willing to compromise.[52] With the Airline Deregulation Act of 1978 and the Motor Carrier Act of 1980, the Carter administration also pushed through legislation that deregulated the airline and trucking industries, ignoring labor objections in the process. In both cases, Carter argued that deregulation would eliminate inefficiencies and reduce costs to the customer, aiding the administration's battle against inflation. Both reforms, however, helped pave the way for the erosion of union power in these industries. There were further differences between the unions and Carter over economic policy, with many union leaders—and their members—alleging that the administration placed too much emphasis on controlling inflation, rather than creating jobs. In October 1978 the Executive Council even blasted Carter's anti-inflation program as "inequitable and unfair" because it gave more emphasis to wage controls than to controlling profits or interest rates.[53]

Leading into the election, Kirkland acknowledged that Carter was not ideal. "We know that Jimmy Carter is not in the pocket of any particular element or force in American society," he told the General Board in September, "a fact that we have, in all candor, had some occasion to regret, when the force was our own." He urged union leaders to put aside these feelings and get behind Carter, but some did not heed this advice. The Firefighters Union and the American Federation of Government Employees (AFGE) both abstained from a General Board vote to endorse Carter. AFGE president Kenneth Blaylock explained that his members were angry with Carter's cuts in the public sector, and did not want to "go out and really fight for" the president. Other delegates doubted whether Carter could win; many Americans felt that he had not achieved a great deal, they noted, and Ronald Reagan was a popular challenger. The endorsement vote still carried easily, partly because Carter addressed the Board and pledged to "stand with" the AFL-CIO until labor law reform was passed. In response, Kirkland asserted that the Federation would do its "absolute utmost" to bring about a Democratic victory.[54]

Carter's weakness with labor supporters was not just a short-term problem. As the records of the Carter administration highlighted, the Teamsters Union—which both Nixon and Ford had cultivated—was drawn to Reagan, but Carter failed to bond with them. "The Carter Administration," admitted labor liaison Landon Butler in May 1979, "has had almost no political relationship with the Teamsters either before or after the 1976 election." The building trades also liked Reagan. Alienated by the Democrats' support of civil rights legislation, and attracted by the Republicans' stronger stance on national security and moral issues, growing numbers of union members were starting to vote Republican. Many of them—the so-called Reagan Democrats—switched in 1980.[55] Furthermore, a number of progressive union leaders, including UAW president Doug Fraser and Machinists leader Bill Winpisinger, were advocates of Senator Edward Kennedy, who ran for the Democratic nomination. While the UAW and Teamsters did not belong to the AFL-CIO at this time, their reluctance to support Carter weakened his campaign. Senator Kennedy refused to withdraw his candidacy after the primaries. Instead, he carried his campaign all the way to the Democratic National Convention in August, where he tried to pass a rule freeing delegates from being bound by the primary results, thus opening up the convention. While this effort failed, the internal fight between Carter and Kennedy hurt the president's campaign, especially as Kennedy had a stronger labor record than Carter and a considerable amount of union support.[56] All of these factors contributed to the disastrous election result. As the *New York Times* summarized, most major unions endorsed the president "reluctantly," while many union members voted for Reagan anyway.[57]

Initially, Kirkland harbored faint hopes—at least publicly—that he might be able to work with the new administration. Soon after the election, he sent a message of congratulations to president-elect Reagan and pledged labor's cooperation, especially in tackling economic problems.[58] The election result still cast a pall over the twenty-fifth anniversary of the AFL-CIO, which passed by with little fanfare in early December. Speaking to reporters on the anniversary, a chain-smoking, nervous Kirkland expressed hope that the new administration would be fair to labor, but he did not seem to believe it. "We're not going to start on the assumption that what might turn out to be bad already has," he noted. "We want to establish as decent and cooperative a relationship as is possible for the good of the country."[59] In private, Kirkland was more apprehensive. In February 1981 he told the Executive Council that the AFL-CIO now operated in a harsh climate. "Many of the programs in which we have been involved will be under attack," he warned.[60]

Although they reflected with the benefit of hindsight, Kirkland's aides felt that Reagan's election represented an important turning point. Even before the PATCO strike, claimed Susan Dunlop, who worked on the *AFL-CIO News* at the time, it was clear that Reagan and his supporters represented "just another world." Once Reagan came into office, she recalled, long lines of limousines were often parked outside the exclusive Hays-Adams Hotel, directly across Sixteenth Street from the AFL-CIO building. "I realized they're here for Reagan," she recalled. "So it was like the limousine crowd came in, and the rest of us, or anybody else, was out, and it was just . . . awful."[61] Out in the field, labor activists witnessed a similar shift. Working as a labor lawyer in New England, Jon Hiatt—who later became the Federation's General Counsel—felt that the climate, while already difficult, shifted when Reagan was elected. "Starting in the late seventies," he recalled, "and really picking up in the early eighties, like particularly when Reagan became president . . . the union-busting industry and trends really started to pick up in a noticeable way . . . the de-stigmatization of antiunion campaigns became the norm." Employers' willingness to take on unions became a defining feature of the decade. "In the eighties we started seeing a lot more of that," concluded Hiatt.[62]

Other former AFL-CIO staffers remembered that the regular access they had enjoyed to the White House stopped when Reagan came into office. "Social visits to [the] White House during the Johnson and Carter administrations were frequent," related lobbyist Ray Denison, "less so during the Reagan years."[63] When Kirkland was elected president of the AFL-CIO, he even received a letter of congratulations from Carter's NLRB chairman, John H. Fanning. In the Reagan era, communication between the AFL-CIO and the labor board dried up.[64]

For Kirkland personally, Reagan's election also represented a turning point. As secretary-treasurer and then president of the AFL-CIO, Kirkland had established a close relationship with Carter. The association went back to the start of the Carter administration, when Kirkland had served on the president-elect's Inaugural Committee, helping to coordinate union involvement in the event. "Your advice on labor matters was indispensable in obtaining the dedicated, competent and timely assistance of the thousands of members of organized labor upon whose work the Inauguration depended," Carter wrote Kirkland shortly afterwards.[65] Following this, the two men remained close. President Carter met with Kirkland regularly, invited him to the National Symphony, and considered him a "friend." The Kirklands also attended private dinners at the White House.[66]

Kirkland also found common ground with Carter in foreign policy. In September 1978 he attended the covert Camp David meetings, thirteen days of negotiations between the leaders of Egypt and Israel that resulted in an historic peace agreement.[67] Carter was pleased when Kirkland became AFL-CIO leader, and during the 1980 election White House aides described Kirkland as "very important," especially in restricting labor support for Edward Kennedy. The contrast with the Reagan years, when Kirkland was ignored by the White

House and treated as out-of-touch with his members, could not have been greater.[68] Even in the final few days of the Carter administration, Kirkland spoke at a reception for Secretary of Labor Marshall, describing the pro-labor economist as "second to none." Kirkland also exchanged friendly toasts with the outgoing president. Things would be very different under Reagan.[69]

The change of climate was immediately apparent in other ways. As early as January 4, 1981—more than two weeks before Reagan's inauguration—a marker was laid down when the new administration unexpectedly announced that Raymond J. Donovan, a former construction company executive, was to be secretary of labor. This was probably the first time that the AFL-CIO had not been consulted about who was to head the Department of Labor. "I look forward to meeting Mr. Donovan," commented Kirkland, displaying his ironic wit.[70] Following this poor start, relations between the AFL-CIO and Donovan deteriorated. In February the new secretary dismissed the Federation's claims that the president's proposed budget cuts would hit low-income Americans hard. "This stuff about the hard-hearted administration picking on the poor should have gone out with high-button shoes," Donovan blasted.[71]

As it struggled to adjust to the election result and the hostility of the new administration, the AFL-CIO received plenty of negative press. Even normally sympathetic observers were critical. In May respected labor reporter William Serrin claimed in the *New York Times* that the AFL-CIO had "turned tame," its strength sapped by the weak economy and a conservative political climate. The Federation had been "curiously docile" in response and was in "disarray."[72] Writing in the *National Review* in April, Arnold Beichman, a former AFL-CIO writer and publicist, was just as harsh, judging that the Federation was experiencing a "crisis of leadership." Like Reagan, Beichman thought that Kirkland was out-of-touch with rank-and-file union members, many of whom had voted Republican for the first time in 1980. He concluded that the AFL-CIO was a "paper tiger" that could not rally its troops effectively. Kirkland carefully filed Beichman's story.[73]

The election gave Reagan a strong political hand that he quickly used against the Federation. Key changes occurred in Congress. In February legislative director Ray Denison told the Executive Council that the enactment of labor's legislative program would now be "more difficult." There were changes in all the Senate staff committees, and Republicans now had a majority on the crucial Senate Labor and Human Resources Committee. Kirkland told the same meeting that he anticipated a "tough Congress," adding that organized labor was on the defensive. In March, when Reagan narrowly survived an assassination attempt, his popularity surged. A profoundly troubled young man,

John Hinckley Jr., fired six times at the president as he left a Washington hotel, seriously wounding Press Secretary James Brady. One bullet also ricocheted off the presidential limousine and lodged in the president's lung, requiring a two-hour operation to remove it. Enduring his brush with death with calm and even humor—"Honey, I forgot to duck," he told his wife Nancy—Reagan enjoyed record poll ratings.[74]

The administration's popularity allowed it to enact important measures. As the *AFL-CIO News* acknowledged, during the early part of the Reagan presidency the administration was able to "steamroller" its harsh economic program through Congress by putting together a working majority of Republicans and conservative southern Democrats.[75] In late July Congress passed Reagan's three-year tax cut in a 235–195 vote, ensuring that the president's entire economic package had been enacted. Reagan also terminated the Comprehensive Employment and Training Act (CETA), a Carter-era jobs program that provided work for some 300,000 people, and he secured more than $130 billion in cuts to social programs through his budget bill. "The Reagan juggernaut has rolled on," commented the *Washington Post*. While Meany had always been a formidable power broker in Washington, Kirkland seemed little more than a spectator.[76]

Kirkland responded to the harsh climate by accelerating his efforts to unify the labor movement. A few weeks after the election, he told the press that he was "making every effort" to bring about the re-affiliations of the Autoworkers and Teamsters, which were now more urgent than ever.[77] In 1981 Kirkland was integrally involved in bringing the UAW back into the Federation after a gap of thirteen years. For several months, he negotiated carefully with UAW president Douglas Fraser, who had to convince a skeptical membership. Kirkland stressed the need for the labor movement to unite at a difficult time, an argument that carried some weight. "The times are a factor," admitted UAW spokesman Don Stillman. "When you're under attack . . . there's a tendency not to want to stand alone but to stand together." Because the UAW's departure had been linked to the rivalry between Meany and Reuther, Kirkland was in a good position. Although some UAW officials still felt that the Kirkland-led Federation was too conservative, particularly in foreign policy matters, Fraser was more conciliatory than Reuther, and he responded to Kirkland's softer leadership style. Announced in July 1981, the re-affiliation brought 1.2 million members into the AFL-CIO, making the UAW the Federation's second-largest affiliate. It was crucial in boosting membership at a difficult time, masking the decline of the early Reagan years, while the extra $2.5 million a year in dues helped to stabilize the Federation's finances.[78]

A few weeks after the UAW came back into the fold, however, another decisive development undermined Kirkland's presidency. On August 3, 1981, just as the Executive Council began its summer meeting in Chicago, 13,000 air traffic controllers walked out on strike, an unexpected action that caught labor leaders off guard. While the Professional Air Traffic Controllers Organization (PATCO) was a small affiliate, its actions, which were linked to calls for better conditions and higher pay, had enormous ramifications. Reagan acted promptly, issuing a forty-eight-hour ultimatum to the strikers to return or be fired. When the deadline passed, most controllers remained on strike, and Reagan declared that military controllers would help keep planes in the sky. Ten days later, after firing the 11,345 controllers who had ignored his order, the president reassured Americans that flight schedules had returned to 80 percent normal.[79]

There were several reasons for Reagan's action. As his papers reveal, most advisers told the president to take a hard line and expressed little sympathy for the controllers. The Office of Management and Budget's Janet Rice, for example, called their demands—including calls for pay increases and a shorter working week—excessive. According to Rice, the controllers earned between $30,000 and $40,000 a year performing work that was "not arduous." They were "perhaps the most overpaid, pampered employees in the Nation." Although moderates in the administration wanted to avoid a costly confrontation with PATCO, they were outvoted by hard-liners like Rice.[80] After taking this advice on board, Reagan—who believed that the strike was illegal—warned the controllers to return if they wanted to keep their jobs. "I never had any doubt how to respond to it," he wrote later. "I don't like firing anybody. But I realized that if they made the decision not to return to work in the full knowledge of what I'd said, then I wasn't firing them, they were giving up their jobs based on their individual decisions."[81]

Behind the scenes, AFL-CIO leaders had warned PATCO president Robert Poli not to strike, insisting that his union could be "destroyed." Federation officials recognized the damaging precedent that would be set—in both the public and private sectors—if the White House permanently replaced the strikers and broke the union. Sympathy for the controllers was initially limited, especially as their union had endorsed Reagan in the election, one of the central ironies of the dispute. There were also tensions between PATCO and the Airline Pilots Association, largely because the controllers had not supported pilots during past airline strikes. As a result, the pilots now refused to respect the controllers' picket lines. Furthermore, Kirkland was annoyed that Poli had not consulted with him about the strike. As former Communication

Workers president Morton Bahr recalled, Kirkland was "really angry at the union because what they had done was go off on their own, and negotiate with the federal government, and thought that Reagan would lay down and play dead." Poli seemed to doubt whether Reagan would carry out his threat, perhaps because government strikes had often been settled without recourse to such action. In addition, he may have felt that Reagan would reward PATCO for its electoral support. New in office, Poli apparently misjudged Reagan, who was keen to show that he was a man of his word.[82] Justifying the walkout, Poli also insisted that it was a last resort for members who had tried to address complaints about stressful working conditions, long hours, and abusive managers for years. "So why did we strike?" he wrote. "The truth is that we are fighting for our profession in the only way left to us to fight . . . we chose to fight to make our profession something more than just a way to draw a paycheck until you are cut short and the check stops coming."[83]

Once Kirkland heard of Reagan's ultimatum, his position shifted. "The bottom line," explained Kirkland's assistant, Ken Young, "is you have to help your sisters and brothers." While the AFL-CIO was caught off guard by the walkout, the Executive Council scrambled together a program to help the strikers. These efforts, while not able to alter the outcome of the dispute, were significant. On August 3 the Council termed Reagan's plans to replace the strikers "repressive" and "vengeful," a strong statement that reassured the controllers.[84] Along with several other Council members, Kirkland also joined the PATCO picket line at Chicago O'Hare Airport, a move that Poli described as "a source of strength" for his embattled members.[85] After Reagan's ultimatum had been carried out, the labor movement helped the PATCO strikers financially. On August 20 the Federation established a support fund to help strikers meet their mortgage payments and other emergency needs. By September 18, the fund had collected $211,000. Helped by contributions from state and local bodies, by February 1982 the Fund had distributed over $646,000 to 1,407 families, many of whom were facing "severe financial problems" because of the walkout.[86]

Kirkland also mobilized members to support the strikers. Initiated in the fall of 1981, an AFL-CIO "Job Employment Program" helped many PATCO strikers find work, with Kirkland calling on all members to pass on news of job openings in their areas. In addition, many Central Labor Councils and state federations passed resolutions in support of the strikers, often arguing that air safety was being jeopardized by the use of inexperienced replacements. While polls showed that a slim majority of Americans—including some union members—supported the government's position, largely because

Lane Kirkland, with Secretary-treasurer Tom Donahue and Irena Kirkland, during the PATCO strike, 1981. Courtesy of Special Collections, University of Maryland Libraries.

the strike was illegal, thousands of AFL-CIO members also wrote letters that supported the strikers and urged a return to the negotiating table. In one typical example, members of the Bloomington Federation of Labor objected to the "repressive measures taken by the government against our brothers and sisters in the Professional Air Traffic Controllers Union." International Chemical Workers Union leader Frank D. Martino even declared that his members stood "shoulder-to-shoulder" with PATCO in its struggle against "a cruel and heartless Administration." The Reagan administration rebuffed all of these appeals, including calls to resume bargaining or give an amnesty to the strikers. Nevertheless, this mobilization of members helped to lay the ground for Solidarity Day, which took protest against the White House a step further. PATCO, summarized staffer Susan Dunlop, had quickly become "a lightning rod, and a focal point."[87]

Reagan's papers highlight how the relationship between the White House and the labor movement hit rock bottom at this time. One example of the rift came in mid-August, when Al Shanker, the president of the 580,000-member American Federation of Teachers, accused President Reagan of "union busting" in the controllers' dispute. Shanker, who had already criticized the administration's economic program, now urged the entire labor movement to help the PATCO strikers.[88] The administration also bristled at labor leaders who compared Reagan's dismissal of the strikers with the way that the Polish Communist regime was suppressing Solidarnosc, a workers' movement that sought the right to strike. In both cases, labor claimed, governments had suppressed legitimate trade union movements, and some union activists felt that it was hypocritical of Reagan to identify with Solidarnosc while he treated unions harshly at home. As Shanker put it, Reagan was a leader "who favors the rights of workers in Poland to go out on strike, but doesn't favor that right for workers in the United States."[89]

Replying to similar criticisms from other union activists, Reagan's aides refused to give ground. White House director of correspondence Anne Higgins drafted a robust form reply: "The President would like you to know that he unqualifiedly rejects the validity of any comparison between his handling of the illegal strike by the Professional Air Traffic Controllers' Organization and recent events in Poland." Poland was "governed by mere force," whereas Reagan had followed the "rule of law" in stopping an unauthorized strike. Implying that Reagan could bypass the labor movement and rely on support from everyday Americans, aides cited polls that indicated public support for his position. "When the government of Poland moves to suppress Solidarity," asserted Higgins, "it faces the resistance of the entire Polish people, who seek to protect the freedoms that they have been able to win. When President Reagan moved to protect the safety of American air travelers from the consequences of PATCO's illegal strike, he enjoyed the overwhelming support of the American people." The administration kept up its hard line throughout the dispute, with the FAA training a new crop of controllers—at an estimated cost of $2 billion—and refusing to take the strikers back. Despite the AFL-CIO's intervention, including efforts to save PATCO by providing it with rent-free office space, the striking controllers went down to a crushing defeat, and in June 1982 PATCO was decertified. For the rest of the 1980s, Kirkland led efforts to get the strikers' jobs back, but they achieved little. The replaced strikers suffered enormously as a result; by 1986, one-third of them were so poor that their families qualified for food stamps.[90]

After the PATCO strike, relations between the Reagan administration and the AFL-CIO deteriorated further. In November the Executive Council issued a statement that spoke out against the administration's "brutal punishment" of the air traffic controllers.[91] Reagan's aides were unimpressed. There was, proclaimed Bob Bonitati—the White House labor liaison who had formerly worked for the Air Line Pilots Association—a state of "all-out war" between the administration and the AFL-CIO, and much of the situation could be blamed on PATCO.[92] Labor leaders were especially angry because during the election campaign Reagan had expressed concern about the "unreasonable" working conditions experienced by many air traffic controllers and had promised to tackle the problem. In a letter to Poli, Reagan had also said that he would "bring about a spirit of cooperation between the President and the air traffic controllers." Citing this commitment, many labor activists felt betrayed.[93]

Reagan's actions had wide-ranging—and long-lasting—consequences. At the time, the leaders of key AFL-CIO affiliates reported a change in employer attitudes. In November 1981 Steelworkers' president Lloyd McBride told the Federation's convention that the labor movement was under attack from a "large section" of American industry. "We are quite likely in a fight for survival," he warned. Since Reagan had taken office, added other union leaders, employer attitudes had hardened considerably. While some of this shift was related to the economic climate, the administration had set the tone.[94] Over time, the importance of PATCO became even clearer. Reagan's dismissal of the controllers, explained CWA leader Morton Bahr in 1988, was "the opening shot in what became an all-out assault on unions by big business and by virtually every agency of the executive branch. . . . The PATCO episode practically established a new industry—union busting—and ushered in an era of takeback bargaining, lockouts and decertification campaigns by employers." As SEIU president John Sweeney added in 1989, Reagan's action sent a "signal [to] the corporate community that union busting was acceptable." In particular, replacing strikers now spread to the private sector. While the NLRA did not allow employers to fire strikers outright, a 1938 Supreme Court decision, *MacKay Radio v. National Labor Relations Board*, upheld their right to permanently replace economic strikers with other workers. Emboldened employers exploited this loophole.[95]

Former Federation staffers also saw Reagan's firing of the PATCO strikers as a crucial action that had encouraged private sector employers to take on organized labor. It was a moment they always remembered. "The PATCO strike began during the Executive Council meeting in Chicago, my first as director, setting an acid tone in relations with the White House," recalled former legislative director Ray Denison. "We were placed into a defensive mode." After PATCO, added Denison, the Reagan administration opposed any legislation that was favored by labor. Experienced staffer Joe Uehlein viewed Reagan's election, and particularly his tough handling of the PATCO strike, as key turning points. "PATCO and all that," he recalled, "it was huge, because that ushered in all the union-busting strategies of the eighties that companies deployed." Crucially, business groups also saw the dispute as decisive. The PATCO strike, summarized the *Wall Street Journal*, was "one of labor's most ignominious defeats."[96]

Other influential observers saw PATCO in a similar light. In 2003 Federal Reserve Chairman Alan Greenspan, speaking about Reagan's legacy, saw PATCO as "perhaps the most important" initiative of the Republican's first term. It had, he claimed, given "weight to the legal right of private employers, previously not fully exercised, to use their own discretion to both hire and discharge workers."[97] The press also saw the strike as very significant. According to veteran reporter A. H. Raskin, the strike initiated a "nightmare" for labor, one in which it suffered a "string of devastating defeats." To be sure, it is possible to exaggerate the influence of PATCO, especially as resistance to unions was already increasing. As historian Joseph A. McCartin has shown in his detailed history of the strike, however, the PATCO dispute, partly because it occurred at a time when employer resistance to unions was on the rise, was the "most significant strike of the late twentieth century." Its implications were "enormous."[98]

For the AFL-CIO—and especially Kirkland—PATCO was a massive blow. Combined with the economic recession, union busting hurt the Federation's bottom line. Between 1981 and 1982, the AFL-CIO lost some 739,000 members.[99] As federal data documented, in 1980–81 labor's ability to strike also turned. According to the Bureau of Labor Statistics, from 1945 to 1979 there were typically 200 to 400 strikes a year involving more than 1,000 workers. After 1980, the number dropped suddenly to ninety-six in 1982 and just forty in 1988, the last year of the Reagan presidency. Clearly, companies' willingness to hire permanent replacements was the main reason for this change. In the early 1970s, about 2.5 million workers were engaged in walkouts involving more than 1,000 people, but in the 1980s only between one and three hundred thousand were. These figures were all-time lows. With its ability to strike eviscerated, American labor had been gravely weakened.[100]

Battered by PATCO, and reeling from the results of the 1980 election, Kirkland's honeymoon was well and truly over. The new AFL-CIO president had to fight back, yet even sympathetic observers doubted whether he could. As one staffer recalled, Kirkland "didn't have the sense of command and authority within the Labor Movement that Meany had." Described by William Serrin as "an inside guy, not an outside guy," Kirkland seemed ill-equipped to go out and build a new AFL-CIO. Personally shy, he was never comfortable pressing the flesh.[101] Even when he took part in rallies or joined picket lines,

Kirkland wore a suit and tie, projecting an image of awkwardness.[102] His use of language also tended to be intellectual and formal. A. H. Raskin called Kirkland a "soft-spoken technocrat," not the type of charismatic leader who could engage with the rank-and-file. Even Tom Donahue acknowledged that Kirkland's personality could be a problem, especially when it came to reaching out to members. Describing his colleague as "very private, and essentially shy, or retiring, in public," Donahue, who was more outgoing and effervescent, had a solution: "My prescription always was if you can get him to sit and give him a drink or two, then everything's going to be perfect with him! Because, with one drink, he would talk to anybody, he'd be happy, and so forth." Talking to strangers, Donahue recalled, "was an effort" for Kirkland.[103]

Even within the AFL-CIO headquarters, Kirkland remained a distant figure to many staff. He rarely walked through the corridors, instead taking the elevator straight from the parking garage to the executive offices on the eighth floor. Equipped with heavy brown velvet curtains that were usually drawn shut, his office was illustrative of his character. "There was no light in there," recalled Denise Mitchell, who came to the AFL-CIO in 1993 to work in communications. "He was across from the White House, but he didn't look out at the White House, he didn't consider himself outward-looking." As Kirkland's General Counsel, Larry Gold, aptly summarized, his boss was "very private, very intellectual, very self-sufficient." Even at AFL-CIO functions, staff recalled that Kirkland would often stand alone, unsure of how to mingle—or not feeling the need to. "After the meetings," recalled Susan Bianchi, who sat on the Executive Council as president of the Association of Flight Attendants, "Lane could be standing alone, in the lobby of a hotel, and everybody else would be in groups of four or five, and he'd be standing there . . . he didn't seek out, I think, the groups, and the groups didn't seek him out." Staffer Markley Roberts had similar memories. "I sometimes wonder if he intimidated people who were not as smart as he was," he reflected, adding that it was "sad" to see Kirkland standing alone. It was a strange look for a leader.[104]

Kirkland also had an uncomfortable relationship with the news media. Criticizing journalism as shallow and inaccurate, he often refused requests for interviews, even on Labor Day. "He was critical of the media," recalled Bianchi. Kirkland's personality and appearance meant that he failed to attract media attention in the way that his predecessor had. "Meany would appear to be pugnacious," remembered Roberts. "I mean partly his appearance, partly the fact that he was identified with a cigar, which made him good cartoon material. Lane did not lend himself to easy cartooning (laugh). I don't know how you could make a successful cartoon of someone being an intelligent introvert."

Kirkland never achieved the same public profile as Meany, who had thrived off verbal battles with reporters. "If you went to his press conferences," added UFCW leader Doug Dority, "he was very meticulous, and very correct in what he said, but he didn't have the kind of charisma that George Meany had had . . . Lane was an intellectual." Despite Kirkland's frosty relationship with journalists, his papers reveal that he read the newspapers regularly, usually at home before traveling to his office. He also kept extensive—and meticulous— clipping files.[105]

Kirkland never accepted press criticism that he was out of touch with the rank and file, the view that he was a "perennial staff man who never held union office." Occasionally answering back, Kirkland argued that staff work had involved him in every aspect of union life, and that he felt at ease in the AFL-CIO. "There's never been a time when I felt out of place in the labor movement," he added. "They had a saying when I was at sea. If you found a good ship with a good cook and a good run, you'd found a home." At one of the most difficult hours in the Federation's history, Kirkland was preparing a mass march that would mobilize both the labor movement and its community allies. Known as Solidarity Day, the protest would stabilize Kirkland's presidency and secure the attention of Congress and the Reagan administration. Involving around 400,000 people, it was the largest U.S. labor march ever held, and one of the biggest mass protests in American history. Kirkland was about to surprise his critics.[106]

CHAPTER THREE

Kirkland Fights Back

The 1981 Solidarity Day Mass March

On the crisp morning of Saturday, September 19, 1981, protesters began to gather near the Washington Monument to take part in Solidarity Day, a mass march that was designed to protest against President Reagan's budget and tax cuts. Although it was initiated by the AFL-CIO, the march mobilized a broad swath of the American population. Its leaders—including civil rights icons such as Jesse Jackson, Bayard Rustin, and Coretta Scott King—were diverse. Closely monitoring events, the Reagan administration estimated that no fewer than 250 organizations were taking part, including 100 unions and a variety of civil rights, religious, and civic groups. Turnout was impressive. According to the National Park Service, 260,000 people attended Solidarity Day, more than the number that had turned out for either the iconic March on Washington in 1963 or the Vietnam War Moratorium in 1969.[1] The crowd stretched for more than a mile down Constitution Avenue as it made its way toward the Capitol. With some justification, organizers claimed that actual attendance was much higher. Park Service crowd estimates tended to be conservative, and several major newspapers—as well as a count from the Washington, DC, mayor's office—recorded that 400,000 people had shown up.[2] Prominent labor writer Joseph Goulden claimed that 500,000 people had taken part.[3] As labor historians Melvyn Dubofsky and Foster Rhea Dulles have noted, Solidarity Day was "perhaps the largest mass march in U.S. history to that time." It was certainly the largest U.S. labor march ever held. Proud of its efforts, the AFL-CIO proclaimed that September 19, 1981, was "a day which will live as a landmark in American history."[4]

Contemporary reporters were also impressed. The *Christian Science Monitor* called Solidarity Day a "spectacular outdoor solidarity rally," adding that the huge crowd represented "a cross-section of middle- and working-class America." The *Washington Post* noted that the march had successfully brought together a "broad slice of America" in a "massive" protest that was "unprecedented in modern labor history," while the *New York Times* saw the march as a significant "achievement" for American labor.[5] Respected political journalist Arch Puddington went further, viewing Solidarity Day as a "stunning success" that suggested that a "reinvigorated labor movement" might be possible. "Virtually every significant union brought members from around the country," he explained, "as did organizations representing blacks, Hispanics, women, environmentalists, the disabled, the elderly, and various organizations of the political left."[6]

Organizers also stressed the protest's significance. The Federation was proud of its role in organizing the largest labor march ever, especially as the political climate in this "era of conservatism" was so hostile. According to the AFL-CIO, half a million workers and their allies had created a "gigantic voice" that signaled "the rebirth of American labor." Once they got home, participants received individually engraved certificates from the AFL-CIO as a marker of the "historic occasion."[7] The success of Solidarity Day meant a great deal to Kirkland, and he deserved much of the credit. The mass protest was largely his idea, and he showed determination and imagination in planning and executing it. Well-funded and well-organized, the march expressed the anger felt by many Americans against Reagan's policies. Moved by the large crowds, Kirkland proclaimed Solidarity Day as "a smashing success" that had strengthened resistance to the Reagan administration's policies. He never forgot the day, seeing it as one of the finest moments of his presidency. Others agreed. When Kirkland stepped down as leader in 1995, the Executive Council recognized Solidarity Day—as well as a "massive" follow-up protest ten years later—as one of the "greatest achievements" of the Kirkland years. Even Gerald McEntee, the AFSCME president who later played a key role in toppling Kirkland, recalled Solidarity Day fondly. "It was just thousands of people, and it was dynamite," he noted later. "It was some day."[8]

The march was important for a number of other reasons. Refuting the White House's public claims, the administration's own records highlight that it closely monitored the protest and was concerned about it. Aides worried about the size of the demonstration and the wide variety of labor and community groups that were involved. They were also concerned about the fact that so many government employees had taken part.[9] Some important political gains also came from Solidarity Day. In the 1982 midterm elections, the Democrats won 27 seats, cementing their hold on the House of Representatives. While these gains largely reflected the impact of the recession, Solidarity Day played a role, especially as it had focused attention on economic issues. The mass protest also mattered because it boosted the morale of many union members and helped to strengthen Kirkland's leadership, ensuring that he was easily reelected in November 1981. The day represented a stunning comeback for the South Carolinian, securing the future of his presidency. For the next decade, Kirkland's leadership was unquestioned.[10]

In a broader sense, Solidarity Day was significant because it showed that the AFL-CIO under Kirkland could connect with workers, as well as with allies outside the labor movement. As the Council put it, the rally demonstrated that labor's leadership "was not out of step with its rank-and-file members." The march set the precedent for a different kind of AFL-CIO, one that was much more connected to its members. While Kirkland proved unable—or unwilling—to fundamentally reorient the Federation toward grassroots activism, John Sweeney ultimately carried through these ideas when he won the presidency. Under Sweeney, the AFL-CIO poured resources into organizing and political mobilization, realizing once more that its real strength lay in its ability to mobilize both its members and its community allies. Even at the time, however, some reformers were disappointed that more was not done to build on the momentum of this remarkable day.[11]

The roots of Solidarity Day lay in the actions of the incoming Reagan administration. Facing a stagnant economy and a budget deficit, the new president initiated sweeping cuts to social programs. In 1981 Congress agreed to slash over $25 billion from welfare programs alone, with further reductions scheduled in the years to come. At the same time, taxes were cut by $750 billion over five years, with high-income earners benefiting the most. These policies were a key part of the broader Reagan Revolution, which used tax cuts to transfer wealth from the middle class to the rich and shifted federal money out of social entitlement programs and into the military. Although the administration argued that these actions would stimulate the economy, many working people—and the AFL-CIO—disagreed. As the Council declared in February, the president's economic policies required "more sacrifice from those who have little, to give more to those who already have much."[12]

The march also reflected the poor relationship between the AFL-CIO and the administration. After taking office, Reagan ignored union leaders, instead appealing directly to rank-and-file members. The tactic annoyed the Federation's leaders, who were used to having access to presidents, even Republican ones. In contrast, Reagan only invited the AFL-CIO's leaders to the White House *after* plans for Solidarity Day had been announced. The administration's actions reflected the confidence it derived from the results of the 1980 presidential election. Having won the vote so comfortably, and with a significant amount of labor backing, the president felt that he had a mandate to speak for American workers.[13]

Reagan played a key role in precipitating Solidarity Day. In February the new president answered labor leaders' criticisms of his proposed social welfare cuts. "I happen to think that sometimes they're (the leaders) out of step with their own rank and file," he told reporters. "They certainly were in the last election." The remarks irked Kirkland, who could bear grudges. "Mr. Reagan has thrown down the gauntlet," he replied. "He claims his victims as allies. He would make working people accomplices in his assault on their interests."[14] AFL-CIO leaders strongly disagreed with the administration's assertion that it spoke for Americans, especially union members. Announcing the march in June, the AFL-CIO pitched it as "the most effective way of responding to the Administration's claim that it has a mandate to reverse the nation's commitment to social and economic justice." In reality, claimed Tom Donahue, "no such mandate exists."[15]

In early May formal plans for the march were laid. Meeting in Baltimore, AFL-CIO leaders agreed to launch a "major demonstration" by "working people" that would be held "around Labor Day." The minutes of the Executive Council meeting suggest that the idea originated with Kirkland, although AFSCME president Jerry Wurf was also instrumental, partly because government employees were heavily affected by Reagan's cuts. In March and April several local labor leaders had also suggested a march on Washington during a series of regional conferences. The march, however, clearly would not have happened without Kirkland; Solidarity Day coordinator John Perkins, for example, recalled that the AFL-CIO president was "the gentleman who decided on Solidarity Day." Kirkland was also the driving force behind the regional conferences, which he pitched as "the vital link that connects our respective AFL-CIO bodies." At the Executive Council meeting, Kirkland set up a committee of five union presidents, authorizing them to work "immediately" on the task of bringing marchers to Washington, DC.[16]

Plans for the march quickly took shape. At the next Executive Council meeting on August 3–5, the special committee reported that it had selected September 19 for the demonstration. The original plan had been to hold a rally around Labor Day, but it was moved back to avoid the worst of the Washington, DC, summer heat and humidity. "The reason we had it September the nineteenth, the first time, is that it's cooler," recalled Susan Dunlop. At the August meeting, the Council added that planning had gone well; many outside groups had pledged their support, and the response from affiliates had been "gratifying." Overall, Kirkland was "looking forward to a large crowd for the demonstration."[17]

Not everything could be planned, however. On the day that the Council convened, the PATCO strike began unexpectedly. While the strike was illegal, many observers felt that the president had gone too far in replacing the controllers so quickly, boosting support for Solidarity Day. The AFL-CIO coordinated support for the PATCO strikers and organized Solidarity Day simultaneously, allowing the two campaigns to complement each other. Solidarity Day now had even greater appeal. "The timing couldn't have been better," recalled Charles Stott, who helped organize the march. "Of course . . . it started as a protest of Ronald Reagan's policies, and the nature of the event picked up momentum when it became evident that Reagan's firing of the Air Traffic Controllers for their illegal strike was a precursor to what private employers would do in the years that followed."[18]

Immediately after the Council meeting, the march was strongly endorsed by a special gathering of the AFL-CIO's General Board, an important step. Justifying the rally, several delegates cited the heavy job losses that their unions were experiencing, blaming the president's economic and trade policies and his hostility to organized labor. In an impassioned speech, United Rubber Workers' president Peter Bommarito voiced his "strong acclaim" for Solidarity Day, saying that labor needed to take to the streets in order to fight back against the "devastating impact" of Reagan's "anti-worker initiatives." Others specifically mentioned the PATCO walkout. According to UAW president Douglas Fraser, Reagan had treated the air traffic controllers in a "cruel and harsh and vicious manner."[19] In closing, the Board urged all affiliates to give "top priority" to Solidarity Day and to commit "all necessary resources" to it. This call was answered. As Secretary-Treasurer Tom Donahue later admitted, affiliates spent "nine or ten million dollars" on organizing the rally. "It was an expensive venture," he noted, "but it had to be done, so we did it."[20]

With Kirkland guiding discussions, Federation leaders agreed that "Solidarity Day" was an appropriate name for the protest. The name acknowledged the example of the Polish labor union, Solidarnosc, which the AFL-CIO strongly supported. In September 1980 the General Board had established a Polish Workers' Aid Fund, and by February 1981 contributions "from every level" of the trade union movement had raised over $200,000. Funds were mainly used to purchase office equipment for the fledgling organization. The Polish workers' willingness to defy an autocratic regime inspired many American labor leaders, particularly Kirkland. "Solidarity is more than just a day," he explained. "As our brothers and sisters in Poland have shown the world, it is a quality of the human spirit that can never be defeated." The name of the march also paid homage to the old labor song "Solidarity Forever," showing that organized labor was trying to reconnect with its radical roots. According to the Federation, Solidarity Day represented "a rebirth of the spirit of the 1930s." For Kirkland, the march offered an opportunity to develop the solidarity theme, the central motif of his presidency.[21]

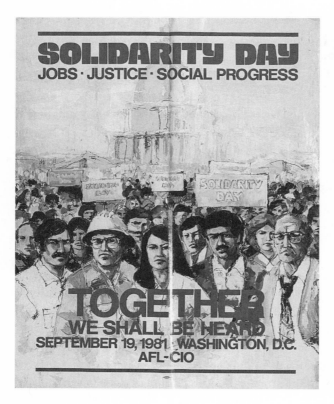

Solidarity Day—
AFL-CIO
promotional poster.
Courtesy of Special
Collections,
University of
Maryland Libraries.

There were other reasons for the demonstration. It was partly designed to celebrate the one hundredth anniversary of the foundation of the American Federation of Labor, a landmark that Kirkland referred to in his address on the day. In calling for the march, Kirkland was also keen to stamp his authority on the AFL-CIO presidency, and especially to show that he was more than a pale imitation of Meany. As labor writer Harry Bernstein noted, the protest was significant because it marked "a major departure" from the AFL-CIO's "traditional policy of avoiding large street demonstrations." A steadfast supporter of the Vietnam War, Meany had refused to countenance AFL-CIO involvement in the antiwar movement, or to endorse the 1963 March on Washington. Taking the helm, Kirkland announced a new direction. "Changing times call for changing tactics," he asserted.[22]

Many in the labor movement noted the shift. "People would say, 'Oh, George Meany would *never* have allowed this,'" observed Susan Dunlop, remembering reaction to the call for a mass march. "I think he (Kirkland) recognized that things were changing," added Charles Stott, "and that we had to go back to

Solidarity Day—protesters enjoying free transport on the Washington, DC, Metro, September 19, 1981. Courtesy of Special Collections, University of Maryland Libraries.

To ensure that the march was a success, the labor movement also drew on its members' expertise. Supplied by the Communication Workers' Union, 1,500 well-trained marshals provided security and supervised press access. At the end of the march, three major unions, including the sanitation workers, cleaned up the entire site.[32]

The parallel with the 1963 March on Washington—where great efforts were expended to prevent violence—was clear. To be sure, as the first march of its kind, the March on Washington did generate more fear and anticipation than Solidarity Day. On both occasions, however, organizers silenced claims that mass marches would end in bloodshed or disorder. The AFL-CIO even planned Solidarity Day by using "how-to" manuals from the 1963 protest. As had been the case at the March on Washington, the lead delegation in 1981 comprised labor and civil rights leaders, walking alongside one another. At the front were Kirkland and Donahue, along with Coretta Scott King, Bayard Rustin, and NAACP leader Benjamin Hooks. The rally even concluded with a singing of "We Shall Overcome," the anthem of the civil rights movement. Several key participants drew explicit links between the two marches. "In a very real sense," professed Mrs. King, "'Solidarity Day' is a continuation of the great march on Washington."[33]

Solidarity Day—main crowd, September 19, 1981. Courtesy of Special Collections, University of Maryland Libraries.

Solidarity Day—march, aerial shot, September 19, 1981. Courtesy of Special Collections, University of Maryland Libraries.

Solidarity Day—lead group, September 19, 1981. Courtesy of Special Collections, University of Maryland Libraries.

Behind the lead group, marchers were drawn from a wide variety of backgrounds. A large contingent came from the union movement, partly because the AFL-CIO had used its Labor Day rallies to publicize Solidarity Day. In New York City, for example, the Labor Day parade—the first in many years— attracted at least 100,000 participants and was led by Kirkland, who acted as grand marshal. The September 7 rally, thought *New York Times'* writer William Serrin, signified the emergence of "a new movement among American trade unionists to oppose President Reagan's economic policies." Twelve days later, many of the same people turned out again for Solidarity Day. According to the AFL-CIO, marchers represented a broad slice of America's working people, illustrating its increasingly diverse membership. "They came from steel mills and textile mills, from food markets and post offices, construction sites and government offices, schools and auto assembly lines, railroad yards and wharfs, everywhere," a press release summarized.[34]

Asked why they were marching, some workers stressed the need to defend hard-won union gains. "I had a grandmother who in 1863 walked from 24th and Fairmount to 22nd and South Street to a knitting mill for $3 a week, 10 hours a day, six days a week," explained John McClay Sr. of Philadelphia.

Solidarity Day—protesters with stickers, September 19, 1981. Courtesy of Special Collections, University of Maryland Libraries.

"It's the unions that changed all that. Now Reagan's trying to bust the unions. He did away with collective bargaining when he fired the air traffic controllers." While many marchers were union members, most were not used to taking part in demonstrations. Some associated protests with "kids who had too much time on their hands," but these marchers were older and had serious economic concerns on their minds. "I'm not a radical," explained Mildred Donahue, a fifty-eight-year-old librarian from Orange, Connecticut. "But Ronald Reagan made me come here. I wanted to make the point that this Administration doesn't have a mandate for what they're doing." According to another demonstrator, Solidarity Day was significant because it had mobilized a broad cross-section of Americans and got them in the streets for the first time: "These people are older. They're all working people. I've been to twenty different demonstrations. There hasn't been one like this before."[35]

The march mobilized people from both near and afar. Public employee unions from Washington, DC, Maryland, and Virginia were particularly well-represented; these workers did not have to travel far, and they were being hit hard by Reagan's cuts. In general, the mid-Atlantic and northeastern states supplied the biggest contingents of protesters, with most traveling by bus.

Showing its support for Solidarity Day, AFSCME's Council 30 sent six bus-loads of marchers from Arlington County, Virginia, and a further four from Richmond. Members were mobilized by flyers reminding them of recent federal budget cuts. "It's Your Job on the Line," they were warned. Hoping that AFSCME could supply more marchers than any other union, its leaders also pushed for a big turnout, especially from local members. In a similar vein, UFCW leader Doug Dority remembered that staffers brought in large numbers of members from the states near Washington, DC. "We had to bring in bus-loads, and busloads, and busloads, of people, and it's sheer logistics . . . you had to get your numbers, as close to Washington as possible. I mean you can't bring a bus from California here very easily, so you can bring one from New Jersey because it's not that far to go."[36]

Solidarity Day was much more than a localized protest, however, and many people traveled long distances to be there. Unwilling to cross PATCO's picket lines, participants showed a lot of creativity. One busload of office workers from Wisconsin journeyed for sixteen hours to take part. "We felt we had to stand up for the principles of the labor movement—to prove that it is not dying," they explained. Another contingent of union members traveled all night by train from Atlanta. While this group paid for their own tickets, others received financial assistance. In Iowa, union members who could not attend donated money so that someone else could go in their place. In the Chicago area, workers who had been laid off by International Harvester raised $50 each so that they could buy bus tickets to the rally. The Minnesota AFL-CIO also paid to bring a delegation of PATCO strikers to the march. A large number of marchers also came by car, with many driving all night so that they could be in Washington by dawn.[37]

Many marchers—including thousands drawn from women's and civil rights groups—did not have labor backgrounds. Almost every protester had a placard, and the variety of slogans that were used illustrated the crowd's diversity. Indeed, one AFL-CIO document showed that twenty-one different slogans were used on the day. The signs were an eclectic mix; while some were labor-based—such as Samuel Gompers' credo, "More Leisure, Less Greed"—others expressed support for the Equal Rights Amendment—which needed to be ratified within the next nine months—or called for the renewal of the Voting Rights Act. Placards also protested against Reagan's cuts and questioned his claims to speak for workers. While a unifying theme was lacking—beyond opposition to the Reagan administration—the mood was determined. As journalist Richard Strout observed, Solidarity Day "was a combination of political rally, strike meeting, religious revival, and outdoor picnic, under chilly skies."[38]

Solidarity Day—protesters, September 19, 1981. Courtesy of Special Collections, University of Maryland Libraries.

Those who addressed the rally illustrated the broad coalition behind it. All leaders of organizations involved in the protest, the eighteen speakers represented a wide variety of citizens, including workers, African-Americans, Latinos, women, young people, senior citizens, and the disabled. NAACP leader Benjamin Hooks declared that his members would "not sit idly by while the bare necessities of life are taken from the needy and given to the greedy," yet he outlined no concrete program of action. In a similar vein, Kirkland—like most speakers—attacked the Reagan's administration policies. He called on those present to "build a new mandate for a humane and just America," yet he included no specifics on how this was to be achieved. In contrast, Rev. Jesse Jackson wanted a campaign of civil disobedience to be directed at the Reagan administration. "Black and white and brown," he urged, "male and female, we must fill the streets, fill the jails, send a message to America: we will not bow." AFSCME leader Jerry Wurf also provided a memorable address. Though he was gravely ill from emphysema, Wurf was determined to address the protesters, especially as large numbers of AFSCME members had turned out. Brought to the stage by ambulance, he told the huge crowd that they would have to keep

Solidarity Day—protesters supporting PATCO, September 19, 1981. Courtesy of Special Collections, University of Maryland Libraries.

working to "turn the country around." By December, the man who had marched alongside Dr. Martin Luther King during the Memphis sanitation workers' strike of 1968 was dead. "Wurf was dying," recalled Gerald McEntee, who succeeded him as AFSCME president, "but he was so proud of the fact that we had all these people." Clearly moved, Kirkland subsequently recalled Wurf's "fierce determination" to rise "from what proved to be his deathbed" and give the speech. It was a memory of Solidarity Day that he always cherished.[39]

Organized in response to Reagan's gibes about out-of-touch union leaders, Solidarity Day was significant because it showed that the Federation could mobilize its members. This achievement was especially notable because affiliates had a lot of autonomy. Looking back, staffers pointed to these gains. According to Jim Baker, Kirkland's former executive assistant, the march provided "visible opposition" to Reagan's policies and "showed that the AFL-CIO could lead its affiliates." It "charged up" those who took part and affected the Democratic-controlled House, which had been acquiescing in Reagan's policies.[40] In oral history interviews, many of those who had taken part stressed the significance—and uplifting effect—of the protest. Solidarity Day, thought

Solidarity Day—sign-bearing protesters, September 19, 1981. Courtesy of Special Collections, University of Maryland Libraries.

African-American staffer Richard Womack, was a "great experience." Demonstrating organized labor's sincerity in working with its "partners," particularly civil rights groups, Womack saw the protest as a "crowning moment" for the labor movement. Susan Dunlop remembered the march as very important because it showed that the labor movement could fight back against the Reagan administration, thus lifting morale at a very difficult time. "That was a demonstration that really meant something to people," she recalled. "People really wanted to come out and say something . . . it helped all of us, tremendously." Solidarity Day, agreed Morton Bahr, a vice president of the CWA, was a "hugely successful" protest that "gave people a boost of energy" and "made the politicians take note."[41]

In the immediate wake of the march, Congress was more responsive to labor's demands. The House overwhelmingly passed a bill to extend the Voting

Solidarity Day—Jesse Jackson speaks, September 19, 1981. Courtesy of Special Collections, University of Maryland Libraries.

Solidarity Day—a gravely ill Jerry Wurf speaks, September 19, 1981. Courtesy of Special Collections, University of Maryland Libraries.

Rights Act and approved funds for the departments of Labor, Education, and Health and Human Services, rejecting the cuts sought by the administration. In addition, Congress blocked the administration's efforts to weaken the Occupational Safety and Health Act (although OSHA enforcement subsequently declined). The momentum generated by the march also boosted the AFL-CIO's successful campaign against tuition tax credits in the District of Columbia, helping to maintain the public schools in the racially polarized District. After the march, Kirkland promised to wield labor's political power to ensure that elected representatives were more responsive to its needs. As the *New York Times* noted, labor was a "visible force" at the Democratic Party's midterm convention in 1982, paving the way for gains in the election.[42]

For the AFL-CIO, Solidarity Day was also significant because it strengthened Kirkland's leadership. Prior to it, labor writers had doubted whether Kirkland could move out of Meany's shadow. In May Kirkland was hurt when *New York Times* reporter William Serrin questioned his leadership, asserting that the labor movement was in crisis.[43] Solidarity Day, however, won over the respected and influential reporter. In November Serrin proclaimed that Kirkland had "begun to place his stamp on the labor federation." Helped by the mass protest, the new AFL-CIO chief had developed "more confidence" and was functioning as a true leader. Kirkland had pushed through a per capita dues increase, had initiated a major organizing project in Houston, and had established the George Meany Memorial Archives in Silver Spring, Maryland. "Whatever success the AFL-CIO may enjoy in the years ahead," he concluded, "it is surely Mr. Kirkland's organization now." The well-regarded *National Journal* agreed. "Kirkland has erased the doubts and won the enthusiastic support of almost all union leaders," wrote columnist James W. Singer shortly after Solidarity Day.[44]

Validating these judgments, Kirkland easily won reelection at the Federation's fourteenth convention in November. As he did so, he drew heavily on the memory of Solidarity Day, calling it "the greatest protest demonstration in our history." A number of speakers lauded Kirkland's leadership in organizing the march, and repeated his mantra, "We have not forgot how to fight." Feeling that he had proved his critics wrong, Kirkland was pleased. "Too often to recount," he told the convention, "we have been written off and left for dead by the fashionmongers of the day only to see them come and go while we remained steadfast on the field of action."[45]

Within the AFL-CIO, Solidarity Day generated other important changes. Widely credited with having organized a successful demonstration, John Perkins became the director of the Federation's political arm, the Committee on

Political Education (COPE). A major improvement on the "crusty" Al Bar-kan, Perkins undertook significant reforms. Copying the New Right's direct mailing techniques, he created a computer mailing list with 12 million mem-bers, hired poll taker Peter Hart to streamline polling and mail operations, and improved communications between the Federation and the Democratic Party. According to Leon Billings, executive director of the Democratic Sena-torial Campaign Committee, Perkins was "going to do in two years what the right wing took 10 years to do. There's no one I've met who's on top of all this as Perkins." Under Perkins, COPE also took on more staff, began to conduct its own national opinion polls, and secured a commitment from all affiliates to pay regular assessments. Perkins' efforts contributed to the gains that the Democrats made in the 1982 elections.[46]

The march also helped to establish a dialogue between the AFL-CIO and the Reagan administration. Soon after the march, Reagan started to talk to labor leaders, even inviting the entire Executive Council to the White House. At the meeting on December 2, which two Council members—Glenn Watts of the Communications Workers and William Winpisinger of the Machinists—refused to attend, the atmosphere was understandably awkward. Drawing from note cards propped up by his coffee cup, Reagan spoke of the need for an improved "dialogue with labor" and promised to pursue an "open door pol-icy" with the Federation. Overseen by Robert Bonitati, aides subsequently laid out a "labor strategy" that involved closer consultation with the Federa-tion. "The AFL-CIO," Bonitati pointed out in one key memo, "is still the dom-inant force in labor's political actions," and the administration had to take it seriously. The following February, Vice President George H. W. Bush ad-dressed an Executive Council meeting in Bal Harbour, Florida. Although his appearance was significant, Bush proclaimed that he was "not happy" with the Federation's criticisms of the administration's economic policies, and he doubted whether the Council would give him a fair hearing. The relationship between Kirkland and Reagan also remained frosty, especially as Reagan re-fused to authorize the rehiring of the PATCO strikers, a major sticking point. The covert aim of the administration's strategy, moreover, was to limit the political gains that the labor movement derived from Solidarity Day.[47]

In public, the Reagan administration tried to downplay Solidarity Day's significance. In a deliberate move, Reagan ignored the protest, leaving for Camp David before the marchers arrived. The president also quipped that more people had attended a Simon and Garfunkel concert than had turned out for Solidarity Day. Held on September 19 in New York City's Central Park, the

President Reagan
Cabinet Room
meeting with
AFL-CIO leaders,
December 2, 1981.
Relations were still
strained after
Solidarity Day.
Courtesy of the
Reagan Library.

free concert by the reunited music duo drew a crowd of between 400,000 and 500,000. Some aides were openly dismissive about the march. "What are they trying to tell us?" asked a Reagan official. "That there are people out there who don't like Ronald Reagan? We know that."[48]

The administration's private records, however, show that aides were concerned about Solidarity Day. As early as June 23, Reagan's special assistant for labor relations, Robert Bonitati, wrote to Public Liaison director Elizabeth Dole about the planned march. "I am sure we will have a massive media event in Washington on September 19," he warned. As a result, key aides needed to meet "at an early date" to "discuss a basic strategy for dealing with 'Solidarity Day' and all of its ramifications." Later, Bonitati informed Dole that the AFL-CIO had undertaken "a major organizational effort" in order to "draw huge throngs to Washington for this event." He estimated that attendance could easily reach 300,000 people, largely because organizers were "convinced that the labor movement's prestige is on the line."[49] Concerned that the march was marshalling opposition to important administration policies, aides kept a close eye on the AFL-CIO, even scrutinizing its logistical arrangements. "It is very difficult to rent a bus on the East Coast," Bonitati reported on September 15.[50]

Aides were also troubled by the march's mobilization of federal employees. In one confidential memo written on September 10, labor relations assistant Baker A. Smith worried that public sector union leaders were planning to "Destabilize the Reagan program" of federal budget cuts. "Solidarity Day," he added, "does represent a significant step in federal employee union officialdom to openly and publicly use their special position of trust to interfere in the process of governance and to thwart the political process." Smith was especially concerned by the activities of the 750,000-member American Federation of Government Employees, which was calling its members, "ALL OUT FOR SOLIDARITY DAY." Coming on the heels of the PATCO walkout, the administration feared that the march might encourage strikes—or a broader protest movement—among federal workers.[51]

Furthermore, advisers worried about the way that the march mobilized African-American groups. A black aide in the Office of Public Liaison, Thelma Duggin recommended to Dole that the administration should "take some positive actions regarding issues of concern to Black America" before September 19. In response, advisers tried to bolster the administration's relationship with African-American groups. These actions were a far cry from the White House's public position. In August, for example, Bonitati told the press that aides were not concerned about Solidarity Day. "I don't think anybody here, officially, has really focused on it," he declared. "There's always some kind of a demonstration here."[52]

The administration's concern about Solidarity Day should not be overstated, as aides also stressed the march's limitations. Advisers found that organizers were struggling to articulate a clear program of action, a downside of the broad coalition behind the rally. According to Bonitati, marchers represented a huge "umbrella" of liberal groups, yet they presented few specific demands. Even the AFL-CIO acknowledged the lack of focus. In August the Executive Council noted that Solidarity Day was concerned with no fewer than fourteen "centerpiece issues": civil rights, education, energy, environment, fair trade, fair taxes, health and safety, housing, jobs, justice, lower interest rates, Social Security, voting rights, and women's rights. All were huge areas in their own right. "Well, at least they're short words," admitted an AFL-CIO spokesperson later. Individual unions also frequently focused on their own issues, while non-labor groups promoted their own, diverse agendas. Organizations represented on the day included the Pittsburgh Central American

Mobilization Committee—which was opposed to American involvement in El Salvador—as well as the Marxist and Leninist USA Party, the DC Area Feminist Alliance, and the National Coalition of Black Gays. As the *New York Times'* David Shribman reported from the rally, "Today's march was a curious potpourri of protest."[53]

In protesting against the Reagan administration's cuts, the AFL-CIO was also on the back foot. A key problem was that the rally was held *after* the administration had enacted its budget and tax programs, robbing it of the ability to block these policies. Addressing the major issues on the Federation's agenda, moreover, was politically difficult at a time of high inflation. To some extent, the march was hurt by the prominent participation of the public sector unions. Anticipating later conservative attacks, many voters blamed these unions for inflation, which stood at 13.5 percent when Reagan took office. Polls also showed that most Americans supported the president's actions in the PATCO dispute, bolstering his confidence.[54]

Despite the large turnout on Solidarity Day, the Reagan administration kept faith in the conservatism of many Americans, including union members. Returning to the results of the 1980 election, they reiterated their belief that labor leaders were out of touch with their members. Their private research also indicated that Reagan remained popular with many union members. In fighting for the long-term support of working Americans, the administration had several advantages, especially as Reagan was a gifted media performer. In interviews and speeches, Reagan stressed his involvement in the labor movement, including a stint as head of the Screen Actors' Guild in the 1940s and 1950s. In an official proclamation, Reagan also designated January 20, 1982, as "Solidarity Day" in order to identify with the Polish labor movement. According to the president, the Poles were "real workers" who were fighting for "fundamental human and economic rights" that included the "right to assemble" and the "right to strike." Reagan skillfully diverted attention from the problems facing American workers and retained—at least among certain unionists—a positive image. As Reagan was aware, some union members praised his handling of the PATCO strike, feeling that he had shown courage in confronting well-paid workers.[55]

While Reagan had regular access to the airwaves, the AFL-CIO had a weak media presence, and Solidarity Day did little to change this. Crucially, PBS canceled an hour-long television special about the march—which was due to be transmitted the following Monday—because of the poor quality of the live broadcast. An estimated audience of 5 million American homes was lost. While some viewers complained that the move reflected pressure from the White House, PBS blamed "technological malfeasance to the worst degree." Put together by Public Interest Video Network, an independent production team, the live broadcast was transmitted to viewers in Washington, DC, for two hours, but it was marred by sound losses, interruptions, and blank pictures. It was almost impossible to hear Kirkland, the main speaker, leading PBS to jettison plans to distribute the special among its 296 member stations. In contrast, Dr. Martin Luther King's stirring speech at the March on Washington has gone down as one of the most memorable in history, partly because it was televised so well. King was also an incredibly gifted orator. Although known primarily as a writer, Kirkland gave a rousing address that stressed that Reagan's opponents were "not alone," but it was not widely preserved for posterity. Given the power of television in forging the national memory, this was a critical problem.[56]

Looking back, however, Solidarity Day stands out as an important episode, an inspiring event that showed that a different kind of labor movement was possible, even at the most difficult of times. As well-regarded journalist Arch Puddington put it, Solidarity Day was an "unalloyed success" that laid "to rest" criticisms that labor was a spent force lacking in creativity. The importance of Solidarity Day was integrally linked to its size, as well as to clever and effective organization. Consequently, outside observers only realized quite late just how big the march would be. Two days before the rally, the Secret Service raised its estimate of "anticipated attendance" from 150,000 to 200,000, yet this calculation still proved to be far too low. Even some participants were surprised by the turnout. "It ended up being bigger than people had expected it to be," recalled marcher Susan Bianchi.[57] A range of nonlabor newspapers— including the Dayton (OH) *Journal Herald,* the *Chicago Sun-Times,* the Charleston (SC) *Evening Post,* and the *Philadelphia Inquirer*—reported that 400,000 people had turned out. America's "Newspaper of Record," the *New York Times,* also used this figure.[58] The number did matter. "They've been saying that we couldn't bring together our rank and file to support our leadership," declared one organizer afterwards. "We've shown them that we can." Solidarity Day, proclaimed the AFL-CIO, was "one of the most memorable and important days in trade union history."[59]

The spirit and determination of those who took part in Solidarity Day deserves to be recognized. The attendance was especially impressive because the PATCO strike led to a boycott of domestic air travel by union members. Organizers had to cancel more than fifty chartered flights. Despite this setback, participants still came from every corner of the United States. One group of union members from Seattle refused to board a direct flight to Washington,

DC, instead flying from Vancouver to Toronto and then taking a thirteen-and-a-half-hour bus ride to the U.S. capital. Other participants finished work on Friday afternoon and rode buses for hundreds—if not thousands—of miles to be at the rally. "Ordinary Americans do not work all day on a Friday, board buses and ride through the night without sleep just to say that they attended a parade or heard speeches," explained Chemical Workers' leader Frank D. Martino. "Not by the hundreds of thousands, they don't."[60]

Occurring at a very difficult time for the AFL-CIO, Solidarity Day was an important morale-booster for many participants. As AFGE president Kenneth Blaylock put it, the demonstration had "given union members hope for change." Several months after the event, the glow was still apparent. In November an upbeat Bill Winpisinger thought that Solidarity Day represented "the beginning of a new day in American trade union history . . . the beginning of a trade union offensive to turn the country around." The march, added UFCW president Bill Wynn, had dispelled the "gloom and the doom" that labor's adversaries concentrated on. "I feel no gloom, I foresee no doom," he enthused.[61]

While sustaining this optimism in the long term would be difficult, the achievement of Solidarity Day did persist. For many participants the mass protest remained one of the highlights of their careers, something that they looked back on with pride. The memory of so many people coming together epitomized what the labor movement was all about. "It was good for everybody," summarized Tom Donahue. When Kirkland resigned in August 1995, Donahue cited Solidarity Day as one of the defining accomplishments of his eight-term presidency. The march, he claimed, had "helped galvanize the labor movement's unity in those years," getting unionists through a very difficult period.[62]

Other activists retained clear—and fond—memories of Solidarity Day. Susan Bianchi stressed its uplifting effects. "I'm more of an introvert than I'm extrovert," she admitted, "but I think it was very motivating, at the end of it you felt very good, you felt very empowered . . . you felt like, 'Okay, yes this is a massive statement, and there's a lot of energy, and we can make change.' It was very positive." Solidarity Day was also a proud moment for Doug Dority. "I remember it *very* well," he stressed, adding that he had marched near the front with other UFCW leaders. "We had a great time. . . . It was a big, big march. . . . Basically, it was a protest, about, 'Hey, treat us all better, this is the working people of this country, they deserve to be treated better.'" Solidarity Day, summarized Charles Stott, was "pretty immense."[63]

Solidarity Day was also important outside the labor movement. It challenged traditional images of organized labor in the 1980s and early 1990s, an era widely associated with defeat and decline. As writer and labor lawyer Thomas Geoghegan noted after one bitter defeat: "Cat was looking around and saying, 'There isn't a strong labor movement . . . so why do we have to put up with one?'"[64] For Geoghegan—and for most observers—labor in these years was "flat on its back," yet the overlooked events of Solidarity Day remind us that the AFL-CIO was also able to fight back. Because it occurred at such a difficult time for American labor, Solidarity Day—rather than being overlooked—is especially deserving of recognition. As the *New York Times* noted, ultimately just the holding of such a large march was a noteworthy accomplishment for a labor movement that had suffered a string of recent defeats. At a very difficult hour, America's beleaguered and decentralized labor movement showed that it still had some solidarity, and it certainly made itself heard. For Kirkland, the challenge was to sustain the energy generated by the one-day protest. It was to prove a massive—and daunting—task.[65]

CHAPTER FOUR

From Solidarity to Defeat

After the euphoria of Solidarity Day, it proved hard to achieve the lasting political change that marchers had dreamed of. As successful as the mass protest had been, in the longer term much hinged on whether Reagan was reelected. For an organization under fire politically, a change in the presidency was very important, and in 1983–84 the Federation mounted a strong campaign behind Democratic challenger Walter Mondale. Reagan, however, had the last laugh, exploiting an improving economy—and his strong personal popularity—to easily win the 1984 election.[1] The economy was Reagan's trump card, helping the GOP to win 59 percent of the vote. The outcome was a bitter blow, especially for those who had marched down the Mall three years earlier. Trying to stay positive, Kirkland noted that union members had voted for Mondale "at least 20 percent better than the general population," partly because of the improved political machine put in place after Solidarity Day. The election proved an important marker, forcing the Federation's leaders—and many members—to realize that they would have to endure at least another four years of a hostile presidency.[2]

Between Solidarity Day and the 1984 election, Kirkland tried to build on the success of the protest. In 1982, 1983, and 1984, he organized Solidarity Day II, III, and IV, and all were large marches. There were some significant internal reforms, as Kirkland oversaw the continued diversification of the Executive Council. Other changes strove to improve the AFL-CIO's image in the media and to increase communication with members. Kirkland also launched a major organizing campaign in Houston, a brave effort in hostile territory. Continuing to see itself as a "People's Lobby," the Federation had some success in defending important social programs, particularly Social Security. In addition, Kirkland took a strong interest in international affairs, providing extensive support for free trade unions in eastern and central Europe, particularly Poland. On the world stage, Kirkland stepped out of Meany's shadow, leading the AFL-CIO back into the ICFTU, which it had left in 1969 after Meany complained that the group was not sufficiently anti-Communist. Finally, Kirkland continued to reunify the Federation, an enduring theme of his presidency.[3]

In many ways, however, Kirkland's reforms did not go far enough. The efforts to diversify the Council were limited and—for many—unsatisfactory. The

Federation struggled to provide effective leadership in the organizing field, and the Houston program was largely a failure. Like many efforts before it, the campaign had been designed to open up the South to unions, but the region remained an Achilles' heel for America's labor movement. While he initiated some reforms, Kirkland was reluctant to openly address the decline in union density, especially in the media. He remained shy and—for critics, at least—disconnected from the rank and file. The follow-up Solidarity Day marches did mobilize large numbers, yet they failed to match the impact of the first one, partly because they were decentralized. In some ways, the "great success" of the first Solidarity Day became a trap for Kirkland. As he admitted to the Council, any subsequent demonstration "would have to be larger or it would be seen as a failure," yet massive demonstrations placed a "heavy financial burden" on affiliates. As the manufacturing sector shed jobs at an unprecedented rate, the large industrial unions became consumed by defensive battles, and were in no position to fund huge demonstrations.[4]

Although they had put the first woman on the Executive Council in 1980, Kirkland and Donahue knew that they needed to go further. In November 1981 the AFGE's Barbara Hutchinson became the second woman—and the second African-American—to serve on the Council. The director of the AFGE's Women's Department, Hutchinson was not the president of an affiliate. According to Council minutes—which were usually summarized—Hutchinson was elected after unspecified "lengthy discussion," suggesting that some members were uneasy with the suspension of "long respected rules with respect to qualification." Kirkland, however, insisted on the change. It would be 1987 before a third woman, Lenore Miller, went onto the Council after she automatically became president of the Retail, Wholesale and Department Store Union following the death of incumbent Alvin Heaps. Again, there was covert resistance, especially from male-dominated unions in manufacturing and the building trades. "It . . . took a while to gain respect," recalled Miller, "but that came." Still, Miller was often mistaken as the wife of another union leader when she attended AFL-CIO meetings.[5]

While there was plenty of work to do, the changes at the top were important, especially in setting an example for the rest of the Federation. Thus, in 1983, UFT official Sandra Feldman became the first female grand marshal of New York City's large Labor Day parade. Three years later, Connecticut became the first state federation to elect a female president, while four other states had chosen women as deputy leaders. Similar changes gradually trickled down to the central labor councils and local unions.[6]

Despite these reforms, the Executive Council remained male-dominated, as both internal and external critics pointed out. While she admired Kirkland, Lenore Miller recalled that it remained hard to get more women on the Council. Although the precedent had been removed by Kirkland, some union leaders continued to believe that Council spots should be reserved for union presidents, positions dominated by men.[7] Kirkland also resisted pressure to create a separate women's department, which could have been used to promote women's issues and connect with female workers. "We used to get a lot of pressure to have a women's department," recalled Susan Dunlop, who came on Kirkland's staff in 1984, "and we talked about it. One of Kirkland's feelings was . . . that women's issues are labor issues, and vice versa, so if you really isolate out [a] women's department, it also can tend to be a place where you can park things you don't want to deal with."[8]

The Federation's record of reaching out to women workers was poor. In the 1980s the proportion of female union members increased, yet this was largely a reflection of the growth of service industries rather than recruitment strategies. In fact, most women workers remained unorganized and poorly paid. In 1979, the year that Kirkland took over, women earned only 59 percent as much as men on average, down from 63.9 percent in 1955. Trapped in low-paying jobs, women were ripe for organizing; in 1981 just 5.5 percent of female workers held managerial positions, and many looked to unions for a better deal. In the same year, there were 20 million office workers in America—most of them women—yet only 10 percent belonged to unions. The Industrial Union Department did document the entry of women into the workforce, and the fact that they had a disproportionate need for union representation, yet there was no apparent follow-up, partly because the IUD's leadership group contained just one woman—Lenore Miller—out of twenty-four vice presidents.[9]

In these years the AFL-CIO did support a drive to organize office and clerical workers, yet this effort was pushed by new SEIU president John Sweeney—who had been elected in 1980—and District 925 leader Karen Nussbaum, rather than by Kirkland. Nussbaum, who had founded her association while working as a clerk-typist at Harvard University, vividly recalled how many male union leaders opposed efforts to organize women. "You can't organize women, because they think with their cunts, not their brains," she recalled being told by a high-ranking Teamsters official. "That was not unique," she added, "we ran into that a lot, actually. But we were determined, and had a mission to organize women workers." Other female union leaders remembered resistance when they fought for more representation within the labor movement. In the 1980s Susan Bianchi served as vice president and president of the Association of Flight Attendants (AFA), a fledgling union that had broken away from the Air Line Pilots Association in 1973. She remembered that the Pilots, along with several other male-dominated unions, fought the AFA's efforts to get a seat on the Executive Council. "I think the AFL, the people who voted on our seat, were influenced, heavily, by the Pilots' positions, and I think some . . . they just didn't support this new, fledgling, female-run, female-dominated . . . organization." It was not until 1989 that the Flight Attendants got their seat.[10]

Kirkland and Donahue were also determined to place more African-Americans on the Council. Efforts moved slowly. In 1984 there were two African-Americans on the key body, yet neither Associated Actors and Artistes of America president Frederick O'Neal, who was in his late seventies, nor Barbara Hutchinson were strong voices for reform. African-American labor activists had wanted a more outspoken candidate, but they had not been successful. It was the large affiliates, particularly in manufacturing and the skilled trades, that held sway, and they continued to be led by white men. In 1982 an analysis by *Black Enterprise* found that just one of the steelworkers' thirty board members was black, while the carpenters and machinists did not have any blacks on their boards. The SEIU and UAW had the highest levels of black representation.[11]

While the leadership remained dominated by white men, the Federation's membership was becoming increasingly diverse, a reflection of the changing nature of the workforce—particularly the growth of the service sector—and the impact of civil rights laws on the workplace. In 1982 the AFL-CIO had around 15 million members; 23 percent were African-American and 29 percent were female. Both groups were generally more responsive to unions than whites. Given this situation, the limited changes at the top did not satisfy many activists. In 1980, when Kirkland announced that he would be reserving Council seats for a woman and a member of a minority group, even O'Neal called it "too little and too late." Other minority leaders called on Kirkland to be more forceful. "It has to come from him, in a determined way," explained AFSCME secretary-treasurer William Lucy, who had headed the Coalition of Black Trade Unionists since its foundation in 1972 but was not put on the Council until October 1995—by John Sweeney. "If Lane said, 'we must do this, I want it done and done now,' then it would happen." Kirkland, however, was apt to defer to affiliates' autonomy, as well as to convention. As Lenore Miller put it, he was "more conciliatory than confrontational." Kirkland's management style, added Kenneth B. Noble in the *New York Times*, favored "compromise and consensus building," but sometimes a firmer hand was needed. Despite the placement of women and African-Americans on the Council, there was no representative from the growing Latino population. Overall, Kirkland feared that a more forceful style might undermine his efforts to unify the Federation, his top priority.[12]

Despite the slow pace of change in Council appointments, Kirkland did initiate one important symbolic reform. In November 1981 he suggested that the AFL-CIO's official seal be changed. Rather than depicting a handshake between two whites, one hand was to be shaded dark. This alteration—which was initially made for a temporary centennial logo—was made permanent at the president's suggestion. "It was a white hand, and a black hand, and he did that . . . it was his decision," recalled staffer Markley Roberts. After 1981, the image of black and white hands embracing—with a map of North America in the background—sent a powerful visual message of racial inclusiveness. It was representative of the Kirkland era that the change was made "without any public notice," and with little fanfare. Kirkland had quietly overseen a major shift in the Federation's image.[13]

Aware of the need for reform, Kirkland took other steps to connect leaders with members. In 1981 he initiated regional conferences, allowing elected union officials to meet with the rank and file and hear their complaints. It was the sort of initiative that was conspicuously absent under Meany. Between 1981 and 1985, the Federation conducted thirty-five conferences in twenty-nine states, meeting with over 20,000 local leaders and members in the process. The conferences influenced a number of important initiatives, including Solidarity Day and the Committee on the Evolution of Work, a high-level body that examined changes in the workplace and their implications for unions.[14] Participants stressed that the gatherings were important. "These conferences," recalled former legislative director Ray Denison, "did much to bring closer the federation leadership to our field operations and made it easier for us to better assist local leadership with state and local legislators." In 1986 the conferences were video-conferenced from Washington, DC, allowing over 4,000 people to participate. While attendees tended to be local union leaders or regional staff, rather than rank and filers, Kirkland had reached out well beyond Washington, DC.[15]

In these years, the AFL-CIO also fought significant defensive battles. In early 1982 it helped to defeat proposed drastic cuts to Social Security, drawing on public opposition in the process. Following this, the Executive Council reaffirmed its pledge to keep Social Security, which provided "fundamental protections" for American workers. More cautious in the wake of Solidarity Day, the Reagan administration was put on notice.[16] Throughout the recession of the early 1980s, the Federation was a steadfast defender of Social Security, viewing it as the cornerstone of the national retirement system. In 1983 it successfully resisted Republican proposals to raise the retirement age. Recognizing the need to fund Social Security on a long-term basis, the Federation instead proposed moderate rises in the payroll tax, with the employee's increase offset by either a refundable tax credit or a general revenue contribution of the same amount. "Thank goodness for the AFL-CIO," recalled Susan Dunlop. "We were big supporters of Social Security."[17]

Other defensive work was equally important. In the Ninety-Seventh Congress, the Republicans pushed for a balanced budget, a move that would have entailed further cuts to social programs. In August 1982, following Senate passage of the Balanced Budget Amendment, the situation became serious. Responding quickly, Kirkland established an Ad Hoc Committee on the Balanced Budget Amendment to wage an "all-out effort" to defeat the measure in the House. A long-standing goal of many conservatives, the amendment imposed strict limits on government spending, but the AFL-CIO hit back with a fourteen-state satellite television conference, as well as radio and newspaper advertising, personal visits by union delegations to key congressional representatives, and other grassroots lobbying initiatives. The AFL-CIO's effort clearly contributed to the House vote of 236–187 for the amendment, forty-six votes short of the two-thirds majority needed to send it to the states for ratification. After the vote, Speaker Tip O'Neill, Majority Whip Tom Foley, and other congressional leaders even credited the AFL-CIO with defeating the amendment.[18]

In these harsh years, when survival was so important, the AFL-CIO continued to speak for all workers. Still viewing itself as a "People's Lobby," the Federation fought for a wide variety of causes. Between 1981 and 1983, the Federation resisted harmful Department of Labor regulations with regard to industrial homework and child labor, and successfully defended the Davis-Bacon and Service Contracts Act, protecting labor standards on public works projects and federal service contracts. It also helped to secure congressional inquiry into proposed guidelines for federal contractors, ensuring that important affirmative action provisions were not undermined.[19] In the 1970s the Federation had pushed OSHA to issue its first regulations about asbestos exposure, and in the Reagan era—in the light of new evidence—it pressed for stronger action. "The standards governing occupational exposure to asbestos in this country have never been adequate," declared staffer Margaret Seminario in 1983. Furthermore, the Federation resisted the Reagan administration's efforts to erode the minimum wage by setting a lower level for teenage workers. "We believe that the minimum wage represents a floor under wages and that no worker, whether young or old, black or white, should be asked to work for less than the wage floor," Kirkland told Congress.[20]

The Federation never forgot its broader mission. In February 1983, for example, at a time when unions were losing members at an unprecedented rate, the Executive Council met and issued statements that went well beyond the economic concerns of its members. Among the issues tackled were civil rights, the Equal Rights Amendment, health care, and occupational safety. On health care, the Federation remained committed to its long-term aim of universal national health insurance. "Until that goal is won," it warned, "we will do all in our power through legislation, collective bargaining and community action to fight cutbacks, to control costs and to improve health services for all Americans."[21] In another example of its wide-ranging interests, the Federation helped to ensure that copyright act protection for American authors was extended for four years. Enacted in 1982, the provisions ensured that books published by American authors had to be published and printed in the United States, saving around 400,000 jobs—union and nonunion—in the process.[22]

On some occasions, the Federation helped to extend important progressive legislation. Indeed, Kirkland moved the AFL-CIO more firmly into a coalition model of relations with its progressive allies, a significant accomplishment. In the spring of 1982 pressure from the AFL-CIO helped to ensure that Congress passed, and President Reagan signed, a twenty-five-year extension to the Voting Rights Act, the landmark legislation that protected black access to the ballot in seven southern states. Drawing on his southern background, Kirkland testified that for almost a century denial of the franchise had been "a way of life in parts of the country." As a result, the law was still badly needed. Kirkland testified at the first congressional hearing on the law's extension, creating pressure to pass what the *New York Times* called "the most important civil rights issue before Congress." As the Federation and its civil rights allies pointed out, the act had been effective in growing the black vote, but it had not yet reached its full potential, and its provisions were still being breached. The AFL-CIO's role was significant in pushing Reagan to support renewal; he had initially refused to commit, even commenting during the election campaign that the federal preclearance requirement—which applied to any changes in voting laws in the affected states—had imposed "unequal burdens on some parts of the nation." The remarks were part of a wider effort by Reagan to gain southern white votes. On June 29, 1982, however, the President signed the historic twenty-five-year extension into law. Reagan's action was, as the *Times* noted, a "bow to political reality," a testament to the strong push for renewal. An extensive campaign by a coalition of labor and civil rights groups—helped by the alliances formed on Solidarity Day—had been effective. The AFL-CIO joined with a wide variety of progressive organizations— including the NAACP, the Leadership Conference on Civil Rights, the Children's Defense Fund, and the American Civil Liberties Union—to ensure that the Voting Rights Act was extended.[23]

At the national level, the Federation forged ongoing links with civil rights groups that built on the Solidarity Day coalition. In the summer of 1983 the AFL-CIO played a major role in organizing the twentieth anniversary of the 1963 March on Washington, which celebrated the Voting Rights Act's renewal and called for more action to tackle ongoing disparities, especially in the economic sphere. While Meany had refused to countenance the original march, under Kirkland the Federation gave strong endorsement. More than thirty major unions gave money to the protest, and two affiliates even donated their Washington office space to organizers. Attitudes had clearly changed. "Labor unions in 1963 were part of the overall pattern of racism in America," commented Cleveland Robinson, a black UAW official. "We have made a lot of progress since then, but we still have a long way to go."[24]

While legislative work remained a high priority, Kirkland understood the need to organize, particularly in the South. Between 1945 and 1970, the South's economy grew about 30 percent faster than the national average, and from 1970 to 1976 alone nearly three million Americans migrated to the region. Growth was concentrated in large metropolitan areas; in Texas, for example, boosters lured scores of companies to the Houston area, partly because there was no state levy on individual or corporate income. Helped by their "right-to-work" laws, southern leaders also attracted outside investment by promising a union-free environment. Furthermore, the South had played a key role in thwarting labor's key political objectives, including passage of labor law reform. Clearly, action was needed.[25]

As he was planning Solidarity Day, Kirkland also launched a major organizing campaign in Houston. The city was selected partly because of its size; it was America's fifth-largest metropolis and its third-largest port. According to Lloyd McBride, who headed the Committee on Organization and Field Services, Houston was "the heart of the 'sunbelt,' " and breakthroughs in organizing could lead to "substantial gains" across the entire South. In 1981 the AFL-CIO committed over $1.6 million to the Houston campaign, using some of the funds to hire seven field representatives and a coordinator. Setting up divisions in several sectors, including construction, government employ-ment, retail, manufacturing, and health care, McBride's department coordi-nated the campaign. Like many organizing drives before it, the Houston project began optimistically. "We expect that there will be thousands of employees in Houston who will become part of the AFL-CIO as a result of this organizing effort," asserted AFT president Al Shanker in November.[26]

Kirkland committed a lot to the campaign. By November, the Federation had assigned thirty-seven staff to the effort, working alongside those from thirty-five affiliates. Shanker's teachers, along with the SEIU and AFSCME, were some of the most enthusiastic supporters. These unions made a monthly contribution of one cent per member to the campaign. In total, at least sev-enty staff worked full-time as organizers in Houston, focusing on forty-five major targets. The campaign, recalled staffer Charles Stott, was "pretty huge," and there were plans to deploy over 100 organizers.[27] Kirkland threw his au-thority behind the drive. Visiting Houston in May 1982, he told a rally that "the primary mission of the AFL-CIO is, now more than ever, to bring more workers within our ranks." At a subsequent area meeting in the city, Kirkland declared that the Federation was committed to the campaign for the long haul, a pledge he later repeated.[28] In order to fund the effort, Kirkland pushed through increases in the per capita dues tax from 19 to 27 cents a month. While it was unpopular with some affiliates, particularly in manufacturing and the skilled trades, the move netted the Federation $14.4 million in revenue over two years.[29]

From the start, however, the Houston campaign was up against it. Previ-ous efforts to organize the South—including the CIO's ambitious "Operation Dixie" in the late 1940s—had been largely unsuccessful, chiefly because of in-tense corporate and community opposition. According to historian James C. Cobb, the South had a "blatantly antiunion political climate," making it hard for any organizing campaign to succeed. To be sure, the Houston effort aroused plenty of opposition from local elites. On top of this, the depressed economy—national unemployment exceeded 10 percent in 1982—hurt badly. "It was unfortunate timing," recalled Stott, "because we kicked off the campaign, just before, or at the same time, as a deepening recession." In November 1982 the AFL-CIO reported that the recession had been "devastating" for construction workers, a key organizing target. In many parts of the country, unemployment in the construction sector exceeded 50 percent, and staff in Houston com-plained about a "massive influx" of construction workers from depressed areas. Many were displaced union members, and they disrupted campaigns by telling nonunion workers that organizers could not be trusted to protect their jobs.

In this climate, drives among health care workers, grocery store staff, teachers, municipal workers, and oil refinery employees were also affected. As new campaign director Alan Kistler reported in May 1983, the economic downturn had "hit all 35 ongoing campaigns in the Houston Organizing Project [HOP]."[30]

Not all of the problems that affected the Houston campaign could be blamed on the harsh economic and political climate. Organizing reports also referred to the need to get a greater number of affiliates involved in the campaign, yet the Federation's decentralized structure militated against this. "The prime responsibility for organizing follow-through will be in the hands of the individual participating unions," reported Lloyd McBride at the start of the campaign. It was a deep-seated philosophy that Kirkland did not challenge, ensuring that unresponsive affiliates were not pressured effectively.[31] In February 1982 the Committee complained about the uneven response of affiliates. It identified a number of problems, including the fact that "not every union" had fulfilled its obligation to place one organizer on the campaign. Others initially assigned a staffer but then withdrew them to fill other needs. Although this practice was "not in conformity" with the concept of a cooperative organizing program, it was tolerated.[32]

These problems persisted. In early 1984 an independent review of the project found that the AFT, SEIU, and AFSCME, unions that already had organizers in the Houston area, were the most committed. In contrast, many other affiliates had failed to assign staff and had not been supportive. "It is very difficult for HOP to coordinate staff activities and to adjust to rapidly changing circumstances when the key international union representative is unavailable for consultation and guidance," asserted the report. The Federation continued to rely heavily on affiliates, partly because it lacked organizers of its own. Observing events, some campaign supporters felt the Federation needed to invest more in organizing. According to Stewart Acuff, a former SEIU organizer who worked on the campaign, the AFL-CIO lacked "organizing capacity" at this time, ensuring that the Houston project represented "unmet potential."[33]

Still, the campaign secured some results. Organizers were able to sign up several sub-contractors, especially in the construction trades, but these were mainly small companies that employed less than twenty workers. Such increases were unlikely to reverse the decline in union density.[34] More impressively, there were sizeable gains among teachers and health care workers. Some of the biggest strides were made by the SEIU, which was successful at organizing several nursing homes. By January 1985, the union had won twelve elections at homes run by Beverly Enterprises in east Texas (and lost only one), results that one campaign leader termed "our most impressive to date." Over 500 workers were brought into the SEIU as a result of these victories, which reflected grassroots work among a heavily female and nonwhite workforce. The Beverly drive was a "huge success," asserted Acuff, partly because these groups were particularly receptive to unions. In addition, the union ran a long-term strategic organizing campaign that exerted leverage on the company.[35]

Overall, however, after a long and costly campaign the results were disappointing. In the South, summarized Tom Donahue, the AFL-CIO had "built a bridgehead, but it never went anyplace." While not all of the problems could be blamed on external factors, the project showed how large-scale organizing was no match for well-funded corporations, who could draw on a huge arsenal of union-avoidance techniques. Large employers, particularly in the private sector, strongly resisted organizing efforts. As the 1984 overview report found, the organizing climate in Houston was very tough, and employer resistance to unions was "firmly entrenched." A right-to-work state, Texas was home to "a horde of antiunion management consultants," and they used every available means at their disposal. In addition, there was no collective bargaining law for public sector workers. "Even with a strong economy," the report concluded, "the HOP faced a difficult task." The downturn in the economy, which affected the local oil industry heavily, represented a "serious obstacle," and the campaign never recovered.[36] After beginning with bold hopes, the Houston campaign gradually petered out. By October 1985, field staff reported that the HOP was running a deficit of $74,013 to the AFL-CIO, and this was projected to increase. Lack of support from affiliates was again cited. "We must reduce payout unless more unions join the Project," staffer Green P. Lewis reported to Kistler. Although the drive limped on until the end of 1985, few active staff remained.[37]

The Houston campaign illustrated how the recession hurt the AFL-CIO. The downturn's effects were widespread. As employers demanded givebacks, many affiliates focused on bargaining rather than organizing. According to NLRB data, the total number of elections fell by 11 percent in 1981 and by a further 28 percent in 1982.[38] The recession also led to falls in membership, undermining the ability to organize. At its meeting in February 1984, the Executive Council reported sharp declines in membership for almost all affiliates. The Electrical Workers had seen membership drop from 835,185 in 1981 to 796,598 in 1983, while even the UFCW had experienced a fall from 1.01 million to 959,150 over the same period. Overall, between 1981 and 1983 the

Federation lost over 1.4 million members. As one union official told the Council, while organizing had achieved some success, much of it was "offset by erosion of membership in local unions as a result of the recession."[39]

Big industrial unions were particularly affected. The membership of the Steelworkers, a talismanic industrial affiliate, slipped from 861,340 in 1981 to 582,298 in 1983, one of the sharpest falls. Job losses were the main culprit. In January 1983, for example, 30,000 of Bethlehem Steel's 82,000 employees were laid off, and the company had also shut its sprawling plant in Lackawanna, New York, permanently. Across the Northeast and Midwest, scores of landmark industrial facilities suffered the same fate, and union officials were consumed by the task of helping their displaced members.[40]

Industrial unions were particularly exposed to broader economic forces. Confronted by what veteran labor reporter A. H. Raskin called "the hammer blows of mass unemployment, savage trade competition and the threatened extinction of highly unionized industries that had been traditional frontrunners in wages and benefits," many affiliates endured hard times. The Federation's research highlighted how globalization proceeded rapidly in the Reagan era. Between 1980 and 1984 alone, the proportion of the U.S. gross national product that consisted of exports and imports jumped sharply, from 10 to over 25 percent. In import-sensitive—and heavily unionized—industries such as autos, steel, and rubber, the effects were severe. As AFL-CIO economist Mark Anderson summarized in 1984, the "internationalization of the U.S. economy" was having an "increasingly negative impact" on American workers. In the first two years of the Reagan presidency, the U.S. dollar also rose on world markets, partly because of the administration's efforts to combat inflation. Imports became cheaper, hurting domestic manufacturers.[41]

Falling membership forced the AFL-CIO to make cuts. Under Kirkland, the Federation launched an early retirement program to reduce staff costs. Between January and May 1983, the number of AFL-CIO staff fell from 419 to 375, helping to ease the budget deficit. "Everybody in the labor movement is hurting as a result of the recession," Kirkland told the Council in May 1983.[42] At the next meeting in August 1983, international union presidents related that they faced the toughest conditions ever. On top of deindustrialization, automation was wiping out many jobs. Some of the membership losses were directly linked to Reagan's policies, especially as the administration aggressively expanded free trade, often cutting assistance for domestic manufacturers in the process. In 1981, for example, Reagan removed cost supports for U.S. shipyards, devastating the heavily unionized sector. Between 1981 and 1993, forty American shipyards closed and over 180,000 workers lost their jobs.[43]

Other Reagan policies also hurt organized labor, especially as the president staffed the NLRB with pro-management figures. "Up until Reagan," recalled Craig Becker, a labor lawyer who later became AFL-CIO General Counsel, "the Labor Board consisted of fairly distinguished neutrals. With Reagan, the Republicans started appointing management lawyers." By August 1983, the Council related that "unfavorable rulings by the National Labor Relations Board" were "making it more difficult to organize and to achieve fair contracts, particularly since the use of the strike is increasingly less effective." In particular, Reagan replaced NLRB chairman John Fanning with Donald L. Dotson, causing a shift that outside observers also noticed. "The NLRB," summarized the *Washington Post* in August 1984, "has reversed a string of pro-labor decisions, making it easier for employers to fight union-organizing efforts."[44]

The problems at the NLRB led to a worrying trend, where workers lost faith in the law's ability to protect their right to organize. A growing number of employers were willing to flout the board's authority, aware that even if they were found guilty of committing unfair labor practices, it would take months—or even years—before dismissed workers were rehired. By the mid-1980s, roughly 75 percent of employers were also hiring labor-management consultants to resist unions, at the cost of $100 million annually. The tactics worked. As organizing director Alan Kistler admitted in one long report to Kirkland, consultants had an "almost flawless" record. "The art of union busting," he concluded, "has reached near perfection with some consultants." Reports from particular campaigns illustrated the problem. "Fear is the biggest obstacle we have to overcome," declared Mike Black, an AFL-CIO organizer based in Charlotte, North Carolina, a largely nonunion city. "If we could overcome fear, we could organize everything. . . . But most people believe if they start organizing, they are going to get fired." Seeing the Board as increasingly impotent, workers continued to avoid it, even when the economy improved. By the mid-1980s, the NLRB was conducting about half the number of representation elections each year compared to a decade earlier.[45]

In the early 1980s, the lack of organizing helped to ensure that union density declined at an unprecedented rate. In 1984 a telling landmark occurred when the proportion of union members fell below 20 percent for the first time in decades. The AFL-CIO cited employer opposition and weak labor law as the main problems, but it was also true that the economy was changing in ways that hurt organized labor. Tellingly, in 1985 unions represented less than 10 percent of the workforce in the service sector, where 90 percent of the job growth was occurring. "The organizing challenge facing the American labor movement today is one of monumental proportions," declared SEIU president John Sweeney in that year.[46]

As the Houston campaign had highlighted, organizing was also held back by internal problems. Elected president of his growing affiliate in 1980, Sweeney led a group of activists in the Federation's progressive wing that wanted to pump more resources into organizing. Concentrated in the service and retail industries, these leaders complained that affiliates in other sectors, particularly the building trades and manufacturing, were unable—or unwilling—to organize. In this period, recalled outspoken SEIU organizer Stewart Acuff, "even unions that wanted to begin organizing, that were progressive, and wanted to do the right thing, didn't know how to organize." The SEIU, added former organizer Gerry Shea, believed in putting "intense resources" into organizing, yet many other unions did not. Even some former SEIU employees, however, also recognized that it was much harder for unions with falling membership to organize, and that the SEIU was—in the words of ex-staffer Bob Welsh— "lucky" to operate in a growing sector of the economy. Some also acknowledged that the SEIU grew because of mergers with smaller unions, as well as organizing.[47]

In the early 1980s, those who felt that Kirkland should have exerted stronger leadership on the organizing issue were still in a minority. As a result, the South Carolinian took the problems in the organizing field—and in domestic affairs generally—in his stride. Kirkland also had other interests. Viewing the AFL-CIO president as an international figure, he was passionate about foreign affairs. This was partly due to Kirkland's time at Georgetown University, where he had attended a special program that the university sponsored for students who were interested in joining the foreign service. Critics would later use Kirkland's Georgetown experience against him, as it bolstered their allegation that his real passion was foreign policy rather than connecting with workers.[48]

Kirkland's interest in foreign affairs, and particularly events in Eastern Europe, increased after 1973, when he married Irena Neumann, a Czechoslovakian Jew who had survived Auschwitz. An earlier marriage to Edith Draper Hollyday, with whom Kirkland had five daughters, ended in divorce. Possessing a strong interest in international affairs, Irena frequently accompanied her husband on overseas trips. Influenced by his wife, Kirkland had a strong interest in the Middle East—he was a forceful supporter of Israel—as well as in European affairs. Overall, Kirkland believed that it was crucial for AFL-CIO leaders to be engaged in international affairs, which were too important to be left to "a tight incestuous breed of economists and diplomats."[49]

Lane Kirkland with his second wife, Irena (née Neumann). Courtesy of Special Collections, University of Maryland Libraries.

Kirkland's personal papers confirm the image of a man who was comfortable at the highest levels in Washington, and his strong interest in foreign policy influenced his friendships. He corresponded regularly with leading politicians and diplomats, including figures on the conservative side of politics, rather than with rank-and-file union members. Among his regular correspondents were Henry Kissinger, Lehman Brothers Chairman Peter G. Peterson, and Jerusalem mayor Teddy Kollek.[50] In June 1981, for example, Kissinger—who had been U.S. Secretary of State during the Nixon and Ford administrations—wrote Kirkland that, "It meant a great deal to me that you were able to be with us for my birthday dinner. It helped make the passing of another year almost painless." When Kissinger celebrated his sixtieth birthday two years later, he thanked Kirkland for his gift of a "beautifully bound" collection of essays by Winston Churchill.[51]

These friendships did not mean that Kirkland was unconcerned about American workers. Former staffers stressed Kirkland's abilities as a writer, and he consistently used fluent prose to defend the interests of everyday Americans. While staff helped him prepare public remarks, Kirkland took an unusually keen interest in the process. "He was a very good writer," remembered former assistant David St. John. "He often wrote his own speeches," added Susan Dunlop. "He was an excellent speechwriter."[52] In his address to the fifteenth convention in October 1983, for example, Kirkland delivered a withering attack on the Reagan administration's economic record that was peppered with references to history and literature; among those quoted were former U.S. president Grover Cleveland, eighteenth-century British statesman Lord Chesterfield, and ancient Greek philosopher Hippocrates. On the eve of the 1980 election, he noted, Reagan had sold a vision of a "shining city, high on a hill," yet three years later reality was very different. Behind the "cold statistics" of high unemployment, he noted, was "a bleak picture of broken lives, blighted communities, ruined enterprises, shattered hopes and lost opportunities." Accusing the administration of "arrogance and indifference," Kirkland promised to "build a city of man and woman that will not shine for the few only . . . where all will share the light and all will find a place in the sun."[53] Congressional hearings were another forum that suited Kirkland, allowing him to deliver well-crafted attacks on Reaganomics and its failure to help most working Americans.[54]

The records of Kirkland's press conferences and media interviews also reveal a man who was capable of holding his own against able opponents. In many ways, Kirkland was at his best in the Reagan era, when the president's hostility pushed him to respond forcefully and cogently. In an unrehearsed appearance on CBS's "Face the Nation" program in October 1982, the AFL-CIO leader refuted the Reagan administration's claims that Americans could "tolerate" an unemployment rate of 6.5 percent. "To talk about 6.5 percent is academic at a time when we have, in effective terms, about 14.5 percent unemployment," Kirkland replied quickly. "I don't know where he got the figure 6.5 percent, perhaps off the back of a cereal box or from *Reader's Digest.*" President Reagan, he concluded, had "promised us a boom, and he brought us a bust." Unafraid of confrontation with the White House, Kirkland repeatedly dubbed the economic downturn "The Reagan Recession." Although he was more quietly spoken than Meany, when challenged, Kirkland was capable of robust—and articulate—responses to reporters. Pressed about his economic vision by a journalist in 1983, Kirkland's reply was clear and prescient. "Are we going to allow our basic industries to disappear, to be transported overseas, and to become some sort of service economy where young people growing up can look to the prospect of taking in one another's laundry or serving junk food?" he asked.[55]

Among those who knew him, the AFL-CIO leader often inspired great loyalty. Staffers stressed Kirkland's intelligence, as well as his decency and sincerity. Jim Baker, who worked as the president's executive assistant, thought

Kirkland was "a brilliant and deep thinker" who liked to receive frank advice.[56] Many Executive Council members also admired Kirkland. According to Lenore Miller, the AFL-CIO leader was very gifted intellectually, and his press conferences were memorable. "He was a *brilliant* man," she recalled. "And I never spent a more satisfying time than being at his press conferences after the meetings, because it was remarkable. He taught reporters what the labor movement was about, what history was, he was brilliant." Susan Bianchi similarly respected Kirkland, stressing qualities that the media missed. While he could be remote, Kirkland was "truly dedicated to the cause."[57]

Kirkland's admirers also remembered that his shyness, especially with the rank and file, was always evident. "He was very comfortable with leaders, I think even more so than with members," recalled Miller. "Lane, as I said, was not someone who could go out and meet workers, he was fundamentally a shy person." In many ways, this reserve was Kirkland's Achilles' heel, because it ensured that few outsiders appreciated his attributes. In addition, Kirkland's reluctance to give regular interviews—or to press the flesh more—ensured that he lacked profile with members. In 1984 a national survey of union members by a conservative foundation found that 60 percent of the rank and file had never heard of Kirkland, while another 21 percent was unsure who he was. The poll may have exaggerated the issue, but it revealed a genuine problem. Ironically, Kirkland had the ability to thrive in interview settings, yet it was not an arena that he coveted.[58]

Those who had worked closely with Kirkland recalled a man with more personality and individuality than he was often given credit for. The *New York Times* once dismissed Kirkland as "unexciting," yet this was not entirely accurate. Working alongside Kirkland, David St. John gained insight into a side of the AFL-CIO president that few saw. Kirkland was a lively travel companion, he recalled, who liked to converse with those he trusted. He would also "sneak cigarettes all the time" because he had promised Irena to give up smoking. Although known as a remote intellectual, Kirkland had a secret passion for fast food, which he indulged when he was on the road. "He very much liked to eat at McDonald's," recalled St. John, "which I think he didn't like to get around, because obviously that's not a union shop. . . . When we were off the radar . . . you could look for a McDonald's. . . . People thought he was erudite and arrogant, and . . . wasn't a real rank-and-file guy, but he had this real love for McDonald's." Kirkland, added aide Charles Stott, also had a "wonderfully dry sense of humor," although it was usually only displayed in private.[59]

Kirkland's other hobbies retained an eclectic edge. As a detailed—and favorable—portrait in the *Washington Post* revealed, Kirkland had several "unlikely pleasures," including going on archaeological digs, studying hiero-glyphics, playing video chess, and quoting the classics. He also enjoyed playing his Marine Band harmonica while his favorite dachshund, Stanley, howled approvingly. Kirkland's work habits were also not those of a conventional bu-reaucrat, as he liked to read the morning newspapers at home and come into the headquarters between 9 and 9.30 A.M. "I used to think he just got up late," recalled former assistant Ken Young. "But then when he got to the office, he'd start asking me questions about what was in the morning papers." Staff knew not to schedule early meetings for the AFL-CIO president. Her husband, ex-plained Irena Kirkland, was a "security risk" before a certain hour.[60]

Drawing on his anticommunism, Kirkland felt strongly about the plight of workers in Eastern and Central Europe, particularly Poland. In the early 1980s, the issue took up a lot of his time, and helped inspire the domestic Solidarity Day movement. Straight after his election, Kirkland got involved in the emerging anticommunist resistance movement in Poland. Working through Leo Labedz, a Polish exile in London, the AFL-CIO helped K.O.R.—a fledgling workers' resistance group—before Solidarnosc was formed. "Of course when Solidarnosc emerged in 1980/81 we were solidly in support," Kirkland explained later. "We organized a Polish aid fund to raise money within the trade union movement to send them assistance . . . in the face of, I might add, some U.S. Government opposition and State Department opposition."[61] In the years that followed, the Federation channeled around $5 million in cash and equipment to Solidarnosc, with the money primarily being used to buy printing equipment and prepare and disseminate publications. The Federa-tion also helped to smuggle into Poland equipment that could not be bought there, including laptop computers and police-band radio scanners. While the CIA initiated a covert policy that included disseminating money to Solidar-nosc, its financial web did not start operating until the end of 1982. As histo-rian Gregory F. Domber has shown, the AFL-CIO was ahead of the CIA in funneling support to Solidarnosc, and was the "highest-profile" American organization to back the group.[62]

Closely monitoring events in Poland, Kirkland ensured that the Executive Council adopted an uncompromising stance that helped the fledgling anti-communist movement. As early as August 1980, when an unprecedented wave of 200 strikes swept across Poland, the Council declared that the pro-tests were "a profoundly important development for human rights, free trade unionism, and democracy in the Communist world." The Federation strongly supported the strikers, who were demanding increased democratic rights as well as better wages. Ten days after the Council meeting, Solidarnosc emerged as a free trade union federation at the Gdansk shipyard, under the leadership of Lech Walesa, a former electrician.[63] In the winter of 1981–82, the Jaruzelski regime retaliated by arresting key union leaders and imposing martial law. In response, the Council pledged that the AFL-CIO would "do everything in its power to help restore Solidarnosc to its place in Polish life." While President Reagan announced sanctions against Poland, the AFL-CIO wanted the United States to impose a trade embargo on the Soviet Union and declare the Polish debt in default. Both recommendations were opposed by the administration, which worried that an embargo would hurt American farmers and businessmen. Fearing disruption to the international banking system, the administration also quietly covered the $71 million owed by the Polish government to American banks.[64]

The pattern had been set. Throughout the early 1980s, the Federation remained one of Solidarnosc's most reliable and important allies. In 1983, as the anticommunist group struggled for existence, the Executive Council vowed to "continue to draw world attention to the Polish government's violation of trade union and human rights." It reiterated its demand for the Reagan administration to end the "complicity" of American banks and declare Poland in default of its loans. At this time, few predicted the success of the anticommunist struggle, yet the AFL-CIO continued to believe in Solidarnosc, and to give it unwavering support.[65]

While Kirkland—like Meany—was a strong anticommunist, he placed his own stamp on the Federation's international work. As was the case domestically, in international matters Kirkland was more conciliatory than Meany. In February 1980 the new AFL-CIO president played an important role in bringing the United States back into the International Labour Organization (ILO), an arm of the UN that focused on social justice. An active member since 1934, the United States had withdrawn from the ILO in 1977 because of concerns about the weakness of its human rights machinery, particularly when it came to placing pressure on Communist countries. Kirkland worked with both the U.S. Council of the International Chamber of Commerce and officials from the Carter administration to ensure that the UN strengthened the independence of worker delegates to ILO meetings, and protected the group's human rights machinery. Thus, in 1978, the ILO censured Czechoslovakia for illegally firing dissidents from their jobs, in violation of UN standards that prohibited employment discrimination.[66]

In 1982 Kirkland also brought the AFL-CIO back into the ICFTU. It was an important step, ensuring that the world's largest trade union federation took its place at the heart of an organization with 85 million members in ninety-four countries. The goal of the ICFTU, Secretary-General John Vanderveken told the Council in 1983, was "to maximize the cohesion of the free labor movement" throughout the world.[67] Kirkland valued the AFL-CIO's participation in these international organizations; in June 1983, for example, he attended the ICFTU Congress in Oslo and the ILO Conference in Geneva, spending the entire month overseas. Kirkland led a delegation of thirteen American union leaders to the ICFTU Congress, the first time that the AFL-CIO had attended since 1964. At the conference, the AFL-CIO focused mainly on issues of "human rights and trade union rights," although it was also interested in economic policy and security questions. Further stressing international work, Kirkland established the George Meany International Award for Human Rights, a major prize that was usually awarded to foreign activists. In 1981 the first award was given to Lech Walesa, although he was unable to travel to the United States to receive it.[68]

Although Kirkland shepherded the AFL-CIO back into the ICFTU, he made few efforts to build genuine partnerships with overseas labor organizations. At this stage, international work focused on high-level alliances rather than the grassroots cooperation that would come later as a response to globalization. In 1982 there were sixteen international labor secretariats, but they functioned as coordinating and research bodies rather than organizations that could use strikes or boycotts to publicize—or disrupt—the transfer of production from one country to another. Part of the problem was the worldwide recession of the early 1980s, which made it harder to build international solidarity. Above all, however, labor movements were organized nationally, hindering efforts to tackle the problems caused by deindustrialization and globalization. As Dan Gallin of the International Union of Food and Allied Workers' Associations explained in 1982, the labor movement's "present state of organization" made it "impossible" for it to challenge capital mobility. Only much later, as capital became increasingly fluid, were stronger international labor partnerships forged.[69] Kirkland also continued to fund several Meany-era initiatives—including the American Institute for Free Labor Development and the Asian-American Free Labor Institute—that reflected Cold War priorities, using labor education to try to undermine support for communism in the developing world. This was another area where Kirkland's reforms had not gone far enough.[70]

While international work was very important to Kirkland, throughout Reagan's first term he recognized that the Federation's main priority was to ensure that the president was not re-elected. In this regard, as an Executive Council resolution put it, Solidarity Day was "only a beginning." The labor movement had to find innovative ways of activating its members, and needed to forge "new bonds" with community allies if Reagan's conservative agenda was to be resisted. In the wake of Solidarity Day, the Federation promoted an economic program that called for increased public spending, lower interest rates, and other stimulatory policies, arguing that a thriving economy would lower inflation. In November 1981 Kirkland also tried to build on the success of the protest by announcing that a second Solidarity Day would be held the following year. According to the Federation, rather than a national march, Solidarity Day II would be a "maximum get-out-the-vote effort on Election Day 1982."[71]

Some important gains came from the second Solidarity Day. There were clear victories from the elections, the focus of activities. Nationally, the Democrats solidified their hold on the House, and there were also positive developments at the state level. In Texas, labor-backed Mark White became governor and all union-backed statewide candidates also won. Labor leaders stressed that such successes were important. "In the march to the polls on Solidarity II, in 1982, we made significant changes in governors, state legislatures, and the composition of the U.S. Congress," summarized Kirkland.[72] At the time of the second Solidarity Day, polls showed that blue-collar workers who had supported Reagan in 1980 were switching to the Democrats. "I thought Reagan was great in 1980, but now I tie him to other Republican candidates and I think the Democrats have the best chance of ending the recession," commented Bill Ferencuha, a Pennsylvanian auto worker. As the *New York Times* summarized, such "blue-collar anger" posed a "threat to Republicans." Buoyed by the results, Kirkland pressed ahead with plans for further Solidarity Days, part of what one reporter termed an aggressive "comeback strategy." As Susan Dunlop recalled, the follow-up Solidarity Days were important to Kirkland, who retained a "slow-burning anger" in the Reagan years that needed an outlet.[73]

Designed to mobilize members ahead of the 1984 presidential election, there were further follow-up marches in 1983 and 1984. In 1983 Kirkland proclaimed that Labor Day would be "Solidarity Day III," and protesters were again mobilized to march against Reagan's economic policies. Organized around the slogan "Across America - We Will Be Heard," about 150 regional rallies replaced a central protest.[74] The level of participation was impressive. In New Haven, Connecticut, for example, more than 100 unions took part in the first statewide Labor Day parade in almost thirty years. "The point of the parade is to participate in the national observance of Solidarity Day III," explained state AFL-CIO representative Roger Clayman. The march had an optimistic air. "There's a resurgence all over the country," claimed seventy-eight-year-old John Rourke, the parade's grand marshal. Some of the demonstrations were very large; police estimated that 100,000 people marched through downtown Detroit, while other industrial cities saw impressive turnouts. Marching in New York and Chicago and ending the day by delivering his main address in Omaha, Nebraska, an energetic Kirkland was integrally involved. The AFL-CIO leader was pleased, insisting that the marches had succeeded in mobilizing large numbers of union members, as well as some community allies. "We were heard!" declared an AFL-CIO summation of press clippings about Solidarity Day III.[75]

Still, the follow-up marches had not been as successful as the first protest. The fusion of "Solidarity Day III" with Labor Day was problematic, reducing participation by community groups and affecting press coverage. While the AFL-CIO marketed the September 5 rallies as "Solidarity Day III," the press often simply reported them as "Labor Day Parades." One *Washington Post* headline, "Solidarity Day Activity Is Joined to Labor Day," said a lot. Reflecting the decentralized nature of Solidarity Day III, press coverage was localized and spotty, and the event lacked broader profile. Many Americans enjoyed the long weekend but failed to reflect on—or notice—the protests. Although there were marches right across the country, the largest occurred in the industrial North, suggesting that labor was mobilizing its base rather than spreading its message. Finally, media coverage often focused on labor's problems rather than on the message of revival that Kirkland wanted to sell, a perennial problem. "American Unions are in trouble this Labor Day," summarized a *New York Times* editorial that briefly mentioned Solidarity Day III, "suffering membership losses, contract setbacks, and political reverses."[76]

Solidarity Day III was preparation for Solidarity Day IV, which was held on the day of the 1984 presidential election. The ultimate aim, explained Kirkland, was to replace the Republican administration with "those who share our conviction that the job of government is to advance the interest of all people, not just the rich and powerful." After reaching a peak of almost 11 percent in November 1982, however, unemployment fell, strengthening Reagan's political position. The president was able to address workers after Solidarity Day III by reassuring them that a "brighter future" lay ahead. Saluting American workers, the president proclaimed, "The resurgence of our economy is bringing real jobs—jobs with a future—in the private sector." The improving economy was Reagan's trump card. By 1984, unemployment had returned to the 7.5 percent it had been in 1980, and inflation was also falling.

When voters went to the polls, these figures helped Reagan enormously. By tying Solidarity Day to the election cycle, moreover, Kirkland had privileged labor's political goals. This reduced participation by nonlabor groups, a defining feature of the first—and most successful—march. Overall, however, the little-known marches had again showed Kirkland's willingness to call his supporters into the streets.[77]

Privately, AFL-CIO leaders knew that they were in trouble long before Americans went to the polls. At the Executive Council meeting in February 1984, research director Rudy Oswald noted that the economic recovery would "likely last through November," allowing President Reagan to take credit for it. Clearly worried, House Speaker Thomas P. O'Neill Jr. also addressed the Council. "If President Reagan is reelected," he warned, "he will step up his assault on issues such as minimum wage, civil rights, social security, health care and education. Poor and middle-income Americans will be hurt." O'Neill asked the AFL-CIO to call out its troops. "Organized labor's support will be a critical factor in defeating President Ronald Reagan in the 1984 elections," he declared.[78]

Kirkland agreed with O'Neill's analysis. Realizing the importance of the election, the Federation backed former Minnesota senator Walter Mondale as early as October 1983, the first time it had made an endorsement before the party primaries. The move confirmed that Kirkland could take risks.[79] According to the *AFL-CIO News*, the endorsement was designed to give the Federation time to mobilize opposition to the Reagan administration's "failed national policies." It was also an effort to avoid a repeat of what had happened in 1980, when Reagan won an unusually large amount of labor support. Then, the AFL-CIO had followed its long-standing policy of leaving affiliates to endorse their own candidates during the primaries, which was now seen as a mistake. Private discussions stressed the need for an early start if labor was to prevail, and reasserted the theme of unity. The pre-primary endorsement of Mondale, noted the Council, "will assure the solidarity that is essential for the labor movement to have an effective voice in the political process." In a General Board vote, 90.9 percent of the ballots cast favored Mondale's endorsement.[80]

Kirkland also believed strongly in Mondale's candidacy. His papers show that he was in regular touch with Mondale, a close friend, and supported his run for the presidency from the outset. The Minnesotan corresponded warmly with Kirkland, thanking him for his "generous" personal—and apparently financial—support of his nascent presidential campaign. "I am so grateful for the friendship such a personal expression as this connotes," he explained. "It means so much to me." Mondale also sent his "love" to Irena Kirkland. On another occasion, Mondale warmly thanked the Kirklands for their "hospitality and continuing friendship."[81]

Kirkland's bold move to back Mondale carried considerable risks, and did not go down well with all union members. Some disliked being told how to vote, while others expressed enthusiasm for alternative candidates, particularly Colorado Senator Gary Hart. In primaries in New Hampshire, Maine, Massachusetts, and Vermont, unionized workers broke ranks and supported Hart. "I'm my own man, I call 'em like I see 'em," explained Al Dovner, a sheet metal worker from Quincy, Massachusetts. Hart ran Mondale close in all of these races.[82] Many African-American workers, meanwhile, supported Rev. Jesse Jackson, a candidate who criticized the labor movement's civil rights record. "A black or a woman will clearly be President of this country before one will even be able to run for head of the AFL-CIO," Jackson quipped in 1984, a prediction that turned out to be true. In May 1984 a *New York Times/ CBS News* poll found that black union members voted overwhelmingly for Jackson in primaries in the heavily unionized states of Illinois, New York, Ohio, and Pennsylvania. In New York, 84 percent of voters in black union households backed Jackson, compared to just 7 percent of whites. Clearly, not all union members were delivering for the Federation's candidate.[83] The early endorsement also gave ammunition to the AFL-CIO's critics. As the *Washington Post* summarized, Kirkland was "condemned as Mondale's would-be puppet-master and champion of a narrow 'special interest.'" When Mondale secured the Democratic nomination in July, the AFL-CIO had to rebut suggestions that it was responsible for the outcome.[84]

To some extent, the early endorsement worked. Mondale claimed later that it was the AFL-CIO's support that had allowed him to win critical primaries and stay in the presidential race. Lacking charisma, Mondale struggled against his rivals, particularly Jackson and Hart, prevailing largely because he had traditional Democratic constituencies behind him. Building on the legacies of Solidarity Day, the AFL-CIO expanded its mobilization of members during the election and engaged in an unprecedented amount of door knocking.[85] After the election, Kirkland defended the move to back Mondale, pointing out that 61 percent of AFL-CIO members had voted for the Democratic ticket, the same margin by which the population as a whole had backed Reagan. "Had the rest of the country voted as union members did," he declared, "the results would have been exactly reversed." Returning to the theme of solidarity, he claimed that the election had again demonstrated the "great strength" that the labor movement could muster when it acted as one.[86] The Federation remained "proud of its efforts," he concluded, especially as Mondale and running mate Geraldine Ferraro had spoken out "for justice and jobs for all Americans."[87]

In February 1985 the Executive Council picked over the results, which brought to an end the four-year Solidarity Day program. In private, several members accepted that Reagan was a skillful adversary who had connected with voters. "President Reagan's campaign painted an optimistic picture of America which is hard to criticize," noted ACTWU's Murray Finley, "and it took the broad theme that America is on the move." Building on this, Mondale told the Council that "a key failure" of his campaign had been "in marketing and the use of television," a forum where the president was a consummate performer. In addition, the Council agreed that Reagan had harnessed the economic recovery to great political advantage.[88] In public, the Federation put on a brave face, stressing that the Democrats still controlled the House and had made gains in the Senate. "Most of the congressional candidates who supported his (Reagan's) program went down to defeat," noted the *AFL-CIO News*. Although he was clearly disappointed, Kirkland tried to remain optimistic. "While it is important to win, it is more important to stand for principles," he asserted.[89]

In reality, the AFL-CIO had little to celebrate. The Federation had banked on a Democratic victory, believing that it was possible after the 1982 midterm elections. Choosing a path of confrontation, its relations with the White House had remained poor. As the *New York Times* reported in August 1984, AFL-CIO leaders shared a "bitter and fearful animosity toward President Reagan" and were terrified of him winning a second term. During the campaign, the Federation had pulled no punches, denouncing the president as a champion of "scab-herders and union-busters." Now, the Federation faced four more years in which it could expect few—if any—favors from the White House. While the Solidarity Day movement had effectively mobilized opposition during Reagan's first term, once he was reelected it lost its focus. It would be 1991 before there was another mass march.[90]

Because the AFL-CIO had been so critical of the Reagan administration, Kirkland's aides now expected the worst. Immediately after the election, Reagan duly moved to solidify a pro-employer majority on the NLRB. "The union busters are in hog heaven now," exclaimed Federation staffer Murray Seeger.[91] At the same time, there were some telling signs of bitterness between the

AFL-CIO and the White House. Revealingly, Kirkland refused to send the customary telegram to the president to congratulate him on his win, and he also let it be known that he would not serve on any bipartisan presidential commissions. Over the next four years, the AFL-CIO would go into survival mode. It was to be one of the most difficult periods in the Federation's history.[92]

CHAPTER FIVE

Defending What We Have

Survival and Decline in Reagan's Second Term

In many ways, Reagan's second term was as dreadful as the AFL-CIO had feared. During these years, there was no letup in the Federation's decline. Between 1979 and 1989, union density fell sharply, from 24.1 percent of the workforce to just 16.8 percent. Almost every other measure of union strength, including the number of strikes and the number of NLRB representation elections, also plummeted. Organized labor, summarized one labor relations expert, had endured a "terrible time" under Reagan. According to scholar Kate Bronfenbrenner, this was a "decade of crisis" for organized labor.[1]

Kirkland and Donahue acknowledged that the Reagan era had been the hardest ever for the AFL-CIO. "On the whole, the best thing that can be said about the 1980s," reflected Donahue in a speech at the end of the decade, "is that they're over."[2] In an address on Labor Day in 1985, Kirkland admitted that the Federation was experiencing "enormous, continuing problems." He continued to blame these troubles primarily on the Reagan administration. "For five years since this Administration took office," he declared, "unfair employers who have never given up the dream of total control over the lives of workers have been reasserting their right to rearrange wage levels and redefine working conditions as they alone see fit." Claiming that the harsh climate of the Reagan years had produced "a new spirit of solidarity and confidence" within the House of Labor, Kirkland again stressed the need to close ranks. Internal unity, rather than reform, remained his primary strategy for dealing with decline. "Solidarity," he explained at the end of the decade, "has been our shield against the most primitive and the most sophisticated assaults by the agents of avarice and exploitation."[3]

Kirkland also emphasized the positive. Here, he had some justification, as it was not all bad news for unions in these years. There were positive developments in international affairs, where the AFL-CIO's resolute support for Solidarnosc in Poland began to pay dividends. Domestically, the sustained economic recovery made it easier to organize, stemming some of the large membership losses of the early 1980s. There were also political victories. In the 1986 midterm elections, the AFL-CIO helped the Democrats to regain control of the U.S. Senate, with 76 percent of the union household vote going to COPE-endorsed candidates. By gaining control of the Senate, the Federation achieved its "number one objective" in the elections. The improved legislative climate contributed to some important gains, including the passage of legislation requiring companies to give adequate notice of plant closures, a long-term Federation goal. Kirkland's continued emphasis on unity also paid off. In 1987 he was proud when the International Brotherhood of Teamsters re-affiliated after a thirty-year absence. The addition of 1.7 million members provided a significant psychological and financial boost. Introducing the Teamsters—along with other re-affiliating unions—to applause at the 1989 convention, Kirkland proclaimed the "reunification of the American labor movement."[4]

In such a harsh climate, Kirkland and his supporters stressed the achievements of the Federation in coming through intact. Even at the end of the disastrous Reagan era, overall membership held steady at around 14 million, validating Kirkland's claims that he had held the Federation together. "I think we've survived as bad as they can do," he commented of the Reagan era, "and in pretty good shape." Many of Kirkland's staff had a similar perspective. "One of the things that I personally give Lane Kirkland credit for was . . . being our ship's captain, steering us through those years, when the labor movement was under attack, and openly," recalled Susan Dunlop. Tom Donahue also stressed the importance of survival. Like other Kirkland supporters, Donahue implicitly contrasted Kirkland's record to that of Sweeney, who had suffered the disaffiliation of over one-third of the membership in the 2005 split. Keeping the Federation together, he insisted, was vitally important.[5]

Critics, however, argued that the emphasis on survival had prevented fundamental changes, especially when it came to connecting with the rank and file. "We are not casting aside the accommodations that have immobilized us," charged Tony Mazzochi, an outspoken vice president of the Oil, Chemical, and Atomic Workers. "Everyone is talking institutional survival, the staff, the institution. Nobody is talking about, or to, the people out there." Mazzochi was unusual, as most of Kirkland's critics were concentrated in the service and public sector affiliates, rather than industrial or craft unions. The organizing director of the SEIU in the 1980s, Andy Stern later castigated Kirkland's approach as "Fortress Unionism." Kirkland's "premise," he explained, "was that we should defend what we have, and that we just needed to wait for the moment." Thus, revival would occur once conditions improved. For Stern, Kirkland was not addressing the harsh realities that the labor movement faced, or recognizing the need for fundamental reform. Some went further; according to *Labor Notes*, a consistent critic of the AFL-CIO, it was the

Federation's "business unionism" that had left American workers "disarmed on the shop floor when the attacks of the Reagan era began."[6]

To be sure, Kirkland initiated some significant reforms in these years. He took steps to improve labor's image in the media, a major source of weakness that was highlighted by Solidarity Day. In February 1982 Kirkland established the Labor Institute of Public Affairs, which was designed to "counter the domination of the public media" by "big business interests." Based within the AFL-CIO headquarters, LIPA was founded with a grant of around $2 million. Headed by Larry Kirkman, a specialist in public service media, the Institute tried to secure a bigger labor presence on television. By October 1983, LIPA was providing nine hours a week of news and information programs to cable TV networks in Seattle, Pittsburgh, and Atlanta, and there was talk of creating a network aimed directly at union families.[7]

Some further successes in the media field followed. In 1987 the AFL-CIO launched its "Union Yes" national advertising campaign, a $13 million effort that was designed to improve labor's public image. "The public generally sees unions in the media mainly through stories about strikes," explained Donahue. "Through this medium of paid advertising, we hope they'll see the positive things a union does—giving an individual a voice in the workplace that is expressed in a collective fashion."[8] The first TV advertising spots featured well-known Hollywood performers, including Jack Lemmon, Tyne Daly, Martin Sheen, Howard Hesseman, and Dionne Warwick. The messages also used "ordinary workers" to broaden their appeal. Helped by its simple and memorable slogan, the Union Yes campaign had some success. In the spring of 1988, after the first run of ads, polling suggested that 39 percent of adults— some 70 million people—recalled the spots. The TV advertising continued, and the campaign was expanded for affiliates to use independently. "We have learned that in this day and age you have to dramatize your issues if you're going to make any progress on them," explained Kirkland.[9] As Frederick O'Neal of the Associated Actors and Artistes of America observed, the commercials were especially important because they tried to dispel the image that the labor movement was a "special interest." Looking back, Kirkman also saw LIPA's work—and especially the Union Yes campaign—as significant because it "brought the AFL-CIO into the information age."[10]

A lot remained to be done, however, especially when it came to creating a stronger national media presence. In the public relations field, the AFL-CIO recognized that it was "badly out-gunned" by its richer adversaries, and it lacked the resources to change this.[11] While the Union Yes campaign proved effective at mobilizing members and appealing to union pride, some also felt that it lacked reach with nonlabor constituencies. Denise Mitchell, who became communications director under John Sweeney, thought the campaign "a little parochial," even though it was "really nice with members." Furthermore, Kirkland did not help LIPA's efforts by his tendencies to refuse interviews. In press conferences, Kirkland could also put down reporters with what William Serrin termed "withering ripostes," and he retained an awkward relationship with the news media. While Federation staff enjoyed Kirkland's press conferences, they did little to enhance the labor movement's public image.[12]

Established in 1984, the Committee on the Evolution of Work also carried out important work, especially as it marked the first organized attempt to address labor's decline. According to the Executive Council, the Committee was a special body that was designed "to review and evaluate changes that are taking place in the United States in the labor force, occupations, industries, and technology and the implications of those changes for workers and for the labor movement." Although Donahue chaired the Committee, he stressed that it had been "Kirkland's idea." "We ought to have a committee, and we ought to look at the future," Kirkland proclaimed. The Committee, which engaged a number of academics and pollsters, aimed to provide the AFL-CIO with a road map that it could use to overcome its problems. It also tried to push the affiliates to do more to tackle decline. For an organization that had traditionally been reluctant to engage in self-reflection, it marked a significant step forward. "Many unions feel that to air their problems in public is to give support to their enemies," summarized William Serrin. "But with unions facing numerous difficulties, the AFL-CIO is taking a candid look at its member unions."[13]

In February 1985 the Committee's most important findings were issued in "The Changing Situation of Workers and Their Unions," a thirty-three-page report. As promised, it was an unusually honest exploration of labor's predicament. Drawing on work by pollsters Louis Harris, Peter D. Hart, and others, the report found that Americans were "ambivalent" about unions, believing that while they were needed to improve wages and working conditions, they were also undemocratic. Some 65 percent of unorganized workers agreed with the statement, "Unions force members to go along with decisions they don't like." The findings highlighted just how much work remained to be done in changing public perceptions, and Kirkland promised increased use of television and other media to tackle the problem. As the report noted, the labor movement faced many other challenges. The workforce now included more than 100 million people, and job growth was concentrated in Sun Belt states, where labor was weak. Increasing numbers of Americans worked part-time or were classified as managers or supervisors, putting them beyond the reach of unions. Moreover, corporate opposition made many workers afraid to organize. It was rare to see the array of problems identified and examined in detail. Overall, the Federation concluded that it was "behind the pace of change," especially in terms of adapting to a shifting workforce. If more workers were to be organized, fundamental reforms were required.[14]

The Committee's private records were even more candid. In one discussion of union density, for example, the Committee noted that union membership was too concentrated in the declining manufacturing sector. "We are part of a shrinking workforce," it admitted. Just maintaining union density at the same level required the Federation to organize 600,000 workers a year, a massive task. In 1982, NLRB figures indicated that just 87,000 workers had been brought into collective bargaining through elections, a figure the Committee termed "dismally impressive."[15]

Parts of the public report still managed an upbeat air. It insisted that there were "seeds of resurgence"; most workers understood the need for unions, and as the economy recovered from the recession, the organizing climate would improve. Some gains were already occurring, especially in the government sector. In a key section, the report contained twenty-eight recommendations, including strengthening links with community groups, changing bargaining tactics to emphasize arbitration and negotiation rather than striking, and increasing members' participation in their unions. Perhaps most significantly, the report called for "new methods of advancing the interests of workers," including new categories of membership, a greater emphasis on organizing, and greater use of corporate campaigns. "It is not enough merely to search for more effective ways of doing what we always have done," acknowledged the report, "we must expand our notions of what it is workers can do through their unions." Donahue emphasized the constructive way in which the twelve-member committee, drawn from across the Federation, had carried out its work. "A major American institution is saying that we have failed in some key ways," he declared. "I am not sure a lot of other institutions have undergone that kind of self-examination."[16]

It was one thing to identify a plan of action, however, and quite another to carry it out. The report identified the solutions but it had a voluntary tone— affiliates were encouraged but not directed to change. New categories of membership, for instance, needed "consideration." In the key area of organizing, the report similarly recognized the need for a "renewed emphasis," yet there was no specific commitment of resources or plan of action from the Federation. While the AFL-CIO president did have limited power—and Kirkland was always keenly aware that affiliation was voluntary—he could have taken a stronger lead. More effort could also have been made to involve members, or even rank-and-file leaders, in the high-level committee's work. "They did do . . . what for them was a pretty groundbreaking report, that report on the future of the Labor Movement," summarized Denise Mitchell, "but they didn't do much about it then, they didn't really try to move a program of change." Another Kirkland critic, Gerry Shea, felt that it was very hard for an organization that had been established in an era of relative union strength to readjust to the harsh climate. "The AFL-CIO," he asserted, "was very organized to *wield* power, not to *build* power, and that's just so true, and when it came to the fact that we were *losing* power, and needed to rebuild it, we were just not structured for it, not equipped for it, not programmed for it."[17]

In key areas, the AFL-CIO under Kirkland proved much better at identifying problems rather than addressing them. One perennial difficulty was the reluctance of many local unions to affiliate with the AFL-CIO's state federations and local central bodies, as there was no constitutional requirement for them to do so. In 1985 the Executive Council reported that affiliations to state federations were "only at 55 percent." This undermined the Federation's work because it deprived the center of funding. The problem epitomized the decentralized nature of the AFL-CIO, especially as each state federation also had a different per capita tax, a different affiliation level, and unique salary and fringe benefits for its officers. Although the Committee on the Evolution of Work proposed the introduction of a per capita payment from international unions directly to the AFL-CIO for transmittal to state and local central bodies, the Federation did not implement the proposal. Ever aware of the need for unity, Kirkland was reluctant to step on toes, particularly those of the powerful and territorial international union presidents. Reformers were frustrated. The problem, noted organizing director Alan Kistler, was that many presidents needed to "become more attentive to suggestions that there must be dramatic changes—in structure, in methodology, in attitude." The problem of decline ultimately applied to "all of them."[18]

Some reforms did grow out of the "Changing Situation" report. Acting on the recommendations, Kirkland pushed an associate member program that was aimed at regaining former union members and enrolling employees in nonunion workplaces. The change was significant, as the Federation's research estimated that 25 million former union members had dropped out because they had lost or changed jobs. By the start of 1989, twenty affiliates were drawing up plans to attract associates, who—in return for a nominal fee—received union-sponsored benefits and publications. In the late 1980s the Federation also broke ground with its Union Privilege Benefit Programs, which offered low-interest credit cards, free legal assistance, guaranteed life insurance coverage, and discounted travel. "These are benefits workers get outside the collective bargaining agreement," explained staffer John Ross, "something the union can offer you that the employer cannot touch." These programs proved popular. By 1991, over 2 million union members and their families carried the Union Privilege Mastercard, which had no annual fee and a competitive interest rate. It also included some innovative features, including the ability to skip up to three months of payment during a strike. Although most of the money generated by the card went to the Bank of New York and a marketing company, it still generated useful revenue for the AFL-CIO. Other members flocked to the Union Privilege mortgage program, which offered savings on down payments, closing costs, and mortgage insurance premiums. This program proved especially helpful in the "right-to-work" states—most of them in the South and West—where union members could not be compelled to pay dues even though they received benefits from the union's contract. "With the mortgage program in effect," explained Union Privilege president David Silverman, "the value of our discounts can easily exceed the cost of union dues."[19]

Some affiliates, particularly in manufacturing and the building trades, resisted these reforms, and they were not penalized. Servicing their members through the labor contract, they argued, was the main priority. Most felt that the associate membership program undermined traditional unionism, hurting those that paid the full amount. "The guy who already pays his union dues may resent it and say, 'Why not get a $5 membership instead of the $12 dues I am paying now,' " admitted a Federation staffer in 1985. "And the building tradesman at the hiring hall is afraid some new guy will walk in with an AFL-CIO membership card and want priority in hiring." Others questioned whether the member services programs were a sound idea. Some agreed with black union activist Bill Fletcher Jr., who asserted that unions must return to their "roots as workers' rights organizations, which means more than just delivering great customer services." Changing the culture of the labor movement, Donahue admitted later, would take a "long time," yet he insisted that the Committee had taken important first steps.[20]

In these years, reforms to the Federation's political program also secured results. During the 1986 midterm elections, COPE ran an effective campaign that featured extensive recruitment of volunteers, effective get-out-the-vote campaigns, and increased education of members. Utilizing new computer technology, the Federation mailed 3.5 million letters to members in forty states, urging support for its candidates. When the votes were counted, labor achieved a crucial objective, helping the Democrats to regain control of the U.S. Senate after six years of Republican dominance. The eight-seat gain built on the two members that the Democrats had picked up in 1984. In the Senate, 70 percent of union-endorsed candidates were successful, compared to 66 percent for all Senate, House, and governors' races. The AFL-CIO also helped the Democrats to gain five seats in the House, solidifying their control.[21]

Despite all the hard work, it was difficult to translate these gains into positive legislation. The Federation continued to fight for a higher minimum wage, for example, providing important advocacy for the millions of Americans who toiled in low-paid jobs. At a congressional hearing in 1987, Kirkland argued that the minimum wage, which had not risen since 1981, was inadequate. "Like social security recipients," he testified, "minimum wage workers are dependent on congressional action. To the extent that Congress fails to adjust their wages, they drop farther into poverty." Republicans in Congress refused to countenance an increase, arguing that it might jeopardize the fragile economy. It was a position supported by some Democrats, particularly in the South, and by the White House. In addition, the Reagan administration pushed for a lower "sub-minimum" for young people, a proposal that the Federation blocked. Even in 1988, when the economy was doing well, the administration opposed the House Education and Labor Committee's proposals to raise the minimum wage over four years from $3.35 an hour to $5.05. According to U.S. Office of Management and Budget (OMB) director James C. Miller III, a higher minimum wage would be inflationary and would "hold down employment of young and inexperienced workers."[22]

The Reagan administration managed to hold the line. In April 1988 a White House brief brushed aside the case for a minimum wage hike, insisting that "increased labor costs for business" would ultimately hurt workers, leading to layoffs, hiring freezes, and fewer jobs. According to the president, young people would be particularly disadvantaged. "Higher minimum wages will surely force young and inexperienced workers into unemployment," declared Reagan. The Federation was outraged. It claimed that, during the Reagan presidency, the cost of living had jumped by 37 percent, yet the minimum wage stayed at $3.35 an hour. "Never, in its 51-year history, has the minimum wage remained unchanged for so long, or its real value dropped so low," summarized the Executive Council. Only later would the Federation's hard work to raise the minimum wage bear fruit.[23]

Although legislative victories were rare, the Federation continued to defend other progressive laws, helping millions of workers in the process.

During Reagan's second term, when the president no longer had to worry about reelection, these efforts were particularly important. In the course of the Ninety-Ninth Congress, the Federation was able to limit cuts to the unemployment insurance program and secure a six-year extension of the Trade Adjustment Assistance (TAA) program, a major Department of Labor initiative that compensated workers who lost their jobs because of imports. During the 1980s, when deindustrialization was widespread, both programs were very important. Originating in the Trade Act of 1962, TAA provided an extra fifty-two weeks of income support to import-affected workers after their unemployment compensation (which lasted twenty-six weeks) was exhausted, as long as they were in an approved training program. There were other defensive victories. In 1986 the AFL-CIO and its allies thwarted a bill that would have introduced punitive penalties for those convicted of picket-line violence. These changes, they argued, would further undermine the right to strike. Sponsored by the National Right to Work Committee—part of a growing number of conservative lobby groups—the bill was killed when the Federation organized a successful filibuster. The Federation was also a steadfast defender of Medicare, and continued to advocate for universal health care. "We long recognized the need to provide proper health care not just for those who can afford it, but for all our citizens," summarized AFL-CIO official Ralph Liborato at a congressional hearing in 1988.[24]

Despite the hostile political climate, the AFL-CIO pushed for the passage of important legislation that went beyond its members' interests. In the One Hundredth Congress, the Federation responded to the demands of the growing number of women workers and tried to pass comprehensive child care legislation. The number of available openings at quality day care centers, it noted, was "ridiculously scarce," while the cost of child care—an average of $3,000 per child per year—was prohibitive. The Federation had been pressing on this issue for some time, with much of the work carried out behind the scenes in congressional hearings. Testifying before the Ninety-Eighth Congress, AFL-CIO vice president Barbara Hutchinson called the lack of child care provision "one of the most serious needs of our day." She pledged that the AFL-CIO would "do everything possible" to achieve adequate child care, "not just for the children of our members, but for all Americans." The Federation proposed the Act for Better Child Care (ABC), which helped fund the development of more child care centers, provided subsidized care for low-income working families, and set standards for child care facilities. The bill was attached to labor-supported legislation that aimed to establish a national minimum standard for family and medical leave. In the fall of 1988, however, the entire package was filibustered by conservatives on the Senate floor. Although the AFL-CIO worked on replacement legislation, its opponents refused to yield.[25]

The Federation also pushed for strengthened safety regulations, particularly with regard to the removal of asbestos from public buildings, a major hazard for many schoolchildren, teachers, and workers. Testifying before Congress in 1985, Federation official Jay Power cited scientific projections that 200,000 Americans would die from asbestos exposure by the end of the century. In addition, there were many other known hazards in the American workplace. "Workplace exposure to toxic substances has taken, and continues to take, a tremendous toll," he asserted, claiming that a quarter of all blue-collar workers would die from occupationally related cancers. As state workers' compensation systems were designed to deal with traumatic injury rather than disease, they had proven "woefully inadequate" in providing compensation, ensuring that a Federal program was needed. The AFL-CIO also supported legislation to provide for medical monitoring of workers who were at risk of contracting occupational diseases, efforts that employers opposed on cost grounds. By fighting on these issues, the AFL-CIO provided important advocacy and laid the groundwork for gains during the Clinton presidency.[26]

Working for the Federation on legislative issues in these years was arduous, especially for staff that remembered the 1960s and 1970s. As veteran employee Markley Roberts recalled, some AFL-CIO lobbyists complained privately that their work was "not fun anymore." Others acknowledged the adversity of working in the labor movement during these years, but insisted that the occasional victories kept them going. "I would compare it to playing golf," recalled Charles Stott, an AFL-CIO field representative in New England at the time. "You might have the worst possible game, and shoot a lot higher score than you wanted to, but you have that one good chip shot, and that's what . . . keeps you coming back."[27]

On some issues, the AFL-CIO did secure legislative breakthroughs. During the One Hundredth Congress, for example, a labor-backed bill to prevent employer abuse of lie detectors passed. Legislation that stopped the federal bankruptcy laws from being used to deprive retirees of health and life insurance benefits was also successful.[28] One of the AFL-CIO's "most crucial victories" occurred in 1988, when it secured the passage of legislation to give workers advance warning of plant closings and mass layoffs. The AFL-CIO had sought passage of this legislation for many years. As early as 1965, the *American Federationist* had called for advance notice of plant closings in order to "minimize the disruptive effects of such major industrial change on the workforce."[29] In the late 1970s, as shutdowns became more common, the issue gained urgency. In 1979 the Federation's lobbyists prepared a package of early notice legislation, but when they introduced it in the early 1980s, the Reagan administration was firmly opposed. Such proposals, the White House insisted, infringed on management rights. In 1987 the president also vetoed a bill mandating that companies with 100 or more workers give their employees at least sixty days' notice of closing. According to Reagan, plant closing legislation was a "sure loser" that would discourage international investment. Following a successful grassroots campaign by the AFL-CIO, labor's congressional allies introduced free-standing plant closing legislation (the previous bill had been part of omnibus trade legislation). Knowing that a second veto would be overridden, and anxious not to damage George H. W. Bush's election campaign, Reagan allowed the bill to become law without his signature.[30]

The president was not happy. In a statement, Reagan blasted the law's congressional supporters, claiming they were "more interested in scoring political points with organized labor than in saving workers' jobs." He had allowed the bill to become law only to end these "political shenanigans" and pursue his broader free trade agenda.[31] The conservative opposition took its toll, as the eventual Worker Adjustment and Retraining Notification Act was diluted, and it only covered companies that employed 100 workers or more. These exemptions meant that the law did not help many workers, and it was later criticized for its ineffectiveness.[32]

Still, the law was significant, particularly when large shutdowns occurred. In addition, this was one of the few times in the 1980s that the AFL-CIO had secured a policy objective over President Reagan's opposition. "The plant closing law was a very important law," recalled Robert McGlotten, the Federation's legislative director at the time. "I really felt a sense of achievement from that." Showing that he could be an able debater, Kirkland was integrally involved. Appearing on NBC's *Meet the Press* in April 1988, Kirkland blasted business suggestions that the law would hurt the American economy, pointing out that Canada, Japan, and West Germany had all built strong economies with such legislation in place. "They all believe that a key to their competitiveness has been the relationship between workers and management in their plants, their companies," he asserted.[33]

Working largely behind the scenes, Kirkland also proved an effective negotiator who was able to reunite the Federation. Apart from the re-affiliation of the UAW and the Teamsters, Kirkland engineered the return of smaller unions such as the Chemical Workers and the West Coast Longshoremen. Some unions were brought into the Federation for the first time; the Brotherhood of Locomotive Engineers, for example, had operated independently for 125 years and was the oldest rail union in the country. In 1988 its leaders were persuaded by Kirkland that they would have a stronger voice inside the AFL-CIO. Pointing to Kirkland's efforts in uniting the Federation, his defenders argued that he had tackled union decline effectively. Despite the hostile political and economic climate, they noted, the Federation's total membership had stayed stable. The AFL-CIO leader was also proud of these achievements. "I was instrumental in bringing to this trade union movement the highest degree of structural solidarity in the entire history of labor in this country," he commented later.[34]

On this issue, Kirkland secured some positive press coverage. "These were important steps," commented the *Chicago Tribune*, "because they helped stay the AFL-CIO's decline in rank-and-file membership." The re-affiliations of the UAW and IBT were particularly significant because these unions—with more than 1 million members each—were two of the largest in the country. As Peter Milius of the *Washington Post* observed, an embattled AFL-CIO badly needed such union "superpowers." In a retrospective assessment of his presidency, the *New York Times* even asserted that Kirkland's success in bringing large independent unions into the AFL-CIO was his "greatest achievement."[35]

In October 1987 Kirkland was integrally involved in bringing the Teamsters back into the Federation after an absence of thirty years. During protracted negotiations, his call for unity prevailed. On October 24, 1987, the Executive Council voted unanimously to accept the IBT's application for re-affiliation, effective November 1. It was a proud moment for Kirkland, who told the Council that he had been working toward "reunification of the labor movement within the AFL-CIO" since 1979. Bringing in 1.7 million members, the Teamsters' re-affiliation allowed Kirkland to mask the membership decline that many affiliates had suffered in the 1980s. Without this boost, the Federation's membership would have been near its all-time low. In addition, it netted an aggressive affiliate with a fast-growing political action committee and an active interest in organizing. Furthermore, re-affiliation reduced competition between the IBT and other international unions during organizing campaigns. The Teamsters were pleased to be back. "The House of Labor is truly under one roof again," exclaimed IBT president Jackie Presser. "Teamsters everywhere are proud to march hand-in-hand with all of our brothers and sisters in the AFL-CIO."[36]

The re-affiliation also had a downside. Remembering the earlier expulsion of the Teamsters and the subsequent imprisonment and mysterious disappearance of Jimmy Hoffa, many Americans continued to associate the trucking union with corruption. Three of Presser's four predecessors had been indicted—including Hoffa for mail fraud and jury tampering—and in 1986 the White House Commission on Organized Crime found that Presser would never have become the Teamsters' president without the assistance of the Genovese organized crime family—particularly its head, Anthony (Fat Tony) Salerno. In 1987 the IBT was being investigated by the Justice Department, who charged that its leaders maintained links to organized crime gangs. The Teamsters wanted to rejoin the AFL-CIO largely to gain political cover against a threatened federal lawsuit, although Presser died from cardiac arrest before he could face the corruption charges. The federal investigation helped to reactivate the issue of union corruption, throwing doubt on the AFL-CIO's conduct. Allowing the "scandal-scarred" Teamsters back into the Federation was a "bold move," wrote Kenneth B. Noble in the *New York Times*, and it attracted internal and external criticism. At a time when Kirkland was trying to improve public perceptions of organized labor, it was especially risky. "Nobody has to tell you the down side," admitted one union leader.[37]

Reiterating his pledge to reunite the House of Labor, Kirkland was unrepentant. "I am committed to do everything I can to bind up the scattered leaves of this movement," he declared. "This is a process of pursuing solidarity and bringing into one house all of labor's children." Kirkland stressed that he would enforce the AFL-CIO's constitution, which barred union members from holding office if they were convicted criminals. He also claimed that none of the IBT's current executive board had criminal links. Continuing to doubt whether Kirkland was capable of strong leadership, some journalists were impressed. Kirkland, summarized Noble, had shown "independent spirit," stamping his authority on the job. "Mr. Kirkland," he proclaimed, "has finally become Mr. Labor."[38] Arguing that potential wrongdoing by top officers did not justify an affiliate's removal, Kirkland proved that he differed from Meany, who had expelled the Teamsters on these grounds. "Individuals in a union may be found guilty," he told a skeptical Council, "but the institution and its members are not."[39]

For the AFL-CIO, even the mixed reaction to the Teamsters' re-affiliation was an improvement on much of the media coverage that it received in these years. In the late 1980s, the sharp decline in union density provoked a slew of gloomy headlines. Examples such as "Unions Losing Workers," "Hard

Times Continue for U.S. Labor," and "Quitting Time for Unions?" annoyed Kirkland, who was an avid collector of clippings.[40] He disliked talking about the decline issue, and grew frustrated with outsiders' focus on it. According to David St. John, Kirkland even parodied the interest in the topic. "Lane used to call it 'whither labor,'" he related. "He used to say, 'Oh God, the whither labor question.' . . . We'd be out on the road somewhere, and arranged a sit-down with some local reporters . . . they would always bring up the 'whither labor' question, which was: 'Aren't unions a thing of the past, aren't they just declining?'" In response, Kirkland emphasized positive developments, particularly in organizing and securing contracts. "I mean anybody could sit there and tick off the problems, and look at some of the declines," explained St. John.[41]

Questioning Kirkland's effectiveness, some reporters also speculated about his future, especially as his sixty-fifth birthday approached. Somewhat piqued, Kirkland brushed off suggestions that he might step down. "Well, those rumors are out of the whole cloth," he told a reporter in late 1986. "I think they started this time of life with Meany, and he went on another 20 years." Kirkland's health problems, however, reactivated the speculation. In February 1987, on the eve of his sixty-fifth birthday, the AFL-CIO president had a malignant tumor removed from a kidney. Because the surgery went well, Kirkland recovered and secured reelection in October. Although he continued to smoke furtively, his health was subsequently robust.[42]

While Kirkland rarely wrote about the decline issue, in 1986 prominent political scientist Seymour Martin Lipset persuaded him to contribute to *Unions in Transition*, an academic volume that probed labor's decline and how it might be averted. Even in a reflective piece, Kirkland's frustration was evident. "It has all been said before," he noted at the start. "Labor's obituary has been written at least once in every one of the 105 years of our existence, and nearly that many causes of death have been diagnosed." Again, Kirkland emphasized good news, stressing that while the big industrial unions were losing members, affiliates representing teachers, government workers, and service employees were growing. Union members earned significantly more than their unorganized counterparts, and they possessed a distinctive "toughness and resilience." In most Western countries, he explained, unions received a much greater level of government protection, but in the United States they had always operated in a harsh political and legislative climate. United and determined, and undertaking important reforms, the labor movement should not be written off. "All in all," he asserted, "the prophets of doom have badly misgauged both the present strength and the future prospects of trade unionism in America."[43]

During Reagan's second term, however, this line became increasingly difficult to maintain. In the crucial organizing area, the crisis worsened; far fewer NLRB elections were taking place, yet labor's winning percentage was not improving. In 1980 there were 8,198 representation elections nationally, of which unions won less than half (3,744). By 1988, there were only 4,152 elections, and unions still won less than half (1,920). The organizing climate had changed sharply since the 1970s, when—despite evidence of rising opposition to unions—the number of representation elections had held steady, at around 8,000 a year. Between 1975 and 1985, the number of successful union decertifications also jumped by 73 percent, from 379 to 654. Employers' willingness to permanently replace strikers, meanwhile, contributed to a dramatic decline in the number of strikes, again transforming long-term patterns. The number of work stoppages involving more than 1,000 workers plummeted, from an annual average of over 200 in the 1970s to 187 in 1980 and just 54 in 1985, around the time that Kirkland penned his essay. Afraid of losing their jobs, and feeling that they had an "empty gun," workers had become reluctant to strike. Despite Kirkland's optimism, the decline of unions had accelerated sharply in the Reagan era. In the words of Ohio AFL-CIO president John Hodges, unions had received a "sad, rude awakening."[44]

In the Executive Council, members candidly discussed how their unions had been weakened in new ways, providing a sharp contrast with Kirkland's public pronouncements. In August 1986 the Council related that there had been a marked "decline in industry-wide bargaining," especially in key industries such as steel, autos, papermaking, and communications. USW president Lynn Williams reported on the new round of bargaining in the basic steel industry, noting that, for the first time since the 1950s, his union had bargained with each company individually. UAW president Owen Bieber added that, in the auto industry, employers were trying to "destroy pattern-bargaining," while ILGWU president Jay Mazur felt that widespread "union-busting" had been "encouraged by the attitudes of the Reagan Administration." Increasing international competition, a product of globalization, was also driving concessionary demands. Many union presidents were stressed and worried, as for the first time it was unclear—with members reluctant to strike—how unions could fight what Vincent Sombrotto of the National Association of Letters Carriers called "efforts toward deindustrialization and deunionization of the American economy."[45]

In some ways, the economic recovery compounded the Federation's problems. The Reagan administration derived a lot of confidence from the upturn, emboldening it to brush aside criticisms from progressive groups. By September 1987, White House aides were boasting that America was enjoying "a history making period of recession-free economic growth." Much of the media also trumpeted the strength of the economic recovery. "The average American has never had it so good," pronounced *Fortune* in the same month, music to the president's ears.[46]

In his second term, Reagan's Labor Day addresses—a good barometer of how he viewed labor issues—became more assured, as he used the recovery to argue that those who criticized his economic policies were wrong. "When we got to Washington six-and-a-half years ago," he declared on Labor Day in 1987, "we put in place economic policies that foster lasting progress." With inflation low and unemployment falling, workers were enjoying sustained economic growth. "In short," concluded Reagan, "the working people of America are better off and what better day to say it than on Labor Day." Reagan also rejected the whole notion of deindustrialization, stressing instead that productivity was increasing. America, he insisted in 1988, was not a nation in decline.[47]

Although the recession was over, economic growth was concentrated in the service and retail sectors, where unions were relatively weak. Buffeted by globalization, heavily unionized manufacturing industries were slow to recover, and rising productivity was offset by job losses. At the AFL-CIO, private records revealed the scale of the crisis. In 1985 the Federation carried out its first detailed investigation into membership falls among affiliates, concluding that there had been "substantial membership losses" for a range of big industrial unions, including the USW, UAW, IAM, ILGWU, and URW. Most of those laid off found work in nonunion industries, accelerating organized labor's decline. After documenting the problems, the AFL-CIO had few answers, and affiliates were not pushed to organize intensively in growing sectors of the economy. Kirkland recognized the challenges caused by globalization, but he struggled to find solutions. "We're in the midst of a major—and I think probably irreversible—shift in our economic base. And that's affecting us very drastically," he commented in 1986. "The industrial sector is still in decline and the only growth is services. I just find it hard to believe that a society on the scale of the American economy can subsist on services alone." In 1987 Kirkland appealed to the Democratic Congress, asserting that the U.S. trade deficit was having a "devastating" impact on employment. The solution, he insisted, lay in reducing the deficit, providing import relief for affected industries, and adopting clear provisions to protect labor rights in trade agreements. With the corporate lobby in the ascendancy, most of these proposals fell on deaf ears. At this stage, the AFL-CIO's trade work was also focused on high-level hearings and testimony, rather than the mobilization of members.[48]

Throughout Reagan's second term, there was little good news for labor. Even when the Federation marked its thirtieth anniversary in 1985, Kirkland admitted to convention delegates that it was hard to celebrate. "The bad news is that our overall growth has been stymied," he noted frankly. "A new labor force has grown up around us and the trade union share of it has dropped." In response, Kirkland tried to focus the convention—held in Anaheim, California—on the task of organizing new members, particularly in the Sunbelt. Labor had "a hell of a lot more people to organize—and we do mean to organize them." Despite the goodwill, there was still no specific organizing plan—or financial commitment—from the top, and results were disappointing. By the time Reagan left office, there were 17 million union members in the United States, but the overall workforce had expanded beyond 100 million. Highlighting how organized labor had stood still while the economy expanded around it, 75 percent of these workers were in the service sector. The need to organize the South, where much of the growth was concentrated, was especially acute. It was telling that, in 1988, just 6 percent of workers in the Carolinas—Kirkland's home area—held union cards.[49]

While many affiliates were consumed with helping their members—especially when they were laid off—the growing service and government sector unions wanted a stronger emphasis on organizing. As the economy changed, these affiliates became more powerful. By 1985, the AFL-CIO had eleven times as many teachers, ten times as many state, county, and municipal workers, and three and a half times as many service workers as it had when it was founded. The relative decline of manufacturing—the share of the workforce employed in this sector had dropped from a third to a fifth—ensured that the AFL-CIO also had fewer auto workers, steelworkers, textile and apparel workers, railroad workers, and deep sea sailors. "What has happened to these unions is a measure of what has happened to America," reflected Kirkland. The roots of the subsequent challenge to Kirkland's leadership were evident, and time favored his future opponents.[50]

Well-connected and increasingly powerful, John Sweeney was one of the main leaders who wanted to commit more resources to organizing. Although Sweeney remained loyal to Kirkland, privately he was not impressed by the regime's organizing record. As was often the case in the Kirkland years, the

AFL-CIO spent a lot of time studying problems in the organizing area and recommending solutions, but game-changing reform was lacking. In the mid-1980s a National Organizing Committee reviewed proposals for the training of organizers and discussed ways of improving results, but there was little evidence that affiliates—especially those who were not part of the Committee—had changed. The Department of Organization and Field Services similarly conducted surveys about rising employer opposition to unions, but these efforts did little more than document that the organizing climate was getting harder. Afraid of rocking the boat, Kirkland refused to demand that affiliates spend more on organizing.[51]

Defensive battles also stopped the AFL-CIO from taking decisive action in organizing. Emboldened by the conservative political climate, more employers took unions on. The replacement of strikers reached a zenith during Reagan's second term; between 1985 and 1989, companies hired permanent replacement workers in nearly one of every five strikes, and high-profile strikes ended particularly badly for labor. In 1985–86, a six-month strike by UFCW members against meatpacking company George A. Hormel in Austin, Minnesota, ended disastrously when the company hired around 1,000 strikebreakers, including 400 union members. Bitter divisions between the local and international union exacerbated the defeat, with strikers alleging that the UFCW—and the AFL-CIO—had not done enough to resist concessionary bargaining. Watching these events, some observers doubted whether labor could win strikes. The Hormel workers, summarized Peter Perl in the *Washington Post*, had "failed to realize that striking in the 1980s is essentially a lost cause."[52]

Even when workers were united, the outcome was often no different. In June 1987 managers at International Paper Company, a corporation that had previously bargained constructively with the union, permanently replaced more than 2,200 union members in Maine, Pennsylvania, and Wisconsin who had gone on strike after resisting demands for extensive concessions. Although very few strikers crossed the picket lines, they still lost their jobs. Most were not rehired, and they also suffered a lot of psychological damage. "It's just like your father and mother kicking you out of the house one day and saying, 'Don't come back, I don't ever want to see you again,'" summarized Dale Martin, a replaced striker from Lock Haven, Pennsylvania. "So that's the way we took it." It was a typical tale; in the mid and late 1980s, most of those who struck were left feeling betrayed, angry, and bitter.[53]

As more and more of its members were replaced, a shell-shocked Federation struggled to respond. By 1984, Kirkland was exploring the introduction of legislation to restrict striker replacement, yet he acknowledged that under the Reagan administration passage was "unlikely."[54] The Federation was also slow to help its striking members. Often, it stood on the sidelines as they were replaced, or—as had been the case in the PATCO dispute—it offered remedial help that softened the blow but failed to alter the outcome. In one indicative early example, the Federation watched as 2,400 striking copper miners at the Phelps Dodge Corporation in Morenci, Arizona, were replaced when they resisted the company's calls for wholesale concessions, including an end to cost-of-living allowances. "The copper strike is an example of the new bargaining climate in America," observed the *Washington Post*. "Financially beleaguered companies with their backs to the wall are demanding cutbacks in wages and benefits and are hiring workers to replace strikers." In November 1984 Kirkland did speak at a rally in Tucson to show support for the workers, yet by this time the mine had been reopened with a mixture of permanent replacements and former strikers. With the workforce replaced, a Federation-backed corporate campaign—including efforts to exert pressure on Phelps Dodge's financial backers—achieved little. The disastrous outcome illustrated broader themes. By 1986, Kirkland was pushing for changes to allow the AFL-CIO to intervene early in any strike, or contract negotiations, of national significance, rather than wait until a local union was on the rocks. "We must be part of the general staff at the inception, rather than the ambulance drivers at the bitter end," he explained. Kirkland hoped to relax "time-hallowed" rules that made it hard for the AFL-CIO to interfere in labor-management disputes until after a strike had begun. Reform moved slowly, however, and time was not on the Federation's side.[55]

Gradually, pressure built from below for a legislative ban on permanent replacements. At the Executive Council meeting in February 1986, Wayne Glenn of the Paperworkers and Bill Bywater of the Electrical Workers expressed concern about "the use of strikebreaking and union-busting tactics by a growing number of employers." They called for federal legislation to address the problem. In response, Kirkland was cautious, arguing that the composition of Congress and the attitude of the current administration made it "unlikely that significant, progressive changes can be accomplished in labor law at this time." Instead, he called on affiliates to build a campaign behind the scenes, especially by educating their members of Congress about the issue. The time to introduce the legislation would come later, once the president who was widely associated with the replacement of strikers had left office. For now, the Federation had to lay the groundwork for subsequent action.[56]

Even when the Federation did help its embattled members, it was unable to secure clear victories. In a long and high-profile battle with Coors Brewery—owned by a conservative family with close links to the Reagans—the AFL-CIO gave assistance to around 1,500 members who belonged to Directly Affiliated Local Union 366. The Coors case became a protracted, ten-year battle that highlighted the depth of corporate resistance to unions, as well as the limitations of union power. Under the leadership of Joseph Coors Sr., a forthright conservative Republican, Coors Co. became what the *Washington Post* called "a nationwide symbol of union busting." The case was important, especially as it illustrated how the climate became increasingly antiunion under Reagan, who often personally sanctioned corporate attacks on organized labor. The Coors battle reached a decisive climax during Reagan's second term.[57]

This time, the AFL-CIO was integrally involved. Because the local union was part of a small group that belonged directly to the Federation without being part of a national affiliate, the AFL-CIO was responsible for providing bargaining support. The dispute dated back to 1977, when the Executive Council initiated a boycott of Coors beer, attracting national attention. Justifying the move, the AFL-CIO cited the company's demands for "regressive contract changes" at its brewery in Golden, Colorado. In particular, the company wanted to gut seniority provisions and wipe out shift differentials and premium pay for weekends. The Council also objected to company demands that workers take lie detector tests or submit to body searches, calling them "a gross violation of human dignity." It noted that the NLRB, which found merit in the local union's charges and issued a complaint against Coors, largely supported its position. The initiation of the boycott also reflected the way that AFL-CIO leaders saw the Coors dispute as very important, as a fight for all American workers. "If the Coors brothers had their way," explained union representative David Sickler, "the legal right to engage in collective bargaining would be denied to America's workers and social justice would be returned to its darker days."[58]

Drawing support from a wide range of labor and community organizations—including gay and civil rights groups—the boycott was impressive. In June 1978 chief executive Bill Coors told shareholders that the boycott was having a "material effect" on sales. Hurt by falling revenue in established markets, the company hit back by expanding into new areas. When the boycott started, Coors' beer was only available in eleven Western states; when it ended, it could be bought in forty-seven states. Coors also retaliated with an aggressive and well-funded marketing campaign that sought to erode support for the union's position. Furthermore, it drew sustenance from the conservative political climate, helping it to turn the tables on the union. Joseph Coors described Reagan as "the greatest President that this country has ever had" and served as part of the president's "kitchen cabinet," advising the White House on presidential appointments and other matters. Clearly, the AFL-CIO could not expect any support from the Reagan administration.[59]

Eventually, both sides tired of the struggle, and in 1987 the Federation secured a partial victory when Coors agreed to settle. In the agreement, Coors said that it would not obstruct union organizing at its plants and would allow the use of union members in the construction of any new facilities, including a planned $70 million packing and distribution plant in Elkton, Virginia. Kirkland trumpeted the agreement as "a resounding success," adding that the labor movement was "immensely proud" of the boycott, which had attracted widespread public support. Of course, any positive news stood out at this time. "Certainly it's a development noteworthy in 1987, when labor is supposed to be dead," acknowledged Federation official Robert Harbrant.[60]

In reality, the Coors settlement was not an unequivocal victory. Coors had not agreed to a union contract in Golden—there would be another vote—and some critics asserted that the boycott was called off prematurely. In charge of the negotiations, Tom Donahue argued that the company would never have recognized the union without an election. He later admitted, however, that the settlement was "not very satisfactory," especially as the company's hostility to unions was unchanged. In November 1987, new chairman William K. Coors, the grandson of the company's founder, reiterated as much. Citing low turnover among his workers, Coors insisted that unions were unnecessary, adding that the company would continue to advocate a "union-free environment" in Golden and Elkton.[61]

These proved to be prophetic words. Although the company agreed to a quick election, in December 1988 its position was upheld when 73 percent of the Golden workers voted against the Teamsters. The AFL-CIO had failed to reinstate bargaining rights, a key objective of the boycott. In Elkton, organizing stalled. Although the IBT gave its brewery division a blank check to organize the new plant, director Charles Klare described the task as "very difficult." Apart from corporate resistance, the Elkton campaign was hindered by competition between the Teamsters and other unions, chiefly the Machinists and Carpenters. Such rivalries still bedeviled many organizing campaigns, wasting precious resources. Overall, despite a national campaign in which it had forged bonds with progressive groups and secured publicity, the AFL-CIO had not made gains on the ground. The story was emblematic. Across America, corporate resistance to unions was uncurbed, and so was the suspicion—or ambivalence—of many workers.[62]

Although they generally kept their views private, a growing number of union presidents wanted the Federation to tackle domestic problems more forcefully. Behind the scenes, there was some disappointment with Kirkland, who continued to place a significant emphasis on international affairs, especially events in Poland. In these years, Kirkland went out of his way to show his support for Polish workers. On September 26, 1985, he spoke at a demonstration organized by the Polish American Congress, pleasing his hosts with a passionate address. "You have truly displayed the heart of the entire movement in urging support for those who are fighting for their freedom and their right to choose their own government," wrote Congress president Aloysius A. Mazewski to Kirkland after the protest.[63] During Reagan's second term—when the Polish struggle dropped out of the headlines—Kirkland never forgot Solidarnosc, and even stepped up assistance. As the Executive Council explained in 1986, Solidarnosc was the "only representative of the voice of Poland's workers." Citing the arrest and convictions of key leaders, the Federation urged affiliates to support the Polish Workers Aid Fund, while state and local central bodies were encouraged to "adopt" regional Solidarnosc organizations.[64]

Domestically, the AFL-CIO experienced setbacks throughout Reagan's second term, culminating in the disappointment of the 1988 presidential election. In August, 96 percent of General Board members endorsed Democratic candidate Michael Dukakis, encouraging hopes of a political change. The late endorsement represented a big shift from 1984, when the AFL-CIO had backed Walter Mondale well before the Democratic Party's convention. This time, Kirkland launched "Democracy at Work," a program that saw the Federation consult carefully with their members—who were sent millions of copies of the candidates' written positions, as well as videotapes and other materials—before a selection was made. In a speech to the Federation in Washington, Dukakis promised to take labor seriously and declared that he would be "an economic leader, not a cheerleader." While the economic recovery made it hard for the Democrats—and Dukakis admitted that more Americans were working than ever before—he criticized the quality of many new jobs. From 1979 to 1985, he stressed, Americans lost jobs that paid an average of $440 a week and replaced them with those that paid "one-third less." This was exactly the kind of message that the AFL-CIO wanted to hear.[65]

After the election, the Council reported that over two-thirds of AFL-CIO members and their families had voted for Dukakis, but this was not enough to stop George H. W. Bush from securing a comfortable victory. Labor still made some gains. The AFL-CIO helped to ensure that pro-labor activist Ron Brown was elected chair of the Democratic National Committee, while Jack Otero from the Transportation Communications Union was elected vice chair for voter participation. There were also important defensive victories. Most notably, in Massachusetts a strong campaign by the labor movement was successful in retaining the state's prevailing wage law, which was very important to the building trades unions.[66] Furthermore, there were indications that labor had helped stem the loss of "Reagan Democrats" to the GOP. According to a national AFL-CIO poll, almost 70 percent of union members voted for Dukakis, a clear improvement on the Democratic vote in the previous two elections. Taking comfort from these results, the Federation approached the Bush era with cautious optimism. Even with another Republican in the White House, there were signs that the next four years would be a little brighter. Above all, Reagan was gone.[67]

CHAPTER SIX

Partial Détente

George H. W. Bush and the AFL-CIO

With the Reagan presidency over, America's beleaguered labor movement hoped for a break. To some extent, it got one. After the Reagan administration—which John Sweeney dubbed "one of the most anti-union administrations in our history"—the Bush era was an improvement. During Reagan's presidency, vice president Bush had forged a workable relationship with the AFL-CIO, and the Federation's leaders viewed him in a more positive light. As Reagan's labor liaison, Robert Bonitati, wrote Bush, "many of the AFL-CIO hierarchy believe you are one of the 'good guys' in the Administration and view you as being less ideological." Bush, agreed former AFL-CIO staffer Charles Stott, "was not viewed as the antiunion president that Reagan was . . . after what Reagan did to the Air Traffic Controllers, that really deepened our resolve to take him on at every turn, whenever he tried to deny the rights of workers."[1]

During Bush's administration, relations between the White House and its labor neighbor were much improved, partly because the new president did a much better job of listening to labor. The two sides found common ground in foreign policy—as they had even under Reagan—but now they shared particular pleasure in the collapse of Communist regimes in Central and Eastern Europe, especially Poland, as well as the demise of apartheid in South Africa. The leaders of the Polish and South African freedom struggles—Lech Walesa and Nelson Mandela—both addressed the AFL-CIO in these years, moments that meant a lot to Kirkland. The strong economic climate—which lasted for most of the Bush presidency—helped the AFL-CIO, spurring gains in organizing and allowing millions of workers to enjoy higher earnings, including an improved minimum wage. Kirkland also carried out some significant internal reforms, establishing an Organizing Institute and initiating recognition of Workers' Memorial Day, which commemorated the Federation's long-standing fight for a safe workplace. In the summer of 1991, he also oversaw the tenth anniversary of Solidarity Day, bringing at least 250,000 people back to Washington to demonstrate labor's unity and press for key legislative goals. For Kirkland and Donahue, these were relatively stable years. At the biennial convention in

November 1991, the long-serving pair were reelected to a two-year term "by acclamation."[2]

At the same time, however, there was no fundamental turnaround in the AFL-CIO's fortunes. Union density continued to decline, albeit more slowly. By 1992, 15.7 percent of American workers belonged to unions, a drop of about one percentage point over the course of Bush's presidency.[3] The White House remained in the hands of Republicans who were hostile to labor's core demands, including comprehensive health care reform and a ban on striker replacements. Brushing aside the AFL-CIO's concerns about job losses and environmental exploitation, Bush was also an avid supporter of a free trade agreement with Canada and Mexico. As a result, globalization continued to undermine the wages and conditions of many American workers. Ultimately, the main differences between Reagan and Bush were slight, but they were still important. Under Bush, summarized former AFL-CIO staffer Susan Dunlop, there was "kind of a détente." These years consequently had a slightly softer tone.[4]

From the start, labor leaders approached the Bush era with guarded optimism. While the climate remained harsh, they were relieved that the Reagan era was over. "I think the situation is still very ugly," summarized Philip McLewin, an AFL-CIO leader in New Jersey, in 1989, "but not as ugly as it has been." In a similar vein, New York union leader Victor Gotbaum commented, "Bush is softer than Reagan, but that doesn't mean he's soft."[5] Bush certainly sent out some signals that he wanted a dialogue with the AFL-CIO. In April 1989 the new president addressed the Federation's Building and Construction Trades, something that Reagan had also done. In his speech, however, Bush promised to be fair and to consult with organized labor, suggesting a more conciliatory tone to his administration. "My door is wide open," he exclaimed. "I want to work with you."[6]

Although this speech was partly a reward to a group that had supported him—and Bush shared long-held Republican goals of getting a bigger slice of the labor vote—it was still a significant marker. Moreover, after the conference a group of building trades leaders were "flabbergasted" to be invited to the White House, where they were "warmly received" by the president and Mrs. Bush. The incident highlighted the positive relationship that Bush forged with the more conservative wing of the labor movement. Charles W. Jones, the president of the International Brotherhood of Boilermakers, later thanked Bush for "an overwhelming and pleasant experience" that he would "always cherish." "The pleasure was ours," replied Bush. Bush also later invited Kirkland and other labor leaders to the White House for a reception in honor of Walesa.

This was a sharp change from Reagan, who failed to establish any rapport with union heads at the start of his presidency.[7]

More significantly, in November Bush agreed to address the AFL-CIO's biennial convention in Washington, DC, something that his predecessor had refused to do. Labor leaders were cautiously optimistic. "Bush says some of the right things, but it still has to be proved that he's a real friend of labor," observed Carpenters' president Wayne Pierce. "At least he wants to sit down and talk."[8] According to Bush's official briefing, his speech was indeed designed to demonstrate "the Administration's desire to forge a partnership with the labor community," differentiating it from the Reagan presidency. In his address, Bush joked about the fact that most union members were Democrats, quipping that those who had voted for him were sitting "in the last row." More seriously, the president stressed that organized labor was a central component of the democratic system, part of the "beating heart of American liberty." Although he had "differences" with the Federation, he was confident that a constructive relationship was possible. Delivering the speech just a few days after the fall of the Berlin Wall—and with Lech Walesa looking on—Bush also found common ground with the AFL-CIO in foreign affairs, where he praised its work "to keep the door to freedom open to all." In closing, he reiterated that he wanted his presidency to see more dialogue between the White House and the AFL-CIO. "I am hopeful," he exclaimed, "that 1989 will be remembered as the year when American labor, business, and government first began to work together, in a real partnership, for the freedom and dignity of workers everywhere."[9]

The speech marked a significant departure from the Reagan years, which had begun with confrontation between the White House and organized labor. Bush's acceptance of the AFL-CIO's invitation, summarized the *New York Times*, represented "a warming in White House relations with the labor movement." After it, Kirkland and Bush corresponded cordially, with the president even sending personal holiday greetings to the Kirklands. Kirkland also thanked Bush for the personal "kindness and courtesy" he had shown during Walesa's visit.[10] Two weeks after the convention, Kirkland accompanied the president on a high-level trip to Poland that was designed to strengthen democracy in Eastern Europe. While the change from the White House's side was significant, so was the willingness of AFL-CIO leaders to listen. "If Reagan had come to speak to us," explained IUE president Bill Bywater in November, "I would have walked out."[11]

There were other important improvements. Relations between the Federation and the Department of Labor, a key agency, were much healthier. As

Lane Kirkland with President George H. W. Bush, who reached out to the AFL-CIO more than Reagan had. Courtesy of Special Collections, University of Maryland Libraries.

To Lane Kirkland
with best wishes,
Lane OK – no more voodoo and no more Kool-Aid.
Hell with the press reports. I enjoyed it!! B.

early as February 1989, new Secretary of Labor Elizabeth Dole addressed the Executive Council, stressing that she saw the DOL as a "people's department" that was designed to ensure that "there is a job for every American who wants to work." A year later, Dole told the Council that she was pleased to have developed "working relationships with leadership of the unions of the AFL-CIO."[12] When Lynn Martin replaced Dole in February 1991, she also fronted the Council, promising to maintain an "open door" policy.[13]

In early 1990, Dole was instrumental in arranging for federal mediation of a major strike between the United Mineworkers (UMW) and the Pittston Coal Group in southwestern Virginia. Although she was pressured by an effective and militant labor campaign—one that was backed by the AFL-CIO—Dole still listened to the union's concerns. Since early 1989, the UMW had fought Pittston's efforts to weaken members' health care and retirement benefits, complaining that the company was refusing to compromise. By ordering mediation, Dole, who had begun her career as a Democrat, acknowledged the value of collective bargaining, something that Reagan had abrogated by refusing to talk to PATCO. Even before the Pittston announcement, Kirkland had declared that he found the Bush administration "a little more civilized" than Reagan's and "less intensely ideological," and he was pleased by the outcome. The settlement was an important victory for labor, as it protected the health and retirement benefits of current and former miners. In return, the company gained greater flexibility in its operating hours. In a broader sense, thought *New York Times'* reporter Peter T. Kilborn, Dole had "taken a step toward ending a bleak period for organized labor in its relations with the Government." Labor leaders were "hardly proclaiming a return to their salad days," he added, "but there is now at least more of the mutual respect that unions experienced with Republican presidents before Reagan." UMW spokesman John Duray even gave Dole some credit. "It's a significant thing that she was willing to take a chance and step out in a different direction than has been the norm of the last 10 years," he declared.[14]

In other ways, Dole was an improvement. Significantly, the new secretary stepped up enforcement of job safety regulations. In 1989 the Occupational Safety and Health Administration's budget went up for the first time in eight years, with Dole using an extra $14.9 million to hire 179 enforcement officers. As a result of the extra staff, the DOL's fines against employers who broke health and safety laws topped $60 million a year, as opposed to $14 million under Reagan. Dole was also willing to consider labor-backed proposals, particularly an increase in the minimum wage and greater assistance for the 35 million Americans who lacked medical insurance.[15]

In other ways, these years began more positively. By 1989, the economy was growing steadily, and both inflation and unemployment were low. The economic climate helped Bush's presidency to assume a softer tone, as expressed by his inauguration call for a "kinder, gentler nation." It also allowed organized labor to recuperate. Unions, declared the *Christian Science Monitor* in 1989, were "getting back on their feet." "After eight years of decline," it added, "the labor movement is entering a period of stability. Membership losses have all but disappeared." The economic recovery particularly helped the manufacturing affiliates, who had hemorrhaged members for most of the 1980s. Between 1982 and 1986, a period in which America's twenty-five biggest steelmakers lost nearly $12 billion, the USW's membership dropped by a quarter. In 1988, however, with the industry recovering, the USW gained 11,000 members, its first membership increase in the decade. Creating a shortage of workers in some sectors, the stronger economy also tipped the balance in collective bargaining. "Whenever you have a tighter labor market," commented labor relations expert George Hagglund in 1989, "unions have more horsepower at the bargaining table."[16]

There were some encouraging developments at the state level. In Pennsylvania and New York—two important union states—affiliates started to gain members. "The climate in Pennsylvania is union," declared Julius Uehlein, the state AFL-CIO president. "Our decline in membership has bottomed out." There were several explanations for the turnaround. After a period of harsh labor-management relations, cooperation was on the rise, while workers' desire for better wages helped unions. Service sector and health care workers were also organizing. Similar optimism was expressed in other states, particularly in the Northeast and Midwest, where unions were strongest. "People are feeling better about the future," explained Ralph Lorenzetti, a UFCW member in Ohio. "The days of concessions and rollbacks are behind us. We're starting to move forward." In November 1988 organized labor also took heart from its defeat of Ballot Question 2 in Massachusetts, which had called for the repeal of the state's prevailing wage law. As the Springfield (Massachusetts) *Sunday Republican* observed, this "big victory" showed that "the labor movement could still flex its political muscle."[17]

Apart from a less hostile presidential administration, there were other reasons why these years were slightly better for labor. Learning from the disastrous defeats of the 1980s, the AFL-CIO began to provide more—and earlier—support to affiliates who were embroiled in labor disputes. Helped by the Federation, workers in a variety of disputes—most notably at Pittston Coal Company, Ravenswood Aluminum Corporation, and AT&T—fought back against company concessions, achieving considerable success. Providing positive headlines, these disputes helped to lift public perceptions of labor. In 1990 a Roper Poll showed that 33 percent of Americans instinctively sided with the union when they first heard of a strike, while 25 percent favored the company. This was the highest level of support for unions, and the lowest for companies, since the poll began in 1979. The proportion of Americans who believed that unions made unreasonable demands had also dropped sharply. "The strikes have let the world know that unions are still here and that they work for the people," summarized Rick Poulette, the president of a CWA local in Palm Beach, California.[18]

The inspiring example of workers in Central and Eastern Europe also lifted perceptions of labor. As Americans saw on television, workers' movements led many of the successful struggles against Communism. Particularly important was the well-publicized example of Poland, where Solidarnosc was re-legalized as a trade union in 1989. Following the first free elections since World War II, Solidarnosc went on to lead a coalition government, placing organized labor at the heart of the new democratic system. It was a remarkable turnaround that inspired many Western observers. "In the space of a few short months in early 1989," noted scholar David Ost, "Solidarity essentially won what it had been fighting for over the past eight years."[19]

Despite these encouraging developments, there was to be no fundamental change in labor's fortunes in the United States, and there were clear limits to the Bush administration's goodwill. The crucial issue of the minimum wage was illustrative. Unlike Reagan, Bush quickly agreed to an increase in the minimum wage, which had been frozen at $3.35 an hour since January 1981. Bush supported raising the minimum to $4.25, while the labor movement and its congressional supporters wanted a hike to $5.05. Like his predecessor, however, Bush also backed a sub-minimum for new employees, a move the AFL-CIO viewed as "a complete undermining of the minimum wage law itself." When it pressed for more, the Federation was unsuccessful. In May 1989 Kirkland told the Executive Council that he had tried to hold discussions with the Bush White House about the minimum wage, but the AFL-CIO was "never contacted or given an opportunity" to express its views.[20]

It was a timely reminder of the limits of change. In the summer of 1989, Bush vetoed a bill that sought to raise the minimum wage higher than he wanted, and the AFL-CIO was unsuccessful in its effort to override the veto. Elizabeth Dole subsequently helped to work out a compromise with Kirkland that saw the minimum increase to $4.25 an hour over two years, a modest victory. While a step in the right direction, the minimum wage now represented 41 percent of average hourly earnings. In contrast, the Federation argued that it should comprise "at least" 50 percent of the average income.[21]

On several other important domestic issues, Bush also disappointed. In June 1990 he vetoed the Family and Medical Leave Act, which would have required businesses with fifty or more employees to grant staff up to three months of unpaid leave at the time of the birth or adoption of a child, or when an immediate family member fell sick. The legislation was strongly supported by union members, particularly female activists such as Joyce Miller, but Bush was more responsive to business lobbying. Although the AFL-CIO fought hard for the bill, which would have covered almost half of all American workers, Bush "strongly objected" to federal intervention in the provision of leave.[22] In 1990 Bush also rejected efforts to allow federal and postal workers the right to choose to participate in political activities after hours, even stopping a compromise proposal from becoming law. Throughout this period, AFL-CIO leaders also knew that the president would veto any legislation that banned permanent striker replacements. On all of these issues, Bush sided with employers.[23]

There were major differences between the administration and the AFL-CIO over trade. Crucially, the North American Free Trade Agreement—which would later have a damaging impact on many unions—originated in the Reagan-Bush era. In the closing days of the Reagan administration, the president had signed a free trade deal with conservative Canadian prime minister Brian Mulroney. The AFL-CIO, along with the Canadian labor movement, opposed the agreement, arguing that it privileged the interests of "investment and services" and threatened jobs, especially in manufacturing. Undeterred, Bush now looked to build on the pact. In the spring of 1990, he initiated discussions with Mexico about an ambitious free trade agreement. The proposal was strongly pushed by Mexican president Carlos Salinas de Gortari, a U.S.-educated free trader. The Bush administration also promoted free trade with great enthusiasm, drawing strength from the domestic economic recovery and world events, where officials saw the collapse of Communism in Eastern Europe as a chance to advance democracy and open markets. Hearing of the talks, in May 1990 the AFL-CIO's Executive Council spoke out: "U.S. trade with and investment in Mexico has already significantly harmed the domestic economy, and a free trade agreement will only encourage greater capital outflow from the United States, more imports from Mexico and a worsened immigration situation." At this stage, however, Bush's officials promised to consult with labor before moving forward.[24]

From the beginning, the strongest opposition within the Federation came from industrial unions, especially those in low-paying industries. According to ACTWU president Jacob Sheinkman, the proposed agreement would cause "massive job losses" in manufacturing industries, as well as health, safety, and environmental problems. By early 1991, the AFL-CIO was working with Congress to "stymie" the Bush administration's efforts to secure fast-track authority to pass the accord. The Federation was also critical of the administration's refusal to include effective workers' rights and environmental protections into the draft agreement.[25] In the end, Bush signed a proposed North American Free Trade Agreement but the Democratic-controlled Congress never endorsed it. During the Clinton presidency, this battle for approval would be bitter and intense.[26]

The AFL-CIO also had strong differences with the Bush administration over China, which was experiencing unprecedented economic growth while maintaining a Communist political system. As the Federation saw it, Bush needed to be more outspoken about Chinese violations of human rights, and stop promoting trade and investment so forcefully. In May 1990 an Executive Council resolution pulled no punches, calling Bush's China policy "morally weak and a strategic shambles." In the wake of the Tiananmen Square massacre of June 1989—when hard-line leaders used the military to kill hundreds, if not thousands, of pro-democracy demonstrators in the center of Beijing—the Federation urged Bush to take a stronger stance against "China's sins."[27] Bush, however, continued to advocate trade expansion; through engagement, he argued, the United States could push China to improve its human rights record. In 1992 the administration also repelled efforts to undermine China's Most Favored Nation trading status. As a result, corporate investment in China rose rapidly. By the end of 1992, as imports surged, the United States had an $18 billion trade deficit with the Asian power. "In some product lines," noted an Executive Council resolution, "American consumers are hard-pressed to find goods that are NOT made in China." According to the AFL-CIO, this deficit was responsible for the loss of 360,000 American jobs, many of them unionized.[28]

When it came to the striker replacement issue, Bush proved no help. Reasoning that the new president might be more sympathetic, the AFL-CIO stepped up its campaign. According to Kirkland, the need to stop strikers from being replaced was a "burning issue" that was "at the heart of the need for labor law reform." As Bush took office, both Kirkland and Donahue testified before Congress to demand an urgent ban.[29] Many affiliates, especially in the industrial sector, felt particularly strongly. "Unions view the use of permanent striker replacements as a deep injustice that will not be tolerated," summarized Bill Bywater of the Electrical Workers. Employers were using permanent replacements to break unions, leading to tragic outcomes for those involved, including loss of income and lasting psychological damage. As an AFL-CIO staffer in Georgia summarized, the issue was "a top priority for all of Organized Labor." Even some employers admitted that striker replacement gave them enormous advantages. "The balance has shifted," commented Mark A. de Bernardo of the U.S. Chamber of Commerce in 1990. "Labor's trump card in a dispute, the strike, is no longer trump."[30]

In the spring of 1989, a labor-backed bill to limit the use of strikebreakers was introduced into the House. The Executive Council was not under any illusions, noting that "a substantial amount of time and effort" would be required "to educate the members of both houses on this issue."[31] Many members of Congress were unaware of the suffering that recent strikes had caused, and they often underestimated how hard it was for replaced workers to find comparable jobs. They were also lobbied heavily by big business, which insisted that the legislation would give unions too much power. In February 1990 legislative director Robert McGlotten told the Council that it would be a "long battle" to get the legislation passed. Although the Federation's polling indicated that there was "strong public support" for a ban, Kirkland admitted that there were "not enough votes in Congress to pass striker replacement legislation or to override a veto at this time."[32]

Building congressional support was a slow process. In July the Executive Council noted that passage of the bill remained "unlikely." "This year's effort," it explained, "is aimed at building strong support for the proposed legislation and possible action in the next Congress." Running an imaginative campaign, the Federation attracted international attention by filing a formal complaint against the United States at the ILO. Lodged with the Committee on Freedom of Association, it alleged that permanent replacement violated the principles of freedom of association and undermined collective bargaining. Although the complaint process contained no sanctions, it did publicize the issue, especially as many overseas unions were shocked that American strikers could be replaced. They also worried that multinational corporations might adopt the tactic in their country.[33]

Committed to the long haul, Kirkland and Donahue authorized a costly campaign on an issue that was very important to many affiliates. By February 1991, fourteen unions had committed full-time staff to work on the campaign in "key states," and most came from the big manufacturing affiliates that still had a lot of influence.[34] As these members saw it, if the labor movement was to remain viable, workers had to have an effective right to strike. According to J. C. Rowe, a member of the Paperworkers' Union in Rome, Georgia, the striker replacement bill was the "most important" of all. "It is time we all work together to restore dignity to all workers in this Great Country," added another worker. The Executive Council also took an uncompromising stance. "The increased use of so-called 'permanent replacement' workers during strikes," it summarized in 1991, "is a direct threat to the vitality of the collective bargaining system."[35]

Labor's campaign provoked a massive backlash from business and conservative groups. Efforts were coordinated by the Alliance to Keep Americans Working, a coalition of 100 business groups and corporations that lambasted the legislation as a "strike breeder bill." While this opposition was evident throughout the country, much of it was concentrated in the South, a crucial region that had blocked other Federation-backed bills, including the labor law reform bill of 1978. By February 8, 1991, extensive work by the AFL-CIO's legislative department had secured 191 co-sponsors of H.R. 5—officially the

Anti-Striker Replacement Act—but just sixteen of these representatives came from former Confederate States (and none from the non-union heartland of the Carolinas). In contrast, there were twenty-three co-sponsors from New York alone.[36] In the South, business groups lobbied politicians relentlessly. Because unions were weak in the region, their voices were drowned out. In Georgia, for example, House Democrats such as Charles Hatcher and J. Roy Rowland received huge stacks of letters from constituents that strongly opposed the bill. Resistance came from individual corporations such as Coca-Cola and International Paper Company, as well as corporate lobby groups such as the Southeastern Poultry and Egg Association and the Georgia Poultry Association. In well-presented letters, writers argued that H.R. 5 represented a dangerous extension of union power, leading to strikes that would undermine the competitiveness of American business in a global age. "The so-called 'strike bill,'" summarized Coca-Cola general manager Wayne W. Purvis in a letter to Hatcher, "is fundamentally unfair, would be devastating to business, and would ultimately lead to more strikes."[37] "An increased number of strikes," added Hugh Sawyer, the president of Wells Fargo Armored Service Corporation, "will not bring value to our country's competitive position in the world economy." Not surprisingly, most of Georgia's Democrats voted against H.R. 5.[38]

Kirkland faced an uphill task. In July 1991, after the House passed H.R. 5 by 247–182, the legislation stalled in the Senate. In May 1992 Kirkland met with Senate Majority Leader George Mitchell, telling him that the bill must come to the Senate floor "in the immediate future." The problem was getting enough votes to end a probable Republican filibuster. Despite covert talks between AFL-CIO leaders and key senators, many legislators would not say whether they supported the bill. Crucially, the Federation knew that Bush would veto striker replacement legislation, and the House vote was well short of veto-proof.[39] Sure enough, in the summer of 1992 the bill fell victim to a Republican-led filibuster in the Senate. Union leaders blamed key southern Democrats—particularly Arkansas senators Dale Bumpers and David Pryor—for failing to vote for the bill after they had promised to do so. It was bitterly disappointing to come so close, and still fail. "We got tons and tons of signatures from, not just members of the union, but from the community too, that we *delivered* to the Congress," recalled George Kourpias, the president of the Machinists Union. "I'll never forget . . . and as usual they just sat there. . . . There again, probably some of our friends left us, and you lose."[40]

Despite the failure, the AFL-CIO pressed on, and the striker replacement issue would re-surface during the Clinton presidency. The campaign also had positive side effects, especially as it focused the Federation's attention on the plight of strikers. As a result, the AFL-CIO became more involved in affiliates' disputes, helping to avert many of the crushing defeats that had characterized the Reagan era. At the end of 1989, for example, the Executive Council noted that it had given "strong national support to strikers," serving notice to employers "that workers continue to have the courage to defend themselves and their movement." Building on these efforts, and seeking to prevent further defeats, all affiliates were now encouraged to negotiate floating "demonstration days" in their contracts, allowing other parts of the labor movement to mobilize support. Affiliates also did a better job of warning the headquarters about potential disputes, and the Federation responded by helping them much sooner than it had before.[41]

Established by Kirkland in 1989, the Strategic Approaches Committee was the main forum for helping strikers. As committee member and Federation staffer Joe Uehlein recalled, the Committee was conceived "as a way to organize better solidarity." It also provided a forum to "brainstorm ideas" when disputes occurred. The Federation was learning hard lessons from the Reagan era. In particular, workers were now encouraged to stay on their jobs, finding other ways—including corporate campaigns—of exerting leverage on their employers. "The whole idea was the strike is the company's weapon," summarized Uehlein.[42]

When workers did strike, the Committee mobilized. In one of its most successful campaigns, it coordinated support during the Pittston dispute. Although they faced long odds, the Pittston strikers were determined to resist the company's demands for "unjustified" wage and benefit concessions. With help from the labor movement, they were largely successful. The AFL-CIO's community services arm provided aid, including food, to the strikers and their families. Along with grassroots members, Federation staff got integrally involved, with many taking part in rallies and protests, including innovative civil disobedience efforts. In an unusual move for Kirkland, he traveled with several Executive Council members to Virginia and met with strikers. Perhaps drawn to its name, Kirkland visited the UMW's "Camp Solidarity," a strike headquarters that was manned by camouflaged workers. In August a T-shirted Kirkland was even arrested during a sit-in. He was part of a group of nineteen labor leaders who locked arms and sat on the steps of the Russell County courthouse, blocking the entrance. "We're with you today, we'll be

Lane Kirkland, along with future AFL-CIO Presidents Richard Trumka and John Sweeney, engaged in civil disobedience during the Pittston coal strike, 1989. Courtesy of the United Mine Workers of America.

with you tomorrow and we'll be with you all the way," Kirkland told the crowd of 1,000. In a union career spanning four decades, it was the first time he had been arrested.[43] In September miners temporarily occupied a coal-preparation plant, and on other occasions they broke civil laws to draw attention to their plight. Overseeing the Pittston campaign, UMW strategist Ken Zinn thought that it was a "momentous dispute" that represented a "turning point for the American labor movement." The strike certainly showed that unions still had muscle, especially if they were willing to embrace innovative tactics and mobilize community support. "Despite what had gone on in the country, despite having Ronald Reagan declare war on workers, you could still win a strike, that was really the importance of Pittston," recalled Richard Trumka, the UMW president during the dispute.[44]

While there was to be no broader turning point, Pittston was not an isolated success. In a range of other high-profile campaigns, the Strategic Approaches Committee helped workers resist concessions. In 1989–90, it supported Communications Workers of America (CWA) and International Brotherhood of Electrical Workers (IBEW) members in a long battle with AT&T. Even before the unions' negotiations with the telecommunications giant had begun, the Committee met with workers to discuss strategy. Resisting the company's efforts to shift health care costs to employees, the unions planned "electronic picketing," enabling supporters to boycott AT&T's long-distance services by using another carrier. The Executive Council also expressed its "full support" for the workers. Once AT&T workers went on strike, the Committee coordinated a program of support, helping the workers to maintain core protections.[45]

In other cases, the Committee helped the Federation to avoid the pattern of strike defeats that had characterized the Reagan era. "The trend started going the other way at that point," noted Trumka, recalling the period after the Pittston strike. "We started winning again." In a 1990 dispute with the *New York Daily News*, the Committee was typically energetic, working with the local unions on an "inside strategy" that brought the company back to the bargaining table. Ultimately, the five unions involved were able to secure new contracts and the paper's owners were thwarted in their efforts to hire permanent replacements. As Kirkland noted, "advance notice" was key to the outcome because it enabled the AFL-CIO to "plan and execute a program of strong, coordinated support."[46] Overseeing the Committee's work, Kirkland authorized the use of innovative tactics. In 1989, for example, he vigorously supported the CWA in strikes against three major telephone companies: Bell Atlantic, NYNEX, and Pacific Telesis. The AFL-CIO even pressed consumers to stop paying their telephone bills until the disputes, which centered around the companies' efforts to weaken health care benefits, had been settled. The tactic was effective, helping telephone workers to retain their benefits.[47]

In the summer of 1992, the Committee secured one of its biggest successes in the unlikely location of Ravenswood, West Virginia, an Ohio River town with a population of less than 4,000. The dispute began in October 1990, when the Ravenswood Aluminum Corporation locked out 1,700 workers after they opposed its demands for far-reaching concessions. In a common pattern, the Ravenswood workers had enjoyed a constructive relationship with the plant's original owners, Kaiser Aluminum, but when Kaiser was bought out in the late 1980s, the new owners downsized the workforce and took on the union. Working together, the United Steelworkers and AFL-CIO hit back with an extensive corporate campaign. With the Strategic Approaches Committee integrally involved, labor staffers researched the company's new owners, uncovering—with the help of a private investigator—a complex chain of holding companies that were ultimately controlled by Marc Rich, an international metals trader and fugitive from U.S. law. Rich became the target of an imaginative union campaign that led to picketing in twenty-two countries and five continents. "We were in his face everywhere, we were costing him real money, and real deals," recalled staffer Joe Uehlein, who was closely involved in the effort. In the course of these activities, the Ravenswood workers, many of whom had never traveled out of the Ohio River Valley, now visited Czechoslovakia, the Netherlands, Romania, Switzerland, and Venezuela. Featuring a giant, ten-foot-high puppet of labor icon Mother Jones, along with a smaller puppet of Marc Rich, the picketing provided memorable street theater and secured press attention. Becoming symbols of the campaign, the puppets were made and manned by theater students from Antioch College in Ohio. Eventually, the pressure on the company told, and the workers got their jobs back, maintained important benefits, and saved their union. According to scholars Tom Juravich and Kate Bronfenbrenner, the Ravenswood campaign suggested that a "revival of American labor" might be possible if similar tactics were used elsewhere. "That's often pointed to as one of the successes of this era," agreed Uehlein. "When those workers, after being locked out for two years, literally marched through town and retook over that mill, it was big."[48]

Some of the elements that had made the Ravenswood campaign a success were repeated elsewhere. International cooperation, for instance, was a key feature of the Pittston fight. In 1989 a delegation from the International Confederation of Free Trade Unions came to the United States to support the Pittston strikers. On their travels, the delegation met with Secretary of Labor Dole, as well as congressional leaders and Pittston CEO Paul Douglas. The effort reflected a change of emphasis for the ICFTU, which had traditionally assisted unions in developing countries. As general secretary John Vandereken explained, increasing attacks on unions in the industrialized world had produced a "new phase" in the confederation's activities.[49] International cooperation, as well as detailed research into corporate weak points, also led to other victories. In 1989 the Oil and Chemical Workers prevailed in a long struggle against German chemical giant BASF, which had locked out workers at its plant in Geismar, Louisiana, in an effort to cut wages, reduce benefits, and contract out jobs. With assistance from the AFL-CIO, workers hit back with an effective campaign that forged bonds with unions in other countries, particularly West Germany. Kirkland helped the international effort, writing to German chemical union I. G. Chemie and appealing for "substantial assistance" in settling the dispute. In addition, labor strategists exposed the company's record of environmental problems, forging new alliances with community members and environmental activists in the process. According to Richard Donaldson, the plant's former industrial relations manager, the union's environmental campaign was "extremely clever" and a "big, big nuisance." The AFL-CIO was upbeat, viewing the BASF settlement as "a hopeful augury for the decade of the '90s."[50]

Refuting the bleak headlines of the Reagan era, both the BASF and Ravenswood disputes showed that American workers still had plenty of fight in them. During the twenty-month Ravenswood lockout, only seventeen of 1,700 union members crossed the picket line. At BASF, workers from a southern "right-to-work" state also held firm, ensuring that the company eventually recalled all of those it had locked out. It also agreed to a new contract that gave workers a wage hike and maintained their health coverage. When this militancy was supported by intelligent corporate campaigns, labor could win. The cost of these victories was, however, considerable; the Ravenswood campaign had a price tag of over $5 million, while labor spent more than $3.5 million during the BASF dispute, much of it on benefits for the locked out workers. In the Pittston strike, the UMW put its entire treasury on the line in order to win. Clearly, the Federation and its affiliates could not afford to run such campaigns very often.[51]

As the Reagan years had highlighted, moreover, determined corporations could still break unions, and labor law remained heavily stacked in companies' favor. Despite labor's success in these international campaigns, globalization was quietly undermining the jobs and working conditions of millions of Americans. Away from the headlines at Ravenswood and Pittston, workers from coast to coast were accepting job cuts and poorer conditions with a mixture of resignation and bitterness. The challenges for the AFL-CIO remained immense.

In the spring and summer of 1990, some of these problems were evident during a bitter and violent dispute between Greyhound Bus Company and the Amalgamated Transit Union. Again responding quickly, the Strategic Approaches Committee coordinated a "program of assistance" to union members, who fought a lengthy battle that highlighted how hard it remained to win strikes. With Greyhound facing increasing competition from both low-cost airlines and Amtrak, the dispute centered on the company's determination to hold down costs, particularly wages. Even before the strike had begun, the Industrial Union Department carried out detailed research into Greyhound, identifying potential weak spots. After March 1, 1990, when over 6,000 union members voted to strike, the Committee provided picket line support, while the Department of Community Services organized food banks and personal counseling referrals. The AFL-CIO also worked in Congress to bring pressure on the company, attracting 160 House sponsors to a resolution that asked managers to resume contract negotiations.[52] All these efforts, however, could not stop the Greyhound strikers from being replaced, and the Federation struggled to get their jobs back. Frustrated, some strikers threatened or attacked the substitute drivers, who were promised top rates of pay after just a few weeks' training. A year after the end of the dispute, Greyhound was in bankruptcy and most of the former strikers had not been re-hired. Many, noted the *New York Times*, felt "forgotten." In 1993, however, the AFL-CIO helped to secure an agreement by Greyhound to pay more than $20 million in back pay to striking drivers. Overall, the Federation had confirmed that it had become more proactive in helping its members during industrial disputes. Without a ban on permanent replacements, however, there was only so much it could do.[53]

Similar lessons were driven home during a major dispute at Eastern Airlines. Once one of the "Big Four" domestic airlines, Eastern struggled to compete after deregulation occurred in the late 1970s. In 1985 airline magnate Frank Lorenzo bought Eastern, precipitating conflict with a unionized workforce that resisted his cost-cutting efforts. Lorenzo also angered workers by selling many of Eastern's most profitable assets, including its reservations system and many of its gates, routes, and aircraft, for a low price to his Continental Airlines and Texas Air operations. On March 4, 1989, a strike began after the Machinists rejected the company's demands for major contract concessions. The IAM, which had bargained for over seventeen months with Eastern's management, wanted the dispute to be referred to a Presidential Emergency Board, but Lorenzo refused to accept this. As a result, pilots and flight attendants also walked off their jobs. Less than a week later, Eastern filed for reorganization under federal bankruptcy laws.[54] Pointing out that they had already given up a lot, workers took a stand. They objected to Lorenzo's asset-stripping, and insisted that his concessionary demands were excessive. "The employees of Eastern built this airline through years of hard work, and now we have the choice of watching Lorenzo tear it down, or take a 50% pay cut," summarized employee Clay Warnock. "How many Americans do you think can stand a 50% pay cut?"[55]

Once again, the AFL-CIO was integrally involved in the Eastern dispute. Well before the strike had begun, the Strategic Approaches Committee launched its "Fairness at Eastern" campaign, which featured picketing at Eastern's headquarters in Miami, as well as rallies and handbills in other key cities. Seeing the strike as an opportunity to demonstrate its opposition to "rampant corporate greed," the AFL-CIO offered extensive support. Kirkland got involved, even castigating Lorenzo as the "Typhoid Mary of union busters in the transportation industry."[56]

Above all, the Federation provided vital financial aid. Within the first two months of the walkout, the "Fairness at Eastern" fund collected $1.2 million from union members. By August, contributions had risen to $1.55 million, of which $1.42 million was "distributed directly" to the strikers. The Federation contributed $150,000, while the rest came from members. This mobilization of support was significant. According to Strategic Approaches Committee Chairman Lynn Williams, the campaign "helped demonstrate to the public, the media and employers that trade union solidarity is a potent force." In addition, union members had experienced the labor movement's power. The Federation's support—especially its commitment to stay with the workers for the long haul—also boosted the strike's effectiveness. Two months after the walkout had begun, labor leaders claimed that Eastern was running fewer than 10 percent of its pre-strike flights. The AFL-CIO was also able to isolate Lorenzo and win backing from a range of public figures, including Richard Gephardt, Jesse Jackson, Michael Dukakis, and Newt Gingrich, the conservative congressman whose district included Atlanta's International Airport, an Eastern hub.[57]

The long dispute at Eastern, however, exposed clear divisions between the Bush administration and the AFL-CIO, reinforcing the limits of any détente. On November 21, 1989, just a week after addressing the Federation's convention, Bush vetoed H.R. 1231, a bipartisan bill that would have established an advisory commission to investigate the Eastern dispute and recommend how it could be resolved. As presidential adviser Roger B. Porter explained, Bush believed that labor-management disputes should be "worked out by the parties themselves, without intervention by or recourse to the President or Congress." Bush saw "no justification" for legislation that mandated government intervention, arguing instead that the "evenhanded" bankruptcy courts would protect the interests of both sides.[58]

In making his decision, Bush ignored appeals from workers, who argued that Lorenzo was using the bankruptcy laws to destroy the unions—and profit from it.[59] Many were angry, especially as Congress's failure to override the veto allowed Eastern to keep selling off its assets. "President Bush and the head of the Department of Transportation . . . have said something about not wanting to get involved in a local labor dispute," wrote Lowell Dietz, an Eastern pilot from Georgia. "I can understand and agree with that. But if this is a local labor dispute, then the Titanic was a boating accident." According to

Dietz, the dispute showed that powerful individuals could "dismantle a company with total disregard for the effect on the lives of the people who made the company what it is." Addressing the Executive Council, Kirkland was also disappointed. The Eastern strike, he commented, involved a "major transportation carrier," justifying national intervention.[60]

The strike ultimately exposed how worker militancy and AFL-CIO support was not enough to defeat a determined employer. It also showed how broader economic forces, particularly deregulation and the increasing fluidity of capital, were encouraging employers to cut labor costs and take on unions. Able to hire permanent replacements, Eastern fought back. In July 1990, after the bankruptcy court appointed a trustee to manage the company, Eastern's managers insisted on keeping the strikebreakers. As the Executive Council summarized in February 1991, the ability of the company to hire permanent replacements had been the "key factor" in preventing a "fair settlement."[61] Like many other workers who went on strike in the 1980s and early 1990s, the Eastern staff paid a heavy price, especially as the bankruptcy meant that they did not receive much-needed benefits, including severance pay. In 1991, moreover, Eastern was liquidated, leaving staff to fend for themselves. Many suffered. "We cannot find jobs," wrote former Eastern employee Joan O'Rourke in June 1991. "Our unemployment checks will stop in July. Many of us are left without health or life insurance and by now are very close to losing our homes. Many of us are in the 50's age group and are helplessly watching everything we have worked so long and hard for slowly disintegrate before our eyes." Still, Federation staffers such as Stewart Acuff, who had helped run the "Fairness at Eastern" campaign, stressed that labor had achieved something through the "historic" mass mobilization, especially in broader terms. "After five or six years of assault," unions were "figuring out how to defend themselves and fight back . . . fighting more effectively, and learning how to organize again." This was clearly an improvement from the dark days of the Reagan era, when the Federation had been slower to help replaced strikers.[62]

In several other areas, Kirkland secured important gains. The president's unfailing efforts to bring unaffiliated unions into the Federation bore particular fruit. Following months of preparatory work, in May 1989 the Brotherhood of Locomotive Engineers formally joined the AFL-CIO. In August the Writers Guild of America, East, which represented writers, editors, and producers at major broadcasters, as well as some staff in the movie industry, was also brought into the Federation. While the Guild was a small union, many of its members were articulate and well-connected. The Guild was soon followed by the United Transportation Union, another relatively small affiliate.[63]

More significantly, in October the UMW voted to affiliate with the AFL-CIO, ending nearly fifty years of self-imposed exile. In 1947, UMW president John L. Lewis had famously left the AFL by slipping a brief note to its president, William Green: "Green—AF of L. We disaffiliate. 12-12-47. Lewis." Two years earlier, Lewis—who was known for being free-spirited and stubborn—also pulled the UMW out of the CIO. In 1989 Richard Trumka mimicked the style of Lewis, letting Kirkland know of his decision in a note that read, "Lane, We affiliate. Rich." At the time, Trumka needed the Federation's support in the Pittston dispute, and Kirkland had also been quietly cultivating the UMW president. Trumka also stressed the need for unity. "A divided labor movement *never* was a good idea," he recalled, "but in a global economy it's even a worse idea, and so . . . I brought the Mineworkers back into the AFL-CIO." According to the *Washington Post*, the affiliation was a "major victory" for Kirkland, who had made great strides in uniting the House of Labor. Now, only two major unions—the United Electrical Workers and the National Education Association—remained outside the Federation. The re-affiliation of the UMW clearly meant a great deal to Kirkland, who called it "one of the greatest pleasures I've had in the trade union movement." As well as bringing unions into the Federation, moreover, Kirkland worked to discourage infighting and rivalry among affiliates. Encouraging union mergers, he also took an active role in using internal machinery to resolve jurisdictional disputes. By the early 1990s, the former barriers between craft and industrial unions were breaking down, and most national trade unions were becoming amalgamated organizations that enrolled workers well outside of their original jurisdictions.[64]

In the Bush years, the ongoing "Union Yes" campaign also improved labor's public image. In February 1989, for example, the Executive Council reported that there was "increasing public recognition and comprehension of the 'Union Yes' logo and the goals of the campaign." Campaign director Larry Kirkman cited independent polls that showed that public perceptions of the labor movement had "improved significantly" since the "Union Yes" advertisements had been broadcast. Featuring actor Edward James Olmos, who was better-known as Lieutenant Martin Castillo in the television series *Miami Vice*, new commercials ran in the spring and fall of 1989, including Spanish language spots. These messages helped to embed the program in the public's consciousness. The simplicity of the "Union Yes" slogan was a masterstroke, and it was backed up by a catchy theme song. Even President Bush joked that he sang the ditty in the shower.[65] In November 1989, AFL-CIO leaders persuaded Lech Walesa to record a "Union Yes" advertisement for national broadcast. It was a significant moment, and many affiliates made use of the recording in their grassroots work. With the commercials proving effective, in May 1990 the Executive Council authorized an extra $4 million to be spent on broadcast advertising.[66]

Kirkland was keen to build on this work. In 1989 the George Meany Memorial Archives began to publish *Labor's Heritage*, a quarterly journal that attracted concise but high-quality work in labor history. Widely placed in libraries and bookstores, the journal—which was beautifully illustrated—helped to improve the public's awareness of labor issues.[67] Housing the AFL-CIO's papers, as well as a rich body of other labor-related material, the archives also established themselves as a premier location for the study of working-class history. Like the "Union Yes" commercials, however, the Meany archives were costly to fund; in 1989 the GMMA's annual budget was $2.45 million, and the figure rose to $3.92 million in 1993. These expenses later became problematic.[68]

Many of the "Union Yes" commercials concentrated on the need for health care reform, a campaign that gathered momentum in these years. Throughout the 1980s and early 1990s, as the economy moved away from manufacturing and toward service sector jobs—many of them part-time—the percentage of Americans without health coverage increased. According to the Census Bureau, between February 1990 and September 1992, a quarter of all Americans, or some 60 million people, had no health insurance for at least one month. Along with other progressive groups, the AFL-CIO was at the forefront of a growing movement that pressed for reform. "The health care tragedy," Kirkland told Congress in April 1991, "is no longer confining itself to the fringes of our society. It's now striking at millions of solid, working, taxpaying families—people who are the backbone of our country, who do their level best to pay their bills and meet their obligations."[69]

In 1990–91 the Federation's Health Care Committee coordinated a yearlong program to raise public awareness of its "strong support for a national health insurance program." For labor the issue had particular urgency, as employers were increasingly shifting health care costs onto workers, triggering disputes. In February 1991 Richard Trumka told the Executive Council that "as many as three-quarters of the strikes that have occurred in recent years have been over health care issues." At this meeting, the Council pledged to continue a grassroots effort to mobilize members and win national health care reform.[70] The Federation was willing to fund an "all-out lobbying effort" to secure its long-held goal of a social insurance national health care program. In the early 1990s, after detailed work by staff, the AFL-CIO formulated proposals for this program to be administered by a national commission of consumers, labor, management, government, and providers. Working largely behind the scenes, the Federation's staff pushed for the adoption of these proposals.[71]

There were other important efforts in the health care area. During the Bush years, SEIU president John Sweeney served on the National Leadership Commission on Health Care, a bipartisan group that investigated the health care system and sought solutions to improve access and care. Beginning the fight for legislative change, the Federation also formulated a "statement of principles" that secured "widespread attention" in Congress. Senate Majority Leader George Mitchell even made health care reform a top priority.[72] Although the Bush administration—and its powerful corporate supporters—remained hostile, the AFL-CIO's campaign prepared the ground for a major reform effort during the Clinton presidency. As Mitchell commented in early 1993, the AFL-CIO had played a "constructive role . . . in working toward comprehensive health care reform even in the face of the Bush administration's resistance to genuine reform."[73]

The AFL-CIO launched other important—and little-known—initiatives in these years. Keen to celebrate the tenth anniversary of Solidarity Day, in 1991 Kirkland organized a mass march in Washington, DC. The protest was needed, he told his colleagues, to dramatize a number of issues, especially striker replacements and health care reform. It would also highlight the right of working people around the globe to join unions of their choosing. As he had in 1981, Kirkland placed John Perkins in charge of the event. This time, however, it was planned for August 31, the Saturday before Labor Day. Each affiliate was instructed to appoint a coordinator to work with the Federation on their union's participation. "It will be important," Kirkland warned the Executive Council, "to match or surpass the 1981 attendance." At its meeting in February 1991, the Council duly sent out a call to the labor movement "to gather in Washington once again to show its solidarity—to demonstrate its continuing commitment to achieving a better life for the working people of this country."[74]

Perkins remained an adept organizer. Under his watchful eye, the Federation chartered 3,500 buses, using them to transport around 200,000 participants, while affiliated groups chartered trains and planes. Union members again flocked to Washington, with many traveling through the night to be there.

Some were motivated by the desire to show their support for a striker re-placement ban. Others cited the need for health care reform, or wanted to show the nation that the labor movement was alive and well. "The union has showed its strength today, brother," commented one participant, summariz-ing the mood. The *Washington Post's* headline—"Labor Sends Politicians a Message Hundreds of Thousands Strong"—highlighted that this was another mobilizing success. Pictures in the *AFL-CIO News* showed a huge body of marchers filling Constitution Avenue as far as the eye could see, a formidable sight. Press reports commented on the healthy levels of participation by racial minorities and women, highlighting that the labor movement was changing. Apart from the labor movement, marchers were drawn from a coalition of more than 180 religious, environmental, civil rights, and civic groups. Again, the level of organization was striking. Perkins thought of every detail, arranging for bus parking at key Metro stations, using union marshals to direct the crowd, and lining the route with portable toilets. Impressively, police reported no arrests on the day.[75]

Although not quite as high as in 1981, turnout was still impressive. The U.S. Park Police estimated that 250,000 people had taken part, while the AFL-CIO put the number at 325,000. Just as he had ten years earlier, Kirkland addressed the large crowd on the Mall. "We're here to remind our elected representa-tives that they were put there to serve, not the faceless marketplace, but real people," he declared. The most rousing speech of the day, however, came from Jesse L. Jackson. Raising his fist in the air as a symbol of solidarity, Jackson called on Bush to "come home now . . . [and] rebuild America." The speech struck a chord with marchers, whose signs called for greater attention to do-mestic issues rather than foreign policy.[76]

Despite the turnout, the march struggled to have the political impact that Kirkland hoped for. This was partly because it was overlooked by much of the media, which was remarkable given its size.[77] The outcome showed that labor still needed to work on improving its public image, and it also suggested that some journalists saw unions as a declining force that lacked the power to back up their legislative demands. When reporters did cover the protest, they often focused on labor's decline, rather than the political issues it was trying to raise. In a detailed piece on the march in the *Washington Post*, for example, Paul Ruffins failed to mention health care reform or striker replacements, in-stead debating whether organized labor could rebuild. "Capitalizing on the changing climate will take creativity and flexibility," he noted, "and critics claim unions are ossified." The protest, noted another reporter, came after a decade in which unions had suffered "devastating membership losses." For participants, this was not what the march was about.[78]

AFL-CIO leaders also made some tactical mistakes, especially in the timing of the rally. Unlike the first Solidarity Day, which was deliberately held when the weather was cooler, the 1991 protest occurred on a hot day in late August. It was easily brushed off by President Bush, who was at his summer home in Maine, and by Congress, which was enjoying a lengthy recess. "I'm sorry no politicians are in town today to see us," admitted marcher Jacky Leach, a UAW member. "They're all on vacation in their nice houses, while we've seen all these people walking the streets out of jobs here." The heat also dampened enthusiasm. After enduring several hours of Washington, DC's notoriously high summer humidity, hundreds of marchers were treated at the scene for heat exhaustion, and at least sixty were hospitalized. "We can't keep as many ambulances in service as people passing out," admitted one National Park Service official. Thus, reports concentrated on the weather as much as the marchers' message.[79] Even within the Executive Council, the holding of the march over a summer holiday weekend, when Washington, DC, was usually quiet, was questioned by AFSCME president Gerald McEntee. Kirkland, however, insisted that many union presidents had wanted to link the march to Labor Day. He also pointed out that August 28, 1991, marked the twenty-eighth anniversary of the March on Washington.[80]

Overall, the final Solidarity Day was a partial success. It helped to inspire Democratic voters ahead of the presidential election, which Bush was predicted to win at the time. Although the president paid little attention to the march, protesters who proclaimed that they were "kicking Bush out in '92" ultimately had the last laugh. While the earlier Solidarity Days had secured more press coverage, they had not prevented Reagan's reelection.[81] As the Atlanta Labor Council summarized in a subsequent document, there were also weaknesses. Held when "few politicians were in Washington," the march had "made no lasting impression on the country's decision-makers." In motivating participants, however, the march was an "unqualified success." Building on this, the Atlanta Council wanted to establish a permanent picket of the White House and Capitol until legislators agreed to solve the health care crisis. Although he considered these proposals, Kirkland refused to endorse them. After affirming his ability to organize mass marches, he again pulled away from extended civil disobedience.[82]

Solidarity Day was not, however, the only mass march of this era. On April 28, 1989, the AFL-CIO organized a large celebration of Workers'

Memorial Day, an event that quickly cemented itself in the labor calendar. Before being adopted by the AFL-CIO, Workers' Memorial Day had originated in Canada a few years earlier. In the United States, the Transport Workers Union (TWU) and the Amalgamated Clothing and Textile Workers—whose members suffered a high rate of workplace injuries and deaths—were particularly keen supporters. Indeed, the idea of marking the day in the United States was suggested by George McDonald, an activist-oriented TWU leader in New York City who wanted to take the issue of workers' safety out of conferences and into "the streets." By coincidence, the Canadian Workers' Memorial Day was commemorated on April 28, the same date that the Occupational Safety and Health Act had gone into effect in the United States, helping the idea to take off. Highlighting the need for the commemoration, the AFL-CIO stressed that 10,000 American workers died on the job each year, while another 50,000 to 100,000 died from occupational diseases resulting from exposure to toxic substances such as asbestos. In 1989 local unions, state federations, and local central bodies from across the country sponsored memorial services and rallies to publicize these tragic facts. Overseeing the efforts, the Federation's Department of Occupational Safety and Health provided advice and materials kits to grassroots coordinators.[83]

The first Workers' Memorial Day was a success, especially as it was a new initiative. In 1989 more than 100 activities—primarily rallies, memorial services, and vigils—were held in forty-four states. In addition, newspaper and radio spots were placed in major cities. According to AFL-CIO safety and health director Margaret "Peg" Seminario, commemorations were deliberately decentralized. They provided "a way to bring focus to these issues" at the grassroots level, and were especially important in communities that had suffered serious industrial accidents. Here, they also provided a sense of closure to families and coworkers of those killed. In a broader sense, the AFL-CIO carried out important work, as it was the only mass-membership national organization to consistently concentrate on workplace safety. It repeatedly highlighted how common workplace accidents were; in the early 1990s, for instance, around 70,000 Americans were permanently disabled in workplace accidents each year, while 6.2 million workers were injured. Occurring incrementally, however, most accidents received little or no reportage. Illustrating this point, public awareness—and media coverage—of Workers' Memorial Day remained limited. The workplace, summarized the *AFL-CIO News* in 1990, was America's "forgotten environment."[84]

In subsequent years, Workers' Memorial Day was commemorated with "hundreds of events" at the local and state level, again coordinated by the

Department of Occupational Safety and Health. In a number of locations where groups of workers had been killed in workplace accidents—including Spokane, Washington, Harrisburg, Pennsylvania, and Pasadena, Texas—the AFL-CIO also oversaw the erection and dedication of permanent memorials. These efforts meant a lot to relatives and community members. Workers' Memorial Day also allowed labor leaders to connect with members, as well as with nonunion workers.[85]

The Federation also used the event to carry out lobbying. "It was always important to have both pieces," explained Seminario, "remembering those who had died and been hurt, but we've got to change things . . . we need to tie this to activism in our goals." On several occasions, the Safety and Health Department brought victims of workplace accidents—or their surviving relatives—to Washington, DC, accompanying them on personal visits to members of Congress. On September 12, 1991, it was the AFL-CIO that transported workers from the Imperial Foods factory in Hamlet, North Carolina to Washington, DC, where they testified before the House Education and Labor Committee. Just a week earlier, twenty-five workers at the chicken processing factory had been killed in a fire because they were trapped behind locked doors. The Federation helped to expose that the Imperial workers had not received any safety training, and that they were afraid to complain in case they lost their jobs. The "awful truth," Seminario told Congress, was that such conditions were not unusual in the United States. This kind of publicity helped to maintain funding for OSHA, especially after the Republican takeover of Congress in 1994. Partly as a result of Seminario's efforts, Workers' Memorial Day began to be observed in other countries, and in 2001 it received official recognition from the ILO. A number of countries, including Brazil, Canada, Spain, Thailand, and the UK, adopted the day formally by law. The AFL-CIO had helped to make this possible.[86]

In another important move, Kirkland oversaw the establishment of the Organizing Institute. Designed to "expand the AFL-CIO's services to affiliates engaged in planning and starting organizing campaigns," the Institute again showed that the Federation was learning from the Reagan era. The idea originated with Richard Bensinger, a young activist who had been an organizer with the Steelworkers' Union for fifteen years. After moving to Washington, DC, Bensinger—with support from several other unions, particularly ACTWU and the UFCW—proposed the idea of an organizing institute to the AFL-CIO's leadership. "We needed a way to recruit more organizers," he recalled, "because there were far many more union representatives than . . . organizers."[87]

Although Bensinger remembered that Kirkland and Donahue were "initially unsure," in time they embraced the idea. In May 1989, following a recommendation from the Organization and Field Services Committee, the Executive Council approved the establishment of the Institute, which was funded by the AFL-CIO but separately incorporated. Seeing the Institute as a way to "change the culture of the labor movement," separate incorporation was Bensinger's idea. Heading the Committee, John Sweeney was a vocal advocate, but Kirkland was also supportive. Operating out of Washington, DC, the Institute was responsible for the recruitment and training of new organizers and the development of associate membership programs. The move was partly a response to decline. As the Council minutes noted, board members recognized the need to help affiliates organize at a time when "antiunion activity" was on the rise. Later, Donahue also told the Council that "membership losses in some sectors help to underscore the need for the growing emphasis on organizing."[88] In recognition of his key role, Bensinger became the Institute's first director. He later paid credit to Kirkland, stating that despite his "conservative" image the AFL-CIO leader had "showed a willingness to experiment" by setting up the Institute. "I remember when I asked him about this, he kind of just laughed, and said, 'Well, why not, we've got to try and do things.' "[89]

The Organizing Institute began at an opportune time. At the biennial convention in November 1989, Sweeney related that there had been an upturn in organizing. "A funny thing has happened as we've reached the end of this decade," he declared. "Not only are we still alive and kicking, but workers are organizing now more than ever in recent years." Helped by the Organizing Institute, and frustrated that their wages were not rising even though the economy was strong, workers were turning to unions. "I don't have enough organizers to keep up," commented Dan Kuschke of the Hotel Employees and Restaurant Employees Union. "I'm hiring." Many unions were indeed getting more serious about organizing, taking on younger, energetic staff with college degrees. On the ground, important breakthroughs had occurred. Sweeney pointed to successes in signing up a wide range of workers, including clerical staff at Harvard, janitors in Los Angeles, textile workers in the South, and government employees in Washington, DC. Covering some 3,300 secretaries and technicians, the Harvard campaign made effective use of radio advertising built around the "Union Yes" slogan. Despite determined opposition from university management—including the use of "captive audience" meetings—AFSCME prevailed. The union's message, "It's not anti-Harvard to be pro-union," was crucial in neutralizing the university's hostility.[90]

Hopes were raised by such victories. The Harvard victory, in particular, secured a lot of press coverage. According to the *Minneapolis Star Tribune*, the vote symbolized "what might be a turning point in the organizing fortunes of the nation's labor unions after a 10-year slump." Other observers were optimistic. Sociologist Dan Clawson even suggested that the victory might presage labor's "next upsurge." In 1991 the organizing discussion at the AFL-CIO convention in Detroit was upbeat. Bucking a "hostile environment," workers were forming unions, and affiliates were "responding" to their concerns.[91]

Importantly, unions began to see success in larger units. The American Federation of Government Employees organized over 1,000 workers at the Social Security Administration, while the UFCW won important victories at Singleton Foods in Florida and Farbest Foods in Indiana. There were also significant breakthroughs in the South; the UAW even organized a Mack Truck plant in South Carolina, a nonunion hotbed. Overall, despite employer hostility and weak labor laws, the AFL-CIO was more positive about organizing than it had been for a decade. In 1990 one report by the Committee on Organizing claimed that unions were "beginning to throw off the widespread pessimism of the 1970s and 1980s." Steps had been taken to increase organizing effectiveness, and the decline in activity "had been reversed." The establishment of the Organizing Institute, the "heroic example" of workers in Eastern Europe, and the increased solidarity that the labor movement had displayed in the strikes at Pittston, Eastern Airlines, and AT&T had all contributed to the change. The Union Privilege Benefit Programs had also been used by affiliates to attract members. Finally, unions were doing a better job of reaching minorities, women, and immigrants, groups that were generally responsive to their message.[92]

Data backed up this optimism. In 1992 the number of NLRB representation elections was the largest since 1985, and unions won 49.9 percent of them, up more than three percent in a year. These gains even continued when the economy weakened. The Organizing Institute helped to secure this turnaround. Between 1989 and 1995, the Institute's budget more than tripled, and it took on new activities, including serving as a consultant to affiliates during organizing drives.[93] Adopting "Organize: Yes We Can!" as its "battle cry," the Institute had brought new energy to the field. Emphasizing the gains, an upbeat Sweeney called the creation of the Organizing Institute "one of the most promising initiatives in recent years." He urged all affiliates to support it.[94]

These successes, however, need to be kept in context. The Federation's public reports, particularly at conventions, tended to be positive. Although organizing had picked up, there was still a long way to go, and it was not just external opposition that was a problem. In August 1990 just six affiliates—out of a total of more than ninety—were participating in the Institute's programs. As Bensinger recalled, there was considerable internal resistance, as just a handful of affiliates devoted at least 10 percent of their budgets to organizing.[95] With 4.5 million members in 1990, the Building and Construction Trades Department represented a powerful conservative bloc within the Federation, and its unions were slow to organize. In a 1991 convention discussion, the AFL-CIO noted the need to create an "organizing culture" among affiliates, hinting at substantial internal resistance. In addition, it was important to reduce "wasteful inter-union rivalry" in organizing, an ongoing problem. Across the Federation, moreover, it was easier to recruit staff for servicing jobs rather than as organizers. "A lot of people discovered that it was more fun to service existing locals than to go out to try to organize new ones," recalled Tom Donahue. Many organizers burnt out, as hours were long and the work demanding. The lack of success could be demoralizing, while the need to travel extensively and work long hours hurt efforts to recruit organizers with families, particularly women. Not enough organizers looked like the workers they were trying to recruit.[96]

In many cases, it also proved difficult to translate election victories into contracts, a thorny problem that the Institute did not directly address. Getting firms to sign a labor agreement was often a Herculean task. In one case, the UFCW was trying to secure a contract with Seafirst Bank more than twelve years after winning representation rights. In the South, election victories were also frequently followed by a lengthy battle to secure a contract.[97] In its private discussions, the Committee on Organizing recognized that organizing remained "arduous and costly," and only "major legislative change" would alter this. It also accepted that an appreciation of the importance of organizing was only "beginning to permeate the labor movement."[98]

In many ways, Kirkland's reforms in organizing—as in other key areas—did not go far enough. The Federation's data indicated that women were particularly keen to organize, yet efforts to recruit them were half-hearted. Joining unions at a faster rate than men, many women saw them as a way of overcoming pay disparities between the sexes. Women were also concentrated in the service sector, the fastest-growing part of the economy. In 1990, AFL-CIO economist Markley Roberts even declared that women were the key to rejuvenating the labor movement, a view that others shared.[99] At the top, however, the AFL-CIO still struggled to reflect its diverse membership. In November 1992, as the Council observed the final days of the Bush presidency, just two of its thirty-five members were women. This was at a time when women comprised

38 percent of union members. In addition, an ILO study found that just two of the Federation's ninety-five affiliates had women presidents, and that the number of women in national leadership positions had increased very little while Kirkland had been in office.[100]

Female pioneers who were elected to the Council in these years recalled the reality behind these statistics. Susan Bianchi, the president of the Association of Flight Attendants, got on the Council in 1989. She recalled the experience as both "very exciting" and "very intimidating." Meetings were "very centralized," and the leaders of the largest unions, particularly AFSCME's Gerald McEntee and SEIU's John Sweeney, tended to dominate discussions. While Bianchi felt respected by Kirkland, she recalled that her assigned seating position—right next to the AFL-CIO president—was odd. "I was probably there for photo-opportunities," she reflected, "so that when a picture of Lane was taken, that there was a female next to him, so that again it was about diversity."[101] Elected to the Council in 1992, Barbara Easterling from the Communication Workers' union agreed that it was still difficult to get more women on the body. Part of the problem was that seniority—a powerful idea in the labor movement—worked against women, who had only come into leadership positions recently. "The Council's made up usually of presidents," she noted. "And that made a big difference, there were not enough women in the titles, to come on board. And then, of course, there's all these men that are waiting for an opening to go on that board, and when the opening comes along and they want to give it to a woman, that creates a big problem, because I've been sitting there waiting: 'Why not me, what are they doing this to me for?'" Efforts to recruit racial minorities also moved slowly. In November 1991 the AFL-CIO elected its first Hispanic vice president, Jack Otero of the Transportation Communications Union. The move only came, however, following complaints from minority delegates, particularly at national conventions.[102]

Despite pressure from female activists, Kirkland remained wary of taking a stand on issues that were important to women, including child care provision and abortion. In the late 1980s, women activists, particularly Lenore Miller, began to push for legislation to improve day care provision and the availability of family leave. These areas were never a high priority for Kirkland, however, and most male leaders shared his view. According to Liz Shuler, who was starting her career in the male-dominated International Brotherhood of Electrical Workers at this time, the labor movement prioritized wages, pensions, and overtime, whereas work-family concerns were seen as "nice little side-issues."[103] In 1990 female activists were also disappointed when the AFL-CIO refused to take a stand on abortion, instead reiterating its neutrality because it feared losing members and creating divisions. While recognizing that many female members believed that abortion was a "union issue," the Federation's Committee on Reproductive Issues—which contained fifteen men and just three women—reacted cautiously.[104] At the Federation's convention a year earlier, member groups had submitted six resolutions on abortion, an unusually high number on a single issue, and all but one explicitly asserted a woman's right to choose. "I think the vast majority of union members are pro-choice," explained one delegate. Many union members wanted a clear alternative to the anti-abortion policies of the Bush administration, but despite this the Federation remained neutral. For many, Kirkland had missed another chance to place organized labor firmly on the left of the Democratic Party.[105]

Instead, Kirkland continued to concentrate on foreign affairs, a choice that many members struggled to appreciate. Determined to give the AFL-CIO a voice on the international stage, Kirkland steadfastly supported U.S. foreign policy; following the outbreak of the Persian Gulf War in early 1991, for example, he instructed the Executive Council to proclaim its "full support of our country and . . . the men and women in our armed forces" in their "courageous" efforts. There was some dissent, with Richard Trumka arguing that there should have been a more rigorous congressional debate on the war before troops were committed. The UFCW's William Wynn and the IUE's William Bywater also spoke out against the administration's continued sale of defense-related products to Iraq after its invasion of Kuwait. Following the passage of Kirkland's resolutions, however, the Council agreed with their leader's call to end debate.[106]

In international affairs this was a successful era for Kirkland, and his confidence showed. In November 1989 the Berlin Wall fell, contributing to the collapse of Communist regimes across Eastern and Central Europe. There were particularly remarkable developments in Poland; in 1990 Solidarnosc leader Lech Walesa was elected president of a free nation. Kirkland's assistant, David St. John, recalled the impact of these events on his boss. "As the Cold War ended, I think Lane felt he was in his element at that point, that things were finally happening," he stated. "We're getting free trade unions in countries that have been denied them for many years . . . it's a new day." The positive mood fed through to Solidarity Day in 1991, which celebrated the victory of workers' movements in Europe. "He felt really good," St. John summarized. At the march, it was emblematic that Kirkland abandoned his suit and wore a neat "Solidarnosc" T-shirt.[107]

The AFL-CIO could certainly take some credit for the collapse of Communism in Poland. In early 1989, an AFL-CIO delegation met with Walesa in Paris, the first time that the Solidarnosc leader had been allowed to leave Poland. At the meeting, Walesa conveyed his "deep appreciation" to the Federation for its "vital support." At an Executive Council meeting in May, Solidarnosc official Jacek Kuron also commented that the AFL-CIO had provided the "greatest help."[108] For Kirkland, however, the crowning moment came in November, when Walesa attended the AFL-CIO's convention in Washington, DC, to accept the George Meany Human Rights Award. The Federation had originally granted Walesa the award in 1981, but he had been unable to leave Poland to accept it. Eight years later, the former electrician told the convention that his organization shared a "bond of friendship" with the AFL-CIO that was "strong and enduring." He added that the democratic movement that was sweeping across his country had only occurred because of "the peaceful struggle of working people, of trade unionists like you and I." Overall, the AFL-CIO had been Solidarnosc's "most steadfast allies." As Walesa received a standing ovation, Kirkland was clearly moved. "Lech, anything I might say in response to your inspiring remarks would be superfluous," he replied quietly.[109]

There were also victories in South Africa, where the Federation had long spoken out against apartheid and called for the release of Nelson Mandela. When Mandela was finally freed in February 1990, and restrictions on trade unions lifted, the Executive Council was upbeat. Mandela, it noted, was "a living symbol of historic proportions of the courage, the will, and the determination of the people of South Africa to end racial inequality." The Federation added, however, that more needed to be done. In particular, the South African government needed to stop its state of emergency, release all political prisoners, and repeal every part of the apartheid legislation. Until these changes were made, the Federation supported sanctions against South Africa.[110]

Mandela was aware of the AFL-CIO's importance. In July the iconic leader addressed the Executive Council in Chicago, acknowledging the role that the Federation had played in undermining apartheid. "The fact that today we are close to the day of liberation is due very largely to the support that we have received here," Mandela told his audience. For many Council members, and especially for Kirkland—who for once displayed a full smile—it was another proud moment. Partly funded by unions, Mandela's visit boosted morale and secured positive press coverage. At its next meeting, the Council pledged to continue its efforts to end apartheid, and urged affiliates to cooperate closely with their South African counterparts.[111]

Lane Kirkland and Lech Walesa, 1989. Courtesy of Special Collections, University of Maryland Libraries.

Despite the common ground that Kirkland had forged with President Bush in foreign affairs, and despite improved relations domestically, overall these years were still difficult ones for the AFL-CIO. Decline had been slowed, not stopped. Key legislative priorities—particularly labor law changes and health care reform—had not been enacted. While it was some improvement over the Reagan years, the partial détente of the Bush years was ultimately unsatisfactory, especially when the chance came to regain control of the White House. Rather than détente—the key feature of these years—after more than a decade of Republican presidencies, most in the labor movement wanted real change, and genuine reform.

When the General Board met in September 1992, they were united in their determination to secure political change. In order to minimize potential support for the Republicans, delegates stressed the damage caused by Reagan and Bush, and deliberately linked the two administrations together. For twelve years, summarized Kirkland, workers' voices had "fallen on deaf ears at the White House." The labor movement, added Gerald McEntee, had been through "twelve long years in which American workers had been beaten and battered." The "dishonor roll" of the Reagan-Bush years stretched from PATCO all the way through to the devastating disputes at Eastern Airlines and Greyhound. "The list goes on and on," declared McEntee. While big industrial unions had suffered the most, white collar workers had not been spared. According to Randy Babbit, the president of the Air Line Pilots Association (ALPA), "the last twelve years of Reagan/Bush has taken a devastating toll on the people I represent, on the airline industry in general, and on this country." Self-consciously traditional, even "conservative," the ALPA had once supported the Republicans, but not anymore. As the election approached, the AFL-CIO stood united. Emerging as the front-runner in the Democratic primaries, forty-six-year-old William Jefferson Clinton was labor's hope to deliver a new political dawn.[112]

CHAPTER SEVEN

He's on Our Side?

Hope and Betrayal in the Clinton Years

After enduring the Reagan-Bush presidencies—dubbed the "years of devastation" by the *AFL-CIO News*—the Federation expected a lot from Bill Clinton. Straight after key Democratic primaries, in which the "Comeback Kid" was able to secure unlikely victories over rivals Jerry Brown and Paul Tsongas, the Federation swung behind Clinton's candidacy. In May 1992 it formally endorsed the emerging front-runner, arguing that he offered a "new start" after a long period of Republican dominance. The Federation noted that the Arkansas governor believed in universal health care, the right to strike without being permanently replaced, and "fair trade"—all key priorities that would now be addressed. Overall, Clinton offered "hope to working Americans seeking to rebuild their communities—be they in the inner cities or the small towns—from the devastation of job loss and official neglect."[1]

During Clinton's crucial first term, these hopes were largely dashed. To be sure, Clinton did much more for the AFL-CIO than his Republican predecessors. Consulting closely with the Federation, he passed the Family and Medical Leave Act, issued a reemployment order for the former PATCO strikers, and appointed more sympathetic officials to the NLRB. Despite these important achievements, Clinton's administration failed on the three key issues that the Federation had identified. It was unable to pass health care reform or workplace fairness legislation, even though support from the AFL-CIO helped both campaigns. Rather than ensuring fair trade, moreover, the administration pushed through the North American Free Trade Agreement (NAFTA) with considerable zeal, largely ignoring the labor movement's concerns in the process. In an effort to stop NAFTA, the Federation launched an unprecedented campaign among its members, but the president's commitment to the agreement won the day. Demoralized after this defeat, the AFL-CIO failed to campaign sufficiently in the 1994 midterm elections, helping the Republicans to make stunning gains. The GOP's clean sweep of Congress destroyed hopes for progressive reform, and led to internal criticism of Kirkland's leadership. After the election, recalled staffer Gerry Shea, many union presidents had a "strong sense" that "something was really

wrong." As a result, Kirkland was overthrown as AFL-CIO president, bringing his eight-term presidency to an ignominious end.[2]

When Clinton had first run for the presidency, it had all been so different.
As the chances of a Clinton victory increased—partly because of ineffective
campaigning by President Bush—the AFL-CIO united behind the challenger. At a packed General Board meeting in September 1992, securing
the required two-thirds majority to endorse Clinton—who addressed the
meeting—proved to be no problem. More than 13 million votes were received,
and of these a resounding 99.81 percent favored the endorsement. Kirkland
was enthusiastic. "Governor Clinton," he commented, "the working people
of this country are confident that you are on their side. They know from bitter
experience that Bush is on the other side. And they're going to be on your
side from here to November, and you can count on it." Right across the Federation, there was a similar mood of optimism. "With the staunch support of
Labor behind the Democratic ticket," wrote A. L. "Mike" Moore of the International Brotherhood of Painters and Allied Trades, "we have the chance to
point our country in a new direction—one in which working people have a
voice, and are truly heard." A headline in the *AFL-CIO News* was even more
emphatic. "Bill Clinton," it declared. "He's on our side."[3]

A consummate campaigner, Clinton connected with everyday Americans in
a way that eluded the reserved George H. W. Bush. Citing the bus trips he had
taken across the country, Clinton claimed that he had been exposed to many
people whose lives had been "broken" by the economic policies of Reagan and
Bush. Claiming a connection with working Americans, he promised to "get our
economy moving again," to build "a high-wage, high-growth, high-opportunity
future," rather than "letting this nation drift as it is now into a hard-work, low-
wage, low-growth future." More specifically, Clinton promised to expand trade
"on terms that are fair to the United States," and suggested that American
workers would enjoy higher wages and better conditions if he were elected.
Focusing on economic issues, he successfully negated Bush's attempts to concentrate on foreign policy, an area where the president had more experience.[4]

In the election, the AFL-CIO worked hard to secure a Democratic victory. In
an analysis for the Executive Council, COPE director John Perkins reported
that union households had "voted overwhelmingly" for Clinton and Al Gore.
Kirkland added that poll data indicated that these households represented
nearly 20 percent of the total popular vote. "Without the margin provided to
Governor Clinton by that union household vote," he declared, "President
Bush would have won a majority of the popular vote." COPE-endorsed

candidates also did well in Congress, winning 274 House and Senate seats, 66.3 percent of those it had contested. Union support was especially influential in heavily populated industrial states.[5] According to the *AFL-CIO News*, the union vote was a "major factor" in Clinton's victory, helping to decide the election in eleven battleground states, including Michigan, New Jersey, and Ohio. Aware of labor's influence over the outcome, some union leaders now demanded payback. According to Teamsters' president Ron Carey, a reformer who had been elected in 1991, politicians needed to appreciate that "the labor movement . . . understands and speaks for the interests of all workers. The support the labor movement was able to generate for the Clinton/ Gore campaign is evidence of that." Carey captured a broader mood. As the *News* put it, a "new era" had begun, and labor's agenda was now at the "top of Capitol Hill."[6]

At a special meeting on November 5, 1992—two days after the election— the Executive Council wasted no time in laying out its "legislative priorities." It was an ambitious catalog of key demands, none of which had been addressed over the previous twelve years. They included comprehensive health care reform, legislation banning the permanent replacement of strikers, passage of a family and medical leave bill, and a major anti-recession program that would rebuild infrastructure and create jobs. The mood of the meeting was upbeat—if not euphoric—with Kirkland adding that the Clinton administration's openness to labor would have "beneficial effects on the climate for organizing."[7] At a full Council meeting held shortly after Clinton's inauguration, there was also lots of optimism. For the first time in over a decade, AFL-CIO leaders reasoned that they could go on the offensive. Capturing the mood, USW president Lynn Williams told the Council that "opportunities [are] now available for the first time in many years to fight positively to advance the labor movement's goals rather than be engaged in a constant defensive battle."[8]

AFL-CIO leaders welcomed the chance to build a closer relationship with the White House and key federal agencies, especially the Department of Labor. As Lenore Miller told Secretary of Labor Robert Reich, she wanted an end to "the adversarial attitude toward the labor movement that has been prevalent in DOL local offices over the past twelve years." In an early address to the Executive Council, Reich—a liberal economist whose work had criticized the increasing mobility of capital—encouraged these hopes. The Clinton administration, he insisted, saw the AFL-CIO "as the voice of working men and women on issues in the workplace and throughout society." The White House wanted a "level playing field" in labor-management relations;

this would be achieved through labor law reform and close consultation with the Federation. Kirkland was encouraged. "The Department of Labor under the Clinton administration," he told the Council, "was returning to its mission of advancing the best interests of workers."[9]

Early on, Clinton and Reich backed up their words. In its first month, the administration rescinded two antiunion Executive Orders that had been issued by Bush. One order had required the posting of signs in workplaces informing employees that they did not have to join a union. According to Kirkland, this had imposed an "extraordinary burden" on local unions, and its removal was significant. Another order had prohibited the use of project agreements, which allowed unions to establish the terms and conditions of employment on federally financed construction jobs. This was now reversed, strengthening unions in the building sector. In addition, President Clinton proposed an extension of federal unemployment benefits for the long-term jobless, pleasing the AFL-CIO, and issued an Executive Order that promoted "partnerships" in federal labor-management relations.[10]

Clinton also unequivocally supported the Family and Medical Leave Act. "Long-backed" by the AFL-CIO, this legislation faced significant opposition from business groups and their powerful congressional supporters, and both Reagan and Bush had vetoed it. The first major legislation signed into law by President Clinton, the new law required companies with more than fifty employees to grant up to twelve weeks unpaid—but job-protected—leave for family medical needs. Worker health benefits would also be continued during the leave. While the legislation had its limitations—it excluded small businesses and many part-time workers—it was a significant advance. Indeed, the law moved the United States closer to the example of other industrial nations, almost all of which provided extended paid leave, closing what Tom Donahue called a "shameful" gap. Despite the exemptions, Census data showed that the law still covered 66 percent of American workers, and the changes were popular. In late 1992, a Gallup poll for *Life* magazine found that 83 percent of adults backed the measure. Legislators who pushed the law through the Democratic-controlled House and Senate understood this grassroots sentiment. "For the parents whose employers do not provide this benefit voluntarily, the choice between keeping one's job or caring for a new child or sick family member is a choice no American should have to make," summarized House majority leader Richard A. Gephardt (D-MO). Once the law was passed, it helped millions of American workers, and it was later seen by the Clinton administration as one of its main accomplishments.[11]

To AFL-CIO leaders, the speedy passage of the Family and Medical Leave Act showed the difference that a friendly White House could make. Indeed, Kirkland and Donahue knew that the new president's role had been crucial. "We had already done work in the Congress and the legislation was there waiting to pass," recalled Kirkland. "It was just a question of having Administration support instead of opposition. That's all we needed to pass it and get it signed." Clinton had moved quickly to enact the bill, which allowed him to fulfill his election promise of "putting people first."[12]

Kirkland reasoned that other key labor aims would now be met, and the administration encouraged these hopes. It promised to support the striker replacement bill, which Bush had said he would veto, and called for a 90-cent increase in the minimum wage, which had stood at $4.25 an hour since 1991. Although Republican opposition delayed a vote on a minimum wage hike, in the summer of 1996 Congress finally approved the 90-cent rise, with Republicans giving in after some of the costs to small business owners were offset through tax breaks. The increase helped more than 10 million low-paid workers. "Robert Reich was terrific from the very outset," recalled Policy Department staffer Christine Owens, who oversaw the campaign, "and then the president really got on board and . . . we were able to move enough Republicans to support the minimum wage . . . increase." As the administration noted proudly, the hike—along with the expansion of tax credits to low-income earners— brought greater "financial independence" to many of America's poorest working families. Although the increase took longer than it would have liked, the AFL-CIO was also pleased. "It was a victory," summarized Owens.[13]

In July 1993 there was more good news. Following a long campaign by the AFL-CIO, as well as pressure from the ICFTU, the Atlanta Committee for the Olympic Games—which were to be held in the Georgia capital in 1996—agreed to a fair-wage agreement. It covered construction workers who were to build the 85,000-seat Olympic stadium, a $210 million project, as well as support facilities. The agreement set a minimum wage of $7.50 an hour, much higher than the federal minimum wage, ensuring that about 90 percent of the construction jobs would be unionized. The agreement also included employer-paid health care benefits and pensions, as well as compulsory training for all contractors and subcontractors. It was a proud moment for Atlanta AFL-CIO president Stewart Acuff, who had spearheaded an extensive grassroots campaign to "make the Olympics righteous." The stadium deal, he wrote, was a "huge victory." New Atlanta mayor Bill Campbell, who had been elected with labor support, also chose Acuff to be his representative on the Olympic Governing Board. While President Clinton had not been directly involved in the campaign, his endorsement of project agreements had helped make the breakthrough possible. Overall, the settlement epitomized the hopeful mood of the early Clinton era.[14]

In the first months of the Clinton presidency, there were other breakthroughs. Significantly, in August 1993 Clinton reversed the Reagan administration's lifetime ban on former PATCO strikers getting jobs at the Federal Aviation Administration (FAA). The move, which followed pressure from both the controllers and the AFL-CIO, also reflected Clinton's desire to hand the unions a symbolic victory at a time when relations were strained over NAFTA. While noting that the Clinton administration did not endorse the "illegal" walkout, a White House statement declared that the dismissed controllers could apply for employment. "The President believes that it is time to put this chapter of labor management relations behind us," it explained. Federation officials were delighted, with staffer John Leyden even declaring that "the era of the all-powerful boss is over." Many former strikers were determined to return to the work they loved, and within a year around 40 percent of them had reapplied. The former controllers found that their applications were processed without preference, however, and in 1994 the FAA implemented a systematic hiring freeze. Subsequent reforms—ironically introduced by the Clinton administration—also hurt the replaced controllers, who now had to compete with younger recruits for jobs. By the second anniversary of Clinton's order, only thirty-seven former strikers had secured FAA posts. According to historian Joseph McCartin, the walkout ultimately helped to win better conditions for America's air traffic controllers—including better pay— yet most of those dismissed in 1981 were excluded from the "fruits of these victories."[15]

Still, the reemployment order was a symbolic victory. Kirkland was proud of his role in helping to negotiate the turnaround, pointing out that he had never accepted Reagan's argument that strikers could be fired, and had not forgotten the PATCO strikers. In an interview given in retirement, Kirkland drew attention to the reemployment order. "I got Clinton," he recalled, "to undo the blacklist on the air traffic controllers . . . they are eligible for reemployment." Some of Kirkland's supporters also cited the order as an important achievement, feeling that it illustrated their leader's quiet tenacity and integrity. "Reagan fired them. Kirkland, to his credit, never accepted that," recalled Tom Donahue. "Lane worked on it for all those years. He kept trying to push the administration to say: 'You've punished them [the fired controllers] enough, get your foot off their neck, and let them at least earn a living.' So some of them did get back in, but not a lot."[16]

As it had promised, the new administration also consulted closely with the AFL-CIO. Coming from a state where unions were weak, Clinton lacked strong labor links, yet he recognized that the Federation was an important Democratic constituency. In May 1993 the president thus invited the entire Executive Council to meet with him in the White House, enjoying what the Council recorded as "an informal dialogue with the President on issues of mutual concern." AFL-CIO leaders also met with vice president Gore and Secretary of Labor Reich.[17] Interactions between staff were also positive. As legislative director Robert McGlotten reported in 1993, the Federation established "good relations" with both White House aides and key cabinet members. "The administration," he concluded, "has sought the AFL-CIO's positions and has been willing to listen to differing points of view." In October 1993 *New York Times* writer Peter T. Kilborn was impressed with the Clinton administration's responsiveness to organized labor. In particular, he cited the passage of the Family and Medical Leave Act, the lifting of the ban on the air traffic controllers, and the effort to overhaul the health care system along lines that unions had long promoted. "Since his election," he concluded, "Mr. Clinton has answered one union prayer after another."[18]

Several AFL-CIO staff also got posts in the Clinton White House. Emphasizing diversity, the new administration was especially receptive to the appointment of women. Those who landed jobs included Karen Nussbaum, who directed the Women's Bureau at the Department of Labor, and Barbara Shailor, who got a high-ranking position in the State Department. In addition, Steve Rosenthal, a staffer with expertise in political mobilization, worked on Clinton's election campaign and subsequently became Associate Deputy Secretary of Labor. "There were openings, there were connections," recalled Nussbaum, summarizing the early Clinton years. "The Department of Labor had lots of good things."[19]

Several other Federation staffers duly got positions in the Department of Labor, something that would have been unimaginable under Reagan or Bush. Ironically, the Clinton administration even poached talented female and minority staff from the AFL-CIO. In 1993 Joyce Miller—the first woman ever elected to the Executive Council—resigned so that she could become director of the Glass Ceiling Commission at the Department of Labor. In the same year, Joaquin Otero, the first Hispanic member of the Executive Council, took a post in International Affairs at the Labor Department. In addition, Clinton appointed Meredith Miller, the Federation's assistant director of Employee Benefits, as his deputy assistant secretary for pension policy. Not surprisingly, relations between the Department of Labor and the AFGE local union that

Lane Kirkland with President Bill Clinton, Vice President Al Gore, Secretary of Labor Robert Reich, and Alexis Herman, Director of the White House Office of Public Engagement. Courtesy of Special Collections, University of Maryland Libraries.

represented its employees were also reported to be "excellent."[20] Aware of the need to continue diversifying its leaders, the committee on Executive Council vacancies selected two women—Linda Chavez-Thompson of AFSCME and Gloria Johnson of the IUE—as the replacements for Miller and Otero. A former bookkeeper who was one of CLUW's founding members, Johnson helped maintain an African-American voice on the Council. A fluent Spanish speaker from a poor Mexican-American background, Chavez-Thompson was proud to be the first Latina elected to the prestigious body. "I broke some ceilings," she recalled.[21]

Clinton himself went out of his way to show that he was consulting with labor. In 1994 he appointed senior advisor George Stephanopoulos as his "special representative to the labor movement." Neither of his Republican predecessors had selected an aide of this type. On symbolic issues, Clinton was particularly responsive. Following a suggestion from an AFSCME local union officer, for example, President Clinton designated May 1994 as "Labor History Month," giving the Federation a platform to raise its media profile.[22]

Clinton staked much of his first term on an ambitious effort to reform the nation's health care system, working closely with the AFL-CIO in the process. As it formulated its proposals, Clinton's health care reform task force held regular meetings with Federation leaders and its Health Care Committee. In charge of the effort, First Lady Hillary Rodham Clinton pledged to discuss the details of the final health care proposal with the Federation before going public. When the administration finally unveiled its health care reform plan on September 22, 1993, the AFL-CIO enthusiastically endorsed it as "good for working people, their families and the country." At the heart of the complex document—which was 1,342 pages long—was a requirement that most employers would pay for 80 percent of their workers' health benefits. The system was underpinned by regional insurance-purchasing alliances that were designed to lower premiums by promoting "managed competition" among private insurers. Meeting the AFL-CIO's long-held goal of universal coverage, the federal government would pay for the uninsured. "We've been for health care since Harry Truman," commented a pleased Federation official, "and we're still for it." The proposals formed the basis of the Health Security Act, which was filed by the administration with Congress.[23]

While these proposals were being formulated, the AFL-CIO mobilized its members. In May 1993 it launched a grassroots public relations campaign to support the administration's reforms. Key activities included the establishment of phone banks, the provision of sample letters to editors, and the scheduling of meetings with elected officials in key districts. Pioneering use was also made of cellular telephones, which the Federation purchased for the campaign. Efforts were extensive; between February and August 1994 alone, the AFL-CIO's Health Care Reform Campaign—which was based in an ad hoc "boiler room" on the first floor of the headquarters building—spent more than $355,000 on direct communications to union members, mostly through targeted mailings. To fund these activities, the Executive Council authorized the establishment of a health care campaign account.[24] Across the country, union activists wrote thousands of letters in support of the campaign, often drawing on materials provided by the Federation. By May 1994, field support director Charles Stott told the Executive Council that the campaign had "been able to effectively target various districts and generate substantial grassroots activity and information." From coast to coast, AFL-CIO staffers were also involved in the effort, often making their case in the national press. "America is on the brink of joining the rest of the industrialized world by insuring quality health care for all," summarized Edward J. Cleary of the New York AFL-CIO in a letter to the *New York Times*. "For our country's future, particularly for its working people, Congress must not squander this opportunity."[25]

The administration appreciated the effort. Addressing the Executive Council in May 1994, Secretary of Health and Human Services Donna Shalala

For Lane Kirkland with appreciation for your support and best wishes — Hillary Rodham Clinton

Lane Kirkland and John Sweeney (foreground) worked closely with Hillary Rodham Clinton, particularly during the fight for health care reform in 1993–94. Courtesy of Special Collections, University of Maryland Libraries.

thanked the AFL-CIO for its "vital" support of health care reform. The administration's proposals were now under consideration by House and Senate committees, and Shalala hoped that "good bills" would result. Reassuring the Federation that he was playing an important role, President Clinton also attended this meeting. The AFL-CIO, along with several affiliates, also participated in the Health Care Reform Project (HCRP), a coalition of organizations representing business, labor, consumers, and providers. The HCRP helped to plan media strategy and shaped efforts to focus lobbying on seventy-two Democrats and eight Republicans who served on three important House committees: Education and Labor, Energy and Commerce, and Ways and Means.[26]

Despite this mobilization, the health care campaign ran into some powerful opposition. Favoring the status quo and disliking government interference in health care provision, the business community was overwhelmingly opposed. One 1994 poll by *Business Week* found that 94 percent of respondents felt that Clinton's health care campaign "gave government too big a role in running health care." Interest groups were especially vociferous. Small insurers worried that larger companies would force them out of business, while small businesses opposed paying 80 percent of their workers' health premiums. In February 1994 Robert McGlotten told the Executive Council that the insurance industry and other "business interest opponents" were exerting "heavy pressure" against health care reform.[27]

Angered by the proposals, opponents invested heavily in TV advertising. The Health Insurance Association spent $14 million on television, radio, and print advertising, including the effective "Harry and Louise" commercials, which featured a fictional suburban married couple who were worried about government intervention into their personal health care matters. The ads ended with a call for viewers to contact their congressional representative. Opponents also organized a letter-writing campaign, swamping key members of Congress with well-crafted appeals. Many letters came from everyday citizens, especially in the South, which again played an important role in blocking a key labor priority. Mirroring the arguments made nationally, but making them with particular force and clarity, southerners argued that the health care changes represented a threat to individual liberty—and were unnecessary. "I do not relish the thought of having the government choose my health care and or physician," wrote Lloyd and Theresa Beasley from Georgia in late 1993. "This is clearly another step toward Socialism and government oppression." They spoke for many. "We have the best health care in the world—bar none," added Scott W. Brown from Albany, Georgia, "and Mr. Clinton wants to make drastic changes?"[28]

Facing this onslaught, health care reformers struggled to respond. Crucially, many Americans with health insurance exerted little pressure for change, allowing opponents to gain the upper-hand. "While direct mail may work on political campaigns," wrote campaign director Stott in an internal document, "when union members were asked to take action on an issue as complex and deeply personal as their health care plan, they did not respond in significant numbers to direct mail appeals to send postcards to their members of Congress." The Building Trades unions, for example, were not enthusiastic about health care reform. Part of the problem was the legislation's complexity, which generated member skepticism. Some union members with generous health benefits also feared that a shift towards a national benefits package could undermine their own plans. Furthermore, recalled Stott, the passage of NAFTA "poisoned" relations between the administration and the AFL-CIO, particularly in the manufacturing sector. Despite what the Executive Council called "extensive congressional activity and lobbying efforts in Washington and in home districts," including a national advertising campaign, large rallies, and letter-writing to elected representatives, the Federation's health care reforms came up short. Clinton's ambitious plan never reached a vote on the floor of the Democratic Congress, and in August 1994 it finally collapsed.[29]

The outcome was devastating for the Clinton administration, and did much to stymie its progressive intentions. As vice president Gore told the Executive Council in February 1995, the failure to enact health care reform was a "bitter disappointment." AFL-CIO leaders were also frustrated, especially as they had hoped that reform would dissuade employers from trying to control costs by cutting wages and benefits. As a result, the Federation remained on the defensive at the bargaining table.[30] Americans, noted the Council, would pay an "enormous" price for the defeat, especially as the numbers of citizens without insurance would increase, putting further pressure on health costs. Still, seasoned activists stressed the value of the struggle. "The whole society has benefited from somebody standing up and saying: 'Yes, health care is a thing we should all have, we need that,'" summarized Susan Dunlop. "It laid the groundwork for Obama's successful effort twenty years later," added Stott. "I think it caused the country to recognize that . . . in the richest country in the world . . . that there's an awful lot of people that are *un*served, or *under*served, by our health care system. It drew attention to that."[31]

While it fell short, the fight for health care reform also strengthened the bonds between the AFL-CIO and the administration. In contrast, the second big campaign of these years—over NAFTA—damaged the relationship. The battle highlighted the substantial differences between organized labor and the White House over trade, a dissonance that traced back to at least the 1960s but which grew as more goods were traded internationally. NAFTA was of enormous importance to the U.S. economy, especially the large manufacturing sectors where millions of union members worked. The treaty aimed to create the world's largest free-trade bloc, one with a population of 370 million and a combined GDP of $6.5 trillion. By eliminating tariffs and other trade barriers between the United States, Canada, and Mexico, NAFTA gave companies in the United States and Canada free access to a rapidly growing Mexican market of 90 million consumers, half of whom were under the age of twenty. It also promised to provide Mexico with much-needed foreign investment. Opponents, however, declared that NAFTA would cause job losses in the United States as companies moved south of the border, or as cheaper Mexican imports replaced American-made products. Low-wage, labor-intensive industries such as apparel and electronics assembly stood to lose the most.[32]

NAFTA originated during the administration of George H. W. Bush. Like his predecessors, particularly—but no means exclusively—on the Republican side of politics, the forty-first president was determined to expand free trade, especially within the Americas. Mexican president Carlos Salinas, who was important in spearheading the agreement, shared this goal, as did conservative Canadian prime minister Brian Mulroney, who had signed a free trade agreement with the United States in 1988. Educated in the United States, Salinas forcefully promoted the agreement, promising that it would mean more jobs for Mexico—and fewer Mexican migrants to the United States and Canada. Insisting that it would boost the U.S. economy and enhance its global competitiveness, the Bush administration also sold the agreement. "We must build on the trend we see toward free markets," declared Bush in 1990, "and make our ultimate aim a free trade system that links all of the Americas— North, Central, and South."[33]

Initially, the AFL-CIO hoped to use its influence with the Clinton administration and persuade it to renegotiate the agreement. Terming Bush's NAFTA "an agreement based solely on exploitation," the Federation pushed the new administration for amendments to protect the rights of working people as well as investors. Specifically, the AFL-CIO asked for violations of workplace standards to be enforced by trade actions. They hoped for a favorable response from Clinton, who had said before the election that, while he supported the concept of free trade to help American exports, he also wanted an agreement that protected workers and the environment. Clinton had specifically criticized Bush's agreement for lacking substantive provisions on "worker retraining" and "environmental cleanup" in Mexico. "I hope we can get the right kind of agreement with Mexico," he declared in September 1992.[34] With a new president in office, Kirkland initially argued that outright opposition from the AFL-CIO would only "shut the labor movement out" of negotiations to improve the agreement. Kirkland gave Clinton the benefit of the doubt, arguing that, "unlike previous presidents," he was willing to hear different perspectives on trade. As he addressed the Council, however, even Kirkland acknowledged that the Clinton administration did "not share all of the views of the labor movement on trade." In February the newly elected president ominously used a speech at American University to endorse "open" commerce. "We must compete and not retreat," he declared.[35]

For much of 1993, the AFL-CIO pressed the Clinton administration, and especially Trade Representative Michael Kantor, to negotiate effective side agreements that addressed workers' rights and environmental issues. Federation leaders reasoned that, by working with the administration, they could get their views across, especially as organized labor had played an important role in electing Clinton.[36] Business interests who favored the agreement, however, also lobbied Clinton, and the president failed to endorse the AFL-CIO's position. In May, Kirkland wrote that Clinton was in a "quandary" over NAFTA because he knew that "any truly effective and enforceable standards will be labeled 'protectionist' by business supporters and will cause them to jump ship." Rather than NAFTA, Kirkland proposed a North Atlantic Free Trade Agreement with the European Economic Community (EEC). Such an agreement would benefit workers, Kirkland argued, because wage levels in the United States and EEC were similar. The idea failed to gain traction, however, as the administration—and its business supporters—repeatedly pressed for a hemispheric trade agreement. Swayed by business arguments, the president stressed the benefits of opening up the Mexican market. "By raising the incomes of Mexicans, which this will do," Clinton declared in August, "they'll be able to buy more of our products and there will be much less pressure on them to come to this country in the form of illegal immigration. I think this will be a very stabilizing, economically healthy agreement."[37]

By August, the administration had negotiated its side agreements on labor rights and environmental protections. Both were difficult to enforce and the labor agreement did not contain meaningful guarantees of the right to organize. Thus, although all three nations promised to uphold the "highest labor standards," enforcement mechanisms—particularly trade sanctions for failing to comply—were lacking.[38] Reporting to the Executive Council, Federation economist Mark Anderson noted that the side agreements did "not appear to be sufficient to enable the AFL-CIO to endorse the pact." Now, the AFL-CIO moved into open disagreement with the White House, launching a "national grassroots publicity and lobby effort" to stop NAFTA. As part of this campaign, the Federation mailed 1,500 letters to state and local union leaders, informing them that the side agreements did not protect workers. Another 700 packages of bumper stickers, pamphlets, and other materials were assembled for mailing. Realizing that it could not defeat the administration on its own, the Federation aimed to expand a coalition of organizations that were opposed to NAFTA into a formidable movement.[39] Like several other AFL-CIO leaders, Tom Donahue saw the agreements as a turning point, and he felt betrayed. "He (Clinton) called me . . . I still remember," he related. "He said that he was going to ensure that there were labor protections, but they would be in a side agreement. I knew what that meant, that means crap. And so we fell out over that . . . and that's why we went on to oppose NAFTA."[40]

Despite the determined mood, the AFL-CIO faced an uphill battle. NAFTA was solidly backed not just by the White House, but by the business community as well. The Federation faced off against a powerful coalition of industry groups, including the Business Roundtable and the U.S. Chamber of Commerce. Many worked through USA-NAFTA, a coalition of over 2,700 corporations that spent over $7 million on its lobbying campaign. As *Business Week* noted candidly, when it came to NAFTA, "Corporate America is united, and its war chest is filled." In slick dossiers mailed to members of Congress, the Chamber argued that NAFTA would "create more U.S. jobs, lower prices for consumer goods, and strengthen competitiveness for American firms at home and abroad." Powerful farm groups also mobilized, especially in the South and Midwest. In Georgia, a major exporter of farm products to Mexico, agricultural interests bombarded their representatives with letters and petitions. "The agriculture industry in the State of Georgia is in full support of NAFTA," summarized P. Jack Davis of Southern Empire Egg Farm in a letter to his congressman.[41]

The Federation's opponents were also in a powerful strategic position. By opposing free trade, the AFL-CIO could be painted as outdated and selfish. As the Executive Council admitted, NAFTA's supporters could "get away with dismissing unions as 'protectionists,'" a term that carried negative connotations. The battle also exposed the limitations of labor's relationship with the Democratic Party, as many pro-labor Representatives also believed in free trade. The AFL-CIO faced a "dilemma," noted IUE president Bill Bywater in Council discussions, "when legislators with otherwise excellent voting records vote wrong consistently on trade issues and fail to understand how these decisions can cost jobs."[42] Further complicating the AFL-CIO's task was Ross Perot, the independent politician who had forcefully criticized NAFTA in his run for the presidency. In a televised presidential debate in October 1992, Perot had grabbed headlines when he declared that NAFTA would lead to a "giant sucking sound of jobs being pulled out of this country" because American workers could not compete with Mexicans paid as little as $1 an hour. While for many Americans Perot became the public face of opposition to NAFTA—helping him to gain nearly 19 percent of the vote in the election—the AFL-CIO was reluctant to work with the populist Texan businessman, who also called for a balanced budget, supported cuts in Social Security, and opposed gun control.[43]

Despite these drawbacks, the Federation launched a massive campaign to stop NAFTA. The effort was underpinned by the belief that the agreement served the interests of multinational corporations rather than working people in either the United States or Mexico. "Our problem is not trade with Mexico, but with this trade deal," explained one AFL-CIO advertisement. "We know NAFTA will cost hundreds of thousands of American jobs. So we oppose it." Anxious to refute the 'protectionist' label, the Federation argued that it was also protecting Mexican workers from multinational companies who were only interested in "exploiting cheap labor."[44] Placed in charge of the effort, international and economic affairs director Mark Anderson threw himself into his work. A former activist from the Food and Allied Service Trades who held a master's degree in political science, Anderson designed a comprehensive campaign with a strong grassroots component. The fight against NAFTA, he recalled, was arguably "the first nationwide political campaign the AFL-CIO had run around a public policy issue," and it was based on the idea of moving beyond "traditional lobbying" and involving workers. With Kirkland's backing, Anderson oversaw a national campaign that "focused an awful lot on our local bodies, state federations, and . . . central labor councils . . . as well as our affiliate unions." Overall, this was another reminder that under Kirkland, the AFL-CIO was capable of mobilizing its members.[45]

Kirkland himself staked a lot on the effort. In early September he ruled out any compromise with the White House, pledging to "go for broke" to defeat NAFTA. The side agreements, he added, were a "bad joke . . . a Rube Goldberg structure of committees all leading nowhere." Building on this rhetoric, the Federation reached out to its community allies. It worked extensively through Frontlash, its outreach program to younger Americans. The AFL-CIO sent campus activists a detailed "ten-step program" to "Kick this NAFTA Habit," with key recommendations including the scheduling of informational "kick off" meetings, the holding of student forums, and seeking appointments with members of Congress. In addition, the Federation forged alliances with several environmental groups, who feared a shift in production from the United States to Mexico, where emission standards were weaker. Church, civic, and civil rights groups were also courted.[46]

As it constructed this movement, the Federation built on the legacy of Solidarity Day. According to the *Washington Post*, the AFL-CIO was the "backbone" of the Citizens Trade Campaign (CTC), a broad coalition of seventy-six labor, consumer, environmental, farm, religious, and civic groups, many of whom had worked together on the earlier marches. The Federation coordinated its campaign from converted offices on the third floor of the headquarters, feeding information to field operations, especially in the 143 congressional districts where House members were undecided.[47] The scale of the campaign was impressive. By early October, the Federation had issued 2 million stickers, 200,000 buttons, and 50,000 posters to members, many of them utilizing the catchy slogan "NAFTA The SHAFTA." The Federation also spent $3.2 million on billboard and radio advertising. Featured prominently in packets of material sent to members,

Kirkland led the fight. "In the end," he explained in the " 'No NAFTA' Action Source Book," a key mobilizing resource, "this issue will not be decided by fringe politicians or corporate lobbyists in Washington, DC. It will be decided by working Americans across this country, and when they are heard, NAFTA will be defeated."[48]

Federation leaders stressed that the campaign was strongly supported by members. The claim was largely valid, especially in manufacturing industries that stood to lose the most. "We see this as a life-and-death issue," summarized Garment Workers' union president Jay Mazur. In strong union states, particularly California, Massachusetts, Michigan, Missouri, Ohio, and Pennsylvania, several affiliates took the unusual step of making the vote of a member of Congress on NAFTA a single-issue test of loyalty to labor. "We won't support people who vote for NAFTA," explained Mazur. "They're steamed up about this," added Machinists president George Kourpias, referring to his members.[49]

Reaffirming its role in representing all workers, the Federation was also able to channel the opposition of many nonunion workers. In the South, for example, nonunion textile and apparel workers put pressure on key Democrats. While some workers acted independently, others were affected by the Federation's high-profile campaign, which called on concerned citizens to express their views. Those targeted included George "Buddy" Darden, a Georgia congressman who was considering how to respond. "The opposition, and the workers who are in greatest peril in my district, apparel and textile workers, are nonunion," commented Darden. Across the country in San Francisco, where most garment workers were also unorganized, labor and nonlabor groups forged a powerful coalition and promised to oust legislators who backed NAFTA. By working through the Citizens Trade Campaign, which had offices in forty-seven states, the Federation was able to reach well beyond its membership. Overseen by Jim Jontz, a former Indiana congressman, the CTC ran an impressive campaign, with state and regional captains—most of them loaned from citizens' groups—organizing rallies, letter-writing, and visits to legislators' district offices.[50]

The grassroots mobilization clearly concerned the Clinton administration. In early October the president addressed the AFL-CIO's biennial convention in San Francisco to try and shore up support for his position. NAFTA, he acknowledged, had become "the symbol of the legitimate grievances of the American working people about the way they've been worked over in the last twelve years." Clinton assured his audience that their fears were misplaced; ultimately NAFTA would "make it better." Although Clinton was a powerful speaker, many in the audience were not convinced. "A lot of the guys were pretty upset," noted UFCW leader Doug Dority, recalling the speech, "and particularly the manufacturing unions." As reporter Gwen Ifill summarized, Clinton's address was greeted with "lukewarm applause," and the president diplomatically described his visit as "an interesting encounter."[51]

As the crucial vote—set for November 17—approached, the Federation stepped up its activities. On November 16 union members shouting, "Dump the NAFTA!" swarmed over Capitol Hill. Some even waved placards that depicted an oversized monkey—dubbed "NAFTA"—sitting on top of a frowning worker. The following morning, the AFL-CIO and its allies placed display ads in the national press that spoke on behalf of "grassroots America." The overall message was clear: "America Wins When This NAFTA loses."[52] As Clinton countered with his own efforts to sway members of Congress, relations with the White House were strained. In the week before the vote, the president even accused the AFL-CIO of using "musclebound" and "roughshod" tactics. In response, Kirkland criticized Clinton for promising Republican representatives that he would defend them if their Democratic opponents used NAFTA against them. "The President has clearly abdicated his role as leader of the Democratic Party," he fumed, adding that Clinton had written "comfort letters" to key Republicans. Kirkland, who could harbor a grudge, also hit back at Clinton's assurances that labor would soon forgive the administration. "Bitterness will linger," he warned.[53]

This period immediately before the vote proved to be crucial. Early on, labor's campaign was producing results. In early September, Majority Whip David E. Bonior predicted that as many as three-quarters of the House would vote against NAFTA.[54] In October and November, however, NAFTA's supporters made a decisive surge, with business groups overwhelming their opponents with advertising and targeted lobbying. Although it was difficult to pinpoint how much each side spent, most observers agreed that the anti-NAFTA forces had been outgunned, with the *Wall Street Journal* estimating that the pro-NAFTA side had spent at least $17 million in 1993, compared to $6 million by their opponents. Much of this expenditure occurred in the final weeks. On November 17 the U.S. House of Representatives thus passed NAFTA by a close—yet clear—vote of 234 to 200. In the end, 102 Democrats, along with 132 Republicans, voted for the agreement, while the "No" vote derived from 156 Democrats, 43 Republicans, and 1 Independent. According to Mark Anderson, the outcome reflected the power of the business community. While it was a "close vote," the campaign had "failed because, at the end of the day, the corporations are hugely powerful, they have unlimited resources."

Kirkland could not hide his frustration. In an address to the press, he termed the vote "a bitter disappointment and a defeat for millions of working Americans."[55]

While Federation staff had expected the business community to mobilize forcefully, they were surprised—and angered—by just how involved the Clinton administration had been. On November 10 Clinton told the national press that NAFTA was a "job winner." Staking a lot on passage of the agreement, Clinton even termed it "the symbol of where we want to go in the world." While conceding that its opposition was effective, Clinton also criticized the AFL-CIO. "I just think they're wrong," he noted bluntly. In these final days, Kirkland hit back, criticizing Clinton's promises to key representatives, including protections for citrus, peanut, sugar, and wheat producers that were written into the text. "The agreement," he charged, "was changed many times in order to buy the votes of representatives seeking protections for their own special interests." Some members of Congress, charged a frustrated Doug Dority, had sold their votes "like a whore on the street" as a result.[56] Clinton and Gore certainly played an important role, especially in their native region, where they charmed—or pressured—wavering Democratic members. Gore even personally thanked representatives—including Darden—who voted for the agreement despite their constituents' concerns. For Gore, these members had taken a "courageous" stand for an "historic pact" that would "create jobs for our people." The successful congressional vote meant a great deal to the administration. As Mickey Kantor summarized, it was "a great victory for the President, as well as for the people of America."[57]

Although the passage of NAFTA was a defeat for the AFL-CIO, some achievements still came out of the campaign. The Federation showed that it could mobilize its members—and many non-members—on a national basis, and the aggressive business response highlighted the effectiveness of these efforts. Even *Business Week* called the opposition to NAFTA "spirited." Addressing the Executive Council after the vote, House Leader Richard Gephardt—who had broken with the administration and opposed NAFTA— declared that the fight had "successfully helped increase public awareness of the dangers of unfair trade." The AFL-CIO, added David Bonior, had "helped many representatives view the effects of unfair trade from the perspectives of workers rather than that of economists and elitists."[58] The struggle also energized many participants. "We found our voice in this fight, as did the American public," declared ACTWU president Jack Sheinkman. "Hundreds and thousands of workers did not have to be pushed or shoved to engage in this battle." Still, many union members felt angry about the outcome. "We put on a hell of a campaign," recalled former IAM president George Kourpias, "and Clinton screwed us."[59]

The strong support that Clinton gave to NAFTA—after promising to negotiate meaningful labor protections—certainly left a legacy of bitterness. As Tom Donahue admitted, the damage was not repaired quickly. "I mean that was a very serious injury I thought Clinton did to us," he recalled. In an effort to improve relations, Al Gore addressed the Executive Council in February 1994, but he got a hostile reception. Summarizing the mood, IUE leader William Bywater told the vice president that many union members were "angry" about the NAFTA vote. The loudest concerns came from the industrial affiliates, who worried that the agreement would cause "the massive loss of good-paying jobs" in their sectors. These jobs, they noted, were not being replaced with comparable positions. Other Council members brought up the president's personal intervention into the NAFTA vote. As Sigurd Lucassen of the United Brotherhood of Carpenters put it, "President Clinton worked hard for passage of the NAFTA pact . . . workers would like to see the same skills applied to passage of the striker replacement ban." Adroitly avoiding discussion of the president's intervention, Gore responded by stressing "mutual concerns," including the ongoing fight to stop striker replacement. Furthermore, he recognized the "legitimate" worries of NAFTA's opponents, especially when they had experienced "the pain of job losses." Also addressing the Council, George Stephanopoulos called for unity, especially if the Health Security Act was to pass. While health care reform and the workplace fairness bill were already in doubt, NAFTA's passage further weakened both campaigns.[60]

A gifted politician, Clinton also tried to repair the damage. In December 1993 he arranged a forty-five-minute meeting with Kirkland in the Oval Office that was designed to, as the *New York Times* put it, "end the bitter public debate over the trade agreement." Kirkland was not won over easily, and the meeting only achieved "mixed results." Highlighting that scars remained, especially on labor's side, neither man spoke to reporters about the meeting nor allowed the news media to photograph them together. Needing labor support, Clinton kept trying. In May 1994 the president was an effusive host when he welcomed the Executive Council to the White House. The two sides needed to put NAFTA behind them, he urged, and work together on other issues, especially the beleaguered health care reform effort. Council members, meanwhile, again pressed Clinton to take a stronger position on the striker replacement legislation.[61]

For many in the labor movement, the resentment left by the administration's support of NAFTA was long-lasting. Even many years later, some staffers felt that Clinton had betrayed them, and they could not move on as easily as the president imagined. "We had just managed to elect a Democratic president, Bill Clinton," recalled Mark Anderson. "The lousy son of a bitch. I spent more hours than I want to think about on the phone with his campaign, before the election, as he was debating what to do about NAFTA." Anderson felt "terrible" after the NAFTA vote, which he viewed as "hugely personal." Like other activists, Anderson had invested a massive amount in the campaign, even taking part in candlelight vigils outside the White House as the vote approached. "We felt very bad about it," he summarized. "It was a very difficult thing, because we were beaten by a Democrat, Democratic president, that we supported in the election." The outcome represented a turning point, especially as labor had gone all out to fight for a crucial issue but had been beaten by a president of its own party. The loss was shocking, and many in the labor movement now felt that something had to change. A defeat that even the *AFL-CIO News* termed a "bitter pill" had set the stage for Kirkland's leadership to be challenged.[62]

For a battered AFL-CIO, passage of striker replacement legislation could have been a meaningful consolation prize. For more than a decade, workers who had resisted corporate demands for concessions—especially cuts to health care benefits—had often struck and been replaced. Banning the hiring of permanent replacements was thus a central Federation aim once Clinton was elected. As the *Washington Post* observed in 1993, the issue was "a political rallying point for organized labor," and the stakes for both business and labor were "high." With a Democratic president in office, the AFL-CIO leadership focused a huge amount of attention on this issue. Its figures indicated that in 1970, permanent replacements were used in only 1 percent of all strikes. By 1992, however, employers hired replacements in 25 percent of all strikes. A 1992 survey by the Bureau of National Affairs also highlighted that 79 percent of employers would try to replace their workers if they struck, or they would give the move serious consideration. For union members, especially in the large industrial affiliates, workers had lost the right to strike, destroying the labor movement's effectiveness. "No issue is more important to the long-term future of organized labor," summarized a resolution at the 1993 AFL-CIO Convention. "We must marshall all our resources to push for passage of the Workplace Fairness Act."[63]

Behind the statistics were the human stories of thousands of American workers who had lost their jobs by striking. The Federation strove to make members of Congress aware of these workers' suffering, and worked to refute allegations that replacing strikers was rare and was usually a defensive response by embattled employers. In early 1993 the Federation brought replaced strikers to Washington, where they testified at congressional hearings. The evidence illustrated that workers had been replaced from coast to coast, and in many different industries. One evocative example was provided by workers from a Champion Auto Parts factory in Hope, Arkansas, President Clinton's birthplace. In September 1991 the workers were permanently replaced after they resisted company demands to gut their health coverage. Without their jobs, workers suffered greatly, but the company refused to bend. "Workers in Hope, Arkansas, are no different from workers in other parts of the country who lose their jobs," explained local union leader Juanita Landmesser. "We have lost a sense of self-worth; we cannot take care of our families; and we don't know what kind of future there will be for us or our families." The Federation claimed that public opinion was behind it, and even in Hope, a conservative southern community, some civic leaders backed the workers. As local minister Rev. Bryan G. Fulwider put it, the Champion story was "about people who have been destroyed by having their jobs taken from them in the midst of a legal strike—a strike not over higher wages, but rather a strike that began as negotiations broke down around the issue of lessened health care coverage." There were plenty of other powerful examples. In one representative case in April 1992, Caterpillar Inc., a leading manufacturer of heavy construction equipment, broke a five-month-long strike by 12,000 UAW members in Peoria, Illinois, when it threatened to replace them. "Announcing permanent replacements is throwing down the gauntlet in a big way," commented an AFL-CIO official.[64]

In Congress, the Federation placed its hopes in H.R. 5 and S. 55, which had been renamed from the Striker Replacement Bill to the Workplace Fairness Bill in an effort to widen its political appeal—and undermine business claims that it was a union power grab.[65] In its core provisions, the bill banned the use of permanent replacements when workers struck over economic issues. At the end of January 1993, veteran Missouri Democrat William Clay reintroduced the legislation right after Clinton's inauguration. As he did so, he referred back to the PATCO strike, claiming that Reagan's seminal move had provided a "green light to similar actions by private employers." Since 1981, Clay claimed, more than 300,000 workers had suffered the "harsh experience" of losing their jobs to permanent replacements. "As workers have felt increasingly unable to strike," he explained, "faith in collective bargaining has been seriously undermined. Legislation is needed to restore confidence in the process which underlies all of labor law." Declaring that the use of replacements had "poisoned the well" and destroyed the "social compact" between management and labor,

Secretary of Labor Reich supported the change. While he was less outspoken, President Clinton declared that he would sign the bill if it passed Congress.[66]

Getting the bill onto Clinton's desk would not be easy. With fifty-seven seats in the Senate, the Democrats lacked the sixty votes needed to end debate and proceed to a floor vote, especially as not all of their senators were reliable labor supporters. In May 1993 the Federation reported privately that it needed to marshal greater support in the upper chamber "in order to offset a likely Republican filibuster." The AFL-CIO also had to push the administration to get more involved, declaring that "verbal commitments" needed to be "translated into action."[67] By October, the Council related that the legislation was "stalled once again" by the threat of a Senate filibuster. Still, the fight went on. "The AFL-CIO will not rest until the Workplace Fairness Act is enacted into law," it asserted. "We pledge our continued, all-out support for the campaign we have waged for the past four years toward that end."[68]

Resistance, however, was fierce. For the business community, the stakes were also high, resulting in what NAM leader Pete Lunnie termed a "vicious battle." On the corporate side, the fight was led by the Alliance to Keep Americans Working, a coalition of more than ninety corporations and business groups, including the National Association of Manufacturers and the U.S. Chamber of Commerce. The battle illustrated the growing power—and unity—of the business lobby, a key cause of declining union density. The influential Chamber of Commerce declared that it was "greatly concerned" by labor's efforts to pass legislation that "would place employers in a position to surrender to union officials' demands." The business community got behind the effort to kill the legislation, which was portrayed as a threat to both economic recovery and stable labor relations. Southern representatives, in particular, were bombarded with letters and petitions urging them to oppose the bill. Business groups also argued that corporate resistance to strikes was linked to foreign competition and consumer demands, rather than to the post-PATCO political climate.[69]

Even in the House, where the Democrats had a majority of 258 to 176, the business campaign caused some damage. On June 15, 1993, the House passed H.R. 5 by a vote of 239–190. Although it was successful, the vote reaffirmed the weakness of labor in the South, an ominous portent. In Georgia, four out of seven house Democrats voted against the bill, while in South Carolina two out of three did so. In contrast, seventeen of New York's eighteen house Democrats supported the bill—and the vote of the other was unknown. Eight of New York's thirteen Republican representatives also backed the legislation.[70] Despite the best efforts of labor's congressional supporters, the corporate backlash took its toll. In February 1994 Senate Majority Leader George Mitchell told the Executive Council that extra votes were still required to get to sixty. Efforts continued to be thwarted, however, by senators who refused to make any commitment before they voted.[71]

When the Senate vote occurred, the Council blamed "conservative elements" for heading off cloture, thus killing the measure "for lack of only a few votes." The final vote was 53 to 47 in favor of ending the filibuster, with most Democrats supporting the bill and most Republicans opposing it. As Robert McGlotten noted in his report to the Council, the parallels with the 1978 labor law reform effort and the 1991 striker replacement vote were glaring, especially as in each case it had been southern senators who had played a key role in blocking the legislation. Sen. Lauch Fairclough (R-NC), for example, charged that the Workplace Fairness bill would return the United States "to the days of forced unionism and widespread strikes." Key southern Democrats David L. Boren (OK), Dale Bumpers (AR), Ernest F. Hollings (SC), Harlan Matthews (TN), Sam Nunn (GA), and David Pryor (AR) voted with 41 Republicans against cloture. Just three Republicans—Alfonse M. D'Amato (NY), Mark O. Hatfield (OR), and Arlen Specter (PA)—also crossed over. Hollings' papers were representative, showing that his vote came after intense lobbying from the business community against the bill, drowning out labor's small voice in the Palmetto State. A philosophical Tom Donahue certainly felt that history was repeating itself. "We tried to get Striker Replacement legislation, and we ran a campaign," he recalled. "We worked the Congress, and spent several million, many millions on it, and we lost it by a handful of votes, again on a filibuster. . . . In each of these cases, we had a majority to pass the legislation, but we didn't have the veto-proof majority."[72]

While there was no denying that the AFL-CIO had suffered another defeat, some gains came from the campaign. After the 1994 congressional elections, when there was no point in re-introducing the legislation, President Clinton issued an Executive Order prohibiting the federal government from doing business with companies that permanently replaced strikers. The order only applied to contracts of more than $100,000, and did not affect companies that had hired permanent replacements in the past. While this was a limited result from a large—and costly—campaign, it was recognition that the effort had made a difference. Indeed, Vice President Gore announced the administration's plan to issue the order at the AFL-CIO's Executive Council meeting in February 1995, and Kirkland was present at the signing in the Oval Office the following month. Republican leaders and business groups were furious, with the U.S. Chamber of Commerce denouncing the move as a "shallow political ploy" to win union support. In 1996, following a legal challenge led by the Chamber, a conservative-dominated federal appeals court voided Clinton's order.[73]

Once again, the Federation had also served the public interest, especially by defending the right to strike. Some activists stressed the intrinsic value of the struggle. "Sometimes it takes a bigger man to take a fight that he can't win, than it does to take one he can win," recalled Doug Dority, referring to the campaign, "and there're some things you just . . . can't not do." AFL-CIO leaders claimed that their efforts had raised "public awareness" of the permanent replacement issue, and employers who used the tactic now risked "adverse publicity and notoriety." There was some evidence to support this assertion. In the 1980s many companies had hired replacements with little negative reaction, but as the AFL-CIO fought back and tried to ban the tactic, there were fewer cases. While this was partly a reflection of a strong economy, and the fact that some workers were now afraid of striking, the AFL-CIO's high-profile campaign had made a difference. Replacing strikers had become more controversial, and many companies—worried about the damage to their reputation—now avoided the tactic. In 1995, when Bridgestone/Firestone Inc. announced plans to replace 4,000 striking rubber workers, the move drew criticism from the White House. "We don't want to involve the equivalent of minor leaguers and rookies making the tires for the next Desert Storm," commented presidential spokesman Michael McCurry.[74]

The failure of the workplace fairness campaign still left a bitter taste among AFL-CIO staffers, especially as they felt that Clinton had not done enough to get the crucial votes. They contrasted the president's hands-off approach—especially his alleged failure to lean sufficiently on Arkansas senator Dale Bumpers—to the way that he personally intervened to get the votes for NAFTA. In the end, Clinton's Executive Order had also turned out to be a bust.[75]

During the first two years of the Clinton presidency, the three big defeats that the AFL-CIO endured took a significant toll. Engrossed in these draining legislative battles, organized labor failed to mobilize sufficiently for the midterm elections. To some extent, labor leaders failed to heed the warning of House Speaker Thomas Foley, who told the Executive Council in February that the "1994 congressional elections will be crucial to maintaining a constructive majority in the House."[76] After the bruising NAFTA battle, in particular, many union members were reluctant to get behind the Democrats. Grassroots activists confirmed that anger over NAFTA was not forgotten easily, or quickly. The agreement, summarized Iowa labor leader James Wengert, was a "big disappointment. We tried to convince him (President Clinton) when he was campaigning that it was a lousy deal. We have members who won't forget it, and I won't either." Clinton, added George Kourpias, "really hurt us" over NAFTA, and many members who had helped elect the Democrat were devastated.[77]

As the election neared, worried AFL-CIO leaders related that it was very hard to get their members to support the Democrats. At a meeting in Washington, DC, on August 9 and 10, 1994, union presidents reported that their members were angry with the Clinton administration over its trade and striker replacement policies. As well as NAFTA, in 1994 Clinton was trying to push through the General Agreement on Tariffs and Trade (GATT), even declaring his "overriding commitment" to free trade as he did so. In response, the Federation argued that GATT did not contain adequate "worker rights and standards." Despite this, Congress ratified the complex treaty just after the 1994 midterm elections.[78] "Union members are still disappointed by President Clinton's support for NAFTA and the new General Agreement on Tariffs and Trade," noted the Council minutes, "and by the Senate leadership's failure to mount a stronger effort to end the filibuster of the striker replacement bill." Significantly, some union presidents reported that their members would not even work on races for incumbents who had supported NAFTA. Some affiliates also threatened to cut funding to Democrats who had voted for the agreement. In the campaign, labor followed what political scientists Steven T. Engel and David J. Jackson have termed a "punishment strategy," with pro-NAFTA Democrats receiving around $25,000 less from labor's Political Action Committees compared to their anti-NAFTA colleagues. In the final vote, some prominent Democratic incumbents who had supported NAFTA—most notably House Speaker Foley—were defeated, although the election result reflected many other issues and plenty of anti-NAFTA Democrats were also victims of the Republican tide.[79]

The loss of labor support certainly hurt the Democrats, especially as a lot of labor's anger had turned inwards. In the end, 29 million fewer Americans voted in the 1994 elections than in 1992, and at least 10 million of these missing votes were from union households. According to a private Federation analysis of exit poll data, union households made up just 14 percent of the vote in 1994, down from 18 percent in 1992. It was an historic low.[80] As George Kourpias told the Executive Council after the election, many union members refused to vote because of their "frustration with the Clinton administration for its failure to stop good-paying jobs from disappearing overseas." Teamsters' leader Ron Carey, meanwhile, related that many of his 1.3 million members were confused about where Clinton stood on labor issues. If these members were to be won back, the administration had to emphasize its "concerns for workers."[81]

Overall, the results were devastating. Every incumbent Republican gubernatorial, senatorial, and congressional candidate was reelected. The Republicans also picked up eleven new governorships, eight seats in the Senate, and fifty-three seats in the House, giving them control of both chambers for the first time in forty years. Frustrated with Clinton's failed initiatives, many voters responded to outspoken Georgia representative Newt Gingrich. A committed conservative activist, Gingrich was also House speaker, using the role to outline a "Contract with America" that promised an assault on budget deficits and steep cuts in social programs. Observing these developments, the AFL-CIO's Construction Trades Department called the 1994 elections a "disaster." Even the *AFL-CIO News* was bereft of positive headlines. "Election imperils progress for workers," it summarized.[82]

Suddenly, the AFL-CIO was back under fire, its hopes for progressive reform stymied after just two years. In April, Tom Donahue told a regional conference that the Federation confronted "the most clever, tenacious, mobilized right-wing power bloc in recent American history." Donahue argued that, for the labor movement to survive, it needed to "work as hard as we can and work in solidarity," a message that Kirkland echoed. The 1994 elections transformed the political climate, effectively killing most of the legislation that the AFL-CIO was seeking. As Kirkland told the Council, "With the changes in the makeup of Congress, the prospect of positive labor law change in the next two years is unlikely." Rather than pushing for health care reform, the Federation now had to fight to defend key social programs, particularly Medicare and Medicaid.[83]

Proposed cuts in Medicare and Medicaid were part of the promised "Contract with America." Republican leaders also sought to relax wage and hour regulations, weaken health and safety rules, and cut the number of government workers. Furthermore, they proposed a balanced budget amendment that threatened Social Security benefits. According to the AFL-CIO, "anti-worker interests" had launched an "assault" on working Americans that promised to "subvert workplace democracy and undermine virtually every social and economic gain the labor movement has ever achieved." The Federation duly pledged to "vigorously oppose" these efforts.[84] For many in the labor movement, however, it was exasperating to be on the defensive again, to see the hopes raised by Clinton's election cut short so quickly. In May 1995, for example, Bill Bywater told the Executive Council that there was a "high level of frustration among many union members with the antiunion climate both of employers and Congress." More had been expected of a Democratic administration.[85]

In the wake of the 1994 elections, the AFL-CIO faced many other problems. As the Federation had feared, deindustrialization accelerated after NAFTA; in 1994, the manufactured goods trade deficit was $156 billion, an all-time record. "America's trade policies are not working," claimed the AFL-CIO. By November 7, 1994, the Labor Department had already received 275 petitions for trade adjustment assistance under NAFTA, representing more than 30,000 workers. Of these, 118 were certified. Actual job losses were higher, as many workers sought assistance through the regular Trade Adjustment Assistance Program, which was less restrictive.[86] In lower-wage manufacturing industries, particularly textiles and apparel, job losses were especially pronounced. To be sure, some of these losses were also caused because a sharp drop in the Mexican peso—which lost 50 percent of its value relative to the dollar during the first year of NAFTA—made Mexican imports cheaper. Federation staffers, however, viewed what was happening as a product of a flawed treaty. "Pretty much everything we predicted was going to happen as a result of this, has happened," recalled Mark Anderson. "Now some people think that's good, but the migration of employment . . . the increase in the trade deficit . . . the downward pressure on wages in the U.S . . . all these things . . . happened." Overall, summarized George Kourpias, most unions were "affected terribly" by NAFTA.[87]

These conclusions were disputed by the business community, which—while implicitly acknowledging that some jobs had been lost, especially in manufacturing—pointed to service sector jobs created by the agreement. "Actually, NAFTA's impact on jobs hasn't approached the debacle that critics had predicted—the famous 'giant sucking sound,'" summarized *Business Week*.[88] With the White House also insisting that NAFTA was a success, tensions with the AFL-CIO continued. In May 1995, for example, Anderson told the Executive Council that the administration was glossing over the true costs of the agreement. "Few economists or government officials had been willing to admit or to say publicly that the data emerging in the aftermath of the NAFTA agreement are showing far greater job losses in the United States than its supporters predicted," he noted. Many labor leaders remained bitter. In June the Federation refused to participate in a hemispheric trade meeting in Miami that Cabinet officers were planning to address. At another meeting in 1995, the Council claimed angrily that they had been let down by the side agreements, which lacked enforcement mechanisms.[89]

The labor side agreement proved to be particularly disappointing. Just as the Federation had feared, enforcement on both sides of the United States-Mexico border was weak—at best. When side agreement complaints were filed, usually alleging failure to protect the right to organize and strike, hearings were duly held. Workers testified, often taking considerable risks to do so. In several cases, the U.S. government office in charge of the hearings concluded that serious violations of the law had occurred. After this, however, nothing happened. Trade sanctions for failing to comply with the side letter were nonexistent, and there were no other meaningful penalties. In Mexico, moreover, the official labor unions were closely aligned with the ruling political party, misleadingly called the Party of Revolutionary Institutions (PRI), and they tended to advance the corporate agenda. Although unofficial workers' organizations challenged NAFTA, exploitative employers used recognition of official unions to undermine their critics. Workers who joined unofficial organizations risked being harassed or fired.[90]

Even many years later, both Kirkland and Donahue felt bitter about this outcome. In an oral history interview in 1996, Kirkland called NAFTA an "atrocity" and admitted that the labor rights side agreement, which he had placed hope in, was "ineffectual." It had "no teeth" and was "a pure façade." Donahue, who had run much of the campaign against NAFTA, was more restrained, yet his disappointment was clear. "Our campaign was to insist that they put in proper labor protections, and environmental protections, and neither of those things happened," he recalled.[91]

For the AFL-CIO, NAFTA was a big blow. Overall, it compounded the severe problems that globalization was already causing the labor movement, especially in the manufacturing sector. By 1996, nearly 24 percent of the world's economic output entered international trade, whereas in 1973 just 12 percent had. Between 1990 and 1997, developing countries' financial flows—or the money that came in and out of their economies—also jumped from $44 billion to $256 billion. Capital had become internationalized, and institutions such as the World Bank, the IMF, and the World Trade Organization—which officially commenced on January 1, 1995, and regulated international trade—were the custodians of the new order. Workers in high-wage labor markets experienced serious disruptions. As economist Jagdish Bhagwati wrote in an influential tome, this was the era in which globalization became a "defining issue," dividing its supporters and critics across the globe.[92]

Privately, AFL-CIO leaders acknowledged that it was not just NAFTA that had caused massive jobs cuts. Indeed, these losses were occurring before the agreement was ratified. At an Executive Council meeting in May 1993, George Kourpias admitted that "even without a NAFTA agreement, thousands of jobs are being exported to Mexico, and the labor movement will need to develop a strategy to prevent even further erosion and losses of American jobs and exploitation of Mexican workers." In the service sector, there were also problems, with Lenore Miller of the Retail, Wholesale, and Department Store union relating that her members were suffering as work was outsourced. Other employers threatened to move if they did not gain major concessions, another common problem.[93] As Tom Donahue reflected later, NAFTA ultimately exacerbated an existing process. "It accelerated damage which was already underfoot," he summarized. "The big leakage of U.S. jobs, in those years, was to Mexico. . . . There's no way we could compete with them, and NAFTA just made that easier." Even before NAFTA had been enacted, the Federation estimated that there were 1,700 maquiladoras (U.S.-owned plants) in Mexico, employing some 450,000 workers. In 1992 workers in these plants were paid an average of $1.64 an hour, making goods that were mainly destined for the United States. There was no doubt, however, that NAFTA had made the situation much worse.[94]

The political disappointments of the early Clinton years also had important internal consequences for the AFL-CIO. For Kirkland and Donahue, these years were bitterly ironic. The steady duo had survived the hostile presidencies of Ronald Reagan and George H. W. Bush without any significant challenge to their authority. When the AFL-CIO had faced a clear external threat, Kirkland's call for solidarity had resonated. During the Clinton presidency, however, both men would be toppled from within. The failed fight against NAFTA, along with the results of the 1994 elections, set the stage for these remarkable events. Within a few months of the election, popular SEIU president John J. Sweeney announced that he would run for the presidency. The result was a bitter internal fight, and the first contested election in the Federation's history. The AFL-CIO would never be the same again.

CHAPTER EIGHT

Saying No to the Status Quo
The 1995 Leadership Challenge

From 1979 to 1995, Lane Kirkland and Tom Donahue brought stability to the AFL-CIO. Both men took pride in holding the Federation together in difficult times, in keeping its membership—in absolute terms—steady. By the end of 1994, however, Kirkland was seventy-two years old and Donahue was sixty-six. They had both served eight terms in office. What the two incumbents—and their supporters—saw as stability was, for others, inaction and lethargy in the face of the ongoing decline in union density and, after 1994, a hostile political climate. Led by John Sweeney, the dissidents' challenge broke an unspoken rule within the AFL-CIO, where protocol proscribed open criticism of Federation leaders or other union presidents. For reformers, however, a healthy AFL-CIO needed to tolerate more robust internal debate. The challenge left a legacy of bitterness, especially among those who lost. At the same time, it also created a reenergized Federation whose leaders were committed to bold new reforms. These were decisive events, especially as the Sweeney-Donahue contest was, as the *Chicago Sun-Times* observed, the first "contested election" for the AFL-CIO presidency. While acrimonious and divisive, the race launched a new era in the Federation's history.[1]

Over the winter of 1994–95, the first stirrings of discontent became public. On January 28, for example, reporter Frank Swoboda broke the story on the front page of the *Washington Post*. According to Swoboda, "influential" members of the Executive Council felt that Kirkland was "unable to meet labor's new needs." Supporting the claim, several union leaders were interviewed. "We need a more dynamic leadership. There are strong feelings it's time for a change," claimed one. Another added: "Lane represents the same old thing, and right now people are demanding change." While the union presidents were all quoted anonymously, it was clear that Sweeney and Gerald McEntee, the president of AFSCME, were integrally involved. "We didn't have a federation that was on the go," McEntee explained later. "It had, institutionally, stood still for any number of years. We had a dwindling of membership without any offsetting activity. We saw our political influence and strength on the wane. We weren't risk takers." McEntee and Sweeney later related that they had begun sounding out other Council members on the need for a leadership change in the fall of 1993, gradually building covert support for the challenge. A forceful activist who had been dissatisfied with Kirkland's leadership for many years, McEntee played the key role. The president of AFSCME since 1981, the plainspoken Philadelphian had never bonded with Kirkland, regarding him as "aristocratic" and aloof. "I disliked him for a variety of reasons," he admitted later.[2]

When the story broke, Kirkland refused to engage with the criticisms in detail. He also stressed that he had not received any formal approach asking him to consider his future. Privately, both Kirkland and Donahue were angry that their critics had vented their frustrations in public. Later in the year, Donahue wrote union presidents that Sweeney and McEntee had acknowledged that they were "the sources" for the leaks. "Call me old-fashioned," he blasted, "but in my book anonymous attacks in the press are neither courageous nor good for the AFL-CIO." Even two decades later, Donahue was clearly hurt by the challenge, pointedly referring to his former opponents only by their surnames. For him, the "split" was initiated by "the dissatisfaction of people like McEntee." Others shared Donahue's resentment. As the *New York Times* summarized, Kirkland's supporters were "outraged that council members had gone public with the federation's dissent."[3]

Defending his conduct, Sweeney emphasized that he had tried to persuade Kirkland to go quietly. On August 31, 1994, and February 3, 1995, he met with Kirkland at the headquarters, telling him about the strong feelings of dissatisfaction in the ranks. Sweeney urged Kirkland to step down so that Donahue could take over. Reacting defensively, Kirkland refused. "I said Tom Donahue would be the candidate," Sweeney wrote later. "He (Kirkland) said, 'I don't want to talk about it.'" As a result, the upcoming Executive Council meeting, scheduled for February 20–23 in Bal Harbour, Florida, became the forum for critics to air their complaints. This was an unprecedented outcome. "Never in the years since World War II," wrote the *New York Times'* Peter T. Kilborn after the meeting, "have the shingles been flying from the house of labor's normally well-ordered façade as they are now."[4]

Kirkland's detractors criticized his record on a number of grounds. The aging leader, they argued, had failed to capitalize on the ending of the Reagan-Bush era, especially as the Democrats controlled both the legislative and executive branches of government for the first time since 1980. The election of Clinton had inspired great hopes, yet these had been largely dashed. In *America Needs a Raise* (1996), where Sweeney laid out his vision of change, he also summed up the case against Kirkland. He cited a number of recent political defeats, including the Federation's failure to stop NAFTA and its inability to ban the permanent replacement of strikers. For Sweeney, the situation high-lighted the need for renewal at the top of the AFL-CIO. "With Bill Clinton's election in 1992," he concluded, "we had, for the first time in twelve years, a president who was not our sworn enemy. Yet labor continued to lose almost as many legislative battles in Washington as we won."[5]

Sweeney and his supporters also pointed to the failure to "move mean-ingful labor law reforms" through the Presidential Commission on the Future of Worker-Management Relations, which had been chaired by former Sec-retary of Labor John Dunlop. Issued in December 1994, much of the Com-mission's 115-page final report was favorable to labor; it called, for example, for more protection of workers' rights during organizing, including the holding of prompt elections. The Commission, however, also pressed for a relaxation of the restrictions on "non-union employee participation pro-grams," which companies used to facilitate worker involvement and discus-sion. While the Commission stressed that "company-dominated forms of representation" should remain illegal, union leaders argued that the Com-mission opened the door to the legalization of company unions, which had been banned since the 1935 National Labor Relations Act. Kirkland, who had helped to engineer the report, was now blamed for its recommendations, as critics argued that the new Republican majority would use them to push their antiunion agenda. The Republican Congress also showed no interest in enacting the Commission's recommendations to make organizing unions easier.[6]

Kirkland's opponents also criticized his focus on foreign policy. "That was one of the beefs *I* had with him," recalled McEntee, "that he didn't care as *much* for the workers here, as he did in . . . foreign countries, in Europe and places like that."[7] Some of the president's supporters also remembered the charge, adding that it gathered force once the Cold War ended. In many ways, Kirkland was a Cold War labor leader, and in a new era he was vulnerable to a challenge. Even a political supporter, Barbara Easterling of the Communica-tion Workers, recalled that many in the Federation thought that Kirkland spent too much time on foreign affairs. "A lot of people felt that he (Kirkland) did too much international work, and too little [domestic] work," she remem-bered. "People resented that." In a tough domestic climate, added Easterling, members "expect[ed] you to be right on the scene, where their problem is." In June 1993, for example, several union presidents were annoyed that Kirkland was in Europe when Congress debated the bill to ban striker replacements.[8]

The criticism annoyed both Kirkland and Donahue. International affairs, they insisted, were an important part of the AFL-CIO president's brief, and domestic union leaders—answerable only to their members—did not understand this. Kirkland, summarized Donahue, "unfairly gets tarred with, 'Well, he spent a lot of time on international affairs.' Well, he's supposed to." The complaints about Kirkland's focus on foreign affairs also revealed deeper dissatisfaction, however. Among many affiliates, there was a strong desire for a different style of leadership, one that was more connected to workers. As Sweeney's chief of staff, Bob Welsh recalled, "I saw the beginning of it . . . it was a lot of frustration, and people kept thinking, 'Well we can do *better* than this.' And I think part of it was Lane's style, Lane was a cerebral guy, he was not somebody who was . . . a *labor* leader." As Denise Mitchell, Sweeney's former campaign manager, put it, Kirkland seemed increasingly "aloof," leading to "a growing sense of frustration that was beginning to boil over." It was time, critics argued, for an AFL-CIO leader who resonated with the membership.[9]

Recalling the charges against Kirkland, even some of his supporters admitted that he should have been a "better politician" and communicated more with union leaders, particularly the presidents of large affiliates. In general, however, the incumbent's team continued to emphasize the constraints facing Kirkland, arguing that he had led the AFL-CIO at a very difficult time and had done a good job in the circumstances. Decline, recalled Kirkland's General Counsel, Larry Gold, was "an issue that . . . haunts everyone who has anything to do with unions." In the circumstances, Kirkland had "responded to it as well as anyone in his position—with his resources and his authority—could."[10]

The result of the 1994 midterm elections strengthened the emerging insurgency. At its meeting in February, which Trumka aide Ken Zinn recalled as "momentous," the Executive Council erupted into dissension, with much of the off-record discussion focusing on the fallout from the disastrous election. The results were a major blow to the labor movement, which had survived the Reagan-Bush years partly because Democratic congresses blunted the hostility of the Republican administrations. In 1994, however, Republicans won control of the House and the Senate for the first time in four decades. This was a "nadir" for the AFL-CIO's political program, thought staffer Michael Podhorzer. Many affiliates now felt that new leadership was needed to revive the Federation. Over the weekend prior to the meeting, eleven union presidents had formed a "Committee for Change" to remove Kirkland. Apart from Sweeney and McEntee, the Committee included Owen Bieber of the Autoworkers, George Becker of the Steelworkers, Ron Carey of the Teamsters, Arthur Coia of the Laborers, Wayne Glenn of the Paperworkers, Frank Hanley of the Operating Engineers, George Kourpias of the Machinists, Sigurd

Lucassen of the Carpenters, and Richard Trumka of the Mineworkers. Although Kirkland retained support in other parts of the Federation—particularly the Building Trades and smaller industrial and craft affiliates—his opponents had amassed a formidable coalition.[11]

Reflecting on the formation of the Committee for Change, other Federation staff also stressed the importance of the 1994 election. Kirkland and Donahue were taken on, recalled Federation lawyer Damon Silvers, because "they had failed in the AFL-CIO's fundamental mission, which was to make sure that working people's voice was heard in Washington. We'd lost the ninety-four elections, right, and I mean it was a perception, [the] political capacity of the labor movement had become unacceptably weak." The election results, thought Bob Welsh, were the "nail in the coffin" for the Kirkland presidency. Many felt, moreover, that Kirkland's response to the poll debacle was inadequate. While the result was "disappointing," he cautioned that it "did not mean that working people have given up hope for better health care, safer workplaces and better treatment on the job." There was no mention of the need for internal reform.[12]

The election was especially important because it undermined Kirkland's legislative strategy and highlighted the necessity of organizing. If decline was to be averted, the main solution seemed to lie in organizing, rather than in political activity. While Kirkland recognized the importance of organizing—as the setting up of the Organizing Institute showed—he had generally followed Meany's approach of focusing the Federation on politics and lobbying, leaving organizing to the affiliates. At the meeting, Kirkland acknowledged that the new Congress was "unlikely" to agree to labor law reform, while other key legislative goals had been thwarted. As a result, it was "increasingly important to advance the cause of organizing." Placed on the defensive, Kirkland announced the appointment of a committee to examine the AFL-CIO's role in organizing. Sweeney was appointed to the body, as were several other leaders who subsequently supported his political challenge.[13]

At the extraordinary Council meeting, which lasted almost five hours and occurred behind closed doors, a brief discussion of organizing also revealed a large gap between Sweeney and Kirkland. While Sweeney pushed for greater involvement by the Federation, Kirkland claimed that organizing was the "responsibility of affiliates." The renewed emphasis on organizing benefited Sweeney, as he had a strong record in the area. Sweeney chaired an AFL-CIO Committee on Organizing, allowing him to formulate new strategies and publicize them to affiliates.[14] Since the 1980s, the energetic SEIU president had also used AFL-CIO conventions to push for a stronger emphasis on organizing.

At the 1987 convention in Miami Beach, for example, Sweeney promoted a resolution that called for more organizing, especially among white-collar workers. "We must make organizing our number one priority," he declared. "Organizing needs to be rebuilt from the bottom up. It takes leadership at the top to recognize this, but the day-in and day-out work must be done at the bottom."[15]

Kirkland did make some response to the 1994 election results. At the February meeting, he announced the launch of new communication activities, particularly "Stand Up for America's Working Families," a media campaign designed to get members more involved in politics so that the Federation could fight back against the "Contract with America." The campaign was quite extensive, with members mobilized through television advertisements and an informational video, as well as badges, bumper stickers, and other materials.[16] Shortly afterwards, "Stand Up" material was distributed through the AFL-CIO's new homepage on the Internet, an important breakthrough. "I believe the popularity of the AFL-CIO's Internet site will continue to grow as more people become aware of it," reported David St. John in 1995. In addition, the Federation established its LaborNet "computer communications network," using it to make electronic contact with staff and some members. In February 1995 Kirkland also pushed through a one cent per capita penalty on affiliates whose affiliation rate with state federations was less than 44 percent. Some thirty-two affiliates were affected, highlighting how Kirkland's presidency—and especially grassroots political work—had been undermined by his reluctance to take prompt action to increase the affiliation rate.[17]

To many in the Federation, however, Kirkland's response to the election results was disappointing. The elections had led to an "acute sense of alarm," wrote Sweeney. "Working Americans had come to a critical point—with corporations downsizing, wages stagnating, unions declining, and our enemies seizing control of Congress." Yet Kirkland did not seem to share this feeling of urgency. "We waited for the top leader of the AFL-CIO to raise his voice or sound his trumpet—but the silence was deafening," alleged Sweeney. When the Council discussed the election results with House minority leader Richard Gephardt, Kirkland was apparently silent, the minutes failing to record any evidence of anxiety or alarm. While several of his challengers—including Kourpias and Becker—did speak, Kirkland seemed at a loss for answers, helping the reformers to gather strength.[18] For UFCW president Doug Dority, the 1994 election results played a key role in pushing him to support the leadership challenge. "Lane was a very intelligent guy, and very articulate, but he went over better with professors and doctors than he did necessarily with union guys," he related. "Then in '94 is when the Republicans won the

Congress . . . Dick Gephardt had been one of our real heroes, and all of a sudden he's a minority leader, instead of a majority leader. Basically, the labor movement was kind of standing still at that time, and so a lot of us got together and started talking about, 'Mm, it's time for a change.' "[19]

The Council meeting left Kirkland gravely weakened. The eleven unions that made up the "Committee for Change" had enough votes to remove him at the upcoming AFL-CIO convention in October. The involvement of Sweeney and McEntee was particularly crucial, as the SEIU and AFSCME were fast-growing unions with memberships of 1.1 and 1.3 million, respectively. The Teamsters also had well over 1 million members. Kirkland knew that he was in serious trouble.[20]

The insurgents hoped that Donahue would be installed as Kirkland's successor, allowing a changing of the guard to occur without major disruption. Well-liked within the Federation, Donahue had escaped some of the fallout from the 1994 elections. He had also been praised for his role in coordinating the fight against NAFTA, as well as his earlier efforts on the Committee on the Evolution of Work. As Donahue had been Kirkland's right-hand man for over fifteen years, and he was younger, most union presidents felt that he deserved the top job. The hope was that Donahue could serve one or two terms before handing over to a younger reformer. Donahue, however, refused to run against Kirkland, his long-term boss and political ally, despite strong pressure from the insurgents. "Sweeney, McEntee, all these other characters, are pressing me to run," recalled Donahue. "They want me to be the president. . . . They were using me, against Kirkland, and that was intolerable, so I was retiring, and that would take me out of the fight. And that pissed off McEntee." On May 8 Donahue surprised many observers by announcing that he would resign as secretary-treasurer at the next convention. At the same time, however, Donahue had not stood and fought with Kirkland, and he admitted later that part of him thought it was time for the president to retire. Yet Donahue insisted that Kirkland—who had served the Federation for nearly fifty years—"was entitled to a gentleman's exit."[21]

These were decisive moments. In April, as the challenge against Kirkland strengthened, Donahue felt that the president came close to stepping down. "I'm convinced," recalled Donahue, "he [Kirkland] was on the verge of dropping out, and saying, 'I'm going to retire.' " After several union presidents, particularly McEntee and Trumka, began to openly criticize the AFL-CIO leader—even telling him to "lead, follow, or get out of the way"—a piqued Kirkland changed his mind, revealing a stubborn streak to his character. "Well, fuck 'em, *I'm* going to run," he told Donahue.[22] Others who were close to Kirkland felt that he was genuinely shocked by the challenge, and found it hard to step aside. "I think in a large measure he never expected that," related Lenore Miller. "He . . . didn't see it coming, and didn't want to recognize it as coming." Just a few months earlier, Kirkland had received the Presidential Medal of Freedom, viewing this as evidence of his successful leadership. At the Executive Council meeting in Washington, DC, on May 9, Kirkland announced that he would be seeking a new term at the convention, while Donahue declared that he would be retiring. As he stood down, Donahue called for solidarity within the ranks.[23]

This appeal was ignored. With Donahue unwilling to run, the rebel unions intensified their search for a strong and effective challenger. "A battle could do some good within the federation," explained McEntee. Given the voluntary nature of the AFL-CIO, any candidate had to achieve consensus and prevent damaging disaffiliations. Though he was popular, Trumka, at forty-five, was considered too young for the presidency, while McEntee was abrasive and not as popular. "McEntee could have gotten one vote," quipped Doug Dority. Sweeney, however, led a large, successful union, giving him activist credentials. In particular, the SEIU's "Justice for Janitors" campaign was gaining contracts for vulnerable workers at this time. In June the high-profile campaign organized a National Justice for Janitors Day, securing positive media attention. Sweeney's calm, reassuring demeanor also meant that he could appeal to more conservative unions. A devout Catholic, the SEIU leader was mild-mannered, a good listener; many of his friends likened him to a priest, while reporters often described him as "avuncular." As a result, even Sweeney's opponents found it hard to disparage him. "I always liked Sweeney," recalled Barbara Easterling, who later ran alongside Tom Donahue. "You're not going to get a milder-looking person than John Sweeney. I mean to get his feathers ruffled, you just had to be a really obnoxious person."[24]

Combined with his successful record as SEIU president, Sweeney's personal qualities made him a formidable candidate. "Not only was he (Sweeney) a Pope-like personality, and very personally reassuring," recalled Andy Stern, who later became SEIU president, "but he had then also sort of remodeled the union, had produced growth, and I think people felt like it was something very much needed in the American labor movement." Sweeney was clearly the right man for the moment. "He was successful, but not threatening," summarized Stern, "a comfortable change agent." Those who were involved in the discussions recalled that they pushed Sweeney to come forward. "John was dragged," related Gerry McEntee. Sweeney was "drafted," added Bob Welsh, because he was "the only logical person who could win election." Pressed by a large number of union presidents, Sweeney concluded that he had to run. "A number of the major unions came to me and urged me to come out strongly, for myself," he recalled.[25]

Alongside Sweeney, Trumka was selected to run as secretary-treasurer, boosting the challengers' activist credentials. Elected president of the UMW in 1982, at the age of just thirty-three, Trumka was respected in the labor movement for his militancy and organizing skills, especially his leadership during the Pittston strike in 1989–90. Trumka was keen to serve alongside Sweeney, whom he described as "one of most humble, best men that I've ever known in my life." The ticket was boosted by the creation of the office of executive vice president, a position designed to mobilize the central labor councils and state federations, as well as reach out to racial minorities and women. The insurgents recruited Linda Chavez-Thompson, a vice president of AFSCME and an activist in the Labor Council for Latin American Advancement, to run for this position. The daughter of Mexican-American farm workers, Chavez-Thompson symbolized the diversity that the reformers promised to bring to the labor movement. If she was elected, Chavez-Thompson would be the AFL-CIO's highest-ranking woman and the first person of color to serve as a top officer. She recalled the significance of her candidacy. "It was a male-dominated labor movement, for years and years," she reflected. "Women were never able to reach high levels of leadership, those that did were very few and far between . . . and . . . were Anglo, Caucasian." Times were changing. On June 13 the insurgents formally announced their triumvirate of candidates, promising that they offered a "New Voice for American Workers."[26]

The formation of the "New Voice" ticket put further pressure on Kirkland. By early June, ten more unions had proclaimed their opposition to his reelection; the rebels now claimed twenty-one affiliates, representing 56 percent of the convention delegates. While these affiliates shared the dissatisfaction generated by the recent political defeats, many also supported Sweeney because they felt that it was time for Kirkland to retire, and for a younger leader to take over.[27] Recognizing that he had little chance of winning, Kirkland announced in mid-June that he was reversing his decision, and would retire on August 1. In a short public statement, Kirkland avoided direct recriminations against his challengers and declared that he wanted Donahue to serve out his term. He still got in some covert barbs, explaining that he was stepping down because he had a "duty" to ensure that "the future direction of the AFL-CIO will be in the hands of one who places the solidarity and best interests of labor as a whole above other considerations." Clearly, Kirkland felt that his critics had disregarded the solidarity that had been the central theme of his presidency. Proclaiming that he had no regrets, Kirkland also implicitly defended his record as president, returning to a seafaring metaphor to do so. "When talking of goals yet unmet," he said, "an old seafarer comrade-at-arms used to say: 'Tomorrow is also a day.' I call upon my successors to make good use of that bright day."[28]

On August 1, 1995, there was also some bitterness in Kirkland's private farewell remarks to the Executive Council. Knowing that his time was up, the departing president tried to be magnanimous. He acknowledged that after "thirty-five years on the bridge of this ship . . . it is now my watch below." At the same time, Kirkland took a swipe at his critics, suggesting that their actions had hurt the AFL-CIO. He spoke out against those who had tried to advance their "own ambitions and interests on the backs of others," making themselves "look better to the gallery by tearing down . . . colleagues." He also claimed that some Executive Council members were "still a rung or two short on the ladder of human perfection, charisma notwithstanding." At the same time, Kirkland appealed for unity, arguing that it was more important than ever. In closing, the exiting leader stood by his record. "I have done it my way," he declared. "There are undoubtedly other ways and quite probably better ways. But it has been the only way I knew that fit me, and I have never faked it."[29]

Those who were close to Kirkland recalled that he never recovered psychologically from these events. According to Susan Dunlop, his long-serving assistant, Kirkland was hurt deeply by "the split," as many Federation staff—particularly Kirkland's supporters—revealingly termed these events. Feeling pushed from office, Kirkland was "angry to the end." The veteran leader felt this way, agreed Tom Donahue, because his opponents had disputed his record, hurting his very core. "If this had been done in a different way," he stated, "if people had challenged Kirkland and said: 'Look, Lane, you're 73, you ought to go,' it might have been a different matter. But they challenged him as an incompetent." Even some of those who had confronted Kirkland admitted that their actions broke an unwritten code governing conduct in the labor movement. "That's the way most of us in the labor movement are brought up," recalled Doug Dority, "you don't go against your leader, unless they're corrupt, or they're so bad that it's incredible. I mean it took a lot." With the AFL-CIO losing members and political ground, Dority—and others—insisted that precedent had to be broken.[30]

The sixteen-year Kirkland presidency thus came to an abrupt end, as the understated South Carolinian slipped quietly away with no fanfare. A short article in the *AFL-CIO News* surveying Kirkland's incumbency—without contributions from current union presidents—was one of the few markers of his departure. "It was a sad end," recalled Dunlop. "Maybe partly he brought it on himself, but I was sorry that it happened to him. . . . It was kind of going with a whimper, and not a bang, and he should have been able to go out with a bang." Kirkland, who had recovered from a previous battle with cancer, died four years later from lung cancer at the age of 77.[31]

Kirkland's resignation allowed Donahue to run for the presidency at the upcoming convention. On the same day as Kirkland's announcement, Donahue duly withdrew his planned retirement and declared that he would run. "I had indicated a month ago that I intended to retire in October," he explained, "but that statement was predicated on the fact that Lane was running for reelection." Justifying his volte-face, Donahue also cited his extensive experience in the union movement, claiming that he had "the unique capacity to unite it at this time."[32] Donahue lacked backing from the key reformers, who were still smarting from his refusal to run against Kirkland. The Sweeney campaign had "gone too far down the road to pull back," declared the president of a major industrial union, speaking anonymously. Although Donahue was annoyed by his opponents' conduct, they insisted that they had no choice. As Richard Trumka commented later, "It was too late, we'd already announced the team, and had a campaign going, and the train left the station, and so Tom decides to run at that point . . . but the die had already been cast."[33]

Donahue retained the votes of pro-Kirkland affiliates, especially the more conservative craft and building trades unions, as well as the backing of Kirkland himself. He also had most of the Executive Council behind him. Recognizing this, the rebels agreed to support Donahue's bid to serve as interim president until an election could be held at the convention. At the August Executive Council meeting, Donahue was elected as the AFL-CIO's third president. Following the vote, Sweeney expressed the first congratulations. Donahue defeated Sweeney by a vote of 21 to 12, while Barbara Easterling beat Richard Trumka in the secretary-treasurer's race by the same margin. Easterling's election was significant, as the former coal-miner's daughter from West Virginia became the first woman to serve as an AFL-CIO executive officer. Straight after the vote, Sweeney urged all affiliates "to join in a dialogue to unify the federation," and he also moved a successful motion that declared the elections unanimous. What followed, however, was the most divisive period in the Federation's history. As the historian Taylor Dark has observed, "The stage was finally set for an epic confrontation at the October convention over the future leadership and direction of the labor movement."[34]

While not lacking a personal element, the battle between Sweeney and Donahue revolved around a number of key issues. There were fundamental differences between the two men and their supporters, especially when it came to how the AFL-CIO should address decline and revive the Federation. Above all, Sweeney wanted a much heavier emphasis on organizing, and his demands pushed Donahue to respond. In August Donahue stressed that the budget of the Organizing Institute had increased 400 percent since 1990. He also claimed that the Institute was being "used extensively" by affiliates to recruit and train organizers. Donahue, however, repeatedly found himself defending the record of the past, whereas Sweeney offered more concrete suggestions for the future. Since 1993, Sweeney had advocated the creation of an AFL-CIO organizing fund that would be used to push affiliates into doing more recruiting, particularly among low-wage workers.[35] For Sweeney and his supporters, particularly in the SEIU, Kirkland's reforms—which Donahue was inextricably associated with—had not gone far enough. Despite the changes, Sweeney pointed out that the labor movement was still spending over 90 percent of all resources on servicing members. "To reverse the change in union density requires a change in resource allocation," charged a resolution submitted by Sweeney's SEIU to the 1993 AFL-CIO convention.[36]

Sweeney's interest in organizing was rooted in his background. Born in 1934, Sweeney was raised in a working-class household in the Bronx, and he claimed that this upbringing motivated him to connect the AFL-CIO with the rank and file. Both of Sweeney's parents were Irish immigrants, and one aide described the labor leader as "Irish as hell." Another termed him a "street guy from New York." Sweeney's father drove a bus in New York City and took his son with him to union meetings. From his father, Sweeney saw firsthand how unions provided important economic benefits for working people. "Because of the union, my father got things like vacation days or a raise in wages," he recalled later. "But my mother, who worked as a domestic, had nobody. It taught me from a young age the difference between workers who are organized and workers who were by themselves." President Sweeney later cited the example of his mother, who had worked for families on the Upper East Side her whole life, as he supported efforts to give greater rights to marginalized workers. "This is personal for me," he explained.[37]

After working as a porter and gravedigger while he was in college, Sweeney entered the labor movement. He quickly worked his way up the Building Service Employees International Union (which later became the SEIU). From his earliest days in the union movement, Sweeney placed a strong emphasis on organizing and grassroots mobilization. "I *always* had a very pro-organizing commitment," he recalled later. "I was always focused on organizing as the backbone of the success of the labor movement."[38] Within months of becoming SEIU president in 1980, Sweeney announced a major organizing campaign among office and clerical workers, a fast-growing—and largely nonunion—segment of the economy. The move marked a departure for the labor movement, and Sweeney pushed the Federation to do more to lead the effort. Led by women's activist Karen Nussbaum, in early 1981 the SEIU itself established District 925, the group's name referring to the working hours of most office workers.[39]

Throughout the 1980s, Sweeney consistently called for the Federation to play a much stronger role in organizing. This, rather than internal unity, was the only long-term solution to decline. At the 1985 convention, he typically submitted a resolution that called for "*mass* organizing," demanding that the Federation "play a stronger role in developing organizing campaigns." Backing up his rhetoric, in 1986 the SEIU was a major supporter of a campaign to organize the Blue Cross/Blue Shield health insurance company. The SEIU, UFCW, AFSCME, and several other unions participated in the effort, while the AFL-CIO provided "staff direction and technical assistance."[40] In the late 1980s—a time when many affiliates were shedding members—the SEIU also launched its innovative "Justice for Janitors" campaign in thirteen large American cities, including Los Angeles, Denver, Atlanta, and Pittsburgh. Relying on signed cards and community pressure rather than NLRB elections, the campaign secured positive media attention and led to organizing gains. Overall, the membership of the SEIU grew from 625,000 to 1.1 million during Sweeney's four-term tenure, giving him a powerful platform from which to challenge.[41]

These campaigns highlighted how the AFL-CIO's membership had been transformed by the influx of service and public sector workers, mirroring the broader changes that had taken place in the economy. In terms of membership, by the time of the 1995 race the SEIU, AFSCME, and UFCW were the biggest affiliates, surpassing former manufacturing stalwarts such as the UAW and USW, which were in decline. As a result, the AFL-CIO was a much more diverse body than it had been a generation earlier, counting huge numbers of white-collar and female workers—as well as racial minorities—among its ranks. As journalist Gary Frank noted, symbols of union membership had changed; whereas a generation earlier, most Americans would have associated union members with "a wrench, a lathe, and a hardhat," by the early 1990s the symbols were just as likely to be "a video display terminal, a nurse's uniform, and a briefcase." Sweeney effectively encapsulated these changes. Although he was—like Meany—an Irish-American from New York City, he

came out of the fast-growing service workers' union, and was much more connected to workers in the new economy. Keen to represent women, Sweeney's
inclusion of Linda Chavez-Thompson was significant, and many of his staffers
were also female.[42]

Overall, Sweeney's supporters insisted that he was an agent of change, and
was best placed to take the AFL-CIO forward. Managing Richard Trumka's
campaign for secretary-treasurer, UMW staffer Ken Zinn summarized how
many Sweeney supporters saw the issues in the election. "It was about whether
the AFL-CIO was going to be the leader of a labor *movement*, or whether it
was going to continue to be an organization that was more of a union *trade*
association. I think it was about whether it was going to reach out to new immigrant workers, people of color . . . whether there was a role for the AFL-CIO,
and the labor movement as a whole, to actually *organize* again. It was about
whether the labor movement had a future. There were some very crucial issues, and finally a rejection of the old way of doing business Meany and Kirkland
had championed." In contrast, Donahue ran on his record, and promised more
gradual change.[43]

Women and racial minorities got behind Sweeney's calls for change with
particular enthusiasm. Many of them felt that Kirkland's efforts to diversify
the Federation, while a step in the right direction, had not gone far enough.
By 1995, women made up over 39 percent of union members, and blacks
15 percent, yet the thirty-five-member Executive Council had thirty white
men, two black men, and three women—one a Latino. Even before Sweeney's
challenge, internal discussions highlighted the demand for reform in this
area. In early 1995, for example, the Federation's Full Participation Committee declared that the AFL-CIO needed strategies to ensure that women, minorities, and younger workers could achieve "greater participation" in their
unions, and secure more leadership positions. It was especially important to
bring about "increasing inclusion of more members in activities at all levels."
The Civil Rights Committee added that affiliates' civil rights and women's
departments often felt "isolated from the work and power of the union and
from avenues to promotion." Many activists hoped that Sweeney would take
diversity much more seriously.[44]

Even during the election process, Sweeney bucked convention and
sought to give a greater voice to members. In particular, he moved debate
beyond the Executive Council. The key decision-making body favored Donahue, largely because each union, regardless of size, had an equal vote. As a
result, a group of twenty or so small unions could make binding decisions
without the backing of most members, and the smaller unions tended to

favor Donahue. Sweeney wanted to transfer decision making to the convention, where each union was allotted a number of delegates in proportion to its membership. Because the insurgents' support was concentrated in the largest affiliates, they knew that this increased their chances of winning. At the convention, each state federation and central labor council was entitled to send one delegate, and the New Voice ticket was also determined to secure these votes. Over the summer and fall of 1995, the rebel unions waged a public, nationwide campaign for grassroots support, forcing Donahue's team to try and do the same. Not only was this the first contested election in the AFL-CIO's history, it was also the first to be conducted in the open, with both sides making their case in public forums.[45]

During the campaign, both sides advanced a number of significant proposals. Sweeney promised to spend at least $20 million a year on the hiring and training of new organizers, particularly women and racial minorities. He also called for a new political program that would be more focused on grassroots activism, with much greater involvement from the state federations and central labor councils. "Our politics," he declared, "must start in the neighborhoods where our members live and vote." Sweeney also faced up to the decline issue with unprecedented candor. Organized labor had declined from "a political powerhouse to a political patsy," and had become "a movement of agonizers, rather than organizers." To turn things around, Sweeney promised a fresh emphasis on organizing and politics, his "twin towers of salvation."[46]

In response, Donahue implemented reforms during his interim presidency. In particular, he approved plans to double the number of organizers trained by the federation each year. He also set aside funds to train 500 local union members to work on key campaigns in the upcoming congressional elections. These changes were part of Donahue and Easterling's "eight-point plan to reform and revitalize the AFL-CIO," a manifesto that also promised increased visibility in the media, a stronger emphasis on diversity, and retooled international programs to help workers take on multinational corporations.[47]

While the two teams generally stuck to the issues in public, the records of the campaign reveal that it also became divisive and personal. In particular, some Donahue supporters attacked the insurgents over their treatment of Kirkland, accusing them of forgetting key labor values such as solidarity and fairness. In July Moe Biller, the president of the American Postal Workers Union, wrote Sweeney to protest about how Kirkland had been removed. His letter captured the strong feelings provoked by the campaign: "I want you to know how I feel about the way you, Gerry McEntee, Rich Trumka and others have treated Brother Lane Kirkland throughout your collective escapade. I personally resent how you and your cabal have demeaned Lane Kirkland as a human being. You have dragged him through the mud, held him up to public scorn, and generally treated him worse than you would a dog in the street. I must ask you, John, what is the labor movement all about if it isn't about human decency?" Other Donahue supporters, including Albert Shanker, the president of the American Federation of Teachers, and Morton Bahr, the president of the Communication Workers, wrote similar letters. Official union publications also took sides, often attacking their adversaries in the process. "Mr. Kirkland's opponents," editorialized the IBEW's *Electrical Union World*, "have done a great disservice to American workers and to Mr. Kirkland personally. . . . These conspirators have much not to be proud of."[48]

In response, Sweeney's supporters criticized the record of the Kirkland-Donahue years. Under Donahue, blasted the leaders of several pro-Sweeney affiliates, the AFL-CIO had focused on "embracing the status quo of inaction on issues and concerns vital to American workers."[49] Sweeney's campaign material also mocked Donahue and Easterling as dull conservatives who were out of touch with grassroots Americans. Only "New Voice," they claimed, had "given so much attention to the plight of American workers," and only they could turn the labor movement around. "It was unfortunate," recalled Denise Mitchell, "but it became extremely bitter."[50]

Donahue's team was keen to dispute their opponents' criticisms. They lambasted the records of both Sweeney and Trumka, challenging claims that they alone had the credentials to reverse union decline. As one Donahue campaign "Fact Sheet" put it, "Department of Labor records show that today the UMWA receives 34% *less dues* than when Trumka was first elected in 1982." The Mineworkers, they pointed out, had suffered its fair share of failed strikes and membership losses. While this was true, it was hardly the kind of publicity that the labor movement needed. Sweeney's record as SEIU president was also scrutinized, with Donahue's team claiming that most of the union's growth came from mergers with independent unions rather than organizing.[51]

In August there were tense exchanges as both sides claimed that their ticket was the more diverse. In particular, Donahue supporters pointed to the fact that they were proposing Barbara Easterling as secretary-treasurer, a position that Sweeney had not offered Linda Chavez-Thompson. They also criticized the creation of the new office of executive vice president. "Why are you running a woman for a nonexistent position?" asked Sandra Feldman, the president of the United Federation of Teachers. "Why didn't you run her for

Secretary-Treasurer, a position which exists?" Sweeney avoided a direct response to these attacks, and in general his campaign material was more restrained, perhaps because he had the numbers to win. Sweeney repeated his message, however, that only his team could take the labor movement forward. "The Federation," he wrote in a resolution that he sent to Donahue, "must be the fulcrum of a vibrant social movement, not simply a Federation of constituent organizations."[52] As members were bombarded with materials and phone calls appealing for their support at the convention, state-level leaders called for calm. "The last thing we need at this crucial time in the labor movement is a civil war," wrote Texas AFL-CIO president Joe D. Gunn in May. "The public upheaval in our leadership must draw to a close before the convention." Both sides also made efforts to stop what Bob Welsh called the "negative campaigning," but met with little success.[53]

By September, Sweeney's supporters were confident of victory, and they pressured Donahue to withdraw. On September 15 a coalition of six union presidents, led by Frank Hanley, wrote the AFL-CIO leader. They defended Sweeney's conduct, pointing out that he had only stepped forward to "lead the campaign for change" after Donahue had refused to run. It was Donahue who had acted dishonorably, they argued, by refusing requests to run against Kirkland and then changing his mind. "Given your feelings about the absolute need for unity in the labor movement and the steadfast, majority support for John Sweeney," they concluded, "we respectfully request that you withdraw your candidacy for president of the AFL-CIO." Donahue remembered that his relationship with Sweeney's supporters deteriorated further at this point, especially when he refused to step aside. He recalled one visit from a delegation of Sweeney supporters that ended particularly badly: "George Kourpias, who was then the president of the Machinists, Hanley, who was the president of the Operating Engineers, and McEntee came to my office. We were going to have a meeting, to talk, I thought. McEntee walked in, stuck his finger in my face, and said, 'You've got to get out of this race.' I said, 'Well, fuck you, no point in talking about this.'"[54]

Although Donahue was determined to see the campaign through, he knew that he was up against it. Later, he reflected on his decision to contest the election to the end even though he lacked the votes. "I kept hoping I'd sway somebody's opinion, bring another group over, but it wasn't there," he admitted. Given his close links to the Kirkland regime, Donahue repeatedly found himself defending the record of his former boss. In particular, he cited Kirkland's success in reuniting the Federation, as well as his efficient management style. In contrast, Sweeney, as an outside candidate, was able to offer a clearer message of change. Appealing directly to the grassroots, he promised to "reenergize the labor movement," to focus attention on the plight of workers who did their jobs with dignity despite declining pay and increasingly demanding working conditions. His "New Voice" slogan offered an effective snapshot of this message. In contrast, Donahue's "Changing Labor Changing America" slogan failed to gain traction, particularly in the media. Although he was only six years younger than Donahue, Sweeney effectively cast his opponent as a man of the past. On Labor Day, for example, the SEIU leader remarked that he was not around when the holiday had been first celebrated in New York 113 years earlier. "However," he quipped, "I understand my friend Tom Donahue was."[55]

Such jibes hurt Donahue. In many ways, moreover, the race was ironic because there were striking similarities between the two men. Both were Irish-Americans from the Bronx. Both were from humble backgrounds; Donahue's father had been a janitor, and as a young man the labor leader had worked as an elevator operator, a school bus driver, a bakery worker, and a doorman. Both Sweeney and Donahue were also in their sixties, and both had spent almost their entire careers in the labor movement. Remarkably, the pair had even come out of the same local union, 32B of the Building Service Employees Union, a 40,000-member organization that represented all of the elevator workers and janitors in New York City. They had become friends when they attended seminars on labor issues at Manhattan College. As Donahue remembered, he had been responsible for selecting Sweeney for his first post at 32B, becoming a mentor to the younger man. Because of this past, Donahue felt betrayed when a man he had "hired" ran against him. Even two decades after the 1995 contest, these feelings lingered. "I had dinner with John, one night, after I had decided to run, and we had a long dinner," he recalled. "I concluded, saying, 'John, I find it incredible that *you* are going to run against *me*. I mean it's just incredible, we've been friends for all these years.' He lived in a house here that I helped him find. . . . We were really quite close. We visited on Easter, and Christmas, and that sort of thing. . . . He kept saying: 'I know, Tom.' I took that to mean that he was agreeing with me. He wasn't! He was saying he knew." Despite Donahue's appeals, Sweeney was aware that he had a lot of support behind him, and he refused to withdraw. Donahue, he recalled, only had a "few" of the larger affiliates behind him.[56] Looking back, Sweeney reemphasized that it was Donahue who had changed his mind about running, forcing the contest. Still, he acknowledged that the race took a heavy toll on both men. "It was a tough, tough time," he related, "and it was tough for me because we had a good friendship, we had a good working relationship."[57]

Declaring publicly that he wanted to have a "spirited contest," Donahue fought on. With a hint of annoyance, he declared that Sweeney should not be allowed to "walk in uncontested in some form of old-style Russian election."[58] Even Donahue's supporters, however, were under no illusions about the result. Many unions were drawn to Sweeney, recalled Lenore Miller, because he tapped the "frustration of the times." There was a strong desire for change, and Sweeney had drawn on it well, laying out a seductive reform message. Fighting back, Donahue tried to cast doubt on Sweeney's ability to deliver on his promises. Speaking from experience, he stressed the limits of the AFL-CIO president's power, especially as affiliation with the Federation was voluntary. Sweeney, however, rejected the idea that the AFL-CIO was a "rope of sand." Rather, it was robust enough to withstand a "rigorous challenge of self-examination."[59]

The race came to a head with the remarkable events at the twenty-first convention. Known for the private nature of its discussions, the Federation had never had a convention like the one that opened on Friday, October 20, 1995, in New York City. There was record media interest and unprecedented attendance, necessitating the use of additional hotels. By Friday, registrations had been received from 527 delegates representing national and international unions, and 530 delegates representing state and local central labor councils. The convention hall could not accommodate all the delegates, alternates, and observers who wanted to attend, forcing the latter group to watch proceedings on television monitors.[60] The convention had been well organized by Sweeney's team, who understood its importance. As Sweeney staffer Stewart Acuff candidly recalled, "I played a big role in helping to pack the convention with central labor council and state fed delegates, which was a key part of the strategy. . . . Even though we knew we had a majority of written ballot votes, we wanted to make sure we had a majority for *hand* counts, and so we made sure. I think 500 central labor councils and states' feds were represented." Whereas previous conventions had featured limited debate, this meeting was characterized by an open discussion of the issues. At its heart, for the first time, was a lengthy debate between the two contenders.[61]

In the debate, which was moderated by the *Wall Street Journal*'s Al Hunt, Sweeney eloquently summarized the need for change in frank terms. The AFL-CIO, he declared, was "caught in a downward spiral of defeat and retreat," having lost the fights over NAFTA, health care reform, and striker replacement. Then came the 1994 election debacle. Citing his record of growth at the SEIU, and stressing the support behind him, Sweeney insisted that only the "New Voice" team could turn things around. "If you want three people who know how to work the streets as well as the suites," he declared, "three people who can walk the walk and talk the talk, then you should choose John Sweeney, Linda Chavez-Thompson, and Rich Trumka and say 'no' to the status quo."[62] These appeals inspired many floor delegates. After years of belonging to a labor movement that was under fire, they wanted fresh—and more aggressive—leadership. "There is an air of excitement and renewal," commented Daniel Knorr, an Ohio delegate. "Labor has been a sleeping dog for too long," added steelworker Don Lance. "We can move forward." Sweeney encouraged these expectations. "I sense from traveling around the country that there is a spirit of enthusiasm that things are going to turn around and improve," he exclaimed.[63]

In response, Donahue stressed the "limitations" of the president's power, a more difficult message to sell. Attempting to hit back, he argued that he could give labor an experienced voice on the national stage, one that did not rely on "crib notes and canned speeches written by others." Offering "nothing but glitzy phrases and old-fashioned rhetoric," Sweeney lacked substance. Donahue also refuted Sweeney's criticisms of the Kirkland years; the SEIU president, he pointed out, had served on the Executive Council throughout this period and could not just blame the problems on others.[64] Overall, the two men offered a sharp contrast, and Sweeney was effective at placing Donahue on the defensive. One exchange epitomized the differences. "I believe in blocking bridges," declared Sweeney, as he outlined how to fight back against aggressive corporations. "We have to worry less about blocking bridges and worry more about building bridges," replied Donahue, who worried that the Federation would "lose sight" of its members if it became part of "some broader protest movement." Sweeney even expressed admiration for French workers, who had shut down much of the country to protest against cuts in pensions and health insurance. His supporters also promised greater militancy. "Something historic's about to happen!" declared Richard Trumka in a memorable convention speech. "You are about to see corporate America's worst nightmare come true!"[65]

When the votes were counted on October 25, Sweeney had won a clear victory. He gained the support of thirty-four unions, representing 7.28 million workers, or 57 percent of the Federation's membership. In contrast, Donahue was endorsed by more affiliates (forty-two), but they only represented 5.7 million workers. Donahue won support from the building trades, the food

and allied trades, and unions in the communications, maritime, and enter-
tainment sectors. Sweeney's strength was concentrated in the very large
unions, especially those in the public, service, transport, and health care sectors. He also received backing from large manufacturing unions, including
the UAW and the Machinists. "New Voice" had triumphed, with Trumka
elected as secretary-treasurer and Chavez-Thompson as executive vice president, the convention approving the creation of this new office. Hearing the
vote count, Sweeney aide Anna Burger remembered a "moment of hope,
optimism, and enthusiasm that we hadn't got in a long time." Feeling that
they had seen "the other side" of the labor movement, Sweeney's supporters
were "very excited." Because a majority of the Council had not backed Sweeney, he quickly expanded the body from thirty-three to fifty-four members.
While it was sold as a means to increase the representation of women and racial minorities, this move strengthened Sweeney's leadership, as he was able
to offer seats to supporters. Many previously unrepresented union presidents
had also wanted to be on the Council for some time, and a few of the seats
were offered to Donahue followers. This helped to ensure that Sweeney's
election was achieved without major disaffiliations from the Federation, a
constant fear.[66]

In his acceptance speech, Sweeney was magnanimous. Calling for unity,
he even quoted "Lane's" advice to the 1989 convention that, "Solidarity has
been our shield against the most primitive and the most sophisticated assaults by agents of avarice and exploitation." Sweeney also signaled, however,
that he was serious about carrying out major reforms. He paid credit to the new
Executive Council, describing it as "truly representative" of the AFL-CIO's
diverse membership.[67] Once the result was known, Sweeney felt that the
Federation rallied behind him and people moved on. "I had great support from
the affiliates at the time," he recalled, "even those who supported Tom, and
Lane, for the most part, all came around, and we got off to a good start."[68]

For those in the Kirkland-Donahue camp, however, the bitter divisions
of 1995 were not easily erased. Because the AFL-CIO president took over
immediately after the vote, the changeover was immediate. Revealingly,
Donahue was not on hand to pass Sweeney the gavel, having left the convention hall before voting began. "He isn't that much of a masochist," commented an aide, speaking anonymously. "He never came back, for the
afternoon session, Tommy," recalled Gerry McEntee, "he just took off and
left. He was so hurt, embarrassed." In the short term, the transition was also
not as smooth as Sweeney recalled, especially for the vanquished. According to Jim Baker, Kirkland's former assistant, Sweeney's staffers "looked at

all of those who had preceded them as if we were war criminals." As Sweeney brought in many new staff, including a large number from the SEIU,
existing employees left in large numbers, often feeling that they had no
choice.[69] Even years later, former staffers remained divided about the race,
and communication between the camps was limited. Almost two decades
on, Tom Donahue also referred to John Sweeney, his former friend and colleague, exclusively by his last name. The relationship between the two men
would never be restored. "We're a movement that doesn't easily forget,"
commented Donahue.[70]

There was also bad feeling on the Executive Council, where UFCW president Doug Dority—who had supported the challenge against Kirkland and
had then backed Donahue against Sweeney—was drafted to mediate between
the two sides. "On the Executive Council," he recalled, "a lot of them were
saying, 'Fuck it, I'm not serving on the Executive Council, with those bas-
tards,' and people were talking about breaking away from the AFL-CIO—
Donahue supporters—and forming a shadow executive board." Such emotive
talk was short-lived, however, and Dority succeeded in persuading both sides
that an embattled AFL-CIO could ill afford further division. As a result, despite their private misgivings Council members united behind Sweeney for
the benefit of the institution. In the end, there was no split—no unions left
the Federation as a result of the 1995 race.[71]

For Kirkland, his short retirement was spent quietly. "After his resignation," summarized William Serrin in the *New York Times*, "Mr. Kirkland was
rarely in the public eye." Kirkland never forgave his opponents, later accusing
them of "mendacity and falsehood." As a result, in the last few years of his life
the former AFL-CIO leader was a lonely—and somewhat forgotten—figure,
and he rarely had contact with the new leadership group. According to Larry
Gold, who served as the Federation's General Counsel from 1980 to 1995,
Kirkland was never the same after being forced from office. "He ceased to be
a fully functioning person of the kind he had been before, once that happened, it was just devastating to him," he summarized.[72]

Although declining health curtailed his travel, Kirkland remained interested in international affairs, particularly in Eastern and Central Europe. In
the summer of 1998, he was invited to represent American trade union members at an international human rights conference in Warsaw. In a rare—and
reserved—letter to "President Sweeney," Kirkland asked if he should deliver a
message on behalf of the AFL-CIO. "If so," he noted, "I would assume the
Federation would be prepared to pay my travel expenses for that mission. If
not, I shall attend, with my wife, at our own expense." There was no record of

a reply from Sweeney.[73] When Kirkland died the following year, it was revealing that *America@Work*, the successor to the *AFL-CIO News*, restricted its
observances to a one-page obituary, quite a contrast to the extensive coverage
that had followed George Meany's passing. In a respectful but restrained
piece, Kirkland was praised as "one of the master builders of the American
union movement." There was no mention of the leadership challenge, the article simply noting that Kirkland had "retired as president in 1995."[74]

For an institution that had been characterized by top-down leadership and
limited debate, the events of 1995 were extraordinary. As Sweeney declared
on the last day of the convention, what had occurred in New York was "historic." For the first time, the AFL-CIO had openly recognized not only that it
was in decline, but that major reforms were needed to try and address this. By
running such an effective campaign, Sweeney had inspired great hopes, both
among his supporters and outside observers. His task now was to translate
these ideas into reality.[75]

CHAPTER NINE

Big Visions and Big Hopes
The Early Sweeney Years

The early Sweeney years were a remarkable time. Hitting the ground running, the new administration poured resources into organizing, securing some impressive early results. In 1998 the Bureau of Labor Statistics reported that union membership had increased by 101,000 over the previous year, a notable turnaround. It seemed that the long-term trend of union decline had been halted, prompting Sweeney to declare that labor was "on the right track."[1] In the political arena, the AFL-CIO won some important victories. During the 1996 elections, it ran an extensive political campaign, turning out a record number of voters from union households. In November 1997 the Federation also helped to block President Clinton's Fast Track trade bill, which threatened further job losses. An air of optimism infused the AFL-CIO headquarters, which was now staffed by an unprecedented number of women, many recruited from outside the labor movement. Among them was Lane Windham, a twenty-seven-year-old Duke University graduate who got a job working as a media aide in the president's office. "Everywhere you looked there was activity, and plans," she recalled. "People had such big visions, and such big hopes. It was just a matter of . . . whose vision got the resources, right. There was no question we were going forward, the question was just in which direction, and how. . . . It was a great time."[2]

The media picked up this air of optimism, providing the labor movement with sustained positive coverage for the first time in decades. In the immediate aftermath of Sweeney's election, many experienced journalists believed that the new leader was capable of reviving the labor movement. According to labor reporter Stephen Franklin, Sweeney may have looked like a "cuddly grandfather," but he made "fiery pronouncements not heard from labor's top leaders in many years." To *Time*, Sweeney was the "rebel of American labor," while the *San Diego Union-Tribune* thought that he was "as tough and as militant as the captain on a picket line."[3] The business press was apprehensive. According to the *Journal of Commerce*, the AFL-CIO's "militant turn" represented "the most dramatic shift in the direction of U.S. labor since the 1930s." Sweeney's candidacy, added the *Wall Street Journal*, represented a "revolution," and employers should be worried.[4] Calling the new AFL-CIO head

"a force for inclusion and activism," President Clinton also welcomed Sweeney's election, and was upbeat about labor's prospects.[5]

The optimism was still evident at the end of 1999, when the AFL-CIO
joined with environmentalists and engaged in mass demonstrations at the
World Trade Organization (WTO) conference in Seattle. To many, the protests were a high point, confirming that Sweeney had transformed organized
labor into a progressive force. Heading into the 2000 presidential election,
the AFL-CIO's revived political machine poured resources into Al Gore's
campaign, helping him pick up the crucial states that made the vote such a
nail-biting affair. Gore's controversial defeat—in what most labor staffers saw
as a "stolen" election—proved a turning point. It resulted in the presidency of
George W. Bush, initiating a hostile era that put the labor movement back on
the defensive. Then, in 2001, the unexpected events of September 11 also
hurt labor, cementing in place a conservative political climate where foreign
policy was prioritized over domestic affairs. Sweeney's presidency never
recovered.[6]

To be sure, even if Gore had secured the presidency, Sweeney would have
found it hard to reverse labor's decline. Corporate opposition to organized
labor was as deep-seated and sophisticated as ever, while labor's ranks continued to be decimated by deindustrialization and globalization. The economic
boom of the late 1990s, which helped organizing, was likely to have ended
anyway. At the same time, the double whammy of Gore's defeat and 9/11
clearly turned the Sweeney presidency. While Clinton had been unable to
deliver on key legislative goals, he had listened to organized labor, even appointing AFL-CIO staff to White House posts. He had also opposed antiunion legislation; in July 1996 he vetoed the "Teamwork for Employees and
Management Act," an effort by the Republican Congress to weaken the NLRA
and allow company-dominated unions. In sharp contrast, Bush's aides ignored
the Federation and pursued antiunion policies. Looking back on the Sweeney
presidency, AFL-CIO staffers repeatedly pointed to the significance of both
the 2000 election and 9/11, seeing them as key turning points. Once Gore
conceded, the positive media headlines about Sweeney's presidency also
stopped. As late as May 2000, labor was reported to be on the "rebound," but
a year later it was chastened. "The labor movement had bet the ranch on Al
Gore," summarized David Moberg in the *Nation*, and his narrow defeat had
catastrophic consequences. After 2001, the second part of Sweeney's presidency would be very different from the first. "The Bush change, and then
September 11th, made the country more inward-looking," recalled staffer
Denise Mitchell, "so suddenly unions were on the defensive. The gains that

were being made, just stopped." By 2009, when a jaded—and noticeably frailer—Sweeney stood down at the age of seventy-five, the hope of the early days was long gone.[7]

Sweeney came into office with considerable momentum. Even before he became AFL-CIO president, the SEIU leader consistently emphasized militancy and worker mobilization, arguing that these were the keys to organizing new groups. In the summer of 1995, Sweeney led a sit-in of striking janitors that blocked rush-hour traffic on Washington, DC's Fourteenth Street Bridge for two hours. In his acceptance speech, Sweeney continued the tough talk, promising to use mass demonstrations and corporate campaigns "to make worker rights the civil rights of the 1990s." Sweeney's team, recalled staffer Craig Becker, "came in committed to make the AFL-CIO a fulcrum for change within the Labor Movement."[8] At a time when real wages were falling and welfare entitlements were being eviscerated, Sweeney promised to give working people a better deal. "America needs a raise," he told a group of New York business leaders.[9]

Sweeney expanded this message in *America Needs a Raise* (1996), an accessible 160-page text, much of it written in the first person. Energetic and clearly argued, the book was written with David Kusnet, a labor journalist and former speechwriter for President Clinton. It confirmed Sweeney's desire to reach out and mobilize public support, raising the AFL-CIO's profile. "I am writing this book," he explained, "to ask you to join the fight for every American's right to contribute—and share in the gains of—a growing economy." Sweeney stressed that while workers were more productive than ever, their wages were falling. Since 1979, productivity had increased by 24 percent but real wages had dropped by 12 percent. Over the same period, the wealthy had gotten richer. Wage gains were restricted to the top 20 percent, but Sweeney's AFL-CIO spoke for the 80 percent of Americans whose real incomes had declined. He promised to "rebuild and revitalize" the labor movement, arguing that this fight would "unite working Americans, and all Americans of goodwill, across the lines of color, class, and culture that divide us today." It was the vision of a labor movement that would achieve both economic security and social justice.[10]

Sweeney realized that in order for the labor movement to be rebuilt, there first needed to be substantial reforms at the top. At the 1995 convention, he pushed through changes that added eighteen seats to the Executive Council, raising the number of vice presidents to fifty-one and opening up places for women, minorities, and smaller unions. As a result, minority representation on the Council jumped from 17 to 27 percent. The key decision-making body now included seven women, nine blacks, two Latinos, and one Asian-American. As the *Pittsburgh Post-Gazette* observed, the union movement was "no longer too pale, too stale, and too male." Although it often received more criticism than big business, in many ways this was misplaced. At the time the federal Glass Ceiling Commission reported that 97 percent of senior managers at Fortune 500 companies were white, and a similar proportion was male. Sweeney had taken an important step in recasting labor's public image.[11]

The new executive vice president, Linda Chavez-Thompson, set a particularly significant example. A former illegal immigrant from Mexico, Chavez-Thompson was the highest-ranking woman and the first person of color to serve as a top officer of the Federation. "I'm a woman and I'm tan and I'm from Texas," she declared proudly. "I represent the American that organized labor has tended to forget: Women, people of color, people in right-to-work states." Like Sweeney, Chavez-Thompson promised to energize the labor movement. "I like to get arrested," she told reporters. Her candidacy, she recalled, was designed to "shake it up a little bit," a role that she clearly enjoyed.[12] As her executive assistant, Chavez-Thompson chose Arlene Holt Baker, an African-American who had risen up the ranks of AFSCME after starting out as a clerical worker. The daughter of a domestic worker and a laborer, Holt Baker had grown up in the racially segregated South of the 1950s. Like Chavez-Thompson, she had seen poverty and racial discrimination firsthand, and both women shared Sweeney's vision of a broadly conceived labor movement. "The workers' struggle, and the struggle for justice anywhere, was so connected," Holt Baker reflected.[13]

In the headquarters building, which had been marked by continuity and low staff turnover, there was a radical shake-up. These changes were necessary because most AFL-CIO staff supported Tom Donahue, who was more familiar to them. Some of those loyal to the old guard, such as David St. John, now left the Federation, while a group of older male staffers retired. Some had little choice. General Counsel Larry Gold, for example, was one of those "let go" as Sweeney took over. Markley Roberts, who had worked for the AFL-CIO since 1962—chiefly in public policy—also departed. "There was encouragement to get old staff out, and new staff in," he recalled. "I would like to think that that changed the results on organizing, and say generally that the new, young blood will achieve more than the tired old people like me."[14] The hiring of new staff did encourage regeneration. "When we had the election in 1995," recalled Susan Dunlop, who was one of the few staff to work for both Kirkland and Sweeney, "things were going to change, and really, I think there was a real interest in completely sweeping out the old AFL-CIO staff and replacing it with new people."[15]

Sweeney also made important physical changes to the building, demolishing a portico that had encouraged arrival by car and creating a new, pedestrian-friendly entrance. Under Kirkland, thought staffer Denise Mitchell, the AFL-CIO headquarters had a "fortress" feel, reinforced by the presence of "tons of black cars outside," whereas under Sweeney there was an "opening up." The new entrance increased access to the lobby and this—along with landscaping outside the entrance—encouraged greater socialization. Unlike Kirkland, who had been chauffeured most places in a town car, Sweeney drove his own vehicle to many appointments. In general, the new president made the building "much more approachable," a representative shift. Thus, Sweeney allowed more outside groups—including the Newspaper Guild and local civil rights organizations—to use the headquarters. For Mitchell, Sweeney's presidency was "premised" on the need to "reach out," not just to members but to all Americans and "the rest of the world too."[16]

Sweeney hired his staff from a much wider range of backgrounds, and included greater numbers of women and racial minorities. Executive appointments set the tone. The new international affairs director, Barbara Shailor, was a former flight attendant who had worked her way up the Machinists Union. In addition, Sweeney hired Karen Ackerman—a former anti-Vietnam War activist and grassroots labor organizer—as his deputy political director, and Denise Mitchell as his director of communications. A native of North Carolina, Mitchell was a communications specialist who had worked for Turner Communications during the early days of CNN, before doing consultancy work for the SEIU. Shailor recalled the fast pace of change. "The leadership, not just at the elected level, but at the senior staff level within the Federation, stayed pretty steady," she noted. "I think almost without exception John appointed new people, and . . . equally appointed women to very senior positions. I think people gasped when he appointed me (laugh), and Karen, and Denise as the head of communications."[17] The appointment of Rosalyn Pelles as director of civil rights and diversity initiatives was also significant. The daughter of African-American tobacco workers from Winston-Salem, North Carolina, Pelles oversaw some important reforms. "When President Sweeney came in," she recalled, "they were looking at both his ticket that he brought in with him, and people he brought into the Executive Council. [It] was the most diverse that it had ever been, so that was a determination to do work around inclusion, and diversity, and full participation, and that work was magnified over time."[18]

Staffers were incredibly optimistic as they started work. "I worked with John Sweeney for many years at the SEIU," recalled Karen Nussbaum, who came to the Federation in 1996, "but I was so excited about the notion of change from inside the labor movement." Nussbaum remembered that she felt "thrilled" at this time, especially as Sweeney was willing to discuss the decline of the labor movement and consider far-reaching solutions.[19] Also hopeful was Marilyn Sneiderman, a former community organizer for AFSCME who was hired to head innovative field mobilization efforts. "When President Sweeney was first elected," she asserted, "there was so much excitement, and so much energy, and so much hope, and so much optimism, that we were going to stem that tide of decline. There was a lot of creativity, a lot of like: 'This is our moment.' . . . It was big." Even experienced staffers such as Joe Uehlein, who had worked for the Federation's Industrial Union Department since the 1970s, remembered the "very exciting times" of the early Sweeney years, when he got a job running the Center for Strategic Campaigns, a new initiative designed to help unions apply economic leverage in organizing campaigns, as well as during bargaining disputes. "A lot of people went to work for John because they believed that was the opportunity to turn the labor movement around, myself included," he explained.[20]

This optimism was understandable. Sweeney was soon delivering on his promises, launching a dizzying array of new initiatives. Some were specifically designed to increase diversity and tap nontraditional constituencies. In 1996, for example, Sweeney established a Working Women's Department, selecting Nussbaum—a key founder of women's group "925"—to head it. Sweeney understood that women were important to labor's future; in 1996 they made up 39 percent of all union members, and the Executive Council reported "continuing strong, positive interest in unions" from female workers. Women also made up over 46 percent of the civilian labor force, and they were coming into the workplace at a faster rate than men.[21] In 1997 the Federation initiated a comprehensive "Ask a Working Woman" survey, polling thousands of women about the issues that troubled them in the workplace. Early surveys showed that women were most worried about the lack of equal pay, although access to affordable health care was also a major concern. Through the surveys and related initiatives, the AFL-CIO gave voice to the frustrations of women workers, their feeling that elected officials had failed to act on key issues. According to Meagan Jeronimo, a legal secretary in Houston, "Women are getting squeezed between stagnant wages and soaring costs, between the need to be involved in our kids' lives and inflexible work schedules . . . and most of us have had just about enough."[22]

Not content with documenting women's views, Federation staff organized "Ask a Working Woman" events; in 1999 alone, there were more than 100 of these, some led by prominent leaders such as Al Gore and Hillary Rodham Clinton. In May 1999, at an "Ask Working Women" event in Buffalo, Clinton told her audience that she would take the issues raised "back with us to Washington." Reform-minded affiliates—especially the SEIU and the UFCW— also began leadership classes for women members, and stepped up organizing efforts. Advocates pointed out that unions could clearly help women workers, especially in overcoming pay disparities. In 1996 unionized women earned 38 percent more than nonunion counterparts, yet the Clinton administration noted that women earned on average only 75 cents for every dollar a man made. Noting that the AFL-CIO was "pushing this issue," Clinton's aides supported legislative efforts to close the gender pay gap but were unable to overcome the opposition of the Republican Congress.[23]

Sweeney's efforts were especially significant in light of the AFL-CIO's history. Under Meany and Kirkland, efforts to diversify the Federation had moved quite slowly. Kirkland had overseen the placement of the first female on the Executive Council, yet five years later the thirty-five-member body contained just two women, at a time when they made up over a third of union members. At the 1985 convention, the AFL-CIO endorsed the status quo by passing over a woman, instead electing four men to the Council. As the *Wall Street Journal*'s Cathy Trost wrote at the time, for most union leaders the AFL-CIO was "still a Brotherhood." Under Sweeney, this was no longer the case.[24]

Sweeney also acted quickly in the organizing area. Soon after coming into office, he created the AFL-CIO Organizing Department, merged the Organizing Institute into the Federation, and started the new Center for Strategic Campaigns. Sweeney committed to sending 1,500 organizers into the field within eighteen months, a remarkable number when measured against past performance. As recently as 1990, the AFL-CIO had not trained any new organizers. By 1997, however, the AFL-CIO was spending $20 million a year on organizing, an eightfold increase compared to the early 1990s. In 1997 alone, the Organizing Institute trained 1,200 new organizers in its three-day programs. At the 1997 convention, the Federation also agreed to raise its percentage of spending on new organizing from 4 to 30 percent.[25] In early 1996, some of the funding for Sweeney's ambitious programs came from a deal with Household International, a finance company. Household agreed to pay the Federation $375 million over five years in exchange for being able to issue and service a special credit card for union members. By now, the Federation's

annual budget was $69 million, and the money was used to fund the new po-
litical program, as well as accelerated organizing efforts. The rapid expansion of organizing efforts enthused staffers. According to Rosalyn Pelles,
Sweeney provided a "new way of thinking" about organizing, and his call for
affiliates to commit more of their resources to it was "an amazing step forward."
The organizing initiatives, added aide Gerry Shea, were "really pioneering
programs."[26]

While Kirkland had often left organizing to the affiliates, under Sweeney
the Federation became much more involved, especially in big, talismanic
campaigns. In 1997 it supported a drive by the United Farm Workers to organize California's $550 million strawberry industry, which employed 20,000
workers. In order to coordinate this effort, Sweeney formed the National
Strawberry Commission for Workers' Rights, a coalition of labor and community groups. Pitched as the biggest organizing drive in the country, the
campaign sought a modest wage increase for the pickers, mainly Latino immigrants who earned just $8,000–$9,000 a year. Workers also had no job security, and conditions were harsh and hazardous, with pickers exposed to
pesticides and often denied access to basic necessities such as clean toilets
and drinking water. Spearheaded by Sweeney, the effort was supported by
many well-known national figures, including Rev. Jesse Jackson and actor
Martin Sheen. "This represents the unity of the labor movement," Sweeney
declared as he led a march of 17,000 people. While the growers bitterly resisted the campaign, it raised awareness of the workers' plight and helped to
re-ignite the organizing zeal of the United Farmworkers, which continued its
efforts across California's strawberry fields for several years.[27]

In general, the renewed emphasis on organizing initially paid off. In
1997 there were some important gains, including the unionization of 10,000
reservation agents at U.S. Airways and 5,000 mechanics at Continental Airlines. The following year, the Hotel Employees and Restaurant Employees
completed a card check recognition campaign at the large Bellagio Hotel in
Las Vegas, while other gains helped the Nevada city to become one of the
most unionized in the country. The change summarized how the Federation
was catching up with the dramatic shifts in the economy. "Las Vegas is the
only place in the U.S. where a hotel maid can afford to buy a house," declared
Hattie Carty, a widowed mother of ten who had risen from maid to local
union president.[28] Visiting Las Vegas in February 1997, Sweeney was upbeat.
At a raucous rally, he pledged to reach out to new members and forge alliances in the community, transforming the AFL-CIO into a "social movement
for economic justice." It was a message that many American workers—

including those in the Culinary Workers' assembly hall—were ready to hear. Journalists were impressed. "In an extraordinary display of class solidarity," related Marc Cooper in the *Nation*, "about 750 Latino dishwashers and gardeners, black maids and housekeepers, white soccer-mom nurses, and potbellied hardhats stood together and shouted, 'Union Power! Union Power!' as they exuberantly received the 62-year-old, baldheaded, banker-suited Sweeney as if he were some sort of rock star."[29]

In the first few years of the Sweeney presidency, some of the biggest gains came among health care workers. Building on his experience in the SEIU, Sweeney hired many staffers from his old union into Federation roles, and they oversaw some significant breakthroughs, especially in the health care sector. In February 1999 the SEIU organized 74,000 home care workers in Los Angeles, the largest union election victory since 1941, when Ford Motor Company had been organized. Capping a long campaign, the SEIU victory was especially significant because most of the new recruits were Latino women, the type of worker that Sweeney had promised to mobilize. Other gains followed, in both the service sector and in manufacturing. Sweeney was integrally involved; in 1998, for example, he was among dozens arrested in San Francisco in support of Marriott workers' right to form a union. Overall, progress was impressive. In 1999 the number of union members increased more than at any other time in the previous two decades. While changes in the economy, particularly the rapid growth of the service sector, meant that union density only held steady, the rise in the absolute number of union members was still significant. "The two-decade hemorrhaging of union membership has been staunched," pronounced the *Nation*.[30]

The gains in organizing also reflected how Sweeney and his staff had been able to revitalize the labor movement at the grassroots level, establishing much stronger links between the Federation and the rank and file. An important program in this regard was Voice@Work, which helped to publicize employer abuses when workers were trying to organize. In June 1999 alone, the Voice@Work campaign organized 120 local activities that were attended by 12,000 union members. The campaign was complemented by the changes taking place in the Federation's official publication. In 1996, *America@Work* replaced the rather staid *AFL-CIO News*, and magazine-style articles now featured workers' voices—and images—much more prominently. "In the magazine," recalled Denise Mitchell, "we would report much more on . . . how members told their stories, in organizing, trying to shine a light on best practices, as part of a change process." In one early story, for example, *America@ Work* publicized the case of the Latino workforce at the Richmark curtain manufacturing plant in Everett, Massachusetts, where the company had fired eight workers in an attempt to stop organizing efforts. As a result of the AFL-CIO's publicity, as well as a local community campaign, managers agreed to recognize the union and reinstated all the workers with back pay. Even the reporting of local stories was now sensitive to broader issues, and the Federation used its publication as a mobilizing tool, encouraging readers to get involved. As *America@Work* asked in its article on the Everett case: "Do workers in this country have a right to organize a union to improve their lives—or not?"[31]

Still, there was also plenty of corporate opposition, and major organizing gains were the exception rather than the rule. In private, AFL-CIO leaders were more circumspect. In January 1998 the Executive Council noted that there was "vicious employer opposition" to organizing. "Much work remains ahead," it concluded. The Federation found that committing resources to the task was insufficient, as intransigent employers would break the law to keep unions out. Ultimately, only labor law reform could really fix the problem, and Sweeney sought to create pressure for this change. In June 1998 he led a nationwide day of action in seventy cities in order to highlight the need for labor law reform. While the Republicans controlled Congress, however, there was little prospect of positive legislation. Employers knew this, and even some of the biggest AFL-CIO campaigns secured mixed results, at best. While it did force growers to raise wages and improve conditions, the strawberry workers' drive failed to produce a single union contract. Across the country, powerful corporations bombarded workers with antiunion propaganda during election campaigns, often relying on labor consultants to great effect. In 1999 one study of 407 private sector companies found that 75 percent of them had hired an outside consultant during an organizing drive. As textile union leader Bruce Raynor noted, at this time many workers—especially in the South—made "pragmatic decisions not to put their job on the line to organize a union" because they knew that it would "get smashed."[32]

Regardless of the results, in light of the AFL-CIO's history the emphasis on organizing was significant. George Meany had famously shown little interest in the area, and the situation only improved moderately under Lane Kirkland. Kirkland had set up the Organizing Institute and called for affiliate support, yet by the time he stood down the Federation's seventy-nine affiliates had a combined income of $6 billion, of which only a minuscule part was devoted to organizing. Furthermore, the topic was rarely discussed by the Executive Council. By the end of August 1996, however, the Organizing Institute had graduated 250 organizers, almost double 1994's 140 graduates, and

Council meetings included extensive discussions of organizing. Sweeney had breathed new life into the House of Labor, especially as organizers were coming from more diverse backgrounds. By the late 1990s, the percentage of female lead organizers was 21 percent, compared to 12 percent in the late 1980s, while the percentage of lead organizers of color had jumped from 15 to 21 percent in the same period. While there was more to do in this area, progress was real.[33]

Modeled on the 1964 Freedom Summer campaign, when thousands of students had traveled to Mississippi to register black voters, "Union Summer" was particularly successful. A four-week educational internship that paid participants $210 a week, Union Summer was designed to be a means through which activists could exercise their commitment to building a new labor movement, one that would empower working people "to address injustice in the workplace, community, and society at large."[34] In early 1996, when the program was launched, it attracted 4,000 applicants for 1,200 places. About half of those accepted were people of color, while an even higher proportion were women. Many found the experience, which included working on the front lines of organizing campaigns, both educational and empowering. "All I knew about unions was what the media fed me—you know, the mob stuff and that they were racist," reflected 20-year-old African-American participant Kenisha Rhone, who completed her internship in East Boston. "Now I wish I could organize my campus." The program broke down barriers between organized labor and the wider community, especially as interns marched with striking newspaper workers in Detroit, led a petition drive to prevent the antiunion Browning-Ferris Industries from getting a municipal contract in Seattle, and helped to organize the luxurious Melrose Resort on Hilton Head Island in South Carolina. Drawing on the civil rights legacy, many interns also took part in a bus tour that helped the UFCW to organize nursing homes in the South. In the course of this tour, interns visited iconic civil rights sites, including Selma, Alabama, and Jackson, Mississippi. Similar activities were carried out in subsequent years, and Union Summer became well known on many college campuses. Sweeney was proud of the program, reflecting that it helped to mobilize young people and had "just been fabulous."[35]

In the early years of his presidency, Sweeney also assumed a high public profile. Traveling extensively, he spoke of organizing as a "crusade." Anxious to improve public perceptions of organized labor, he declared that AFL-CIO conventions would be held in urban centers rather than glitzy vacation spots, helping affiliates to connect with their members and avert press criticism. In

1997 the biennial convention was held in gritty Milwaukee, pleasing local workers. "Just look around—you can see the change in the labor movement," declared delegate Mike Murphy. "This isn't some resort in Florida. This is a union city, a place that working people can identify with. Look at the delegates—young people, women, mothers with children." In a similar fashion, Sweeney moved Executive Council meetings from the Bal Harbour yacht resort in Florida to a variety of urban centers, including Los Angeles and Chicago. Not content to deal solely with traditional union constituencies, he also reached out to new groups. In 1999, for example, he made headlines when he "put aside thoughts of class struggle" and rang the opening bell at the New York Stock Exchange. "We like to do what's counterintuitive," explained Denise Mitchell.[36]

Striving to fulfill his commitment to make labor rights as important as civil rights, Sweeney connected the AFL-CIO with the Left, restoring ties that had been shattered by the Federation's enthusiastic support of U.S. foreign policy during the Cold War. Encouraged by Sweeney's election, in January 1996 more than thirty prominent intellectuals, including Betty Friedan, Henry Louis Gates, Arthur Schlesinger Jr., and Barbara Ehrenreich, wrote the *New York Review of Books* and promised to support labor's rebirth. Following this, Sweeney worked with left-leaning academics and launched more than two dozen teach-ins at universities, raising students' awareness of labor issues. As Steven Greenhouse observed in the *New York Times*, labor and the Left were "getting cozy again."[37]

Helped by his new staff, Sweeney also worked to build alliances with an emerging anti-globalization movement. In November 1999 union members joined with environmentalists, students, religious groups, and anarchists and engaged in mass demonstrations at the WTO Ministerial Conference in Seattle. Under Barbara Shailor's leadership, the AFL-CIO brought more than 20,000 unionists from around the world to Seattle for the protests. Rather than taking a protectionist tone, as they had in the past, union activists insisted that free trade agreements needed to protect workers' rights across the globe. As part of the protests, the AFL-CIO organized a large march from Seattle Center to downtown, with participants carrying signs that proclaimed, "Labor Rights Not Trade Wrongs" and "End Corporate Rule." Becoming known as the "Battle of Seattle," the protests, which brought the city to a standstill, overshadowed the conference. They even forced the postponement of the meeting's opening ceremonies, disrupting President Clinton's plans to use the gathering—which was part of a new millennial round of trade negotiations—to showcase American commitment to free trade. Sweeney was delighted. "We've been working on building this coalition for a few years now," he explained, "and we'll now put our heads together to see how we build on this."[38]

For many in the Federation, Seattle was a high point. Staffers who took part felt energized, regarding the protests as a prime illustration of the broad movement that they were trying to construct. "This was a moment when the environmentalists, and the labor movement, and the community groups, were interacting at a *whole* new level," recalled aide Lane Windham, who participated in the demonstrations. "I mean building a whole new level of progressive leadership. Now that's not to say there weren't differences. . . . But there's all these kinds of alliances happening that you wouldn't necessarily have thought of, and I thought held great promise." Marilyn Sneiderman, who helped to organize the protests, remembered that she worked effectively with local groups, symbolizing Sweeney's mantra of connecting the Federation with the grassroots. A strong local labor council already had good ties with community and environmental groups, and the AFL-CIO built on this. Overall, the Seattle protests represented "one of those moments when you could feel like people were together and could fight back against something that was wrong." Media reports were similarly upbeat. According to the *New York Times*, the "surprisingly large" protests had led to the emergence of a "new and vocal coalition" that could disrupt the president's plans for trade liberalization.[39]

The Federation moved to build on the Seattle movement. The following year, it worked with students, environmentalists, and religious groups who were opposed to the Clinton administration's plans to extend permanent trade ties with China. According to protesters, China had to improve its human rights record before it was made a lasting trading partner. The Clinton administration, however, remained committed to a trade policy based on "open markets under the rule of law." Around the same time, Sweeney also spoke at a rally in favor of writing off Developing World debt and announced an alliance with the Sierra Club. It was all a sharp departure from the Kirkland era. As Sweeney supporters proclaimed, this was "not your father's labor movement!" Overall, Sweeney had placed organized labor firmly on the left side of the Democratic Party and the political spectrum, whereas for the previous forty years this had not been the case. Organized labor in the United States now stood in much the same place politically as European labor, a considerable accomplishment.[40]

The Seattle protests also illustrated the important changes taking place in the AFL-CIO's international work. Sweeney underpinned these efforts, using a 1998 visit to Mexico City to announce a "new internationalism" that featured stronger bonds with unions in other countries, particularly in the Americas. It was especially important to fight the harshest aspects of globalization, which depressed wages and undermined workers' rights across the globe. "We are reaching out to allies across the world to pursue our common mission more aggressively and imaginatively than before," he declared.[41]

Related to these efforts, Sweeney also oversaw a striking change in immigration policy. Traditionally, the AFL-CIO had supported strict immigration controls. As recently as February 1995, the Executive Council had declared that immigration should be controlled by "orderly methods" that included "deterring unauthorized entries." With the emphasis on protecting the standards of American workers, immigrants—especially illegal ones—were seen as a threat. In February 2000, however, the Executive Council issued a historic statement that called for a "new amnesty program" for undocumented immigrants. According to the Council, these illegal arrivals were welcome, as most were making "enormous contributions to their communities and workplace."[42]

This was a bold shift, especially as it alienated many members. Just fifteen years earlier, the AFL-CIO had helped to pass legislation that punished employers who hired illegal immigrants, a move supported by many unionists. The Federation had to do "tons of education with our members" to convince them to accept the change, recalled Lane Windham, who oversaw large immigration forums in key locations. Clearly influenced by his experiences in the "Justice for Janitors" campaign, a committed Sweeney took the lead. Just a few days before 9/11, he led a march along Pennsylvania Avenue that reaffirmed the Federation's new immigration stance. The change also reflected Sweeney's own background, as well as his outgoing personality, as he enjoyed meeting with immigrant workers. "Mr. Sweeney was *leading* that work, which I think is huge," thought former associate general counsel Ana Avendano. As Windham added, given the AFL-CIO's history, the new immigration policy was "one of *the* central changes" of these years. This was an historic shift, and one that it is difficult to imagine Tom Donahue bringing about so rapidly.[43]

While the change reflected Sweeney's leadership, it also came about because of pressure from affiliates with large immigrant memberships, who appreciated that immigrant recruits could revive the labor movement. "By the year 2000 it was clear that a large number of unions were organizing immigrant workers," recalled Avendano, adding that employer requests to see workers' papers—policies that the AFL-CIO had previously supported—were a powerful "union-busting" tool. Even if undocumented workers were dismissed for union activity, they were not entitled to back pay or reinstatement, the two most powerful remedies available under the NLRA. Leaders such as articulate Hotel Employees and Restaurant Employees Union (HERE) president John Wilhelm had pushed for immigration reform for some time, and Sweeney was pleased to endorse the change. "You made me the proudest labor leader in the world by rewriting the AFL-CIO's policy on immigration," he told the 2001 convention.[44]

There were also important changes in international affairs, where Sweeney abolished the American Institute for Free Labor Development—a classic Cold War body—along with the Federation's institutes for Africa and Asia, merging their functions into the American Center for International Labor Solidarity. Many of the Center's new staff were sympathetic to the Left in Central America, a clear shift from the Kirkland era. Sweeney oversaw innovative programs to build solidarity with unions in other countries, particularly in Latin America and Europe, finding common ground in the struggle against globalization. In particular, workers had to cope with capital flight and the increasing dominance of multinational corporations on the world economy. "In the AFL-CIO the focus became on . . . multinational companies," recalled Barbara Shailor, "on pension funds and politics. That was being done with our affiliates, but it eventually sort of transferred into a discussion at the global level." Shailor oversaw a series of conferences where the AFL-CIO forged bonds with federations in other countries, sharing information on union pension funds and building a stronger global labor movement. Labor writers were again impressed. According to Harold Meyerson, Shailor had transformed the International Affairs Department into an "effective proponent of global social democracy."[45]

Domestically, Sweeney's political work also secured results. Sweeney came into office promising a "massive political effort" to mobilize Americans around the issue of falling wages and corporate downsizing. Shortly before the 1996 election, the Federation secured an important breakthrough when President Clinton signed a bill that raised the federal minimum wage from $4.25 to $5.15 an hour, while states were allowed to increase it even further. As he agreed to the hike, Clinton paid tribute to the AFL-CIO, especially its "tireless" president. The move was a victory for Sweeney's "America Needs a Raise" campaign, which had overseen grassroots lobbying and town hall meetings in twenty cities, as well as national advertising and public education.[46]

In the 1996 congressional elections, the AFL-CIO spent $35 million on political activities, a sharp increase that yielded results. Much of the money was used to increase labor's voice in the media, as well as boost its grassroots political programs. The campaign was funded by a dues increase that Sweeney pushed through. In the election, exit polls showed that union households contributed 24 percent of the vote, compared to just 14 percent in 1994. The union vote also helped to bring important labor issues—such as education, pensions, and Medicare—to the fore. While the Republicans kept control of both the House and Senate, after the disaster of 1994 the results were encouraging; not only did President Clinton come back to win an unlikely second term, but the Democrats also gained two House seats. Sweeney, declared *New York Times* reporter Francis X. Clines, was "a newly discovered national political force."[47] The Federation was proud of the outcome, which reinforced a sense that the early reforms were working—even though much more remained to be done. Led by Steve Rosenthal, Sweeney's new political team had increased the AFL-CIO's political power. "The labor movement was seen as a toothless tiger at that point, particularly coming off the ninety-four elections," recalled Rosenthal, a former community organizer who became political director in December 1995. "Our mission really was to try to figure out how to rebuild labor's political clout.... We built the political organization that put labor back on the map."[48]

Overseen by the field mobilization department, a new "Union Cities" program also increased the Federation's political effectiveness. The program sent out staff to work with central labor councils across the country, encouraging them to get more involved in politics and organizing. "Union Cities is this whole thing about building," explained Marilyn Sneiderman, the energetic staffer who headed the program. "Basically, Union Cities was: 'How do we transform the culture of the local labor movements, so that they are reaching out?'" The effort secured real results, particularly in large metropolitan areas. "Basically, most of the labor councils said to me, they'd never had this kind of support," added Sneiderman. Union Cities epitomized Sweeney's desire to connect with the grassroots, his understanding that the labor movement needed to be built from the ground up. By 2001, with Union Cities still growing, Sweeney anticipated further political gains.[49]

Following the 1996 election, the AFL-CIO won some important early victories. In November 1997 it helped to block President Clinton's Fast Track trade bill, which would have allowed Clinton to negotiate trade agreements that Congress could only accept or reject, not amend. Working closely with Congress, the Federation helped to ensure that the bill was withdrawn after an estimated 70 House Republicans declared against the president and their own party leadership. Worried about the prospect of further deindustrial-

ization, the Building Trades Department lobbied hard against the bill, persuading many Republican members to oppose it. Although Clinton made
extensive promises to representatives who would support him, against a reenergized AFL-CIO this was no longer enough.[50] In what Sweeney called a
"big win," the Federation conducted a well-financed campaign that targeted
Democratic candidates in key congressional districts and exploited voters'
concerns about job losses after NAFTA. In the course of the campaign, the
AFL-CIO made 800,000 phone bank calls, distributed 750,000 postcards,
and organized hundreds of rallies. According to the *New York Times*, this was
"labor's biggest legislative victory in years."[51]

Further victories followed. In June 1998 the AFL-CIO defeated California's Proposition 226, which would have required unions to get annual written permission from every member for political action, including voluntary
contributions to political action committees. According to labor leaders, the
provision would have stymied their political work. The following year, it
knocked back similar "paycheck deception" efforts—laws to create burden-
some restrictions on union members' rights to participate in the political and
legislative process—in eighteen states.[52]

At the national level, the Federation also carried on vital defensive work.
In 1998 it defeated congressional attacks on important protective legislation,
including wage and hour laws and health and safety provisions. The AFL-CIO
successfully protected OSHA's ergonomics standard—a key initiative of
Clinton's Department of Labor—from congressional interference, helping
millions of union and nonunion workers as a result. It also continued to fight
hard for an effective OSHA, a battle that secured results. By the end of the
twentieth century, fatalities in the American workplace had been halved since
OSHA was created forty years earlier, and occupational injury and illness
rates had declined by 40 percent. While there were many reasons for these
improvements—especially improved enforcement by OSHA and the decline
of the heavy industrial sector, where accidents were rife—the AFL-CIO's vigilance had also played its part. "We've had a very significant reduction [in
workplace fatalities], and I think it's basically the fact that we have laws and
enforcement," reflected Peg Seminario, the AFL-CIO's long-serving safety
and health director. The Federation's "pressure to maintain things" had made
a difference.[53]

At the same time, the Federation pursued key legislative goals with increased vigor. In 1998 it launched an extensive grassroots lobbying campaign
for health care reform and a Patient's Bill of Rights, organizing rallies at select
HMOs and at senate offices in forty different cities. Through such efforts, the

AFL-CIO helped maintain pressure for legislative action in this high-priority area.[54] Nationally, more aggressive use of members' voices in the media—particularly in the 1998 "Day to Make Our Voices Heard" campaign, and the 1999 "7 Days in June" program—also boosted the Federation's political work. Both programs concentrated on the "quiet war" that employers waged against workers who wanted to join a union, highlighting the ongoing need for labor law reform.[55]

These efforts were certainly noticed by labor's opponents, and conservative commentators were apprehensive about the AFL-CIO's political rebirth. "The real worry in GOP cloakrooms is the return of the relentless AFL-CIO," declared the *Wall Street Journal*'s Paul Gigot in April 1997. Under Sweeney, labor was "running a permanent election campaign" that concerned its opponents, who complained that it was unfair to spend members' dues on political activities. In the fall of 1997, *Fortune* ranked the AFL-CIO as the third most powerful lobby group in the nation, well ahead of the fifteenth-placed U.S. Chamber of Commerce. In the 1998 midterm elections, the AFL-CIO helped to ensure that, although union households accounted for just 17 percent of the population, they comprised 23 percent of voters. The Federation's figures also indicated that 71 percent of union voters had backed labor's candidates. Sweeney's staff claimed that they had reversed the trend of the Kirkland years, when labor had often struggled to stem the loss of its voters—especially white men—to the Republicans. Overall, the Federation asserted that working families had won some "major victories" in the elections; the anticipated Republican gains did not materialize, and the GOP actually lost five House seats. This was only the second time since the Civil War that the president's party had gained seats in a midterm election.[56]

In the early part of his presidency, Sweeney even oversaw victories in large labor disputes. In the summer of 1997, he gave high-profile backing to the Teamsters when it undertook an inspiring nationwide strike against United Parcel Service. Just three days into the walkout, the Executive Council pledged that the AFL-CIO would provide "whatever it takes in terms of time, energy, and resources to help the Teamsters win," crucial backing to an embattled affiliate. Involving 180,000 workers, the strike ended with workers securing a range of improvements, including pay increases and more full-time positions. The labor movement effectively publicized the company's increasing reliance on part-time workers, mobilizing support from a public that worried about declining job security. As Teamsters leader Ron Carey put it, "Part-time America won't work—that's the issue." Brokering the deal that settled the dispute, Secretary of Labor Alexis Herman also played an important role.[57]

Media observers were impressed, with many predicting that labor was on the upswing. For the *Washington Post*, this was "the labor movement's biggest victory in thirty years," while the *Nation* termed it a "big win" and a moment where history had "changed gears." Even President Clinton—who had refused demands to seek an injunction under the 1947 Taft-Hartley Act—was upbeat, declaring at the end of the dispute that "labor is back." For the first time in decades, organized labor had resisted wholesale concessions and won a major national strike. Polls showed that a majority of Americans had favored the strikers, a sharp contrast with the PATCO walkout. Sweeney was delighted. "We will use the energy of the UPS defeat to renew the fight for good jobs," he proclaimed.[58]

Around this time, other Sweeney initiatives began to bear fruit, and the AFL-CIO leader received lots of outside praise. Unions, declared the *New York Times* in September 1997, were "at their strongest position in nearly a generation." Another 1997 headline, "Organized Labor Mounts Comeback," said a lot.[59] In October, Sweeney, Trumka, and Chavez-Thompson were easily reelected, and their terms were extended to four years. They now pushed ahead with their mantra of "Organize, Mobilize, Energize." In October 1999 labor reporter Steven Greenhouse declared in the *Times* that labor had been "revitalized" under Sweeney, who had taken over a federation that was "spiraling downward." With new political power and organizing momentum, the Federation's fate had "turned around."[60]

At its biennial convention in 1999, the Federation was upbeat as it took stock of what Sweeney had achieved. In August, when the Executive Council reported to the convention, it claimed that there was "a new momentum and renewed energy within our movement." The Council was buoyed by the latest figures from the Bureau of Labor Statistics, which showed that over 500,000 workers had joined unions in 1998, leading to a net gain of 100,000 members. The Federation had "stemmed what had been a decline in union strength."[61] In October, the AFL-CIO launched Workingfamilies.com, a low-cost Internet service for active and retired union members, a potential market of 17 million households. Union members would pay no more than $14.95 a month, about one-third less than the commercial rate, and they also received low-cost computers. The Federation could now use the Internet—which at the time was much more widely available to high-income households—to reach working families, and it got the system running ahead of the 2000 presidential election. As the new millennium dawned, the AFL-CIO was still receiving positive headlines.[62]

The AFL-CIO thus went into the 2000 election with considerable momentum. After endorsing Gore early on, the Federation ran a long and intensive campaign, and the results were impressive. In all, the Democrats received a record 26.3 million votes from union households, 4.1 million more than in 1996. This represented 26 percent of all voters, almost double the proportion of union members. Organized labor, acknowledged *Industry Week*, had "brought Democrats to within a whisker of sweeping Congress and the White House." Through the Federation's "2000 in 2000" program—designed to elect union members to public office—more than 2,600 rank and filers actually won office, exceeding the target. The program typified the Sweeney presidency's emphasis on grassroots mobilization. Further reflecting this, "Labor 2000" volunteers mobilized tens of thousands of working people to knock on doors, make phone calls, disseminate literature, and talk with coworkers. Available from its website, the AFL-CIO's "Working Families Toolkit," which allowed local unions, state federations, and central labor councils to customize flyers for their members, was a great success. In all, union members ordered over 3.5 million flyers through the website.[63]

Sweeney again led from the front, even joining Rev. Jesse Jackson on "people-powered" bus tours that were designed to get out the vote in key states. Other changes made under Sweeney's leadership, especially the establishment of permanent staff in each congressional district, a renewed emphasis on voter registration, and the setting up of a new media fund, all made a difference. As political scientist Peter Francia wrote in 2000, "Organized labor's recent successes are attributable to the strategic changes and reallocation of union resources brought about by the Sweeney leadership."[64]

The AFL-CIO was at the forefront of the movement to challenge the election result. Immediately following the incomplete Florida vote count, it dispatched staff to the Sunshine State. Some arrived before their counterparts from the Democratic National Committee, helping to organize rallies, run a hotline, and build infrastructure for the campaign. The Federation also put a "Texas Truth Squad" of local union members on the road, using them to spread dire warnings—based on Bush's record as governor of Texas—of how workers would suffer under a Bush presidency. These actions indicated how much was at stake for the Federation. As Steve Rosenthal recalled, the AFL-CIO was "*deeply* invested" in Gore's campaign. It was a painful blow when, on December 12, the conservative U.S. Supreme Court controversially ruled in

Bush v. Gore that Bush had won Florida, and therefore the election. Many union members never accepted the ruling. As Sweeney wrote later, the AFL-CIO had "arguably" elected a president.[65]

Looking back, AFL-CIO staff saw the outcome as a crushing blow. "We had an enormous number of lawyers, staff, mobilization experts, on the ground, *in* Florida," recalled Rosenthal, "and it was heartbreaking, because there was so much at stake." Devastated and exhausted, Rosenthal relinquished his position as political director soon afterwards. The labor movement was "very disappointed," added chief of staff Bob Welsh, especially as many wanted Gore to fight on. Instead, Gore conceded straight after the Supreme Court decision, even though many legal analysts—and the four dissenting judges—believed that the decision was flawed, and that the case should be remanded to the Florida court for a recount. According to Rosenthal, Gore and Sweeney had a "very, very good" relationship. The two leaders had conferred about strategy in Florida, but Gore disappointed labor activists by not doing more to challenge the result.[66] "It was sad," recalled Sweeney. "Al Gore would have been a good president, but it was unfortunate. . . . We think that Al Gore should not have conceded as early as he did, and we think that if he held out, that there were enough questions out there, that this needed further examination."[67]

Several former staffers believed that these were decisive moments for the Sweeney presidency. "I think the defeat of Gore, and the Gore team's unwillingness to fight in Florida, was a turning point," stressed Stewart Acuff, who was the Federation's Midwestern director at the time, "because they outfought us in Florida . . . and Gore was too afraid to turn us loose. We could have made that much harder for them to steal Florida than we did . . . I mean they just weren't cold-blooded enough in the Gore campaign." While it seems unlikely that a Gore presidency would have produced conditions allowing the labor movement to grow—and NAFTA's effects would continue to be felt—the AFL-CIO would have had a stronger voice in Washington, including more access to the White House. The political climate would also have been friendlier. General Counsel Jon Hiatt recalled the abrupt shift in climate. "In 2000 when Bush won," he reflected, "then . . . for the last half of the Sweeney presidency, it was playing defense, completely."[68]

In the wake of the election, not all of the energy of the early Sweeney years was lost. Harnessing the anger generated by the result, the Federation launched several new programs. Building on the 2000 in 2000 initiative, it established Target 5000, which aimed to train union members and place 5,000 of them in office "over the next few election cycles." It also launched the Alliance for Retired Americans, a 2.5 million-member group that was designed to give union retirees a stronger political voice.[69]

Just as these reforms were being enacted, however, the unexpected terrorist attacks of September 11, 2001, occurred. Because the AFL-CIO building was practically adjacent to the White House, it was caught up in the attacks, and staff had vivid memories of the day. On the morning of the attacks, senior Sweeney staffers were holding a meeting on the eighth floor of the headquarters, overlooking the White House. Steve Rosenthal vividly recalled how the meeting was aborted soon after the Pentagon was hit by one of the hijacked planes, killing 184 people and causing a large fire. "We were beginning to see some smoke across the Mall, and they ended the meeting," he remembered. Soon afterwards, the area around the White House, including the AFL-CIO building, was closed, and staff joined a panicked exodus from the city. "People were stunned, and trying to figure out what to do," continued Rosenthal. "They closed the building, this whole area downtown, was immediately closed, because they were worried about an attack on the White House. We all had to go home. I remember it was hysteria leaving the city, because it was just gridlock everywhere." Lane Windham, who had to cancel a press conference announcing further alliances between the AFL-CIO and community and environmental groups to protest against globalization, also recalled the panicked scenes, as Secret Service agents with machine guns and tear-gas masks scurried outside the AFL-CIO building. "I started sending out notices to *cancel* the press conference, and *then* we started to see smoke, and we couldn't tell where the smoke was coming from," she related. With the cell phone network overloaded, staffers were unable to get messages to their families. Instead they had to drive home, with many taking several stressful hours to reach the outer suburbs. As the *New York Times* noted, the scenes in Washington, where a state of emergency was declared for four days, were "apocalyptic."[70]

In New York City, the attacks hurt and shocked the labor movement, especially as many unionized firefighters, police officers, and emergency workers died as they sought to rescue those trapped inside the World Trade Center. At the AFL-CIO's convention in December, large billboards honored the 600 union members who had perished on 9/11.[71] Also killed inside the Center were a sample of the twenty-first-century American workforce, including an unknown number of undocumented immigrants who worked as delivery staff, maintenance workers, and window washers. Some of these service employees had been delivering food to office workers on the upper floors when the first plane hit. Their plight highlighted why the AFL-CIO had changed its immigration policy. "The World Trade Center was more than just steel and concrete," commented Sweeney, a native New Yorker, at a convention meeting overshadowed by the attacks. "It was a microcosm of our city. . . . The immigrants from eighty-six different nations who were killed will always be a reminder of our tradition of welcoming all people to our shores." Sweeney also praised the actions of the slain union members; their spirit of sacrifice was part of "the fiber of our nation and our movement."[72]

In the longer term, 9/11 had a significant impact on American politics and culture that hurt the AFL-CIO. On January 20, 2001, when Bush was inaugurated, many Americans still perceived him as an illegitimate, "unelected president." In the wake of the attacks, however, Bush's popularity soared; a Gallup poll on September 23 showed that 90 percent of Americans approved of the way Bush was handling his job, the highest rating ever recorded by Gallup for a president. As Bush launched a "War on Terror" in the months that followed, his popularity remained high.[73] Looking back, some former staffers saw 9/11 as even more important than the 2000 election in turning the tide against the Sweeney presidency. "*That* is when he won his legitimacy," asserted Lane Windham. "What September the eleventh did, it legitimized Bush on one hand, which was the place where we didn't have power, and at the same time stripped this growing community coalition, growing global fairness coalition, of power. Those two things basically, I think, meant that the Sweeney administration became somewhat unmoored, from some of the direction it had been heading." Others thought that it was the combined effects of the two events that really undermined the Sweeney presidency. The election of Bush was "awful," thought Bob Welsh. "Then we had 9/11 right after that, so you suddenly have the environment of the United States changing to this one that's still haunting us, where economic issues, however important they might be . . . were completely surpassed by security issues. . . . We had no chance of getting anything done." The AFL-CIO's efforts to build alliances with academics, clergy, community groups, and environmentalists—a feature of the early Sweeney years—had now been "chilled," summarized Marilyn Sneiderman.[74]

The terrorist attacks also hurt the labor movement because they led to a sharp economic downturn. As a result, conditions were no longer as favorable for organizing. By April 2003, unemployment stood at 6 percent, an eight-year high.[75] Unionized sectors were hit hard; the airlines cut more than 70,000 jobs, and the hotel trade, where organizers had been making gains, was devastated. In Las Vegas alone, business fell so sharply that the casinos laid off 15,000 workers. In New York City, economists calculated that 80,000 people were thrown out of work by the attacks, while a further 75,000—mainly service workers such as bellhops, limousine drivers, and nannies—experienced a sharp drop in income as wealthy residents tightened their belts. Within a month of 9/11, the drop in travel and tourism had caused one-third of HERE's 265,000 members to be laid off. "The situation is catastrophic," declared President John Wilhelm.[76] Even the upbeat Sweeney admitted that the climate had changed sharply. The terrorist attacks, he summarized in December, had left a legacy of "hellish terror, economic disaster, and massive layoffs."[77]

Of course, it is important not to exaggerate the success of Sweeney's reforms. Even without the setbacks of 2000 and 2001, some hard questions should be asked about the results of Sweeney's efforts. Political mobilization could only achieve so much, especially when organized labor was fighting employers whose industrial relations policies were insulated from political processes by the courts, as well as by their own autonomy. Organized labor's predicament could also not be blamed entirely on outside enemies. Infighting and alleged corruption in the Teamsters' union, for example, hurt the AFL-CIO's efforts to capitalize on their victory in the UPS strike, especially as a court-appointed review board later expelled Ron Carey from the union because of alleged financial mismanagement during his 1996 election victory over James P. Hoffa. The case generated a lot of negative headlines, reviving what the *Washington Post's* Frank Swoboda adroitly termed labor's "image problem."[78]

The scandal had a direct effect on the AFL-CIO. According to federal prosecutors, three political consultants working for Carey allegedly used various groups, including the Democratic National Committee and the AFL-CIO, to illegally funnel money to finance Carey's campaign. Sweeney and Trumka both appeared before the federal grand jury investigating the Teamsters election, with the AFL-CIO secretary-treasurer accused by prosecutors of being complicit in the efforts to channel money to Carey's campaign. Trumka invoked his Fifth Amendment rights during the investigations, forcing Sweeney to announce an interpretation of the 1957 AFL-CIO resolution—which barred any union official who invoked the amendment from holding office—that effectively exempted Trumka from being removed. Although the AFL-CIO denied any involvement, the scandal took its toll. As labor writer Jane Slaughter noted in early 1998, the Teamsters' impressive victory was "soon wiped off the front pages by revelations about internal chicanery." The decision by a federal oversight panel to permanently bar Carey from holding any office in the Teamsters also hurt Sweeney. The two New Yorkers were close allies—both were institutional reformers—and Carey's election had helped pave the way for Sweeney's challenge. Carey's fall, declared the *Washington Post*'s Thomas B. Edsall, was "a significant setback to the progressive wing of organized labor that has taken control of the AFL-CIO." In contrast, Sweeney lacked strong ties to James P. Hoffa (the son of the late James R. Hoffa), who in 1998 won the rerun election for the Teamsters' presidency.[79]

As Sweeney sought to reform the AFL-CIO, there were other internal issues. In the organizing field, one of the key problems was resistance from *within* the Federation. At the national convention in 2001, Sweeney admitted that he had not come close to organizing one million new members a year, a major target. A key reason was the fact that only a small number of unions were devoting 30 percent of their resources to organizing, as demanded from above.[80] While some affiliates struggled to find the necessary resources, others were content to service their members and were reluctant to change. "They don't know how to organize," one official told journalist Jo Ann Wypijewski, "they don't want to organize."[81]

A large part of the problem was the AFL-CIO's decentralized structure. Many affiliates resisted Sweeney's calls to organize, and the Federation lacked the power to compel them. In 1999 the Executive Council decreed that "all national unions" should shift "significant resources into organizing" but there was no mention of sanctions or penalties for those that failed to comply. As a result, the next year the Council was still discussing the "need for unions to make a commitment to organizing." Because affiliation with the Federation was voluntary, Sweeney was loath to push the issue. Another ongoing problem was the reluctance of some local unions to join local central councils or state federations, further weakening the center's authority. Sweeney was successful at mobilizing more union members, especially during election cycles, yet some of them still lacked formal affiliation with the AFL-CIO, depriving it of badly needed funding. According to Brad Burton, Richard Trumka's executive assistant, the affiliation issue was "always a problem."[82]

Behind the scenes, there were sharp debates between Sweeney's staffers and affiliates about the organizing mantra. Some staff remembered how hard it was to get the affiliates onboard. According to Susan Washington, Sweeney's assistant, "The one area everybody seemed to agree on was the political activity. The one area that there was almost never agreement on, was what is the role of the AFL-CIO in organizing." Many affiliates, she noted, seemed unsure of how the Federation could help them organize. Others lacked expertise, or were put off by the cost. Organizing "was and still is a huge resource issue," she concluded. Brad Burton also remembered that the call to organize faced significant internal resistance, especially as organizing was still carried out primarily by the affiliates. "We had a very small number of unions that did organizing very well, and Sweeney's union was one of them, SEIU," he recalled candidly, "but boy, a lot of unions just did not put much effort into organizing. And their cultures would be [to] reward cronies. . . . You'd look at their organizers, even if they had organizers, they'd be older white guys, that had maybe some political influence within the union, and they were being rewarded for that. What you really need are organizers that look like the people you were trying to organize." After interviewing Organizing Institute alumna, sociologist Daisy Rooks reached similar conclusions, exposing a "cowboy mentality" among white men that celebrated the intense and family unfriendly working environment of organizing. As a result, many women and people of color were still excluded from the ranks of lead organizers.[83]

The debate about organizing exposed broader tensions. Even among staff at the headquarters, there were conflicting views about whether the Federation should focus on organizing or concentrate on servicing its members. "There's always an internal debate, in this building, about who we are," summarized Ana Avendano. "Are we a leadership organization, or are we a *service* organization? And many feel that we should exist, the AFL-CIO should exist, to service our affiliates, period." While Sweeney felt that the AFL-CIO needed to take a stronger leadership role, changing the culture of labor—even inside the Beltway—was difficult.[84]

When organizing was successful, deindustrialization wiped out many of the gains. In February 1997, Federation economist Mark Anderson estimated that "hundreds of thousands" of jobs had been lost because of NAFTA, especially in manufacturing industries. Since the treaty had passed, employment in the maquiladora facilities in Mexico had also jumped from 450,000 to 867,000. "For those of us who expressed some reservations about NAFTA," he concluded, "the three years since enactment have sadly brought no surprises." Across the country, executives were also using the threat of moving to Mexico to stymie organizing campaigns.[85] Even when the AFL-CIO oversaw successful organizing efforts, it was struggling just to break even. Despite a massive commitment of resources, Sweeney was only able to secure a slight rise in union density overall, from 14 percent in 1994 to 14.5 percent in 1996. The figure then dropped slightly, to 13.9 percent in 1998 and 13.5 percent in 2000. Still, the sharp falls of the Reagan era had not been repeated.[86]

In the new millennium, however, there was no doubting that the problems facing the Sweeney presidency got a lot worse. The infectious enthusiasm of the early years disappeared, and momentum was lost. As they looked back on the fourteen-year Sweeney presidency, AFL-CIO staff repeatedly viewed the 2000 election and 9/11 as turning points. An articulate Marilyn Sneiderman captured well how the hope of the early Sweeney years ended abruptly with the election, causing frustrated aides to attack one another. "That was a really rough time," she recalled. "I think people really started pointing fingers at each other, and inwardly . . . it was painful. It wasn't the election itself, but it's what it represented." The election initiated the Bush presidency, an era that would be marked by more rapid union decline, increased difficulties in organizing, and a damaging—and unprecedented—internal split. Overall, the second half of the Sweeney presidency would be much more difficult than the first. By 2009, when a tired John Sweeney stepped down, the big vision and big hopes of his early presidency were distant memories.[87]

CHAPTER TEN

Our Job Has Never Been Harder

The Sweeney Presidency in the Bush Era, 2001–2009

During the presidency of George W. Bush, the national political climate changed dramatically. The relationship between the Federation and the White House symbolized this shift. Despite major differences over NAFTA, labor leaders had enjoyed a productive relationship with Bill Clinton, rebuilding trust in the later years of the presidency. As Lane Kirkland once commented, on all issues apart from NAFTA he "got along with Clinton very well." During the Clinton years, AFL-CIO staff visited the White House regularly, and some of them even got jobs there. Under Bush, these contacts stopped. Rather, staffers remembered the Bush presidency as a disaster for the Federation, a period of unprecedented isolation. "We never met with Bush," summarized chief of staff Bob Welsh. "I mean he was just on another planet." Under Bush, added director of government affairs Bill Samuel, "we were always on defense."[1] Even the mild-mannered Sweeney was affected by the shift, later describing the Bush presidency as "tough days." Laborers' leader Terry O'Sullivan was less circumspect, terming the Bush presidency "eight years of torture and hell."[2]

The AFL-CIO endured many setbacks in these years. Constrained by internal and external resistance, as well as the rapid decline of the manufacturing sector, organizing stalled. A major campaign to secure labor law reform again fell short, while health care reform never got off the ground. Disappointment fed dissension in the ranks. By early 2005, Sweeney had become a target for reformers who demanded fundamental changes. Ironically spearheaded by SEIU leader Andy Stern—in many ways Sweeney's protégé—the critics promised to centralize the Federation and secure better organizing results. After the two sides were unable to resolve their differences—partly because of a personality clash between the leaders—Stern took almost 40 percent of the AFL-CIO's members into Change to Win, a rival federation. This was the biggest schism in organized labor since the creation of the CIO in the 1930s, and it generated plenty of negative publicity. While even sympathetic observers proclaimed that the union movement was in "turmoil" and "crisis," labor's opponents wrote it off. As conservative journalist Michael Barone put it, "Big Labor, RIP." The headlines were a dramatic contrast to the optimism that had greeted the start of Sweeney's presidency.[3]

The reports of labor's demise were premature. Despite all the problems—especially the way that the AFL-CIO was forced to carry out severe cuts after the disaffiliations—the Federation retained a lot of political power. Helped by Sweeney's reforms, its political operations remained very effective, especially during national elections. In 2006 the AFL-CIO played a crucial role as the Democrats regained control of the House and Senate, and won a majority of the governorships and state legislatures. In 2008 the Federation launched an unprecedented campaign to help the Democrats regain the presidency, convincing many white members to put aside their racial fears and vote for Barack Obama. Coming at a time of declining union density, this political mobilization was some achievement. As special counsel Damon Silvers put it: "The AFL-CIO's political program during the Sweeney years did something almost miraculous, which was to basically maintain the labor movement's political power, while our private sector membership was declining."[4]

Even organized labor's opponents paid tribute to its reinvigorated political program. "Politically, the labor movement is still very strong, especially on Capitol Hill where they exercise power that is far beyond their numbers in the workplace," declared Randel Johnson, a vice president of the U.S. Chamber of Commerce, in 2004. More sympathetic observers were also impressed. "Whatever labor's problems," summarized Steven Greenhouse in the *New York Times*, "few deny that unions remain one of the most formidable forces in politics, especially because of their ability to turn out the vote." Given the failure to pass labor law reform, as well as other key measures, critics would question whether the AFL-CIO was adequately rewarded for its political support. Ultimately, however, the big electoral victories, especially in 2008, meant that these difficult years were not without a silver lining.[5]

From the start, the relationship between the AFL-CIO and the Bush administration was poor. There was clearly baggage from the election, with Bush aware that organized labor had been one of his most vociferous opponents. Shortly after the presidential inauguration, Sweeney voiced dismay when the administration blocked regulations that stopped federal contracts from being awarded to companies that violated labor laws. Clearly piqued, Sweeney promised that the AFL-CIO would "hold him (Bush) responsible" for policies that hurt workers. Then, 9/11 undermined Sweeney's reforms, initiating both an economic recession and an intellectual climate of patriotic conformity. "Our job has never been harder," he told the Executive Council soon afterwards. The attacks undermined protests against unfettered global-ization, dampened labor's fight for immigration reform, weakened a new anti-sweatshop campaign, and helped to secure passage of Bush's Fast Track trade bill, which gave the president new powers to negotiate trade deals, including plans to further expand free trade within the Americas. Labor strongly op-posed the controversial trade measure, which squeaked through the House by one vote on December 6. Tellingly, Bush drew upon his popularity to se-cure the votes he needed, especially in the Republican-dominated South, and the AFL-CIO lost another crucial trade battle.[6] In early 2002, Sweeney told the Council that the AFL-CIO now faced a number of "urgent challenges," and the period ahead would not be easy. These challenges, he noted, were "brought about by the continued recession, an antiunion administration, and the continuing impact of the global economy." As Sweeney spoke of difficul-ties rather than opportunities, it was clear that the entire tone of his presi-dency had shifted.[7]

In the year or so after 9/11, AFL-CIO staffers disliked the way that Bush was able to use the terrorist attacks to bolster his political position, shifting attention away from pressing domestic issues, particularly the state of the economy. "George Bush of course became a very popular president after 9/11, and he could do no wrong," recalled executive vice president Linda Chavez-Thompson. "Everything he wanted, he got." In 2002, for example, the Bush administration pressed ahead with plans to contract out more federal work, threatening many union jobs and forcing the AFL-CIO onto the defensive. The administration, it argued, had a "gross misunderstanding of the special role of public employees in performing governmental activities." Such protests made little difference. Between 2000 and 2006, spending on federal contractors jumped from $207 billion to $400 billion. As the *New York Times* noted, private contractors were becoming a "virtual fourth branch of government," sitting next to federal employees at almost every agency. Most of these contractors were nonunion.[8]

In the 2002 midterm elections, the president exploited concern about ter-rorism and used it to shore up his political position. Although the incum-bent's party usually lost support in midterm contests, in 2002 the Republicans gained eight House and two Senate seats. Reflecting on the campaign, Swee-ney's anger at the administration was palpable. Despite its best efforts, the AFL-CIO had been unable to match the "obscene levels of spending by cor-porate special interests," or counter the influence of a president who "beat the war drums" and raised record amounts of campaign funding. "To be fair,

Democratic leaders did try very aggressively to raise [the] working family economic issue," Sweeney wrote. "But they were no match for the President's focus on Iraq."[9]

In 2003 tensions increased when Sweeney abandoned the Federation's traditional support of U.S. foreign policy and criticized Bush's war in Iraq. The 9/11 attacks paved the way for the American-led invasion of Iraq, the central initiative of the administration's "War on Terror." Starting in March 2003, the war created a highly patriotic atmosphere that inhibited unions, whose resistance to pay and benefit cuts could be portrayed as un-American, especially if it involved work stoppages. After backing administrations in the Vietnam and Persian Gulf Wars—and its predecessor organizations had also upheld U.S. involvement in the Korean War—the AFL-CIO broke with tradition and criticized Bush's invasion of Iraq. It was the first time in its history that the AFL-CIO had openly broken with a sitting president's war policy, a move driven primarily by the lack of evidence that Iraqi leader Saddam Hussein was a genuine threat to peace. In early 2003, for example, the Executive Council boldly declared, "The president has not fulfilled his responsibility to make a compelling and coherent explanation to the American people and the world as to the need for military action against Iraq."[10]

It was a bold move that attracted criticism, especially from conservatives. "The antiwar resolution," proclaimed the *Wall Street Journal*, "shows how far left Big Labor has swayed since John Sweeney and his fellow partisans took control in 1995." Undeterred, some affiliates went even further, insisting that the Iraq issue was being used to distract Americans from the poor state of the economy. In the months before the invasion, thousands of trade unionists also took part in antiwar protests. Once the war began, Sweeney tacitly supported the administration's war goals, yet he also acknowledged the right of "people of good conscience" to express opposition. As the conflict dragged on, organized labor played a central role in the burgeoning antiwar movement, pleasing progressives but alienating the administration.[11] In the summer of 2005, as many Americans worried about the length and cost of the war, Sweeney publicly called the Bush administration "horrible," widening the chasm between himself and the president.[12]

The administration made no effort to repair the relationship. Indeed, White House Press Secretary Ari Fleischer dismissed the Federation's leaders as "appendages of the Democratic National Committee" who were out of step with rank-and-file workers. Everyday union members, he insisted, supported the war in Iraq. The administration insisted that it would only work with labor leaders who could cross the "partisan divide."[13] Federation leaders felt alienated and shut out. "I think we were hurt during the Bush years, because during that period of time there was no communication whatsoever between the White House and organized labor," explained Chavez-Thompson. "Even during the senior Bush years, he would at least visit with Lane Kirkland." Ironically, following office renovations, the AFL-CIO president's view of the White House was clearer than ever. "Every day when I look out at the White House," commented Sweeney, "it's like an insult."[14] In order to cope, AFL-CIO staff even joked about their political isolation. Sweeney, recalled Lane Windham, "Used to say . . . the only time he was invited to the White House under Bush was when the Pope invited him." In April 2008 the visit of Pope Benedict XVI was indeed the one time that Sweeney—a keen Catholic—was invited to the Bush White House, yet there was no discussion of labor issues.[15]

Any hope that sympathetic officials in the Department of Labor might be more helpful was soon crushed. In sharp contrast to the sympathetic appointments of the Clinton years, Bush selected Elaine Chao, a conservative Taiwanese-American who lacked any relationship with the union movement, as his secretary of labor. Serving in the role for the entire Bush presidency, Chao concentrated on relaxing regulations for businesses and tightening them for unions. In particular, she substantially increased the number of investigators working for the Office of Labor Management Standards, a department agency that regulated unions. In terse correspondence with Sweeney, Chao rejected suggestions that there was "inadequate dialogue" between her department and the AFL-CIO. The Bush administration, she insisted, was interested in hearing labor's views. Federation staffers were unconvinced. Chao, asserted Barbara Shailor, "was aggressively anti-organized labor."[16]

Determined to confront this challenging climate, Sweeney pressed ahead with his reforms. It was crucial, he told the Executive Council in 2002, to "focus more resources on the priority areas of organizing and politics." Sweeney made some progress in convincing affiliates to invest more in organizing. By 2005, twenty-five of the fifty-eight AFL-CIO unions committed 10–50 percent of their budgets to organizing, compared to an estimated average of just 3 percent in the early 1990s.[17] Despite this, the results were disappointing, especially in the service sector, where several big campaigns were launched. Generally, low-paid service workers responded positively to labor organizers, yet corporate resistance prevented wholesale gains. The hostile political and economic climate also took its toll. "Organizing," summarized Andy Stern to the Council, "is hard work."[18]

Launched in 2002, a major UFCW drive against Wal-Mart was emblematic. The world's largest corporation responded by intimidating or firing key activists, and it also closed its store in Jonquiere, Quebec, the only unionized Wal-Mart in North America, effectively chilling organizing efforts. Heading off union criticisms, the company also made positive changes to improve conditions, giving staff more breaks and improving compliance with state employment laws. By 2007, Wal-Mart employed more than 1.3 million workers in the United States alone, yet none of them were protected by a union contract. As *Business Week* noted, Wal-Mart typified how, "over the past two decades, Corporate America has perfected its ability to fend off labor groups."[19]

With Bush in office, the Federation found that employers became more willing to violate labor laws. One labor-based study of over 1,000 representation elections held between 1999 and 2003 found that 34 percent of the companies had fired pro-union workers and 47 percent had threatened to cut the wages and benefits of those who were trying to organize.[20] Under Bush, the "union avoidance" industry flourished; in 2003, employers utilized their legal right to make workers attend antiunion meetings in 92 percent of organizing drives, while in 78 percent of such cases, supervisors pressured workers in one-on-one sessions. In these meetings, managers often threatened to close plants if the union won, a menacing move at a time when record numbers of jobs were moving offshore. For the AFL-CIO, it was clear that the law needed to be changed. According to Stewart Acuff, who became organizing director in 2002, workers faced a "vicious assault" from employers, especially in the burgeoning parts of the economy. "The service sector, the hotel sector, the health care sector, the cleaning sector, all were growing, but workers effectively weren't allowed to organize," he recalled. It was, he admitted, the "worst possible time" to be organizing director.[21]

Many of the campaigns launched during Acuff's tenure bore out his prognosis. In 2004–2005, an effort to organize coffee giant Starbucks achieved little after top management hired consultants. As a result, only a few stores in New York City were organized.[22] Elsewhere, the gains that affiliates did make, such as a successful SEIU effort to sign up Houston janitors and the CWA's breakthrough at Cingular Wireless stores in the South, mostly came when firms agreed to recognize unions without an election. When employers took a harder line, unions rarely prevailed.[23]

Although it was supposed to protect the right to organize, the NLRB became even more ineffective under Bush. Just as he had done at the Department of Labor, the president stacked the NLRB with pro-business appointments, and the Board consequently issued a series of anti-labor rulings. This was illustrated well in 2006, when the NLRB promulgated new guidelines that greatly expanded the definition of supervisory staff, who by federal law were not allowed to join a union. This ruling came in the "Kentucky River" cases, which dated back to a dispute involving Kentucky River Community Health Care Inc. in Hazard, Kentucky. The NLRB ruled that charge nurses, who headed units but did not have the authority to hire and fire, were to be considered as supervisory staff. As a result of the ruling, an estimated eight million workers lost their right to be represented by a union. A disappointed Sweeney lambasted the "latest" effort by the "Bush-appointed NLRB" to hurt organized labor. "The NLRB," he declared, "should protect workers' rights—not eliminate them."[24]

Several other NLRB decisions particularly hurt labor. In September 2007 a key ruling made it more difficult for illegally fired workers to collect back pay. As congressional investigations found, workers who were fired for union activity could take over ten years to secure back pay. Earlier, the Board had strengthened employers' rights to lock out staff and denied nonunion employees the right to have a coworker present when managers called them in for investigative or disciplinary meetings. The latter ruling affected 87 percent of American workers. "This board has undermined collective bargaining at every turn, putting the power of the law behind lawbreakers, not law victims," claimed veteran Democratic senator Edward M. Kennedy. As the Federation saw it, under Bush the NLRB had been "perverted into a dangerous enemy of workers' rights."[25] Federal data highlighted how the organizing climate had turned as workers lost faith with the NLRB. Under Bush, the number of elections for union representation fell steadily, from 2,896 in 2000 to 2,099 in 2005. By 2009, the figure was just 1,304. Unions, moreover, only won about half of the elections they contested.[26]

Major organizing campaigns illustrated the problems. In 2007 the Board found that Starbucks had broken the law thirty times in fighting union activity, with two employees being fired for supporting the union. Despite this ruling, the penalties for ignoring the law were insufficient, especially as discharged employees often waited years to get their jobs back. As a result, virtually all of Starbuck's 6,900 stores remained unorganized. In its high-profile effort to organize Wal-Mart, labor also won ten favorable NLRB rulings, yet they made little difference to the company's conduct.[27]

While the AFL-CIO tried to link the failure of organizing to the hostility of the Bush administration and the weakness of labor laws, it is clear that these were not the only factors. Structural shifts in the economy, for example, also hurt. Across the country, employers increasingly relied on temporary workers or undocumented immigrants, groups that were notoriously difficult to organize. As *New York Times* reporter Louis Uchitelle documented in *The*

Disposable American (2006), millions of American workers, in both blue- and white-collar fields, now had little job security, reducing morale and eroding labor's influence. By 2004, the Bureau of Labor Statistics' count of "worker displacement"—which it had started in 1984—recorded that at least 30 million full-time workers had been permanently separated from their jobs against their wishes. Many more had been forced into early retirement or had suffered what Uchitelle termed a "disguised layoff."[28]

The economic climate undermined the labor movement in other ways. As many affiliates were devastated by layoffs and plant closings, they lacked the will—or resources—to focus on organizing. This was especially true in the heavily unionized industrial sector. Although the decline of manufacturing was a long-standing problem, it accelerated dramatically under Bush. Combined with the longer-term effects of globalization, the severe economic recession hit workers hard. In the first decade of the twenty-first century, the United States lost 5.5 million manufacturing jobs, about one-third of the total number of workers in the sector. This unprecedented rate of decline had a dramatic effect on the AFL-CIO.[29] In 2007 Sweeney told the General Board that recent years had witnessed "the destruction of millions of good union jobs and the hopes and dreams and contributions of millions of union members." For Sweeney, deindustrialization was the "basic cause" of organized labor's decline.[30]

Federation staff remembered how the loss of jobs hurt organizing. According to Susan Washington, manufacturing affiliates often spent large sums on organizing campaigns "only for the factory or the place to close down." This was a particular problem for the steelworkers' and textile unions. Unions in these sectors were also impelled to spend much of their time trying to prevent shutdowns or helping their displaced members. With a huge stack of plant closures to deal with, union leaders had little time for organizing.[31] In this climate, corporate threats to move production abroad possessed extra menace. As Mark Anderson related, "I remember being in organizing campaigns, where a company would, in negotiations, shrink-wrap equipment, and put it on a pallet, and put a mailing label on it: 'Juarez.'" Although it remained technically illegal to move plants to Mexican towns such as Juarez to avoid unionization, companies no longer had to make explicit threats. "So this greatly increased their bargaining power," concluded Anderson. As even *Business Week* acknowledged, because NAFTA had made it safer to invest in Mexico, it also "made the threat of plant relocations more real."[32]

In these years, several manufacturing affiliates were devastated by deindustrialization. In 1996, when Sweeney was newly elected, the textile and apparel industry employed 1.5 million workers, but plant closures and layoffs ensured that this number fell to just 407,000 in 2010. While the industry had never been heavily unionized, the impact on the Union of Needletrades, Industrial and Textile Employees (UNITE) was immense. As southern director Harris Raynor recalled, plant closures hit like a "tidal wave," devastating workers and weakening the union. "In an incredibly rapid period of time, we lost just about everything," he admitted.[33] The UAW and USW—once two of the largest AFL-CIO affiliates—were also hit hard by deindustrialization. As steelworkers' president Leo Gerrard explained in 2009, "The industrial base of the country has been shredded. And that clearly undermines the auto sector, it undermines the steel industry, it undermines all of manufacturing." Membership of the UAW fell from 1.5 million in 1979 to less than 500,000 in 2009. The AFL-CIO, summarized staff member Bob Baugh, took "huge hits" from deindustrialization in these years.[34]

The losses had a disproportionate impact on African-Americans. Particularly reliant on industrial jobs, blacks had used unions—once they became more responsive to them—to climb into the middle class. "African Americans are some of the most loyal trade-unionists you could find," asserted Tefere Gebre, an African-American union activist. "The labor movement has been one of the biggest vehicles, providing and creating . . . a black middle class in this country." In the 1980s, one out of every four black workers was a union member, but by 2005 the figure was closer to one in seven. Because of deindustrialization, the Federation had lost strength among one of the most pro-union segments of the population. "The percentage of black workers who have been knocked out of union jobs is one of the little-known tragedies of the last five years," commented Sweeney.[35]

With so many affiliates shedding members, it was not possible to replace them all through organizing. In Executive Council meetings, union presidents candidly discussed these problems. In December 2001, for example, Electrical Workers' leader Edward L. Fire related that many of his members had been "victimized by trade." His union—like others—had been "unable to organize new members to compensate for losses." Leo Gerrard related that the situation in the steel industry was "very serious," adding that, "no one can say that the USWA will continue to exist three or four years from now." The discussion typified the gloomy tone that had descended upon the AFL-CIO, a sharp contrast from the early Sweeney years. Indeed, Vincent Sombrotto of the National Association of Letter Carriers claimed that the meeting had "been a catharsis rather than a debate." He urged Council members to work out a plan and fight back.[36]

The main strategy that emerged was an even greater emphasis on politics. Priority had to be given to political action, concluded the Council, especially as it was estimated that four million union members were still not registered voters. If these voters could be tapped, favorable political results could lead to labor law reform, boosting organizing. Promising that it would avoid a repeat of the "2000 election disaster," the AFL-CIO began mobilizing for 2004. "We won't let them steal it again," summarized *America@Work*.[37]

After the disappointing 2002 vote, Sweeney poured resources into politics. In the fall of 2003, he oversaw the creation of Working America, which allowed Americans who were not union members to join the Federation and support its work, particularly during elections. Sweeney set up the group because he was convinced that "the AFL-CIO must represent the interests of all working people." Within two years, the nonprofit association had become the fastest-growing organization for working people in the country. While some people joined because membership was free, there was no doubt that Working America bolstered the AFL-CIO's political efforts—and its public profile. This was highlighted in the 2004 election, when union households represented only 17 percent of the voting age population but 24 percent of those who voted. National exit polls showed that four million more votes came from union households in 2004 than in 1992, despite labor's decline. Clearly, the AFL-CIO was tapping many of the previously unregistered voters. "[John] Kerry would not have come close without the union vote," declared Sweeney. Although the war in Iraq gave Bush an advantage in national security issues, the Federation helped to elevate economic issues to center stage. As a result, Bush's winning percentage of the popular vote—50.7 to 48.3—was the narrowest ever for an incumbent president.[38]

Although Bush's reelection was a blow—and the Republicans also made small gains in the House and Senate—the 2004 election provided a platform for labor's unlikely political revival. Even at a time of declining membership, voters living in union households turned out at higher levels and were more likely to vote Democratic. In crucial swing states, labor played an especially important role. In Michigan, members of union households made up 37 percent of the vote, and they also comprised 34 percent in Ohio and 30 percent in Pennsylvania, significantly higher than levels of union membership in those states. Among white members of union households, Kerry performed about 30 percentage points better in those states than among other white working-class voters. "We were the force that made the 2004 election so close," asserted Doug Burnett, an AFSCME political director. "Without union members we would have lost Wisconsin, Minnesota, Michigan, and Pennsylvania in 2004."[39]

The 2004 campaign had been extensive and expensive, with internal records indicating that the AFL-CIO spent $50 million on the presidential race alone.[40] Sweeney was confident, however, that the political program was heading in the right direction. In particular, the Federation was carrying out important work among its white membership—and their families. Its data showed that among white voters, 61 percent of members voted for Kerry, compared to just 41 percent of nonunion whites. Overall, AFL-CIO members voted for Kerry by a margin of 65 percent to 33 percent, and in the key battleground states of Florida, Iowa, Minnesota, Missouri, Ohio, and Oregon, the gap was even larger—68 to 31 percent, an 11-point improvement over 2000. Helped by the Federation's work, union members were the largest group of white men who were still voting Democratic. In an America where the white vote was an increasingly conservative one, this was some achievement. As assistant political director Michael Podhorzer recalled, in these years the AFL-CIO planted a lot of the "seeds" that bore fruit later, particularly in 2008.[41]

Following the 2004 race, Sweeney expanded the Working America program. Emerging out of senior staff discussions, the initiative built on Kirkland-era debates about associate membership programs. Working America was very important because it reached nonunion constituencies, helping to overcome the problems caused by shrinking union density. The group specifically targeted working-class voters—especially whites—who were likely to support the Republicans. "The mission of Working America," recalled Karen Nussbaum, the talented staffer chosen by Sweeney to direct the group, "was to go into working-class neighborhoods, talk to working-class people who don't have a union on the job about jobs, and the economy, and engage, give them information that otherwise they weren't getting." Nussbaum recalled that many of these voters were watching the conservative Fox News network when her staff first met them. By giving these voters an alternative message, Working America made important breakthroughs, and many got involved in the Federation's grassroots political programs. Within eighteen months, the group had one million members, and the number rose steadily thereafter. Even Nussbaum found the level of success "surprising."[42]

Although the AFL-CIO took some positives from the 2004 election, it had still suffered another defeat. The labor movement knew that it faced four more years of a hostile presidential administration. The difficult climate—especially the lack of success in the organizing field—took its toll. A climate of doubt, and introspection, increasingly clouded labor's debates, and internal dissatisfaction increased. The first stirrings of a split occurred in 2003, when five unions—SEIU, HERE, the Laborers, the Carpenters, and UNITE—joined together in an informal "New Unity Partnership" to push for more reforms, particularly a greater emphasis on organizing. In 2003 and 2004, the five presidents met regularly to discuss ways of expanding union membership, raising speculation of a pending leadership challenge. Andy Stern, the most vocal figure within New Unity, declared in 2004 that he was not considering abandoning the AFL-CIO, but warned that fundamental reforms to address union decline and the changing nature of the workforce—especially the Wal-Mart business model of low wages, few benefits, and downward price pressure on suppliers—were needed. Thrown on the defensive, Sweeney accepted that his reforms had lost momentum. "There is no question that we have some serious problems," he acknowledged. The AFL-CIO leader blamed deindustrialization as the main culprit, pointing to the loss of three million manufacturing jobs over the previous three years. "As aggressively as we have been organizing more workers, we've not been able to keep up with the job loss," he explained. Arguing that the AFL-CIO needed to become more innovative, Sweeney's critics were not satisfied. The recent loss of a 138-day dispute involving 59,000 California supermarket workers, in which the Safeway, Kroger, and Albertson chains beat the union and obtained a two-tier contract providing lower wages and fewer benefits for new workers, added to the sense of crisis. Some Executive Council members openly suggested that they might break away. "As a matter of survival, it is imperative for the labor movement to organize on a much greater scale," commented energetic HERE leader John Wilhelm. "If the present structure of the labor movement can't grow much faster, history shows that workers will invent something else."[43]

This was no idle threat, especially after the 2004 election, which Sweeney had described as a crucial contest. In the wake of Bush's reelection, a number of unions put forward proposals to boost organizing, consolidate unions, and tackle the decline in union density more directly. As Harold Meyerson noted in the *Washington Post*, Sweeney's critics did not dispute his success in "turning around" the political program, yet they felt that more needed to be done to recruit new members, especially in light of the rapid decline in manufacturing. Charismatic and outspoken, Stern emerged as the leader of the reform movement. Just one week after the election, he proposed a range of solutions for labor's problems, including rebating half the $25 million that the AFL-CIO received from its credit card into the organizing campaign at Wal-Mart, forcing small unions (who often tended to be resistant to organizing) to merge with large ones, and cutting affiliates' dues to the Federation so that more money could be spent on organizing. In the wake of the election, the reform movement was boosted when the Teamsters expressed their support. "Until the Teamsters came forward, a lot of people believed this was just something between Andy [Stern] and John [Sweeney]," one union official commented, referring to rumors that Stern, who had been hired into the SEIU by Sweeney twenty years earlier, wanted to challenge his former boss. "Now, it's really about the direction of the AFL-CIO."[44]

At the Executive Council meeting in November, which was dominated by the election postmortem, Stern pressed his proposals. He was, however, only allotted ten minutes at the end of the day to do so. Clearly dissatisfied, Stern announced that the SEIU was setting up a committee to examine the possibility of leaving the AFL-CIO if it failed to embrace the reform movement's demands. As the New York Times reported, Stern's threat to withdraw his 1.8 million members generated "widespread anger" within the Federation. In response, Stern insisted that Sweeney was unwilling to carry out the "structural change" that the labor movement needed to address decline. In a similar vein, SEIU secretary-treasurer Anna Burger stressed that reformers had tried to "push an agenda, with the AFL-CIO, about reengagement and organizing," but their demands were repeatedly "stymied." The battle lines were being drawn.[45]

In the first half of 2005, as Stern built support and pressed his demands with increasing intensity, the crisis grew. Early in the year, it became apparent that Stern's proposals, particularly his call to put more resources into organizing, had attracted strong support. Sweeney, however, claimed that he had the necessary votes to secure reelection in July.[46] In early March, the president's position was strengthened when the Executive Council rejected, by a vote of 15 to 7, a proposal put forward by five large unions—including the Teamsters and SEIU—to halve affiliates' contributions to the Federation in order to free up more funds for organizing. Stern pledged to fight on. "What I want to do and what we all want to do," he explained, "is restore the strength of workers in our country, and we can't do it by growing smaller. We have to grow stronger." His demands were bolstered by the latest figures from the Bureau of Labor Statistics, showing that the percentage of unionized workers had slipped from 13.5 percent in 2000 to 12.5 percent in 2004.[47]

In response, Sweeney sought to head off the reform movement by putting more resources into both organizing and political mobilization. He forcefully implemented his proposals, which led to 105 of the Federation's 450 staff members being laid off in order to free up $15 million to give to affiliates to help with organizing. Among the changes, America@Work was discontinued as a print publication, and the field mobilization department—which had helped to build key grassroots programs in the early Sweeney years—was merged into the political program, eliminating thirty positions. In order to increase the emphasis on organizing, the Policy and Legislative departments were also amalgamated. Angry staff were told that the blame lay with the insurgent unions. Those who left included younger people who were attracted by the buy-out deal on offer. "It was done in a way that it drained a lot of the young people out, because you could take a buy-out if you'd been here *any* time," recalled Denise Mitchell. "So it just sucked a lot of the energy out of the labor movement."[48]

The dissidents were unrepentant. Backed by several powerful affiliates— especially the Teamsters, the SEIU, and the UFCW—reformers dismissed Sweeney's proposals as inadequate. Stern pressed Sweeney to stand down in July, claiming that he had already enjoyed ten years to turn around labor's fortunes. Stern, who was only fifty-four, was also reported to be angry that Sweeney had gone back on an earlier promise to retire when he turned seventy. Claiming that he was in good health and that he had changed his mind, Swee- ney instead announced that he would seek another four-year term. Sweeney also wanted to retire on his own terms, and he worried about walking away when many affiliates were strongly opposed to Stern's efforts.[49]

Many observers felt that while the issues were important, Stern's demands also reflected personal ambition. It was an allegation that Stern denied. "That'd be the fucking worst job in the world!" he exclaimed later, adding that the AFL-CIO president had limited power and had to manage "all these egoma- niac people" in national unions. Other members of Change to Win unions stressed that they respected Sweeney, but felt that he was focusing too much on politics rather than organizing. According to Laborers' president Terry O'Sullivan, John Sweeney was "one of the finest labor leaders" around. "We just had a difference of opinion," he added, "that politicians and politics were going to fix all our problems. Change to Win, to me, was more about *organizing* than about politics."[50]

It was true that the split came largely from the top, with little involvement from grassroots members. At the local level, union members were generally bemused and saddened by these events. "Mostly," summarized John Ryan from the Cleveland Central Labor Council, "we feel like we're children of some great parents who are getting divorced at the worst time of our lives." According to AFL-CIO staffer Mike Cavanaugh, who oversaw efforts to limit fallout at the state and local level, members saw the fight as "frankly insane . . . and about some people's egos, really."[51] Reflecting the lingering bitterness from the 1995 race, some former Donahue supporters felt that Sweeney had helped to create the conditions that led to the subsequent split, especially as he had made it acceptable to challenge the president's record. "Exactly what happened in 1995 was really the precursor to 2005," thought Susan Bianchi, the former president of the Association of Flight Attendants. "It was the people who saw all this disunity, in 1995, saw that, 'Oh, now we've broken the code' [and] . . . that sort of opened the gates. . . . Andy Stern learned at the feet of John Sweeney how to break things apart."[52]

In explaining the broader reasons for the split, Sweeney's staffers returned to the 2000 election and 9/11. Without access to the White House, they explained, the labor movement had turned inward. "Had Al Gore won," asserted Bob Welsh, "there would have been no split in the labor movement. Change to Win would not have happened if there was a Democratic president, wouldn't have happened, because there wouldn't have needed to be a second voice." Lane Windham also saw Change to Win as a reflection of the harsh climate. "After September the eleventh, when Bush was gaining power in the U.S., the labor movement was losing power," she explained. "It basically opens up this moment for the labor movement to say: 'We have to do something, we have to change it, we are getting stomped, basically. . . . We've given it nearly a decade, it's not turned around, [and] we have to do something different.'" After Bush's reelection, moreover, Stern's reform proposals, which had previously been pushed internally by the New Unity Partnership, gained wider exposure. Clearly, the political climate had helped to decide the fate of Sweeney's presidency.[53]

In June 2005 Stern announced plans to form Change to Win. The five original members were the SEIU, the Teamsters, the UFCW, the Laborers, and the newly merged UNITE HERE. Although they were rather an eclectic mix—and there was never much cohesion between them—these unions comprised well over a third of the Federation's 13 million members. The dispute came to a head at the AFL-CIO's convention in July, where the reformers called for the Federation to triple the amount it spent on organizing. This was labor's "summer of discontent," thought Steven Greenhouse, and the seventy-one-year-old Sweeney was placed under enormous pressure.[54] As the convention began, the SEIU and Teamsters—with a combined membership of 3.2 million—withdrew from the Federation. "This was not an easy or happy decision," claimed Stern. "It represents . . . a recognition that we are in the midst of the most rapid transformative moment in economic history, and workers are suffering." The other members of Change to Win boycotted the convention, ensuring Sweeney's election. Even in his acceptance speech, Sweeney struck a downcast tone, referring to recent events as "contentious and stressful." It was vital, he concluded, for labor to "stick together."[55]

Following the convention, the reformers looked to strengthen their ranks. They were soon joined by the United Brotherhood of Carpenters, which had quit the Federation in 2001. On September 27, the breakaway unions formally founded Change to Win. In doing so, they promised to organize many of the 50 million workers whose jobs could not be sent overseas or automated, including janitors, nursing home workers, security guards, and cashiers. Sweeney reacted sadly to the news. "There's nothing the Change to Win unions are doing today they couldn't have done in unity with the entire labor movement," he claimed. In contrast, Change to Win's leaders claimed that they were rebuilding the labor movement rather than destroying it. "American workers play by the rules, but the rules no longer work," declared Anna Burger. The reformers would "rekindle the American Dream," ensuring that workers were "valued and rewarded" once more. A former welfare worker from Pennsylvania who had risen up the ranks of the SEIU, Burger broke ground as the first woman to head an American labor federation when she was elected as chair of Change to Win. It was a proud moment for Burger, who would serve in the prominent position for five years. "I think that when I was in a public place," she recalled, "that it helped. I would get letters from people, I would get emails from people; I think it kind of changed the idea of what the labor movement could be."[56]

At the AFL-CIO, the split had a number of negative consequences, especially for staff morale. "There was a lot of apprehension, and some anxiety," recalled aide Christine Owens. "We certainly believed that a unified labor movement . . . would be able to exercise the most power, at a time of declining resources . . . and so we were concerned about the implications of a split." The economic impact on the Federation was considerable. "Our finances suffered very significantly," admitted Bill Samuel. The Federation could not afford to lose four of its biggest unions, as they contributed about one-third of its income. Moreover, Sweeney's ambitious reforms were costly to fund.[57]

Apart from the financial cost, the split undermined Sweeney's programs in other ways. It damaged the Federation's political work, especially as Samuel and his staff "didn't talk" to their Change to Win counterparts "for some time." The split also cost the Federation much of its support from intellectuals, who were now attracted by Change to Win's reformist ideas. In May 2006 a distracted AFL-CIO failed to give cohesive support to May Day immigrant rights demonstrations, the sort of initiative that had characterized Sweeney's early presidency. A series of massive demonstrations—including a turnout of an estimated 400,000 people in Chicago—were designed to influence congressional debate about whether to grant legal status to undocumented immigrants living in the United States. The marches were also a response to House proposals to build a 700-mile-long wall along the Mexican border and make illegal presence in the United States a felony. Although some workers took part in the protests—and the Federation participated in the Washington, DC, march—most unions did not get involved, and some of them told their immigrant members to go to work. Finally, the split created a massive amount of negative publicity, tainting the labor movement once more with what aide Gerry Shea called a "sense of failure." The positive stories of the early Sweeney years became a distant memory. What Harold Meyerson termed "Labor's Civil War" generated plenty of copy, and conservatives reacted gleefully. The 2005 split, summarized John Zogby in the *Wall Street Journal*, could very well be labor's "epitaph." This was no way to celebrate the AFL-CIO's fiftieth anniversary, which passed almost unnoticed in the midst of the bitter political battle.[58]

The AFL-CIO's private records offer further insights into the problems caused by the departure of some of its biggest—and most energetic—affiliates. In February 2007 Sweeney told his colleagues on the General Board that, over the previous eighteen months, they had lived through "one of the TOUGHEST internal struggles in the history of our movement," and these "DISTRACTIONS and DEFECTIONS" had come at the worst possible time. The use of capitals confirmed Sweeney's anger and sense of betrayal.[59] At the Executive Council meeting the following month, Sweeney acknowledged that the Federation was struggling for relevancy. "We have many battles to fight," he proclaimed, "but the biggest is over the very survival of the labor movement as a force in the American economy and the American workplace." The last two years, Sweeney summarized in July, had been a "huge test."[60]

Most significantly, the split led to sizeable reductions in the funding of the AFL-CIO's programs, further undermining Sweeney's reforms. At the Executive Council meeting in May 2007, Sweeney admitted that the Federation had been forced to make "major cuts in spending because of the disaffiliations." Health insurance and pension contribution costs were also rising, and membership was falling. The situation was grim, especially in light of ongoing industrial decline and the contraction of the public sector due to cuts. "The industrial unions are still reeling from plant closures and off-shoring," he admitted, "and the growth in the public sector that used to compensate for that loss has disappeared." Overall, the AFL-CIO had a $3 million deficit, and the situation was projected to worsen. "Without an increase in membership—or a major cut in spending," he warned, "we will be seeing annual deficits of per-haps seven million [dollars] by the time of our 2009 convention."[61]

The Council was particularly concerned about the fate of the National Labor College, which the AFL-CIO had established in 1997 on its campus in Silver Spring, Maryland. The nation's only labor college, the NLC taught pio-neering courses to grassroots unionists, forging the connections between the Federation and the membership that characterized Sweeney's presidency. By this time, however, the AFL-CIO was spending about $5 million annually to support the college, which had borrowed heavily to make capital improve-ments. Although the campus survived, these costs were increasingly unsus-tainable. In order to reduce the Federation's overheads, publication of *Labor's Heritage* and the *American Federationist* had ceased. After December 2001, the AFL-CIO's constitutional conventions were also held every four years, rather than two, thus saving considerable expense.[62]

The split also affected Sweeney personally. As he admitted later, any AFL-CIO president was accustomed to "tough days." The internal split, however, was particularly hard to bear. "That one hurt," he acknowledged.[63] Although he was reluctant to elaborate, Sweeney clearly felt betrayed by Stern. Stern was more forthcoming, recalling that his relationship with Sweeney never re-covered. "John Sweeney personally was very hurt," he reflected almost a de-cade after the split. "In John Sweeney's mind . . . since he had been very good to me, and he had, he couldn't believe this wasn't an attack on him politically." This sense of betrayal never left Sweeney, who felt deflated. As a result, the defensive tone of the second half of his presidency was reinforced.[64]

In the wake of the split, there were some efforts to repair the damage, par-ticularly at the local level. In August 2005, following pressure from grassroots leaders, Sweeney allowed local unions from the departed internationals to rejoin state and local labor bodies as special affiliates if they signed a "solidar-ity charter." The effort was designed to allow unions from the two Federa-tions to cooperate, especially during political campaigns. As the 2006 election approached, both sides recognized the importance of working together, and relations began to thaw, even in Washington.[65]

The 2006 midterm elections showed that the split, for all of its negative consequences, had not undermined labor's political clout. Both sides agreed on the importance of political campaigning, and by early 2006 they had started to work together. Sweeney continued to give especially high priority to political work, seeing it as even more important as organizing stalled. In the weeks leading up to the elections, the AFL-CIO spent over $100 million on campaigning. "The mobilization effort was enormous. It's like nothing I've seen before," declared political scientist Bob Bruno. Terming its effort the "largest, broadest mobilization in history," the AFL-CIO organized 30 million phone calls to union voters and distributed 20 million pieces of mail. In the last four days alone, it mobilized more than 13.4 million union voters in thirty-two states and 515 electoral races. The results were impressive, as nearly three-quarters of union members voted for the labor-endorsed candidate. The AFL-CIO helped the Democrats to make important gains, especially as they captured control of both the U.S. House and Senate.[66] The Democrats also won some important gubernatorial races and secured the passage of minimum wage initiatives in six states. The results, claimed Sweeney, represented "a great political victory." Others agreed. At an Executive Council meeting in 2007, Senator Chuck Schumer (D-NY) commented, "Without labor, we wouldn't have taken back the U.S. Senate."[67]

It was notable that Sweeney's political reforms, especially the creation of Working America, had continued to bear fruit. Working America was at the heart of the election effort, signing up 700,000 members in the crucial swing state of Ohio alone. Nationally, less than half of those who joined Working America came from union families. One-third were "born-again" Christians and one-third belonged to the National Rifle Association. The Federation was winning over voters that it would otherwise have lost, allowing it to exert considerable leverage.[68] In the wake of the vote, Sweeney was upbeat again. "We reminded our nation and our elected officials that the working men and women of the AFL-CIO are an UNPARALLELED POLITICAL FORCE in our country," he told his colleagues. He was especially proud of Working America, describing it as "one of the great innovations of the AFL-CIO and the labor movement."[69]

After the election, Sweeney's top priority was to secure passage of the Employee Free Choice Act (EFCA). The Federation launched a "national fight" to pass the EFCA, which allowed workers to choose whether they formed a union based on signed cards or through the NLRB election process. In its two other core provisions, the law guaranteed workers a first union contract through mediation and conciliation, and strengthened penalties for violations against workers who were trying to organize or negotiate their first contract.[70] The card check provisions, in particular, allowed workers to avoid NLRB elections, which employers used to undermine support for the union. In 2007 the AFL-CIO's research indicated that over half of companies threatened to close their plants if the union won an NLRB election. Many more fired or intimidated union supporters in the period just before the vote, or they called workers into meetings where they disseminated antiunion propaganda. The EFCA was thus a crucial measure, promising to break the logjam in organizing that had weakened Sweeney's presidency. At a General Board meeting in February 2007, Sweeney called for a "major movement-wide campaign" to pass the EFCA. "No bill is more important to us as a movement," he explained.[71]

Placed in charge of the fight, Stewart Acuff recalled that it was a "huge campaign" that involved intense lobbying in Washington and mass mobilization at the grassroots. Building on Sweeney's reforms—as well as the legacy of Solidarity Day—the campaign mobilized allies in the churches and in liberal organizations. Following a positive start, several polls indicated that the majority of Americans supported labor law reform. Reflecting this, on March 1, 2007, Congress passed the EFCA by a margin of 241 to 185. "Make no mistake: Employee Free Choice will become law," proclaimed Sweeney. After "a terrific legislative win," organized labor was "on a high."[72]

The celebrations were premature. As political staffer Michael Podhorzer summarized, defeating the EFCA was a "high priority" for the business community. After intense lobbying from corporate interests, the House vote fell short of the two-thirds majority needed to override a promised veto by President Bush, and in June, Senate Republicans blocked the Federation's top legislative priority. The outcome underlined the limitations of labor's political power, showing that increased mobilization of supporters could only achieve so much when union density was declining and Republicans controlled the White House. "Winning change for working people is the hardest it's been in many, many years," Sweeney admitted.[73]

The defeat prompted a bout of self-reflection. At an Executive Council meeting in March 2007, Sweeney admitted to his colleagues, "The reality is that we're still not growing . . . and we still can't get a big enough majority in the Senate to pass the Employee Free Choice Act." Looking back, Sweeney blamed employer opposition—and especially the power of the "conservative right wing"—for undermining support, scaring many Americans into believing that the legislation would make unions too powerful. "It was too bad," he noted sadly. Some labor activists also felt that the card check provisions were a mistake, however, especially as they had allowed opponents to attack unions as undemocratic. As former UFCW president Doug Dority put it, "When we tried to get certified without having elections, all of a sudden . . . you are favoring something that goes against the fabric of what's right, and what we fight for in this country." By inserting the card check provisions, labor had opened itself up to business attacks that it would remove confidentiality from organizing drives. It proved a fatal flaw, especially as the business campaign against the bill was unprecedented in scale and cost. Card check also made it hard to sell the bill to citizens, including some union members. "With faith in democracy deeply ingrained in the national psyche, it was almost impossible to convince the general public that card check was as democratic as a secret ballot election," observed *Labor Notes.*[74]

Despite this disappointment, the 2006 election left Sweeney confident that, with the AFL-CIO's help, the Democrats could win back the White House. If labor was to push its key legislative goals, particularly labor law and health care reform, a change in the presidency was essential. In the 2008 election, the Federation consequently carried out what it termed "its largest, broadest mobilization in history." Once again, the record commitment of 2006 was surpassed.[75] Liberal columnist Harold Meyerson agreed with the Federation's claims, calling its effort "the most massive and sophisticated electoral campaign that labor has ever waged." In particular, the Federation played a key role in the election of America's first African-American president, convincing their white members to back Obama in much greater proportions than white Americans did as a whole.[76]

The AFL-CIO's campaign was well planned and generously funded. As early as September 2007, the Executive Council authorized the spending of $53.4 million on a broad program in the upcoming election. As well as securing the election of a Democratic president, the operation was aimed at expanding the Democrats' majorities in the House and Senate, electing key governors, and being competitive in hundreds of state legislative races. To fund this commitment, the AFL-CIO set aside $20 million a year for two years from its General Fund, as well as transferring $5 million from the Solidarity Fund and the Organizing Fund. The rest of the money was produced by a special one dollar per member assessment. Despite the loss of several large affiliates, the Federation claimed that it would be mobilizing 25 percent more members than it had in 2004, largely because of the expansion of household members and Working America. Sweeney also planned to mobilize an "army" of 200,000 union volunteers, using them mainly to get out the vote.[77]

Justifying this program, the Federation argued that the election represented "an historic opportunity to change America." Fresh from the victories of 2006, and with the Republicans hobbled by an unpopular president and an increasingly controversial war in Iraq, labor had "a rare opening to lead an historic realignment."[78] Sweeney was confident about the outcome, especially when the economy weakened significantly in the months before the election. In 2007–2008, the Global Financial Crisis was widely regarded as the worst economic downturn since the Great Depression. Ending five years of job growth, it boosted calls for political change. In November 2007 unemployment was 4.7 percent, but it jumped above 7 percent within a year. Moreover, the AFL-CIO's political program had "been on a roll" since 2006, and this fed through to unprecedented interest in the presidential race. "We have seen there is a greater interest on the part of this campaign," Sweeney told the press in June. "More people want to be involved, more folks are knowledgeable about the issues, all of them recognize the problems with the economy. . . . It's making folks angry and wanting to be involved."[79]

In the end, the campaign was even bigger than Sweeney anticipated. When the financial contribution of affiliates was included, the AFL-CIO estimated that it had spent $200 million on election activities. Some informed observers thought that the cost was even higher, especially when Change to Win was included. According to the *New York Times*, organized labor had spent "more than $300 million" to help elect Barack Obama and increase the Democratic majority in Congress.[80] The AFL-CIO's effort to reach voters was extensive; during the campaign its records claimed that staff and volunteers had knocked on the doors of at least 10 million union households, made 70 million phone calls, and dropped 20 million leaflets at work sites. Although this was a nationwide campaign, it focused heavily on twenty-four battleground states that were home to 13 million voters.[81]

The AFL-CIO's political drive was no last-minute effort. Prior to the endorsement of a presidential candidate in June, the Federation spent four months working to discredit Republican front-runner John McCain with union voters. "Everywhere John McCain goes in the coming months, union activists will be there to confront him on his economic positions and plans and demand that he speak to working families' concerns," explained political director Karen Ackerman. In particular, the Federation exposed McCain's "unwavering" support for George W. Bush's "failed" economic agenda.[82] Focused on high-priority states, this effort avoided some of the mistakes of the 1980s, when the Federation had failed to sufficiently challenge growing political conservatism among its membership. The headquarters created a popular "McCain Revealed" website, while campaigners showed up at McCain events, distributed fliers, and knocked on doors. The effort worked; between February and June, the Federation's research found that McCain's favorable rating among union members plunged from 57 percent to 33 percent.[83]

While these efforts were going on, the Federation refrained from endorsing a Democratic candidate. During a lively primary contest, the AFL-CIO mirrored the reaction of other liberal constituencies, with many unions, including AFSCME, originally backing front-runner Hillary Clinton, who had more political experience than Obama. AFSCME, summarized Gerald McEntee, was a "Clinton union." Across the labor movement, the New York senator was particularly popular with women unionists.[84] As Barack Obama's campaign gathered force, however, affiliates began to switch. As a community organizer and state senator in Illinois, Obama had forged good relations with organized labor, and during the primaries he won endorsements from several large unions, including the SEIU and the Teamsters. As a result, Change to Win endorsed Obama as early as February, helping him to capture the Democratic nomination. "We did a lot of work within our unions around the endorsement of Barack Obama," recalled Anna Burger proudly. "I think it was a significant thing, the fact that Change to Win existed, and was able to get out there and endorse Barack Obama."[85]

As the battle for the Democratic nomination came to a climax, Obama reached out to the AFL-CIO. On June 18, 2008, he attended a special General Board meeting. The next day, he hosted a large town hall meeting for union leaders. A gifted campaigner, Obama sold his pro-labor credentials, including his support for legislation to raise the minimum wage and strengthen the right to unionize. These moves sealed the deal. In justifying its endorsement of Obama, the AFL-CIO cited his 98 percent voting record on labor issues in the U.S. Senate.[86] This compared to McCain's lifetime score of just 16 percent—and McCain had sat in the Senate for over twenty years. According to a Federation analysis, Hillary Clinton's score was 93 percent. Obama's record inspired grand hopes, with Sweeney's office describing the Illinois senator as a "champion for working families."[87]

After formally endorsing Obama in June, the AFL-CIO undertook fresh initiatives to undermine McCain's support. Several efforts focused on educating potentially conservative constituencies within the labor movement. In July the Federation launched the AFL-CIO Veterans Council, a group designed to connect with more than two million union veterans. At the same time, it ran television ads in six battleground states—including the key industrial states of Michigan, Ohio, Pennsylvania, and Wisconsin—that focused attention on McCain's record as a senator, rather than his past as a decorated Vietnam War veteran. "Every vet respects John McCain's war record," noted veteran Jim Wasser in one of the ads. "It's his record in the Senate that I have a problem with." McCain, the ads continued, had consistently voted with Bush, supporting his flawed economic policies and opposing higher health benefits for veterans.[88] Other AFL-CIO messages got personal, exposing McCain's extensive private wealth—the Republican candidate was said to be worth more than $100 million—and picturing him as a remote plutocrat with little understanding of workers. Shortly before the election, the Federation also launched a sportsmen's group, reassuring them that organized labor—and Obama—supported gun ownership.[89]

Despite these efforts, as an African-American candidate Obama faced unique obstacles. Obama's "biggest challenge," summarized the *Washington Post*, was to win over white working-class voters in crucial Rust Belt states where unions were still strong.[90] For forty years white voters had preferred Republican presidential candidates. In 2004 exit polls by CNN showed that 58 percent of white voters had backed President Bush. In the summer of 2008, about 15.4 million workers still belonged to unions, and 73 percent of them were white. If Obama was to win, the AFL-CIO needed to reach its white members.[91]

Early results graphically illustrated the problem. In March and April, Obama lost the Ohio and Pennsylvania primaries. He was "struggling to connect with working-class white voters," concluded the *Post*'s Shailagh Murray. In Indiana in early May, Obama also narrowly lost the primary to Hillary Clinton, despite belated appeals for the AFL-CIO's help. "You guys are pretty persuasive," he told a group of union members in Evansville. "I need you to tell your membership this is something worth fighting for."[92] In April, Harold Meyerson detailed how Obama was struggling to win the white working-class vote. "As Obama is still the likely nominee," he noted, "many Democrats fear that come November, working-class whites will pull Obama and their party down to defeat." Meyerson predicted, however, that unions offered Obama his "best shot" at securing white votes, especially from men.[93]

Out in the field, union staffers reported that many white members were reluctant to support Obama. "I think race is playing a major part," acknowledged MacDavis Slade, a political activist with the painters' union. "I think that's why some people say, 'Isn't he a Muslim?'" Other union members refused to acknowledge the race issue but were still hesitant to embrace Obama. "The main reason you get is, 'I don't trust him because I don't know him,'" explained Anthony Rainey, a UAW leader in Wisconsin. AFL-CIO strategists worked to address this resistance. "We're very conscious of the fact that many voters have never voted for an African-American for any office," commented Karen Ackerman. "For some voters, including union voters, particularly older voters, there is a reluctance." To combat these fears, canvassers stressed Obama's support of tax cuts for the middle class, his commitment to protect Social Security (and McCain's prior support for its privatization), and his call for trade agreements to include more workers' rights. The idea was to "peel away" voters' objections to Obama and emphasize his positive record on crucial labor issues.[94]

Some of these efforts, however, met the race issue head-on. "The Truth about Barack Obama," an AFL-CIO flyer that was distributed in the steel districts of Pennsylvania, was indicative. "Is he a Christian?" it asked of Obama. "Yes. Was he sworn in on a Bible? Yes. Was he born in America? Yes." Backing up these materials, local union activists carried out a lot of educational work, including regular meetings with workers. In these gatherings, leaders stressed some "basic facts" about Obama, emphasizing that he was raised by a single mother and had paid his own way through college.[95] The overall aim of the educational campaign, explained Karen Ackerman, was to combat "fear and hesitancy" among white members. Important work was also carried out by Working America. As Karen Nussbaum recalled, over 80 percent of Working America's membership—which now topped 2.5 million—were white, making the group a "trusted messenger" for the Obama campaign within white neighborhoods.[96]

Setting an example from the top, AFL-CIO leaders also played an important role. One crucial moment occurred in July, when Richard Trumka—who was known as an eloquent orator—traveled to Las Vegas to address the USW's convention. Speaking to a gathering dominated by middle-aged white men, the former coal miner was candid. There were, he noted, "a lot of white folks," including "many good union people," who "just can't get past this idea that there's something wrong with voting for a black man." These voters, he urged, should be educated rather than judged. In particular, he urged workers to focus on Obama's labor record, and to contrast it with McCain's. It was also time, however, to make amends for labor's past. As he explained in an inspiring conclusion: "There's no evil that's inflicted more pain and suffering than racism—and it's something we in the labor movement have a special responsibility to challenge." Following his remarkable speech, Trumka received a standing ovation from an audience that saw him as one of their own. Many USW delegates returned to key Midwestern states—where their membership was concentrated—energized. They now urged their family and friends to get behind Obama. The speech also had a broader impact; going viral, it attracted more than half a million views on YouTube. As the *Washington Post* observed, this was "surely the first YouTube moment" in the AFL-CIO's history.[97]

Trumka's speech was no isolated event. The secretary-treasurer made the same pitch many times, but the Las Vegas speech made news because it was filmed. "What I saw was," he recalled, "that there're a bunch of our members that I think wanted to get involved, but they had this real reluctance, and I thought that I had to create some space for them . . . to be able to point and say, 'Trumka said we ought to do this.' . . . Also, I wanted to start the dialogue—or the conversation—in the labor movement about racism, and in the country, quite frankly." Through the summer and fall of 2008, scores of other union leaders made the same pitch, especially to the predominantly white industrial affiliates. In one major speech to the Machinists union, AFSCME secretary-treasurer Bill Lucy—one of the most prominent African-Americans in the AFL-CIO—again urged workers to focus on labor issues rather than race. Despite these efforts, some union presidents were candid about the scale of the task they faced. According to Gerald McEntee, the AFL-CIO had to "fight our own members" over the race issue, particularly in Appalachian areas.[98]

While the task often seemed overwhelming, this work gradually reaped rewards. "It started having a positive effect," recalled Trumka, "and opened things up." Executive vice president Arlene Holt Baker agreed, and recalled how white and black workers reacted very differently to Obama's candidacy. "Now, for our members of color, let me be clear, they were going to be voting for it," she explained. "That's where they were." Among whites, the Federation's educational work, including Trumka's speech, helped convince "the necessary percentage" to support Obama. "It wasn't the white women," thought Holt Baker, the highest-ranking African-American leader in the AFL-CIO, "it was the white men . . . they could see their leader, leaders, whom they trusted [backing Obama] . . . but you also needed to have the local leaders, have the conversation with their members. . . . I think that that education, to be honest, I don't believe President Barack Obama would have been president, the first term, without that." African-American staffer Susan Washington also asserted that the Federation had played a "huge role" in getting workers, especially white males, to rethink their attitudes. Trumka's speech, she concluded, was a decisive moment.[99]

Other factors ensured the success of labor's election drive. The AFL-CIO cooperated effectively with Change to Win, especially in the swing industrial states where unions were strong. The Laborers' International Union, a Change to Win affiliate, even participated in the AFL-CIO's political program. At the grassroots level, hundreds of local unions from the departed affiliates continued to work with the AFL-CIO's city, county, and state labor councils, ensuring that the split did not undermine organized labor's political program.[100] Change to Win's leaders also tackled their members' racial fears. "You have to go out and educate voters," proclaimed James P. Hoffa. "People will vote against their own economic interests out of fear, out of demagoguery, out of racism. Those are the things we've got to penetrate . . . to look them in the eye and say, 'This is your life; this is your pocketbook; this is your home.' "[101]

The two federations also marshalled their resources well. Both used Catalist, a company founded by Democratic operative Harold M. Ickes, to provide personal data on targeted voters. As Change to Win political director Jeffrey Lerner summarized, the overall goal was to "maximize impact." These efforts were important, especially as the Republicans were utilizing their own "voter vault" of personal data. The AFL-CIO also played an active part in America Votes, a liberal coalition that brought together nearly fifty unions and liberal groups, including EMILY's List, the NAACP Voters Fund, Planned Parenthood, and the Sierra Club. With a budget of $25 million, America Votes coordinated the efforts of its member groups, ensuring that they didn't "walk on top of each other."[102]

The Obama campaign was also successful because it utilized a network of local volunteers. In 2004 the Republicans had used a similar strategy to secure record turnout. Four years later, union members were integrally involved as the Democrats adopted the same tactics. In the 2008 election, explained Steve Rosenthal, neighbor-to-neighbor outreach was "more important than in any recent one, because of, without mincing words, the race factor. Having white validators, people working these neighborhoods who live in those neighborhoods and are of those neighborhoods, who are saying, 'Get out and vote for this guy,' is really important." Some outside observers agreed. According to Yale political scientist Donald Green, an expert on the topic, face-to-face contact increased a voter's chance of turning out by 7 to 10 percent.[103]

In the closing stages of the campaign, the AFL-CIO also funded a massive direct mail campaign that forcefully attacked John McCain, effectively linking him to the economic policies of the Bush administration. By October 26, the Federation had sent more than 57 million pieces of political mail, an effort that it called the "largest and most targeted" in its history. In 2004 the Federation's mail program had concentrated on thirteen states, but by 2008 it had expanded to twenty-one battleground states. The mail messages were well thought out, having been extensively tested on groups of 20,000 union members. In short, sharp messages, ads referred to the Global Financial Crisis (GFC) as the "Bush/McCain financial crisis," while McCain's three-point economic plan was mockingly summarized as: "Send jobs overseas. Put Wall Street first. Ignore Main Street." According to the *Washington Post*, the AFL-CIO's mail campaign was "sophisticated" and effective.[104]

The 2008 economic collapse assisted the AFL-CIO. In an election where the poor state of the economy was, as two leading commentators have observed, "by far the dominant issue," the Federation's material was very effective. In 2007–2008, the GFC boosted the Democratic Party's chances, especially as real unemployment climbed to double-digit levels.[105] On September 15, 2008, Lehman Brothers, one of the world's biggest financial institutions, failed, further undermining confidence in the Republican administration. As he struggled to respond, McCain made errors. Just after the Lehman Brothers story broke, he claimed that the "fundamentals of our economy are strong." Within an hour of McCain uttering the phrase at a rally in Florida, Obama was using it against him, implying that the Republican nominee, like Bush, was out-of-touch on economic issues. The AFL-CIO also made effective use of the stumble. "It certainly helped Obama's campaign, and ours," recalled Denise Mitchell. "I mean people couldn't believe he said that, it was mind-boggling, and it was like Lehman was falling at the moment he said it." As political journalists Chuck Todd and Sheldon Gawiser observed, McCain had voiced a phrase that he would "regret for the rest of his life."[106]

While Obama's victory ultimately reflected many broader factors—including his mobilization of young and nonwhite voters, his success in raising money, and his ability to cast himself as best-placed to tackle the country's severe economic problems—the AFL-CIO's campaign made an important difference. On October 19, Matthew Mosk wrote in the *Washington Post* that the Federation's mail drive and phone bank had been crucial as Obama gained a clear lead.[107] Conducted on election night for the AFL-CIO, an exit poll by Peter D. Hart Associates also showed that across the swing states union members had supported Obama by an impressive 68–30 margin. "In the critical battleground states," agreed Gerald McEntee, "workers gave Sen. Obama the winning edge." For Sweeney, this was a great moment, and he captured the euphoria aroused by Obama's victory well. "Led by a candidate with an uncommon ability to inspire hope, we reclaimed our country from those who are serving corporate interests and the privileged at the expense of everyone else," he declared straight after the election. "And what we've seen—the stunning voter participation and the common call for change—is an indication of the history we can continue to make together."[108]

For many in the AFL-CIO, this victory also meant a lot, especially as it came at such a difficult time. Sweeney's staffers recalled the election fondly. "The Obama stuff was just, 'Wow, we did it!'" remembered Karen Ackerman. "We were able to really have a role in pushing back on very bigoted attitudes, racist attitudes, among some members. So I think that was a very unique . . . and very, very important role." The campaign to elect Obama was "unique in American history," added Stewart Acuff, especially as the labor movement had stood up for racial justice. Staffer Charles Stott, who had held various roles at the Federation since 1978, worked on the campaign in the key state of Ohio. When the result came in, Stott sat in his hotel room, "with tears running down my face, just so proud of the American electorate, for what they did. It was just a great moment . . . far outweighing anything else that I think I've ever done." Clearly, this was a landmark event in the AFL-CIO's history.[109]

Revealingly, Obama's opponents also asserted that the AFL-CIO had played a crucial role in the election. Obama, they argued, was a captive of union forces, a puppet who would implement labor priorities such as the EFCA and national health care reform. "This last election the labor bosses spent $400 million to $500 million getting the other side elected," blasted House Republican leader John Boehner, "and they just didn't do that for their good health. They've been making investments in the other side so they can control the policy-making side." The risk, added Randel Johnson of the U.S. Chamber of Commerce, was that the Obama administration would be "controlled" by organized labor. Despite the result, labor's opponents were far from cowed. While the AFL-CIO had run a very effective campaign, it now had to convince Congress to act on its legislative demands. Past experience, especially during the Clinton presidency, had also highlighted that Democratic politicians did not always meet labor's expectations.[110]

Following the 2008 election, however, hopes were revived that the EFCA would finally pass. As a candidate, Obama had expressed support for the legislation. "If a majority of workers want a union, they should get a union; it's that simple," he asserted in April 2008.[111] The administration quickly drafted a fresh version of the bill, which promised card checks and stronger penalties for labor law violations. The fight to pass the legislation was intense, with one union official terming it "the biggest battle between labor and corporations in this country since the Taft-Hartley Act of 1947." Heading the charge, the Chamber of Commerce denounced the bill as "payback" to "union bosses" that would signal the death of "workplace democracy." Powerful corporations, including Wal-Mart and Home Depot, also spoke out. As Bill Samuel acknowledged, the "heavy pressure" from corporations, particularly retailers and drugstores, took its toll. By the time the bill was introduced into Congress in March 2009, it faced opposition from sixteen well-funded conservative groups. The Democratic Party was also divided on the issue, as well-heeled supporters saw the legislation as too pro-labor. An inexperienced legislator, Obama struggled to unite the party behind the legislation.[112]

The opportunity to pass the bill soon passed. After the fall of 2009, when the Democrats lost their sixty-vote super-majority in the Senate due to the death of Senator Edward Kennedy and his replacement by Republican Scott Brown, the bill's fate became bleak. Given that Massachusetts had not elected a Republican senator since 1972, this turn of events was surprising. Eventually, the labor movement had to agree to shelve its proposals. Shortly before Sweeney stood down, an AFL-CIO statement claimed that organized labor was "closer than we have been in a generation" to securing labor law reform. Given the scale of the Federation's campaign, however, its inability to pass the EFCA was a major failure. The limitations of Sweeney's strategy had been highlighted.[113]

The fight over the bill illustrated how Sweeney had transformed the AFL-CIO into a formidable political machine, yet in doing so he had also spurred his opponents into action. All during the Sweeney years, business groups outspent organized labor, and the period witnessed a conservative revival that stymied much of the Federation's work. Inspired by the AFL-CIO's example, corporate groups began to stress grassroots mobilization, with the American Enterprise Institute even promising "hand-to-hand combat" with its labor adversary. Just after Sweeney left office, the U.S. Supreme Court's decision in *Citizens United v. Federal Election Commission* (2010)—where the conservative-led court held that the expenditure of money in federal elections was, by any entity, a form of free speech—encouraged the spending spree. Although union election spending was also uncapped, it was corporations— with much deeper pockets—that benefited the most.[114] Organized labor found itself in a political quandary; breaking with the Democrats and launching an independent party was unlikely to succeed in a winner-takes-all, two-party electoral system, and most of labor's political problems stemmed from the hostility of the Republicans—who regained control of the House of Representatives in 2010—rather than weak support from the Democrats. Proposals calling for workers to look to socialism were also up against it in a country where workers had long rejected radical ideas.[115] After Sweeney left office, moreover, the AFL-CIO agreed to Obama's directive that the Affordable Care Act should be passed before the EFCA. As Bill Samuel recalled, this turned out to be "a very fateful mistake" by the Federation. In the years that followed, the fight to pass—and defend—the Affordable Care Act was very time-consuming, overshadowing other issues.[116]

Still, some positives came out of the labor law campaign. "The Employee Free Choice Act campaign got the entire labor movement focused on organizing, right, and that was huge," recalled Stewart Acuff. Right across the country, campaign activists had made public officials more aware of the problems that workers faced in the field. Nevertheless, without labor law reform, organizing remained very difficult. According to Elizabeth Bunn, who became Organizing Director in the wake of this campaign, workers who tried to form unions continued to face a "brutal, unrelenting attack" that was led by multinational employers. Overall, this was the "number one reason" for the continued problems in the organizing area.[117]

The failure of organizing could not simply be attributed to mounting external resistance and the weakness of labor law. Some former staffers were candid about the fact that many international unions resisted the call to organize more, even in the latter years of the Sweeney presidency. "It is true that many unions used deindustrialization, and automation, and all kinds of reasons, for not investing in growth," recalled Bob Welsh, "and many unions . . . were completely content to be the size they were. It's all working fine, we can pay the bills . . . so what?" In the building trades, in particular, the emphasis was on finding work for those who came to the hiring hall rather than going out and recruiting. Organizing was expensive, making it unpopular with many struggling affiliates. Because of the AFL-CIO's long-standing policy of letting affiliates organize, some union leaders disliked 'outside' interference in the area, leading to complex—and fiery—debates about how to proceed. For many unions, the imperative of servicing members also took precedence over organizing. Those tasked with encouraging affiliates to put more emphasis on organizing stressed that the task was not easy. "My role was in part to try to get affiliates to resource organizing," recalled Ken Zinn, who became deputy director of organizing in 2003. "There were experiments, and some of them worked, and some of them didn't."[118]

In the final analysis, other staffers agreed that the record of Sweeney's presidency in the organizing arena was mixed, at best. As Gerry Shea put it, the organizing programs "never really matured . . . despite lots and lots of attempts." The failure in organizing meant that there was no dramatic turnaround in labor's fate. Between 1995 and 2009, the years that Sweeney was in office, union density dropped from 14.5 to 12 percent.[119] This was a slower rate of decline than had occurred under Kirkland, when density had fallen 10 percent—from around 24 percent—over a slightly longer period. Given that Sweeney had promised to stop union decline, however, the results were disappointing.[120]

Sweeney must bear some of the blame. As the failure to pass the EFCA showed, even his political strategy had limitations, especially when labor confronted powerful opponents who were free to fight unions with few—or no—political costs. Reflecting on his presidency, Sweeney admitted that his record was mixed. "Of course I would like to be able to say, in my last official report as your president, that we've reached all the goals we set out for ourselves," he wrote in 2009. "We've set the right foundations, but our movement still has a great deal of building to do on them." Sweeney's resigned—and somewhat defensive—tone was a far cry from the optimism and energy that had swept across the AFL-CIO when he had taken office. As labor relations scholar Richard W. Hurd commented in 2009, "Based on the optimism that supporters of the labor movement felt in 1995 when he [Sweeney] was elected, I think it's hard not to be disappointed with the results." As former Kirkland supporters quietly pointed out, the split also clouded Sweeney's legacy.[121]

Although Sweeney was unable to secure a fundamental change in the labor movement's fortunes, his presidency was very important. A number of permanent shifts had occurred. Prior to the Sweeney era, the AFL-CIO had shown that it could mobilize the membership for specific events—particularly the successful Solidarity Day marches—yet there had been little sustained interest in connecting with the grassroots, particularly through organizing. By the end of the Sweeney era, this had fundamentally changed; while the tension between organizing and servicing members remained, the ground had shifted. Both the AFL-CIO and Change to Win gave a high priority to organizing, with the latter establishing its Strategic Organizing Center to oversee its efforts. In another clear break with the past, Sweeney built a more inclusive and diverse labor movement, and these changes also had a lasting impact. By 2008, there were ten women on the Executive Council, and women also headed a number of state federations. While full equality had not been achieved, important ground had been broken. Sweeney's efforts to forge links with global unions, his landmark policy shift on immigration, his links with progressive allies, and his opposition to the war in Iraq were also highly significant.[122]

Sweeney's reforms were also significant because they inspired the next generation of AFL-CIO leaders. "John Sweeney played a huge role in my life," noted Tefere Gebre, an African immigrant who became executive vice president in 2013, "because *he* inspired me, and I became a believer in the labor movement when the Sweeney, Trumka, Linda Chavez-Thompson team got elected." Like many others, Gebre was drawn to Sweeney's focus on organizing and building power at the local level. Sweeney's successor, Richard

Trumka, recognized his important legacies. "I think John put a lot of things in place, for a lot of us to build on," he reflected. "He immediately started drawing the attention to organizing and the need to increase organizing, and . . . I think he took us out of the era where we looked like an elite club, and brought us back into creating a movement." Under Sweeney, added Trumka's political director, Michael Podhorzer, the labor movement had become "more grassroots" and "engaged." This was a permanent "cultural shift."[123]

Ultimately, perhaps the most impressive legacy was in politics, especially as an unprecedented Federation campaign had helped to secure the election of America's first black president. As Sweeney saw it, labor's political clout had "grown tremendously" during his tenure. Sweeney, summarized Denise Mitchell, left behind a "powerhouse political program." When Sweeney retired, columnist Harold Meyerson—along with many other commentators—agreed with these positive assessments. "Give Sweeney credit where credit is due," he concluded. "Under his leadership, the unions' political program became so adept that labor was punching well above its weight." At a time when union density had continued to fall, this was some achievement.[124]

Epilogue
Holding On in the Trumka Years

Well before Sweeney's retirement, it was no secret that Richard Trumka would be the next president of the AFL-CIO. For fourteen years, "Rich," as he was known within labor circles, had served as secretary-treasurer, giving him the inside track on the presidency. The only other obvious challenger, the talented but divisive Andy Stern, had already left the Federation. Running unopposed, and with Sweeney's endorsement, Trumka took over with little fanfare at the AFL-CIO's twenty-sixth convention. The contrast with the dramatic events of 1995 could not have been greater. Trumka took office on September 16, the day after President Obama spoke to delegates. In his address, Obama praised Trumka as a "friend" and a "fiery advocate for America's ideals." His eloquence helped to ease the former Mineworkers' leader into office. The convention itself was held in Pittsburgh, just up the Monongahela River from Nemacolin, Pennsylvania, the small town where Trumka had grown up. Addressing the convention, Trumka referred back to the "little mining town," claiming that it had taught him the importance of "hard work, respect for workers and the power in each of us to challenge the injustice that we see."[1]

In his nomination speech, Trumka outlined an ambitious agenda. Under him, the AFL-CIO would not just win elections, but legislative battles as well. In particular, the dream of health care reform would finally be achieved. The Federation would also reconnect with the most vulnerable workers hurt by the recession, particularly the young. "Our message to America is that just as unions built the middle class once before, if you give us a chance, we can build it again," he proclaimed. "We need a labor movement that's not afraid of new ideas—and understands that nostalgia for the past is no strategy for the future." Trumka's AFL-CIO would look out, not in. He promised to spread his vision to the millions of Americans—especially freelance workers and contractors—who were "trapped in the twilight of the contingent economy," usually without health insurance and pensions.[2]

There were clear parallels with the Sweeney presidency, which had also begun with grand plans. As Steven Greenhouse observed in the *New York Times*, the AFL-CIO was "promising a new day, again." Like Greenhouse, seasoned observers doubted how much could be achieved, especially as Trumka faced many of the same forces that had thwarted Sweeney, including factory closures, increasingly antiunion corporations, and workers afraid that they would lose their jobs if they organized. To be sure, in his first five years in office Trumka did not achieve a dramatic turnaround in the Federation's fortunes. In many ways labor's problems deepened, especially in the wake of the "Tea Party" election of 2010. Having made stunning gains at the national and state levels, a buoyant Republican Party took on the labor movement and forced it to endure a series of concessions, particularly at the bargaining table.[3]

Once again, however, the AFL-CIO fought back, and the Trumka years were not without their victories. Like Kirkland, another secretary-treasurer who had taken over unopposed, Trumka was able to reunite the Federation. In particular, he coaxed back several affiliates from Change to Win. As a result, the Federation maintained a membership of more than 11 million, allowing it to function as an effective national workers' center. Reawakening the spirit of Solidarity Day, Trumka's AFL-CIO also took part in mass protests, mobilizing behind beleaguered government workers in Wisconsin and taking part in the promising "Occupy Wall Street" movement. At a time of crisis, Trumka also showed a willingness to innovate, placing an unprecedented number of women and nonwhites on the Executive Council. In an important symbolic shift, he also seated the first representative from a workers' advocacy group, rather than a formal trade union.[4]

To some outside observers, Trumka seemed an unlikely reformer. Conservative critics were especially skeptical, questioning whether the tough third-generation coal miner was the man to reform organized labor. "The burly and mustachioed Mr. Trumka physically epitomizes the image of an old-time labor leader," thought the *Wall Street Journal*'s Kris Maher, who used Trumka's appearance to reactivate the "Big Labor" trope.[5] A former high school football star, Trumka had an imposing physical presence. Even in middle age, noted another reporter, Trumka tended "more to linebacker heft than safety leanness," and this build—together with a thick mane of hair—led to physical comparisons with legendary football coach Mike Ditka. Trumka was also sixty years old when he took over the AFL-CIO presidency, and his ascendancy continued the pattern of white men holding the top job. Critics who saw the Federation as "male, pale, and stale" wondered how much had really changed. Like Sweeney, Trumka's interest in social justice partly derived from his Catholicism. Both men also came out of blue-collar backgrounds, and Trumka's past as a coal miner connected him directly to the traditional industrial unions. Although he had lived in Washington, DC, for many years, Trumka had never forgotten his roots. Even as AFL-CIO president,

Trumka continued to relax by hunting and shooting, as well as by riding a motorcycle.[6]

Trumka, however, was more complex and talented than appearances suggested. A college graduate, he was a keen reader who was especially interested in learning about labor's decline. Working his way up the labor movement, Trumka had forged a reputation for militancy and innovation, especially during his leadership of the UMW during the Pittston strike. One of the few successful high-profile strikes of the Kirkland era, Pittston established Trumka's credentials as a serious contender for national office. "It showed the entire labor movement that they could win strikes," he asserted later. As secretary-treasurer of the AFL-CIO, Trumka forged bonds with progressive organizations; in the summer of 2001, for example, he spoke at the NAACP convention in New Orleans and led a joint labor and civil rights rally afterwards.[7] Like Sweeney, Trumka was also candid about the labor movement's problems and the need to try out new ideas. As the *Washington Post's* Alec MacGillis concluded, Trumka could not be reduced to a simple stereotype. Rather, he was "a mix of inside and outside man," an experienced Washington operator who also knew how to connect with the rank and file. Above all, he was "defined by flexibility" rather than the brute force that his physique suggested.[8]

Clear and forthright in person, Trumka had a cogent vision. Feeling that the AFL-CIO had become too inward-looking and "ossified" in the latter years of the Sweeney presidency, he wanted to restore the correct balance between "institution" and "movement." Trumka was proud of his blue-collar background, and it exerted a heavy influence on his thinking. "I'm a product of a coalfield," he noted in 2015. "I think it gives you a different perspective; when you come from the rank and file you have a greater appreciation of the rank and file. I really look at the labor movement from the bottom level up, not the top level down . . . you make the rank and file stronger, and better educated, and you always win." In his office overlooking the White House, Trumka displayed memorabilia from his mining days, including his battered underground helmet. "I keep that there so I remember, every day, where I came from and what I am," he explained. Other eclectic materials—including books on labor history, the Civil War, and economics—sustained the AFL-CIO president. A large placard on his desk proclaimed, "Nothing was ever accomplished by a reasonable person." Even in his mid-sixties, Trumka exuded energy and self-belief. Convinced that the labor movement could rebound, he rose at 4.30 A.M. every day, got to the AFL-CIO building by 6 A.M., and often worked through to 6 P.M. Trumka, thought General Counsel Craig Becker, had experienced adversity, both as a coal miner and the leader of an affiliate that had lost members. As a result, he had an "incredibly compelling personal history" that made him a "good leader for the times."[9]

Trumka quickly implemented some important changes, especially in terms of reaching out to young workers. When he took over, the average AFL-CIO member was forty-seven years old. "We've lost touch with a whole generation," he admitted.[10] Trumka insisted that these workers needed a voice, especially as they were more likely to hold insecure contract jobs. In order to try to reach the young, the AFL-CIO made much greater use of Facebook and Twitter, and commissioned several studies on the changing nature of the workforce. There was a youth summit, as well as listening tours aimed at younger workers. Early on, Trumka also established a large digital department in the headquarters, staffing it with young people who developed the Federation's texting capacity and redesigned its website. The department was deliberately experimental. "People work sitting on the floor, with their laptops there," explained Ana Avendano, Trumka's assistant. "It's very informal . . . they have a, what they call a war room, it's not hierarchical . . . so that has energized (the AFL-CIO), and brought in a fresh perspective."[11]

Trumka's leadership choices also sent a clear message. To give the labor movement a fresher face, Trumka boldly chose 39-year-old Liz Shuler, a former clerical worker from Oregon, as his deputy. Designated as an ambassador to young workers, Shuler was the youngest ever secretary-treasurer of the AFL-CIO. Trumka showed a willingness to disregard seniority, which remained a powerful concept in the labor movement. An important envoy to poorly paid minority workers, Arlene Holt Baker was elected as executive vice president. For the first time, two of the Federation's top three officials were women. "We made history with that ticket," recalled Holt Baker proudly. "I think it was a good way to get people's attention, that the labor movement is changing, and open for business," added Shuler.[12]

From the start, Trumka's speaking ability also grabbed attention. Forged in the tough environment of mine workers' bath houses—where he emphasized that any speaker had to grab their audience's attention very quickly—Trumka had exceptional oratorical skills. Trumka, recalled Doug Dority, was "forthright, and very strong, and . . . dynamic. . . . I've got to admit to you that there were times that I didn't invite him to things, because I didn't want to have to compete with him, as a speaker!" Trumka was recognized as a superior speaker to Sweeney, who had read out his public remarks and rarely offered extemporaneous comments. Under Sweeney, quipped Dority,

Executive Council meetings had been "pretty boring," but Trumka was much more engaging.[13]

As soon as he became president, Trumka laid out his vision of a more assertive AFL-CIO. "The labor movement is the best vehicle out there to make broad social change that creates an America where everyone gets a chance to win once in a while, not just the people on Wall Street but every American out there," he declared in September 2009. "It's a big, big task, it's a big, big fight, and all the people that are arrayed against us are going to try to prevent us from changing anything. But with every fiber of my body, I look forward to that fight."[14] While accepting that workers and unions were experiencing a "historic collapse," Trumka claimed that there were "historic opportunities" to fight back, especially as he took office with a new administration and a new Congress. Trumka's vision was of an AFL-CIO that spoke up for all working Americans, rather than just its members. As he took office, Trumka also won attention by threatening to punish Democratic congressmen and others who took labor's support for granted. It was, however, unclear whether he would—or could—follow through on this threat.[15]

Trumka's optimism was partly justified. As the *Washington Post* observed, under George W. Bush the AFL-CIO had been "frozen out," with Sweeney invited to the White House once in eight years. In the first six weeks of the Obama presidency, however, Sweeney visited the White House at least once a week for receptions, bill signings, and meetings. It was a pattern that continued under Trumka, who was keen to exploit the opportunity.[16] Other labor leaders knew that they had to act fast. Together with the election of a Democratic Congress, Obama's election was "an opportunity of a lifetime," summarized Laborers' leader Terry O'Sullivan. Hopes were high, and Obama encouraged them. In September 2009, when the president spoke at the AFL-CIO convention, he pledged his commitment to comprehensive health care reform, delighting most of his audience. He also identified openly with the AFL-CIO. "You know," he remarked, "the White House is pretty nice, but there's nothing like being back in the House of Labor." On several subsequent occasions, Obama was fulsome in his praise of organized labor. "I don't think any president since Roosevelt has been rhetorically as open about his support for the labor movement," reflected Craig Becker.[17]

In the early part of his presidency, Obama backed up his words with action. He signed an Executive Order that made it harder for federal contractors to discourage union activities and appointed Hilda Solis, a committed labor supporter, as Secretary of Labor. A former state representative from California,

Solis was the daughter of a Mexican father and a Nicaraguan mother, both of whom had been active in unions. "Labor voices were muffled for eight years under the Bush administration," summarized the *Kansas City Star* in 2009, "but there's no question now that unions are being heard at the White House on a host of issues."[18] Obama's appointments to the NLRB were also more pro-labor, and key board rulings encouraged the AFL-CIO. The Board became more aggressive in reinstating union activists who were fired during organizing drives, declared that graduate teaching assistants should have the right to unionize, and imposed restrictions on employers' ability to campaign against unions on the eve of elections. Soon, conservatives were complaining that the NLRB was a pro-union, liberal body that needed to be reformed.[19] In another break with Bush, President Obama explicitly reached out to workers, spending his first three Labor Days in office at union functions. Furthermore, Obama made Trumka a member of his Council on Jobs and Competitiveness, and appointed SEIU official Patrick Gaspard as his first political director.[20]

Both Obama and Trumka staked much on health care reform, an area where action was long overdue. By 2009, a record 50.7 million Americans were without health insurance, up from 46.3 million the year before, largely because recession-hit employers were laying off workers or eliminating health benefits.[21] The AFL-CIO worked closely with the administration on health care reform, and its mobilization of members—as well as high-level lobbying—clearly made a difference. In early 2010, labor backing helped Obama to squeeze his plan through Congress despite highly effective opposition from the Republican Party and its corporate supporters. It was a significant achievement, and supporters lauded the fact that the law expanded Medicaid for the poor, mostly at the federal government's expense, and provided subsidies for middle-income workers to help buy policies on new insurance exchanges. "The health care bill alone is the most significant and far-reaching piece of domestic social policy in my lifetime," declared Neera Tanden, the CEO of the liberal Center for American Progress. "A new season in America" had begun, added Obama.[22]

In order to secure a deal, Obama had to accept significant amendments to the public insurance plan that unions wanted, largely because of effective opposition from business groups. He subsequently granted frequent exemptions to the law's requirement that employers provide at least $750,000 in coverage to each person in their health plans. By 2013, there were also union concerns about the postponement of an employer mandate to ensure coverage for workers and the potential damage that the coming health insurance exchanges might inflict on existing plans. Still, health care reform had passed, fulfilling a long-term AFL-CIO goal. The Federation also helped to ensure that the plan got off the ground and that it stayed on the books, despite efforts by congressional Republicans to derail it. Obama and his supporters—including the AFL-CIO—had succeeded where Presidents Truman, Johnson, Nixon, and Clinton had all failed, putting America on a path to universal health insurance coverage.[23]

In other areas, Obama was more of a disappointment. The failure to secure labor law reform while the Democrats had control of Congress was a major blow, and some commentators saw the outcome as decisive. For Harold Meyerson, the battle over the EFCA in 2009–10 was "labor's last stand." Others doubted that the law would have made a massive difference in a workforce that was changing so rapidly, especially as jobs were increasingly contracted out. Corporate resistance to organizing was deep-seated, and union decline was caused by many other factors, including structural shifts in the workforce. The EFCA had been a high priority for the AFL-CIO, however, and some activists felt that Obama should have provided a stronger lead.[24]

To some extent, the AFL-CIO was to blame for its disillusionment with Obama. "People invested *far* too much in this guy," summarized Bob Welsh in 2013.[25] At the time, it was difficult to be so philosophical, especially after hopes had been raised so high. By 2010, many in the Federation were demoralized, feeling that the AFL-CIO had not been adequately rewarded for its electoral support. As a result, the Federation failed to campaign as enthusiastically in the midterm elections as they had two years earlier. Some were still disappointed about the EFCA, while the poor state of the economy also hurt Obama. As a result, many voters listened more to influential conservative critics—especially Glenn Beck and Bill O'Reilly—rather than Working America. In midterm elections, voters also tended to be older and whiter, adding to labor's problems. The election results were a disaster for the AFL-CIO, as the Republicans gained sixty-three seats in the House and six in the Senate, as well as securing control of twenty-nine of the fifty state governorships.[26]

These results had far-reaching consequences. At the state level, several newly elected Republican governors went after unions, blaming them for financial deficits and the recession. Their actions reflected a breakdown in bi-partisanship, and a hardening of attitudes to organized labor on the Right. "The relationships between Labor and the Republicans have become almost nonexistent, at every level," summarized Craig Becker. In the past, some Republicans had supported—or at least respected—labor, but this was no longer the case. Rather, the new governors saw public sector unions as prime examples of inefficiency and bureaucratic inertia, traits they associated with virtually all government activity. Decisive events took place in Wisconsin, a state where, ironically, public employee unionism had been born in the 1930s. In February 2011, Tea Party-endorsed Governor Scott Walker put forward a legislative package that severely curtailed public workers' collective bargaining rights. In many ways, events in Wisconsin highlighted the AFL-CIO's dire predicament, as its opponents now took on unions in the public sector, where they retained real strength. In 2010 unions represented 37.4 percent of public employees, and, for the first time, there were more union members in the public sector (7.9 million) compared to the private (7.4 million). If labor was broken in its key stronghold, the consequences would be far-reaching.[27]

What happened in Wisconsin, however, also illustrated the AFL-CIO's ability to fight back, even when times were desperate. In the spirit of Solidarity Day, unlikely mass protests would become a feature of the Trumka years. In October 2010, for example, a labor rally in Washington, DC, drew more than 100,000 people, far more than the more-publicized Occupy Wall Street rallies the following year. Organized by unions and allied organizations and demanding fair and decent jobs, the "One Nation" rally had striking parallels with Solidarity Day. Many participants came to Washington on buses, there was widespread participation from community organizations, and the focus was on securing more equitable economic policies. "We are going to be marching for jobs for all," explained George Gresham, an SEIU leader from New York City. An experienced African-American activist, Gresham thought up the march with NAACP director Benjamin Jealous, and the AFL-CIO threw its support behind the initiative. In a further parallel—especially with Solidarity Day in 1991—media coverage of the "One Nation" rally was very limited.[28]

In Wisconsin, Walker's attack triggered mass labor protests that attracted widespread media attention. The Wisconsin protests were long lasting, and they featured a compelling confrontation between a conservative governor and public sector workers that resonated in many other states. In February 2011 the Federation was at the heart of a week-long standoff in Madison that attracted thousands of union members. The campaign, claimed Gerald McEntee, "showed our ability to put boots on the ground." Some rallies drew 100,000 participants, helping to reinvigorate unions throughout the state—and nation. Trumka was integrally involved. On February 18, the AFL-CIO president stood in the entrance of the Wisconsin state capitol, an imposing sight. Walker, he explained, was "standing in the doorway of our country's most basic values and cherished aspirations." Collecting nearly 1 million signatures, the Federation helped to force a recall election in Wisconsin, and it also organized rallies in several other state capitals. Trumka was encouraged.

"We've never seen the incredible solidarity that we're seeing right now," he explained during the protests, which attracted union members from a wide geographical area. Helped by extensive media coverage, many Americans had become more supportive of labor. Bearing this out, a *New York Times*-CBS poll indicated that the public opposed efforts to weaken the collective bargaining rights of public employees by nearly a 2-to-1 margin. "It'll be up to us to keep it going and continue defining ourselves in ways the American public will support," concluded Trumka.[29]

Helped by a massive corporate counter-mobilization, Walker survived the recall vote. The election was not held until June 2012, giving Walker's supporters time to hit back. Still, some gains came from the Wisconsin campaign, and Walker's antiunion legislation was modified by subsequent court rulings. Helped by the protests, polls showed that most Wisconsinites—and most Americans—supported collective bargaining rights for government workers. In other states, there were also positive consequences. In Ohio, a labor campaign helped to ensure that, in 2012, voters repealed antiunion legislation that had been initiated by new Republican governor John Kasich.[30]

Overall, however, labor remained under attack in a wide range of states, especially where the Tea Party had helped secure GOP control of the governorship and the legislature. Pushing an agenda to expand privatization of the schools, conservatives launched legal and legislative attacks on the large teaching unions, particularly the AFT and NEA. Although the unions hit back, they were fighting a defensive battle to maintain their wages and benefits, particularly tenure and seniority provisions. Many private sector workers felt that government employees were cosseted and out-of-touch, a jealousy that was skillfully exploited by conservatives to undermine organized labor.[31]

In the wake of the midterm elections, organized labor came under unprecedented attack. As Denise Mitchell admitted, following the elections labor suffered "a very assiduous pummeling." Density continued to decline, there were frequent defeats in organizing drives, and unions were forced to suffer humiliating multiyear wage freezes. The labor movement made headlines as it broke a series of unwanted records. In 2010 unions represented just 6.9 percent of private sector workers—lower than the level in 1929, before the passage of the NLRA.[32] By the end of 2013, the Bureau of Labor Statistics reported that overall union density had slipped to just 11.3 percent, an historic, ninety-seven-year low. "These numbers are very discouraging for labor unions," observed industrial relations scholar Gary N. Chaison.[33] The problems also affected Change to Win, which did not achieve the organizing success it had envisaged. While Andy Stern refused to accept that the split had been a mistake, he admitted that he "ran out of ideas," and that his organization had "drifted backwards, after a burst of energy." In 2010 Stern gave up the SEIU presidency and his position in the Change to Win leadership group, retiring from the labor movement at the age of just 59.[34]

Exploiting labor's problems, its opponents pushed to expand the coverage of antiunion legislation. Crucially, right-to-work laws began to spread beyond the South and West, penetrating the union heartland in the Midwest for the first time. In the aftermath of the 2010 election, Indiana enacted a right-to-work law. Less than two years later, Michigan's Republican-controlled legislature pushed through several bills designed to cripple the state's beleaguered unions. Enacted on December 12, 2012, the most important was a right-to-work measure. Given that Michigan was the birthplace of the UAW, and had always been one of the most unionized states in the nation, the move was highly symbolic. As the *Christian Science Monitor* asked, "if the Republicans can enact laws limiting union power in Michigan, where might they turn next?" In passing its law, Michigan became the twenty-fourth right-to-work state. Many Republicans now pushed for a national Right-to-Work law, a long-held GOP goal that the AFL-CIO continued to resist.[35]

The state-level attacks were ominous, especially as it was public sector unions that had sustained the AFL-CIO when it was under fire. In candid interviews, former and current AFL-CIO leaders admitted the gravity of the situation. "I really do worry," acknowledged Secretary-treasurer Liz Shuler in 2015. "Being the finance person, it's rough out there, because with membership losses, all these state attacks that are happening, in the legislatures . . . it's just like, 'Bam, Bam, Bam!' You get pretty beat down." Former staffer Christine Owens was also concerned, especially as the Federation's political program was under threat. "The attack on public sector unions has really drained them of resources," she admitted, "and so, in reality, the unions probably are not going to have the resources to put into the *political* campaigns, which is part of the objectives of these attacks. . . . Definitely, for the opposition it's an effective strategy."[36]

In the wake of the 2010 elections, organizing became even harder. In a sharp shift from the early days of the Obama presidency, Republicans looked to take on the NLRB. After 2011, when the Board annoyed conservatives by charging that Boeing's plan to open an assembly plant in South Carolina retaliated against its workers in Washington State for going on strike, the Republicans declared war on the labor board. Over the next two years, they blocked Obama's appointments, leaving the NLRB without its full slate of five members. As the *New York Times* observed, the crucial labor agency was left "rudderless." The AFL-CIO saw the move as representative, symptomatic of a breakdown in long-standing beliefs that collective bargaining was beneficial and that workers' right to organize should be protected by the government.[37] Not surprisingly, corporate resistance to organizing also increased. "There's just been this exponential increase of employer opposition," asserted AFL-CIO organizing director Elizabeth Bunn in late 2013. "Huge companies that make millions, and billions, of dollars, opposing unions, and that's made the climate very, very difficult."[38]

Organizing was held back by many other problems. In the South and West, where companies were increasingly locating, resistance to unions came not just from corporations but from local political and economic leaders, who worried that unions were bad for business. In early 2014, the UAW suffered what *USA Today* called a "devastating defeat" in an NLRB election at a Volkswagen plant in Chattanooga, Tennessee, despite the fact that the company had not opposed the union. Instead, decisive opposition came from state Republican politicians and from business groups. The UAW, they argued, had caused the downfall of Detroit, a claim that influenced many workers.[39] The ongoing problems in Detroit—the entire city was forced to file for bankruptcy in July 2013—battered labor's image, undermining organizing efforts. Hurt by the recession, and by corporate attacks on their members, many AFL-CIO affiliates found it impossible to prioritize organizing. In addition, the economy became increasingly dependent on temporary workers and on undocumented immigrants, two groups that were very difficult to organize. "Instead of signing up for a long career as an auto worker or a coal miner," summarized the *Washington Post*, "more people now work on contract for no benefits, rupturing the relationship between labor and management that unions had evolved to exploit."[40]

Even at the AFL-CIO's headquarters, the harsh climate took its toll. To stem financial losses, Trumka was forced to undertake an internal restructure, robbing him of the resources he needed to carry out his reforms. Although some of the deficit was linked to the costs of the 2008 election campaign, there were many other causes, including the rising health care costs of employees. At an Executive Council meeting in September 2007, then Secretary-Treasurer Trumka reported that premium payments for the Federation's health care plan were increasing by around 10 percent a year. In the years that followed, the problem continued.[41] Home to the National Labor College and the AFL-CIO archives, the forty-seven-acre campus in Silver Spring, Maryland, also proved increasingly costly to maintain. In August 2012, the Federation put the entire campus on the market, claiming that it could no longer afford to subsidize the college, which had been running annual deficits of more than $6 million. It was later sold to the Amalgamated Transit Union, which used it to train workers.[42]

The financial problems made it increasingly important to reunify the labor movement. With Sweeney gone, the prospects for healing improved. Trumka placed a strong emphasis on unity, while his activist credentials were widely admired within labor circles. As soon as he took office, Trumka forged a closer relationship with Change to Win, gradually convincing several of its affiliates to return to the AFL-CIO. In 2009, UNITE HERE, which was beset by internal divisions and a dispute with SEIU, decided to come back. In 2010, the Laborers' International Union, looking to promote unity across the labor movement, also agreed to re-affiliate. The move brought in 800,000 much-needed members. "We are very excited that the labor movement is headed toward becoming more unified just as we need it the most," explained Trumka.[43]

The biggest prize of all came in 2013, when the 1.3-million-member UFCW returned to the fold following lengthy negotiations. In explaining the move, UFCW president Joe Hansen cited the need for unity at a difficult time, yet he also praised Trumka's "bold leadership." There were also efforts to get the 3-million-member National Education Association—which was not part of either Federation—to join the AFL-CIO. As Liz Shuler summarized, because the loss of the Change to Win unions had hurt "big time," the re-affiliations were a significant achievement.[44] Apart from the financial benefits, the return of these affiliates boosted morale. Watching events in retirement, John Sweeney felt vindicated. "From the very beginning I said, 'Don't worry too much, they'll be back,'" he declared in 2013.[45]

While Sweeney insisted that the labor movement was healing, some significant divisions remained, particularly within his former union. In the aftermath of the 2008 presidential election, the SEIU consumed itself in lengthy "civil wars," including a territorial fight with a northern Californian local that had broken away. The union also suffered an embezzlement scandal involving Stern's protégés and fought with some of its Change to Win partners.[46] The SEIU remained outside the AFL-CIO, a major source of weakness as it remained the fastest-growing union in the country. Even after Stern stepped down as president, SEIU leaders stubbornly refused to rejoin.[47] Although some of the SEIU's growth came in controversial circumstances—with *Labor Notes* accusing Stern of making "chummy deals" with employers—by 2013 the union claimed more than two million members. New president Mary Kay Henry—a talented leader who beat Stern's heir apparent, Anna Burger— repeatedly asserted that unions could work together without being part of the same federation. In a similar vein, the Teamsters and United Farm Workers also refused Trumka's overtures. As such, Trumka's work to reunite the Federation remained unfinished. "The split obviously continues to be a difficult issue," admitted Craig Becker in 2015, "in terms of the resources of the Federation, in terms of coordination of important parts of the Labor Movement, in terms of duplication of effort . . . so it's not an easy role, as to the AFL-CIO."[48]

Trumka continued to work hard to make the AFL-CIO more innovative and edgy. In the fall of 2011, he mobilized the AFL-CIO behind the "Occupy Wall Street" protests, a movement that expressed the frustration of many Americans with high unemployment, greed on Wall Street, and increasing income inequality. In October, Trumka even made an unexpected stop at Zuccotti Park in Lower Manhattan, the movement's base. "I'm the head of the AFL-CIO," he told protesters. "We're here because we're going to support you guys." Along with the Federation, affiliates provided a variety of help, including legal assistance, food, and office space, to the Occupy movement. "Our members have been trying to have this discussion about Wall Street and the economy for a long time," explained Trumka. "This movement is providing us the vehicle." Illustrating his flexibility, Trumka sat down with Obama administration officials in the same week that he delivered hundreds of fresh bagels to the Occupy protesters. Although its concrete achievements were limited—and it always sought to avoid making specific demands—the Occupy movement was one of the bright spots of the Trumka era. As labor historians Daniel Katz and Richard A. Greenwald wrote in 2012, the inspiring protests suggested that the labor movement could be "saved."[49]

In other areas, Trumka was characteristically bold. He consistently pushed for comprehensive immigration reform, including a path to citizenship for the 11 million undocumented immigrants already in the United States. Emphasizing that this was "the moral thing to do," Trumka also admitted that undocumented immigrants drove down wages. Although efforts to pass these reforms stalled in the Republican-led House, the AFL-CIO continued to press the issue.[50] In 2011 Trumka also oversaw an historic Council statement that condemned the wars in Iraq and Afghanistan as a "costly mistake." This was a "victory for the progressive movement," thought the *Nation*, especially in light of the Federation's history. Trumka also spoke out against mass incarceration, especially of African-American men. Stressing that many potential union members were either locked up in jail or frozen out of the job market because they had committed felonies, Trumka made mass incarceration a labor issue.[51]

To revitalize the Federation, Trumka was willing to take risks. In September 2013 he announced bold plans to let millions of nonunion workers—as well as environmental, immigration, and civil rights groups—join the AFL-CIO. "The crisis for labor has deepened," he explained. "It's at a point where we really must do something differently. We really have to experiment." Although the press emphasized the novelty of Trumka's ideas, they drew on Sweeney and Kirkland's associate membership programs, as well as the deeper bonds forged with progressive groups—particularly the NAACP and the Sierra Club—during the Solidarity Day movement. Still, Trumka pushed the envelope much further. He even set up a dozen committees, including groups for young workers, web experts, historians, pollsters, and Wal-Mart workers, to propose ways to revive labor. Trumka gave outside constituencies a greater voice over labor questions than had been the case in the past, when alliances had often been forged during labor disputes but then withered. As Liz Shuler put it, the aim was to make labor a "transformational" partner rather than a "transactional" one.[52] Self-consciously experimental, Trumka was more open-minded than his predecessors. "We're asking academics, we're asking our friends in other movements, 'What do we need to become?'" he explained. "We'll try a whole bunch of new forms of representation. Some will work, some won't, but we'll be opening up the labor movement."[53]

Trumka oversaw dramatic changes at the AFL-CIO's convention, which had once been formal and staid. In September 2013 reporter Steven Greenhouse thought that the twenty-seventh convention in Los Angeles was reminiscent of a "mass group therapy session," as delegates—including scores of nonunion groups who had been invited—debated a raft of new initiatives designed to revive organized labor. Delegates passed a resolution that redefined the labor movement as comprising "all workers who want to take collective action to improve wages, hours, and working conditions," rather than just union members. In addition, the convention elected Tefere Gebre, a forty-five-year-old former refugee from Ethiopia, as its executive vice president. After settling in California as a teenager, Gebre worked in a variety of insecure jobs—including stints as a valet parker, a liquor store clerk, and a door-to-door knife salesperson—before landing a position with UPS. At UPS, Gebre joined the Teamsters, and from there he worked his way up the local labor movement, transforming the Orange County Labor Federation into a potent force. His election sent a signal that the labor movement was "reorienting itself" and taking notice of the "growing power" of immigrant workers. "People who look like me," he added, "who talk like me, have never aspired to be in places like this in the labor movement, and I think that that's the signal to send ... (to) the child of immigrants who's struggling right now, and to an

African-American little boy, that there is an opportunity, as long as we have this thing called the labor movement, to move up and lead." The Convention also approved the election of Bhairavi Desai, director of the New York Taxi Workers Alliance, to the Executive Council. Desai became the first representative from a nonunion advocacy group, rather than a trade union, to sit on the Council. Initiated by Kirkland, and significantly expanded by Sweeney, reforms to diversify the Council had been taken forward in new ways.[54]

In politics, there were also successes. In 2012 organized labor played an important role in securing President Obama's reelection and maintaining Democratic control of the Senate, despite a determined—and well-funded— Republican campaign. "When you look at how close the election returns were, the president did benefit substantially from organized labor," commented Charles B. Craver, a labor law expert.[55] As in 2008, the AFL-CIO carried out vital work in the battleground states, especially with white working-class voters. In Ohio, widely seen as the most decisive state of all, the AFL-CIO reached two million potential voters in the last four days of the campaign, up from 1.2 million four years earlier. Nationally, 54.5 percent of white working-class men who were union members voted for Obama, compared to just 27.5 percent of their nonunion counterparts. According to one expert, the swing of 27 points among this group was "monumental." While *Citizens United* had allowed corporate groups to increase their spending, it had also helped the AFL-CIO, especially as it made it easier to visit nonunion households. "Tuesday was a very good day for America's unions," summarized Harold Meyerson, "which demonstrated yet again their power at the polls."[56]

During Obama's second term, the economy continued to recover, helping the AFL-CIO. Unemployment, which stood at almost 8 percent in November 2012, had fallen to 6.2 percent by April 2014, and it continued to drop thereafter. Reflecting his background in an industrial union, Trumka pushed hard for a stronger manufacturing sector. "You can't be a world-class country and have a world-class economy unless you produce things," he declared.[57] Partly responding to labor pressure—the AFL-CIO did a good job of putting economic issues at the heart of the 2012 election—President Obama pledged to create one million manufacturing jobs during his second term. Although the rate of job creation suggested that this goal would not be met, the manufacturing sector made a partial comeback in these years, helping the labor movement.[58]

Although there were positive developments for the AFL-CIO, the media continued to concentrate heavily on labor's decline. In 2011, *Washington Post* columnist Robert Samuelson used the widespread attacks on public sector unions to pronounce the "death knell of Big Labor." Many academic studies had a similar focus. "Today the only thing big about 'Big Labor' is its problems," asserted sociologist Jake Rosenfeld in *What Unions No Longer Do* (2014), which probed the drop in density and its negative consequences for American workers.[59] While Kirkland had been annoyed by the focus on decline, Sweeney had faced up to the issue and discussed it openly. Some of Trumka's staff were even more candid about the Federation's problems. In 2013, for example, executive vice president Arlene Holt Baker admitted that the AFL-CIO was "teetering," and desperately had to "grow as a movement" if it was to remain viable.[60]

Keen to take a broader perspective, other AFL-CIO staff emphasized the significant reforms that had taken place under Sweeney and Trumka. "If the metric is density, then things look grim," admitted Ana Avendano, "but if you look at the way that the Federation has changed since 1995, in terms of the role that it plays in civil society, it's made huge advances." Trumka also refused to get discouraged. Preferring to read the density figures another way, he emphasized the considerable power that the AFL-CIO still had. "We punch way beyond our weight," he asserted. "But think about this, even if we only punched our weight, that's 13 percent, what other group in the United States . . . has 13 percent of the population?"[61]

Although Trumka and his staff looked for solutions to the density problem, there was no easy answer. In many ways, the AFL-CIO was the victim of broad forces that were largely beyond its control, and it is worth remembering that union federations around the world shared much of its predicament. In Australia, for instance, union density declined from 50 percent in 1980 to 22.4 percent in 2005, a dramatic drop. In 1997 a detailed ILO report found that unions represented less than 20 percent of the workforce in more than half the world's countries. In the United States, the report blamed changes in the composition of the workforce, rather than union tactics, as one of the main causes of falling membership. In other countries, including the UK, Australia, and New Zealand, changes in employment legislation played a bigger role. Covering ninety-two nations, the report also found that, despite declines in membership, unions retained significant influence, a point that the AFL-CIO's history had repeatedly illustrated.[62] Even by international standards, however, the AFL-CIO operated in a hostile climate. In 2012 the watchdog Freedom House rated the United States as less free for labor than forty-one other nations, largely because of the NLRA's ineffectiveness.[63]

Probing labor's decline and placing it in a broader context, informed American commentators provided some answers. "The good news," wrote Katz and Greenwald in 2012, "is that we have been here before and the rumor of labor's demise has often been exaggerated."[64] Many authors suggested helpful solutions for labor's revival. While there was widespread agreement that labor law reform remained crucial, some argued that to achieve it organized labor had to become more militant and define its core ideology. It was especially important to find new ways of making workers' rights resonate with a national audience, perhaps by stressing that they were a form of civil rights. Organizing had to be more focused on women, as well as African-Americans and new immigrants, all groups that were generally responsive to labor's message. Alliances between labor and community-based immigrants' rights groups—a strategy that had been used successfully in California—were also widely advocated. In general, labor had to connect more with transformative social movements and find innovative ways of making strikes effective again. As activist scholar Michael Yates wrote in 2009, at a time of economic insecurity unions mattered more than ever because they remained the "one institution" in American life that had significantly improved the lives of most citizens. According to two other authors, organized labor was "the only player even remotely competing with corporate America," especially when it came to electoral politics.[65]

Despite all the problems facing the AFL-CIO, after five years of the Trumka presidency it remained one of the biggest union federations in the world. Its history is a story of survival, of providing a national voice for working Americans regardless of whether they belonged to unions or not. Given that affiliation was entirely voluntary, holding the Federation together, especially when it was under fire in the 1980s and early 1990s, was truly a notable achievement. As the decline in union density accelerated, moreover, the Federation had to speak for all working Americans because it knew that it was increasingly unlikely to win legislation just for its members. Like Yates, former staffers stressed the significant role that the Federation performed in providing a voice for all working people, especially in an America increasingly dominated by corporate capitalism. As such, it remained very relevant, and it continued to make important history. "The AFL-CIO is the only organization in this country that's speaking for *workers*," summarized Brad Burton, Trumka's former executive assistant, in 2013. "Who the hell is looking out for workers in this country, other than the AFL-CIO? . . . We don't have as much as we want, need, or should have, but we do have influence."[66] Trumka put it even better. "That's why I love the labor movement," he reflected in

2015, "because it's still the best opportunity, perhaps the only opportunity, to make massive social change on the scale that's needed, to make the country work for everybody in the country, and not just the rich. . . . We speak for the 90 percent that works every day for a living . . . and we're going to make sure that they get a fair shake as well."[67]

Notes

Introduction

1. See, for example, "History Calls; Barack Obama's Landmark Nomination by the Democratic Party Will Have Been Well Earned," *Washington Post*, June 5, 2008, A18; Shailagh Murray, "Two Candidates, Two States and One Big Day: Indiana and North Carolina Shape Up as Big Pieces of the Democratic Puzzle," *Washington Post*, May 6, 2008, A9; Harold Meyerson, "Can He Be a Working-Class Hero?" *Washington Post*, August 27, 2008, A13.

2. "Remarks by Richard L. Trumka, USW Convention," July 1, 2008, 15, 16, transcript supplied by the AFL-CIO (in author's possession); Alec MacGillis, "No Getting around This Guy: AFL-CIO's Richard Trumka Aims to Hold That Line on Health Care," *Washington Post*, September 7, 2009.

3. MacGillis, "No Getting around This Guy," (quotation). Trumka's speech is available online at "AFL-CIO's Richard Trumka on Racism and Obama," https://www.youtube.com/watch?v=7QIGJTHdH50 (accessed February 15, 2015).

4. Michael A. Fletcher, "Labor Seeks Election Rewards; Union Organizing Rights Could Be Early Obama Test," *Washington Post*, November 6, 2008, D1 (quotation); "Pennsylvania AFL-CIO's Massive Mobilization of Union Voters Puts PA in Win Column for Barack Obama," *PR Newswire*, November 5, 2008; Robert H. Zieger, "'Labor Did It' Again," Gainesville (FL) *Sun*, November 9, 2008.

5. Richard Trumka interview; Andres quoted in Rosenfeld, *What Unions No Longer Do*, 178.

6. For important books on the 2008 election that give little or no coverage to labor's contribution, see Balz and Johnson, *Battle for America 2008*, esp. 89, 93; Abramson, Aldrich, and Rohde, *Change and Continuity*; Heilemann and Halperin, *Game Change*, 143; Traister, *Big Girls Don't Cry*, 72; Kenski, Hardy, and Jamieson, *The Obama Victory*.

7. Kennedy quoted in Patterson, *Restless Giant*, xiii. While the literature on the labor movement is much less extensive than that on the civil rights movement, Meany and his era have been covered more than the subsequent period. For important works, see Goulden, *Meany*; Robinson, *George Meany*; Taft, *Organized Labor*; Lichtenstein, *Most Dangerous Man*. In contrast, the only work focused specifically on Kirkland is Puddington's hagiographical *Lane Kirkland*. There are no biographies of Tom Donahue or John Sweeney, and their era is also under-represented in the literature.

8. Patterson, *Restless Giant*; Rogers, *Age of Fracture*; Wilentz, *Age of Reagan*; Chafe, *Unfinished Journey*. Unless otherwise noted, all references to Chafe's *Unfinished Journey* in the notes are to the second edition.

9. Solidarity Day has been particularly overlooked. Although they both give good coverage to social movements, there is no coverage of Solidarity Day, for example, in the popular surveys of recent American history by Patterson, *Restless Giant*, and Chafe, *Unfinished Journey*. The protest is also not mentioned in detailed, encyclopedic textbooks such as Tindall and Shi, *America*; Brinkley, *American History*; Foner, *Give Me Liberty*; and Norton et al., *A People and a Nation*. Solidarity Day is not covered in standard labor history surveys such as Lichtenstein, *State of the Union*; Babson, *The Unfinished Struggle*; and Zieger and Gall, *American Workers, American Unions*. It is also not mentioned in key works on the contemporary labor movement, even when scholars argue that organized labor needs to become more of a social movement—as it did on Solidarity Day—in order to improve its fortunes. See, for example, Fletcher, Jr. and Gapasin, *Solidarity Divided*; Getman, *Restoring the Power of Unions*; Clawson, *The Next Upsurge*. The follow-up Solidarity Day marches have been even more neglected, and extensive newspaper searches—even on the 250,000-participant 1991 effort—yielded very few results. The *New York Times*, for example, had just one story on Solidarity Day II. For limited coverage, see "Big Questions, on Labor's Big Day," *New York Times*, September 6, 1982, 16; "Labor Day, Labor's Challenge," *New York Times*, September 5, 1983, 18; Frank Swoboda, "Pro-Labor Rally Set for Mall," *Washington Post*, August 30, 1991, D1; Frank Swoboda and Sandra Torry, "Labor Sends Politicians a Message Hundreds of Thousands Strong," *Washington Post*, September 1, 1991, A1.

10. When this project began the AFL-CIO Papers were held at the George Meany Memorial Archives in Silver Spring, Maryland, although in October 2013 the vast collection reopened, after a brief closure, at the Hornbake Library, University of Maryland at College Park. Most of the post-1979 material in the AFL-CIO Papers is restricted, and the author secured permission from the AFL-CIO to access it. All citations from the Papers follow the format used at the time of consultation. For examples of works that use the AFL-CIO Papers for the earlier period, see Draper, *Conflict of Interests*; Zieger, *The CIO*; and Cowie, *Stayin' Alive*.

11. Donahue served as secretary-treasurer of the AFL-CIO from 1979 to 1995 and also as president in 1995. He was integrally involved in many of the events described here. The former international and economic affairs director of the AFL-CIO, Anderson led the fight against the North American Free Trade Agreement (NAFTA) in the early 1990s, as well as several other related campaigns. Both allowed me to make extensive copies from their papers. Copies of all documents cited in their paper collections are in the author's possession.

12. Trumka took over from Sweeney in 2009.

13. Most of those interviewed were former AFL-CIO staff and elected leaders, with some key figures interviewed more than once. I also interviewed some figures from outside the AFL-CIO, including several leaders of Change to Win. The bibliography contains further details of those interviewed. Requests to interview leading figures from management organizations, particularly the U.S. Chamber of Commerce, were declined, but I have tried to provide some representation of the management viewpoint through other sources, including congressional collections.

14. Hill quoted in Zieger, *For Jobs and Freedom*, 168. Hill's arguments were put forth in his landmark *Black Labor*, as well as in numerous journal articles, including: "Race, Ethnicity and Organized Labor," 31–82; "The Problem of Race in American Labor History," 189–208; and "Myth-Making as Labor History," 132–200.

15. See especially Gould, *Black Workers*; Goldfield, *The Color of Politics*; Nelson, *Divided We Stand*; Roediger, *Wages of Whiteness*; Roediger, *Working toward Whiteness*.

16. Radosh, *American Labor*, 4, 452; Scipes, *AFL-CIO's Secret War*, xi, xii, xxiv. For another work in this vein, see Sims, *Workers of the World Undermined*.

17. Buhle, *Taking Care of Business,* 206; Wehrle, *Between a River and a Mountain*, 2.

18. See, for example, Waters and Van Goethem, eds., *American Labor's Global Ambassadors*; Richards, *Maida Springer*; Hughes, *In the Interest of Democracy*. Hughes' work focuses on the AFL, one of the predecessor organizations of the AFL-CIO.

19. For examples of works in this genre, see Moody, *An Injury to All* and *US Labor in Trouble and Transition*; and Goldfield, *The Decline of Organized Labor*.

20. Buhle, *Taking Care of Business*, 3, 9, 205, 209, 263; Moody, *An Injury to All*, xx.

21. See, for example, Lane Kirkland, interview by James F. Shea and Don R. Kienzle, November 13, 1996, Labor Diplomacy Oral History Project, transcript in folder 8, box 4, RG95-007, Lane Kirkland Files, AFL-CIO Papers.

22. For histories of the Australian Council of Trade Unions, for example, see Donn, *The Australian Council of Trade Unions*; and Hagan, *The History of the A.C.T.U.* For the British TUC, see Martin, *TUC*. For work on the All-China Federation of Trade Unions, see Lee, *Trade Unions in China, 1949 to the Present*; and Pringle, *Trade Unions in China*. On the Canadian Labour Congress, see Kwavnick, *Organized Labour*. For a comparative study of the TUC and its West German counterpart, see Clark, *Trade Unions*.

23. A. H. Raskin, "CIO Favors Huge Fund for a Post-Merger Drive," *New York Times*, August 1, 1955, 1 (Meany quotation); "AFL-CIO, with 15,000,000, Largest Free World Labor Unit," *New York Times*, December 1, 1955, 27.

24. Seth S. King, "Organized Labor Faces an Uncertain Election Year," *New York Times*, August 11, 1982, A18 (quotation); "Distinguished Speaker Address by Thomas R. Donahue: IRRA Meeting," ca. 1989–1990, "Press Releases and Speeches, '95 (3), folder," Tom Donahue Papers, Washington, DC, personal collection shared with author, hereafter cited as "Donahue Papers." The Donahue papers are unprocessed. Folder details are provided here where they were available, but some material was also filed without folders. Copies of all documents cited here are in the author's possession.

25. Robert Fitch, "The Fat Cats of Labor," Melville (NY) *Newsday*, October 22, 1995, A42; John D. Schulz, "New AFL-CIO Leadership Teams with Carey in Fight over Fired Overnite Organizer," *Journal of Commerce*, November 6, 1995, 31; AFL-CIO, "About Us," available at http://www.aflcio.org/aboutus (accessed August 1, 2011, copy in author's possession). Membership dropped after 2005 partly because an internal split caused several large affiliates to leave the Federation—tragic events that are covered further below.

26. Craig Becker interview; "Meany Lays Down AFL-CIO Policy," *New York Times*, November 5, 1955, 1; closing quotation in George Meany's Address to the 16th Constitutional Convention of the United Steelworkers of America, September 18, 1972, "AFL-CIO Convention (Meany) 11/19/71 (1 of 8)," 10, box 28, Charles W. Colson Files, White House Special Files-Staff Member Office Files, Richard Nixon Presidential Library, Yorba Linda, California (hereafter cited as "Nixon Library").

27. The AFL-CIO's international activities, especially in the Cold War era, have received a lot more attention from writers than its domestic history has. See, for example, Puddington, *Lane Kirkland*, 191–238; Scipes, *AFL-CIO's Secret War*; Wehrle, *Between a River and a Mountain*.

28. "AFL-CIO 21st Constitutional Convention—New York City 1995 Election Results—National and International Unions," folder 3, Donahue Papers.

29. *Constitution of the AFL-CIO and Other Official Documents Relating to the Achievement of Labor Unity* (Washington, DC: American Federation of Labor and Congress of Industrial Organizations, 1956), 3. Highlighting the AFL-CIO's centrality to American life, its constitution was printed in full in the *New York Times*. See "Text of Constitution Agreed on for Merger of AFL and CIO into Federation," *New York Times*, May 3, 1955, 24.

30. Kirkland quoted in Report to the 1993 AFL-CIO Convention from the AFL-CIO Executive Council, 1; John B. Judis, "Strife in the AFL-CIO," *New Republic*, March 21, 2005, clipping in "The Split—2003-4-5," Donahue Papers; "AFL-CIO Leaders Buoyed by Better Image in Poll," Roanoke (VA) *Times*, February 22, 1990, A9; Jon Hiatt interview.

31. Quotation in John J. Driscoll, "How U.S. Labor Is Tackling the 'Fix' It Is In," *New York Times*, December 19, 1983, A18.

32. Jimmy Carter to George Meany, September 4, 1978, "AFL-CIO 6/3/78–12/18/78 [C/F, O/A 564]," box 86, Chief of Staff Files (Landon Butler Files), Jimmy Carter Presidential Library, Atlanta, Georgia (hereafter cited as "Carter Library"). The quotation from Johnson, and the description of the pen display, is based on the author's visit to view this item, which is on display in the AFL-CIO's headquarters in Washington, DC.

33. Jim Kennedy interview; Susan Dunlop interview (2013).

34. Paul A. Gigot, "Terminator II: Why Big Labor Keeps on Coming," *Wall Street Journal*, April 11, 1997, A14; Dawn Kopecki, "Grassroots Lobbies Bygone Era's Cigar Chompers," *Washington Times*, November 24, 1997, D6; "Building and Construction Trades Department, AFL-CIO, Executive Council Report," 38, in "Trade and Industrial Department Reports to the Executive Council, August 1998," box 1, AR2001-0031, AFL-CIO Papers; Lane Windham interview (2013).

35. Steven Greenhouse, "Reshaping Labor to Woo the Young," *New York Times*, September 1, 1985, A1.

36. Ken Ibold, "Last Stand or Comeback? Unions, Experts Disagree," *Palm Beach Post*, September 4, 1989, 16; "Ohio Labor Leaders Say They See End of Lean Membership Times," Akron (OH) *Beacon Journal*, September 5, 1989, B5.

37. Cowie, *Stayin' Alive*, 1–19 (quotations on 11); Stein, *Pivotal Decade*; Lichtenstein, *State of the Union*, 212–45. Broader literature on the 1970s includes older works such as

Carroll, *It Seemed Like Nothing Happened*; Hurup, ed., *The Lost Decade*; Schulman, *The Seventies*; and influential recent accounts such as Ferguson et al., eds., *The Shock of the Global*; Schulman and Zelizer, eds., *Rightward Bound*; and Borstelmann, *The 1970s*. For an excellent overview of the literature on the 1970s, and insights into the strong interest in the decade, see Keys, Davies, and Bannan, "The Post-Traumatic Decade," 1–17 ("hot" quotation on 5).

38. Sharon Cohen, "Can John Sweeney Bring Back Labor?" *Tampa Tribune*, September 15, 1996, 1; "Talking Points for JJS: Transportation Trades Department Executive Board Meeting," March 4, 2007, "3/4/07 TTD Executive Committee Meeting Las Vegas," box 1, AR2009-0024-B05/G/25, AFL-CIO Papers; "President's Report to the AFL-CIO Convention, 2009," 3, available at www.aflcio.org/about us/thisistheaflcio/convention /2009/ (accessed February 21, 2012, copy in author's possession).

39. Barrie Clement, "Union Membership Still Falling," *Times* (London), July 22, 1985; Shane Green, "Trade Union Membership Keeps Falling, Say Figures," *The* (Melbourne) *Age*, November 23, 1993, 3; Alan Mitchell, "The Unions' Hidden Membership Crisis," *Sydney Morning Herald*, August 20, 1987, 12. For a detailed examination of the international nature of union decline, and suggestions about how to tackle it, see the essays in Phelan, ed., *Trade Union Revitalisation*.

40. Mark Anderson interview; George Kourpias interview.

41. "Talking Points for JJS: Transportation Trades Department Executive Board Meeting," March 4, 2007, "3/4/07 TTD Executive Committee Meeting Las Vegas," box 1, AR2009-0024-B05/G/25, AFL-CIO Papers; John Sweeney interview; Bob Welsh interview; Lane Windham interview (2013).

42. Meany quoted in Proceedings of the Thirteenth Constitutional Convention of the AFL-CIO, November 15–20, 1979, 8, 9.

43. Kenneth B. Noble, "Kirkland's Teamster Decision: Pulling a Meany," *New York Times*, December 1, 1987, A22.

44. Sweeney quoted in Proceedings of the 2001 AFL-CIO Convention, December 3–6, 2001, 66.

45. Susan Dunlop interview (2013); Barbara Shailor interview.

46. Richard Womack interview.

Chapter One

1. A. H. Raskin, "AFL and CIO to Unite Today; Discords Arising," *New York Times*, December 5, 1955, 1.

2. Proceedings of the First Constitutional Convention of the AFL-CIO, December 5, 1955, 7 (Reuther quotation), 25 (Meany quotation), 32 (Eisenhower quotation), 107–9, 136–40, 143–45 (Roosevelt quotations on 143).

3. "Dedication: Home of American Labor," June 4, 1956, folder 39, box 1, RG21-001, Legislation Department Files, AFL-CIO Papers.

4. C. P. Trussell, "Union Heads Say Merger Creates Political Strength," *New York Times*, September 6, 1955, 1 (first quotation); "President Doubts Unions Can 'Boss':

Eisenhower Discusses Effect of AFL-CIO Merger on U.S. Politics," *New York Times,* March 3, 1955, 16 (other quotations).

5. "Meany Defends Labor in Politics," *New York Times,* October 9, 1958, 40 ("bunk" quotation); A. H. Raskin, "Merged Labor Unions Face Many Problems: Drive to Organize More Workers to Meet Strong Opposition," *New York Times,* December 4, 1955, E9 ("colossus" quotation).

6. "Message from President Eisenhower to the 1st Annual Convention of the AFL-CIO, New York City," December 5, 1955, box 783, White House Central Files (President's Personal File 47), Dwight D. Eisenhower Presidential Library, Abilene, Kansas (hereafter cited as "Eisenhower Library").

7. Denison, *Growing Up in the Great Depression,* 164; "Remarks by Jimmy Carter to the AFL-CIO General Board Meeting," August 31, 1976, "Remarks-AFL-CIO, 8/31/76" folder, box 67, Jimmy Carter Speech File, Carter Library; Jim Kennedy interview; closing quotation from Robert McGlotten interview.

8. Peter T. Kilborn, "Prospective Labor Leaders Set to Turn to Confrontation," *New York Times,* October 25, 1995, 41; Chafe, *Unfinished Journey,* 448; Philip Shabecoff, "AFL-CIO Acts to Coordinate Union Recruiting," *New York Times,* February 24, 1980, 24.

9. Steven Greenhouse, "Reshaping Labor to Woo the Young," *New York Times,* September 1, 1985, A1; Kathleen Lynn, "For Labor, a Decade of Decline: Factory Jobs Went Overseas," *The Record (New Jersey),* September 4, 1989, C1.

10. Proceedings of the Sixteenth Constitutional Convention of the AFL-CIO, October 28–31, 1985, 163; Lynn, "For Labor, a Decade of Decline," C1; Greenhouse, "Reshaping Labor," A1.

11. "AFL-CIO Paid Membership, 1955–1977," in Proceedings of the Twelfth AFL-CIO Constitutional Convention, December 8–13, 1977, 47–52; William Serrin, "The Mobility of Capital Disperses Unions' Power," *New York Times,* March 21, 1982, E8.

12. "AFL-CIO Paid Membership, 1955–1977," in Proceedings of the Twelfth AFL-CIO Constitutional Convention, December 8–13, 1977, 47–52; Serrin, "The Mobility of Capital," E8.

13. "Discontent Shakes Labor's Solid Front," *Business Week,* February 26, 1972, 63, clipping in folder 11, box 28, Charles W. Colson Files, White House Special Files-Staff Member Office Files, Nixon Library.

14. "Dedication: Home of American Labor," June 4, 1956 (quotations); District of Columbia Permit, May 17, 1956; W. C. Hushing to Robert E. McLaughlin, May 15, 1956—all in folder 39, box 1, RG21-001, Legislation Department Files, AFL-CIO Papers.

15. AFL-CIO Executive Council Minutes, August 12–15, 1957, 17, box 83, AFL-CIO Papers.

16. For a fine overview of the emergence and growth of the CIO, see Zieger, *American Workers, American Unions,* 66–103. For more detail, see Zieger, *The CIO,* esp. 6–41.

17. A. H. Raskin, "Behind the AFL-CIO Merger—Three Basic Reasons," *New York Times,* February 13, 1955, 174 (first quotation); Meany quoted in Proceedings of the Second Constitutional Convention of the AFL-CIO, December 5–12, 1957, 7.

18. First quotation in "Agreement for the Merger of the American Federation of Labor and the Congress of Industrial Organizations," February 9, 1955, 67, in AFL Executive Council Minutes, February 1–10, 1955, box 82, AFL-CIO Papers; Gerry Shea interview; Zieger, *The CIO*, 362.

19. "Agreement for the Merger of the American Federation of Labor and the Congress of Industrial Organizations," February 9, 1955, 68, in AFL Executive Council Minutes, February 1–10, 1955, box 82, AFL-CIO Papers (quotations); Zieger, *The CIO*, 363.

20. *Constitution of the AFL-CIO and Other Official Documents Relating to the Achievement of Labor Unity* (Washington, DC: American Federation of Labor and Congress of Industrial Organizations, 1956), 13.

21. "Agreement for the Merger of the American Federation of Labor and the Congress of Industrial Organizations," February 9, 1955, 69–70 (quotation on 70), in AFL Executive Council Minutes, February 1–10, 1955, box 82, AFL-CIO Papers.

22. Ibid., 71; AFL-CIO Executive Council Minutes, August 27–30, 1956, 15, box 83, AFL-CIO Papers; Robinson, *George Meany*, 163.

23. A. H. Raskin, "Crusader for Clean Unionism," *New York Times*, October 20, 1957, SM18; Kenneth B. Noble, "Kirkland's Teamster Decision: Pulling a Meany," *New York Times*, December 1, 1987, A22.

24. Tom Donahue interview (2013).

25. Susan Dunlop interview (2013) (first quotation); AFL-CIO Executive Council Minutes, February 16–24, 1959, 19–20, 32, box 85, AFL-CIO Papers (other quotation); Alan Kistler, "New Hope for the Farm Workers," *American Federationist*, September 1975, 1; Goulden, *Meany*, 399. For more detail on the long farm workers' campaign, see Ferriss and Sandoval, *The Fight in the Fields*. For background to the campaign, see Daniel, *Bitter Harvest*.

26. Jim Kennedy interview.

27. Zieger and Gall, *American Workers, American Unions*, 208.

28. "A Code of Ethical Practices with Respect to Racketeers, Crooks, Communists and Fascists," in AFL-CIO Executive Council Minutes, January 28–February 6, 1957, 60, box 83, AFL-CIO Papers.

29. Proceedings of the Second Constitutional Convention of the AFL-CIO, December 5–12, 1957, 57; AFL-CIO Executive Council Minutes, September 24–25, 1957, 123, box 83, AFL-CIO Papers ("racketeer" quotation).

30. AFL-CIO Executive Council Minutes, May 20–23, 1957, 37, box 83, AFL-CIO Papers.

31. Proceedings of the Second Constitutional Convention of the AFL-CIO, December 5–12, 1957, 59, 66 ("blackened" quotation); AFL-CIO Executive Council Minutes, October 24–25, 1957, 5, box 83, AFL-CIO Papers.

32. AFL-CIO Executive Council Minutes, December 10, 1957, 3, box 83; AFL-CIO Executive Council Minutes, February 3–11, 1958, 23, box 84; AFL-CIO Executive Council Minutes, May 3–6, 1960, 3, box 86—all in AFL-CIO Papers.

33. AFL-CIO Executive Council Minutes, February 20–28, 1961, 5–6, box 86, AFL-CIO Papers; Proceedings of the Third Constitutional Convention of the AFL-CIO, September 17–23, 1959, 283 ("loss" quotation).

34. "Meany Lays Down AFL-CIO Policy: Promises Strenuous Political Action to Get Legislation United Labor Wants," *New York Times*, November 5, 1955, 1. Illustrating the unwanted attention the Teamsters case brought the AFL-CIO, it was also the subject of several books. See, for example, Sheridan, *Fall and Rise of Jimmy Hoffa*; James and Dinnerstein James, *Hoffa and the Teamsters*; Hutchinson, *Imperfect Union*.

35. Proceedings of the Second Constitutional Convention of the AFL-CIO, December 5–12, 1957, 320 (first quotation); AFL-CIO Executive Council Minutes, May 3–6, 1960, 2, box 86, AFL-CIO Papers (other quotations).

36. A. H. Raskin, "CIO Favors Huge Fund for a Post-Merger Drive," *New York Times*, August 1, 1955, 1; "Union Members Total 18,000,000; Million Added Since 1952—One of Four in Country's Labor Force Belongs," *New York Times*, November 14, 1955, 51.

37. "AFL-CIO Resolution on Women Workers: Adopted by the AFL-CIO Convention," December 1955, folder 1, box 26, RG1-027, President's Files, 1944–1960; and AFL-CIO Executive Council Minutes, May 20–23, 1957, 10, box 83 (Megel data)—both in AFL-CIO Papers; "AFL-CIO Paid Membership, 1955–1977," in Proceedings of the Twelfth AFL-CIO Constitutional Convention, December 8–13, 1977, 47–48.

38. Proceedings of the First Constitutional Convention of the AFL-CIO, December 5, 1955, 145–48; A. H. Raskin, "Merged Labor Unions Face Many Problems: Drive to Organize More Workers to Meet Strong Opposition," *New York Times*, December 4, 1955, E9; Reuther quoted in "Eisenhower's Talk, Excerpts from Meany and Reuther Speeches," *New York Times*, December 6, 1955, 22.

39. "Agreement for the Merger of the American Federation of Labor and the Congress of Industrial Organizations," February 9, 1955, 69, in AFL Executive Council Minutes, February 1–10, 1955, box 82, AFL-CIO Papers; "Union Members Total 18,000,000; Million Added Since 1952," 51; Raskin, "CIO Favors Huge Fund," 1; "AFL-CIO, with 15,000,000, Largest Free World Labor Unit," *New York Times*, December 1, 1955, 27.

40. Raskin, "Merged Labor Unions Face Many Problems," E9 (quotation); Proceedings of the First Constitutional Convention of the AFL-CIO, December 5, 1955, 150; "Agreement for the Merger of the American Federation of Labor and the Congress of Industrial Organizations," February 9, 1955, 69–70, in AFL Executive Council Minutes, February 1–10, 1955, box 82, AFL-CIO Papers.

41. Raskin, "Behind the AFL-CIO Merger," February 13, 1955, 174; AFL-CIO Executive Council Minutes, August 27–30, 1956, 17, box 83, AFL-CIO Papers (Livingston quotation).

42. AFL-CIO Executive Council Minutes, February 16–24, 1959, 20, box 85, AFL-CIO Papers.

43. AFL-CIO Executive Council Minutes, May 3–6, 1960, 3, box 86, AFL-CIO Papers.

44. AFL-CIO Executive Council Minutes, February 16–24, 1959, 21, box 85, AFL-CIO Papers (Livingston quotation); AFL-CIO Executive Council Minutes, May 3–6, 1960, 3, box 86, AFL-CIO Papers (other quotation).

45. AFL-CIO Executive Council Minutes, February 6–14, 1956, 2, 21, 29, box 83, AFL-CIO Papers.

46. AFL-CIO Executive Council Minutes, May 1, 1956, 26, box 83, AFL-CIO Papers.

47. AFL-CIO Executive Council Minutes, May 20–23, 1957, 69, box 83, AFL-CIO Papers.

48. AFL-CIO Executive Council Minutes, February 16–24, 1959, 13, 60, box 85, AFL-CIO Papers.

49. AFL-CIO Executive Council Minutes, January 28–February 6, 1957, 223–25 (quotations on 225), box 83, AFL-CIO Papers.

50. AFL-CIO Executive Council Report, September 17–23, 1959, 210; AFL-CIO Executive Council Report, December 5–12, 1957, 234.

51. AFL-CIO Executive Council Report, September 17–23, 1959, 224.

52. Ibid., 244.

53. Dwight Eisenhower to Raymond F. Leheney, April 27, 1955, box 783, White House Central Files (President's Personal File 47), Eisenhower Library (Eisenhower quotation); "Speakers' Handbook on Labor Law Reform," AFL-CIO Task Force on Labor Law Reform, July 26, 1977, 35, "Labor Law Reform, 1977," file 33–9, box 33, RG98-002, AFL-CIO Papers; Gerry Shea interview.

54. AFL-CIO telegram to Lyndon Johnson, September 2, 1961; and Lyndon B. Johnson to George Meany, September 3, 1964—both in "George Meany 1/1/63–12/31/64," box 337, White House Central Files-Name File (George Meany), Lyndon Baines Johnson Presidential Library, Austin, Texas (hereafter cited as "Johnson Library").

55. AFL-CIO Executive Council Minutes, August 3–5, 1970, 49, 51, box 91, AFL-CIO Papers.

56. Rudy Oswald interview; "History of Federal Minimum Wage Rates under the Fair Labor Standards Act, 1938–2009," available from the U.S. Department of Labor at http://www.dol.gov/whd/minwage/chart.htm (accessed November 15, 2013, copy in author's possession); Robinson, *George Meany*, 244; Quotation in Rudy Oswald to author, July 20, 2013 (correspondence in author's possession).

57. Claude Desautels to Marvin Watson, August 9, 1965; and Invitation of August 5, 1965—both in "George Meany 1/1/65–12/31/65," box 337, White House Central Files-Name File (George Meany), Johnson Library.

58. Lyndon B. Johnson signing invitation, April 10, 1965, "George Meany 1/1/65–12/31/65," box 337, White House Central Files-Name File (George Meany); and Lyndon B. Johnson signing invitation, August 18, 1964, "George Meany 1/1/63–12/31/64," box 337, White House Central Files-Name File (George Meany)—both in Johnson Library; "Labor-endorsed" quotation in David L. Perlman, "House Votes School Aid 'Breakthrough'" *AFL-CIO News*, April 3, 1965, 1.

59. Report of the AFL-CIO Executive Council, December 9–15, 1965, 209–10; AFL-CIO Executive Council Minutes, February 20–23, 1995, A19, box 105, AFL-CIO Papers; Rudy Oswald interview (closing quotation).

60. The union shop required workers to join a union after employment. While the Taft-Hartley Act authorized the union shop under certain conditions, as a way of producing stability, it also contained the provision allowing the states to outlaw the union

shop even with respect to workers engaged in interstate commerce. See "'Right to Work' Laws," *Washington Post and Times-Herald*, December 9, 1954, 16.

61. "'Right-To-Work' Drive: 15 More States to Be Asked to Ban Union Shops," *New York Times*, April 2, 1956, 26; "Will You Let Reuther Get Away With It?" (Committee for Constitutional Government advertisement), *Wall Street Journal*, September 22, 1958, clipping in folder 63, box 13, RG21-001, Legislation Department Files, AFL-CIO Papers (quotations).

62. "Keep the Taft-Hartley Act Intact and Protect Fundamental American Rights" (Citizens Committee to Preserve Taft-Hartley advertisement), *Time*, May 14, 1965, E16, clipping in folder 54, box 85, RG21-001, Legislation Department Files, AFL-CIO Papers; Robinson, *George Meany*, 244–47; Brody, *Workers in Industrial America*, 232–33; closing Meany quotation in David L. Perlman, "14(b) Repeal Vote Stalled As Filibuster Grips Senate," *AFL-CIO News*, October 9, 1965, 1.

63. David L. Perlman, "Indiana Legislature Scraps State 'Right-to-Work' Law," *AFL-CIO News*, January 30, 1965, 1.

64. "Pennsylvania" (AFL-CIO Study), ca. 1965, folder 24, box 83, RG21-001, Legislation Department Files, AFL-CIO Papers.

65. AFL-CIO Executive Council Minutes, November 24, 1964, 2, box 89, AFL-CIO Papers; Cobb, *The South and America*, 157–58, 205–6.

66. Haberland, "Women's Work," 154–55; Lopez, "Low-Wage Lures South of the Border," *American Federationist*, June 1969, 1.

67. Stein, *Running Steel, Running America*, 26–30, 203–5.

68. Douglass Cater to The President, March 17, 1967, "American Federation of Labor, 1/1/67–12/31/67," box 125, White House Central Files-Name File (American Federation of Labor), Johnson Library. Proceedings of the Seventh Constitutional Convention of the AFL-CIO, December 7–12, 1967, 84–94, quotations on 84, 85.

69. Proceedings of the Eighth Constitutional Convention of the AFL-CIO, October 2–7, 1969, 435–67.

70. Proceedings of the Eighth Constitutional Convention of the AFL-CIO, October 2–7, 1969, 435–36; closing Meany quotation in Goulden, *Meany*, 402.

71. For a detailed account of the Meany-Reuther split, see Goulden, *Meany*, esp. 264–69, 371–403 (quotations on 264).

72. W. Willard Wirtz to the President, November 14, 1966, "American Federation of Labor, 1/1/66–12/31/66," box 125, White House Central Files-Name File (American Federation of Labor), Johnson Library (quotation); Joe Califano to the President, June 6, 1967, "American Federation of Labor, 1/1/67–12/31/67," box 125, White House Central Files-Name File (American Federation of Labor), Johnson Library.

73. Walter P. Reuther et al. to George Meany, July 1, 1968; and George Meany to Walter P. Reuther et al., July 10, 1968—both in AFL-CIO Executive Council Minutes, September 16–17, 1968, 38–46 (quotations on 38, 41, and 46), box 91, AFL-CIO Papers.

74. AFL-CIO Executive Council Minutes, September 16–17, 1968, 23, box 91, AFL-CIO Papers.

75. AFL-CIO Executive Council Minutes, May 12–13, 1970, 16, box 91, AFL-CIO Papers.

76. Zieger, *For Jobs and Freedom*, 125–27.

77. AFL-CIO Executive Council Minutes, February 6–14, 1956, 19, box 83; and AFL-CIO Executive Council Minutes, August 12–15, 1963, 6, 26, box 88—both in AFL-CIO Papers; Susan Dunlop interview (2013). For a fine account of Rosa Parks' arrest and its role in precipitating the Montgomery Bus Boycott, see Branch, *Parting the Waters*, 128–35.

78. Andrew J. Biemiller to Henry B. Mann, January 31, 1964 (first quotation), and Andrew J. Biemiller to Fred B. Rooney, January 31, 1964, folder 13, box 9, RG21-001, Legislation Department Files, AFL-CIO Papers (second quotation).

79. Samuel Stratton to Evelyn Dubrow, August 9, 1963, folder 11, box 9, RG21-001, Legislation Department Files, AFL-CIO Papers; Andrew J. Biemiller to Sir and Brother, January 23, 1964, folder 13, box 9, RG21-001, Legislation Department Files, AFL-CIO Papers (quotation).

80. Minchin and Salmond, *After the Dream*, 14–15.

81. Jim Kennedy interview; Rudy Oswald interview; David L. Perlman, "Johnson Signs Rights Act; Meany Pledges Labor's Aid," *AFL-CIO News*, July 4, 1964, 1 (Meany quotations).

82. Zieger and Gall, *American Workers, American Unions*, 221, 223; Proceedings of the Fourth Constitutional Convention of the AFL-CIO, December 7–13, 1961, 463 (first quotation), 464 (second quotation), 467, 492.

83. Proceedings of the Fourth Constitutional Convention of the AFL-CIO, December 7–13, 1961, 475, 476.

84. Proceedings of the Fifth Constitutional Convention of the AFL-CIO, November 14–20, 1963, 206 (Randolph quotation), 240 (Meany quotation).

85. Ibid., 216.

86. Zieger and Gall, *American Workers, American Unions*, 179, 223; Goulden, *Meany*, 313.

87. "AFL-CIO Resolution on Women Workers: Adopted by the AFL-CIO Convention," December 1955, "Civil Rights, 1954–1958" ("substandard" quotation); and "The AFL-CIO and Women Workers," December 1956 (Policy Statement), "Civil Rights, 1954–1958"—both in folder 1, box 26, RG1-027, President's Files, 1944–1960, AFL-CIO Papers.

88. Boris Shiskin to George Meany, May 27, 1957, folder 1, box 26, RG1-027, President's Files, 1944–1960, AFL-CIO Papers.

89. "Coalition of Labor Union Women Fact Sheet—That Stupid Commercial, 'You've Come a Long Way Baby' Is a Lie!" March 19, 1974, "Coalition of Labor Union Women, 1974–1979," box 2.325/P25, Steve Russell and Donna Mobley Papers, held at the Dolph Briscoe Center for American History, University of Texas at Austin (hereafter cited as "Russell and Mobley Papers"); "Statement of Coalition of Labor Union Women," before House Labor Subcommittee on Labor-Management Relations (on

Administration's Labor Law Reform Bill), September 8, 1977, in "Labor Law Reform, 1977," file 33-9, box 33, RG98-002, AFL-CIO Papers.

90. "Come to the Founding Meeting of the New York Coalition of Labor Union Women," (CLUW flyer), June 17, 1974, "Coalition of Labor Union Women, 1974–1979," box 2.325/P25, Russell and Mobley Papers (quotations); "CLUW Statement of Purpose," March 23–24, 1974, "Coalition of Labor Union Women, 1974–1979," box 2.325/P25, Russell and Mobley Papers.

91. See, for example, "Coalition of Labor Union Women Fact Sheet—That Stupid Commercial, 'You've Come a Long Way Baby' Is a Lie!" March 19, 1974, "Coalition of Labor Union Women, 1974–1979," box 2.325/P25, Russell and Mobley Papers.

92. "Coalition of Labor Union Women: Resolution on Participation within Unions—National Coordinating Committee," September 22, 1974, "Coalition for Labor Union Women, 1974–1975," box 2.325/P29, Russell and Mobley Papers; Barbara Easterling interview.

93. "Coalition of Labor Union Women Statement of Purpose," March 1974, in "Coalition of Labor Union Women 1977 Convention," box 2.325/P35, Russell and Mobley Papers; Celia W. Dugger, "Woman to Join AFL-CIO Council," *Washington Post*, August 22, 1980, clipping in "AFL-CIO—1980 (3)," box 87, Chief of Staff (Landon Butler) Files, Carter Library; Goulden, *Meany*, 372 (Meany quotation).

94. Donna Mobley handwritten notes, undated, in "Donna Mobley: Coalition of Labor Union Women, 1979, undated," box 2.235/P36, Russell and Mobley Papers (Mobley quotation); Robert A. Georgine to Sir and Brother, May 16, 1977, "Women in Unions, 1977–1978," box 2.325/P36, Russell and Mobley Papers; Lenore Miller interview (other quotations).

95. Zieger and Gall, *American Workers, American Unions*, 168–78; founding convention resolution quoted in AFL-CIO Executive Council Minutes, February 17–24, 1975, 56, box 94, AFL-CIO Papers; Tom Donahue interview (2015); Proceedings of the Second Constitutional Convention of the AFL-CIO, December 5–12, 1957, 9, 11 (Meany quotation).

96. George Meany, "Meany Looks Into Labor's Future," *New York Times*, December 4, 1955, SM11 (first quotation); AFL-CIO Executive Council Minutes, April 29–May 1, 1958, 33–34, box 84, AFL-CIO Papers (other quotation).

97. AFL-CIO Executive Council Minutes, February 16–24, 1959, 103–4, box 85, AFL-CIO Papers.

98. Lyndon Baines Johnson to George Meany, July 2, 1964, "George Meany 1/1/63–12/31/64," box 337, White House Central Files-Name File (George Meany), Johnson Library (quotations); Puddington, *Lane Kirkland*, 193–94.

99. AFL-CIO Executive Council Minutes, September 16–17, 1968, 5, box 91, AFL-CIO Papers (first quotation); Puddington, *Lane Kirkland*, 194; Robinson, *Meany*, 395 (other quotations); Scipes, *AFL-CIO's Secret War*, 32–34.

100. Gervase N. Love, "'Unstinting' Support Pledged to Nation's Viet Nam Effort," *AFL-CIO News*, December 18, 1965, 1 (first quotation); AFL-CIO Executive Council Minutes, August 22–24, 1966, 110, box 90, AFL-CIO Papers (second and third quota-

tions); George Meany to President Johnson, December 29, 1967, untitled George Meany folder, White House Central Files-Name File (George Meany), box 337, Johnson Library (other quotations).

101. De Groot, *A Noble Cause?* 233–34; Goulden, *Jerry Wurf*, 207; AFL-CIO Executive Council Minutes, February 19–26, 1973, 121, box 93, AFL-CIO Papers (first four quotations); Wehrle, *Between a River and a Mountain*, 2 (other quotations).

102. "George Meany: Philosopher of Labor," *New York Times*, December 7, 1957, 14.

103. Saul Miller, "Meany Calls on Convention to Build on 10-Year Gains," *AFL-CIO News*, December 11, 1965, 1, 16.

104. Memorandum for the President, June 15, 1965, "George Meany 1/1/65–12/31/65," box 337, White House Central Files-Name File (George Meany), Johnson Library.

105. Zieger and Gall, *American Workers, American Unions*, 193; AFL-CIO Executive Council Report, October 2–7, 1969, 1 (quotation).

106. "Rubber Union Wins 28c in 3 New Tire Contracts," *AFL-CIO News*, April 24, 1965, 1; Meany quoted in AFL-CIO Press Release, April 14, 1971, "Meany Quotes," folder 3, box 77, Charles W. Colson Files, White House Special Files-Staff Member Office Files, Nixon Library.

107. AFL-CIO Executive Council Report, November 18–22, 1971, 2 (first quotations); Proceedings of the Eleventh Constitutional Convention of the AFL-CIO, October 2–7, 1975, 20 (other quotations).

108. Report of the AFL-CIO Executive Council, November 18–22, 1971, 220–21.

109. Nixon, *RN*, 672 (first two quotations); Charles W. Colson memorandum for the President, November 30, 1970, folder 5, box 23, Charles W. Colson Files, White House Special Files-Staff Member Office Files, Nixon Library (other quotations); George T. Bell to Charles W. Colson, November 12, 1971, folder 15, box 28, Charles W. Colson Files, White House Special Files-Staff Member Office Files, Nixon Library.

110. "Address by Louis Stulberg, AFL-CIO Fraternal Delegate to the Trades Union Congress, Brighton, England," September 4–8, 1972, folder 4, box 73, Charles W. Colson Files, White House Special Files-Staff Member Office Files, Nixon Library.

111. AFL-CIO Executive Council Minutes, February 17–24, 1975, 155, box 94, AFL-CIO Papers; Richard Nixon, "Statement on Signing the Fair Labor Standards Amendments of 1974," April 8, 1974, online by Gerhard Peters and John T. Woolley, The American Presidency Project, available at http://www.presidency.ucsb.edu/ws/?pid =4169 (accessed February 5, 2015); AFL-CIO Executive Council Minutes, November 16, 1989, B1, box 103, AFL-CIO Papers.

112. AFL-CIO Executive Council Minutes, February 15–22, 1982, 30, box 98, AFL-CIO Papers; Goulden, *Jerry Wurf*, xv–xvi, 3–5, 207; Karen Ackerman interview (quotation).

113. "AFL-CIO Paid Membership, 1955–1977," in Proceedings of the Twelfth AFL-CIO Constitutional Convention, December 8–13, 1977, 50; Bob Welsh interview; David L. Perlman, "Food and Commercial Union Links 1.3 Million Members," *AFL-CIO News*, June 9, 1979, 1, 3.

114. Minchin, "Organizing a Labor Law Violator," 27–28 (first quotation); AFL-CIO Executive Council Minutes, February 19–26, 1979, 100, box 96 (second quotation); and AFL-CIO Executive Council Minutes, February 21–28, 1977, 52, box 95 (other quotations)—both in AFL-CIO Papers.

115. Speech by George Meany, July 6, 1977, "Labor Law Reform Conference, 1977, July 6," box 85, RG1-038, Labor Reform, 1977, AFL-CIO Papers (first two Meany quotations); George Meany to Trade Unionist, ca. 1977, "Labor Law Reform, 1977," file 33-8, box 33, RG98-002, AFL-CIO Papers (other Meany quotations).

116. "Humphrey Heads Coalition for Labor Law 'Justice,'" AFL-CIO Press Release, September 14, 1977; and George Meany to Trade Unionist, ca. 1977—both in "Labor Law Reform, 1977," file 33-8, box 33, RG98-002, AFL-CIO Papers (quotation).

117. "Employer Objections to H.R. 77," n.d., in "Labor Law Reform [O/A 6342] (2)," box 231, Domestic Policy Staff (Stu Eizenstat) Files, Carter Library.

118. Jimmy Carter to George Meany, June 12, 1978, "AFL-CIO 6/3/78–12/18/78 [C/F, O/A 564]," box 86, Chief of Staff (Landon Butler) Files, Carter Library (first quotation); Richard Reiman to Landon Butler, June 9, 1978, "Labor Law, 5/16/78–9/28/79," box 176, Chief of Staff (Steve Selig) Files, Carter Library (other quotation).

119. "News from NAM," National Association of Manufacturers Press Release, September 23, 1977, "Labor Law Reform, 1977," file 33-9, box 33, RG98-002, AFL-CIO Papers; Remarks by George Meany at White House Breakfast, May 9, 1978, "Labor Law (2)," box 112, Chief of Staff (Landon Butler) Files, Carter Library (Meany quotations).

120. AFL-CIO Executive Council Minutes, October 31, 1978, 26, box 96, AFL-CIO Papers; "The Death of Labor Law Reform," undated *New York Times* editorial in "Labor Law Reform, 1975–1979," box 43, RG1-038, Labor Reform, 1977, AFL-CIO Papers.

121. Gerry Shea interview; Report of the AFL-CIO Executive Council, October 18–23, 1973, 415. For a full account of the AFL-CIO's struggle to pass full employment legislation—officially titled the Humphrey-Hawkins Full Employment Act—see Cowie, *Stayin' Alive*, 270–88.

122. Proceedings of the Eleventh Constitutional Convention of the AFL-CIO, October 2–7, 1975, 25.

123. AFL-CIO Executive Council Minutes, February 19–26, 1979, 21, box 96, AFL-CIO Papers (Kistler quotation); Meany quoted in AFL-CIO Executive Council Report, November 15–20, 1979, 1.

124. This conclusion is based on my detailed reading of the Council minutes in the Meany era. See, for example, AFL-CIO Executive Council Minutes, February 20–27, 1978, I–V. Despite a full agenda at this meeting, there is no item on organizing.

125. Proceedings of the Thirteenth Constitutional Convention of the AFL-CIO, November 15–20, 1979, 112–13, 371.

126. Proceedings of the Twelfth Constitutional Convention of the AFL-CIO, December 8–13, 1977, 460.

127. "Speakers' Handbook on Labor Law Reform," AFL-CIO Task Force on Labor Law Reform, July 26, 1977, 25–26, "Labor Law Reform, 1977," file 33-9, box 33, RG98-002, AFL-CIO Papers.

128. Stu Eizenstat to Frank Moore, September 5, 1977, "AFL-CIO [CF, O/A40]," box 136, Domestic Policy Staff (Stu Eizenstat) Files (Eizenstat quotation); and "Remarks by the President to the AFL-CIO General Board," September 4, 1980, "AFL-CIO—1980 (3)," box 87, Chief of Staff (Landon Butler) Files (Carter quotation)—both in Carter Library. For an insight into the tensions that did exist between the Carter administration and the AFL-CIO over inflation policy, see Stein, *Pivotal Decade*, 219–23.

129. Ray Marshall to President Jimmy Carter, April 27, 1977, White House Central Files-Name File (Lane Kirkland), Carter Library; AFL-CIO General Board Minutes, September 4, 1980, 11, box 1, AR2002-0106, AFL-CIO Papers ("largest" quotation); "Remarks of the President at the 13th Constitutional Convention of the AFL-CIO," November 15, 1979, "AFL-CIO Convention, 11/79," box 87, Chief of Staff (Landon Butler) Files, Carter Library (Carter quotation); Bill Johnston to Landon Butler, January 12, 1978, "AFL-CIO [O/A6245]," box 136, Stuart Eizenstat Files, Carter Library.

130. Landon Butler and Bill Johnston to President Jimmy Carter, January 13, 1978 (quotations); and Bill Johnston to Landon Butler, January 12, 1978—both in "AFL-CIO [O/A6245]," box 136, Stuart Eizenstat Files, Carter Library.

131. Noble, "Kirkland's Teamster Decision," A22; Tom Donahue interview (2015).

Chapter Two

1. Joe J. Bradshaw to Jimmy Carter, May 16, 1980, "AFL-CIO (2)," box 87, Chief of Staff (Landon Butler) Files, Carter Library.

2. Jimmy Carter to George Meany, September 25, 1979 (first quotation); and "Remarks of the President at the 13th Constitutional Convention of the AFL-CIO," November 15, 1979 (other quotations)—both in "AFL-CIO Convention, 11/79," box 87, Chief of Staff (Landon Butler) Files, Carter Library.

3. Susan Dunlop interview (2013); Morton Bahr interview.

4. Markley Roberts interview; Proceedings of the Thirteenth Constitutional Convention of the AFL-CIO, November 15–20, 1979, 284–87 (quotations on 284, 285); Testimony of Tom Donahue before the U.S. Senate Labor and Human Resources Committee, "Amending the National Labor Relations Act and the Railway Labor Act to Prevent Discrimination Based on Participation in Labor Disputes," June 6, 1990, folder 36, box 16, series 30, AFL-CIO Legislation Department Files, RG21-002, AFL-CIO Papers.

5. Lyndon B. Johnson to Lane Kirkland, November 19, 1960, folder 28, box 2, RG95-007, Lane Kirkland Files, AFL-CIO Papers (quotations); Joe Califano memorandum for the President, February 24, 1967, "American Federation of Labor, 1/1/67–12/31/67," box 125, White House Central Files-Name File (American Federation of Labor), Johnson Library.

6. Lane Kirkland biography by "Rathbun," n.d., folder 17, box 4, RG95-007, Lane Kirkland Files, AFL-CIO Papers; Tom Donahue interview (2013).

7. Charles W. Colson Memorandum for the President, May 12, 1970, folder 14, box 21, Charles W. Colson Files, White House Special Files-Staff Member Office Files, Nixon Library (first quotation); AFL-CIO Executive Council Minutes, May 14–15, 1969, 11, box 91, AFL-CIO Papers (other quotation).

8. George Meany to Murray H. Finley, December 4, 1974, folder 2, box 1 (Meany quotation); and Lane Kirkland biography by "Rathbun," n.d., folder 17, box 4—both in RG95-007, Lane Kirkland Files, AFL-CIO Papers (Kirkland quotation).

9. Charles W. Colson Memorandum for the President, May 12, 1970, folder 14, box 21, Charles W. Colson Files, White House Special Files-Staff Member Office Files, Nixon Library (quotation); "Allies and Adversaries Alike Offering Remembrances of George Meany; 'His Legacy is the AFL-CIO,'" *New York Times*, January 12, 1980, 25.

10. Susan Dunlop interview (2013); Proceedings of the Thirteenth Constitutional Convention of the AFL-CIO, November 15–20, 1979, 287.

11. Lane Kirkland biography by "Rathbun," n.d., folder 17, box 4, RG95-007, Lane Kirkland Files, AFL-CIO Papers; Kenneth B. Noble, "Kirkland's Teamster Decision: Pulling a Meany," *New York Times*, December 1, 1987, A22 (quotations).

12. AFL-CIO Executive Council Minutes, November 20, 1979, 2, box 96 (Volume 24) (quotation); and AFL-CIO Executive Council Minutes, May 26–27, 1982, box 98— both in AFL-CIO Papers.

13. "Statement by the President," January 11, 1980; and Jimmy Carter to Postmaster General William Bolger, January 15, 1980—both in "AFL-CIO (1)," box 87, Chief of Staff (Landon Butler) Files, Carter Library.

14. J. Y. Smith, "AFL-CIO's Kirkland Dies at 77," *Washington Post*, August 15, 1999, folder 1, Donahue Papers.

15. Kathy Sawyer, "Lane Kirkland: Made in America and Proud to Wear the Union Label," *Washington Post*, July 15, 1984.

16. Joseph Lane Kirkland, "Continuous Discharge Book," folder 16, box 4, RG95-007, Lane Kirkland Files, AFL-CIO Papers; Donahue interview (2015).

17. "Lane Kirkland's Farewell Remarks to the Executive Council," n.d. (ca. 1995), Donahue Papers (quotation); Joseph Lane Kirkland, "Continuous Discharge Book," folder 16, box 4, RG95-007, Lane Kirkland Files, AFL-CIO Papers; Puddington, *Lane Kirkland*, 24–26.

18. "Report of Lane Kirkland, Summer Quarter, 1946," School of Foreign Service, Georgetown University; and James F. Leahigh to Lane Kirkland, May 3, 1948—both in folder 14, box 4, RG95-007, Lane Kirkland Files, AFL-CIO Papers.

19. Lane Kirkland, interview by James F. Shea and Don R. Kienzle, November 13, 1996, 2, Labor Diplomacy Oral History Project, transcript in folder 8, box 4, RG95-007, Lane Kirkland Files, AFL-CIO Papers.

20. Lane Kirkland to Alexander Moore, November 4, 1997, "Correspondence, 1995–98," box 8, RG95-007, Lane Kirkland Files, AFL-CIO Papers.

21. "Former AFL-CIO President Dies," AFL-CIO Press Release, August 14, 1999, folder 1, Donahue Papers; Ray Denison to the author, June 23, 2013 (copy in author's possession).

22. Kirkland, interview, Lane Kirkland Files, AFL-CIO Papers; Susan Dunlop interview (2015); Joseph Lane Kirkland to Sirs, October 7, 1992, folder 16, box 4, RG95-007, Lane Kirkland Files, AFL-CIO Papers.

23. Proceedings of the 1989 AFL-CIO Convention, November 13–16, 1989, 10; Puddington, *Lane Kirkland*, 24. For vivid insights into the poor conditions in the southern textile industry in the early 1930s when Kirkland was growing up, see Hall et al., *Like a Family*, esp. 295–307; Hodges, *New Deal Labor Policy*, 8–21.

24. AFL-CIO Executive Council Minutes, May 23–24, 1990, 17, box 104, AFL-CIO Papers (first quotation); Frank Swoboda, "Unions Hope New Solidarity Will Cancel Decade-Long Slide," *Washington Post*, story reprinted in *Austin-American Statesman*, September 3, 1989, D3 (solidarity quotation); Tom Donahue interview (2015); Susan Dunlop interview (2015).

25. "Former AFL-CIO President Dies," AFL-CIO Press Release, August 14, 1999, folder 1, Donahue Papers.

26. Jim Baker to author, April 30, 2013 (correspondence in author's possession); "Years of Devastation," *AFL-CIO News*, August 31, 1992, 6.

27. David St. John interview; Joe Uehlein interview.

28. Philip Shabecoff, "New Touch is Shown at Labor's Helm," *New York Times*, February 22, 1980, A12.

29. Philip Shabecoff, "A Low-Key Heir to George Meany," *New York Times*, October 14, 1979, F9; Susan Dunlop interview (2013); closing quotation in "AFL-CIO President Lane Kirkland Message to Trade Unionists," June 8, 1995, 6, Donahue Papers.

30. Saul Miller, "New Leaders Steer Course As Labor Tackles the '80s," *AFL-CIO News*, November 24, 1979, 1.

31. Ephraim Evron to Lane Kirkland, November 19, 1979, folder 6, box 3 (Begin's message included in Evron's letter); T. A. Murphy to Lane Kirkland, December 7, 1979, folder 6, box 3; Malcolm S. Forbes Jr. to Lane Kirkland, January 4, 1990, folder 29, box 2; Thomas J. Watson Jr. to Lane Kirkland, October 23, 1979, folder 3, box 3 (Watson quotations)—all in RG95-007, Lane Kirkland Files, AFL-CIO Papers.

32. R. J. Hawke to Lane Kirkland, November 12, 1979, folder 6, box 3, RG95-007, Lane Kirkland Files, AFL-CIO Papers; Jimmy Carter to Lane Kirkland, November 19, 1979, Lane Kirkland Name File, White House Central Files, Carter Library.

33. "The Most Powerful Boss Visiting LO," *Dagens Nyheter*, May 24, 1980, translated clipping in untitled folder, OS box 3, RG95-007, Lane Kirkland Files, AFL-CIO Papers.

34. AFL-CIO Executive Council Minutes, February 18–25, 1980, 30–31, box 97, AFL-CIO Papers; Report of the AFL-CIO Executive Council, October 28–31, 1985, 7.

35. See, for example, Alexander E. Barkan, "The Union Member: Profile and Attitudes," *American Federationist*, August 1967, 1–6.

36. Denise Mitchell interview; Tom Donahue interview (2015).

37. Tom Donahue interview (2013); AFL-CIO Executive Council Minutes, February 6–14, 1956, 1, box 83, AFL-CIO Papers.

38. AFL-CIO Executive Council Minutes, November 19, 1979, 2 (Kirkland quotation); and AFL-CIO Executive Council Minutes, November 20, 1979, 3, both in box 96 (Volume 24), AFL-CIO Papers.

39. AFL-CIO Executive Council Minutes, February 18–25, 1980, 13, box 97, AFL-CIO Papers.

40. Joyce Miller, "Allies in the Future," *American Federationist*, December 1979, 24.

41. AFL-CIO Executive Council Minutes, May 4–5, 1993, 2, box 106, AFL-CIO Papers; Celia W. Dugger, "Woman to Join AFL-CIO Council," *Washington Post*, August 22, 1980, clipping in "AFL-CIO—1980 (3)," box 87, Chief of Staff (Landon Butler) Files, Carter Library.

42. AFL-CIO Executive Council Minutes, February 18–25, 1980, 56 (quotation); and AFL-CIO Executive Council Minutes, May 6–7, 1980, 31–32—both in box 97, AFL-CIO Papers.

43. "Statement by Kirkland," October 19, 1980, "J. P. Stevens 1980–," box 104, ACTWU-Cornell Papers; 1981 ACTWU Convention Proceedings, 33.

44. AFL-CIO General Board Minutes, September 4, 1980, 8, 9, 15, 16, box 1, AR2002-0106 (quotations); AFL-CIO Executive Council Minutes, November 16, 1989, B1, box 103, both AFL-CIO Papers.

45. AFL-CIO General Board Minutes, September 4, 1980, 21, 23–24, box 1, AR2002-0106, AFL-CIO Papers.

46. Howell Raines, "Labor and Reagan Remain Far Apart," *New York Times*, September 6, 1981, 21; Chafe, *Unfinished Journey*, 455 (quotation).

47. "Labor's Day, Labor's Challenge," *New York Times*, September 5, 1983, 18 (first quotation); Philip Shabecoff, "Labor Worries over Decline in Its Influence," *New York Times*, June 4, 1981, E3 (next two quotations); Philip Shabecoff, "AFL-CIO to Seek Bigger Voice on Political Issues and Candidates," *New York Times*, February 19, 1981, A28 (closing quotation).

48. Rex Hardesty, "The Republican Comeback," *American Federationist*, November 1980, cover page (quotation); Rex Hardesty, "Election '80: A Pivotal Decision for America," *American Federationist*, October 1980, cover page; Seth S. King, "Organized Labor Faces an Uncertain Election Year," *New York Times*, August 11, 1982, A18.

49. Lane Kirkland, "Labor and Politics after 1980," *American Federationist*, January 1981, 18–20 (quotations on 18 and 19).

50. Philip Shabecoff, "Voter Shifts and Conservatives' Gains Worry Labor," *New York Times*, November 9, 1980, A30.

51. Jim Kennedy interview.

52. "Statement of Secretary of Labor Ray Marshall at U.S. Department of Labor Press Briefing," August 11, 1978, "AFL-CIO 6/14/78–8/28/78 [CF, O/A 621]," box 86, Chief of Staff (Landon Butler) Files, Carter Library.

53. "Statement by the President," October 24, 1978, "10/24/78—Signing-Airline Deregulation Act of 1978 (S. 2493)," box 34, Speechwriting File; and "Statement by the

President," July 1, 1980, "Trucking Deregulation—Statements, Jimmy Carter," box 93, Domestic Policy Staff (Richard Neustadt) Files—both in Carter Library; closing quotation in "Anti-Inflation Program," AFL-CIO Executive Council Statement, October 31, 1978, folder 7, box 27, series 1, subseries F, Professional Air Traffic Controllers Organization Records, Georgia State University, Atlanta (hereafter cited as "PATCO Papers"); accessed online on February 1, 2014, at http://digitalcollections.library.gsu.edu/cdm/ref/collection/PATCO/id/47413.

54. Minutes of the 1980 AFL-CIO General Board Meeting, September 4, 1980, 22, 32, 54–55, 64, 73, box 1, AR2002-0106, AFL-CIO Papers.

55. Landon Butler to Hamilton Jordan, May 1, 1979, "Labor-Political" folder, box 79, Chief of Staff (Hamilton Jordan) files, Carter Library. There is a massive amount of literature on the broader rise of the Republican Party and the New Right in this era, especially in the South. See, for example, Carter, *From George Wallace to Newt Gingrich*. For a helpful national overview, see Patterson, *Restless Giant*, 130–51.

56. Landon Butler to Hamilton Jordan, May 1, 1979, "Labor-Political," box 79, Chief of Staff (Hamilton Jordan) Files, Carter Library.

57. King, "Organized Labor," A18.

58. Hardesty, "The Republican Comeback," 1.

59. "AFL-CIO Weighing New Campaign," *New York Times*, December 7, 1980, A43.

60. AFL-CIO Executive Council Minutes, February 16–23, 1981, 23, box 97, AFL-CIO Papers.

61. Susan Dunlop interview (2013).

62. Jon Hiatt interview.

63. Denison, *Growing Up*, 165.

64. John H. Fanning to Lane Kirkland, November 20, 1979, folder 6, box 3, RG95-007, Lane Kirkland Files, AFL-CIO Papers.

65. Jimmy Carter to Lane Kirkland, March 4, 1977, White House Central Files-Name File (Lane Kirkland), Carter Library.

66. Landon Butler to Lane Kirkland, April 18, 1977, and Signed Photograph of Carter and Kirkland, October 1977; Gretchen Poston to Mrs. Carter, June 5, 1979; Hamilton Jordan to Lane Kirkland, August 13, 1979; Jimmy Carter Signed Photograph, July 23, 1980—all in White House Central Files-Name File (Lane Kirkland), Carter Library.

67. Jimmy Carter to Lane Kirkland, April 28, 1978, White House Central Files-Name File (Lane Kirkland), Carter Library.

68. Jimmy Carter to Lane Kirkland, November 19, 1979; and Landon Butler to the President and Mrs. Carter, July 23, 1980 (quotation)—both in White House Central Files-Name File (Lane Kirkland), Carter Library.

69. "Reception for Secretary of Labor Ray Marshall," January 13, 1981 (quotation); and "Exchange of Toasts between Lane Kirkland and Jimmy Carter," January 13, 1981—both in folder 1, box 1, RG95-007, Lane Kirkland Files, AFL-CIO Papers.

70. Shabecoff, "Labor Worries over Decline," E3.

71. Philip Shabecoff, "Economic Plan Rejected by Labor Chiefs as Unfair," *New York Times*, February 20, 1981, A10.

72. William Serrin, "Where Are the Pickets of Yesteryear?" *New York Times*, May 31, 1981, F1.

73. Arnold Beichman, "Lane Kirkland's Crisis of Leadership," *National Review*, April 3, 1981, 348, 352, clipping in untitled folder, OS box 4, RG95-007, Lane Kirkland Files, AFL-CIO Papers.

74. AFL-CIO Executive Council Minutes, February 16–23, 1981, 4 (Denison quotation), 23 (Kirkland quotations), box 97, AFL-CIO Papers; Patterson, *Restless Giant*, 156 (Reagan quotation).

75. "Republicans Fall Short in Bid for House Gains," *AFL-CIO News*, November 10, 1984, 1.

76. Patterson, *Restless Giant*, 156–57; Warren Brown, "AFL-CIO Rally: To Belabor Reagan's Points," *Washington Post*, August 2, 1981, H1 ("juggernaut" quotation).

77. "AFL-CIO Weighing New Campaign," *New York Times*, December 7, 1980, A43.

78. Iver Peterson, "After 13 Years, Auto Union Joins AFL-CIO Again," *New York Times*, July 2, 1981, A14 (Stillman quotation); "Auto Union to Rejoin AFL-CIO in July," *New York Times*, June 18, 1981, A22.

79. McCartin, *Collision Course*, 290–93, 300–305; Patterson, *Restless Giant*, 157–58.

80. Janet Rice to Annelise Anderson, March 3, 1981, "PATCO Strike (2 of 2)," series 4, box 10, OA8982, Craig Fuller Files, Ronald Reagan Presidential Library, Simi Valley, California (hereafter cited as "Reagan Library"); McCartin, *Collision Course*, 11.

81. Reagan, *An American Life*, 283.

82. Jim Kennedy interview ("destroyed" quotation); A. H. Raskin, "The Air Strike is Ominous for Labor," *New York Times*, August 16, 1981, A1; Morton Bahr interview; Reagan, *An American Life*, 283; McCartin, *Collision Course*, 291, 307–10.

83. Robert E. Poli and Robert E. Meyer to Brothers and Sisters, October 8, 1981, folder 4, box 32, series 1, subseries F, PATCO Papers (accessed online on February 1, 2014, at http://digitalcollections.library.gsu.edu/cdm/ref/collection/PATCO/id/51154).

84. Young quoted in McCartin, *Collision Course*, 293–94; other quotations in AFL-CIO Executive Council Minutes, August 3–5, 1981, 57, box 97, AFL-CIO Papers.

85. AFL-CIO Executive Council Minutes, August 3–5, 1981, 57, box 97, AFL-CIO Papers; Poli quoted in Robert E. Poli to Lane Kirkland, August 5, 1981, folder 2, box 26, series 1, subseries F, PATCO Papers (accessed online on February 1, 2014, at http://digitalcollections.library.gsu.edu/cdm/ref/collection/PATCO/id/45627).

86. AFL-CIO Executive Council Minutes, September 18, 1981, 2, box 97, AFL-CIO Papers; Robert E. Poli and Robert E. Meyer to Brothers and Sisters, October 8, 1981, folder 4, box 32, series 1, subseries F, PATCO Papers (accessed online on February 1, 2014, at http://digitalcollections.library.gsu.edu/cdm/ref/collection/PATCO/id/51154); AFL-CIO Executive Council Minutes, February 15–22, 1982, 76, box 98, AFL-CIO Papers.

87. First quotation in PATCO Presidential Update (PATCO Newsletter), September 25, 1981, folder 7, box 26, series 5, PATCO Papers (accessed online on February 2, 2014, at http://digitalcollections.library.gsu.edu/cdm/ref/collection/PATCO/id

/23930); Resolution of Greater Boston Labor Council, AFL-CIO, August 21, 1981, folder 5, box 12, series 5, PATCO Papers (accessed online on February 2, 2014, at http://digitalcollections.library.gsu.edu/cdm/ref/collection/PATCO/id/8196); Robert Williams et al. to Robert E. Poli, September 14, 1981, folder 1 (Bloomington quotation); and Frank D. Martino to Robert Poli, August 27, 1981—both in folder 1, box 13, series 5, PATCO Papers (accessed online on February 2, 2014, at http://digitalcollections .library.gsu.edu/cdm/ref/collection/PATCO/id/8724); closing quotation in Susan Dunlop interview (2013).

88. "AFT President Shanker Criticizes Reagan's Handling of PATCO Strike," AFT News Release, August 11, 1981 ("union busting" quotation); and Bob Bonitati to Elizabeth Dole, April 23, 1981—both in "American Federation of Teachers," box 10, series 1, OA6847, Robert Bonitati Files, Reagan Library.

89. Minutes of the 1980 AFL-CIO General Board Meeting, September 4, 1980, 47, box 1, AR2002-0106, AFL-CIO Papers. For a useful overview of the rise of Solidarnosc and its significance, see Cirautas, *Polish Solidarity Movement*.

90. Anne Higgins Form Reply, February 22, 1982, "PATCO 1 of 4," box 8, OA6846, Robert Bonitati Files, Reagan Library; McCartin, *Collision Course*, 331–32; Gary W. Eads to Brothers and Sisters, March 19, 1982, folder 11, box 20, series 1, subseries E (Gary Eads Files), PATCO Papers (accessed online on February 1, 2014, at http://digitalcollections.library.gsu.edu/cdm/ref/collection/PATCO/id/42970).

91. Damon Stetson, "Labor Chiefs Seek Organizing and Political Funds," *New York Times*, November 15, 1981, 40.

92. "Talking Points," undated memo, in "AFL-CIO July 1981–January 1983 (5)," box 1, series 1, OA6841, Robert Bonitati Files, Reagan Library.

93. Ronald Reagan to Robert E. Poli, October 20, 1980, "PATCO Strike (1 of 2)," box 10, series 4, OA8982, Craig Fuller Files, Reagan Library.

94. Proceedings of the Fourteenth Constitutional Convention of the AFL-CIO, November 16–19, 1981, 75 (McBride quotation); Bill Keller, "Labor Chiefs United by Fear of 2nd Reagan Term," *New York Times*, August 19, 1984, 32.

95. Bahr quoted in Philip Dine, "Closing Ranks . . . Labor Unions Trying to Reunify in Face of Mounting Woes," *St. Louis Post-Dispatch*, March 6, 1988, 1B; Proceedings of the 1989 AFL-CIO Convention, November 13–16, 1989, 323 (Sweeney quotation); Albert R. Karr, "Senate Panel Votes Bar on Replacing Striking Workers," *Wall Street Journal*, June 20, 1991, A5.

96. Ray Denison to author, June 23, 2013 (copy in author's possession); Joe Uehlein interview; closing quotation in Laurie McGinley, "PATCO's Ghost Haunts Air Controller Activists," *Wall Street Journal*, May 15, 1987, 1.

97. Greenspan quoted in Cowie, *Stayin' Alive*, 445.

98. A. H. Raskin, "Big Labor Tries to End Its Nightmare," *New York Times*, May 4, 1986, A1 (quotations); Peter T. Kilborn, "Dole Winning Applause for Labor Dept. Actions," *New York Times*, January 4, 1990, A16; McCartin, *Collision Course*, 10. For recent work that stresses the importance of the 1970s in turning labor's fortunes, see Cowie, *Stayin' Alive*; Stein, *Pivotal Decade*.

99. AFL-CIO Executive Council Minutes, February 20–24, 1984, D94, box 99, AFL-CIO Papers. These are twelve-month average figures.

100. Cowie, *Stayin' Alive*, 363; Patterson, *Restless Giant*, 158.

101. Larry Gold interview; William Serrin, "Lane Kirkland, Who Led Labor in Difficult Times, Is Dead at 77," *New York Times*, August 15, 1999 (quotation); Norman Kempster, "Former AFL-CIO President Lane Kirkland Dies," *Los Angeles Times*, August 15, 1999, A8, reprint in folder 1, Donahue Papers.

102. See, for example, the images that accompany the following stories: James M. Shevis, "10.1% Joblessness Tied to Reagan: Double-Digit Rate Highest since 1940," *AFL-CIO News*, October 16, 1982, 1; "Leaflet Day Opens Drive for Heavy Voter Turnout: Labor Takes Message to Plant Gates," *AFL-CIO News*, October 23, 1982, 1.

103. A. H. Raskin, "Labor's Grand Illusions," *New York Times*, February 10, 1985, 305; Tom Donahue interview (2013).

104. Markley Roberts interview; Denise Mitchell interview; Larry Gold interview; Susan Bianchi interview.

105. Susan Bianchi interview; Markley Roberts interview; Doug Dority interview; Serrin, "Lane Kirkland, Who Led Labor"; Tom Donahue interview (2013). For Kirkland's clipping files, see especially boxes 054, 057, 0511, and 0512, RG95-007, Lane Kirkland Files, AFL-CIO Papers.

106. Sawyer, "Lane Kirkland: Made in America."

Chapter Three

1. Bob Bonitati to Elizabeth H. Dole, September 9, 1981, "Solidarity Day 09/19/1981," box 6, series 1, Joseph W. Canzeri Files, Reagan Library; Eric Pianin and Warren Brown, "Crowd Proclaims Labor's Solidarity," *Washington Post*, September 20, 1981, A1; Dray, *There Is Power*, 638.

2. "Solidarity Day Sends Powerful Message from Workers," AFL-CIO Press Release, September 24, 1981, file 5-27, box 5, RG98-002, Vertical Files, 1881–1999, AFL-CIO Papers. For examples of press reports that use the 400,000 figure, see Noreen Wilhelm, "Labor Makes It Day of Protest," Dayton (OH) *Journal Herald*, September 6, 1983, and Catherine Woodard, "Unions Working Today—to Beat Reagan," *Fort Worth Star-Telegram*, September 5, 1983, clippings in "Solidarity Day 1981," box 6, RG95-009, Alan Kistler Files, AFL-CIO Papers.

3. Goulden, *Jerry Wurf*, xiii.

4. Dubofsky and Rhea Dulles, *Labor in America*, 389 (first quotation); McCartin, *Collision Course*, 318; closing quotation in "Solidarity Day: A Worker Record" (AFL-CIO Flyer), "AFL-CIO Solidarity Day, 1982–1983," file 5-27, box 5, series 3, Vertical Files, 1881–1999, AFL-CIO Papers.

5. Richard L. Strout, "'Solidarity Day' in Washington Gives Reagan Foes a Lift; Protesters Call Economic Policies Their No. 1 Concern," *Christian Science Monitor*, September 21, 1981, 3 (first two quotations); Pianin and Brown, "Crowd Proclaims," A1; "Solidarity Today; What Tomorrow?" *New York Times*, September 19, 1981, 22.

6. Puddington, *Lane Kirkland*, 129 (first and third quotations), 130 (second quotation).

7. Wilentz, *Age of Reagan*, 1–4 (first quotation on 1); second and third quotations in "Solidarity Day: A Worker Record" (AFL-CIO Flyer); and other quotation in "Solidarity Day Memento Tied to Social Security Fight" (AFL-CIO Press Release), January 7, 1982—both in "AFL-CIO Solidarity Day, 1982–1983," file 5-27, box 5, series 3, Vertical Files, 1881–1999, AFL-CIO Papers.

8. First quotation in "Solidarity Day Memento Tied to Social Security Fight," (AFL-CIO Press Release), January 7, 1982, "AFL-CIO Solidarity Day, 1982–1983," file 5-27, box 5, series 3, Vertical Files, 1881–1999, AFL-CIO Papers; second and third quotations in AFL-CIO Executive Council Report, October 23–26, 1995, 176, in "Exec. Council Reports, Lane Kirkland Years, '95," Donahue Papers; closing quotations in Gerald McEntee interview.

9. For the way that Reagan's aides collected materials on Solidarity Day and expressed concerns about it, see the large collection of rally material in "Solidarity Day (09/19/1981)," folders 1-5, box 24, Morton Blackwell Files, Reagan Library. The administration's specific concerns about the march are discussed further below.

10. Tom Donahue interview (2013); Richard Womack interview.

11. AFL-CIO Executive Council Report, October 23–26, 1995, 176–77, in "Exec. Council Reports, Lane Kirkland Years, '95," Donahue Papers (quotation on 176); John Sweeney interview; Joe Uehlein interview.

12. Chafe, *Unfinished Journey*, 473; Dray, *There is Power*, 637; Rudy Oswald, "The Economic Outlook: A Report to the Executive Council, AFL-CIO," AFL-CIO Executive Council Minutes, May 7–8, 1981, 20–28; and closing quotation in AFL-CIO Executive Council Minutes, February 16–23, 1981, 74—both in box 97, AFL-CIO Papers.

13. Howell Raines, "Labor and Reagan Remain Far Apart," *New York Times*, September 6, 1981, 21; Harry Bernstein, "AFL-CIO Planning Huge Protest in Capital Against Budget Cuts," *Los Angeles Times*, July 15, 1981, B13; Ed Townsend, "Union Leadership Ponders Ways to Build On 'Solidarity Day' Success," *Christian Science Monitor*, September 25, 1981, 5.

14. Reagan quoted in Richard L. Strout, "Worried Unions Aim for Biggest Mass Rally Ever in Capitol," *Christian Science Monitor*, September 15, 1981, 3; other quotations in Lane Kirkland, "Solidarity for a Fair and Humane America," *American Federationist*, August 1981, 3.

15. "AFL-CIO Issues Call for 'Solidarity Day' Demonstration to Counter Reagan Claims of Mandate," AFL-CIO Press Release, June 19, 1981, "Solidarity Day (3)," OA6847, Robert Bonitati Files, Reagan Library (first quotation); Donahue quoted in "Solidarity Day Offers Chance to Stand Up Against 'Mandate'" *AFL-CIO News*, July 1981, clipping in "Solidarity Day (09/19/1981), 1 of 5," box 24, Morton Blackwell Files, Reagan Library.

16. Perkins quoted in transcript of "Labor News Conference," September 29, 1981, file 5-27, box 5, RG98-002, Vertical Files, 1881–1999; Kirkland regional conference quotation in Lane Kirkland to Trade Unionist, December 7, 1982, folder 2, box 11, series

6, Alan Kistler Files; AFL-CIO Executive Council Minutes, May 7–8, 1981, 4, box 97 (all other quotations)—all in AFL-CIO Papers.

17. AFL-CIO Executive Council Minutes, August 3–5, 1981, 14, box 97, AFL-CIO Papers; Susan Dunlop interview (2013).

18. McCartin, *Collision Course*, 290–93, 300–5; Charles Stott interview.

19. Speech by Peter Bommarito, August 6, 1981, in "Solidarity Day (3)," OA6847, Robert Bonitati Files, Reagan Library; "General Board Members Speak Out on Solidarity Day," *American Federationist*, August 1981, 7 (Fraser quotation), 8.

20. "A Powerful Expression of Protest," *American Federationist*, August 1981, 1 (first two quotations); Tom Donahue interview (2013) (Donahue quotations).

21. "Every level" quotation in "Statement by the AFL-CIO Executive Council on Poland," February 17, 1981, 60, box 97, AFL-CIO Papers; Kirkland quoted in Dubofsky and McCartin, *American Labor*, 301; Puddington, *Lane Kirkland*, 128; "rebirth" quotation in "Solidarity Day: A Worker Record" (AFL-CIO Flyer), "AFL-CIO Solidarity Day, 1982–1983," file 5-27, box 5, series 3, Vertical Files, 1881–1999, AFL-CIO Papers.

22. Dubofsky and McCartin, *American Labor*, 300; "AFL-CIO Issues Call For 'Solidarity Day' Demonstration to Counter Reagan Claims of Mandate," AFL-CIO Press Release, June 19, 1981, "Solidarity Day (3)," OA6847, Robert Bonitati Files, Reagan Library; Bernstein, "AFL-CIO Planning Huge Protest" (first two quotations), B13. For Meany's unwillingness to endorse the March on Washington, see AFL-CIO Executive Council Minutes, August 12–15, 1963, 6, 26, box 88, AFL-CIO Papers.

23. Susan Dunlop interview (2013); Charles Stott interview; Tom Donahue interview (2015).

24. Puddington, *Lane Kirkland*, 39–42, 55–57; Kirkland, "Solidarity for a Fair," 3 (first quotation), 4 (second quotation); closing quotation in "Together We Shall Be Heard: Solidarity Day," AFL-CIO Flyer, September 19, 1981, in "Solidarity Day (3)," OA6847, Robert Bonitati Files, Reagan Library.

25. "AFL-CIO Mass Rally in Washington, September 19," unidentified labor press clipping in "Solidarity Day (09/19/1981), 1 of 5" (NAACP quotations), box 24, Morton Blackwell Files, Reagan Library; "Seniors Rally for Social Security," *AFL-CIO News*, July 25, 1981; "A Call to Join Solidarity Now," undated Peace Movement Flyer in "Solidarity Day (09/19/1981), 5 of 5" (Peace Movement quotations), box 24, Morton Blackwell Files, Reagan Library.

26. AFL-CIO "Fact Sheet on Solidarity Day," July 30, 1981, "Solidarity Day 09/19/1981," box 6, series 1, Joseph W. Canzeri Files, Reagan Library; Philadelphia City Council Resolution No. 553, August 6, 1981, "Petitions-Resolutions from Local Government Officials," White House Office of Records Management (hereafter referred to as "WHORM") Open Files, PR013-02-038746, Reagan Library.

27. Bob Bonitati to Elizabeth H. Dole, September 9, 1981, "Solidarity Day 09/19/1981," box 6, series 1, Joseph W. Canzeri Files; first quotation in "National Non-AFL-CIO Organizations that Have Endorsed Solidarity Day," August 1981, "Solidarity Day (09/19/1981), 1 of 5," box 24, Morton Blackwell Files; second and third quotations in Elizabeth H. Dole to Edwin Meese III et al., September 11, 1981, "Solidarity Day (2),"

F009, Elizabeth Dole Files—all in Reagan Library; Brock quotation in Warren Brown, "AFL-CIO Rally: To Belabor Reagan's Points," *Washington Post*, August 2, 1981, H1.

28. Susan Bianchi interview; AFL-CIO "Fact Sheet on Solidarity Day," July 30, 1981; and "Solidarity Day—Advisory Board Members," n.d.—both in "Solidarity Day 09/19/1981," box 6, series 1, Joseph W. Canzeri Files; Thelma Duggin to Elizabeth Dole, August 17, 1981, "Solidarity Day (2)," F009, Elizabeth Dole Files—all in Reagan Library.

29. Kathy Sawyer, "Big Labor Going High-Tech in Battle for Votes of Working People," *Washington Post*, September 9, 1982, A8; Joann L. Lublin and Robert S. Greenberger, "Labor Gambles Its Political Clout on Saturday's Anti-Reagan Rally," *Wall Street Journal*, September 15, 1981 ("double plan" quotation), and "AFL-CIO Solidarity Day," *AFGE Challenger*, September 19, 1981—both clippings in "Solidarity Day (09/19/1981), 3 of 5," box 24, Morton Blackwell Files, Reagan Library; Rudy Oswald interview.

30. "Solidarity Day Transportation Guide," September 19, 1981, in "Solidarity Day (3)," OA6847, Robert Bonitati Files, Reagan Library (first three quotations); Strout, "Worried Unions," 3; "over 5,000" quotation in AFL-CIO Executive Council Minutes, September 18, 1981, 2, box 97, AFL-CIO Papers; Hughes quoted in John Burgess, "Union Makes Sept. 19 Day to Ride Subways," *Washington Post*, September 9, 1981, B6; closing quotations in Proceedings of the Fourteenth Constitutional Convention of the AFL-CIO, November 16–19, 1981, 15.

31. AFL-CIO "Fact Sheet on Solidarity Day," July 30, 1981, "Solidarity Day 09/19/1981," box 6, series 1, Joseph W. Canzeri Files, Reagan Library; "Traffic Restrictions in Effect for Demonstration," *Washington Post*, September 19, 1981, B8; Pianin and Brown, "Crowd Proclaims," A1.

32. "AFL-CIO 'Solidarity Day' May Backfire," *Human Events*, September 12, 1981, 5; Pianin and Brown, "Crowd Proclaims," A1; Puddington, *Lane Kirkland*, 130; "AFL-CIO Update: Solidarity Day," September 15, 1981, file 5-27, box 5, RG98-002, Vertical Files, 1881–1999, AFL-CIO Papers.

33. Lublin and Greenberger, "Labor Gambles Its Political Clout," *Wall Street Journal*, September 15, 1981 ("how to" quotation); Pianin and Brown, "Crowd Proclaims," A1 ("We Shall Overcome" quotation); Coretta Scott King, "The Cynical Politics of Selfishness," *American Federationist*, October 1981, 14 (King quotations).

34. William Serrin, "Solidarity on Parade: Labor March Rekindles Union Spirit Despite the Movement's Big Problems," *New York Times*, September 8, 1981, B9 (first quotation); "Solidarity Day Sends Powerful Message from Workers," AFL-CIO Press Release, September 24, 1981, file 5-27, box 5, RG98-002, Vertical Files, 1881–1999, AFL-CIO Papers (second quotation).

35. McClay quoted in Lucinda Fleeson, "Phila. Labor: In Step with the March," *Philadelphia Inquirer*, September 20, 1981, A15; other quotations in David Shribman, "A Potpourri of Protesters," *New York Times*, September 20, 1981, 1.

36. "AFSCME Council 30 Solidarity Day Bus Schedule," "Solidarity Day (09/19/1981), 1 of 5," box 24, Morton Blackwell Files, Reagan Library; Gerald McEntee

interview; closing quotation in "It's Your Job on the Line," AFSCME Flyer, "Solidarity Day (3)," OA6847, Robert Bonitati Files, Reagan Library; Doug Dority interview.

37. "Solidarity Day Revisited," *White Collar* (OPEIU journal), January–March 1982, 6, clipping in "AFL-CIO Solidarity Day, 1982–1983," file 5-27, box 5, series 3, AFL-CIO Papers; "AFL-CIO Update: Solidarity Day," August 24 and September 11, 1981; and "Bus, Auto Caravans Set for Solidarity Day," AFL-CIO News Service Release, September 3, 1981—both in file 5-27, box 5, RG98-002, Vertical Files, 1881–1999, AFL-CIO Papers.

38. "Solidarity Day Slogans," in file 5-27, box 5, RG98-002, Vertical Files, 1881–1999, AFL-CIO Papers (slogan quotation); closing quotation in Strout, " 'Solidarity Day' in Washington," 3.

39. "In This Issue," *American Federationist*, October 1981, 2 (first Kirkland quotation), 16 (Jackson quotation); Pianin and Brown, "Crowd Proclaims," A1 (Hooks and Wurf "turn" quotation); Goulden, *Jerry Wurf*, xiii–xv, 289–92; AFL-CIO Executive Council Minutes, February 18–22, 1991, 22, box 104, AFL-CIO Papers; McEntee quoted from Gerald McEntee interview; closing Kirkland quotations in "AFSCME" (Kirkland Speech), June 22, 1982, RG98-003, File MSS 212, Lane Kirkland Files, AFL-CIO Papers.

40. Lublin and Greenberger, "Labor Gambles Its Political Clout"; quotations in Jim Baker to author, April 30, 2013 (correspondence in author's possession).

41. Richard Womack interview; Susan Dunlop interview (2013); Morton Bahr interview.

42. "Did Organized Labor's 'Solidarity Day' Sway Congress?" *Christian Science Monitor*, October 16, 1981, 2; AFL-CIO Executive Council Minutes, November 14, 1981, 18, box 97, AFL-CIO Papers; closing quotation in "Big Questions on Labor's Big Day," *New York Times*, September 6, 1982, 16.

43. William Serrin, "Where Are the Pickets of Yesteryear?" *New York Times*, May 31, 1981, F1; Arnold Beichman, "Lane Kirkland's Crisis of Leadership," *National Review*, April 3, 1981, 348, 352.

44. William Serrin, "The Kirkland Influence: After Two Years, the AFL-CIO Carries His Stamp and Changes Seem More Likely," *New York Times*, November 21, 1981, 1; James W. Singer, "A Man for All Unions," *National Journal*, September 27, 1980, 1623.

45. Proceedings of the Fourteenth Constitutional Convention of the AFL-CIO, November 16–19, 1981, 13, 15, 288; McCartin, *Collision Course*, 321–23.

46. Howell Raines, "Moving to Regain Labor's Lost Power," *New York Times*, January 17, 1983, A12 (first quotation); David Burnham, "New Means to Mobilize Labor Tried," *New York Times*, October 12, 1983, B9; Sawyer, "Big Labor Going High-Tech," A8 (Billings quotation).

47. "Notes—AFL-CIO Executive Board Meeting with President," December 2, 1981, "AFL-CIO Executive Council with the President 12/2/1981 (2)," box 1, series 1, OA6841, Robert Bonitati Files, Reagan Library (Reagan quotations); McCartin, *Collision Course*, 320–21; "A Suggested Labor Strategy," n.d., "Labor Strategy (1)," box 6, series 1, Robert Bonitati Files, Reagan Library (Bonitati quotations); AFL-CIO Executive

Council Minutes, November 18, 1981, 1, box 97 and February 15–22, 1982, 6, box 98—both in AFL-CIO Papers.

48. McCartin, *Collision Course*, 318; Tom Sherwood, "Labor Expects 100,000 for Solidarity Day," *Washington Post*, September 13, 1981, B1; "Solidarity Day 1981: 250,000 March on Washington," *Labor Notes*, September 8, 2009; "Art Garfunkel Chronology," at http://www.artgarfunkel.com/chrono/1984-1980.html (accessed December 2, 2014, copy in author's possession); Paul L. Montgomery, "Simon-Garfunkel Reunion Jams Central Park," *New York Times*, September 20, 1981, 1; unidentified Reagan aide quoted in Lublin and Greenberger, "Labor Gambles Its Political Clout," *Wall Street Journal*, September 15, 1981. Exact attendance at the Simon and Garfunkel concert is unclear. As noted in the sources above, New York City Mayor Ed Koch estimated the crowd size at 500,000, but the Police Department used a figure of 400,000. Art Garfunkel's website, cited above, also uses the 500,000 figure.

49. Robert F. Bonitati to Elizabeth H. Dole, June 23, 1981, "Solidarity Day (3)," OA6847, Robert Bonitati Files (first three quotations); and Bob Bonitati to Elizabeth H. Dole, September 9, 1981, "Solidarity Day 09/19/1981," box 6, series 1, Joseph W. Canzeri Files (other quotations)—both in Reagan Library.

50. Quotation in Bob Bonitati to Elizabeth H. Dole, September 15, 1981, "Solidarity Day (2)," OA6847, Robert Bonitati Files, Reagan Library. See also the large collection of material collected by aides on the march in "Solidarity Day (09/19/1981)," folders 1–5, box 24, Morton Blackwell Files, Reagan Library.

51. Baker A. Smith to Morton Blackwell, September 10, 1981, "Solidarity Day (09/19/1981), 3 of 5," box 24, Morton Blackwell Files, Reagan Library; "ALL OUT" quotation in "AFL-CIO Solidarity Day," *AFGE Challenger*, September 19, 1981, clipping in "Solidarity Day (09/19/1981), 3 of 5," box 24, Morton Blackwell Files, Reagan Library.

52. First quotation in Thelma Duggin to Elizabeth Dole, August 17, 1981, "Solidarity Day (2)," F009, Elizabeth Dole Files, Reagan Library; Bonitati quoted in Brown, "AFL-CIO Rally," H1.

53. Bob Bonitati to Red Cavaney and Jack Burgess, June 19, 1981, "Solidarity Day (3)," OA6847, Robert Bonitati Files, Reagan Library ("umbrella" quotation); AFL-CIO Executive Council Minutes, August 3–5, 1981, 14, box 97, AFL-CIO Papers; AFL-CIO spokesman quoted in Lublin and Greenberger, "Labor Gambles Its Political Clout"; Shribman, "A Potpourri," 1 (closing quotation).

54. Brown, "AFL-CIO Rally"; Foner, *Give Me Liberty*, 988; Lydia Saad, "Americans Backed UPS Workers in Strike," *Gallup News Service*, August 23, 1997.

55. "Framing Solidarity Day—Point II," n.d., "Solidarity Day (09/19/1981), 3 of 5," box 24, Morton Blackwell Files; and Reagan quoted in "Solidarity Day: A Proclamation by the President of the United States of America," January 1982, "1982 Solidarity Day," box 3, Office of White House Correspondence Files (Proclamations)—both in Reagan Library; McCartin, *Collision Course*, 293.

56. Lucinda Fleeson, "PBS is Hoping to Air Special on 'Solidarity Day'" *Philadelphia Inquirer*, September 26, 1981, B1 ("malfeasance" quotation); "AFL-CIO Update:

Solidarity Day," August 31, 1981, file 5-27, box 5, RG98-002, Vertical Files, 1881–1999, AFL-CIO Papers; William Serrin, "Solidarity Day's Enigmatic Organizer," *New York Times*, September 19, 1981, 11; Kirkland quoted in "Today is Just a Start," *American Federationist*, October 1981, 2.

57. Puddington, *Lane Kirkland*, 129, 130; "attendance" quotation in Bob Bonitati to Elizabeth H. Dole, September 17, 1981, "Solidarity Day (1)," OA6847, Robert Bonitati Files, Reagan Library; Susan Bianchi interview.

58. Wilhelm, "Labor Makes It"; "Union Leaders Gearing Up for 150 Anti-Reagan Rallies," *Chicago Sun-Times*, September 5, 1983; "Lowcountry, Nation Celebrate Labor Day," Charleston (SC) *Evening Post*, September 5, 1983; "Unions Plan Anti-Reagan Labor Day Rallies," *Philadelphia Inquirer*, September 5, 1983, A2; Paul Bass, "Labor Day Parade is First Since 1966," *New York Times*, September 4, 1983, 9. Covering Solidarity Day III, all of these articles also discuss the original march.

59. Townsend, "Union Leadership Ponders," 5 ("shown" quotation); "Solidarity Day Section for Speeches," June 24, 1981, file 5-27, box 5, RG98-002, Vertical Files, 1881–1999, AFL-CIO Papers ("memorable" quotation).

60. Warren Brown, "Solidarity Day May Fall Prey to Air, Hotel Union Strikes," *Washington Post*, September 7, 1981, WB3; Pianin and Brown, "Crowd Proclaims," A1; "AFL-CIO Update: Solidarity Day," August 20, 1981; and Martino quoted in "Reflections from a Solidarity Day Marcher," *Chemical Worker*, October 1981, 2—both in file 5-27, box 5, RG98-002, Vertical Files, 1881–1999, AFL-CIO Papers.

61. AFL-CIO Executive Council Minutes, February 17–21, 1986, 6, box 101, AFL-CIO Papers; Winpisinger and Wynn quoted in Proceedings of the Fourteenth Constitutional Convention of the AFL-CIO, November 16–19, 1981, 289, 290–91.

62. Tom Donahue interview (2013) (first quotation); AFL-CIO Executive Council Minutes, August 1–2, 1995, 2, box 108, AFL-CIO Papers.

63. Susan Bianchi interview; Doug Dority interview; Charles Stott interview.

64. Moody, *An Injury to All*, 4; Zieger and Gall, *American Workers, American Unions*, 257 (Geoghegan quotation), 258. For examples of studies that detail some of the big labor strikes of the 1980s, see McCartin, *Collision Course*; Getman, *Betrayal of Local 14*; Geoghegan, *Which Side Are You On?*

65. Geoghegan, *Which Side Are You On?* (first quotation in book title); Zieger and Gall, *American Workers, American Unions*, 257, 258; Juravich and Bronfrenbrenner, *Ravenswood*, esp. ix–xi; Minchin, *Forging a Common Bond*; "Solidarity Today," *New York Times*, September 19, 1981, 22.

Chapter Four

1. For an overview of Reagan's triumph in the 1984 presidential election, see Chafe, *Unfinished Journey*, 480–81; Tindall and Shi, *America*, 1244–45.

2. Chafe, *Unfinished Journey*, 476, 481; quotation in AFL-CIO Executive Council Minutes, February 18–22, 1985, 5, box 100, AFL-CIO Papers; Tom Donahue interview (2013).

3. Robinson, *George Meany*, 394. As well as the Communist issue, Meany also accused the ICFTU of financial irregularities.

4. AFL-CIO Executive Council Minutes, February 17–21, 1986, 7, box 101, AFL-CIO Papers.

5. AFL-CIO Executive Council Minutes, November 18, 1981, 2, box 97, AFL-CIO Papers (first two quotations); Lenore Miller interview; Susan Dunlop interview (2015).

6. Edward A. Gargan, "Jobs are Key Issue for City's Labor Day Marchers," *New York Times*, September 6, 1983, B2; Laurent Belsie, "Women Progress Slowly in Heading Unions," *Christian Science Monitor*, January 6, 1987.

7. Lenore Miller interview.

8. Susan Dunlop interview (2013).

9. Philip Shabecoff, "Women's Group Set to Organize Office Workers: Joins Forces with Union in Drive for Membership," *New York Times*, March 4, 1981, A12; "Fact Sheet on Women Workers" (Industrial Union Department document), n.d., folder 16, box 6, series 4, Alan Kistler Files, RG95-009, AFL-CIO Papers.

10. Karen Nussbaum interview; Susan Bianchi interview.

11. Bill Keller, "The Uneasiness between Blacks and Union Leaders," *New York Times*, May 13, 1984, D2; Steve Askin, "Turmoil in the Ranks," *Black Enterprise*, September 1982, 60, 62, 64.

12. Philip Shabecoff, "New Touch is Shown at Labor's Helm," *New York Times*, February 22, 1980, A12 (O'Neal quotation); Lenore Miller interview; "Minorities Frustrated by Union Representation," *Philadelphia Daily News*, November 21, 1989, 20 (Lucy quotations); William Serrin, "Study Finds Racial Bias in Union Movement," *New York Times*, June 6, 1982, 28; Kenneth B. Noble, "Kirkland's Teamster Decision: Pulling a Meany," *New York Times*, December 1, 1987, A22.

13. Markley Roberts interview; AFL-CIO Executive Council Minutes, November 14, 1981, 6, box 97, AFL-CIO Papers (second quotation). There was no record of any opposition to this change.

14. Established in 1984 and issuing its main findings in 1985, the Evolution of Work Committee will be discussed further in the next chapter, on Reagan's second term. See Puddington, *Lane Kirkland*, 258–59.

15. Report of the AFL-CIO Executive Council, October 28–31, 1985, 1–2; quotations in Ray Denison to author, June 23, 2013 (copy in author's possession); AFL-CIO Executive Council Minutes, February 17–21, 1986, 25, box 101, AFL-CIO Papers.

16. AFL-CIO Executive Council Minutes, February 15–22, 1982, 73, 74 (quotation), box 98, AFL-CIO Papers.

17. AFL-CIO Executive Council Minutes, February 21–28, 1983, 78–79, box 99, AFL-CIO Papers; Susan Dunlop interview (2013).

18. AFL-CIO Executive Council Minutes, February 21–28, 1983, 96–99, box 99, AFL-CIO Papers (quotation on 96); David L. Perlman, "Labor Hails Defeat of Balanced Budget Amendment Move," *AFL-CIO News*, October 9, 1982, 1, 3.

19. AFL-CIO Executive Council Minutes, May 24–25, 1983, 23, box 99, AFL-CIO Papers.

20. "Testimony of Margaret Seminario before the House Committee on Government Operations, on Regulation of Occupational Exposure to Asbestos," June 28, 1983, folder 98, box 13, series 30; and "Statement of Lane Kirkland before the Labor Subcommittee of the Senate Committee on Labor and Human Resources, on Legislation to Establish a Sub-Minimum Wage," March 25, 1981, folder 7, box 12, series 29—both in AFL-CIO Legislation Department Files, RG21-002, AFL-CIO Papers.

21. AFL-CIO Executive Council Minutes, February 21–28, 1983, i–iv, 129 (quotation), box 99, AFL-CIO Papers.

22. AFL-CIO Executive Council Minutes, August 3–5, 1982, 5, box 98, AFL-CIO Papers.

23. AFL-CIO Executive Council Minutes, May 26–27, 1982, 3, box 98, AFL-CIO Papers; Minchin and Salmond, *After the Dream*, 210–11, 232–33 (Reagan and "bow" quotations on 233); Kirkland quoted in "Statement of Lane Kirkland before the Subcommittee on Civil and Constitutional Rights, Committee on the Judiciary, of the House of Representatives on Extending the Voting Rights Act of 1965," 25, box 12, series 29, AFL-CIO Legislation Department Files, RG21-002, AFL-CIO Papers; Robert Pear, "Civil Rights and Labor Leaders Urge a 10-Year Extension of Voting Act," *New York Times*, May 7, 1981 (other *Times* quotation).

24. Peter Perl, "Labor Unions Get in Step for March on DC," *Washington Post*, August 7, 1983, B1.

25. Cobb, *The South and America*, 59–60, 157–58.

26. "Report by Lloyd McBride, Chairman, Committee on Organization and Field Services," February 1981, in AFL-CIO Executive Council Minutes, February 16–23, 1981, 129–35 (quotations on 130), box 97, AFL-CIO Papers; Proceedings of the Fourteenth Constitutional Convention of the AFL-CIO, November 16–19, 1981, 78 (Shanker quotation).

27. AFL-CIO Executive Council Minutes, November 14, 1981, 24, box 97; and Donald Slaiman to Melvin H. Roots, February 8, 1983, "Houston Organizing Project: 1983," file 4.19, series 4, subseries 1, RG95-009, Alan Kistler Files—both in AFL-CIO Papers; closing quotation in Charles Stott interview.

28. Kirkland quoted in "Text of a Speech by AFL-CIO President Lane Kirkland at Houston Organizing Rally," May 6, 1982, "Houston Organizing Project: 1981–1985," file 4.18, series 4, subseries 1, RG95-009, Alan Kistler Files, AFL-CIO Papers; Donald Slaiman to Melvin H. Roots, February 8, 1983, "Houston Organizing Project: 1983," file 4.19, series 4, subseries 1, RG95-009, Alan Kistler Files, AFL-CIO Papers.

29. William Serrin, "The Kirkland Influence: After Two Years, the AFL-CIO Carries His Stamp and Changes Seem More Likely," *New York Times*, November 21, 1981, 13.

30. Griffith, *The Crisis of American Labor* ("Operation Dixie" quotation in subtitle); Cobb, *The South and America*, 206 ("political climate" quotation); Charles Stott interview (Stott quotations); AFL-CIO Executive Council Minutes, May 24–25, 1983, 8, box 99 (closing quotation); "AFL-CIO Houston Organizing Project: Travelers' Assistance Seminar," November 6 and 7, 1982, "Houston Organizing Project: 1981–1982," file 4.17, series 4, subseries 1, RG95-009, Alan Kistler Files—all in AFL-CIO Papers (other quotations).

31. Lloyd McBride, "Houston Cooperative Organizing Program Progress Report," August 1981, "Houston Organizing Project: 1981–1982," file 4.17, series 4, subseries 1, RG95-009, Alan Kistler Files, AFL-CIO Papers.

32. AFL-CIO Executive Council Minutes, February 15–22, 1982, 80, box 98, AFL-CIO Papers.

33. Ruttenberg, Friedman, Kilgallon, and Associates, "A Review of the Houston Organizing Project Prepared for the AFL-CIO," February 1984, 21, "Houston Organizing Project: 1984," file 4.20, series 4, subseries 1, RG95-009, Alan Kistler Files, AFL-CIO Papers (first quotation); Stewart Acuff interview.

34. See, for example, "Monthly Organizing Tally Sheet: Roofers Local Union #116," March 9, 1982, and "Monthly Organizing Tally Sheet: Pipefitters Local Union #211," March 3, 1982—both in "Houston Organizing Project: 1983," file 4.19, series 4, subseries 1, RG95-009, Alan Kistler Files, AFL-CIO Papers.

35. "A Brief Summary of Activities within the PE and HC Division," January 22, 1985, "Houston Organizing Project: 1985," file 4.21, series 4, subseries 1, RG95-009, Alan Kistler Files, AFL-CIO Papers; Stewart Acuff interview.

36. Ruttenberg, Friedman, Kilgallon, and Associates, "A Review of the Houston Organizing Project Prepared for the AFL-CIO," February 1984, 3–4, "Houston Organizing Project: 1984," file 4.20, series 4, subseries 1, RG95-009, Alan Kistler Files, AFL-CIO Papers.

37. Tom Donahue interview (2015); Green P. Lewis to Alan Kistler, October 24, 1985, "Houston Organizing Project: 1985," file 4.21, series 4, subseries 1, RG95-009, Alan Kistler Files, AFL-CIO Papers.

38. AFL-CIO Executive Council Minutes, May 24–25, 1983, 8, box 99, AFL-CIO Papers.

39. AFL-CIO Executive Council Minutes, February 21–28, 1983, 31, box 99, AFL-CIO Papers; AFL-CIO Executive Council Minutes, February 20–24, 1984, 20 (closing quotation), D90–92 (membership statistics), box 99, AFL-CIO Papers.

40. AFL-CIO Executive Council Minutes, February 20–24, 1984, D93, box 99, AFL-CIO Papers; "Unhappy New Year," *AFL-CIO News*, January 8, 1983, 1.

41. A. H. Raskin, "Frustrated and Wary, Labor Marks Its Day," *New York Times*, September 5, 1982, A1; "Speech Given by Mark A. Anderson, Department of Economic Research, AFL-CIO," January 12, 1984, Mark Anderson Papers, Washington, DC, personal collection shared with author (hereafter cited as "Anderson Papers"); Murray L. Weidenbaum, "Assessing Reagan's Economic Program," *New York Times*, August 22, 1982, 4.

42. AFL-CIO Executive Council Minutes, May 24–25, 1983, 25, 31 (Kirkland quotation), box 99, AFL-CIO Papers.

43. AFL-CIO Executive Council Minutes, August 3–4, 1993, B2, box 105, AFL-CIO Papers.

44. Craig Becker interview; AFL-CIO Executive Council Minutes, August 8–10, 1983, 29, box 99, AFL-CIO Papers; closing quotation in Pete Earley, "Teamsters Go Often to NLRB: Activists Find Road Gets Rougher," *Washington Post*, August 24, 1984.

45. Peter Perl, "AFL-CIO Admits Failures, Prepares to Change Tactics," *Washington Post*, February 25, 1985, 5; Black quoted in Minchin, *Fighting Against the Odds*, 151;

Kistler quotations in Alan Kistler to Lane Kirkland, n.d., folder 16, box 6, series 4, Alan Kistler Files, RG95-009, AFL-CIO Papers.

46. Proceedings of the Sixteenth Constitutional Convention of the AFL-CIO, October 28–31, 1985, 163–64, 169 (Sweeney quotation).

47. Stewart Acuff interview; Gerry Shea interview; Bob Welsh interview ("lucky" quotation).

48. Puddington, *Lane Kirkland*, 30.

49. Susan Dunlop interview (2013); AFL-CIO Executive Council Minutes, February 21–28, 1983, 81, box 99, AFL-CIO Papers; closing quotation in William Serrin, "Lane Kirkland, Who Led Labor in Difficult Times, Is Dead at 77," *New York Times*, August 15, 1999.

50. See, for example, Teddy Kollek to Lane Kirkland, July 4, 1983, folder 4, box 3, RG95-007, Lane Kirkland Files, AFL-CIO Papers.

51. Henry A. Kissinger to Lane and Irena Kirkland, June 10, 1981, folder 28, box 2; and Henry A. Kissinger to Lane and Irena Kirkland, July 6, 1983, folder 4, box 3—both in RG95-007, Lane Kirkland Files, AFL-CIO Papers.

52. For Kirkland's revisions, see, for example, Murray Seeger to Katy Vogel, May 30, 1985 (with attached press statement), in RG98-003, File MSS 121, 193, 213, AFL-CIO Papers; David St. John interview (quotation); Susan Dunlop interview.

53. Proceedings of the Fifteenth Constitutional Convention of the AFL-CIO, October 3–6, 1983, 9–18 (quotations on 10, 18); Ronald Reagan, "Election Eve Address: 'A Vision for America'" November 3, 1980, available at http://www.reagan.utexas.edu/archives/reference/11.3.80.html (accessed December 5, 2014, copy in author's possession).

54. See, for example, "Statement by Lane Kirkland to the Joint Economic Committee of Congress," July 20, 1982, folder 9, box 13, AFL-CIO Legislation Department Files, RG21-002, AFL-CIO Papers.

55. *Face the Nation* (transcript), October 10, 1982, 2, 3, in "Transcripts," 1, box 1, RG95-007, Lane Kirkland Files (first four quotations); AFL-CIO Executive Council Minutes, May 26–27, 1982, 1, box 98 ("recession" quotation); "AFL-CIO President Lane Kirkland's Interview with Associated Press reporters Merrill Hartson and Donald M. Rothberg," March 10, 1983, 3, in "Transcripts," 1, box 1, RG95-007, Lane Kirkland Files (closing quotation)—all in AFL-CIO Papers.

56. Jim Baker to author, April 30, 2013 (correspondence in author's possession).

57. Lenore Miller interview; Susan Bianchi interview.

58. Lenore Miller interview; Kathy Sawyer, "Lane Kirkland: Made in America and Proud to Wear the Union Label," *Washington Post*, July 15, 1984.

59. Opening quotation in "Who Will Lead Labor, Where?" *New York Times*, June 19, 1995, A12; David St. John interview; Charles Stott interview.

60. Sawyer, "Lane Kirkland: Made in America"; Susan Dunlop interview (2015).

61. Lane Kirkland, interview by James F. Shea and Don R. Kienzle, November 13, 1996, 18, Labor Diplomacy Oral History Project, transcript in folder 8, box 4, RG95-007, Lane Kirkland Files, AFL-CIO Papers.

62. Frank Swoboda, "AFL-CIO Looks to Militancy at Home after Survival Decade," *Washington Post*, November 12, 1989, A13, clipping in untitled folder, OS box 12, RG95-007, Lane Kirkland Files, AFL-CIO Papers; Domber, *Empowering Revolution*, 69 (quotation), 109–10.

63. AFL-CIO Executive Council Minutes, August 20–21, 1980, 25, box 97, AFL-CIO Papers.

64. AFL-CIO Executive Council Minutes, February 15–22, 1982, 63–64, box 98, AFL-CIO Papers.

65. AFL-CIO Executive Council Minutes, May 24–25, 1983, 11, 61, box 99, AFL-CIO Papers (quotations); AFL-CIO Executive Council Minutes, May 7–9, 1984, 19, B36–37, box 99, AFL-CIO Papers.

66. "Statement by the President," February 13, 1980, and "Questions and Answers" (Carter Administration Fact Sheet), n.d., "ILO," box 196, Chief of Staff (Bernie Aronson) Files, Carter Library.

67. AFL-CIO Executive Council Minutes, February 21–28, 1983, 4, box 99, AFL-CIO Papers.

68. Ibid., 8 (quotation), 26.

69. William Serrin, "The Mobility of Capital Disperses Unions' Power," *New York Times*, March 21, 1982, E8.

70. AFL-CIO Executive Council Minutes, February 16–23, 1981, 26, box 97, AFL-CIO Papers; AFL-CIO Executive Council Report, October 3–6, 1983, 185.

71. AFL-CIO Executive Council Minutes, November 14, 1981, 18, box 97 (first two quotations); "The Reagan Recession and Its Victims," AFL-CIO statement, AFL-CIO Executive Council Minutes, August 3, 1982, 31, box 98; closing quotation in AFL-CIO Solidarity Day III Press Release, August 26, 1983, "AFL-CIO Solidarity Day, 1982–1983," box 5, series 3, file 5-27, Vertical Files, 1881–1999—all in AFL-CIO Papers.

72. Tindall and Shi, *America*, 1239; Catherine Woodard, "On Holiday, Labor Parades Its Resolve," *Fort Worth Star-Telegram*, September 6, 1983, clipping in "Solidarity Day 1981," box 6, RG95-009, Alan Kistler Files; and Kirkland quoted in "Labor Gears Up for Solidarity Day," *AFL-CIO News*, June 4, 1983, 1–2, clipping in "AFL-CIO Solidarity Day, 1982–1983," file 5-27, box 5, series 3, Vertical Files, 1881–1999—both in AFL-CIO Papers.

73. "Labor Beats Drum for Big Vote," *Christian Science Monitor*, October 29, 1982, 2; first three quotations in William Serrin, "Blue-Collar Anger at Reagan Poses Threat to Republicans," *New York Times*, October 28, 1982, A1; "comeback" quotation in Kathy Sawyer, "Big Labor Going High-Tech in Battle for Votes of Working People," *Washington Post*, September 9, 1982, A8; closing quotation in Susan Dunlop interview (2015).

74. "Labor Gears Up for Solidarity Day," *AFL-CIO News*, June 4, 1983, 1–2, clipping in "AFL-CIO Solidarity Day, 1982–1983," file 5-27, box 5, series 3, Vertical Files, 1881–1999 (quotation); and "Union Leaders Gearing Up for 150 Anti-Reagan Rallies," *Chicago Sun-Times*, September 5, 1983, clipping in "Solidarity Day 1981," box 6, RG95-009, Alan Kistler Files—both in AFL-CIO Papers.

75. Paul Bass, "Labor Day Parade Is First since 1966," *New York Times*, September 4, 1983, 9 (Rourke quotation); "Unions Plan Anti-Reagan Labor Day Rallies," *Philadelphia Inquirer*, September 5, 1983, A2; Tim Belknap, "Unionists Rally in City, Blast Reagan," *Detroit Free Press*, September 6, 1983; closing quotation in "Press Reaction Solidarity Day III," folder 4, box 6, series 4, Alan Kistler Files, AFL-CIO Papers.

76. Don Bean, "Labor Wants Reagan Out of Job," *Cleveland Plain Dealer*, September 6, 1983 ("parades" quotation); "Union Bosses Blast Policy: Meanwhile, Vacationers Relish Holiday," *Wichita Eagle-Beacon*, September 6, 1983, 3A; and Ann Wead Kimbrough, "Unions Planning Labor Day March," *Atlanta Journal and Constitution*, September 4, 1983—all clippings in "Solidarity Day 1981," box 6, RG95-009, Alan Kistler Files, AFL-CIO Papers; closing quotation in "Labor's Day, Labor's Challenge," *New York Times*, September 5, 1983, 18. The *Washington Post* headline is from Peter Perl, "Solidarity Day Activity Is Joined to Labor Day," *Washington Post*, September 5, 1983, A12.

77. Kirkland quoted in Jim Strong, "Labor Leaders Speak Out on 3rd Solidarity Day," *Chicago Tribune*, September 5, 1983, 12, section 4; and Reagan quoted in "Reagan Target of Labor Day Rallies," *Chicago Tribune*, September 5, 1983, 4, section 1—both clippings in "Solidarity Day 1981," box 6, RG95-009, Alan Kistler Files, AFL-CIO Papers; Chafe, *Unfinished Journey*, 476.

78. AFL-CIO Executive Council Minutes, February 20–24, 1984, 2, 4, box 99, AFL-CIO Papers.

79. John M. Barry, "Endorsement of Mondale Begins New Era for Labor," *AFL-CIO News*, October 15, 1983, 1.

80. Barry, "Endorsement of Mondale," 1; Hedrick Smith, "AFL-CIO, Shaken by Hart, Trying to Regroup for Mondale," *New York Times*, March 11, 1984, B9; AFL-CIO Executive Council Minutes, October 1, 1983, 34 ("solidarity" quotation); and AFL-CIO Executive Council Minutes, May 7–9, 1984, 3—both in box 99, AFL-CIO Papers.

81. Walter F. Mondale to Lane Kirkland, May 29, 1984; and Walter F. Mondale to Lane and Irena Kirkland, May 25, 1983—both in folder 2, box 3, RG95-007, Lane Kirkland Files, AFL-CIO Papers.

82. Smith, "AFL-CIO, Shaken by Hart," B9.

83. Keller, "The Uneasiness," D2.

84. Sawyer, "Lane Kirkland: Made in America" (quotation); Robert Pear, "Labor Leaders Play It Low Key at Convention," *New York Times*, July 20, 1984, A11.

85. AFL-CIO Executive Council Minutes, February 18–22, 1985, 2, box 99, AFL-CIO Papers; Charles Stott interview.

86. Report of the AFL-CIO Executive Council, October 28–31, 1985, 2.

87. David L. Perlman, "Split-Ticket Voting Tribute to Reagan, Rebuff to Program," *AFL-CIO News*, November 10, 1984, 1 (first quotation); "Kirkland Voices Pride in Labor's Effort," *AFL-CIO News*, November 10, 1984, 1 (second quotation).

88. AFL-CIO Executive Council Minutes, February 18–22, 1985, 4, 5, box 98, AFL-CIO Papers.

89. Perlman, "Split-Ticket Voting," 1 (first quotation); "Republicans Fall Short in Bid for House Gains," *AFL-CIO News*, November 10, 1984, 1; AFL-CIO Executive Council Minutes, February 18–22, 1985, 5, box 98, AFL-CIO Papers.

90. A. H. Raskin, "Labor's Grand Illusions," *New York Times*, February 10, 1985, 305 ("scab-herders" quotation); Bill Keller, "Labor Chiefs United by Fear of 2nd Reagan Term," *New York Times*, August 19, 1984, A32 (other quotation).

91. Raskin, "Labor's Grand Illusions," 305.

92. Ibid.

Chapter Five

1. Kate Bronfenbrenner, "The Role of Union Strategies in NLRB Certification Elections," *Industrial and Labor Relations Review* 50, no. 2 (January 1997): 195; Kathleen Lynn, "For Labor, A Decade of Decline: Factory Jobs Went Overseas," *The Record* (New Jersey), September 4, 1989, C1 (closing quotation from Charles R. Perry of the Wharton School of Business); "Kirkland Sees a Resurgence for Troubled Labor Unions," *New York Times*, September 1, 1985, A26.

2. "Distinguished Speaker Address by Thomas R. Donahue: IRRA Meeting," ca. 1989–1990, "Press Releases and Speeches, '95 (3)," Donahue Papers.

3. "Kirkland Sees a Resurgence for Troubled Labor Unions," *New York Times*, September 1, 1985, A26; closing Kirkland quotation in Proceedings of the 1989 AFL-CIO Convention, November 13–16, 1989, 10.

4. Report of the AFL-CIO Executive Council, October 26, 1987, 104–5 (quotation on 104); Kirkland quotation in Proceedings of the 1989 AFL-CIO Convention, November 13–16, 1989, 11.

5. Susan Bianchi interview; Kirkland quoted in Peter T. Kilborn, "Dole Winning Applause for Labor Dept. Actions," *New York Times*, January 4, 1990, A16; Susan Dunlop interview (2013); Tom Donahue interview (2013).

6. Mazzochi quoted in William Serrin, "Organized Labor Is Increasingly Less So," *New York Times*, November 18, 1984, E3; Andy Stern interview; Judy Ancel, "To Build International Solidarity, AFL-CIO Needs to Dump Old Baggage," *Labor Notes*, April 30, 2002. The term "fortress unionism" is a reference to Rick Yeselson's influential "Fortress Unionism," *Democracy* 29 (Summer 2013), available at http://democracyjournal.org/29 /fortress-unionism.php (accessed September 24, 2015, copy in author's possession), which argues that the labor movement should concentrate on buttressing the areas where it is already strong and making alliances with progressive groups—which was very similar to Kirkland's approach.

7. AFL-CIO Executive Council Minutes, May 26–27, 1982, 11, box 98, AFL-CIO Papers (quotations); David Burnham, "New Means to Mobilize Labor Tried," *New York Times*, October 12, 1983, B9.

8. Donahue quoted in "AFL-CIO to Try Ads to Polish Image," *San Francisco Chronicle*, October 26, 1987, A7.

9. Report of the AFL-CIO Executive Council, November 13–16, 1989, 5 (Kirkland quotation); "Stars Sign Up for Union Commercials," *San Francisco Chronicle*, March 15, 1988, E1; other quotation in Larry Kirkman profile at http://www.american.edu/soc/faculty/larry.cfm (accessed October 20, 2014, copy in author's possession).

10. AFL-CIO Executive Council Minutes, October 24, 1987, 5, box 102, AFL-CIO Papers; closing quotation in Larry Kirkman profile at http://www.american.edu/soc/faculty/larry.cfm (accessed October 20, 2014, copy in author's possession).

11. AFL-CIO Executive Council Minutes, February 15–22, 1982, 50 (quotation); and AFL-CIO Executive Council Minutes, May 24–25, 1983, 13—both in box 98, AFL-CIO Papers.

12. Denise Mitchell interview; William Serrin, "Lane Kirkland, Who Led Labor in Difficult Times, Is Dead at 77," *New York Times*, August 15, 1999.

13. Tom Donahue interview (2013) (Donahue quotations); Puddington, *Lane Kirkland*, 258; Committee quotation in "The New American Workplace: A Labor Perspective," A Report by the AFL-CIO Committee on the Evolution of Work, February 1994, "New American Workplace—Labor Perspective," folder, Donahue Papers; William Serrin, "Labor Conference Focuses on Need For Changes to Reinvigorate Unions," *New York Times*, September 22, 1985, 42.

14. Peter Perl, "AFL-CIO Admits Failures, Prepares to Change Tactics," *Washington Post*, February 25, 1985, 5; "The Changing Situation of Workers and Their Unions," A Report by the AFL-CIO Committee on the Evolution of Work, February 1985, 5, 9, 12, 13, "Changing Situation of Workers and Their Unions" in Donahue Papers (other quotations).

15. Evolution of Work Committee Minutes, n.d., folder 10, box 4, series 4, Alan Kistler Files, AFL-CIO Papers.

16. "The Changing Situation of Workers," February 1985, 17–29 (report quotations on 14, 17, and 18), Donahue Papers; Perl, "AFL-CIO Admits Failures," 5.

17. "The Changing Situation of Workers," February 1985, 19, 27, Donahue Papers; Denise Mitchell interview; Gerry Shea interview.

18. Untitled Memo by Wayne Glenn and Don Slaiman, May 8, 1985, folder 9, box 4, series 4, Kistler Files, AFL-CIO Papers; Kistler quoted in Alan Kistler to Charlie McDonald, folder 9, box 4, series 4, Kistler Files, AFL-CIO Papers.

19. Peter Perl, "AFL-CIO Unveils Tactics: 'Associate' Membership Has Special Benefits," *Washington Post*, October 28, 1985, A4; John McLaren, "Organized Labor Regrouping after Reagan, Economic Losses," *San Diego Evening Tribune*, January 30, 1989, 8 ("Perspective" section) (Ross quotation); closing Silverman quotation in Paul Ruffins, "Why American Unions Believe Their Future Is Now," *Washington Post*, September 1, 1991, C5.

20. AFL-CIO official quotation in Perl, "AFL-CIO Unveils Tactics," A4; Fletcher quoted in Ruffins, "Why American Unions Believe," C5; closing Donahue quotation in William Serrin, "Labor Sees Gains in Effort to Change," *New York Times*, February 17, 1986, A10.

21. Report of the AFL-CIO Executive Council, October 26, 1987, 104–6.

22. Kirkland quoted in U.S. Congress, House, Committee on Education and Labor, *Hearings on H.R. 1834, The Minimum Wage Restoration Act of 1987*, 100th Congress, 1st session, 160; James C. Miller III to Robert H. Michel, April 18, 1988, "Labor—Minimum Wage (1)," box 2, OA18896, Thomas G. Moore Files, Reagan Library (other quotations).

23. "The Case against a New Minimum Wage Law," April 19, 1988, "Minimum Wage 04/20/1988," box 22, OA19206, White House Office of Public Affairs Files, Reagan Library (first two quotations); Report of the AFL-CIO Executive Council to the 1989 Convention, 108 (other quotation).

24. Report of the AFL-CIO Executive Council, October 26, 1987, 111, 113–14; Liborato quotation in U.S. Congress, Senate, Committee on the Budget, *Catastrophic and Long-Term Health Care*, 100th Congress, 1st Session, 1988, 64. For more explanation of how both the unemployment compensation and TAA programs worked to assist "trade-displaced" workers, see Kletzer, *Job Loss from Imports*, 80–81.

25. Report of the AFL-CIO Executive Council to the 1989 Convention, 102–3 (first quotation on 103); Hutchinson quoted in U.S. Congress, House, Select Committee on Children, Youth, and Families, *Improving Child Care Services: What Can Be Done?* 98th Congress, 2nd session, 1984, 235, 237.

26. Report of the AFL-CIO Executive Council to the 1989 Convention, 111; U.S. Congress, House, Committee on Education and Labor, *Hearings on Compensation for Occupational Disease*, 99th Congress, 1st session, 1985, 155–58 (Power quotations on 156); U.S. Congress, House, Committee on Small Business, *Occupational Disease Notification: Potential Liability Problems*, 100th Congress, 1st Session, 1988, 1–4.

27. Markley Roberts interview; Charles Stott interview.

28. Report of the AFL-CIO Executive Council to the 1989 Convention, 101.

29. Ibid., 100. *American Federationist* article summarized in "Prior Shutdown Notice Urged in Union Pacts," *AFL-CIO News*, December 25, 1965, 1.

30. AFL-CIO Executive Council Minutes, February 19–26, 1979, 111, box 96, AFL-CIO Papers; Report of the AFL-CIO Executive Council to the 1989 Convention, 100; Reagan quoted in "Mandatory Advance Notice of Layoffs and Plant Closings" (White House Talking Points), May 16, 1988, "Plant Closings TP 5/16/1988 (1)," box 1, OA18689, Roger Bolton Files, Reagan Library.

31. "Statement by the President," August 2, 1988, "Plant Closings TP 5/14/1988 (4)," box 1, OA18689, Roger Bolton Files, Reagan Library.

32. Renee L. Reymond to Roger Bolton, August 10, 1988, "Plant Closings TP 5/14/1988 (4)"; and John S. Irving to Randolph M. Hale, August 24, 1988, "Plant Closings TP 5/14/1988 (4)"—both in box 1, OA18689, Roger Bolton Files, Reagan Library.

33. Robert McGlotten interview; *Meet the Press* (transcript), April 24, 1988, 2, in "Transcripts," 1, box 1, RG95-007, Lane Kirkland Files, AFL-CIO Papers.

34. "Former AFL-CIO President Dies," AFL-CIO Press Release, August 14, 1999, folder 1, Donahue Papers; Philip Dine, "Closing Ranks . . . Labor Unions Trying to Reunify in Face of Mounting Woes," *St. Louis Post-Dispatch*, March 6, 1988, 1B; closing

quotation in "AFL-CIO President Lane Kirkland Message to Trade Unionists," June 8, 1995 (Chicago Speech), Donahue Papers.

35. Stephen Franklin, "Lane Kirkland, 77; Led AFL-CIO in Difficult 1980s," *Chicago Tribune*, August 15, 1999, 6, clipping in folder 1, Donahue Papers; Peter Milius, "Labor Movement Is Deeply Divided Following Election," *Washington Post*, November 24, 1972, A26; closing quotation in "Who Will Lead Labor, Where?" *New York Times* (editorial), June 19, 1995, A12.

36. Kirkland quoted in AFL-CIO Executive Council Minutes, October 24, 1987, 5, 7, box 102, AFL-CIO Papers; Laurent Belsie, "AFL-CIO Celebrates New Solidarity," *Christian Science Monitor*, November 14, 1989, 7; Report of the Building and Construction Trades Department (1990), 104, in AFL-CIO Executive Council Minutes, July 31–August 1, 1990, box 104, AFL-CIO Papers (Presser quotation).

37. First two quotations in Kenneth B. Noble, "Kirkland's Teamster Decision: Pulling a Meany," *New York Times*, December 1, 1987, A22; James Barron, "Jackie Presser, President of Besieged Teamsters' Union, Dies in Cleveland at 61," *New York Times*, July 11, 1988; closing quotation in Laurent Belsie, "Labor Tries to Brush Up Its Image, but with Teamsters Back in Fold, It Will Be Tough," *Christian Science Monitor*, October 30, 1987, 3; Tom Donahue interview (2015).

38. Kenneth B. Noble, "Teamsters Gain a Readmittance to AFL-CIO," *New York Times*, October 25, 1987, A1; Noble, "Kirkland's Teamster Decision," A22 (quotations).

39. AFL-CIO Executive Council Minutes, October 24, 1987, 6, box 102, AFL-CIO Papers.

40. "Unions Losing Workers: Membership Down 62,000," Akron (OH) *Beacon Journal*, January 23, 1988, A8; Steve Kaufman, "Hard Times Continue for U.S. Labor," *Journal of Commerce*, August 17, 1989, 2A; "Quitting Time for Unions?" Owensboro (KY) *Messenger-Inquirer*, August 20, 1989, 1G.

41. David St. John interview.

42. Kenneth B. Noble, "Q and A: Lane Kirkland," *The New York Times*, December 14, 1986, A76 (quotations); Irvin Molotsky and Warren Weaver Jr., "Kirkland on the Mend," *New York Times*, February 28, 1987, 1; David St. John interview.

43. Lane Kirkland, " 'It Has All Been Said Before . . . ,' " in *Unions in Transition*, ed. Lipset, 393 (first quotation), 396–99, 403 (closing quotation).

44. Kathleen Lynn, "For Labor, A Decade of Decline: Factory Jobs Went Overseas," *The Record* (New Jersey), September 4, 1989, C1; "Labor's Ultimate Weapon, the Strike, is Mostly Failing," *Wall Street Journal*, October 13, 1986, 1; "Kirkland Sees a Resurgence for Troubled Labor Unions," *New York Times*, September 1, 1985, A26; "gun" quotation from a Machinists' official in Zieger and Gall, *American Workers, American Unions*, 258–59; closing quotation in "Ohio Labor Leaders Say They See End of Lean Membership Times," Akron (OH) *Beacon Journal*, September 5, 1989, B5.

45. AFL-CIO Executive Council Minutes, August 5–7, 1986, 3–4, box 101, AFL-CIO Papers.

46. Both quotations in U.S. Department of Labor, "Working in America: A Chart Book," September 23, 1987, "Labor (3)," box 20, OA18018, Public Affairs Files, Reagan Library.

47. "Presidential Radio Talk: Labor Day," September 5, 1987, "09/05/1987 Radio Address: Labor Day," box 339 (1987 quotations); and "Signing Ceremony for Trade Bill, Long Beach, California," August 23, 1988, "08/23/1988 Signing Ceremony for Trade Bill (1)," box 395—both in Speechwriting Files (research), Reagan Library.

48. Kenneth B. Noble, "Decline in Industrial Unions Cited," *New York Times*, October 25, 1985, A18; first two Kirkland quotations in Noble, "Q and A," A76; other Kirkland quotation in "Testimony of Lane Kirkland before the Senate Finance Committee on the Goals of U.S. Trade Policy," January 20, 1987, folder 13, box 15, series 30, AFL-CIO Legislative Department Files, RG21-002, AFL-CIO Papers.

49. Report of the AFL-CIO Executive Council, October 28–31, 1985, 8 (Kirkland quotations); Kenneth Eskey, "Declining Unions Face Newest Threat: Job Loss," *Houston Chronicle*, September 3, 1989, A1; Louis Uchitelle, "Economic Scene: Service-Sector Wage Issues," *New York Times*, December 19, 1986, D2; Tammy Joyner, "Unions Push Past Former Boundaries," *Charlotte Observer*, February 22, 1988, 1C.

50. Report to the AFL-CIO Executive Council, October 28–31, 1985, 9.

51. Proceedings of the Fifteenth Constitutional Convention of the AFL-CIO, October 3–6, 1983, 59–60; John Sweeney interview.

52. Zieger and Gall, *American Workers, American Unions*, 258; Peter Perl, "The Hormel Strike Was Doomed to Fail," *Washington Post*, February 16, 1986, C5; "Hormel Fires Meatpackers At 3 Plants," *Washington Post*, January 28, 1986, A3; penultimate quotation in Perl, "The Hormel Strike Was Doomed," C5. See also "Labor's Ultimate Weapon," 1.

53. Timothy J. Minchin, "'Labor's Empty Gun': Permanent Replacements and the International Paper Company Strike of 1987–88," *Labor History* 47, no. 1 (February 2006): 21–22; Dale Martin interview.

54. AFL-CIO Executive Council Minutes, August 8–10, 1983, 27, 28, box 99, AFL-CIO Papers; Joe Uehlein interview; AFL-CIO Executive Council Minutes, February 20–24, 1984, 34, box 99, AFL-CIO Papers (Kirkland quotation).

55. A. H. Raskin, "Big Labor Tries to End Its Nightmare," *New York Times*, May 4, 1986, A1 (Kirkland quotations); "Union Leaders Gather to Back Copper Strikes," *New York Times*, November 19, 1984, B11; Paul Taylor, "Striking Copper Workers Find They Can't Go Home to 'Mother,'" *Washington Post*, December 14, 1983, A2 ("financially beleaguered" quotation); Peter Perl, "Unions Try New Tactic on Phelps Dodge," *Washington Post*, February 20, 1985, D3.

56. AFL-CIO Executive Council Minutes, February 17–21, 1986, 6–7, box 101, AFL-CIO Papers.

57. Susan Kelleher and T. R. Reid, "Teamsters Defeated at Coors: Workers Soundly Reject Affiliation," *Washington Post*, December 17, 1988, D11.

58. Council quotations in "Boycott of Coors Beer," AFL-CIO Executive Council statement, May 4, 1977, 34, box 95, volume 22; and Sickler quoted in A. David Sickler to Joseph F. Hancock, August 5, 1985, RG95-009, series 4, SS3, file 8-8 (Coors Boycott)—both in AFL-CIO Papers.

59. First quotation in Douglas R. Sease, "Uncertain Weapon: Some Union Boycotts Have a Lot of Impact, but Most of Them Flop," *Wall Street Journal*, June 26, 1978,

clipping in RG95-009, series 4, SS3, file 8-8 (Coors Boycott); and "National Incentive Covenant between Adolph Coors Company and a National Black Economic Development Coalition," September 18, 1984, RG9-003, series 7, file 43-10 (Coors Boycott)—both in AFL-CIO Papers; John Gallagher, "Coors Makes Push vs. 10-Year Boycott," Syracuse (NY) *Post-Standard*, June 5, 1987, A1; Lynda Richardson and Mary Jordan, "AFL-CIO Agrees to End Its Boycott of Coors Beer," *Washington Post*, August 20, 1987, A2; closing quotations in Joseph Coors to Elizabeth H. Dole, July 20, 1982, case file 087492, box 63 (first quotation), and John S. Herrington to Joseph Coors, August 29, 1983, case file 160912, box 4—both in WHORM Files, Reagan Library.

60. Richardson and Jordan, "AFL-CIO Agrees to End Its Boycott," A2 (first Kirkland quotation); Lane Kirkland, Coors Boycott Press Statement (Draft), August 19, 1987, RG98-003, File MSS 212, Lane Kirkland Files, AFL-CIO Papers; Richardson and Jordan, "AFL-CIO Agrees to End Its Boycott," A2 (Harbrant quotation).

61. Jonathan Tasini, "The Beer and the Boycott," *New York Times*, January 31, 1988, SM18; Tom Donahue interview (2013) (first quotation); "Coors: Va. Plant Won't Need Union," *Washington Post*, November 2, 1987, WB26 (other quotation).

62. Lane Kirkland to Patrick J. Campbell et al., January 19, 1988, folder 107, box 13, series 9, Alan Kistler Files, RG95-009, AFL-CIO Papers; Kelleher and Reid, "Teamsters Defeated at Coors," D11; AFL-CIO Executive Council Minutes, August 22–23, 1988, 2, box 103, AFL-CIO Papers; Klare quoted in "Union Plans to Organize Coors Plant," Richmond (VA) *Times-Dispatch*, November 7, 1986, 8; "The Changing Situation of Workers," February 1985, 12, Donahue Papers.

63. Aloysius A. Mazewski to Lane Kirkland, October 4, 1985, "Correspondence, 1975–1992," folder 3, box 3, RG95-007, Lane Kirkland Files, AFL-CIO Papers.

64. AFL-CIO Executive Council Minutes, February 17–21, 1986, 18, C7, box 101, AFL-CIO Papers.

65. AFL-CIO Executive Council Minutes, August 22–23, 1988, 17, box 103, AFL-CIO Papers; "Democracy at Work" quotation in "Lane Kirkland: Opening Press Conference Remarks," August 18, 1987, RG98-003, File MSS 121, 193, 213, AFL-CIO Papers; "Reagan, Bush Debut as Campaign Duo; Dukakis Gets AFL-CIO Endorsement," *Atlanta Journal-Constitution*, August 25, 1988, A19.

66. AFL-CIO Executive Council Minutes, February 20–24, 1989, 19, box 103, AFL-CIO Papers.

67. Gary Frank, "WMass Leaders See Growth in the Next Decade," Springfield (MA) *Sunday Republican*, January 22, 1989, F22.

Chapter Six

1. Proceedings of the 1989 AFL-CIO Convention, November 13–16, 1989, 323 (Sweeney quotation); Robert Bonitati to George H. W. Bush, May 18, 1981, "AFL-CIO, February-June 1981 (1)," box 1, series 1, OA6841, Reagan Library; closing quotation in Charles Stott interview.

2. "AFL-CIO Re-Elects Kirkland," *New York Times*, November 14, 1991, A20.

3. "Union Affiliation of Employed Wage and Salary Workers by Selected Characteristics," U.S. Bureau of Labor Statistics, data available at http://www.bls.gov/cps/cpslutabs.htm (accessed January 10, 2014, copy in author's possession).

4. Susan Dunlop interview (2013).

5. Kathleen Lynn, "For Labor, a Decade of Decline: Factory Jobs Went Overseas," *The Record* (New Jersey), September 4, 1989, C1 (McLewin quotation); Peter T. Kilborn, "Dole Winning Applause for Labor Dept. Actions," *New York Times*, January 4, 1990, A16 (Gotbaum quotation).

6. George H. W. Bush remarks at AFL-CIO Building and Construction Trades Legislative Conference, April 18, 1989, 23, "SP540, National Conference of Building and Construction Trades, AFL-CIO," 19395-007, WHORM Speech File, George H. W. Bush Presidential Library, College Station, Texas (hereafter cited as "Bush Library").

7. Charles W. Jones to Mr. President and Mrs. Bush, April 24, 1989 (first three quotations), and George Bush to Charles W. Jones, May 10, 1989—both in "SP540, National Conference of Building and Construction Trades, AFL-CIO," 19395-007, WHORM Speech File, Bush Library; Richard Benedetto, "Bush Courts Labor Unions," *USA Today*, November 14, 1989.

8. Benedetto, "Bush Courts Labor."

9. Bobbie Kilberg to George H. W. Bush, November 15, 1989, and George H. W. Bush speech to AFL-CIO Convention, November 15, 1989, 1–17 (quotations on 1, 3, 4, 13, and 16)—both in "SP623, AFL-CIO Convention, Washington, DC, 11/15/89," 19415-010, WHORM Speech File, Bush Library.

10. First quotation in Peter T. Kilborn, "Back Abortion Rights, AFL-CIO Is Asked," *New York Times*, November 14, 1989, clipping in untitled folder, box OS12, RG95-007, Lane Kirkland Files, AFL-CIO Papers; and Kirkland quoted in Lane Kirkland to George Bush, December 6, 1989, and George Bush to Lane Kirkland, December 20, 1989—both in "SP623, AFL-CIO Convention, Washington, DC, 11/15/89, Case Number 096884," WHORM Speech File, 19415-011, Bush Library.

11. George H. W. Bush speech to AFL-CIO Convention, November 15, 1989, 5, "SP623, AFL-CIO Convention, Washington, DC, 11/15/89," 19415-010, WHORM Speech File, Bush Library; Benedetto, "Bush Courts Labor" (Bywater quotation).

12. AFL-CIO Executive Council Minutes, February 20–24, 1989, 8–9, box 103 (first two quotations); and AFL-CIO Executive Council Minutes, February 19–22, 1990, 7, box 104 (second quotation)—both in AFL-CIO Papers.

13. AFL-CIO Executive Council Minutes, February 18–22, 1991, 13, box 104, AFL-CIO Papers.

14. Kilborn, "Dole Winning Applause," A16; Kenneth Zinn interview.

15. Kilborn, "Dole Winning Applause," A16; John McLauren, "Organized Labor Regrouping after Reagan, Economic Losses," *San Diego Evening Tribune*, January 30, 1989, 8.

16. Laurent Belsie, "Industrial Unions on the Rebound," *Christian Science Monitor*, January 23, 1989, 7; Norton et al., *A People and a Nation*, 950 (Bush quotation); Scott Lautenschlager, "Unions See New Life in the '90s: Membership Has Declined, but Influence Hasn't," *Wisconsin State Journal*, September 3, 1989, 1F (Hagglund quotation).

17. Mary Klaus, "State's Labor Leaders Say Future is Brighter," Harrisburg (PA) *Patriot-News*, September 4, 1988, D1 (Uehlein quotation); "Ohio Labor Leaders Say They See End of Lean Membership Times," Akron (OH) *Beacon Journal*, September 5, 1989, B5 (Lorenzetti quotation); Gary Frank, "WMass Labor Leaders See Growth in the Next Decade," Springfield (MA) *Sunday Republican*, January 22, 1989, F22 (last two quotations).

18. "AFL-CIO Leaders Buoyed by Better Image in Poll," Roanoke (VA) *Times*, February 22, 1990, A9; Ken Ibold, "Last Stand or Comeback? Unions, Experts Disagree," *Palm Beach Post*, September 4, 1989, 16 (Poulette quotation).

19. McLauren, "Organized Labor Regrouping," January 30, 1989, 8; Ost, *Solidarity and the Politics of Anti-Politics*, 205–7 (quotation on 206).

20. "Statement by the AFL-CIO Executive Council on Minimum Wage," May 2, 1989, in AFL-CIO Executive Council Minutes, May 2–3, 1989, A5 (first quotation); and AFL-CIO Executive Council Minutes, May 2–3, 1989, 3 (second quotation)—both in box 103, AFL-CIO Papers.

21. AFL-CIO Executive Council Minutes, August 8–9, 1989, 6, box 103; and AFL-CIO Executive Council Minutes, February 18–22, 1991, 12 (quotation), B5, box 104—both in AFL-CIO Papers; Kilborn, "Dole Winning Applause," A16.

22. AFL-CIO Executive Council Minutes, February 18–22, 1991, 14, box 104, AFL-CIO Papers; Steven A. Holmes, "Bush Vetoes Bill on Family Leave," *New York Times*, June 30, 1990, 1 (Bush quotation).

23. AFL-CIO Executive Council Minutes, July 31–August 1, 1990, 17; and AFL-CIO Executive Council Minutes, February 18–22, 1991, 3–4, 7—both in box 104, AFL-CIO Papers.

24. U.S. Congress, House, Committee on Energy and Commerce, *U.S.-Canada Free Trade Agreement*, 100th Congress, 2nd Session, 1988, 110–11 (first quotation from Rudy Oswald on 111); AFL-CIO Executive Council Minutes, May 23–24, 1990, 18 (other quotation), B2–B3, box 104, AFL-CIO Papers; Minchin, *Empty Mills*, 187.

25. AFL-CIO Executive Council Minutes, February 18–22, 1991, 2 (Sheinkman quotation), 21 (other quotation), box 104, AFL-CIO Papers.

26. AFL-CIO Executive Council Minutes, February 15–18, 1993, C1–C3, box 105, AFL-CIO Papers; Mark Anderson interview.

27. AFL-CIO Executive Council Minutes, May 23–24, 1990, A27, box 104, AFL-CIO Papers (quotations); Patterson, *Restless Giant*, 228.

28. AFL-CIO Executive Council Minutes, February 15–18, 1993, C6, box 105, AFL-CIO Papers.

29. AFL-CIO Executive Council Minutes, May 23–24, 1990, 2, 3, box 104, AFL-CIO Papers (quotations); "Testimony of Thomas R. Donahue, before the U.S. Senate Labor and Human Resources Committee, Amending the National Labor Relations Act and the Railway Labor Act to Prevent Discrimination Based on Participation in Labor Disputes," June 6, 1990, folder 36, box 16, series 30; and "Lane Kirkland Testimony before the U.S. House of Representatives Committee on Education and Labor," March 6, 1991, folder 52, box 16, series 30—both in AFL-CIO Legislative Department Files, RG21-002, AFL-CIO Papers.

30. AFL-CIO Executive Council Minutes, February 18–22, 1991, 15, box 104, AFL-CIO Papers (Bywater quotation); "priority" quotation in M. J. Flynn to Charles Hatcher, April 4, 1991, "Labor Strike (2 of 3)," box 68, series 1, subseries C, Charles F. Hatcher Papers, held at Richard B. Russell Library for Political Research and Studies, University of Georgia, Athens (hereafter cited as "Hatcher Papers"); Peter T. Kilborn, "Replacement Workers: Management's Big Gun," *New York Times*, March 13, 1990, A24.

31. AFL-CIO Executive Council Minutes, May 2–3, 1989, 3, box 103, AFL-CIO Papers.

32. AFL-CIO Executive Council Minutes, February 19–22, 1990, 10 (McGlotten quotation), 28 (Kirkland quotations), box 104, AFL-CIO Papers.

33. AFL-CIO Executive Council Minutes, July 31–August 1, 1990, 13–14, box 104, AFL-CIO Papers.

34. AFL-CIO Executive Council Minutes, February 18–22, 1991, 5, box 104, AFL-CIO Papers.

35. J. C. Rowe to George Darden, August 31, 1990, and Joe G. Tippett to George Darden, August 18, 1990—both in folder 8, box 42, series 1, George W. "Buddy" Darden Papers, held at Richard B. Russell Library for Political Research and Studies, University of Georgia, Athens (hereafter cited as "Darden Papers"); AFL-CIO Executive Council Minutes, February 18–22, 1991, A1, box 104, AFL-CIO Papers (closing quotation).

36. "Breeder" quotation in Frank Swoboda, "Bill Banning Permanent Replacement of Strikers Faces Test," *Washington Post*, July 17, 1991, D1; "Co-Sponsors of H.R. 5 as of February 8, 1991," in AFL-CIO Executive Council Minutes, February 18–22, 1991, A3–A5, box 104, AFL-CIO Papers.

37. Abit Massey to Charles Hatcher, April 24, 1991, Wayne W. Purvis to Charles Hatcher, April 22, 1991 (quotation), Carey K. Williamson III to Charles Hatcher, April 9, 1991, and Don Dalton to Charles F. Hatcher, March 29, 1991—all in folder 1, box 68, series 1, Hatcher Papers.

38. Hugh Sawyer to Charles Hatcher, June 7, 1991, folder 1, box 68, series 1, Hatcher Papers (quotation); form reply of J. Roy Rowland, n.d., folder 26, box 50, series 3, J. Roy Rowland Papers, held at Richard B. Russell Library for Political Research and Studies, University of Georgia, Athens (hereafter cited as "Rowland Papers").

39. Albert R. Karr, "Bill to Bar the Permanent Replacement of Strikers is Cleared by House, 247–182," *Wall Street Journal*, July 18, 1991, A2; AFL-CIO Executive Council Minutes, May 5–6, 1992, 6, box 105, AFL-CIO Papers (quotation).

40. Minchin, "'It Tears the Heart Right out of You': Memories of Striker Replacement at International Paper Company in De Pere, Wisconsin, 1987–88," *Oral History Review* 31, no. 2 (Summer–Fall 2004): 26; Tom Donahue interview (2013); George Kourpias interview.

41. AFL-CIO Executive Council Minutes, November 11, 1989, 3–4, box 103, AFL-CIO Papers.

42. Joe Uehlein interview.

43. AFL-CIO Executive Council Minutes, August 8–9, 1989, 8–9 (first quotation on 8), box 103, AFL-CIO Papers; Kirkland quotation in "Labor Leaders Arrested at Rally Backing Union Workers on Strike," *New York Times*, August 25, 1989.

44. Kenneth Zinn interview; Richard Trumka interview. For more insight into the Pittston strike, especially the legal and civil disobedience tactics used by the strikers, see Brisbin Jr., *A Strike Like No Other Strike.*

45. AFL-CIO Executive Council Minutes, May 2–3, 1989, 2, box 103, AFL-CIO Papers (quotations); AFL-CIO Executive Council Minutes, February 19–22, 1990, 25, box 104, AFL-CIO Papers.

46. Richard Trumka interview; AFL-CIO Executive Council Minutes, May 23–24, 1990, A19 (third quotation); AFL-CIO Executive Council Minutes, May 8, 1991, 5 (fourth and fifth quotations)—both in box 104, AFL-CIO Papers.

47. AFL-CIO Executive Council Minutes, August 8–9, 1989, 10, box 103, AFL-CIO Papers.

48. Joe Uehlein interview; Juravich and Bronfenbrenner, *Ravenswood,* ix–xi (quotation in title), 193–95.

49. AFL-CIO Executive Council Minutes, February 19–22, 1990, 11, D9, box 104, AFL-CIO Papers.

50. Minchin, *Forging a Common Bond,* 1–3, 24–37, 143; Richard Donaldson interview; "Resolution on Union Victories," January 5, 1990, "Incoming Correspondence," box 3, Oil, Chemical, and Atomic Workers' International Union (OCAW) Local 4-620 Papers, PACE Local 4-620, Gonzales, Louisiana.

51. Juravich and Bronfenbrenner, *Ravenswood,* xi; Minchin, *Forging a Common Bond,* 1–2, 139, 148, 150; Joe Uehlein interview.

52. AFL-CIO Executive Council Minutes, May 23–24, 1990, 9, A18, box 104, AFL-CIO Papers; Peter T. Kilborn, "Money Isn't Everything in Greyhound Strike," *New York Times,* April 9, 1990.

53. AFL-CIO Executive Council Minutes, February 18–22, 1991, 38, box 104, AFL-CIO Papers; "Strikers at Greyhound Feel Forgotten," *New York Times,* March 4, 1991 (quotation); Frank Swoboda, "Battle over Striker Replacement Bill Resuming; Neither Organized Labor nor Management Seems Willing to Compromise," *Washington Post,* April 22, 1993, B11.

54. "Statement by the AFL-CIO Executive Council on the Eastern Air Lines Strike," May 3, 1989, in AFL-CIO Executive Council Minutes, May 2–3, 1989, B1, box 108, AFL-CIO Papers.

55. Clay Warnock to George (Buddy) Darden, February 20, 1989, folder 4, box 26, Darden Papers.

56. AFL-CIO Executive Council Minutes, February 20–24, 1989, 5, box 103, AFL-CIO Papers (first quotation); "For Labor, Eastern is Chance to Stem Decline," *Philadelphia Daily News,* March 7, 1989, 3 (other quotations).

57. AFL-CIO Executive Council Minutes, August 8–9, 1989, 8, box 103, AFL-CIO Papers ("distributed" quotation); "Statement by the AFL-CIO Executive Council on the Eastern Air Lines Strike," May 3, 1989, in AFL-CIO Executive Council Minutes, May 2–3, 1989, B1, B3, box 103, AFL-CIO Papers; AFL-CIO Executive Council Minutes, May 2–3, 1989, 10–12, box 103, AFL-CIO Papers ("demonstrate" quotation on 11); Paulette Thomas, Bob Davis, and John E. Yang, "Airline Backfire: Texas Air Triggered

Investigation of Itself with Shuttle Gambit—Lorenzo Plan Led Regulators to Worry about Viability of Remainder of Eastern," *Wall Street Journal*, April 15, 1988, 1.

58. Roger B. Porter to William H. Bywater, November 29, 1989, document number 091438 (LA005-15), WHORM Files, Bush Library.

59. See, for example, Perry J. Chapin to George Bush, March 8, 1989, document number 024978 (LA005-15), WHORM Files, Bush Library.

60. Lowell Dietz to Buddy Darden, March 10, 1989, folder 4, box 26, series 1, Darden Papers (Dietz quotations); AFL-CIO Executive Council Minutes, February 19–22, 1990, 8, box 104, AFL-CIO Papers (Kirkland quotation).

61. AFL-CIO Executive Council Minutes, July 31–August 1, 1990, 8; and AFL-CIO Executive Council Minutes, February 18–22, 1991, 38 (quotations)—both in box 104, AFL-CIO Papers.

62. Joan O'Rourke to Ed Jenkins, June 8, 1991, "Eastern Airlines Benefits 1991," box 43, series 2, Edgar L. Jenkins Papers, held at Richard B. Russell Library for Political Research and Studies, University of Georgia, Athens; Stewart Acuff interview.

63. AFL-CIO Executive Council Minutes, May 2–3, 1989, 4; and AFL-CIO Executive Council Minutes, August 8–9, 1989, 1–2—both in box 103, AFL-CIO Papers.

64. Richard Trumka interview (Trumka quotation); "UMW Rejoins AFL-CIO to End 42-Year Break," Lexington (KY) *Herald-Leader*, October 13, 1989, D7 (Kirkland quotation); Frank Swoboda, "Mine Workers Decide to Affiliate with AFL-CIO," *Washington Post*, October 5, 1989, A4, clipping in "AFL-CIO Convention, 11/13/89," Office of Speechwriting Files, 13694-008, Bush Library (other quotations); Lichtenstein, *State of the Union*, 249–50; Lane Kirkland to Sigurd Lucassen, May 13, 1994, in AFL-CIO Executive Council Minutes Files (1995), box 1, AR2002-0106, AFL-CIO Papers.

65. AFL-CIO Executive Council Minutes, February 20–24, 1989, 14–15, box 103, AFL-CIO Papers; George H. W. Bush speech to AFL-CIO Convention, November 15, 1989, 2, "SP623, AFL-CIO Convention, Washington, DC, 11/15/89," 19415-010, WHORM Speech File, Bush Library.

66. AFL-CIO Executive Council Minutes, November 16, 1989, 3, box 103; and AFL-CIO Executive Council Minutes, May 23–24, 1990, 4, box 104—both in AFL-CIO Papers.

67. AFL-CIO Executive Council Minutes, February 20–24, 1989, 34, box 103, AFL-CIO Papers.

68. Ibid.; AFL-CIO Executive Council Minutes, February 15–18, 1993, 34, box 106, AFL-CIO Papers.

69. Robert Pear, "Gaps in Coverage for Health Care," *New York Times*, March 29, 1994, D23; Kirkland quoted in "Testimony of Lane Kirkland before the Senate Finance Committee on National Health Care Reform," April 9, 1991, folder 56, box 16, series 30, AFL-CIO Legislative Department Files, RG21-002, AFL-CIO Papers.

70. AFL-CIO Executive Council Minutes, February 18–22, 1991, 2 (Trumka quotation), 7 ("strong support" quotation), 8, box 104, AFL-CIO Papers.

71. AFL-CIO Executive Council Minutes, February 18–22, 1991, B2, box 104, AFL-CIO Papers.

72. AFL-CIO Executive Council Minutes, February 20–24, 1989, 21, box 103, AFL-CIO Papers; AFL-CIO Executive Council Minutes, May 8, 1991, 9, box 104, AFL-CIO Papers (quotations).

73. AFL-CIO Executive Council Minutes, February 15–18, 1993, 2, box 105, AFL-CIO Papers.

74. AFL-CIO Executive Council Minutes, February 18–22, 1991, 22, C9 (closing quotation), box 104, AFL-CIO Papers.

75. Frank Swoboda, "Pro-Labor Rally Set for Mall: Organizers Expect More Than 200,000," *Washington Post*, August 30, 1991, D1; Frank Swoboda and Saundra Torry, "Labor Sends Politicians a Message Hundreds of Thousands Strong," *Washington Post*, September 1, 1991, A1 (quotations); "Many Faces, One Voice," *AFL-CIO News*, September 9, 1991, 5.

76. Swoboda, "Pro-Labor Rally Set," D1; Swoboda and Torry, "Labor Sends Politicians a Message," A1 (quotations); "Many Faces," 5.

77. Extensive searches in newspaper databases found almost no articles on this mass march. Only the *Washington Post* gave it detailed coverage, particularly in Swoboda and Torry, "Labor Sends Politicians a Message," A1.

78. Paul Ruffins, "Why American Unions Believe Their Future Is Now," *Washington Post*, September 1, 1991, C5; closing quotation in Swoboda and Torry, "Labor Sends Politicians a Message," A1.

79. Jeff Gerth, "Thousands Rally in Washington, Calling for Action on Social Issues," *New York Times*, September 1, 1991, 1; quotations in Swoboda and Torry, "Labor Sends Politicians a Message," A1.

80. AFL-CIO Executive Council Minutes, February 18–22, 1991, 22, box 104, AFL-CIO Papers.

81. Swoboda and Torry, "Labor Sends Politicians a Message," A1.

82. "Solidarity III" resolution in AFL-CIO Executive Council Minutes, February 15–18, 1993, D18–19, box 106, AFL-CIO Papers.

83. Margaret "Peg" Seminario interview; Report of the AFL-CIO Executive Council, November 13–16, 1989, 5.

84. Arlee C. Green, "The Workplace: Forgotten Environment," *AFL-CIO News*, April 16, 1990, 1; Margaret "Peg" Seminario interview (quotation).

85. AFL-CIO Executive Council Minutes, February 21–24, 1994, 24, box 105 (quotation); and AFL-CIO Executive Council Minutes, May 23–24, 1990, A9, box 104—both in AFL-CIO Papers.

86. AFL-CIO Executive Council Minutes, February 21–24, 1994, 24, box 105; AFL-CIO Executive Council Minutes, May 9–10, 1995, 9, box 108; "Testimony of Margaret Seminario before the House Education and Labor Committee on the Imperial Food Products Fire and Reform of the Occupational Safety and Health Act," September 12, 1991, folder 83, box 16, series 30, AFL-CIO Legislative Department Files, RG21-002 ("awful truth" quotation)—all in AFL-CIO Papers; Margaret "Peg" Seminario interview (other quotations).

87. AFL-CIO Executive Council Minutes, May 2–3, 1989, 15, box 103, AFL-CIO Papers (first quotation); Richard Bensinger interview (other quotations).

88. AFL-CIO Executive Council Minutes, May 2–3, 1989, 15, box 103 ("antiunion" quotation); and AFL-CIO Executive Council Minutes, February 18–22, 1991, 17, box 104 ("membership" quotation)—both in AFL-CIO Papers; Richard Bensinger interview (other quotations).

89. Richard Bensinger interview.

90. Proceedings of the 1989 AFL-CIO Convention, November 13–16, 1989, 323–24 (Sweeney quotation on 323); AFL-CIO Executive Council Minutes, February 19–22, 1990, 18, 20 (Kuschke quotation), box 104, AFL-CIO Papers; Clawson, *The Next Upsurge*, 81–83 ("it's not" quotation on 83).

91. Dave Hage, "Unions Launching New, Aggressive Organizing Efforts," *Minneapolis Star Tribune*, May 23, 1988, 1A; Clawson, *The Next Upsurge* (quotation in title), 89; Proceedings of the 1991 AFL-CIO Convention, November 11–14, 1991, 319. For another example of the positive press coverage produced by the Harvard victory, see Allan R. Gold, "Union's Victory at Harvard Seen as Spur to Labor Drive," *New York Times*, May 19, 1988, 150.

92. John Sweeney, "Report of the AFL-CIO Executive Council Committee on Organizing," February 21–22, 1990, in AFL-CIO Executive Council Minutes, February 21–22, 1990, C57–C61 (quotations); and AFL-CIO Executive Council Minutes, May 23–24, 1990, 13—both in box 104, AFL-CIO Papers.

93. AFL-CIO Executive Council Minutes, August 3–4, 1993, 6; and AFL-CIO Executive Council Minutes, February 20–23, 1995, 31—both in box 105, AFL-CIO Papers.

94. Report of the AFL-CIO Executive Council to the 1991 Constitutional Convention, 99 (first two quotations); Proceedings of the 1989 AFL-CIO Convention, November 13–16, 1989, 324 (third quotation).

95. AFL-CIO Executive Council Minutes, July 31–August 1, 1990, 15, box 104, AFL-CIO Papers; Richard Bensinger interview; David Moberg, "Labor Debates Its Future," *The Nation*, March 14, 2005, 12.

96. Report of the Building and Construction Trades Department (1990), 64, in AFL-CIO Executive Council Minutes, July 31–August 1, 1990, box 104, AFL-CIO Papers; Proceedings of the 1991 AFL-CIO Convention, November 11–14, 1991, 319, 320 (first two quotations); AFL-CIO Executive Council Minutes, February 18–22, 1991, 16, box 104, AFL-CIO Papers; other quotation in Tom Donahue interview (2015).

97. AFL-CIO Executive Council Minutes, February 19–22, 1990, 18, box 104, AFL-CIO Papers; Nick Atkins interview.

98. Sweeney, "Report of the AFL-CIO Executive Council," C57–C61, box 104, AFL-CIO Papers.

99. "More Women Are Joining Unions," Madison (WI) *Capital Times*, February 8, 1990, 21; Karen Nussbaum interview.

100. AFL-CIO Executive Council Minutes, November 5, 1992; and AFL-CIO Executive Council Minutes, February 15–18, 1993, 32—both in box 105, AFL-CIO Papers;

Frank Swoboda, "Women Aspiring to Union Leadership Roles Find Limits There Too," *Washington Post*, February 14, 1993, H2.

101. Susan Bianchi interview.

102. Barbara Easterling interview; "AFL-CIO Reelects Kirkland," *New York Times*, November 14, 1991, A20.

103. AFL-CIO Executive Council Minutes, August 8–9, 1989, 3, box 103, AFL-CIO Papers; Liz Shuler interview.

104. "Report of the AFL-CIO Committee on Reproductive Issues," July 31, 1990, A3–A8 (quotations on A6–A7), box 104, AFL-CIO Papers.

105. Kilborn, "Back Abortion Rights," clipping in untitled folder, box OS12, RG95-007, Lane Kirkland Files, AFL-CIO Papers.

106. AFL-CIO Executive Council Minutes, February 18–22, 1991, 29–30, box 104, AFL-CIO Papers.

107. Tindall and Shi, *America*, 1258–62; David St. John interview.

108. AFL-CIO Executive Council Minutes, February 20–24, 1989, 12–13 (Walesa quotations); AFL-CIO Executive Council Minutes, May 2–3, 1989, 7 (Kuron quotation)—both in box 103, AFL-CIO Papers.

109. Proceedings of the 1989 AFL-CIO Convention, November 13–16, 1989, 124–30 (quotations on 124, 125, 130).

110. AFL-CIO Executive Council Minutes, February 19–22, 1990, 14, C40–C41, box 104, AFL-CIO Papers.

111. Magda Lynn Seymour and Michael Byrne, "Unions Give Nelson Mandela a Hero's Welcome," *AFL-CIO News*, July 9, 1990, 1 (Mandela quotation); AFL-CIO Executive Council Minutes, July 31–August 1, 1990, 12–13, box 104, AFL-CIO Papers; Kenneth Zinn interview.

112. Transcript of the Proceedings of the AFL-CIO General Board Meeting, September 3, 1992, 2, 9–10, 15–16, box 1, AR2002-0106, AFL-CIO Papers.

Chapter Seven

1. "Years of Devastation," *AFL-CIO News*, August 31, 1992, 6; AFL-CIO Executive Council Minutes, February 17–20, 1992, A1, box 105, AFL-CIO Papers (other quotations).

2. John F. Meese et al. to William J. Clinton, May 20, 1996, Clinton White House Archived Websites available from the Clinton Presidential Library Online (hereafter cited as "Clinton Library") at http://www.clintonlibrary.gov/_previous/KAGAN%20COUNSEL/Counsel%20%20Box%20008%20-%20Folder%20010.pdf (accessed August 6, 2013); Gerry Shea interview (quotations).

3. Transcript of the Proceedings of the AFL-CIO General Board Meeting, September 3, 1992, 27 (Kirkland quotation); and A. L. "Mike" Moore to Thomas R. Donahue, September 4, 1992, in "1992 General Board Meeting Minutes," September 3, 1992—both in box 1, AR2002-0106, AFL-CIO Papers (Moore quotations); "Bill Clinton: He's On Our Side," *AFL-CIO News*, September 14, 1992, 1 (closing quotations).

4. Transcript of the Proceedings of the AFL-CIO General Board Meeting, September 3, 1992, 19–20, 25, 26, box 1, AR2002-0106, AFL-CIO Papers.

5. AFL-CIO Executive Council Minutes, November 5, 1992, 1–2, box 105, AFL-CIO Papers.

6. "Labor Shares Clinton Victory," *AFL-CIO News*, November 9, 1992, 1; AFL-CIO Executive Council Minutes, May 4–5, 1993, 5, box 106, AFL-CIO Papers (Carey quotation); "Labor Agenda Rises to Top of Capitol Hill," *AFL-CIO News*, February 1, 1993, 1 (final two quotations).

7. AFL-CIO Executive Council Minutes, November 5, 1992, 5, 7, box 105, AFL-CIO Papers.

8. AFL-CIO Executive Council Minutes, February 15–18, 1993, 24, box 106, AFL-CIO Papers.

9. Ibid., 8, 11.

10. Ibid., 7; Lane Kirkland, interview by James F. Shea and Don R. Kienzle, November 13, 1996, 36, Labor Diplomacy Oral History Project, transcript in folder 8, box 4, RG95-007, Lane Kirkland Files, AFL-CIO Papers (Kirkland quotation); closing quotation in "A Report to the President on Progress in Labor-Management Partnerships" (National Partnership Council Document), December 1997, available from the Clinton Library at http://www.clintonlibrary.gov/assets/DigitalLibrary /AdminHIstories/Box%2051-060/Box%2054/1505033-opm-office-merit-systems -oversight-effectiveness-5.pdf (accessed August 5, 2013).

11. Report to the 1993 Convention from the AFL-CIO Executive Council, October 4–7, 1993, 125 (first quotation), 145; Donahue quoted in U.S. Congress, House, Committee on Education and Labor, *The Parental and Medical Leave Act of 1986*, 99th Congress, 2nd session, 1986, 12; Susan Chira, "Family Leave is Law; Will Things Change?" *New York Times*, August 15, 1993, A3; Gallup poll and Gephardt quotation in Adam Clymer, "Family-Leave Bill Sent to President," *New York Times*, September 11, 1992, A26; "Five Years of Success: Report on the Family and Medical Leave Act," in "A History of the U.S. Department of Labor during the Clinton Administration, 1993– 2001," Clinton Administration Oral History Project, 2000, appendices [3], L0017–L0022, available from the Clinton Library at http://www.clintonlibrary.gov/assets/storage /Research%20-%20Digital%20Library/ClintonAdminHistoryProject/31-40/Box%2033 /1497349-department-of-labor-appendices-3.pdf (accessed September 8, 2013).

12. Kirkland quoted in Kirkland, interview, Lane Kirkland Files, AFL-CIO Papers; Clinton quoted in "A History of the U.S. Department of Labor during the Clinton Administration, 1993–2001," Clinton Administration Oral History Project, 2000, appendices [3], L0001, Clinton Library.

13. AFL-CIO Executive Council Minutes, February 15–18, 1993, 12, box 106; and AFL-CIO Executive Council Minutes, February 20–23, 1995, A9, box 108—both in AFL-CIO Papers; Richard W. Stevenson, "Clinton Signs a Bill Raising Minimum Wage by 90 Cents," *New York Times*, August 21, 1996, B6; "financial independence" quotation in "A History of the U.S. Department of Labor during the Clinton Administration,

1993–2001," Clinton Administration Oral History Project, 2000, 8, Clinton Library; Christine Owens interview.

14. John R. Oravec, "Workers Win Gold with Olympics Pact," *AFL-CIO News*, July 26, 1993, 1; Acuff, *Playing Bigger Than You Are*, 41–42 (quotations on 42).

15. AFL-CIO Executive Council Minutes, February 21–24, 1994, 10, box 107, AFL-CIO Papers; McCartin, *Collision Course*, 356–58 (quotations).

16. Tom Donahue interview (2013); Kirkland, interview, Lane Kirkland Files, AFL-CIO Papers.

17. AFL-CIO Executive Council Minutes, May 4–5, 1993, 1, 9 (quotation), box 106, AFL-CIO Papers.

18. AFL-CIO Executive Council Minutes, May 4–5, 1993, 1, 9 (first quotation), 13 (McGlotten quotation), box 106, AFL-CIO Papers; Peter T. Kilborn, "Unions Gird for War over Trade Pact," *New York Times*, October 4, 1993, A14.

19. Karen Nussbaum interview; Barbara Shailor interview; Steve Rosenthal interview.

20. AFL-CIO Executive Council Minutes, May 4–5, 1993, 2, 19, box 106; AFL-CIO Executive Council Minutes, August 3–4, 1993, 23, box 106; AFL-CIO Executive Council Minutes, February 21–24, 1994, 19, box 107 ("excellent" quotation)—all in AFL-CIO Papers.

21. AFL-CIO Executive Council Minutes, August 3–4, 1993, 1–2, box 106, AFL-CIO Papers; Linda Chavez-Thompson interview.

22. AFL-CIO Executive Council Minutes, February 21–24, 1994, 7 (first quotation); and AFL-CIO Executive Council Minutes, May 10–11, 1994, 20 (second quotation)—both in box 107, AFL-CIO Papers.

23. AFL-CIO Executive Council Minutes, May 4–5, 1993, 8–9; and AFL-CIO Executive Council Minutes, October 2, 1993, A23 ("good for" quotation)—both in box 106, AFL-CIO Papers; Patterson, *Restless Giant*, 329 ("managed competition" quotation); closing quotations in Thomas L. Friedman, "President Confers with Labor Leader for Fence Mending," *New York Times*, December 11, 1993, 1.

24. AFL-CIO Executive Council Minutes, May 4–5, 1993, 10, box 106, AFL-CIO Papers; AFL-CIO Executive Council Minutes, February 21–24, 1994, 22, box 107, AFL-CIO Papers; "Cost Benefit Analysis of Selected Elements of the AFL-CIO Health Care Reform Campaign," n.d., and "AFL-CIO Health Care Reform Field Operations 1993–1994," November 12, 1994 ("boiler room" quotation)—material supplied to the author by Charles Stott (copy in the author's possession).

25. AFL-CIO Executive Council Minutes, May 10–11, 1994, 3, box 107, AFL-CIO Papers (Stott quotation); "Health Care for All, if Congress Doesn't Weaken," *New York Times*, March 6, 1994, E14 (Cleary quotation).

26. AFL-CIO Executive Council Minutes, May 10–11, 1994, 1, 2, box 107, AFL-CIO Papers; "AFL-CIO Health Care Reform Field Operations 1993–1994," November 12, 1994, document supplied to author by Charles Stott (copy in author's possession).

27. "Why Business Hates Clinton," *Business Week*, October 10, 1994, 38–39; AFL-CIO Executive Council Minutes, February 21–24, 1994, 22, box 107, AFL-CIO Papers.

28. "Even Cheerleaders Get the Blues," *Business Week*, May 30, 1994, 60; Lloyd Z. Beasley and Theresa Beasley to J. Roy Rowland, October 22, 1993, and Scott W. Brown to J. Roy Rowland, October 16, 1993—both in folder 1, box 149, series 2, Rowland Papers.

29. "Cost Benefit Analysis of Selected Elements of the AFL-CIO Health Care Reform Campaign," material supplied to the author by Charles Stott (copy in the author's possession); "Even Cheerleaders," 60; Charles Stott interview ("poisoned" quotation); Patterson, *Restless Giant*, 329–30; closing quotation in AFL-CIO Executive Council Minutes, May 10–11, 1994, 3; and AFL-CIO Executive Council Minutes, August 9–10, 1994, 7–8—both in box 107, AFL-CIO Papers.

30. AFL-CIO Executive Council Minutes, February 20–23, 1995, 7 (Gore quotation); and AFL-CIO Executive Council Minutes, February 20–23, 1995, 14—both in box 108, AFL-CIO Papers.

31. AFL-CIO Executive Council Minutes, February 20–23, 1995, A10, box 108, AFL-CIO Papers; Susan Dunlop interview (2013); Charles Stott interview.

32. Zieger, *American Workers, American Unions*, 2nd ed., 203; Karl Kahler, "Dissolving the Borders on Trade," San Jose (CA) *Mercury News*, October 3, 1993, 20A; Cynthia Mitchell, "Textile, Apparel Industries Now Favor Free Trade," *Atlanta Journal-Constitution*, October 1, 1992, D1.

33. "Address by the President of Mexico, Carlos Salinas de Gortari, during the annual meeting of the American Society of Newspaper Editors" (at Harvard University), April 10, 1991, "Trade-US-Mexico FTA and Fast Track Extension Parts 1 and 2," box 33, Marilyn Lloyd Papers, held at Lupton Library, University of Tennessee at Chattanooga (hereafter cited as the "Lloyd Papers"); "Text of Remarks by the President on the Enterprise for Americas Address," June 27, 1990 (Bush quotation), "GATT," box 8, series 5780/150, International Ladies' Garment Workers' Union (ILGWU) Papers-Cornell (held at Kheel Center); Stuart Auerbach, "Farm, Textile and Labor Groups Oppose Goals of Bush, Big Business," *Washington Post*, March 2, 1991, A8.

34. AFL-CIO Executive Council Minutes, February 15–18, 1993, C1, box 105, AFL-CIO Papers (first quotation); Gwen Ifill, "Clinton is Pressed to Take Stand on Pact," *New York Times*, September 7, 1992, 9 ("right kind" quotation); "Clinton Criticizes Provisions in Trade Pact," *New York Times*, September 11, 1992, A31 (other quotations).

35. AFL-CIO Executive Council Minutes, May 4–5, 1993, 8, box 105, AFL-CIO Papers (Kirkland quotations); closing Clinton quotations in *Public Papers of the Presidents of the United States: Administration of William J. Clinton* (Washington, DC: U.S. Government Printing Office, 1993), 210.

36. AFL-CIO Executive Council Minutes, August 3–4, 1993, 20, box 105, AFL-CIO Papers.

37. Lane Kirkland, "A Trade Marriage Made in Heaven," *Washington Post*, May 19, 1993, A19; Clinton quoted in Keith Bradsher, "Last Call to Arms on the Trade Pact," *New York Times*, August 23, 1993, D1.

38. Zieger and Gall, *American Workers, American Unions*, 264.

39. AFL-CIO Executive Council Minutes, August 3–4, 1993, 20–21, box 105, AFL-CIO Papers (Anderson quotations); Bradsher, "Last Call to Arms," D1.

40. Tom Donahue interview (2013); George Kourpias interview.

41. Kevin Goldman, "NAFTA Supporters and Foes Pitch Views to Public in Ad Campaigns," *Wall Street Journal*, September 16, 1993, B6; "NAFTA" *Business Week*, September 13, 1993, 26 (first quotation); U.S. Chamber of Commerce, "North American Free Trade Agreement: Implications for U.S. Business," September 1991, i, "NAFTA B," box 33, Lloyd Papers ("create" quotation); P. Jack Davis to Don Johnson, November 1, 1993, folder 17, box 1, series 1, Don Johnson Papers, held at Richard B. Russell Library for Political Research and Studies, University of Georgia, Athens (hereafter cited as "Johnson Papers").

42. AFL-CIO Executive Council Minutes, May 4–5, 1993, 7 (first quotation); and AFL-CIO Executive Council Minutes, February 21–24, 1994, 29 (other quotations)—both in box 105, AFL-CIO Papers.

43. "The 1992 Campaign: Transcript of 3rd TV Debate between Bush, Clinton and Perot," *New York Times*, October 20, 1992, 20 (quotation); Bradsher, "Last Call to Arms," 1; Chafe, *Unfinished Journey*, 7th ed., 482–83, 488.

44. "Why Are Multinational Corporations and the Mexican Government Spending Over $50 Million to Push NAFTA through Congress?" (AFL-CIO and Citizens Trade Campaign advertisement), *Washington Post*, November 10, 1993, A24.

45. Mark Anderson interview.

46. Kilborn, "Unions Gird for War," A14; "Organizing Guide to Defeat NAFTA," n.d., "9–10 NAFTA Action Items," box 9, Frontlash Records, 1968–1997, RG50-001, AFL-CIO Papers (quotations).

47. Frank Swoboda, "President Woos Labor on NAFTA; Unions Tap Job Fears in Leading Opposition," *Washington Post*, October 5, 1993, C1.

48. Ibid.; Peter T. Kilborn, "The Free Trade Accord; Little Voices Roar in the Chorus of Trade-Pact Foes," *New York Times*, November 13, 1993, 1; "NAFTA The SHAFTA" button in oversize box 3, RG95-007, Lane Kirkland Files, AFL-CIO Papers; Kirkland quoted in Lane Kirkland to Trade Unionists, n.d., Anderson Papers.

49. Frank Swoboda, "Kirkland: No Compromise on NAFTA," *Washington Post*, September 1, 1993, F3.

50. Kilborn, "The Free Trade Accord," 1.

51. Frank Swoboda, "President Woos Labor," C1; Doug Dority interview; two closing quotations in Gwen Ifill, "Clinton Defends Trade Pact to Skeptical AFL-CIO," *New York Times*, October 5, 1993, B10.

52. Thomas L. Friedman, "The Free Trade Accord: The President; Adamant Unions Zero in on Clinton," *New York Times*, November 16, 1993, B10; "NAFTA: Who Wins? Who Loses?" (display ad), *Washington Post*, November 17, 1993, A20.

53. Friedman, "The Free Trade Accord," B10.

54. Swoboda, "Kirkland: No Compromise," F3.

55. Jill Abramson and Bob Davis, "Expensive Battle over NAFTA Has Each Side Claiming Its Being Outgunned and Outspent," *Wall Street Journal*, November 15, 1993, A14; NAFTA vote breakdown in *AFL-CIO News*, November 29, 1993, 7; Mark

Anderson interview; Kirkland quoted in "AFL-CIO Press Conference" (transcript), November 18, 1993, Anderson Papers.

56. Clinton quoted in "Press Conference by the President," November 10, 1993, available from the Clinton Library at http://www.clintonlibrary.gov/assets/storage/Research%20 %20Digital%20Library/Reed%20Crime/77/647420-potus-speeches.pdf (accessed August 6, 2013, copy in author's possession); Kirkland quoted in "AFL-CIO Press Conference" (transcript), November 18, 1993, Anderson Papers; Doug Dority interview.

57. Al Gore to Buddy Darden, November 17, 1993, and Michael Kantor to George Darden—both in November 23, 1993, folder 10, box 92, series 2, Darden Papers.

58. "Why Business," 40; AFL-CIO Executive Council Minutes, February 21–24, 1994, 6–7, box 105, AFL-CIO Papers.

59. Sheinkman quoted in "AFL-CIO Press Conference" (transcript), November 18, 1993, Anderson Papers; Tom Donahue interview (2013); George Kourpias interview.

60. AFL-CIO Executive Council Minutes, February 21–24, 1994, 7–10 (all quotations on 9 and 10), box 105, AFL-CIO Papers.

61. Thomas L. Friedman, "President Confers with Labor," 1 (quotations); AFL-CIO Executive Council Minutes, May 10–11, 1994, 4, box 105, AFL-CIO Papers.

62. Mark Anderson interview; closing quotation in Michael Byrne, "Clinton-Republican Coalition Passes NAFTA," *AFL-CIO News*, November 29, 1993, 1.

63. Frank Swoboda, "Battle over Striker Replacement Bill Resuming; Neither Organized Labor nor Management Seem Willing to Compromise on Issue," *Washington Post*, April 22, 1993, B11 (first two quotations); AFL-CIO Executive Council Minutes, February 20–23, 1995, D14, box 108, AFL-CIO Papers (other quotations).

64. Congressional testimony extracted in Michael Byrne, "Story of Hope: Strikebreaker Use 'Defies Morality, Justice,'" *AFL-CIO News*, April 12, 1993, 4 (Landmesser and Fulwider quotations); Gregory A. Patterson and Robert L. Rose, "Showdown: Labor Makes a Stand in Fight for Its Future at Caterpillar Inc.," *Wall Street Journal*, April 7, 1992, A1 (closing quotation).

65. For an example of the union power-grab allegation, see Robert T. Thompson, "An Anti-Worker Labor Bill," *Wall Street Journal*, August 31, 1990, A10.

66. "Donahue, Reich Rebut Foes of Workplace Fairness," *AFL-CIO News*, April 12, 1993, 4; Clay quoted in Conrad O. Spratlin to Don Johnson, April 12, 1993, "H.R. 5 Striker Replacement Bill," box 2, series 1, subseries B, Johnson Papers.

67. AFL-CIO Executive Council Minutes, May 4–5, 1993, 4, box 106, AFL-CIO Papers.

68. AFL-CIO Executive Council Minutes, October 2, 1993, A22, box 106, AFL-CIO Papers.

69. Swoboda, "Battle over Striker," B11 (Lunnie quotation); Frank Swoboda, "AFL-CIO Begins Campaign on Replacement Workers," *Washington Post*, June 21, 1991, F2; John R. Poole to Don Johnson, April 22, 1993, folder 21, box 2, series 1, Johnson Papers; Thompson, "An Anti-Worker," A10.

70. 1993 Voting Record, First Session—103rd Congress (American Federation of Government Employees document), folder 88, box 33, series 2, Johnson Papers.

71. AFL-CIO Executive Council Minutes, February 21–24, 1994, 4–5, box 107, AFL-CIO Papers.

72. AFL-CIO Executive Council Minutes, August 9–10, 1994, 4, box 107, AFL-CIO Papers; Fairclough quoted in Helen Dewar, "Senate Fails to Break Filibuster on Striker Replacement Bill," *Washington Post,* July 13, 1994, A6; Ernest F. Hollings to Harry Gibson, May 9, 1991, and Ted Maness to David Rudd, June 23, 1992—both in "Striker Replacement," box 422, Ernest F. Hollings Papers, held at the South Carolina Political Collections Library, University of South Carolina, Columbia; Tom Donahue interview (2013).

73. AFL-CIO Executive Council Minutes, February 20–23, 1995, 7, box 108, AFL-CIO Papers; Asra Q. Nomani, "Clinton Bans Use of Firms that Replace Strikers; GOP and Business Vow Battle," *Wall Street Journal,* March 9, 1995, A5; Peter T. Kilborn, "Clinton Order Discouraging Striker Replacement is Voided," *New York Times,* February 3, 1996. In their 1996 ruling, a three-judge panel of the U.S. Court of Appeals for the District of Columbia held that the president's order had the effect of undermining the 1935 National Labor Relations Act, under which the courts had held that employers could permanently replace strikers.

74. Doug Dority interview; AFL-CIO Executive Council Minutes, August 9–10, 1994, 3–4, box 107, AFL-CIO Papers; McCurry quoted in Nomani, "Clinton Bans Use," *Wall Street Journal,* March 9, 1995, A5.

75. Wayne Glenn interview.

76. AFL-CIO Executive Council Minutes, February 21–24, 1994, 6, box 105, AFL-CIO Papers.

77. Dale Kueter, "Unions Looking for Strike Bill, Health Care Reform," *The Gazette* (Cedar Rapids-Iowa City), January 9, 1994, 4; George Kourpias interview.

78. Clinton quoted in "Statement of the President in Response to Rep. Gephardt's Decision to Support the Uruguay Round Implementing Legislation," December 21, 1993, available from the Clinton Library at http://clinton6.nara.gov/1993/12/1993-12-21-presidents-statement-on-gephardt-support-of-gatt.html (accessed August 29, 2010); "Statement of Thomas R. Donahue," Senate Commerce, Science, and Transportation Committee on the Uruguay Round of Implementing Legislation, October 14, 1994, Anderson Papers (AFL-CIO quotation).

79. AFL-CIO Executive Council Minutes, August 9–10, 1994, 4, box 105, AFL-CIO Papers; Steven T. Engel and David J. Jackson, "Wielding the Stick Instead of the Carrot: Labor PAC Punishment of Pro-NAFTA Democrats," *Political Research Quarterly* 51, no.3 (Sept. 1998): 813–28 (quotation on 813, statistic on 821).

80. "Building and Construction Trades Department, AFL-CIO, Executive Council Report," 37, in "Trade and Industrial Department Reports to the Executive Council, August 1998," box 1, AR2001-0031, AFL-CIO Papers; "Union Household Share of Vote and Workforce Percentage, 1992–2012," Steve Rosenthal Papers, Washington, DC, personal collection shared with author (hereafter cited as "Rosenthal Papers").

81. AFL-CIO Executive Council Minutes, February 20–23, 1995, 4, 8, box 108, AFL-CIO Papers.

82. Kennedy, Cohen, and Bailey, *The American Pageant,* 992–93; "Building and Construction Trades," 37, in "Trade and Industrial Department Reports," AFL-CIO Papers ("disaster" quotation); Michael Byrne, "Election Imperils Progress for Workers," *AFL-CIO News,* November 14, 1994, 1.

83. AFL-CIO Executive Council Minutes, February 20–23, 1995, 34, A11 (quotation), box 108, AFL-CIO Papers.

84. AFL-CIO Executive Council Minutes, February 20–23, 1995, A2, box 108, AFL-CIO Papers.

85. AFL-CIO Executive Council Minutes, May 9–10, 1995, 4, box 108, AFL-CIO Papers.

86. AFL-CIO Executive Council Minutes, February 20–23, 1995, A14, box 108, AFL-CIO Papers; David Kameras, "NAFTA Labor Promises Empty," *AFL-CIO News,* November 28, 1994, 3.

87. AFL-CIO Executive Council Minutes, February 20–23, 1995, A17, box 108, AFL-CIO Papers; Mark Anderson interview; George Kourpias interview.

88. "NAFTA: Where's That 'Giant Sucking Sound'?" *Business Week,* July 7, 1997, 45. Voiced during the second presidential debate in 1992, the "giant sucking sound" was candidate Ross Perot's colorful phrase for what he feared would be the negative impact of NAFTA on the U.S. economy, as American jobs whooshed across the border to cheap labor markets in Mexico. For more information, see Patterson, *Restless Giant,* 251.

89. AFL-CIO Executive Council Minutes, May 9–10, 1995, 16 (Anderson quotation); and AFL-CIO Executive Council Minutes, February 20–23, 1995, 25—both in box 108, AFL-CIO Papers.

90. Zieger and Gall, *American Workers, American Unions,* 263–64.

91. Kirkland, interview, Lane Kirkland Files, AFL-CIO Papers; Tom Donahue interview (2013).

92. Zieger and Gall, *American Workers, American Unions,* 262; Bhagwati, *In Defense of Globalization,* 3.

93. AFL-CIO Executive Council Minutes, May 4–5, 1993, 7, box 105, AFL-CIO Papers.

94. Tom Donahue interview (2013); Mark Anderson, "U.S.-Mexican Free Trade Agreement: An AFL-CIO Perspective," n.d., Anderson Papers; "Hourly Compensation Costs for Production Workers in Manufacturing, 1980–1992," AFL-CIO Task Force on Trade Fact Sheet, 1993, Anderson Papers.

Chapter Eight

1. Barbara Shailor interview; Taylor Dark, "Debating Decline: The 1995 Race for the AFL-CIO Presidency," *Labor History* 40, no. 3 (1999): 327; quotation in Janet Kidd Stewart, "Labor Looks to Regain Influence," *Chicago Sun-Times,* September 3, 1995, 41.

2. "On the go" McEntee quotation in Harry Bernstein, "Gerald McEntee: Bringing Labor into the National Political Debate," *Los Angeles Times,* March 2, 1997, 3 (magazine); Frank Swoboda, "Key Union Leaders Want Kirkland to Leave," *Washington Post,* January 28, 1995, A1 (other quotations); Peter T. Kilborn, "Bringing Down Labor's

Giant Leader: Union Presidents Recount 2-Year Plan to Unseat Lane Kirkland," *New York Times*, September 4, 1995, 7; last two quotations in Gerald McEntee interview.

3. Thomas R. Donahue to General Presidents, September 20, 1995, folder 5, Donahue Papers; Tom Donahue interview (2013); closing quotation in Kilborn, "Bringing Down Labor's Giant Leader," 7.

4. Kilborn, "Bringing Down Labor's Giant Leader," 7 (Sweeney quotations); Dark, "Debating Decline," 329; closing quotation in Peter T. Kilborn, "Retiring Labor Chief Supports Deputy," *New York Times*, June 13, 1995, A16.

5. Sweeney, *America Needs a Raise*, 90.

6. Ibid. (first quotation); Dunlop commission quotations in Dark, "Debating Decline," 327; "The Dunlop Commission on the Future of Worker-Management Relations— Final Report," December 1, 1994, available at http://digitalcommons.ilr.cornell.edu /key_workplace/2/ (accessed June 4, 2014); "An Unbalanced Labor Law Proposal," *New York Times*, July 10, 1996, 14.

7. Gerald McEntee interview. Richard Trumka similarly recalled, "Lane was so fixated on international affairs," Richard Trumka interview.

8. David St. John interview; Barbara Easterling interview; William Serrin, "Lane Kirkland, Who Led Labor in Difficult Times, Is Dead at 77," *New York Times*, August 15, 1999.

9. Tom Donahue interview (2013); Bob Welsh interview; Denise Mitchell interview.

10. Markley Roberts interview ("politician" quotation); Larry Gold interview.

11. Ken Zinn interview; Dark, "Debating Decline," 329; "nadir" quotation in Michael Podhorzer interview.

12. Damon Silvers interview; Bob Welsh interview; Kirkland quoted in Michael Byrne, "Election Imperils Progress for Workers," *AFL-CIO News*, November 14, 1994, 1.

13. AFL-CIO Executive Council Minutes, February 20–23, 1995, 31, box 108, AFL-CIO Papers.

14. Ibid.; John Sweeney, "Report of the AFL-CIO Executive Council Committee on Organizing," February 21–22, 1990, in AFL-CIO Executive Council Minutes, February 21–22, 1990, C57–C61, box 104, AFL-CIO Papers.

15. Proceedings of the 1987 AFL-CIO Convention, October 26–29, 1987, 326–27.

16. AFL-CIO Executive Council Minutes, February 20–23, 1995, 19, box 108, AFL-CIO Papers.

17. AFL-CIO Executive Council Minutes, May 9–10, 1995, 6, box 108, AFL-CIO Papers; David St. John to Thomas Donahue, June 26, 1995, folder 4, Donahue Papers; AFL-CIO Executive Council Minutes, May 9–10, 1995, 17, box 1, AR2002-0106, AFL-CIO Papers.

18. Sweeney, *America Needs a Raise*, 90; AFL-CIO Executive Council Minutes, February 20–23, 1995, 3, box 108, AFL-CIO Papers.

19. Doug Dority interview.

20. Dark, "Debating Decline," 329, 330; Bernstein, "Gerald McEntee," 3 (magazine).

21. Dark, "Debating Decline," 330; Tom Donahue interview (2013) (first and second quotations); closing quotation in Tom Donahue interview (2015).

22. Tom Donahue interview (2013).

23. Lenore Miller interview; AFL-CIO Executive Council Minutes, May 9–10, 1995, 1, box 108, AFL-CIO Papers.

24. "'Stop Kirkland' Mutiny Breaks Out within AFL-CIO," *St. Louis Post-Dispatch*, May 10, 1995, 5C (McEntee quotation); Doug Dority interview; Zieger and Gall, *American Workers, American Unions*, 259–60; "avuncular" quotation in Alec MacGillis, "No Getting Around This Guy: AFL-CIO's Richard Trumka Aims to Hold That Line on Health Care," *Washington Post*, September 7, 2009; George F. Will, "Arise, Ye Prisoners," *Newsweek*, November 27, 1995, 98; Barbara Easterling interview.

25. Gerald McEntee interview; Andy Stern interview; George Kourpias interview; Bob Welsh interview; Denise Mitchell interview; John Sweeney interview.

26. Dark, "Debating Decline," 330; Richard Trumka interview; Linda Chavez-Thompson interview.

27. George Kourpias interview; Gerald McEntee interview.

28. "Lane Kirkland Announces Retirement" (AFL-CIO Press Release), June 12, 1995, folder 11, Donahue Papers.

29. Frank Swoboda, "Kirkland Will Leave AFL-CIO; Struggle Brewing over Labor's Future," *Washington Post*, June 13, 1995, A1; "Lane Kirkland's Farewell Remarks to the Executive Council," n.d., "Lane Kirkland's Farewell Remarks to the Executive Council," Donahue Papers (quotations); AFL-CIO Executive Council Minutes, August 1–2, 1995, 1–2, box 108, AFL-CIO Papers.

30. Susan Dunlop interview (2013); Tom Donahue interview (2013); Doug Dority interview.

31. Rex Hardesty, "Aug. 1 to Mark End of Historic Kirkland Era," *AFL-CIO News*, July 31, 1995, 1, 12; Susan Dunlop interview (2013).

32. "AFL-CIO Secretary-Treasurer Tom Donahue News Conference," June 12, 1995, folder 3, Donahue Papers.

33. First quotation in Louis Uchitelle, "2 Rivals in AFL-CIO Are Seeking Its Presidency," *New York Times*, June 11, 1995, 22; Richard Trumka interview.

34. AFL-CIO Executive Council Minutes, August 1–2, 1995, 3, box 108, AFL-CIO Papers; closing quotation from Dark, "Debating Decline," 331.

35. AFL-CIO Executive Council Minutes, August 1–2, 1995, 10 (quotation), 13, and October 20, 1995, 7—all in box 108, AFL-CIO Papers.

36. AFL-CIO Executive Council Minutes, February 20–23, 1995, 31, box 108, AFL-CIO Papers.

37. Francis X. Clines, "For Big Labor, and New Chief, a Time to Smile," *New York Times*, October 29, 1996, A1; Robert L. Rose, "John Sweeney Plots a Revolution at AFL-CIO," *Wall Street Journal*, June 14, 1995, B1 ("Irish" quotation); Charles Stott interview ("street guy" quotation); Steven Greenhouse, "Labor Leader Is Stepping Down Both Proud and Frustrated," *New York Times*, September 13, 2009, A32 (main Sweeney quotation); closing Sweeney quotation in "Statement of AFL-CIO President John Sweeney, Domestic Workers Bill of Rights Press Conference," May 20, 2008, box 6, AR2009-0024-B05/G/30, AFL-CIO Papers.

38. Bob Welsh interview; John Sweeney interview.

39. Philip Shabecoff, "Women's Group Set to Organize Office Workers: Joins Forces with Union in Drive for Membership," *New York Times*, March 4, 1981, A12.

40. Proceedings of the Sixteenth Constitutional Convention of the AFL-CIO, October 28–31, 1985, 163, 164 (first two quotations); AFL-CIO Executive Council Minutes, February 17–21, 1986, 28, box 101, AFL-CIO Papers (other quotation).

41. Dave Hage, "Unions Launching New, Aggressive Organizing Efforts," *Minneapolis Star-Tribune*, May 23, 1988, 1A; Frank Bass, "'A Defining Moment'; AFL-CIO Election Described as Bellwether for Labor Movement," *Fort Worth Star-Telegram*, October 22, 1995, 1.

42. Gary Frank, "Labor Movement Negotiating Troubled Waters," Springfield (MA) *Sunday Republican*, September 3, 1989, A1.

43. Ken Zinn interview.

44. Frank Swoboda, "Kirkland Expected to Step Down; Coalition Threatened Union Election Defeat," *Washington Post*, June 10, 1995, A1; AFL-CIO Executive Council Minutes, February 20–23, 1995, 29–30, box 108, AFL-CIO Papers (quotations).

45. Dark, "Debating Decline," 332–33; Stewart Acuff interview.

46. "Our politics" quotation in John J. Sweeney to Thomas R. Donahue, August 1, 1995, folder 6, Donahue Papers; other Sweeney quotations in Bob Minzesheimer, "New Union Chief Vows Turnaround," *USA Today*, October 26, 1995, 4A; Dark, "Debating Decline," 334.

47. Dark, "Debating Decline," 335; "Changing Labor Changing America" (Donahue-Easterling Campaign Pamphlet), Donahue Papers (quotation).

48. Moe Biller to John J. Sweeney, July 19, 1995, folder 5, Donahue Papers (quotation); Dark, "Debating Decline," 331–32; closing quotation in "Qualities of Leadership," *Electrical Union World*, August 29, 1995, 4, clipping in folder 5, Donahue Papers.

49. Frank Hanley et al. to Thomas R. Donahue, September 15, 1995, folder 5, Donahue Papers.

50. "Campaign Fax (Sweeney Campaign Newsletter)," September 5, 1995, folder 5, Donahue Papers; Denise Mitchell interview.

51. "Fact Sheet: Trumka Campaign Statements/Trumka Record," May 1995 (emphasis in original); and "SEIU's Growth under John Sweeney," n.d.—both in folder 4, Donahue Papers.

52. Sandra Feldman to John J. Sweeney, August 8, 1995, folder 5; and John J. Sweeney to Thomas R. Donahue, August 1, 1995, folder 6—both in Donahue Papers.

53. Joe D. Gunn to The Committee, May 29, 1995; and closing quotation in Bob Welsh to Jay Foreman, August 23, 1995—both in folder 6, Donahue Papers.

54. Frank Hanley et al. to Thomas R. Donahue, September 15, 1995, folder 5, Donahue Papers; Tom Donahue interview (2013).

55. Dark, "Debating Decline," 333–34; Donahue quotation in Tom Donahue interview (2015); first Sweeney quotation in John J. Sweeney, Linda Chavez-Thompson, and Rich Trumka to "Trade Union Leader," September 8, 1995, folder 5; "Changing

Labor Changing America" (Donahue-Easterling Campaign Pamphlet); closing Sweeney comment in "Campaign Fax (Sweeney Campaign Newsletter)," September 5, 1995,
folder 5—all in Donahue Papers.

56. Steven Greenhouse, "Working Men: Old Friends, New Rivals," *New York Times*,
October 24, 1995, 131; Tom Donahue interview (2013) (Donahue quotations).

57. John Sweeney interview.

58. Proceedings of the 1995 AFL-CIO Convention, October 23–26, 1995, 123.

59. Lenore Miller interview; Dark, "Debating Decline," 335; Tom Donahue interview (2015).

60. AFL-CIO Executive Council Minutes, October 20, 1995, 1, box 108, AFL-CIO
Papers.

61. Proceedings of the 1995 AFL-CIO Convention, October 23–26, 1995, 116; Stewart
Acuff interview.

62. Proceedings of the 1995 AFL-CIO Convention, October 23–26, 1995, 118, 119.

63. Anna Burger interview; Knorr and Lance quotations in William Hershey,
"Union Delegates Return Hopeful," Akron (OH) *Beacon Journal*, October 27, 1995, B1;
Sweeney quoted in Susan Sward, "New Leader of AFL-CIO Unveils Plan," *San Francisco
Chronicle*, December 9, 1995, A14.

64. Proceedings of the 1995 AFL-CIO Convention, October 23–26, 1995, 120–23
(quotations on 121).

65. Tim Shorrock, "Sweeney Poised to Oust Donahue at AFL-CIO," *Journal of
Commerce*, October 25, 1995, 6B; Sweeney and Donahue "bridge" exchange in Peter
T. Kilborn, "Prospective Labor Leaders Set to Turn to Confrontation," *New York Times*,
October 25, 1995; other Donahue quotations in Proceedings of the 1995 AFL-CIO
Convention, October 23–26, 1995, 121; Steven Greenhouse, "For Labor, a Nation to
Envy," *New York Times*, December 24, 1995, E5; Trumka quoted in Kilborn, "Prospective
Labor Leaders," 41.

66. "AFL-CIO 21st Constitutional Convention—New York City 1995 Election
Results—National and International Unions," 3, Donahue Papers; Anna Burger interview; Dark, "Debating Decline," 336–37, 340–41.

67. Proceedings of the 1995 AFL-CIO Convention, October 23–26, 1995, 301 (first
quotation); AFL-CIO Executive Council Minutes, October 26, 1995, 1, box 108, AFL-CIO
Papers (second quotation).

68. John Sweeney interview.

69. First quotation in Frank Swoboda, "AFL-CIO Elects New Leadership; Activist Challenger Vows to Remake Union," *Washington Post*, October 26, 1995, A1; Gerald
McEntee interview; Jim Baker to author, April 30, 2013 (correspondence in author's
possession); Rudy Oswald interview.

70. Tom Donahue interview (2013); closing quotation in Frank Swoboda, "AFL-CIO
Chief in Close Contest for Top Union Post," *Washington Post*, September 4, 1995, A4.

71. Doug Dority interview.

72. Serrin, "Lane Kirkland, Who Led Labor"; Larry Gold interview.

73. Serrin, "Lane Kirkland, Who Led Labor"; Lane Kirkland to John Sweeney, July 14, 1998, folder 8, box 3, RG95-007, Lane Kirkland Files, AFL-CIO Papers (quotations).

74. "Remembering Lane Kirkland," *America@Work*, September 1999, 4.

75. AFL-CIO Executive Council Minutes, October 26, 1995, 1, box 108, AFL-CIO Papers.

Chapter Nine

1. AFL-CIO Executive Council Meeting Minutes, October 13–14, 1998, 6, "October 13–14, 1998," box 1, AR2002-0106/AO/E/04, AFL-CIO Papers; Sweeney quoted in Glenn Burkins, "Number of Workers in Labor Unions Grew Last Year," *Wall Street Journal*, January 26, 1999, B3.

2. Lane Windham interview (2013).

3. Stephen Franklin, "John Sweeney: Taking Aim," *Journal of Commerce*, May 10, 1996, 7A; John Greenwald, "The Battle to Revive the Unions," *Time*, October 30, 1995, 64; Frank Green, "New AFL-CIO Leader Gives No-Nonsense Speech Here," *San Diego Union-Tribune*, March 20, 1996, C1.

4. Tim Shorrock, "AFL-CIO Takes Militant Turn, Elects Sweeney," *Journal of Commerce*, October 26, 1995, 1A; Robert L. Rose, "John Sweeney Plots a Revolution at AFL-CIO," *Wall Street Journal*, June 14, 1995, B1.

5. Clinton quoted in "Sweeney Elected AFL-CIO Leader," *New Hampshire Union Leader*, October 26, 1995, A2.

6. Quotation in Michael Podhorzer interview. See also Lane Windham interview (2013); Gerry Shea interview.

7. "Teamwork for Employees and Management Act of 1995" (congressional report), May 1, 1996, available from the Clinton Library at http://www.clintonlibrary.gov/_previ ous/KAGAN%20COUNSEL/Counsel%20%20Box%20008%20-%20Folder%20010 .pdf (accessed August 6, 2013); Steven Greenhouse, "Despite Defeat on China Bill, Labor Is on Rise," *New York Times*, May 30, 2000, A1 (first quotation); David Moberg, "The Six-Year Itch: John Sweeney Sees the AFL-CIO through Some Growing Pains," *The Nation*, September 3, 2001, 11; Denise Mitchell interview.

8. Peter T. Kilborn, "Prospective Labor Leaders Set to Turn to Confrontation," *New York Times*, October 25, 1995; Sweeney quotation in Frank Swoboda, "After Tough Talk, a Leadership Test for Labor," *Washington Post*, October 29, 1995, H1; Craig Becker interview.

9. Sweeney quoted in Steve Fraser and Nelson Lichtenstein, "New Life for the Labor Movement," *Washington Post*, December 31, 1997, C7.

10. Sweeney, *America Needs a Raise*, 2–5, quotations on 5; M. E. Sharpe, "America Needs a Raise," *Challenge* 40, no. 1 (Jan./Feb. 1997): 127; "America Needs a Raise," AFL-CIO Executive Council Statement, February 19, 1996. All AFL-CIO Executive Council statements cited below have been digitized on the AFL-CIO website at http://www.aflcio.org/About/Exec-Council/EC-Statements. Hard copies of all statements

cited here are also in the author's possession. Only Council statements from the Sweeney era onwards are available on the AFL-CIO's website; earlier statements need to be
accessed in hard copy.

11. Jim McKay, "AFL-CIO: No Longer Too Pale, Too Stale, Too Male," *Pittsburgh
Post-Gazette*, October 29, 1995, C1. The Glass Ceiling Commission was established by
the 1991 Civil Rights Act.

12. AFL-CIO Executive Council Meeting Minutes, September 21, 2007, 6,
"8/5–6/08—Executive Council Meeting, Chicago, IL," box 7, AR2009-0024/BO5/G/31,
AFL-CIO Papers; McKay, "AFL-CIO: No Longer," C1 (first two quotations); "New
Leader for Labor," *Journal of Commerce*, October 27, 1995, 6A ("arrested" quotation);
Linda Chavez-Thompson interview (final quotation).

13. Arlene Holt Baker interview.

14. David St. John interview; Rudy Oswald interview; Markley Roberts interview;
Larry Gold interview.

15. Susan Dunlop interview (2013).

16. Denise Mitchell interview.

17. Barbara Shailor interview; Denise Mitchell interview.

18. Rosalyn Pelles interview.

19. Karen Nussbaum interview.

20. Marilyn Sneiderman interview; Joe Uehlein interview; Mike Cavanaugh interview.

21. AFL-CIO Executive Council Meeting Minutes, March 19–20, 1998, 5, "Executive
Council, March 19–20, 1998," box 1, AR2002-0106/AO/E/04, AFL-CIO Papers (quo-
tation); Diane E. Lewis, "9 to 5 Founder to Launch AFL-CIO Women's Unit," *Boston
Globe*, June 4, 1996, 42; Amy Waldman, "Labor's New Face: Women Renegotiate Their
Role," *The Nation*, September 22, 1997, 11.

22. Margarita Bauza, "Health Care, Pay Top Concerns of Working Women," Norfolk
(VA) *Virginian-Pilot*, August 13, 2006, K1; "Working Women 'Stir the Pot' on Economic
Security, Urge Women to Vote Nov. 7," *U.S. Newswire*, September 21, 2006, 1 (Jeronimo
quotation).

23. Waldman, "Labor's New Face," 11; Clinton quoted in "AFL-CIO 'Ask Working
Women' Event: Concluding Remarks by First Lady Hillary Rodham Clinton," May 7,
1999, available from the Clinton Library at http://www.clintonlibrary.gov/assets/stor
age/Research%20%20Digital%20Library/FLOTUS-speeches/2011-0415-S/Box-024
/2011-0415-S-flotus-statements-speeches-%205-99-10-12-99-binder-ask-working
-woman-buffalo-ny-5-7-1999.pdf (accessed August 5, 2013); "Chronology of AFL-CIO
and Sweeney Initiatives, 1995–2009," n.d., AFL-CIO document provided to the author
by the AFL-CIO (copy in author's possession); closing quotation in Tom Freedman and
Mary L. Smith to Bruce Reed and Elena Kagan, February 19, 1988, available from the
Clinton Library at http://www.clintonlibrary.gov/assets/storage/Research%20%20
Digital%20Library/Reed-Subject/109/647386-equal-pay.pdf (accessed August 6, 2013).

24. Wilfrid C. Rodgers, "New Voices to Sound in Labor, Management," *Boston
Globe*, February 22, 1980, 1; Cathy Trost, "To the Union Chiefs, It's Still a Brotherhood,"
Wall Street Journal, November 20, 1985, 1 (quotation).

25. "Chronology of AFL-CIO and Sweeney Initiatives, 1995–2009"; Louis Uchitelle, "AFL-CIO Candidates Prod Each Other to Move Unions toward Change," *New York Times*, August 7, 1995; Jan M. Rosen, "Unions Gather Strength, But So Do Executives," *New York Times*, September 7, 1997, F2; John Nichols, "Labor Unions Put Dramatic New Emphasis on Organizing," Madison (WI) *Capital Times*, September 25, 1997, 13A.

26. Steven Greenhouse, "Labor Sees Fiscal Hope in Credit Card Deal," *New York Times*, February 23, 1996, 4; Rosalyn Pelles interview; Gerry Shea interview.

27. Sweeney quoted in "Union Rallies in California to Organize Berry Pickers," *New York Times*, April 14, 1997, A14; "Chronology of AFL-CIO and Sweeney Initiatives, 1995–2009"; Lisa Fernandez and Maria Alicia Gaura, "Strawberry Union Decision Hinges on 60 Disputed Votes," *San Francisco Chronicle*, May 28, 1999, A26.

28. AFL-CIO Executive Council Meeting Minutes, October 13–14, 1998, 6, "October 13–14, 1998," box 1, AR2002-0106/AO/E/04, AFL-CIO Papers; Burkins, "Number of Workers," B3; Carty quoted in Steven Greenhouse, "Labor Rolls on in Las Vegas, Where Hotel Union Is a National Model," *New York Times*, April 27, 1998, 10.

29. Sweeney quotation in Fraser and Lichtenstein, "New Life," C7; Marc Cooper, "Labor Deals a New Hand," *The Nation*, March 24, 1997, 11.

30. "Chronology of AFL-CIO and Sweeney Initiatives, 1995–2009"; "Labor's Labors," *The Nation*, November 1, 1999, 3 (closing quotation). For another similarly positive story, see "Labor Ends Its Long Slide," *New York Times*, January 22, 2000, A14.

31. "Chronology of AFL-CIO and Sweeney Initiatives, 1995–2009"; Denise Mitchell interview; "Out in the Open: The Richmark Story," *America@Work*, November/December 1996, 10–11 (quotation on 10).

32. AFL-CIO Executive Council Meeting Minutes, January 29–30, 1998, 4, 5, "Executive Council, January 29–30, 1998," box 1, AR2002-0106-AO/E/04, AFL-CIO Papers; "Chronology of AFL-CIO and Sweeney Initiatives, 1995–2009"; Eric Brazil, "Slim Pickin's for Would-Be Strawberry Union: Central Coast Growers Continue to Keep the UFW Out," *San Francisco Examiner*, October 13, 1997, D1; Kris Maher, "Unions' New Foe: Consultants," *Wall Street Journal*, August 15, 2005, B1; Bruce Raynor interview (closing quotation).

33. AFL-CIO Executive Council Meeting Minutes, February 20–23, 1995, 31, box 1, AR2002-0106/AO/E/04, AFL-CIO Papers; Patterson, *Restless Giant*, 65; Kenneth C. Crowe, "For Unions, No Resting on Laurels," Melville (NY) *Newsday*, September 2, 1996, A25; Eric Alterman, "Labor and Academe," *The Nation*, October 14, 1996, 5; Kate Bronfenbrenner and Dorian T. Warren, "Race, Gender, and the Rebirth of Trade Unionism," *New Labor Forum* 16, no. 3/4 (Fall 2007): 145–46.

34. "Answers to Common Questions about Union Summer," n.d., "Union Summer," box 1, AR2003-0086, AFL-CIO Papers.

35. Nancy Harvin to AFL-CIO Staff, April 16, 1999, "Union Summer," box 1, AR2003-0086, AFL-CIO Papers; Muriel H. Cooper and James B. Parks, "What I Did on my Summer Vacation," *America@Work*, October 1996, 14–17 (Rhone quotation on 15); closing Sweeney quotation in John Sweeney interview.

36. G. Pascal Zachary, "AFL-CIO Places Big Bet on Las Vegas, Its Largest Organizing Drive in Decades," *Wall Street Journal*, January 27, 1997, 1 ("crusade" quotation); Cooper, "Labor Deals," 11; Steven Greenhouse, "Labor Goes to Capitalism's Citadel, and the Sky Doesn't Fall," *New York Times*, September 4, 1999, C3 (Mitchell quotation).

37. Steven Greenhouse, "Labor and the Left: Getting Cozy Again but Common Goals May Not be Enough to Revive a Potent Alliance," *New York Times*, September 5, 1998, A1; "Labor Goes to College," *The Nation*, October 28, 1996, 4.

38. Sam Howe Verhovek and Steven Greenhouse, "Seattle is Under Curfew after Disruptions: Thousands of Protesters Disrupt Seattle Trade Talks," *New York Times*, December 1, 1999, A1 (slogan quotations); Sweeney quoted in Steven Greenhouse, "After Seattle, Unions Point to Sustained Fight on Trade," *New York Times*, December 6, 1999, A28; Harold Meyerson, "Labor's Civil War," *The American Prospect*, June 2005, 45–46.

39. Lane Windham interview (2013); Marilyn Sneiderman interview; Greenhouse, "After Seattle," A28.

40. Clinton administration quotation in "From the Cold War to the Wired World: Trade Policy in the Clinton Era," November 2000, 3, available from the Clinton Library at http://www.clintonlibrary.gov/assets/storage/Research%20%20Digital%20Library /ClintonAdminHistoryProject/101111/Box%20107/1756308-history-ustr-from-cold -war-to-wired-world-trade-policy-clinton-era.pdf (accessed August 6, 2013); Joseph Kahn and Steven Greenhouse, "Unions Prepare to Hit the Street in Washington," *New York Times*, April 12, 2000, A16; "father" quotation in "Labor and Protest in DC," *The Nation*, May 1, 2000, 3.

41. "Remarks by John J. Sweeney, National University, Mexico City," January 22, 1998, in "Globalization 1998–2000," box 17, 6000/010 (President's Office files), Union of Needletrades, Industrial and Textile Employees Papers, held at the Kheel Center, ILR School, Cornell University.

42. "Immigration and the American Dream," AFL-CIO Executive Council statement, February 23, 1995 (first two quotations); "Immigration," AFL-CIO Executive Council statement, February 16, 2000 (other quotations).

43. Eunice Moscoso, "Labor Groups Rally for Immigration," *Atlanta Constitution*, September 6, 2001, A16; Steven Greenhouse, "Labor Backs Amnesty for Migrants: In Policy Reversal, AFL-CIO, Employers Say that Illegal Immigrants Deserve Protection," *Austin American Statesman*, February 17, 2000, D1; Ana Avendano interview ("leading" quotation); Lane Windham interview (2013).

44. Ana Avendano interview; closing Sweeney quotation in Proceedings of the Twenty-Fourth Biennial Convention of the AFL-CIO, December 3–6, 2001, 46.

45. Puddington, *Lane Kirkland*, 212–13; Barbara Shailor interview; Meyerson, "Labor's Civil War," 45–46.

46. Tim Shorrock, "US Labor Readying Campaign to Mobilize Workers," *Journal of Commerce*, December 18, 1995, 2A ("massive" quotation); Crowe, "For Unions, No Resting," A25 (Clinton quotation); "Chronology of AFL-CIO and Sweeney Initiatives, 1995–2009."

47. Steven Greenhouse, "AFL-CIO Vows to Spend More Than Ever Before on Candidates," *New York Times*, February 16, 2000, A21; Francis X. Clines, "For Big Labor, and New Chief, a Time to Smile," *New York Times*, October 29, 1996, A1 ("political force" quotation).

48. "Union Household Share of Vote and Workforce Percentage, 1992–2012," Rosenthal Papers; Steve Rosenthal interview; "Working Families *Are* Back," *America@Work*, November/December 1996, 13, 15.

49. Marilyn Sneiderman interview; Proceedings of the Twenty-Fourth Biennial AFL-CIO Convention, December 3–6, 2001, 46.

50. "Building and Construction Trades Department, AFL-CIO, Executive Council Report," 33, in "Trade and Industrial Department Reports to the Executive Council, August 1998," box 1, AR2001-0031, AFL-CIO Papers.

51. Steven Greenhouse, "After Derailing Trade Bill, Labor Sets Ambitious Goals," *New York Times*, January 30, 1998, 10; quotations in Jill Abramson and Steven Greenhouse, "Labor Victory on Trade Bill Reveals Power," *New York Times*, November 12, 1997, A1; "Chronology of AFL-CIO and Sweeney Initiatives, 1995–2009."

52. Executive Council Report to the AFL-CIO Convention (draft), August 2, 1999, 1, "August 3–4, 1999, Executive Council Meeting, Chicago, IL," box 1, AR2001-0031, AFL-CIO Papers (quotation); "Chronology of AFL-CIO and Sweeney Initiatives, 1995–2009."

53. "Chronology of AFL-CIO and Sweeney Initiatives, 1995–2009"; "A History of the U.S. Department of Labor during the Clinton Administration, 1993–2001," Clinton Administration Oral History Project, 2000, 83–90, Clinton Library; Margaret "Peg" Seminario interview (quotations).

54. "Chronology of AFL-CIO and Sweeney Initiatives, 1995–2009."

55. Executive Council Report to the AFL-CIO Convention (draft), August 2, 1999, 1, "August 3–4, 1999, Executive Council Meeting, Chicago, IL," box 1, AR2001-0031, AFL-CIO Papers.

56. Paul A. Gigot, "Terminator II: Why Big Labor Keeps on Coming," *Wall Street Journal*, April 11, 1997, A14 (first two quotations); Dawn Kopecki, "Grassroots Lobbies Replace Bygone Era's Cigar Chompers," *Washington Times*, November 24, 1997, D6; closing quotation in "Reports to the AFL-CIO Convention," August 2, 1999, 5, "August 3–4, 1999, Executive Council Meeting, Chicago, IL," box 1, AR2001-0031/ EO2/F/21, AFL-CIO Papers.

57. Timothy J. Minchin, "Shutting Down 'Big Brown': Reassessing the 1997 UPS Strike and the Fate of American Labor," *Labor History* 53, no. 4 (November 2012): 545 (Carey quotation), 546; Steven Greenhouse, "UPS and Union Break Off Negotiations," *New York Times*, August 10, 1997, 1, 26; "Teamsters and UPS Agree on a 5-Year Contract Plan to End Strike after 15 Days," *New York Times*, August 19, 1997, A1.

58. Minchin, "Shutting Down 'Big Brown,'" 542, 544. For a more detailed study of the UPS strike, see Kumar, *Outside the Box*.

59. Rosen, "Unions Gather Strength," F2; Richard Cowan, "Organized Labor Mounts Comeback," Greensboro (NC) *News Record*, August 31, 1997, E1.

60. Jo Ann Wypijewski, "Union Time," *The Nation*, October 20, 1997, 3 (first quotation); Steven Greenhouse, "Labor, Revitalized with New Recruiting, Has Regained Power and Prestige," *New York Times*, October 9, 1999, 14.

61. Executive Council Report to the AFL-CIO Convention (draft), August 2, 1999, 1, "August 3–4, 1999, Executive Council Meeting, Chicago, IL," box 1, AR2001-0031, AFL-CIO Papers.

62. Frank Swoboda, "AFL-CIO to Offer Access to Internet for Members," *Washington Post*, October 11, 1999, A8; Greenhouse, "Despite Defeat," A1; Moberg, "The Six-Year Itch," 11.

63. William H. Miller, "Sweeney Sees Organization Gains," *Industry Week*, March 5, 2001, 12 (first quotation); John B. Judis, "Labored Steps: Strife in the AFL-CIO," *The New Republic*, March 21, 2005, 10; other quotations in "Chronology of AFL-CIO and Sweeney Initiatives, 1995–2009."

64. First quotation in "Chronology of AFL-CIO and Sweeney Initiatives, 1995–2009"; Peter Louis Francia, "Awakening the Sleeping Giant: The Renaissance of Organized Labor in American Politics" (PhD diss., University of Maryland, 2000), 157. For similar, updated conclusions, see also Francia, *The Future of Organized Labor*.

65. Lane Windham interview (2013); Sweeney quoted in "President's Report to the AFL-CIO Convention, 2009," 5, available at www.aflcio.org/about us/thisistheaflcio /convention/2009/ (accessed February 21, 2012, copy in author's possession); Steve Rosenthal interview (2015). For an overview of the 2000 election and the crucial Supreme Court decision, see Patterson, *Restless Giant*, 404–21.

66. Steve Rosenthal interview (2013) (first two quotations); Bob Welsh interview; Patterson, *Restless Giant*, 416–17; closing Rosenthal quotation in Steve Rosenthal interview (2015).

67. John Sweeney interview.

68. Stewart Acuff interview; Gerry Shea interview; Damon Silvers interview; Jon Hiatt interview.

69. "Chronology of AFL-CIO and Sweeney Initiatives, 1995–2009."

70. Steve Rosenthal interview (2015); Lane Windham interview (2015); Steve Twomey, "Security Heightened in DC; Government Shuts Down, Employees Sent Home," *Washington Post*, September 11, 2001, A2; closing quotation in Adam Clymer, "An Altered Landcsape: The Capital as 3 Cities, Each One Now a Fortress," *New York Times*, September 11, 2002, 18.

71. Steven Greenhouse, "During a Blue-Collar Upswing, Labor Seeks a Lift," *New York Times*, December 5, 2001, A16; Steven Greenhouse, "Labor Leaders Hail Workers for 9/11 Sacrifices," *New York Times*, September 4, 2002, B3.

72. Steven Greenhouse and Mireya Navarro, "After the Attacks: The Hidden Victims; Those at Towers' Margin Elude List of Missing," *New York Times*, September 17, 2001, A11; Sweeney quoted in Proceedings of the Twenty-Fourth Biennial Convention of the AFL-CIO, December 3–6, 2001, 44–45.

73. Patterson, *Restless Giant*, 423 ("unelected" quotation); "A Snapshot Gives Bush 90% Approval," *New York Times*, September 24, 2001, B6.

74. Lane Windham interview (2013); Bob Welsh interview; Marilyn Sneiderman interview.

75. David Leonhardt, "Jobless Rate Rose to 6% Last Month," *New York Times*, May 3, 2003, A1.

76. Steven Greenhouse, "Toll Mounts as Northwest Plans to Cut 10,000 Jobs," *New York Times*, September 22, 2001, C5; Steven Greenhouse, "Behind Las Vegas's Glitter, Heavy Losses and Layoffs," *New York Times*, October 19, 2001, A14; Steven Greenhouse, "As the Rich Do Without Extras, Service Workers Do Without," *New York Times*, November 29, 2001, D1; Wilhelm quoted in Steven Greenhouse, "A Labor Leader on the Rise as His Workers Are Down," *New York Times*, October 13, 2001, A8.

77. Sweeney quoted in Proceedings of the Twenty-Fourth Biennial Convention of the AFL-CIO, December 3–6, 2001, 46.

78. Charlotte Ryan, "It Takes a Movement to Raise an Issue," 483–511, 489; Frank Swoboda, "Teamsters Scandal Revives Labor's Image Problem; Union Gains in Public Opinion from UPS Strike Threatened by Recent Turmoil," *Washington Post*, November 23, 1997, A16 (quotation).

79. Frank Swoboda and Sharon Walsh, "U.S. Says Carey Used DNC, AFL-CIO; Consultants Plead Guilty to Funneling Money to Teamsters President's Reelection Campaign," *Washington Post*, September 19, 1997, A1; Thomas B. Edsall, Sharon Walsh, and Frank Swoboda, "Teamsters Election Scandal: Liberal Activism Gone Awry," *Washington Post*, October 6, 1997, A1; Jane Slaughter, "UPS and Detroit Newspaper Strikes," *Monthly Review* 49, no. 8 (1998): 53; Thomas B. Edsall, "Carey Expulsion Hurts Progressives; But AFL-CIO's Sweeney Remains Secure," *Washington Post*, July 28, 1998, E4 (closing quotation).

80. AFL-CIO Executive Council Meeting Minutes, May 3–5, 2000, 7, "May 3–5, 2000," box 1, AR2002-0106/AO/E/04, AFL-CIO Papers; Peter Olney, "The Arithmetic of Decline and Some Proposals for Renewal," *New Labor Forum* 10 (Spring 2002), 7; Nelson Lichtenstein, "A Race between Cynicism and Hope," *New Labor Forum* 10 (Spring 2002), 71.

81. AFL-CIO Executive Council Meeting Minutes, August 4–5, 1998, 7–8, "August 4–5, 1998," box 1, AR2002-0106/AO/E/04, AFL-CIO Papers; Wypijewski, "Union Time," 3 (quotations).

82. "Organizing Priorities and Strategies," AFL-CIO Executive Council Statement, May 4, 1999 (first and second quotations); AFL-CIO Executive Council Meeting Minutes, May 3–5, 2000, 7, "May 3–5, 2000," box 1, AR2002-0106-AO/E/04, AFL-CIO Papers (third quotation); Brad Burton interview.

83. Susan Washington interview; Brad Burton interview; Daisy Rooks, "The Cowboy Mentality: Organizers and Occupational Commitment in the New Labor Movement," *Labor Studies Journal* 28, no. 3 (2003): 33–62.

84. Ana Avendano interview; Richard Trumka interview.

85. Mark Anderson Speech Notes, NAFTA Panel, Columbia University, February 28, 1997, Anderson Papers; Mike Cavanaugh interview.

86. "Union Household Share of Vote and Workforce Percentage, 1992–2012," Rosenthal Papers (copy in author's possession).

87. Marilyn Sneiderman interview.

Chapter Ten

1. Lane Kirkland, interview by James F. Shea and Don R. Kienzle, November 13, 1996, 35, Labor Diplomacy Oral History Project, transcript in folder 8, box 4, RG95-007, Lane Kirkland Files, AFL-CIO Papers (first quotation); Bob Welsh interview; Gerry Shea interview; Bill Samuel interview.

2. John Sweeney interview; Laborers' president Terry O'Sullivan quoted in Alec MacGillis, "For Unions, A Time of Opportunity and Worry; Obama to Address AFL-CIO as Labor Faces Its Divisions," *Washington Post*, September 15, 2009, A15.

3. Steven Greenhouse, "Among Dissident Union Leaders, the Backgrounds May Vary but the Vision is the Same," *New York Times*, July 22, 2005, A15; John B. Judis, "Labored Steps: Strife in the AFL-CIO," *The New Republic*, March 21, 2005, 10; Steven Greenhouse, "As Labor Leadership Gathers, Head of Largest Union Issues Call for Major Changes," *New York Times*, November 10, 2004, A18 (first two quotations); Jonathan Cutler and Thaddeus Russell, "Workers of the World . . . Disunite!" *Christian Science Monitor*, July 6, 2005, 9; Michael Barone, "Big Labor, RIP," *Wall Street Journal*, July 28, 2005, A10 (final quotation).

4. Damon Silvers interview.

5. Steven Greenhouse, "Labor is Feeling Embattled as Union Leaders Convene," *New York Times*, March 9, 2004.

6. Steven Greenhouse, "Labor Looks for Common Ground with Bush," *New York Times*, February 6, 2001, A14 ("responsible" quotation); Joseph Kahn, "As Vote Nears, Bush Presses for New Trade Powers," *New York Times*, December 5, 2001; David Moberg, "Labor: In Fighting Trim," *The Nation*, December 31, 2000, 4; "Our job" quotation in *AFL-CIO Executive Council Report*, 24th Biennial Convention (2001), 7.

7. John J. Sweeney to AFL-CIO Executive Council, February 8, 2002, "2002/02/28," box 1, AR2003-096, AFL-CIO Papers.

8. Linda Chavez-Thompson interview; Christine L. Owens to David C. Childs, December 19, 2002, George W. Bush White House Files available from the George W. Bush Presidential Library at http://georgebush-whitehouse.archives.gov/omb/circulars /a076/comments/a76-299.pdf (accessed August 16, 2013, copy in author's possession); Scott Shane and Ron Nixon, "In Washington, Contractors Take On Biggest Role Ever," *New York Times*, February 4, 2007, 1.

9. "Remarks by John Sweeney, Post-Election Press Briefing," November 6, 2002 (first two quotations), and Sweeney handwritten notes on "Remarks by John Sweeney, Post-Election Press Briefing," November 6, 2002—both in "11/7/02—Post Election Press Briefing, Phone Calls, Washington, DC," box 5, AR2003-0096, AFL-CIO Papers.

10. Steven Greenhouse, "Labor, Breaking Tradition, Criticizes War Preparations," *New York Times*, February 28, 2003, A14.

11. "So Much for Solidarity," *Wall Street Journal*, March 6, 2003, A12 (first quotation); Tim Shorrock, "Labor's Cold War," *The Nation*, May 19, 2003, 15 (second quotation); Michael Luo, "Antiwar Groups Use New Clout to Influence Democrats on Iraq," *New York Times*, May 6, 2007, 1.

12. "Debating Labor's Future: A Forum with Janice Fine," *The Nation*, August 1/8, 2005, 22 (Sweeney quotation); "Iraq," AFL-CIO Executive Council statement, February 27, 2003; "End Our Military Involvement in Iraq," AFL-CIO Executive Council statement, March 7, 2007.

13. Quotations in "Press Gaggle by Ari Flesicher," September 2, 2002, George W. Bush White House Files, available at http://georgebush-whitehouse.archives.gov/news/releases/2002/09/20020902-1.html (accessed August 16, 2013, copy in author's possession). See also "Press Gaggle by Ari Flesicher," February 28, 2003, George W. Bush White House Files, available at http://georgebush-whitehouse.archives.gov/news/releases/2003/02/20030228-5.html (accessed August 16, 2013, copy in author's possession).

14. "Draft Opening Remarks by John J. Sweeney, AFL-CIO Meeting with Sen. Barack Obama," June 18, 2008, "6/18 and 19/08 Meetings w/Barack Obama, Washington, DC," box 6, AR2009-0024, AFL-CIO Papers; Linda Chavez-Thompson interview.

15. Lane Windham interview (2013) (quotation); "Schedule for John J. Sweeney," April 16, 2008, and White House Invitation to John J. Sweeney, April 16, 2008—both in "4/16–17/08—Pope Benedict XVI's Visit, Washington, DC," box 6, AR2009-0024, AFL-CIO Papers.

16. Elaine L. Chao to John Sweeney, February 22, 2002, "2002/02/28," box 1, AR2003-096, AFL-CIO Papers; Barbara Shailor interview.

17. John J. Sweeney to AFL-CIO Executive Council, February 8, 2002, "2002/02/28," box 1, AR2003-096, AFL-CIO Papers (Sweeney quotation); David Moberg, "Labor Debates Its Future," *The Nation*, March 14, 2005, 12.

18. The White House, "Press Briefing by National Economic Adviser Gene Sperling and U.S. Trade Representative Charlene Barshefsky," November 24, 1999, 5, Clinton Presidential Papers available from the Clinton Presidential Library at http://clinton4.nara.gov/WH/New/WTO-Conf-1999/briefings/19991124-1245.html (accessed August 29, 2010); Stern quoted in AFL-CIO Executive Council Minutes, December 3–4, 2001, 13, "2002/02/28," box 1, AR2003-096, AFL-CIO Papers.

19. Steven Greenhouse, "Trying to Overcome Embarrassment, Labor Opens a Drive to Organize Wal-Mart," *New York Times*, November 8, 2002, A28; Steven Greenhouse, "Report Assails Wal-Mart Over Unions," *New York Times*, May 1, 2007, C3; Constance L. Hays, "Wal-Mart Plans Changes to Some Labor Practices," *New York Times*, June 5, 2004, C2; *Business Week* quotation in Paul Krugman, "State of the Unions," *New York Times*, December 24, 2007, A17. For a fine, broader analysis of Wal-Mart's growth and its labor relations policies, see Lichtenstein, *Retail Revolution*, esp. 118–48.

20. "Why Workers Need Unions, and Better Laws Protecting Their Rights to Organize," Economic Policy Institute Press Release ca. 2011, available at http://www.epi.org/news/why-workers-need-unions-and-better-laws-protecting-their-rights-to-organize/#.TO_b5WY4Ks.email (accessed March 6, 2012, copy in author's possession).

21. Steven Greenhouse, "Unions to Push to Make Organizing Easier," *New York Times*, August 31, 2003, N22; Stewart Acuff interview (quotations).

22. Robin Finn, "Rebel Barista with a Cause," *New York Times*, June 11, 2004, B4; Anthony Ramirez, "Union Steps Up Drive to Organize Starbucks," *New York Times*, November 26, 2005, B5; Steven Greenhouse, "Board Accuses Starbucks of Trying to Block Union," *New York Times*, April 3, 2007, B2; Daniel Gross, "Latte Laborers Take on a Latte-Liberal Business," *New York Times*, April 8, 2007, 4.

23. Matt Richtel, "In Wireless World, Cingular Bucks the Antiunion Trend," *New York Times*, February 21, 2006, C1; Steven Greenhouse, "Employers Sharply Criticize Shift in Unionizing Method to Cards from Elections," *New York Times*, March 11, 2006, A9; Steven Greenhouse, "Janitors' Union, Recently Organized, Strikes in Houston," *New York Times*, November 3, 2006, A18; Steven Greenhouse, "Cleaning Companies in Accord with Striking Houston Janitors," *New York Times*, November 21, 2006, A18.

24. For an overview of this important case, see Sean Lengell, "NLRB Decision Angers Unions," *Knight Ridder Tribune Business News*, October 4, 2006, 1 (quotations); Will Lester, "Labor Board Redefines Employee Eligibility for Legal Protections on Union Membership," *Associated Press Archive*, October 4, 2006.

25. Steven Greenhouse, "Labor Board's Detractors See a Bias against Workers," *New York Times*, January 2, 2005, 12; Steven Greenhouse, "Critics Say Labor Board Favors Business," *New York Times*, December 14, 2007, A33 (Kennedy quotation); "The Bush NLRB's Attack on Workers' Rights," AFL-CIO Executive Council Statement, August 11, 2004 (closing quotation).

26. "Employee Union Representation Elections, 1997–2009," data from the Bureau of Labor Statistics, available at http://www.bls.gov/opub/ted/2010/ted_20100709 _data.htm (accessed December 15, 2014, copy in author's possession).

27. Finn, "Rebel Barista," B4; Ramirez, "Union Steps Up," B5; Greenhouse, "Board Accuses Starbucks," B2; Gross, "Latte Laborers," 4; Greenhouse, "Critics Say Labor Board," A33.

28. Alec MacGillis, "5 Myths about the Labor Movement," *Washington Post*, February 21, 2010, B3; closing quotation in Louis Uchitelle, *The Disposable American*, 4–5 (quotations on 5). Although I have here used the 2007 edition, *The Disposable American* was originally published by Knopf in 2006.

29. Steven Greenhouse, "Labor Leader Is Stepping Down Both Proud and Frustrated," *New York Times*, September 13, 2009, A32. For insight into the long-term roots of deindustrialization, see Stein, *Pivotal Decade*, and Bluestone and Harrison's landmark *The Deindustrialization of America*.

30. Sweeney quotations in "Remarks by John J. Sweeney at the AFL-CIO General Board Meeting," February 8, 2007, "2/8/07 AFL-CIO General Board Meeting, Silver Spring, MD," box 1, AR2009-0024-BO5/9/25, AFL-CIO Papers.

31. Susan Washington interview; Bob Welsh interview.

32. Mark Anderson interview; "NAFTA: Where's That 'Giant Sucking Sound'?" *Business Week*, July 7, 1997, 45.

33. Mark Mittelhauser, "Employment Trends in Textiles and Apparel, 1973–2005," *Monthly Labor Review* 120, no. 8 (August 1997): 24; Bureau of Labor Statistics employment data at http://www.bls.gov/iag/tgs/iag_index_alpha.htm (accessed October 25, 2010); Harris Raynor interview.

34. Leo Gerrard interview; Greenhouse, "Labor Leader Is Stepping Down," A32; Bob Baugh interview. At the time of the interview, Baugh was the leader of the AFL-CIO's industrial union council.

35. Tefere Gebre interview; Louis Uchitelle, "For Blacks, a Dream in Decline," *New York Times*, October 23, 2005.

36. AFL-CIO Executive Council Minutes, December 3–4, 2001, 5, 6, box 1, AR2003-0096, AFL-CIO Papers.

37. Ibid.; quotations in "We Won't Let Them Steal It Again," *America@Work*, September/October 2004, 3.

38. "Talking Points/WA Core Staff Meeting—January 18, 2007," January 18, 2007, "1/18/07—Working America Leadership Training, Washington, DC," box 1, AR2009-0024-B05/G/25, AFL-CIO Papers (opening Sweeney quotation); Karen Nussbaum, "A 'Shadow PAC'? Not Us—We're Growing by the Day," *Wall Street Journal*, April 19, 2006, A13; "Country's Fastest-Growing Labor Organization," *Management Report*, February 2008, 6; closing Sweeney quotation in "Debating Labor's Future," 17.

39. Alec MacGillis, "Labor Leaders Stress Unions' Importance for Obama," *Washington Post*, August 29, 2008, A27; Steven Greenhouse, "Union Leaders Confronted by Resistance to Obama," *New York Times*, September 29, 2008, A17 (Burnett quotation).

40. John J. Sweeney to All National Unions, September 25, 2007, "9/21/07 AFL-CIO Executive Council, Washington, DC," box 3, AR2009-0024, AFL-CIO Papers.

41. "Working Families: A Leading Political Force for a Better America" (AFL-CIO Press Release), "8/7/07—Presidential Forum, Chicago," box 3, AR2009-0024, AFL-CIO Papers; Michael Podhorzer interview.

42. Karen Nussbaum interview.

43. Greenhouse, "Labor is Feeling Embattled," A16 (quotations); Lane Windham interview (2013); Thomas B. Edsall, "Union Leader Urges AFL-CIO Reform; Federation is Outdated, SEIU Head Says," *Washington Post*, June 22, 2004, A2; Steven Greenhouse, "Though United in Politics, Unions Face Internal Turmoil," *New York Times*, August 1, 2004, 19. Although they joined the New Unity Partnership, the United Brotherhood of Carpenters were not part of the AFL-CIO.

44. Greenhouse, "Labor is Feeling Embattled," A16; Harold Meyerson, "For Labor, Tough Choices," *Washington Post*, December 15, 2004, A33 (quotations).

45. Harold Meyerson, "New Labor?" *American Prospect*, February 2005, 12–14; quotation in Steven Greenhouse, "Labor Chief Emerges from Meeting a Winner, but for How Long?" *New York Times*, March 4, 2005, A16; Stern quotation in Stern, *A Country That Works*, 97; Anna Burger interview.

46. Meyerson, "New," 12–14; Steven Greenhouse, "Unions Want to Cut Dues to AFL-CIO," *New York Times*, February 19, 2005, A10.

47. Steven Greenhouse, "Labor Leaders Reject Rival Plan to Shift More Money to Organizing," *New York Times*, March 3, 2005, A14 (Stern quotation); "Union Household Share of Vote and Workforce Percentage, 1992–2012," Rosenthal Papers (copy in author's possession).

48. Harold Meyerson, "Labor's Civil War," *American Prospect*, June 2005, 45–46; Denise Mitchell interview; Christine Owens interview.

49. Steven Greenhouse, "Sweeney to Seek New 4-Year Term as Head of AFL-CIO," *New York Times*, September 18, 2003, A24; Greenhouse, "Labor Chief Emerges," A16; Stern, *A Country That Works*, 97.

50. Andy Stern interview; Anna Burger interview; Terry O'Sullivan interview.

51. Katherine Stapp, "Labour: AFL-CIO Crisis Ignores Us, Workers Complain," *Global Information Network*, July 27, 2005, 1; Ryan quoted in David Moberg, "Labor Splits Open," *The Nation*, July 11, 2005, 5; Mike Cavanaugh interview.

52. Susan Bianchi interview.

53. Bob Welsh interview; Lane Windham interview (2013); Meyerson, "For Labor, Tough Choices," A33.

54. Steven Greenhouse, "AFL-CIO Is Urged to Oust Its Leader," *New York Times*, May 17, 2005, A12; Steven Greenhouse, "A Summer of Discontent for Labor Focuses on Its Leader's Fitness for His Job," *New York Times*, May 31, 2005, A13 (quotation); Steven Greenhouse, "Five Unions to Create a Coalition on Growth," *New York Times*, June 13, 2005, A12.

55. "Solidarity in Pieces," *New York Times* (editorial), July 27, 2005, A22 (Stern quotation); Sweeney quoted in AFL-CIO 2005 Convention Proceedings, July 25–28, 2005, 335.

56. Steven Greenhouse, "Labor Leaders Offer Locals 'Solidarity'," *New York Times*, August 11, 2005, A21; Sweeney and Burger quoted in Steven Greenhouse, "Breakaway Unions Start New Federation," *New York Times*, September 28, 2005, A17; Anna Burger interview.

57. Christine Owens interview; Bill Samuel interview; Gerry Shea interview.

58. Randal C. Archibold, "Immigrants Take to U.S. Streets in Show of Strength," *New York Times*, May 2, 2006; Katz and Greenwald, eds., *Labor Rising*, 6; Meyerson, "Labor's Civil War," 45–50; closing quotation in John Zogby, "Disorganized Labor," *Wall Street Journal*, August 9, 2005, A10; Robert J. Grossman, "Unions Follow Suit," *HR Magazine*, May 2005, 46.

59. "Remarks by John J. Sweeney," February 8, 2007, AFL-CIO Papers.

60. "Talking Points for JJS: Transportation Trades Department Executive Board Meeting, Las Vegas, NV," March 4, 2007, "3/4/07—TTD Executive Committee Mtg. Las Vegas," box 1, AR2009-0024, AFL-CIO Papers; "Talking Points for Officers—All Field Staff Meeting," July 17, 2007, "7/17/07 Field Staff Meeting, Washington, DC," box 3, AR2009-0024-B05/G/27, AFL-CIO Papers (closing Sweeney quotation).

61. John Sweeney's Address to the AFL-CIO Executive Council, May 30, 2007, "5/30/07 Executive Committee Meeting, Washington, DC," box 2, AR2009-0024, AFL-CIO Papers.

62. "Chronology of AFL-CIO and Sweeney Initiatives, 1995–2009," n.d., AFL-CIO document provided to the author by the AFL-CIO (copy in author's possession);

Eugene L. Meyer, "A Campus Built by Labor is Going on the Block," *New York Times*, August 1, 2012, B6.

63. John Sweeney interview.

64. Andy Stern interview.

65. Greenhouse, "Labor Leader Offers Locals," A21.

66. Bruno quoted in Philip Dine, "Strength in Numbers: Unions Got Up from Their Deathbed and Delivered in the Election," *St. Louis Post-Dispatch*, November 10, 2006, A1; "Working Families: A Leading Political Force for a Better America," n.d., "8/7/07—Presidential Forum, Chicago," box 3, AR2009-0024-B05/G/27, AFL-CIO Papers; "AFL-CIO Announces Huge 'Final Four' GOTV Push," *U.S. Newswire*, October 30, 2006.

67. "Remarks by John J. Sweeney," February 8, 2007 (Sweeney quotation); and closing quotation in AFL-CIO Executive Council Minutes, September 21, 2007, "8/5–6/08—Executive Council Meeting, Chicago, IL," box 7—both in AR2009-0024, AFL-CIO Papers.

68. Steven Greenhouse, "Labor Goes Door to Door to Rally Suburban Voters," *New York Times*, October 8, 2006, 1, 20; Jane M. Von Bergen, "Labor Movement Gets a Face-Lift," *Knight Ridder Tribune Business News*, February 11, 2006, 1; "Country's Fastest-Growing," 6.

69. First Sweeney quotation in "Remarks by John J. Sweeney," February 8, 2007; and other quotation in "John Sweeney Talking Points," August 6, 2007, "8/6/07 Working America Meeting, Chicago," box 3, AR2009-0024-B05/G/27—both in AFL-CIO Papers.

70. "Employee Free Choice Act: A Campaign for Hope and Progress," AFL-CIO General Board Statement, February 8, 2007, "2/8/07 AFL-CIO General Board Meeting, Silver Spring, MD," box 1, AR2009-0024-BO5/G/25, AFL-CIO Papers (quotation). For a fine discussion of the battle to pass the EFCA and its broader importance, see the "Up for Debate" section of *Labor: Studies in Working-Class History of the Americas*, 7, no. 3 (Fall 2010): 7–32, especially Nelson Lichtenstein, "Despite EFCA's Limitations, Its Demise Is a Profound Defeat for U.S. Labor" (29–32).

71. "General Board Meeting," February 8, 2007 (Sweeney's address), "2/8/07—AFL-CIO General Board Meeting, Silver Spring, MD," box 1, AR2009-0024, AFL-CIO Papers (Sweeney quotations).

72. Stewart Acuff interview (first quotation); "Talking Points for JJS," March 4, 2007, AFL-CIO Papers.

73. Michael Podhorzer interview; "Employer Interference by the Numbers," December 2007, "12/10–11/07 Global Organizing Conf.—Washington, DC," box 4, AR2009-0024-BO5/G/28, AFL-CIO Papers; "The Employee Free Choice Act: Two Steps Closer to Becoming Law," AFL-CIO Executive Council Statement, August 7, 2007; closing Sweeney quotation in "Remarks by John J. Sweeney," February 8, 2007, AFL-CIO Papers.

74. "Talking Points for JJS," March 4, 2007, AFL-CIO Papers (first quotation); John Sweeney interview (other Sweeney quotations); Doug Dority interview; Steven

Greenhouse, "Democrats Drop Key Part of Bill to Assist Unions," *New York Times*, July 16, 2009, A1; closing quotation in Rand Wilson, "The Labor Law Reform We Need," *Labor Notes*, July 11, 2012.

75. "Working Families: A Leading Political Force for a Better America" (AFL-CIO Press Release), "8/7/07—Presidential Forum, Chicago," box 3, AR2009-0024, AFL-CIO Papers ("largest" quotation); Lane Windham interview (2013).

76. Harold Meyerson, "Can He Be a Working-Class Hero?" *Washington Post*, August 27, 2008, A13.

77. John J. Sweeney to All National Unions, September 25, 2007, "9/21/07 AFL-CIO Executive Council, Washington, DC," box 3, AR2009-0024, AFL-CIO Papers; Don Frederick and Andrew Malcolm, "Democrats' Well-Timed Remarks," *Los Angeles Times*, September 30, 2007, A21 (quotation).

78. "Labor 2008: AFL-CIO Membership Mobilization Program" (AFL-CIO document), "9/21/07 AFL-CIO Executive Council, Washington, DC," box 3, AR2009-0024, AFL-CIO Papers (quotations); "Draft Opening Remarks by John J. Sweeney, AFL-CIO Meeting with Sen. Barack Obama," June 18, 2008, "6/18 and 19/08 Meetings w/Barack Obama, Washington, DC," box 6, AR2009-0024, AFL-CIO Papers.

79. Sweeney quoted in "Swing States an Edge for Obama," *Washington Post*, June 27, 2008, A4; unemployment data from the Bureau of Labor Statistics at http://data.bls .gov/timeseries/LNS14000000 (accessed November 14, 2014, copy in author's possession).

80. "TPs for Pres. Sweeney for Greenhouse, *Chicago Tribune*, Major Interviews," June 26, 2008, "6/18 and 19/08 Meetings w/Barack Obama, Washington, DC," box 6, AR2009-0024, AFL-CIO Papers; Meyerson, "Can He Be," A13; Steven Greenhouse, "Unions Look for New Life in World of Obama," *New York Times*, December 29, 2008, B6 (quotation).

81. MacGillis, "Labor Leaders Stress," A27; "TPs for Pres. Sweeney for Greenhouse, *Chicago Tribune*, Major Interviews," June 26, 2008, "6/18 and 19/08 Meetings w/Barack Obama, Washington, DC," box 6, AR2009-0024, AFL-CIO Papers.

82. "AFL-CIO Protesters to Follow McCain Around," *Los Angeles Times*, March 13, 2008, A13.

83. "Draft Opening Remarks by John J. Sweeney, AFL-CIO Meeting with Sen. Barack Obama," June 18, 2008, "6/18 and 19/08 Meetings w/Barack Obama, Washington, DC," box 6, AR2009-0024, AFL-CIO Papers.

84. "Remarks by John J. Sweeney," February 8, 2007, AFL-CIO Papers; Gerald McEntee interview.

85. MacGillis, "Labor Leaders Stress," A27; Michael Finnegan, "AFL-CIO Backs Obama Candidacy," *Los Angeles Times*, June 27, 2008, A22; Anna Burger interview.

86. "Notice to AFL-CIO General Board—General Board Meeting to Consider a Presidential Endorsement," June 19, 2008; and "Draft Opening Remarks by John J. Sweeney, AFL-CIO Meeting with Sen. Barack Obama," June 18, 2008—both in "6/18 and 19/08 Meetings w/Barack Obama, Washington, DC," box 6, AR2009-0024, AFL-CIO Papers.

87. AFL-CIO General Board Statement: Endorsement of Senator Barack Obama for President of the United States, June 2008, "6/18 and 19/08 Meetings w/Barack Obama, Washington, DC"; and "Talking Points: AFL-CIO Endorsement of Barack Obama," June 2008, "6/26/08 Obama Endorsement" (quotation)—both in box 6, AR2009-0024, AFL-CIO Papers. See also the untitled AFL-CIO analysis of candidates' voting records in "5/30/07 Executive Committee Meeting, Washington, DC," box 2, AR2009-0024, AFL-CIO Papers.

88. "Presidential Elections," *Washington Post*, July 10, 2008, A4.

89. Shailagh Murray and Jonathan Weisman, "Obama Tells Allies He is Ready to Hit Back: As GOP Attacks Grow, He Links McCain, Bush," *Washington Post*, August 19, 2008, A4; *Washington Post*, October 15, 2008, A3.

90. MacGillis, "Labor Leaders Stress," A27.

91. "Selling the Man to the Membership: Calling Union Members Who Don't Vote Democratic 'Racist' is Risky," Charleston (WV) *Daily Mail*, September 1, 2008, 4A; Alexandra Berzon and Michael Mishak, "Tackling Race to Negate It," *Las Vegas Sun*, September 10, 2008.

92. Shailagh Murray, "Two Candidates, Two States, and One Big Day: Indiana and North Carolina Shape Up as Big Pieces of the Democratic Puzzle," *Washington Post*, May 6, 2008, A9.

93. Harold Meyerson, "Landing the White Whale," *Washington Post*, April 30, 2008, A19.

94. Steven Greenhouse, "Union Leaders Confronted by Resistance to Obama," *New York Times*, September 29, 2008, A17.

95. Michael Powell, "Democrats in Steel Country See Skin Color, and Beyond It," *New York Times*, October 27, 2008, A1 (first two quotations); Shailagh Murray, "Democratic Candidates Begin Touring Rust Belt; Campaign Caught off Guard by McCain's Pick," *Washington Post*, August 30, 2008, A10 (third quotation).

96. MacGillis, "Labor Leaders Stress," A27 (Ackerman quotation); "TPs for Pres. Sweeney for Greenhouse, *Chicago Tribune*, Major Interviews," June 26, 2008, "6/18 and 19/08 Meetings w/Barack Obama, Washington, DC," box 6, AR2009-0024, AFL-CIO Papers; Karen Nussbaum interview (Nussbaum quotation).

97. "Remarks by Richard L. Trumka, USW Convention," July 1, 2008, transcript supplied by the AFL-CIO (in author's possession); "AFL-CIO's Richard Trumka on Racism and Obama," available at http://www.youtube.com/watch?v=7QIGJTHDH50 (accessed November 21, 2014, copy in author's possession); closing quotation in Alec MacGillis, "No Getting around This Guy," *Washington Post*, September 7, 2009.

98. Richard Trumka interview; Lucy quoted in Acuff, *Playing Bigger Than You Are*, 115; Christi Parsons and Rick Pearson, "Democratic National Convention: Union Chief Rails at Racism," *Los Angeles Times*, August 27, 2008, A14.

99. Richard Trumka interview; Arlene Holt Baker interview; Susan Washington interview.

100. Steven Greenhouse, "Politics Has Dissidents Talking to AFL-CIO," *New York Times*, July 19, 2008, A9.

101. MacGillis, "Labor Leaders Stress," A27.

102. Wayne Leslie, "Democratic Groups Turn to Foot Soldiers," *New York Times*, September 21, 2008, A24.

103. Alec MacGillis, "Obama Camp Relying Heavily on Ground Effort," *Washington Post*, October 12, 2008, A4.

104. Eli Saslow, "Mailed Ads Have Become Mostly Negative, Experts Say," *Washington Post*, October 26, 2008, A13.

105. Todd and Gawiser, *How Barack Obama Won*, 43; unemployment data from the Bureau of Labor Statistics at http://data.bls.gov/timeseries/LNS14000000 (accessed November 14, 2014, copy in author's possession).

106. Kenski, Hardy, and Jamieson, *The Obama Victory*, 1; Denise Mitchell interview; Todd and Gawiser, *How Barack Obama Won*, 23 (closing quotation).

107. Matthew Mosk, "Economic Downturn Sidelines Donors to '527' Groups," *Washington Post*, October 19, 2008, A9.

108. "AFL-CIO Union Voters Help Drive Historic Victory for Obama," *PR Newswire*, November 5, 2008.

109. Karen Ackerman interview; Acuff, *Playing Bigger Than You Are*, 115; Denise Mitchell interview; Charles Stott interview.

110. Steven Greenhouse, "In Obama, Labor Finds the Support it Expected," *New York Times*, March 2, 2009, B3.

111. Esther Kaplan, "Can Labor Revive the American Dream?" *The Nation*, January 26, 2009, 12.

112. AFL-CIO Organizing Director Stewart Acuff quoted in "Which Side Are You On?" *The Nation*, April 6, 2009, 4–5 (first quotation); Kaplan, "Can Labor Revive," 13, 14 (other quotations).

113. "Employee Free Choice Act," AFL-CIO Executive Council Statement, March 3, 2009.

114. Adam Liptak, "Court Declines to Revisit Its Citizens United Decision," *New York Times*, June 26, 2012, A14; Greg Hitt, "Big Business Takes Page from Labor's Playbook, Focusing on Grass-Roots Contacts in Campaigns," *Wall Street Journal*, November 1, 1999, A56 (quotation from Karlyn Bowman); "Labor's Lies," *Wall Street Journal*, July 18, 1996, A12.

115. Francia, *The Future of Organized Labor in American Politics*, 146–49.

116. Bill Samuel interview.

117. Stewart Acuff interview; Elizabeth Bunn interview.

118. Bob Welsh interview; Susan Washington interview; Ken Zinn interview.

119. Gerry Shea interview; Barbara Shailor interview; Sharon Cohen, "Can John Sweeney Bring Back Labor?" *Tampa Tribune*, September 15, 1996, 1; "Talking Points for JJS," March 4, 2007, AFL-CIO Papers.

120. Kathleen Lynn, "For Labor, A Decade of Decline: Factory Jobs Went Overseas," *The Record* (New Jersey), September 4, 1989, C1.

121. Hurd quoted in Greenhouse, "Labor Leader Is Stepping Down," A32; Tom Donahue interview (2013).

122. Bob Welsh to President Sweeney, July 18, 2008, "8/5–6/08—Executive Council Meeting, Chicago, IL," box 7, AR2009-0024/BO5/G/31, AFL-CIO Papers. For examples of important breakthroughs by women, see Wyatt Olson, "AFL-CIO Boss: Union Support Growing," Bangor (ME) *Daily News*, September 6, 1999, 1; John Reynolds, "Blackshere Wins Illinois AFL-CIO Election," Springfield (IL) *State Journal Register*, January 9, 2000, 11; Ned Randolph and John LaPlante, "Black Woman Takes Helm of AFL-CIO," Baton Rouge (LA) *Advocate*, November 16, 2004, 1C; Steve Alexander, "Minnesota AFL-CIO Picks First Woman as President," *Minneapolis Star Tribune*, August 19, 2009, D1.

123. Tefere Gebre interview; Richard Trumka interview; Michael Podhorzer interview.

124. "Debating Labor's Future," 17 (Sweeney quotation); Denise Mitchell interview; Harold Meyerson, "John Sweeney's Real Triumphs," *Washington Post*, September 16, 2009, A23.

Epilogue

1. Andy Stern interview; Steven Greenhouse, "Labor Leader is Stepping Down Both Proud and Frustrated," *New York Times*, September 13, 2009, A32; Obama quoted in Proceedings of the Twenty-Sixth Constitutional Convention of the AFL-CIO, September 13–17, 2009, 326; Trumka quoted in Proceedings of the Twenty-Sixth Constitutional Convention of the AFL-CIO, September 13–17, 2009, 13–14.

2. Michael Mishak, "AFL-CIO Sees Young as Challenge, Opportunity," *Las Vegas Sun*, September 20, 2009.

3. Steven Greenhouse, "Promising a New Day, Again," *New York Times*, September 15, 2009.

4. Ibid.; Richard Trumka interview.

5. Kris Maher, "Big Labor Leader is Old School Writ Large," *Wall Street Journal*, September 1, 2009, A13.

6. Alec MacGillis, "No Getting around This Guy," *Washington Post*, September 7, 2009; Greenhouse, "Promising a New Day."

7. Richard Womack to President Sweeney (Department of Civil and Human Rights Report), August 14, 2001, "Monthly Reports, AFL-CIO Department (2001)," box 1, AR2003-0084, AFL-CIO Papers; Richard Trumka interview.

8. David Moberg, "One Hat for Labor?" *The Nation*, May 18, 2009, 18–21; MacGillis, "No Getting around This Guy"; Greenhouse, "Promising a New Day."

9. Richard Trumka interview; Craig Becker interview.

10. Maher, "Big Labor Leader," A13 (quotation); Mishak, "AFL-CIO Sees Young."

11. Greenhouse, "Promising a New Day"; Ana Avendano interview.

12. Arlene Holt Baker interview; Liz Shuler interview.

13. Doug Dority interview.

14. Richard Trumka interview; Trumka quoted in MacGillis, "No Getting around This Guy."

15. Proceedings of the Twenty-Sixth Constitutional Convention of the AFL-CIO, September 13–17, 2009, 14.

16. "Frozen out" quotation in MacGillis, "No Getting around This Guy"; Steven Greenhouse, "In Obama, Labor Finds the Support it Expected," *New York Times*, March 2, 2009, B3.

17. Alec MacGillis, "For Unions, A Time of Opportunity and Worry; Obama to Address AFL-CIO as Labor Faces Its Divisions," *Washington Post*, September 15, 2009, A15 (O'Sullivan quotation); Proceedings of the Twenty-Sixth Constitutional Convention of the AFL-CIO, September 13–17, 2009, 325–34 (Obama quotation on 325).

18. David Stout, "With a Swipe at Bush, Obama Acts to Bolster Labor," *New York Times*, January 31, 2009, A14; Esther Kaplan, "Can Labor Revive the American Dream?" *The Nation*, January 26, 2009, 12–13; closing quotation in Randolph Heaster, "Obama and Unions Still Working It Out," *Kansas City Star*, September 7, 2009, A1.

19. Steven Greenhouse, "U.S. Proposes Posted Notice of the Right to Unionize," *New York Times*, December 22, 2010, B3; Steven Greenhouse, "Labor Board Case against Boeing Points to Fights to Come," *New York Times*, April 23, 2011, B1; Paul H. Derrick, "Labor Board Edges to Pro-Union Stance," Raleigh (NC) *News and Observer*, November 17, 2010, A15; Diana Furchtgott-Roth, "Americans Dodge Unions, but Feds Insist Anyway," *Washington Examiner*, December 24, 2010, 29.

20. Jackie Calmes, "For Obama, a Familiar Labor Day Theme," *New York Times*, September 6, 2011, A19; "Obama Pitches for Big Labor's Backing at Ohio Gathering, President Exhorts AFL-CIO to Join Him in Health Care Battle," Newark (NJ) *Star-Ledger*, September 8, 2009; Reid Wilson, "Why Labor is Vulnerable," *National Journal*, March 2, 2011; Alec MacGillis, "Officials: Stern to Resign from Union President Post," *Washington Post*, April 13, 2010, A3.

21. Reed Abelson, "Employers Pushed Costs for Health on Workers," *New York Times*, September 3, 2010, B1; "The Recession's Awful Impact" (editorial), *New York Times*, September 17, 2010, A26.

22. Tanden quoted in David Leonhardt, "Job Losses Outweigh Successes," *New York Times*, October 27, 2010, B1; Obama quoted in "Obama Makes His Mark," *The Daily Astorian* (Astoria, Oregon), March 23, 2010.

23. "The Public Plan," (editorial) *New York Times*, August 19, 2009, A26; Robert Pear, "Making Exceptions in Obama's Health Care Act Draws Kudos, and Criticism," *New York Times*, March 20, 2011, A21; Steven Greenhouse and Jonathan Martin, "Unions' Misgivings on Health Law Burst Into View," *New York Times*, September 12, 2013, B1.

24. Harold Meyerson, "Labor's Last Stand," *Washington Post*, May 25, 2011, A19.

25. Bob Welsh interview.

26. Harold Meyerson, "Labor Rows against an Angry Tide," *Washington Post*, September 1, 2010, A17; Perry Bacon Jr., "As Elections Near, Voter Outreach Intensifies," *Washington Post*, November 1, 2010, A6.

27. Craig Becker interview; Alec MacGillis, "5 Myths about the Labor Movement," *Washington Post*, February 21, 2010, B3; Zieger, Minchin, and Gall, *American Workers, American Unions*, 295–96.

28. Steven Greenhouse and Cara Buckley, "Seeking Energy, Unions Join Wall Street Protest," *New York Times*, October 6, 2011, A1; Mariya Strauss, "'One Nation' to March on Washington Oct. 2," *Labor Notes*, September 10, 2010.

29. Sam Hananel, "AFL-CIO Leader: Wisconsin Fight Energizing Unions," *Associated Press Archive*, March 2, 2011; Dennis Brady, "Supporters Rally for Wis. Governor's Bill," *Washington Post*, February 20, 2011, A3; McEntee quoted in Peter Whoriskey and Dan Balz, "Governor's Triumph Deals Major Blow to Unions," *Washington Post*, June 7, 2012, A4; Trumka quoted in Dennis Brady, "Wisconsin Budget Impasse Deepens," *Washington Post*, February 19, 2011, A1.

30. Zieger, Minchin, and Gall, *American Workers, American Unions*, 296–97.

31. Ibid.

32. Denise Mitchell interview; Steven Greenhouse, "The Ecumenical Union," *New York Times*, September 7, 2013, B1; Robert J. Samuelson, "Big Labor's Big Decline," *Washington Post*, February 28, 2011, A15.

33. Michael A. Fletcher, "Organized Labor Cheers New Effort to Streamline Unionization Efforts," *Washington Post*, February 6, 2014, A12; Steven Greenhouse, "Share of the Work Force in a Union Falls to a 97-Year Low, 11.3%," *New York Times*, January 23, 2013 (Chaison quotation).

34. Andy Stern interview.

35. Zieger, Minchin, and Gall, *American Workers, American Unions*, 309–10 (*Monitor* quotation on 310).

36. Mark Ballard, "Unions Being Demonized," Baton Rouge (LA) *Advocate*, December 16, 2012, 7B; Amy Gardner, "Union Leaders Support Obama Despite Tension," *Washington Post*, September 6, 2012, A9; Liz Shuler interview; Christine Owens interview; Craig Becker interview.

37. Mark Landler and Steven Greenhouse, "Vacancies and Partisan Fighting Put Labor Relations Agency in Legal Limbo," *New York Times*, July 16, 2013, A14.

38. Elizabeth Bunn interview.

39. Brent Snavely, "VW's Tennessee Workers Reject Union," *Detroit Free Press*, February 15, 2014, reprinted in *USA Today* at http://www.usatoday.com/story/money/cars/2014/02/14/vw-workers-vote-against-uaw/5500897/(accessed November 26, 2014, copy in author's possession).

40. Monica Davey, "Michigan: Union Leaders Seek Government Money for Detroit," *New York Times*, July 26, 2013, A17; MacGillis, "5 Myths about the Labor Movement," B3; Lydia DePillis, "Can Damon Silvers Save Organized Labor?" *Washington Post*, November 19, 2013 (quotation).

41. Mishak, "AFL-CIO Sees Young"; AFL-CIO Executive Council Minutes, September 21, 2007, 18, "8/5–6/08 Executive Council Meeting, Chicago, IL," box 7, AR 2009–0024, AFL-CIO Papers.

42. Eugene L. Meyer, "A Campus Built by Labor Is Going on the Block," *New York Times*, August 1, 2012, B6; Daniel J. Sernovitz, "Transit Union Pays $31.4 Million for Former National Labor College Campus," *Washington Business Journal*, July 30, 2014, available at http://www.bizjournals.com/washington/breaking_ground/2014/07/transit

-union-pays-31-4-million-for-former-national.html (accessed November 26, 2014, copy in author's possession).

43. "Union to Rejoin the AFL-CIO," *New York Times*, August 15, 2010, A19; Jack Katzanek, "Construction Union Rejoins AFL-CIO," *McClatchy-Tribune Regional News*, August 18, 2010; Terry O'Sullivan interview.

44. "UFCW Joins AFL-CIO" (UFCW Press Release), August 8, 2013, available at http://www.ufcw.org/2013/08/08/ufcw-joins-afl-cio/ (accessed November 20, 2014, copy in author's possession); Liz Shuler interview.

45. John Sweeney interview.

46. MacGillis, "For Unions, A Time," A15; Early, *The Civil Wars in U.S. Labor*, xi–xii; Jane Slaughter, "Has Andy Stern Reunited Labor?" *Labor Notes*, September 8, 2009.

47. MacGillis, "Officials: Stern to Resign," A3; Andy Stern interview.

48. Slaughter, "Has Andy Stern?" ("chummy" quotation); "Unions Ramp Up Support," *New York Times*, June 12, 2013, A20; "Union to Rejoin," A19; Andy Stern interview; Craig Becker interview.

49. Eli Saslow, "Occupied by What's Next," *Washington Post*, October 10, 2011, A1 (first two Trumka quotations); Peter Wallsten, "Lending a Little Organized Labor to Occupy Wall Street," *Washington Post*, October 21, 2011, A1 (other Trumka quotations); Katz and Greenwald, eds., *Labor Rising* (closing quotation on book cover).

50. Richard Trumka interview; Ashley Parker and Steven Greenhouse, "Labor and Business Reach Deal on Immigration Issue," *New York Times*, March 31, 2013, A14; Julia Preston, "Immigration Vote Unlikely This Year, Lawmaker Says," *New York Times*, November 9, 2013, A13.

51. "The AFL-CIO Says Enough," *The Nation*, September 12, 2011, 5; Tefere Gebre interview; Richard Trumka interview.

52. Greenhouse, "The Ecumenical Union," B1; Liz Shuler interview.

53. Harold Meyerson, "Laboring for the Future," *Washington Post*, May 10, 2013, A25.

54. Steven Greenhouse, "At Labor Group, a Sense of a Broader Movement," *New York Times*, September 14, 2013, B3; Tefere Gebre interview.

55. Steven Greenhouse, "Labor Leaders Have Obama's Back, and Are Ready to Help," *New York Times*, November 13, 2012, A12.

56. Zieger, Minchin, and Gall, *American Workers, American Unions*, 307–9 (Meyerson quotation on 309); Rosalind S. Heiderman, "Unions Ramp Up Ohio Ground Game," *Washington Post*, October 10, 2012, A8.

57. AFL-CIO Executive Council Minutes (draft), May 22, 2002, 3, "8/6–07/02—Executive Council Mtg., Chicago, IL," box 4, AR2003-0096, AFL-CIO Papers; Greenhouse, "Promising a New Day" (Trumka quotation); unemployment data from the Bureau of Labor Statistics at http://data.bls.gov/timeseries/LNS14000000 (accessed January 30, 2015, copy in author's possession).

58. "Don't Let Washington Forget: No TPP Trade Deal at any Cost," *Alliance for American Manufacturing News*, March 22, 2013 (copy in author's possession); "We're Talking Manufacturing, and Washington is Listening," *Alliance for American Manufacturing News*, March 29, 2013 (copy in author's possession).

59. Samuelson, "Big Labor's," A15; Rosenfeld, *What Unions No Longer Do*, 1. See also Hogler, *The End of American Labor Unions*.

60. Arlene Holt Baker interview.

61. Ana Avendano interview; Richard Trumka interview.

62. Phelan, ed., *Trade Union Revitalisation*, 17; Philip Bassett, "Union Membership Slips Worldwide" *(London) Times*, November 4, 1997, 33.

63. Richard D. Kahlenberg and Moshe Z. Marvit, "The Right to Unionize Should be a Civil Right," *Washington Post*, September 2, 2012, B4.

64. Katz and Greenwald, eds., *Labor Rising*, 6.

65. Getman, *Restoring the Power of Unions*, xv; Yates, *Why Unions Matter*, 11; Dray, *There Is Power*, 674; Dean and Reynolds, *A New New Deal*, 1 ("only player" quotation); Jane Slaughter, "Rolling Sympathy Strikes Harass Food-Service Giant," *Labor Notes*, November 25, 2011.

66. Brad Burton interview.

67. Richard Trumka interview.

Bibliography

Manuscripts

Abilene, Kansas
  Dwight D. Eisenhower Presidential Library
  White House Central Files (President's Personal File)
Athens, Georgia
  Richard B. Russell Library for Political Research and Studies, University of
    Georgia
  George W. "Buddy" Darden Papers
  Charles F. Hatcher Papers
  Edgar L. Jenkins Papers
  Don Johnson Papers
  J. Roy Rowland Papers
Atlanta, Georgia
  Jimmy Carter Presidential Library
  Bernie Aronson Files (Chief of Staff)
  Landon Butler Files (Chief of Staff)
  Stuart Eizenstat Files (Domestic Policy Staff)
  Hamilton Jordan Files (Chief of Staff)
  Steve Selig Files (Chief of Staff)
  White House Central Files-Name File (Lane Kirkland)
  Southern Labor Archives, University Library, Georgia State University
  Professional Air Traffic Controllers Organization Records (accessed digitally)
Austin, Texas
  Dolph Briscoe Centre for American History, University of Texas at Austin
  Steve Russell and Donna Mobley Papers
  Lyndon Baines Johnson Presidential Library
  White House Central Files-Name File (American Federation of Labor)
  White House Central Files-Name File (George Meany)
Chattanooga, Tennessee
  Lupton Library, University of Tennessee at Chattanooga
  Marilyn Lloyd Papers
College Park, Maryland
  Hornbake Library, University of Maryland
  AFL-CIO Papers
College Station, Texas
  George H. W. Bush Presidential Library

White House Office of Records Management (WHORM) Files
Office of Speechwriting Files
Columbia, South Carolina
South Carolina Political Collections Library, University of South Carolina
Ernest F. Hollings Papers
Gonzales, Louisiana
Oil, Chemical, and Atomic Workers' International Union (OCAW) Local 4-620
Papers, PACE Local 4-620, Gonzales, Louisiana
Ithaca, New York
Kheel Center for Labor-Management Documentation and Archives, School of
Industrial and Labor Relations, Cornell University
Amalgamated Clothing and Textile Workers' Union Papers
International Ladies' Garment Workers' Union Papers
Union of Needletrades, Industrial, and Textile Employees Papers
Little Rock, Arkansas
William Jefferson Clinton Presidential Library
Clinton White House Archived Websites (accessed digitally)
Simi Valley, California
Ronald Reagan Presidential Library
Morton Blackwell Files
Roger Bolton Files
Robert Bonitati Files
Joseph W. Canzeri Files
Elizabeth Dole Files
Craig Fuller Files
Thomas G. Moore Files
Michael L. Mussa Files
Office of White House Correspondence Files
Speechwriting Files (research)
White House Office of Public Affairs Files
White House Office of Records Management—Open Files
Washington, DC
Mark Anderson Papers (Personal collection shared with author)
Tom Donahue Papers (Personal collection shared with author)
Steve Rosenthal Papers (Personal collection shared with author)
Yorba Linda, California
Richard Nixon Presidential Library
Charles W. Colson Files
White House Special Files

Author's Interviews

Karen Ackerman, Washington, DC, October 7, 2013
Stewart Acuff, Washington, DC, October 8, 2013

Mark Anderson, Washington, DC, July 17, 2013

Nickolas Atkins, Atlanta, Georgia, November 22, 1995

Ana Avendano, Washington, DC, April 17, 2015

Morton Bahr, Washington, DC, July 19, 2013

Bob Baugh, Washington, DC, June 18, 2009

Craig Becker, Washington, DC, April 21, 2015

Richard Bensinger, October 13, 2013 (telephone interview)

Susan Bianchi, Washington, DC, April 23, 2015

Elizabeth Bunn, Washington, DC, October 11, 2013

Anna Burger, Washington, DC, November 5, 2015

Brad Burton, Washington, DC, July 15, 2013

Mike Cavanaugh, Washington, DC, April 17, 2015

Linda Chavez-Thompson, July 26, 2013 (telephone interview)

Tom Donahue, Washington, DC, July 16, 2013, and November 3, 2015

Richard Donaldson, Baton Rouge, Louisiana, November 7, 2000

Doug Dority, Washington, DC, April 21, 2015

Susan Dunlop, Washington, DC, July 19, 2013, and November 5, 2015

Barbara Easterling, Washington, DC, October 7, 2013

Tefere Gebre, Washington, DC, April 17, 2015

Leo Gerrard, Pittsburgh, Pennsylvania, June 17, 2009

Wayne Glenn, Nashville, Tennessee, June 17, 1998

Larry Gold, Washington, DC, April 23, 2015

Jon Hiatt, Washington, DC, October 9, 2013

Arlene Holt Baker, Washington, DC, July 26, 2013

Jim Kennedy, Washington, DC, July 23, 2013

George Kourpias, Washington, DC, October 10, 2013

Gerald McEntee, Washington, DC, November 4, 2015

Robert McGlotten, Washington, DC, July 24, 2013

Lenore Miller, October 11, 2013 (telephone interview)

Denise Mitchell, Washington, DC, April 15, 2015

Karen Nussbaum, Washington, DC, July 23, 2013

Terry O'Sullivan, Washington, DC, November 6, 2015

Rudy Oswald, Rockville, Maryland, July 18, 2013

Christine Owens, Washington, DC, April 20, 2015

Rosalyn Pelles, July 26, 2013 (telephone interview)

Michael Podhorzer, May 7, 2015 (telephone interview)

Bruce Raynor, Greensboro, North Carolina, July 28, 1995

Harris Raynor, Union City, Georgia, June 18, 2010

Markley Roberts, Washington, DC, April 13, 2015

Steve Rosenthal, Washington, DC, July 18, 2013, and November 4, 2015

Bill Samuel, Washington, DC, July 22, 2013

Margaret "Peg" Seminario, Washington, DC, October 10, 2013

Barbara Shailor, Washington, DC, July 25, 2013

Gerry Shea, Washington, DC, July 16, 2013
Elizabeth Shuler, Washington, DC, April 14, 2015
Damon Silvers, Washington, DC, July 15, 2013
Marilyn Sneiderman, Washington, DC, July 26, 2013
Andy Stern, Washington, DC, October 11, 2013
David St. John, Washington, DC, July 22, 2013
Charles Stott, April 14, 2015 (telephone interview)
John Sweeney, Washington, DC, July 15, 2013
Richard Trumka, Washington, DC, April 23, 2015
Joe Uehlein, Takoma Park, Maryland, October 10, 2013
Susan Washington, July 19, 2013 (telephone interview)
Bob Welsh, Arlington, Virginia, July 17, 2013
Lane Windham, Takoma Park, Maryland, July 24, 2013, and November 5, 2015
Richard Womack, Washington, DC, July 22, 2013
Ken Zinn, Silver Spring, Maryland, October 9, 2013

Newspapers and Journals

Akron (OH) *Beacon Journal*
American Prospect
Associated Press Archive
Astoria (OR) *Daily Astorian*
Atlanta Journal-Constitution
Austin-American Statesman
Bangor Daily News
Baton Rouge (LA) *Advocate*
Black Enterprise
Boston Globe
Business Week
Cedar Rapids-Iowa City (IA) *Gazette*
Charleston (SC) *Evening Post*
Charleston (WV) *Daily Mail*
Charlotte Observer
Chicago Tribune
Chicago Sun-Times
Christian Science Monitor
Cleveland (OH) *Plain Dealer*
Dagens Nyheter
Dayton (OH) *Journal Herald*
Detroit Free Press
Fort Worth Star Telegram
Gainesville (FL) *Sun*
Gallup News Service

Global Information Network
Greensboro (NC) *News Record*
Harrisburg (PA) *Patriot-News*
Houston Chronicle
Human Events
Journal of Commerce
Kansas City Star
Knight Ridder Tribune Business
Labor Notes
Las Vegas Sun
Lexington (KY) *Herald-Leader*
London *Times*
Los Angeles Daily News
Los Angeles Times
Madison (WI) *Capital Times*
Management Report
McClatchy-Tribune Regional News
Melbourne *The Age*
Melville (NY) *Newsday*
Minneapolis Star Tribune
Monthly Labor Review
Nation
National Journal
National Review
New Jersey *The Record*

New Republic
New York Times
Newark (NJ) *Star-Ledger*
Newsweek
Norfolk (VA) *Virginian-Pilot*
Owensboro (KY) *Messenger-Inquirer*
Palm Beach Post
Philadelphia Daily News
Philadelphia Inquirer
Pittsburgh Post-Gazette
PR Newswire
Richmond (VA) *Times-Dispatch*
Roanoke (VA) *Times*
San Diego Evening Tribune
San Diego Union-Tribune
San Francisco Chronicle
San Francisco Examiner

San Jose (CA) *Mercury News*
Springfield (IL) *State Journal Register*
Springfield (MA) *Sunday Republican*
St. Louis Post-Dispatch
Sydney Morning Herald
Syracuse (NY) *Post-Standard*
Tampa Tribune
Time
U.S. Newswire
USA Today
Wall Street Journal
Washington Business Journal
Washington Examiner
Washington Post
Washington Times
Wichita (KS) *Eagle-Beacon*
Wisconsin State Journal

Trade and Union Journals

AFGE Challenger
AFL-CIO News
Alliance for American Manufacturing News
American Federationist
America@Work

Chemical Worker
Electrical Union World
HR Magazine
Industry Week
White Collar

Government Documents

U.S. Congress, House, Select Committee on Children, Youth, and Families. *Improving Child Care Services: What Can Be Done?* 98th Congress, 2nd Session, 1984.

U.S. Congress, House, Committee on Education and Labor. *Hearings on Compensation for Occupational Disease*, 99th Congress, 1st Session, 1985.

U.S. Congress, House, Committee on Education and Labor. *The Parental and Medical Leave Act of 1986*, 99th Congress, 2nd Session, 1986.

U.S. Congress, House, Committee on Education and Labor. *Hearings on H.R. 1834, The Minimum Wage Restoration Act of 1987*, 100th Congress, 1st Session, 1987.

U.S. Congress, House, Committee on Small Business. *Occupational Disease Notification: Potential Liability Problems*, 100th Congress, 1st Session, 1987.

U.S. Congress, Senate, Committee on the Budget. *Catastrophic and Long-Term Health Care*, 100th Congress, 1st Session, 1987.

U.S. Congress, House, Committee on Energy and Commerce. *U.S.-Canada Free Trade Agreement*, 100th Congress, 2nd Session, 1988.

Books, Articles, and Dissertations

Abramson, Paul R., John H. Aldrich, and David W. Rohde. *Change and Continuity in the 2008 and 2010 Elections.* Washington, DC: CQ Press, 2012.

Acuff, Stewart. *Playing Bigger Than You Are: A Life in Organizing.* Minneapolis: Levins, 2012.

Babson, Steve. *The Unfinished Struggle: Turning Points in American Labor, 1877–Present.* Lanham, MD: Rowman and Littlefield, 1999.

Balz, Dan, and Haynes Johnson. *The Battle for America 2008: The Story of an Extraordinary Election.* New York: Viking, 2009.

Bhagwati, Jagdish. *In Defense of Globalization.* New York: Oxford University Press, 2004.

Bluestone, Barry, and Bennett Harrison. *The Deindustrialization of America: Plant Closings, Community Abandonment, and the Dismantling of Basic Industry.* New York: Basic Books, 1982.

Borstelmann, Thomas. *The 1970s: A New Global History from Civil Rights to Economic Inequality.* Princeton, NJ: Princeton University Press, 2012.

Branch, Taylor. *Parting the Waters: America in the King Years, 1954–63.* New York: Simon and Schuster, 1988.

Brinkley, Alan. *American History: A Survey, Vol. 2, since 1865.* 11th ed. Boston: McGraw-Hill, 2003.

Brisbin, Richard A., Jr. *A Strike Like No Other Strike: Law and Resistance during the Pittston Coal Strike of 1989–1990.* Baltimore: Johns Hopkins University Press, 2002.

Brody, David. *Workers in Industrial America: Essays on the Twentieth Century Struggle.* New York: Oxford University Press, 1980.

Bronfenbrenner, Kate. "The Role of Union Strategies in NLRB Certification Elections." *Industrial and Labor Relations Review* 50, no. 2 (January 1997): 195–212.

Buhle, Paul. *Taking Care of Business: Samuel Gompers, George Meany, Lane Kirkland, and the Tragedy of American Labor.* New York: Monthly Review Press, 1999.

Carew, Anthony, Michel Dreyfus, Geert Van Goethem, Rebecca Gumbrell-McCormick, and Marcel van der Linden, eds. *The International Confederation of Free Trade Unions.* Bern, Switzerland: Peter Lang, 2000.

Carroll, Peter N. *It Seemed Like Nothing Happened: America in the 1970s.* New Brunswick, NJ: Rutgers University Press, 1990.

Carter, Dan T. *From George Wallace to Newt Gingrich: Race in the Conservative Counterrevolution, 1963–1994.* Baton Rouge: Louisiana State University Press, 1996.

Chafe, William H. *The Unfinished Journey: America since World War II.* 2nd ed. New York: Oxford University Press, 1991.

———. *The Unfinished Journey: America since World War II.* 7th ed. New York: Oxford University Press, 2011.

Cirautas, Arista Maria. *The Polish Solidarity Movement: Revolution, Democracy, and Natural Rights.* London: Routledge, 1997.

Clark, Jon. *Trade Unions, National Politics and Economic Management: A Comparative Study of the TUC and the DGB*. London: Anglo-German Foundation for the Study of Industrial Society, 1980.

Clawson, Dan. *The Next Upsurge: Labor and the New Social Movements*. Ithaca, NY: ILR Press, 2003.

Cobb, James C. *The South and America since World War II*. New York: Oxford University Press, 2011.

Cowie, Jefferson. *Stayin' Alive: The 1970s and the Last Days of the Working Class*. New York: The New Press, 2010.

Daniel, Cletus E. *Bitter Harvest: A History of California Farmworkers, 1870–1941*. Ithaca, NY: Cornell University Press, 1981.

Dark, Taylor. "Debating Decline: The 1995 Race for the AFL-CIO Presidency." *Labor History* 40, no. 3 (1999): 323–43.

Dean, Amy B., and David B. Reynolds. *A New New Deal: How Regional Activism Will Reshape the American Labor Movement*. Ithaca, NY: ILR Press, 2009.

DeGroot, Gerard J. *A Noble Cause? America and the Vietnam War*. Harlow, UK: Pearson, 2000.

Denison, Ray W. *Growing Up in the Great Depression*. Port Sanilac, MI: The Denison Arts, 2003.

Domber, Gregory F. *Empowering Revolution: America, Poland, and the End of the Cold War*. Chapel Hill: University of North Carolina Press, 2014.

Donn, Clifford B. *The Australian Council of Trade Unions: History and Economic Policy*. Lanham, MD: University Press of America, 1983.

Draper, Alan. *Conflict of Interests: Organized Labor and the Civil Rights Movement in the South, 1954–1968*. Ithaca, NY: ILR Press, 1994.

Dray, Philip. *There Is Power in a Union: The Epic Story of Labor in America*. New York: Anchor Books, 2011.

Dubofsky, Melvyn, and Foster Rhea Dulles. *Labor in America: A History*. 7th ed. Wheeling, IL: Harlan Davidson, 2004.

Dubofsky, Melvyn, and Joseph A. McCartin, eds. *American Labor: A Documentary Collection*. New York: Palgrave Macmillan, 2004.

Early, Steve. *The Civil Wars in U.S. Labor: Birth of a New Workers' Movement or Death Throes of the Old?* Chicago: Haymarket Books, 2011.

Ferguson, Niall, Charles S. Maier, Erez Manela, and Daniel J. Sargent, eds. *The Shock of the Global: The 1970s in Perspective*. Cambridge, MA: Harvard University Press, 2010.

Ferriss, Susan, and Ricardo Sandoval. *The Fight in the Fields: Cesar Chavez and the Farmworkers Movement*. New York: Harcourt Brace, 1997.

Fink, Leon, and Brian Greenberg. *Upheaval in the Quiet Zone: A History of Hospital Workers' Union, Local 1199*. Urbana: University of Illinois Press, 1989.

Fletcher, Bill, Jr., and Fernando Gapasin. *Solidarity Divided: The Crisis in Organized Labor and a New Path Toward Social Justice*. Berkeley: University of California Press, 2008.

Foner, Eric. *Give Me Liberty: An American History.* New York: W. W. Norton, 2009.

Francia, Peter Louis. "Awakening the Sleeping Giant: The Renaissance of Organized Labor in American Politics." PhD diss., University of Maryland, 2000.

———. *The Future of Organized Labor in American Politics.* New York: Columbia University Press, 2006.

Geoghegan, Thomas. *Which Side Are You On? Trying to Be for Labor When It's Flat on Its Back.* New York: Farrar, Straus and Giroux, 1991.

Getman, Julius G. *The Betrayal of Local 14: Paperworkers, Politics, and Permanent Replacements.* Ithaca, NY: ILR Press, 1998.

———. *Restoring the Power of Unions: It Takes a Movement.* New Haven, CT: Yale University Press, 2010.

Goldfield, Michael. *The Color of Politics: Race and the Mainsprings of American Politics.* New York: New Press, 1997.

———. *The Decline of Organized Labor in the United States.* Chicago: University of Chicago Press, 1987.

Gould, William B. *Black Workers in White Unions: Job Discrimination in the United States.* Ithaca, NY: Cornell University Press, 1977.

Goulden, Joseph C. *Meany.* New York: Atheneum, 1972.

———. *Jerry Wurf: Labor's Last Angry Man.* New York: Atheneum, 1982.

Griffith, Barbara S. *The Crisis of American Labor: Operation Dixie and the Defeat of the CIO.* Philadelphia: Temple University Press, 1988.

Haberland, Michelle. "Women's Work: The Apparel Industry in the United States South, 1937–1980." PhD diss., Tulane University, 2001.

Hagan, Jim. *The History of the A.C.T.U.* Melbourne, Australia: Longman Cheshire, 1981.

Hall, Jacquelyn Dowd, James Leloudis, Robert Korstad, Mary Murphy, Lu Ann Jones, and Christopher B. Daly. *Like a Family: The Making of a Southern Cotton Mill World.* Chapel Hill: University of North Carolina Press, 1987.

Heilemann, John, and Mark Halperin. *Game Change: Obama and the Clintons, McCain and Palin, and the Race of a Lifetime.* New York: HarperCollins, 2010.

Hill, Herbert. *Black Labor and the American Legal System: Race, Work and the Law.* Madison: University of Wisconsin Press, 1977.

———. "Myth-Making as Labor History: Herbert Gutman and the United Mine Workers of America." *International Journal of Politics, Culture and Society* 2, no. 2 (Winter 1988): 132–200.

———. "The Problem of Race in American Labor History." *Reviews in American History* 24, no. 2 (June 1996): 189–208.

———. "Race, Ethnicity and Organized Labor: The Opposition to Affirmative Action." *New Politics,* 1, no. 2 (Winter 1987): 31–82.

Hodges, James A. *New Deal Labor Policy and the Southern Cotton Textile Industry, 1933–1941.* Knoxville: University of Tennessee Press, 1986.

Hogler, Raymond L. *The End of American Labor Unions: The Right-to-Work Movement and the Erosion of Collective Bargaining.* Santa Barbara, CA: Praeger, 2015.

Hughes, Quenby Olmstead. *In the Interest of Democracy: The Rise and Fall of the Early Cold War Alliance between the American Federation of Labor and the Central Intelligence Agency.* Oxford: Peter Lang, 2011.

Hurup, Elsebeth, ed. *The Lost Decade: America in the Seventies.* Aarhus, Denmark: Aarhus University Press, 1996.

Hutchinson, John. *The Imperfect Union: A History of Corruption in American Trade Unions.* New York: Dutton, 1970.

James, Ralph C., and Estelle Dinnerstein James. *Hoffa and the Teamsters: A Study of Union Power.* Princeton, NJ: Van Nostrand, 1965.

Juravich, Tom, and Kate Bronfenbrenner. *Ravenswood: The Steelworkers' Victory and the Revival of American Labor.* Ithaca, NY: ILR Press, 1999.

Katz, Daniel, and Richard A. Greenwald, eds. *Labor Rising: The Past and Future of Working People in America.* New York: The New Press, 2012.

Kennedy, David M., Lizabeth Cohen, and Thomas A. Bailey. *The American Pageant: A History of the Republic, Volume 2, since 1865.* 13th ed. Boston: Houghton Mifflin, 2006.

Kenski, Kate, Bruce W. Hardy, and Kathleen Hall Jamieson. *The Obama Victory: How Media, Money, and Message Shaped the 2008 Election.* New York: Oxford University Press, 2010.

Keys, Barbara, Jack Davies, and Elliott Bannan. "The Post-Traumatic Decade: New Histories of the 1970s." *Australasian Journal of American Studies* 33, no. 1 (2014): 1–17.

Kletzer, Lori G. *Job Loss from Imports: Measuring the Costs.* Washington, DC: Peterson Institute for International Economics, 2001.

Kumar, Deepa. *Outside the Box: Corporate Media, Globalization, and the UPS Strike.* Urbana: University of Illinois Press, 2007.

Kwavnick, David. *Organized Labour and Pressure Politics: The Canadian Labour Congress, 1956–1968.* Montreal: McGill-Queen's University Press, 1972.

Lee, Lai To. *Trade Unions in China, 1949 to the Present; The Organization and Leadership of the All-China Federation of Trade Unions.* Singapore: Singapore University Press, 1986.

Lichtenstein, Nelson. "Despite EFCA's Limitations, Its Demise Is a Profound Defeat for U.S. Labor." *Labor: Studies in Working-Class History of the Americas* 7, no. 3 (Fall 2010): 29–32.

———. *The Most Dangerous Man in Detroit: Walter Reuther and the Fate of American Labor.* New York: Basic Books, 1995.

———. *The Retail Revolution: How Wal-Mart Created a Brave New World of Business.* New York: Metropolitan Books, 2009.

———. *State of the Union: A Century of American Labor.* Princeton, NJ: Princeton University Press, 2002.

Lipset, Seymour Martin, ed. *Unions in Transition: Entering the Second Century.* San Francisco: Institute for Contemporary Studies, 1986.

Martin, Ross. *TUC: The Growth of a Pressure Group, 1868–1976.* Oxford, UK: Oxford University Press, 1980.

McCartin, Joseph A. *Collision Course: Ronald Reagan, the Air Traffic Controllers, and the Strike That Changed America*. New York: Oxford University Press, 2011.

Minchin, Timothy J. *Empty Mills: The Fight against Imports and the Decline of the U.S. Textile Industry*. Lanham, MD: Rowman and Littlefield, 2013.

———. *Fighting Against the Odds: A History of Southern Labor since World War II*. Gainesville: University Press of Florida, 2005.

———. *Forging a Common Bond: Labor and Environmental Activism in the BASF Lockout*. Gainesville: University Press of Florida, 2003.

———. "'It Tears the Heart Right out of You': Memories of Striker Replacement at International Paper Company in De Pere, Wisconsin, 1987–88." *Oral History Review* 31, no. 2 (Summer–Fall 2004): 1–27.

———. "'Labor's Empty Gun': Permanent Replacements and the International Paper Company Strike of 1987–88." *Labor History* 47, no. 1 (February 2006): 21–42.

———. "Organizing a Labor Law Violator: The J. P. Stevens Campaign and the Struggle to Unionize the US South, 1963–1983." *International Review of Social History* 50, no. 1 (April 2005): 27–51.

———. "Shutting Down 'Big Brown': Reassessing the 1997 UPS Strike and the Fate of American Labor." *Labor History* 53, no. 4 (November 2012): 541–60.

Minchin, Timothy J., and John A. Salmond. *After the Dream: Black and White Southerners since 1965*. Lexington: University Press of Kentucky, 2011.

Moody, Kim. *An Injury to All: The Decline of American Unionism*. New York: Verso, 1988.

———. *US Labor in Trouble and Transition: The Failure of Reform from Above, the Promise of Revival from Below*. New York: Verso, 2007.

Nelson, Bruce. *Divided We Stand: American Workers and the Struggle for Black Equality*. Princeton, NJ: Princeton University Press, 2001.

Nixon, Richard M. *RN: The Memoirs of Richard Nixon*. Melbourne: The Macmillan Company of Australia, 1978.

Norton, Mary Beth, David M. Katzman, David W. Blight, Howard P. Chudacoff, Thomas G. Paterson, William M. Tuttle Jr., and Paul D. Escott. *A People and a Nation: A History of the United States*. 6th ed. Boston: Houghton Mifflin, 2001.

Ost, David. *Solidarity and the Politics of Anti-Politics: Opposition and Reform in Poland since 1968*. Philadelphia: Temple University Press, 1990.

Patterson, James T. *Restless Giant: The United States from Watergate to Bush v. Gore*. New York: Oxford University Press, 2005.

Phelan, Craig, ed. *Trade Union Revitalisation: Trends and Prospects in 34 Countries*. Oxford, UK: Peter Lang, 2007.

Pringle, Tim. *Trade Unions in China: The Challenge of Labour Unrest*. Abingdon, UK: Routledge, 2011.

Puddington, Arch. *Lane Kirkland: Champion of American Labor*. Hoboken, NJ: John Wiley, 2005.

Radosh, Ronald. *American Labor and United States Foreign Policy*. New York: Random House, 1969.

Reagan, Ronald. *An American Life*. London: Arrow Books, 1991.

Richards, Yevette. *Maida Springer: Pan-Africanist and International Labor Leader*. Pittsburgh: University of Pittsburgh Press, 2000.

Robinson, Archie. *George Meany and His Times*. New York: Simon and Schuster, 1981.

Roediger, David R. *The Wages of Whiteness: Race and the Making of the American Working Class*, rev. ed. London: Verso, 1999.

————. *Working toward Whiteness—How America's Immigrants Became White: The Strange Journey from Ellis Island to the Suburbs*. New York: Basic Books, 2005.

Rogers, Daniel T. *Age of Fracture*. Cambridge, MA: Belknap Press, 2011.

Romano, Renee C., and Leigh Raiford, eds. *The Civil Rights Movement in American Memory*. Athens: University of Georgia Press, 2006.

Rooks, Daisy. "The Cowboy Mentality: Organizers and Occupational Commitment in the New Labor Movement." *Labor Studies Journal* 28, no. 3 (2003): 33–62.

Rosenfeld, Jake. *What Unions No Longer Do*. Cambridge, MA: Harvard University Press, 2014.

Ryan, Charlotte. "It Takes a Movement to Raise an Issue: Media Lessons from the 1997 UPS Strike." *Critical Sociology* 30, no. 2 (2004): 483–511.

Schulman, Bruce J. *The Seventies: The Great Shift in American Culture, Society, and Politics*. New York: Free Press, 2001.

Schulman, Bruce J., and Julian E. Zelizer, eds. *Rightward Bound: Making America Conservative in the 1970s*. Cambridge, MA: Harvard University Press, 2008.

Scipes, Kim. *AFL-CIO's Secret War Against Developing Country Workers*. Lanham, MD: Lexington Books, 2010.

Sheridan, Walter. *The Fall and Rise of Jimmy Hoffa*. New York: Saturday Review Press, 1972.

Sims, Beth. *Workers of the World Undermined: American Labor's Role in U.S. Foreign Policy*. Boston: South End Press, 1992.

Slaughter, Jane. "UPS and Detroit Newspaper Strikes." *Monthly Review* 49, no. 8 (1998): 53–57.

Stein, Judith. *Pivotal Decade: How the United States Traded Factories for Finance in the Seventies*. New Haven, CT: Yale University Press, 2010.

————. *Running Steel, Running America: Race, Economic Policy, and the Decline of Liberalism*. Chapel Hill: University of North Carolina Press, 1998.

Stern, Andy. *A Country That Works: Getting America Back on Track*. New York: Free Press, 2006.

Sweeney, John J. *America Needs a Raise: Fighting for Economic Security and Social Justice*. Boston: Houghton Mifflin, 1996.

Taft, Philip. *Organized Labor in American History*. New York: Harper and Row, 1964.

Tindall, George Brown, and David Emory Shi. *America: A Narrative History*. 5th ed. New York: W. W. Norton, 2000.

Todd, Chuck, and Sheldon Gawiser. *How Barack Obama Won: A State-by-State Guide to the Historic 2008 Presidential Election*. New York: Vintage Books, 2009.

Traister, Rebecca. *Big Girls Don't Cry: The Election That Changed Everything for American Women*. New York: Free Press, 2010.

Uchitelle, Louis. *The Disposable American: Layoffs and Their Consequences*. New York: Vintage Books, 2007.

Waters, Robert Anthony, Jr., and Geert Van Goethem, eds. (with foreword by Marcel van der Linden). *American Labor's Global Ambassadors: The International History of the AFL-CIO during the Cold War*. New York: Palgrave Macmillan, 2013.

Wehrle, Edmund F. *Between a River and a Mountain: The AFL-CIO and the Vietnam War*. Ann Arbor: University of Michigan Press, 2005.

Wilentz, Sean. *The Age of Reagan: A History, 1974–2008*. New York: HarperCollins, 2008.

Yates, Michael D. *Why Unions Matter*. 2nd ed. New York: Monthly Review Press, 2009.

Zieger, Robert H. *American Workers, American Unions*. 2nd ed. Baltimore: Johns Hopkins University Press, 1994.

———. *The CIO, 1935–1955*. Chapel Hill: University of North Carolina Press, 1995.

———. *For Jobs and Freedom: Race and Labor in America since 1865*. Lexington: University Press of Kentucky, 2007.

Zieger, Robert H., and Gilbert J. Gall. *American Workers, American Unions*. 3rd ed. Baltimore: Johns Hopkins University Press, 2002.

Zieger, Robert H., Timothy J. Minchin, and Gilbert J. Gall. *American Workers, American Unions*. 4th ed. Baltimore: Johns Hopkins University Press, 2014.

Index